AS & A2
Geography

Exam Board: AQA

Complete Revision
and Practice

AS-Level Contents

Published by CGP

Editors: Claire Boulter, Joe Brazier, Jo Sharrock.

Contributors: Margaret Collinson, Kevin Cooper, Chris Critchlow, Michael F. Dean, Paddy Gannon, Thomas Leverage (M. A.), Helen Nurton, Sophie Watkins, Dennis Watts, Eileen Worthington BSc hons.

Proofreader: Rosie McCurrie

With thanks to Laura Collar for the copyright research.

ISBN: 978 1 84762 906 7

Groovy website: www.cgpbooks.co.uk
Jolly bits of clipart from CorelDRAW®
Printed by Elanders Ltd, Newcastle upon Tyne.

Based on the classic CGP style created by Richard Parsons.

Photocopying — it's dull, grey and sometimes a bit naughty. Luckily, it's dead cheap, easy and quick to order more copies of this book from CGP — just call us on 0870 750 1242. Phew!

A2-Level Contents

Exam Structure

The road is long... with many a winding meander... so just to make sure you don't get lost along the way, here's a page that tells you a bit about all the different exams for both AS and A2 Geography.

You Have to Sit **Two Exam Papers** for **AS**...

Unit 1 Exam — *Physical and Human Geography*

1) It's **2 hrs** long and there are **120 marks** to be had (worth 70% of your AS grade).
2) It tests **all** the topics you've studied.
3) There are **two sections** — **A** and **B**. Both sections have the **same structure**:

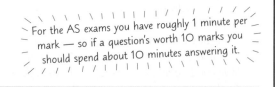
For the AS exams you have roughly 1 minute per mark — so if a question's worth 10 marks you should spend about 10 minutes answering it.

- You **have to answer** the first question in Section A (on **Rivers, Floods and Management**), the first question in Section B (on **Population Change**) and **ONE other** question in **each section**.
- For each question there are a couple of **short-answer parts** — some test your **knowledge** of the topic and some test your **understanding** by getting you to **interpret** a **resource**.
- The **last part** of each question is an **'essay' question**, which often needs **case study** material.

Unit 2 Exam — *Geographical Skills*

1) It's **1 hr** long and there are **50 marks** in total (worth 30% of your AS grade).
2) This paper tests your **investigative**, **map-reading**, **graph-reading**, **statistical** and **fieldwork skills**.
3) The questions will be based on your knowledge from **Unit 1** and on **your own fieldwork**.

...and **Two Exam Papers** for **A2**

See the Exam Skills section (p. 248-259) for more advice on answering exam questions and writing about fieldwork.

Unit 3 Exam — *Contemporary Geographical Issues*

It's **2 hrs 30 mins** long, there are **90 marks** in total and it's worth **30%** of your overall A level. There are **three sections**:

SECTION A

- You have to **answer questions** on **ONE physical option** — either Plate Tectonics, Weather and Climate or Ecosystems. There will be questions where you have to use your **understanding** to **interpret resources** (like photos, maps and graphs) and questions that **test your knowledge** of the topics.
- There will be **three questions** that add up to **25 marks in total**. Spend about **45 minutes** on this section.

SECTION B

- You have to **answer questions** on **ONE human option** — either World Cities, Development and Globalisation or Contemporary Conflicts and Challenges.
- The structure of this section is **exactly the same as Section A**, so spend about 45 minutes on it.

SECTION C

- You have to answer **ONE essay question** worth **40 marks**. You get a choice of **six** — one on each topic.
- You should spend about **60 minutes** penning your finest answer.
- You **can't answer the essay question on an option you've already answered in Section A or B**, so you should **choose your essay question first**, before you decide which options you'll answer in Sections A and B.

Unit 4 Exam — *Geography Fieldwork Investigation* <u>OR</u> *Geographical Issue Evaluation*

1) You **either** sit the **Geography Fieldwork Investigation exam**, or the **Geographical Issue Evaluation exam**.
2) Whichever one you're doing, you have to answer **all the questions**. It's **1 hr 30 mins** long and there are **60 marks** in total. It's worth **20%** of your overall A level grade.

GEOGRAPHY FIELDWORK INVESTIGATION

- There are **two sections** in this paper — **A** and **B**.
- In Section A you'll have to answer questions about **your fieldwork**. Spend about an **hour** on this bit.
- In Section B you'll have to answer **general investigation questions**, e.g. comment on a particular method used. Spend about **30 mins** on this part.

GEOGRAPHICAL ISSUE EVALUATION

- For this exam you're **given a resource booklet** to study about **two months before** your exam.
- In the exam you'll get questions on things like **data analysis**, **data interpretation**, **fieldwork to investigate the issue** and **theory** to do with the issue.

AS-Level

Geography

Exam Board: AQA

The Hydrological Cycle

What better way to start off a lovely new geography book than with some nice rivers...

Drainage Basins are Local Open Systems

Water doesn't **come into** or **leave** planet Earth — it's continuously **cycled** between the **oceans** and the **atmosphere**, returning to the ocean when it falls as **rain** (or other forms of **precipitation**, e.g. snow). This is known as the **global hydrological cycle**. The global hydrological cycle is a **closed system** — there are no **inputs** or **outputs**. There are also **local** hydrological cycles, e.g. **drainage basin hydrological cycles**:

1) A river's **drainage basin** is the area **surrounding** the river where the rain falling on the land **flows** into that river. This area is also called the river's **catchment**.

2) The **boundary** of a drainage basin is the **watershed** — any precipitation falling **beyond** the watershed enters a **different drainage basin**.

3) Drainage basins are **open systems** with **inputs** and **outputs**.

4) Water comes **into** the system as **precipitation** and **leaves** via **evaporation**, **transpiration** and **river discharge**.

A Typical Drainage Basin System

You Need to **Learn** All This **Drainage Basin Terminology**

Inputs — Water Coming into the System

Precipitation includes **all** the ways moisture **comes out** of the atmosphere.
Precipitation is mainly **rain**, but don't forget the other types like **snow**, **hail**, **dew** and **frost**.

Storage — Water Stored in the System

1) **Interception** is when some precipitation **lands on vegetation** or other structures, like **buildings** and **concrete** or **tarmac** surfaces, before it reaches the soil. Interception creates a **significant store** of water in **wooded areas**. **Interception storage** is only **temporary** because the collected water **evaporates** quickly.

2) **Vegetation storage** is water that's been **taken up** by **plants**. It's all the water **contained** in plants at any one time.

3) **Surface storage** includes water in **puddles** (depression storage), **ponds** and **lakes**.

4) **Groundwater storage** is water stored in the ground, either in the **soil** (**soil moisture**) or in **rocks**. The **water table** is the top surface of the **zone of saturation** — the zone of **soil** or **rock** where **all** the **pores** in the soil or rock are **full of water**. **Porous rocks** (rocks with lots of **holes** in them) that hold water are called **aquifers**.

5) **Channel storage** is so obvious that it's often overlooked — it's the **water** held in a **river** or **stream channel**.

The Hydrological Cycle

Flows and Processes — Water Moving from One Place to Another

1) **Surface runoff** (also called **overland flow**) is water **flowing over** the land. It can flow over the **whole surface** or in **little channels**. Surface runoff is common in **arid areas** where **torrential rain** falls on **hard baked** land.

2) **Throughfall** is water **dripping** from one **leaf** (or other plant part) to **another**.

3) **Stemflow** is water running down a plant **stem** or a **tree trunk**.

4) **Throughflow** is water moving slowly **downhill** through the **soil**. Throughflow is **faster** through **"pipes"** — things like **cracks** in the **soil**, or **animal burrows**.

5) **Infiltration** is water **soaking** into the soil. **Infiltration rates** are influenced by **soil type**, **soil structure** and how much water's **already in** the soil. In a **heavy storm**, water **can't** infiltrate fast enough, so it **flows** over the surface.

6) **Percolation** is water **seeping down** through soil **into the water table**.

7) **Groundwater flow** is water flowing **slowly below** the **water table** through **permeable rock**. Water flows **slowly** through most rocks, but rocks that are **highly permeable** with lots of **joints** (gaps that water can get through) can have **faster** groundwater flow, e.g. limestone.

8) **Baseflow** is groundwater flow that **feeds** into rivers through river **banks** and river **beds**.

9) **Interflow** is water flowing **downhill** through **permeable rock above** the water table.

10) **Channel flow** is the water flowing in the **river** or **stream** itself. This is also called the **river's discharge**.

Outputs — Water Leaving the System

1) **Evaporation** is water turning into **water vapour** — **turning** from a **liquid** to a **gas**.

2) **Transpiration** is **evaporation** from **plant leaves** — plants and trees **take up** water through their roots and **transport** it to their **leaves** where it evaporates into the atmosphere.

3) **Evapotranspiration** is the process of evaporation and transpiration **together**.

4) **River discharge**, or **river flow**, is another **output**.

Potential evapotranspiration (PET) is the amount of water that **could** be lost by evapotranspiration. **Actual evapotranspiration** is what **actually** happens. For example, in a **desert** potential evapotranspiration is **high** (because **heat increases** the amount of **evaporation**) but actual transpiration is **low** (because there **isn't** that much moisture in the first place).

The **Water Balance** Shows the Balance Between **Inputs** and **Outputs**

Water balance is worked out from **inputs** (precipitation) and **outputs** (channel discharge and evapotranspiration). The water balance affects how much water is **stored** in the basin. The general water balance in the **UK** shows **seasonal patterns**:

1) In **wet seasons**, precipitation **exceeds** evapotranspiration. This creates a **water surplus**. The **ground stores fill** with water so there's **more surface runoff** and **higher discharge**, so **river levels rise**.

2) In **drier seasons**, precipitation is **lower than** evapotranspiration. **Ground stores** are **depleted** as some water is **used** (e.g. by plants and humans) and some flows into the **river channel**, but **isn't** replaced by precipitation.

3) So, at the **end** of a dry season, there's a **deficit** (**shortage**) of water in the ground. The ground stores are **recharged** in the next **wet season** (i.e. autumn).

Water balance for a temperate zone, e.g. UK

- = ET
- = P
- = water surplus
- = ground store depletion
- = ground store recharge

Practice Questions

Q1 List five ways in which water is stored in the hydrological cycle.

Q2 Water vapour evaporates from the leaves of plants. What is this process called?

Exam Question

Q1 Describe how the water balance of the UK changes with the seasons. [4 marks]

My grandad has issues with water flow...

There are loads of words that you need to remember on these pages. It might seem like a pain, but if you learn them all now it'll mean the rest of the section will make a lot more sense. And you thought geography was just about colouring in maps...

River Discharge

Phew, I'm glad those last two pages are over — too many definitions for my liking.
None on this page thankfully... OK, when I said none, I actually meant a few.

River Discharge is the Volume of Water Flowing in a River

River discharge is simply the **volume** of water (in cubic metres, **m³**) that **flows** in a river **per second**. Unsurprisingly, it's measured in **cubic metres per second** (**m³/s**) — this is a bit of a mouthful, so geographers usually just shorten it to **cumecs**. River discharge is **affected** by:

1) **Precipitation** — the **more** precipitation, the **higher** the **discharge**.

2) **Hot weather** — the **higher** the temperature, the **lower** the **discharge** because the rate of **evaporation** is **higher**.

3) **Removal of water** from the river (**abstraction**) — also **reduces** the **discharge**.

Nelly was an abstraction master when she had a thirst on.

Hydrographs Show River Discharge Over a Period of Time

Hydrographs are graphs of river **discharge** over **time**. They show how the **volume of water** flowing at a certain point in a river **changes** over a **period of time**. Storm hydrographs show river discharge around the time of a **storm event**. They only cover a relatively **short time period** (hours or days, rather than weeks or months).

1 **Peak discharge** — this is the **highest** point on the graph, when the **river discharge** is at its **greatest**.

2 **Lag time** — this is the delay between **peak rainfall** and **peak discharge**. This delay happens because it takes **time** for the rainwater to **flow** into the river. A **shorter** lag time can **increase peak discharge** because more water reaches the river during a **shorter period of time**.

3 **Rising limb** — this is the part of the graph **up to** peak discharge. The river discharge **increases** as rainwater flows into the river.

4 **Falling limb** — this is the part of the graph **after** peak discharge. **Discharge** is **decreasing** because **less water** is flowing into the river. A **shallow** falling limb shows water is flowing in from **stores** long after it's **stopped raining**.

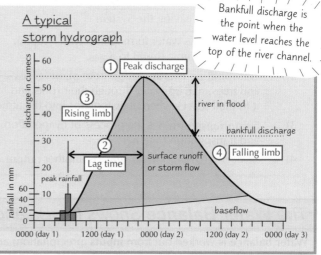

A typical storm hydrograph

Bankfull discharge is the point when the water level reaches the top of the river channel.

The **exact shape** of the hydrograph varies with each **river drainage basin** and each individual **storm event** (see below). A basin with **rapid runoff** and not much **storage** capacity gives a hydrograph with a **short lag time** and **high peak discharge**. This is called a "**flashy**" hydrograph — the graph has **steep**, roughly **symmetrical** rising and falling limbs.

The Storm Hydrograph is Affected by Physical Factors

Not all **drainage basins** are the **same** and the **weather** tends to vary too — these **physical factors** affect the storm hydrograph:

1) **Drainage basin characteristics** — the **physical features** of the drainage basin affect **lag time** and **peak discharge**.

   • **Larger drainage basins** can catch **more precipitation**, so they have a **higher peak discharge** compared to smaller basins. But **smaller basins** generally have **shorter lag times** because precipitation has **less distance** to travel, so reaches the main channel **quicker**.

   • **Steep-sided** drainage basins have **shorter lag times** than shallower basins — water flows **more quickly** downhill into the river on steep slopes. This can also **increase peak discharge**.

   • **Circular** basins are more likely to have a **flashy** hydrograph than **long, narrow** basins. This is because all points on the **watershed** are roughly the **same distance** from the point of discharge **measurement**. This means lots of water will reach the measuring point at the **same time**, **increasing peak discharge**.

   • Basins with **lots of streams** (high **drainage density**) drain **quickly**, so have **shorter lag times**.

2) The **amount** of water **already present** in the drainage basin ("**antecedent moisture**") — affects **lag time**.

   • If the ground's already **waterlogged** (the soil can't **absorb** any more water) then **infiltration** is **reduced** and **surface runoff increases**. Surface runoff is much **faster** than **throughflow** or **baseflow**, so rainwater reaches the river **more quickly**, **reducing lag time**.

River Discharge

3) **Rock type** — affects **lag time** and **peak discharge**.

- **Impermeable rocks** don't **store** water or let water flow through them. This **reduces infiltration** and **increases surface runoff, reducing lag time**. **Peak discharge** also **increases** as **more water** reaches the river in a shorter period.

See pages 2-3 for definitions.

4) **Soil type** — affects **lag time** and **peak discharge**.

- **Sandy soils** allow a lot of **infiltration**, but **clay soils** have very **low infiltration rates**. Low infiltration rates **increase surface runoff, reducing lag time** and **increasing peak discharge**.

5) **Vegetation** — affects **lag time** and **peak discharge**.

- Vegetation **intercepts** precipitation and **slows its movement** to the river channel, **increasing lag time**. Interception is **highest** when there's **lots of vegetation** and **deciduous trees** have their **leaves**.
- The **more vegetation** there is in a basin, the **more water** is **lost** (through **transpiration** and **evaporation** directly from the vegetation) before it reaches the river channel, **reducing peak discharge**.

6) **Precipitation** — affects **peak discharge**.

- **Intense storms** will generate **more precipitation** and so **greater peak discharges** than **light rain showers**.
- The **type** of precipitation also affects **lag time** — e.g. snow that's fallen in a **winter storm** can **melt** (**meltwater**) and flow into the river in **spring**, giving a **very long lag time**.

7) **Temperature** — affects **lag time** and **peak discharge**.

- **Hot**, **dry** conditions and **cold**, **freezing** conditions both result in **hard ground**. This **reduces infiltration** and **increases surface runoff** — **reducing lag time** and increasing **peak discharge**.
- **High temperatures** can **increase evapotranspiration**, so **less water** reaches the river channel, **reducing peak discharge**.

Human Activity Also Affects the Hydrograph

1) In **urban areas**, much of the **soil** is covered with man-made **impermeable** materials like **concrete**. Water **can't infiltrate** into the soil, which **increases surface runoff**, so water flows **more quickly** into the river. This makes the **lag time short** and **increases peak discharge**.

2) Man-made **drainage systems** affect the hydrograph in a similar way. Water flows down **drains** into the river before it can **evaporate** or **infiltrate** into the soil, causing a **shorter lag time** and **increased peak discharge**.

Practice Questions

Q1 What is river discharge?

Q2 What is the unit of measurement for river discharge?

Q3 How can human activity affect the storm hydrograph?

Exam Question

Q1 a) Give the lag time and peak discharge for the storm hydrograph shown above. [2 marks]

b) How might deforestation of the river Riggs drainage basin affect its storm hydrograph? Explain your answer. (Assume all other features, including precipitation, stay the same.) [4 marks]

I ain't saying she's a gold digger, but she loves her flashy hydrographs...

Storm hydrographs can look quite confusing, but they're not so bad once you've got your head round them. If you can explain how and why all the physical factors and human activities affect river discharge and lag time then you've nailed it, good and proper.

River Processes

I could try and come up with an amusing introduction to erosion, but I'm only four pages into this section and rivers are really starting to wear me down.

Erosion Can Affect the Length, Depth and Width of a River

The **energy** of a river flowing **downhill** causes **erosion**. The **bed** (the **bottom** of the river channel) and **banks** (the **sides** of the river channel) of a river can be **eroded** — making the river **longer**, **deeper** and **wider**:

Headward erosion	Vertical erosion	Lateral erosion
Headward erosion makes the river **longer**. It happens near a river's **source** as **throughflow** and **surface runoff** causes **erosion** at the point the water **enters** the river channel (the **valley head**).	**Vertical erosion** deepens river channels. It happens in the **upper stages** of a river.	**Lateral erosion** makes the river **wider**. It happens in the **middle** and **lower** stages of a river.

There are **five** main ways in which river erosion happens:

1) **Hydraulic action** — the **pressure** of the **water** breaks **rock particles** away from the bed and banks. It's strongest in **rapids** and **waterfalls** (see p. 10), and during **floods**.

2) **Abrasion (corrasion)** — eroded pieces of rock in the water **scrape** and **rub** against the bed and banks, **removing material**. **Most erosion** of river beds and banks happens by abrasion.

3) **Attrition** — eroded rocks **smash** into each other and break into **smaller** fragments. Their edges also get **rounded off** as they rub together. Attrition **doesn't erode** the bed and banks — it just makes the particles of rock in the river **smaller** and **more rounded**.

The more eroded material a river carries, the more erosion it can cause by abrasion.

4) **Cavitation** — **air bubbles** in turbulent stretches of water **implode** causing **shockwaves** that **break** pieces of rock off the banks and bed.

5) **Corrosion (solution)** — the dissolving of rock by **chemical processes**. Carbon dioxide dissolves in water to form a **weak acid**, which reacts with rocks like **limestone** and **chalk**, breaking them down.

Transportation is the Process of Eroded Material Being Carried in a River

The **velocity** of a river provides the **energy** needed for it to **transport eroded material**. The eroded material carried in a river is called its **load**, and it can be carried in **four** ways:

1) **Solution** — substances that can **dissolve** are carried along **in** the water. E.g. **limestone** is dissolved into river water that's slightly **acidic**.

2) **Suspension** — very **fine** material, like **silt** and **clay** particles, is whipped up by **turbulence** (erratic swirling of water) and carried along in the water. **Most** eroded material is transported this way.

3) **Saltation** — **larger particles**, like **pebbles** or **gravel**, are **too heavy** to be carried in suspension. Instead, the **force** of the water causes them to **bounce** along the river bed.

4) **Traction** — very **large** particles, e.g. **boulders**, are **pushed** along the river bed by the force of the water.

Material transported by **traction** or **saltation** is called the river's **bedload**.

Solution   Suspension

Saltation

Traction

River Processes

Deposition is the Process of Dropping Eroded Material

Deposition happens when the river **loses energy**. When it **slows down**, it loses energy and **drops** some of its load. The speed and energy of a river can be reduced in many ways:

1) **Reduced rainfall** causes **lower discharge**, which means the river **slows down** and has **less energy**.
2) **Increased evaporation** or **abstraction** (taking water out of a river for human use) also causes **lower discharge**.
3) **Friction**, e.g. in **shallow** areas of the river and **close to the banks**, reduces the **speed** of the river, reducing its **energy**.
4) When the river is forced to **slow down**, e.g. before a **narrow section** of the channel, it **loses energy**.
5) A lot of energy is **lost** when the river meets the **sea** (the sea **absorbs** the energy).

The Capacity of a River is the Total Amount of Material It Can Carry

1) The capacity is the **total load** (measured in volume, weight or mass) that a river can **transport** at a given point.
2) The load of a river can be **divided** into **different categories** according to **particle size**.
   The particle sizes range from fine **silt** and **clay** (less than 0.1 mm in diameter) to **big boulders**.
3) The **competence** describes the **maximum particle size** that a river is capable of **transporting** at a given point.

The Hjulström Curve Shows the Link Between River Velocity and Competence

The **competence** of a river is affected by the amount of **energy** it has, which is related to its **velocity** — generally, the greater the velocity, the greater the energy. The **Hjulström curve** shows the **relationship** between river velocity and competence. It also shows how the **processes** of **erosion**, **deposition** and **transportation** vary with river velocity:

- The **critical erosion velocity curve** on the graph shows the **minimum velocity needed** for the river to **pick up** (erode) and **transport** particles of **different sizes** (in suspension or as bedload). It takes a **higher velocity** to **erode** material than it does to just **transport** material.

- The **mean settling velocity curve** shows the velocities at which particles of **different sizes** are **deposited**, i.e. it shows the **competence** of the river at different velocities.

The curves vary with river depth and characteristics.

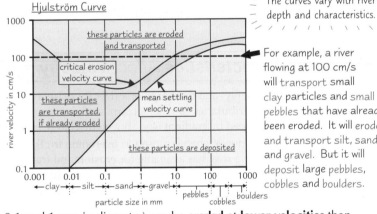

For example, a river flowing at 100 cm/s will transport small clay particles and small pebbles that have already been eroded. It will erode and transport silt, sand and gravel. But it will deposit large pebbles, cobbles and boulders.

The graph also shows that particles of **sand** (between 0.1 and 1 mm in diameter) can be **eroded** at **lower velocities** than **finer particles** such as **silt** and **clay**. This is because **silt** and **clay** particles **stick together more** than sand, which means they're **harder** to dislodge, so it requires **more energy** (greater velocity) to erode them.

Practice Questions

Q1 Name the four ways a river can transport its load.
Q2 Briefly describe two reasons why a river drops its load.
Q3 What is meant by the competence of a river?

Exam Questions

Q1 Describe the five main ways in which river erosion can happen.   [5 marks]

Q2 Outline how the critical erosion velocity curve on a Hjulström graph varies with particle size.   [6 marks]

Hjulström curve — sounds more like something you'd find in IKEA®...

OK, apart from that scary-looking diagram, this is all pretty simple. Bits of river beds and banks get knocked and scraped into the water (erosion). The river carries the material along while it's got enough speed and energy (transportation) and then drops it when it slows down (deposition). The faster the river is going, the more energy it has, so the more stuff it can carry. Not too bad...

The Long Profile and Channel Characteristics

The long profile — well, it's long and, erm, a profile. And that's all I have to say about that. Well, not quite...

The **Long Profile** Shows the **River's Gradient** from Its **Source** to the **Sea**

1) A **long profile** shows you how the **gradient** of the river channel **changes** from the river's **source** to its mouth by showing the **height of the river bed** above the **base level** for the whole length of the river.

2) The **base level** is the **lowest point** that the river **can erode to** — usually **sea level** (or the level of a **lake** or **reservoir**).

3) The **total amount** of erosion and deposition along the **full course** of a river are **balanced**. But the **rates** of **erosion** and **deposition change** along the course of a river. This can result in the formation of **landforms** such as **waterfalls** (where the rate of **erosion** is **higher** than the rate of **deposition** — see p. 10), which make the profile **uneven**.

4) Because the **total** amount of erosion and deposition is **balanced**, the rate of erosion of landforms like waterfalls is **equal** to the rate of deposition elsewhere along the river. This means that **over time** the long profile will **change** from being uneven to a **smooth curve**. This is called a **graded profile** (but it hardly ever happens).

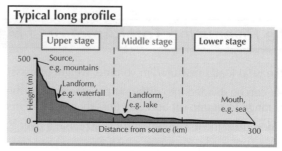

Typical long profile

Upper stage | Middle stage | Lower stage

Source, e.g. mountains

Landform, e.g. waterfall

Landform, e.g. lake

Mouth, e.g. sea

Height (m)

Distance from source (km)

Graded profile

Erosion has 'smoothed out' the waterfall.

Deposition has 'filled in' the lake.

Height

Distance from source

Royal profile

A river's course can be split into **three stages** — **upper** (near the source), **middle**, and **lower** (near the mouth). The **energy** of a river **varies** in each stage:

1) In the **upper stage**, the **gradient** is **steep** and the river is **high** above sea level, which gives it lots of **potential energy** (energy that can be **converted** into **other forms**, e.g. kinetic).

2) As the gradient **decreases** towards the **middle stage**, potential energy is converted to **kinetic energy** (movement) — the river **gains velocity**.

3) In the **lower stage**, the river has **little** potential energy, but **lots** of kinetic energy — it flows **faster**.

Channel Characteristics Affect **Velocity** and **Discharge**

The **velocity** (kinetic energy) and **discharge** of a river **increase** as you go **downstream** from source to mouth. Discharge **increases** as **tributaries** (smaller streams and rivers) and **more surface runoff** join the main channel. **River velocity** is influenced by **gradient** (see above), **discharge** and **channel characteristics** — the **shape** and **roughness**.

1) Most of a river's kinetic energy is used to **overcome friction** — the rest causes **erosion**. The **more energy** a river has available for **erosion** and **transportation**, the **more efficient** it is. An efficient river will have a **high velocity**, **high discharge** and **little friction**.

2) **Efficiency** is measured by **hydraulic radius**. The **larger** its hydraulic radius the **more efficient** a river is.

- The **hydraulic radius** is the channel's **cross-section area divided** by the **length** of its **wetted perimeter** (the **total length** of the **banks** and river **bed** that are in contact with the water).
- **Contact** between the water and the wetted perimeter creates **friction**, which **increases energy loss** and **slows the river down**.
- A **larger hydraulic radius** means that a **smaller proportion** of water is in contact with the wetted perimeter. So **friction is lower**, which **reduces energy loss**, increasing **velocity** and **discharge**.
- **Smooth, narrow, deep** channels (like channel **A**) have a **larger hydraulic radius** and so are **more efficient** than **shallow, broader** ones (like channel **B**).

A — Banks 5 m — Bed 5 m
Wetted perimeter = 15 m
Cross-section area = 25 m²
Hydraulic radius = 1.7

B — Banks 2 m — Bed 7 m
Wetted perimeter = 11 m
Cross-section area = 14 m²
Hydraulic radius = 1.3

3) **Channel roughness** also affects the efficiency. **Protruding banks** and **large, angular boulders** on the river bed **increase the wetted perimeter** and cause **more friction**. This **reduces** efficiency, velocity and discharge.

4) As channel roughness **increases**, so does **turbulence** (erratic swirling of the water in the main flow). Turbulent flow is **more effective** at **picking up** particles from the river bed than smooth flow — so turbulence causes **greater erosion**.

5) Channel roughness is **greatest** in the **upper stages** of the river. So although the **gradient** is steep, the river **loses** a lot of energy to **friction**, so discharge and velocity are **lowest** here during **normal conditions**.

6) In the **lower stages**, the banks and bed of the river are **smooth**, so there's much **less friction**. This means **less energy** is lost, so discharge and velocity are the **highest** in this stage.

The Long Profile and Channel Characteristics

River Processes Change as the River Flows from Source to Mouth

Upper stage

EROSION
Mainly **vertical** and by **abrasion** (there's also some **hydraulic action**). Erosion occurs when there are **high-energy conditions** (i.e. when **velocity** and **discharge** are high after **heavy rain** or **ice melt**). The **rough channel** causes **turbulence** and the **large, angular bedload** is **dragged along** the **river bed**, causing **intense downwards (vertical) erosion**.

TRANSPORTATION
Mainly **large particles** such as **boulders** carried by **traction** or **saltation** during high-energy conditions.

DEPOSITION
Little deposition — mainly **largest particles** deposited in the **river bed** as **energy levels drop**.

Middle stage

EROSION
Mainly **lateral** and by **abrasion**. **Attrition** of **larger particles** in this stage means that sediment **particle size decreases** from source to mouth.

TRANSPORTATION
More material carried in **suspension** as particle size **decreases**. Some larger particles moved by **saltation**.

DEPOSITION
Sand and **gravel** are deposited across the **flood plain** as the river floods and **friction reduces** the river's **energy**.

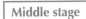

There's more about these processes on page 6.

Lower stage

EROSION
Although **velocity** and **discharge** are **highest** in this stage, there's **less erosion** because **turbulence is lower** and sediment particle size is **reduced** (reducing abrasion). Some **lateral erosion** occurs during the **formation of meanders**.

TRANSPORTATION
Mainly **smaller particles** such as **silt** and **clay** carried by **suspension**, or substances carried **in solution**.

DEPOSITION
Smaller particles such as **sand, silt** and **clay** are deposited on the **flood plain** when the river **floods** and in the **river mouth** as the **sea absorbs river energy**.

The Cross Profile Shows the Shape of the River Channel and Valley

The **cross profile** of a river shows you what a **cross-section** of the **river channel** or the **river valley** looks like. The **valley** cross profile changes during the **different stages** of a river's **long profile**.

1) **Upper stage** valleys are **steep V shapes**. **Vertical** erosion creates **narrow** valley floors and **steeply sloped** sides.
2) **Middle stage** valleys are **wider**, caused by **lateral** erosion. **Deposition** creates a **flood plain** on the valley floor.
3) **Lower stage** valleys are **wide** with **gently sloping** sides. There's a much **wider flood plain** caused by **deposition**.

Practice Questions

Q1 What does the long profile of a river show?

Q2 Describe the features of a lower stage river valley.

Exam Questions

Q1 What does the hydraulic radius tell you about a river, and how is it calculated? [3 marks]

Q2 Outline how the processes of erosion, transportation and deposition change along a river's long profile. [6 marks]

It's not the length of your wetted perimeter that counts, it's the hydraulic radius...

Phew, there's quite a lot of terms to learn on these pages: wetted perimeter, hydraulic radius, efficiency, roughness and turbulence. Learn what they all mean and how they affect velocity, discharge, erosion, transportation and deposition during the river's stages.

River Landforms

Hurrah! After a few pretty dull pages, you get to learn about all kinds of brilliant river landforms.

Fluvial just means it's caused by rivers and streams.

Waterfalls, Rapids and Potholes are Caused by Fluvial Erosion

Waterfalls

1) Waterfalls form where a band of **hard** rock meets **softer** rock. The soft rock is **eroded more** than the harder rock, causing a 'step' in the river bed.

2) The water flowing over the step **speeds up** due to the **lack of friction** as it drops over the step. This increase in speed gives the water **greater erosive power**, causing further erosion of the soft rock and **undercutting** of the harder rock.

3) As the hard rock is **undercut**, it can **collapse**. A deep **plunge pool** is carved out by **abrasion** at the foot of the waterfall as the bits of **collapsed rock** are **swirled** round by **turbulence**.

4) **Over time**, **more undercutting** causes **more collapse**. The waterfall will **retreat** (move **back up** the channel), leaving behind a **steep-sided gorge**.

Potholes

Potholes are **small circular hollows** in the river bed. They're formed by **abrasion** as **turbulence** swirls a river's **bedload** round in a **circular motion**, causing it to **rub** and **scrape** out holes.

Rapids

Rapids are relatively steep sections of river with **turbulent flow** where there are **several sections** of **hard rock**. They're a bit like **mini-waterfalls**.

Meanders are Formed by Combined Erosion and Deposition

Large, **sweeping curves** in a river's middle and lower stages are called **meanders**. They're formed by **erosion** and **deposition**.

1) **Meanders** form where **alternating pools** (areas of **deep** water) and **riffles** (**shallow** water) develop at **equally spaced intervals** along a stretch of river. The distance between pools is **5-6 times** the **width** of the river bed.

2) Because the river channel is **deeper** in pools it's more **efficient** (see p. 8), so it has **greater energy** and **more erosive power**. Energy is **lost** as the river flows over a riffle because of **friction**.

3) The **spacing** and **distance** between riffles and pools causes the river's flow to become **uneven** and **maximum flow** to be concentrated on **one side** of the river.

4) **Turbulence increases** in and around **pools** as the **water speeds up**, so the flow of water begins to **twist** and **coil**.

5) This causes **corkscrew-like** currents in the river called **helicoidal flow**, which **spiral** from bank to bank between pools.

6) The helicoidal flow causes more **erosion** and **deepening** of the pools. It also causes **eroded material** to be **deposited** on the **inside** of the **next bend**, where the river **loses energy**.

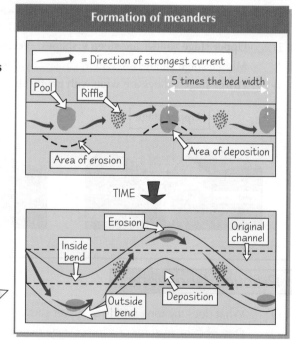

7) The **combination** of erosion and deposition **exaggerates** the bends until large **meanders** are formed. The combined processes also create the meanders' distinctive **asymmetric cross-section**.

8) **Oxbow lakes** are formed when the **neck** of the loop of a meander is **broken** through, often during **flooding**. **Deposition** dams off the loop, leaving an oxbow lake.

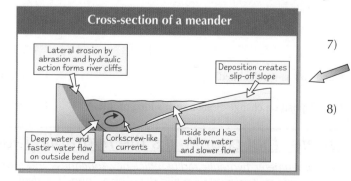

River Landforms

Braiding, Flood Plains, Levees and Deltas are Caused by Fluvial Deposition

Braiding

1) **Braiding** occurs when rivers are carrying a **vast** amount of **eroded sediment** (e.g. in meltwater).

2) If the river's **velocity drops**, or the sediment **load** becomes **too much** for the river to carry, sediment is **deposited** in the channel.

3) This causes the river to **divide** into many **small, winding** channels that eventually rejoin to form a single channel.

River channel

Deposited sediment

Flood plains

1) When a river **overflows** its banks and floods the flat land either side of the river (the **flood plain**), there's an **increase** in the **wetted perimeter** and **reduction** in **hydraulic radius**.

2) This **increases friction**, reducing the velocity of the river and causing fine **silt** and **sand** to be **deposited** across the flood plain.

Levees

1) Levees are natural, **raised embankments** formed as a river **overflows** its banks.

2) During a flood, material is deposited across the **whole flood plain** as the river **loses velocity** and **energy** due to **increased friction**.

3) The **heaviest** material (e.g. sand and gravel) is dropped first, **closest** to the river channel.

4) Over time, this material **builds up** on the river bank, creating a **levee**.

Levees   Flood plain

River channel

Deltas

1) When a river reaches the **sea** (or a **lake**), the **energy** of the **river** is **absorbed** by the **slower** moving water of the sea (or lake).

2) This causes the river to **deposit** its load. These deposits **build up** on the sea bed, until the **alluvium** (deposited sediment) **rises above** sea level, **partially blocking** the mouth of the river.

3) The river has to **braid** into several **distributaries** in order to reach the sea, forming a **delta**.

Alluvium   Sea

River channel

Rejuvenation Allows a River to Resume Vertical Erosion

See page 8 for the long profile.

1) A river is said to be **rejuvenated** if its base level is **lowered**. This can be caused by either the **ground level rising** (**crustal uplift**) or by a **drop in sea level**.

2) The drop in base level gives the river greater **potential energy**, increasing its **vertical erosion** potential.

3) The **long profile** of the river is **extended** and a **knickpoint** (a sharp change in gradient, often a **waterfall**) will form and mark the junction between the **original** long profile and the new one.

Original long profile

Knickpoint

Original base level

New long profile

New base level

Source   Mouth

There are distinctive **landforms** associated with rejuvenation:

1) **River terraces** are former **flood plains** which have been left **above** the level of **present-day** flooding following increased **vertical erosion**.

2) **Incised meanders** are formed when a river keeps its meandering course as **vertical erosion** increases. The result is a **deep, winding valley** with **steep sides**. The river is left **far below** the level of the **former flood plain**.

Practice Questions

Q1   Briefly describe how waterfalls are formed.

Q2   Name two river landforms associated with rejuvenated rivers.

Exam Question

Q1   Describe the formation of levees.   [4 marks]

Drove my Chevy to the levee — but the levee was just an old riverbank...

Don't be too rapid in going over the stuff on these pages — you'll only end up in deep water. But don't spend forever meandering around the facts. Slip off and take a break if you need to and come back rejuvenated. That's the best way to nick points in the exam.

Causes and Impacts of Flooding

Right... time to learn what causes rivers to go wild (but not in a good way, unless you're a kayaker) and what happens when they do.

Prolonged Rainfall and Heavy Rainfall are the Main Causes of Flooding

1) **Flooding** occurs when the **discharge** of a river is **so high** that the **river spills over** its **banks** onto the **flood plain**.

2) A **major cause** of **flooding** is **prolonged rainfall**. After a **long period** of **rain**, the **ground** becomes **saturated** (it **can't absorb** any more water). Any further rainfall **can't infiltrate**, which **increases surface runoff**, which **increases discharge**.

3) **Heavy rainfall** (e.g. the rain you get with **thunderstorms**) can lead to **rapid surface runoff** if the rainfall is **too intense** for **infiltration** to occur. This can lead to a **sharp rise** in **river discharge** called a **flash flood**.

4) **Melting snow** and **ice** also lead to a **huge increase** in a river's **discharge**. For example, **melting snow** in the **Himalayas** contributes to the **annual summer flooding** of the **River Ganges** in **Bangladesh**.

If you don't know what any of these terms mean see pages 2-3.

There are Physical Factors That Increase the Risk of Flooding...

Some **physical characteristics** of **drainage basins** can **increase** the **risk** of **flooding**:

Lag time is the time between peak rainfall and peak discharge.

Sparse vegetation or deciduous trees

- **Sparse vegetation** in the drainage basin means **little rainfall** is **intercepted**, so **more rain** reaches the **ground**. This **increases** the **volume of water** reaching the river, which **increases discharge**.

- **Deciduous trees** have **no leaves** in **winter**, which has the **same effect** as sparse vegetation — little rainfall is intercepted.

Impermeable ground

- **Clay soils** and some **rocks**, such as **granite** and **shale**, are **impermeable** — they **don't allow** **infiltration** of **surface water**. This **increases surface runoff**, which **increases discharge**.

- If the ground has been **baked hard** by the heat of the summer, or it's **frozen**, the **same thing happens** — water can't infiltrate, increasing surface runoff and discharge.

Circular drainage basins

Water draining into the main river channel will **all arrive** in a **short space of time** because all points in the basin are a similar distance from the river. This **increases discharge**.

High drainage density

Drainage basins with a **high drainage density** (lots of streams) drain **quickly**, so have **short lag times**. Lots of **water** flows from the streams into the main river in a **short space of time**, **increasing discharge**.

Steep slopes

If the **drainage basin has steep-sided valleys**, water will reach the **river channel** much **faster** because water flows **more quickly** on **steeper slopes**. This **increases discharge**.

...and Human Factors

A lot of these factors are the same as those that reduce lag time and increase the peak discharge on a flood hydrograph — see pages 4-5.

Humans often make flooding more **frequent** and more **severe** by **changing things** in the **drainage basin**:

Urbanisation

- **Urban areas** have **large areas** of **impermeable tarmac** and **concrete**, so when it rains **surface runoff** is **very rapid**.

- **Gutters** and **drains** quickly take **runoff** to **rivers**.

- Both of these things **reduce lag time** and so **increase discharge**.

Deforestation

- **Clearing trees** and plants **reduces interception** and **evapotranspiration**. This **increases** the **volume of water** that reaches the channel, which **increases discharge**.

- Deforestation leaves the soil **loose**. The soil is **eroded** by rainwater and **carried** to the **river**, which **raises the river bed**. This **reduces** the **channel capacity**, so it takes **less water** for the river to **flood**.

Flood management strategies

Flood management strategies (see pages 16-17) can actually end up making **flooding worse**. For example, if **dams fail** they release a **huge volume** of **water all at once** — giving a huge **increase** in **discharge**.

Agriculture

Overgrazing leaves areas with **less vegetation**, so has the **same effect** as deforestation (see above). **Overgrazing** and **ploughing** also **increase soil erosion**.

Climate change

Climate change could cause an **increase** in **rainfall** and **more storms** in some areas, which could **increase flooding**.

Causes and Impacts of Flooding

Flooding Affects People, the Economy and the Environment

Here are some of the **possible** impacts:

Social impacts

1) **People** and **animals** can be **killed**.
2) **Floodwater** is often **contaminated** with **sewage**, which can lead to a **lack of clean drinking water**.
3) **Contaminated water** can also put people at **risk of diseases** (e.g. **diarrhoea** and **dysentery**)
4) **Possessions** can be **damaged** by floodwater or **lost** (washed away).
5) People can be made **homeless** as their **properties** are **inundated** or **damaged**.

Economic impacts

1) **Businesses** often have to shut down as premises are **inundated** and **power supplies** are affected.
2) **Rescue work** and **repairs** are usually **costly**. **Insurance premiums** go **up** after floods.
3) **Unemployment levels** often **rise** as **businesses shut down** because they can't recover from the flooding.
4) **Public transport, roads** and **bridges** can be **destroyed**.
5) **Crops** can be **destroyed**. This can lead to a **rise** in the **price** of **food**.

Environmental impacts

1) Floodwater **contaminated** with sewage and rubbish can **pollute rivers**.
2) **River banks** are **eroded**.

Positive impacts include:

1) **River sediment** is **deposited** on the **flood plain**. This makes the land **more fertile**.
2) **Wetlands** can be created, e.g. **marshes** and **ponds**, which are **habitats** for many species.

The **social** impact is usually **higher** in **poorer countries** because flood defences are poorer, people are less able to evacuate, sanitation systems aren't as good and buildings are of a poorer quality. The **absolute economic** impact is usually **higher** in **richer countries** as they have more high value buildings and infrastructure. However, the **relative economic** impact is usually **higher** in **poorer countries** — the buildings and crops that are damaged are worth less money, but this affects the economy more because they have less money to recover from it (e.g. to rebuild homes).

Flood Frequency Can be Calculated

1) Floods of a **very large size** (**magnitude**) don't happen very often — they're **not very frequent**.
2) **Small floods** happen more often — they're **more frequent**.
3) Large floods usually occur due to **unusually** heavy or prolonged rainfall.
4) By keeping **records** over many **years**, people can **predict how often** a flood of a certain magnitude may **occur** — this is called the **flood return interval** (**RI**).

   For example, if a **2 m** high flood occurred along a river in **1701**, **1806** and **1899** — then the **return interval** of a 2 m high flood is about **100 years**.

5) A **small flood** may have an **RI** of **one** or **two years**, whereas a **huge flood** may have an **RI** of **100 years** or more.

There are exceptions to this rule — large floods occur frequently when they're caused by annual snow melt or annual monsoons, e.g. a large flood happens in Bangladesh every year.

Henry made sure he was definitely prepared for the flood this time.

Practice Questions

Q1 Why is prolonged rainfall a major cause of flooding?

Q2 Name two human activities that increase the risk of flooding.

Q3 Briefly describe the possible social impacts of flooding.

Q4 Briefly describe the possible economic impacts of flooding.

Q5 What is a flood return interval?

Exam Questions

Q1 Outline the physical characteristics of a drainage basin that would have a high risk of flooding. [6 marks]

Q2 Explain two ways in which urbanisation increases the risk of flooding. [5 marks]

If only the "getting wet" part of flooding were the worst part...

It's normal for rivers to flood occasionally, but us humans have made it more of a problem. You need to learn all the causes and impacts of flooding — use boring old list-making to help you. List the causes under two headings (natural and human) and the impacts under three headings (social, economic and environmental). Colour them nice and prettily. Oh yeah — then learn 'em.

Causes and Impacts of Flooding — Case Studies

Just to make learning case studies more difficult, the causes and impacts of flooding are different in different places.
Flooding in poorer areas tends to have a much bigger impact on people's lives and health than flooding in wealthier areas...

Case Study 1 — Flooding of South Asia, 2007

Parts of **South Asia** flood **most years**, usually in **late summer**. This is **because**:

1) **South Asia** has a **monsoon climate** — **80%** of **rain** falls in just **four months**.

2) Much of **South Asia** is **low-lying land**, particularly **Bangladesh** where **90%** of **land** is **less** than **10 m above sea level**.

3) **Melting snow** and **ice** from the **Himalayas** in the **late summer** months **increase** the **Brahmaputra River discharge**.

In **July** and **August 2007**, the **flooding** was **particularly severe** in **Bangladesh** and **India**.

Physical factors were the **main cause...**
1) The **monsoon** came **suddenly** after a **very dry, early summer**.
2) There was **heavy rainfall** — **Assam** had a **record 169.5 mm** in **24 hours** on **22nd July**, and **900 mm** in total for July.
3) The **long duration** of **heavy rainfall** completely **saturated** the soil, increasing surface runoff and increasing discharge.
4) The **peak discharges** of the **River Ganges** and **Brahmaputra** coincided, which **increased** the river **discharge downstream**.

...but human activities made the **flooding worse**
1) **Deforestation** in **Nepal** and the **Himalayas** meant less rainfall was intercepted, which **increased discharge**.
2) The **growth** of **urban areas**, due to **migration**, also **increased surface runoff**.
3) **Collapse** of old **earth dams** in **Madhya Pradesh**, **India**, caused **further flooding**.

The Flooding Had Major Impacts, Especially on People

SOCIAL IMPACTS
1) **Over 2000 people died**. The **death toll** was **high** for many reasons, e.g. many people were **reluctant** to **evacuate** (as they'd have to **leave** their **land** and **livestock unattended**) and many **children drowned** because they **couldn't swim**. **Poor transport links** meant evacuation was slow.
2) As **wells** became **polluted** with **sewage**, there was a **lack of clean drinking water**. **Over 100 000 people** caught **water-borne diseases** (e.g. dysentery and diarrhoea).
3) An estimated **25 million people** were made **homeless**.
4) **112 000 houses** were **destroyed** in **India**, as **porous mud bricks** became **saturated** by **floodwater**.
5) **Dhaka** (Bangladesh's capital) was **inundated**, especially the **poorer districts** and **shanty towns** near the river.
6) Children **lost out** on **education** as **4000 schools** were **affected** and **44 schools** were totally **destroyed**.

ECONOMIC IMPACTS
1) The **cost** of the **flood** was estimated at **US$ 1 billion**, including damage to **crops** and **property**.
2) **Factories** were **closed** around **Dhaka**, due to **flood damage** and **loss of raw materials** (e.g. **rice**). Many of the **poorest workers** became **unemployed**.
3) There was **widespread loss of livestock** (e.g. **cattle**). Since **80%** of Bangladeshis rely on **agriculture**, many **lost** their **livelihoods**.
4) **550 000 hectares** of **land couldn't** be **planted** with **rice** at peak time, because of **flooded fields**. A **lower rice crop** meant the **world price** of basmati rice rose by **10%**.
5) **10 000 km** of **roads** were **destroyed**. Landslides blocked roads in the **highlands** of Nepal and Assam.
6) **Debt increased**, both **individually** (e.g. farmers borrowed money for food and seeds) and **nationally** (e.g. governments imported food and medicine).

ENVIRONMENTAL IMPACTS
1) The flood deposited **fertile silt** on the **flood plain**.
2) **Rivers** were **polluted** with **sewage**.

Human Factors Made the Impacts Worse

1) **Bangladesh** is a **poor country** so there **aren't** many **flood defences** or **flood warning systems** in place.

2) **Low incomes**, **few savings** and **little insurance** limited people's **ability** to **recover** after the flood.

3) **Corrupt officials diverted aid money** away from the people most in need.

Causes and Impacts of Flooding — Case Studies

Case Study 2 — *Flooding* of *Carlisle*, *Cumbria*, *2005*

The **River Eden** runs through **North Cumbria** and reaches the sea near **Carlisle**.

1) The **drainage basin** of the River Eden is **very large** so it **catches** a **large volume** of **rainfall**, leading to a **high river discharge**.

2) Some parts of the basin have **steep sides**, so water **runs quickly** down to the **river**.

3) There are **many streams** that **drain quickly** into the river, making the **lag time short**.

On **8th January 2005**, the **River Eden** flooded Carlisle.
The **flood return interval** (RI) of such a large flood is about **200 years**.

Physical factors were the main cause...

1) There was **heavy rainfall** on the **6th** January, for **36 hours**. **200 mm** of **rainfall** was recorded, which was the **equivalent of four months** rain.

2) Rain fell on **saturated ground** so the water **didn't soak** into the ground but **ran straight off** into the **river**.

3) This caused a **very high peak discharge** (**over 1520 cumecs**), compared to an **average discharge of 52 cumecs**.

...but human activities made the flooding worse

1) Carlisle is a **large built-up area**, with **impermeable concrete** and **tarmac surfaces**, and **little soil** or **vegetation**. This meant there was **little infiltration** of rainfall and **high surface runoff**, which **increased discharge**.

2) **Drains** and **sewerage systems overflowed** in some areas — becoming a **source** of **flooding** themselves. **25%** of the **flooding problems** were associated with **overflowing drains**.

The *Flooding* Had Major *Impacts*, Particularly on Carlisle's *Economy*

SOCIAL IMPACTS

1) **Three people died** in the floods.

2) **Over 3000 people** were made **homeless** for up to a **year** and thousands of **personal possessions** were **damaged**. Living in **temporary accommodation disrupted lives** in many ways, e.g. **travel arrangements** were **disrupted**, people were **separated** from **community networks** and friends, and they had **problems receiving post**.

3) Children **lost out on education** as **four schools** were **severely flooded**. **Newman Catholic School** didn't re-open until **Easter**.

4) There was an **increase in stress-related illnesses** following the floods.

ENVIRONMENTAL IMPACTS

1) The flooding **increased river bank erosion** in some areas.

2) **Rivers** were **polluted** with rubbish and sewage.

ECONOMIC IMPACTS

1) It took about a **year** to **repair the damage** to homes and repairs **cost over £100 million**.

2) **350 businesses** had to **shut down** as there was **no electricity**, **telephone service** or **transport**. Trade activities from Carlisle **railway** station were **suspended**.

3) **United Biscuits**, the **largest employer** in Carlisle, was **flooded** with **3 m** of water that caused **over £5 million damage**. 33 out of 1100 employees **lost their jobs**.

4) **70 000 addresses** had **no power**. The **sewage works**, **police station**, **fire station** and **council offices** were **severely flooded**.

5) **80 buses** (most of the public transport fleet) were **destroyed**. Many **roads** and **bridges** were **damaged**, e.g. **Warwick Road**.

Practice Questions

Q1 Briefly describe the physical reasons why the 2007 floods in South Asia were particularly severe.

Q2 Briefly describe the economic impacts of the 2005 Carlisle flood.

Exam Question

Q1 Using two named examples, compare the impacts of flooding in poorer and wealthier countries. [10 marks]

Rain, rain, go away — come again another day but not all at once in one big downpour...

Flooding can cause havoc, and it takes a lot of time and money to get things back to normal again. And it's not just the sheer amount of water — don't forget the knock-on effects, like contaminated water supplies, landslides, job losses, food price rises...

Flood Management Strategies

Flooding can cause major disasters, so unsurprisingly people try to stop it happening. There are various ways of doing this, but as usual there are various problems associated with each way.

There's **Not Enough Money** to **Protect Everywhere** from **Flooding**

1) The aim of flood management is to **protect homes**, **businesses** and the **environment** from **flooding**.

2) This is because flooding can have severe **social**, **economic** and **environmental impacts** (see p. 13).

3) It's **tricky** trying to **manage flooding** though — there **isn't enough money** available to **protect everywhere**.

4) Choosing **which** places are protected (and **how** they're protected) is done using **cost-benefit analysis**.

5) **Large settlements** and **important industrial sites** (e.g. power plants) are **more likely** to be protected than small settlements or farmland.

Flood Management Includes Hard Engineering and Soft Engineering

① Hard Engineering Defences Involve Built Structures

Hard engineering defences are **man-made structures** that **reduce flooding**.
General disadvantages of hard engineering defences include:

1) They're **expensive** to **build** and **maintain**, and need **technical skill**. **Poorer countries** often **can't afford** these flood defences.

2) **Floods** happen **less often**, but they can be **more hazardous** if they do happen. E.g. if a **dam breaks** then a **huge** amount of water will **rapidly flood** the land.

3) **Natural processes** are **disrupted**, e.g. **crops** don't get **fertile silt** from river sediment during **low-level flooding**.

4) Some people think they're **ugly**.

Fortunately, flood defence strategies have progressed somewhat over the years.

Here are some of the **most common** types of **hard engineering defences**:

Scheme	How it works	Extra benefits	Disadvantages
Dams	Dams are huge walls built across rivers. A reservoir (artificial lake) is formed behind the dam. Flood water is caught by the dam, which prevents flooding downstream. The water is released as a steady flow throughout the year.	• Turbines are often built into the dams, which generate electricity. • Steady water release allows irrigation of land below the dam throughout the year. • People can use the reservoir for recreational activities, e.g. sailing.	• They're very expensive. • Land is flooded when a reservoir is created. This often destroys farmland and forces people to move elsewhere. • They affect wildlife, e.g. they can prevent salmon migrating upstream to breeding grounds. • They trap sediment normally carried in rivers. This can cause the dam to fail. It can also cause increased erosion downstream, as there's less protective sediment being deposited.
Channel straightening	Channel straightening is where meanders are removed by building artificial cut-throughs. This makes the water flow faster, which reduces flooding because water drains downstream more quickly and doesn't build up to a point where the river channel can't contain it any more.	It takes less time to navigate the river because it has been made shorter.	• Flooding may happen downstream instead, as flood water is carried there faster. • More erosion occurs downstream because the river flows faster. • Altering river channels disturbs wildlife habitats.
Levees	Levees are embankments built along rivers. The river can hold more water without overflowing and so it floods less often.	They allow the flood plain to be built upon.	• They're quite expensive. • There's a risk of severe flooding if the levees are breached.
Diversion spillways	Diversion spillways are channels that take water elsewhere if the water level in the river is too high. Water is normally diverted around an important area or to another river. They prevent flooding because river discharge is reduced. The spillways often have gates that can be opened, so the release of water can be controlled.		• An increase in discharge when the diverted water joins another river (or rejoins the same one) could cause flooding below that point. • If spillways are overwhelmed, water will flood areas not used to flooding, which could cause even bigger problems.

Flood Management Strategies

2 Soft Engineering Defences Work With, Not Against, the Basin Processes

Soft engineering defences use **knowledge** of the **whole river basin** and its **processes**, to try to **work with nature**. General **advantages** are:

1) They're **cheaper** to **maintain** than hard engineering defences — this is **especially important** for **poorer countries**.
2) **Flooding** is more **predictable**, **reducing** the **risk** of an **unexpected disaster**.
3) They can **improve opportunities** for **recreation**, such as **fishing**.
4) Some people think they're **more attractive** than hard engineering schemes.

Here are some of the **most common** types of **soft engineering defences** that **reduce flooding**:

Scheme	How it works	Extra benefits	Disadvantages
Land use management	Planning restrictions prevent buildings or roads being constructed on the flood plain. Use of the flood plain is restricted to things like playing fields, allotments or parks. More water can infiltrate so there's less surface runoff, which reduces discharge and flooding.	• There are no new buildings or roads on the flood plain to be damaged, so the impact of any flooding is reduced. • It provides recreational opportunities, e.g. football fields.	• It restricts development. This is especially a problem where there's a shortage of housing. • It can't be used in areas that are already urbanised.
Wetland and river bank conservation	Wetlands store flood water and also slow it down. This reduces flooding downstream. So conserving or re-establishing wetlands gives natural protection from flooding. Planting trees and shrubs along the river bank increases interception and lag time, and reduces discharge. This also decreases flooding.	• Vegetation protects the surface soil from erosion. • The vegetation provides habitats for wildlife.	Less land is available for farming.
River restoration	River restoration involves making the river more natural, e.g. by removing man-made levees. The flood plain can then flood naturally. As the water spreads out over the flood plain the river's discharge is reduced (because less water is in the channel), which reduces flooding downstream.	• Little maintenance is needed, as the river's left in its natural state. • The river provides a better habitat for wildlife.	Local flood risk can increase, especially if nothing's done to prevent major flooding.
Alteration of urban surfaces	Building porous pavements or soakaways increases infiltration, which reduces rapid surface runoff to the river channel. This increases lag time, which reduces discharge and flooding.	Any pollutants in the water are filtered out by the soil before the water reaches the channel.	It's expensive.

Areas of trees and shrubs along river banks are called riparian buffers.

Soakaways are hollows or trenches filled with gravel.

The **impact** of **flooding** can also be **reduced**:

Scheme	How it works	Disadvantages
Weather forecasts and flood warnings	The Environment Agency monitors weather forecasts, rainfall and river discharge. They warn people about possible floods through TV, radio, newspapers and the internet. This means people can evacuate before the flood happens, saving lives. People can also move possessions and use sandbags to help reduce damage if flooding occurs.	• Some people might not be able to access the communication network. • Flash floods may happen too fast for warnings. • People may ignore warnings if they were inaccurate in the past.

Soft Engineering is More Sustainable than Hard Engineering

Hard engineering is often **expensive** and **disrupts natural processes**. Soft engineering tends to be **cheaper** and requires **much less time** and **money** to **maintain** than hard engineering. Soft engineering is designed to **integrate** with the natural **environment** and it creates areas like **wetlands**, which are important **habitats** for **wildlife**. So soft engineering's a **more sustainable management strategy** than hard engineering because it has a **lower economic cost** and **environmental impact**.

Practice Questions

Q1 What is hard engineering? Give an example of a hard engineering flood defence.

Q2 What is soft engineering? Give two advantages of using soft engineering rather than hard engineering defences.

Exam Question

Q1 Explain how flooding can be reduced without the use of major man-made structures. [8 marks]

Flood management strategies — let the ideas come flooding in...

Flood management is a pretty difficult task — whatever scheme you decide on, there are drawbacks. Also, saving your own neck often causes a flood somewhere else — usually downstream of you (which isn't a very neighbourly thing to do, really)...

Flood Management Strategies — Case Studies

Here are two beautiful case studies for you — showing you how different places manage floods in different ways.

Hard Engineering *is Used on the* Yangtze *to* Control Flooding

1) The **Yangtze River** flows through **China**. At 6380 km long, it's the **third longest** river in the world.

2) **Seasonal flooding** is **common** around the Yangtze — China has a **rainy season** that lasts from about **June** until **August** and the huge **increase** in **river discharge** during this time often causes flooding. Flooding causes **huge problems** as there's lots of **farmland** and loads of **major cities** next to the river, e.g. **Wuhan** and **Nanjing**.

3) **Five major floods** have happened over the **last century** — in 1931, 1935, 1949, 1954 and 1998.

4) The flood of **1954** covered **193 000 km²** of land and **killed 33 169 people**. Over **18 million people** had to **move**. It covered the city of **Wuhan** for **over 3 months**.

5) The flood in **1998 killed** around **3000 people** and made **14 million** people **homeless**.

6) **Flood protection** is mostly done through **hard engineering** defences.

Defences *Include* Dams *and* Levees

Daning River
Three Gorges Dam
Area of reservoir
Wuhan
Yangtze River
East China Sea
Temple of Zhang Fei

There are many **levees** along the river. E.g. there are **3600 km** of levees along the **middle** and **lower parts** of the river.

There are many **dams** on the Yangtze that reduce flooding (**46** are planned or under construction at the moment). The biggest of these is the **Three Gorges Dam**:

1) Work began on the **101 m high** Three Gorges Dam in **1994**.

2) A **reservoir** is building up behind the dam (it takes years to build up as the dam is huge). The reservoir **catches** any **flood water**, which can then be slowly released over time. The reservoir can store around **22 km³** of flood water.

3) It's also the largest **hydroelectric power station** in the world. The flow of water turns **26 turbines** built into the dam.

4) **Locks** have been built alongside the dam so **ships** can get past it.

Hard Engineering *Has* Reduced Flooding *but Has Also* Caused Problems

The construction of the **Three Gorges Dam** has had many **positive effects**, but also plenty of **negative effects**:

Positive effects

1) It's thought that the dam has **reduced major flooding** from **once every 10 years**, to once every **100 years**.

2) The turbines in the dam produce a lot of **electricity** — capacity is likely to reach **22.5 gigawatts** (enough to supply about **3%** of China's demand, which is loads).

3) The **reduction in flooding** has made it much **safer** to **navigate** up the Yangtze. **River shipping** has also **increased** as **bigger ships** can now travel up the river because the reservoir is deeper than the old river.

Levees have also caused problems:

1) In the **1998 floods** many levees **broke**, which contributed to **devastating flooding**.

2) After this, many levees were **reinforced**. They were **effective** at **reducing flooding** in the **2002 floods** (though the floods were **less severe** than the 1998 ones).

Negative effects

1) People have had to **relocate** as the water level in the reservoir has risen. It's thought that between **1.3** and **2 million people** in total will have to **relocate** by the time it's full — **13 cities** and **1352 villages** will be submerged.

2) The reservoir will also flood **farmland**, **657 factories**, and **1300** sites of **cultural** and **historic interest**. For example, as the water rises the **Temple of Zhang Fei** will be submerged.

3) A huge amount of **sediment** is normally carried down the Yangtze River. The dam will **trap** the sediment, which could lead to **failure** of the dam and cause **catastrophic flooding**.

4) The dam could **destroy habitats** and **endanger species**. E.g. the endangered **Siberian crane** spends the winter in wetlands below the dam, which are expected to be affected by less flooding. Fewer than 100 **baiji dolphins** are left in the Yangtze, and the dam could **reduce their food supply**.

5) The Three Gorges Dam **doesn't protect everyone** — rising water levels in the reservoir will **increase flooding** along the **tributaries** that lead into it, e.g. the **Daning River**. The increased water levels in the tributaries will also increase **erosion** of **riverbanks**, causing collapses and landslides.

Flood Management Strategies — Case Studies

Soft Engineering is Used in Abingdon to Control Flooding

1) **Abingdon**, a town in South-east England, was **built** on the **flood plains** of the **River Thames** and the **River Ock**.

2) **1500 properties** in Abingdon have a **1% chance** of **flooding** in a given year.

3) Abingdon has had **regular floods** over the years — in 1947, 1968, 1977, 1979, 1992, 2000 and 2007.

4) **Intense storms** in **July 2007** caused particularly bad **flash floods**. The **River Thames** and **Ock** burst their banks, flooding **660 properties** in **Abingdon**. **Increased surface runoff** in built-up areas made the flooding **even worse**.

5) **Hard engineering** defences have been considered but have been **rejected** for various reasons. E.g. a **diversion spillway** to transport Ock floodwater south of Abingdon was **too expensive**, and **flood barriers** to protect properties along the Ock would **increase flood risk downstream**. Flood protection is mostly done through **soft engineering** defences.

Defences Include Land Use Management, Flood Warnings and Soakaways

Gravel soakaways have been built along the **A34 road**.

Low-value land is allowed to flood, e.g. **Tilsley Park sports ground** is being considered as an additional **flood storage area**.

There are **planning restrictions** on **new housing developments** built on the **Ock flood plain**, stating they must have **improved drainage systems**.

Improvements have been made to **riparian buffers** along smaller rivers. Planting trees **reduces** the **volume** of **water** reaching the **Thames** and **Ock** rivers where the **flood problem** is **greater**.

Local voluntary **flood wardens** communicate **advice** and **warnings**.

There's **detailed advice** on the **internet** about **reducing flood damage**, e.g. by raising cupboards and using water-resistant plaster.

Map labels: A34, Tilsley Park, Abingdon boundary, River Thames, Ock flood plain, Thames flood plain, Tesco, River Ock, River Thames

Tesco were forced to **revise** recent extension plans — they had to add **drainage improvements** such as **soakaways** and **permeable tarmac**.

The Environment Agency's **Local Flood Warning Plan** warns **specific areas** at risk and provides a **24 hour Floodline**.

There are **restrictions** on **land use**, e.g. planning permission was **refused** for buildings on the **Thames flood plain**.

Soft Engineering Reduces Damage but Floods Still Happen

1) It's **difficult** to **measure** the **success** of flood defences because it's hard to figure out if any reduction in flooding was because of the **success** of new defences, or because the weather conditions were **less severe**.

2) Several **flood warnings** were issued by the **Environment Agency** in early **2008**.

3) The **Ock flood plain**, which has developments on, **didn't get flooded**. The Thames flood plain did get **flooded** but it's largely **clear of development**, due to **land use management** and **planning restrictions**.

4) The **2008 floods** did **less damage** than in previous years, with **minimal cost**, **little disruption** to community services, **no lives lost** and only a **few injuries**. However, **flooding** does still happen in **Abingdon**.

Practice Questions

Q1 List the types of hard engineering used on the Yangtze.

Q2 List the types of soft engineering used around Abingdon.

Exam Question

Q1 With reference to named examples, discuss the success of different engineering approaches to flood prevention. [10 marks]

Maybe if we all get together and ask the clouds to please not rain...

You can't ask for two case studies more different than these. You need to know who's built what, where, and why — and if it's successful.

Introduction to Coastal Environments

Coastal environments are the areas where the land meets the sea. And they're almost as exciting as they sound...

Coasts are Systems — They Have Inputs, Processes and Outputs

Sediment cells in England and Wales

1) **INPUTS** — **river sediment**, sediment from **cliffs** that have been **eroded** or suffered **landslides**, and sediment that has been **transported** by waves from **offshore** (out at sea).

2) **PROCESSES** — **wave action**, **tidal movement**, **erosion**, **weathering**, **transportation**, **deposition**.

3) **OUTPUTS** — sediment **washed out to sea**, or deposited **further along** the coast.

> **Coastal sediment cells** (also called **littoral cells**) are lengths of coastline that are pretty much entirely **self-contained** for the movement of sediment. Each one is a **coastal system**. So **processes** going on in **one cell** don't affect the movement of sediment in **another** cell.

Waves are Responsible for Erosion and Deposition of Beach Sediment

1) **Waves** are created by the **wind** blowing over the surface of the sea. The **friction** between the wind and the surface of the sea gives the water a **circular motion**.

2) The **effect of a wave** on the **shore** depends on its **height**. Wave height is affected by the **wind speed** and the **fetch** of the wave. The fetch is the **maximum distance of sea** the wind has blown over in creating the waves. A **high wind speed** and a **long fetch** create **high** waves.

3) As waves approach the shore they **break**. **Friction** with the sea bed **slows** the bottom of the waves and makes their motion more elliptical (squashed and oval-shaped). The **crest** of the wave rises up and then **collapses**.

4) Water washing **up** the beach is called the **swash**. Water washing **back** towards the sea is called the **backwash**.

5) There are **two types** of wave:

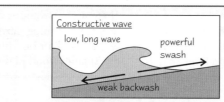

Constructive waves have a **low frequency** (only around **6-8** waves per minute). They're **low and long**, which gives them a more **elliptical** cross profile. The powerful swash carries material up the beach and **deposits** it.

Destructive waves are **high** and **steep**, with a more **circular** cross profile. They have a **higher frequency** (**10-14** waves a minute). The strong backwash **removes** material from the beach.

Wave frequency is how many waves pass a point in a particular time.

6) The waves in an area are usually mainly constructive or mainly destructive.

Tides Affect Where Waves Break

Tides are the periodic **rise** and **fall** of the **ocean surface**. They're caused by the gravitational pull of the **Moon** and the **Sun**. Tides affect the **position** at which **waves break** on the beach (at high tide they break higher up the shore). The area of land between **maximum high tide** and **minimum low tide** is where landforms are created and destroyed.

See page 52 for more on weathering.

Sub-aerial Weathering Occurs Along the Coastline

1) **Sub-aerial weathering** describes coastal processes that are **not linked** to the action of the sea. It includes **freeze-thaw weathering** and **salt weathering**. Weathering **weakens cliffs** and makes them **more vulnerable** to **erosion**.

2) **Throughflow** (the flow of water through the cliffs) and **runoff** (the flow of water over the land) caused by **heavy rain** can also make cliffs more **unstable** and increase the likelihood of **mass movement**.

3) Mass movement is the **movement** of material **downhill** due to gravity. It includes **landslides**, **slumping** (a type of landslide) and **rockfalls**.

Introduction to Coastal Environments

There are **Five** Main Ways **Waves Erode** the **Coastline**

Waves don't just erode beaches — they also erode **rocks** and **cliffs**. Here are the five main ways they do it:

1) **Abrasion/corrasion** — Bits of rock and sediment transported by the waves smash and grind against rocks and cliffs, breaking bits off and smoothing surfaces.

2) **Hydraulic action** — Air in cracks in cliffs is **compressed** when waves crash in. The pressure exerted by the compressed air breaks off rock pieces.

3) **Quarrying** — The energy of a wave as it breaks against a cliff is enough to detach bits of rock.

4) **Corrosion/solution** — **Soluble rocks** (e.g. limestone, chalk) get gradually **dissolved** by the seawater.

5) **Attrition** — Bits of rock in the water smash against **each other** and break into smaller bits.

The **Rate** at Which a Stretch of Coastline is Eroded Depends on **Several Factors**

1) **The width of beach** — i.e. the distance between high and low tide marks. Beaches slow down waves, reducing their erosive power. So a wide, flat beach will protect cliffs more than narrow, steeper beaches.

2) **The breaking point of the waves** — a wave that breaks directly at the foot of a cliff transfers the most energy to the cliff and causes the most erosion. Waves that hit the cliff before they break, or break further offshore will erode much less.

3) **The aspect** — if the coastline faces the dominant wind and wave direction, erosion will be faster.

4) **The fetch of the waves** — waves with a longer fetch are much higher and steeper, and have more energy, so will cause the most erosion.

5) **Rock type** — hard rocks like granite are much more resistant to erosion than softer rocks, e.g. clay.

See page 25 for a case study of coastal erosion.

Currents Transport **Sediment**

1) A **current** is the general flow of water in one direction.

2) Currents move material **along** the coast — this is called **longshore drift**.

3) **Swash** carries sediment (e.g. shingle, pebbles) **up** the beach, **parallel** to the prevailing wind. **Backwash** carries sediment back **down** the beach, at **right angles** to the shoreline.

4) When there's an **angle** between the prevailing wind and the shoreline, a few rounds of swash and backwash move the sediment **along** the shoreline.

Longshore Drift: waves following prevailing wind

longshore drift

← = swash
← = backwash

Practice Questions

Q1 Draw a table to show the main inputs, processes and outputs of a coastal system.

Q2 Sketch a diagram to show how longshore drift works.

Exam Questions

Q1 Describe the characteristics of constructive and destructive waves.   [4 marks]

Q2 Outline how cliffs are eroded along the coastline.   [6 marks]

What did the sea say to the beach — nothing, it just waved...

You really need to get your head around all the processes going on at the coast — cliffs are eroded and weathered, currents carry sediment about and constructive waves deposit it. Then there are destructive waves that annoyingly remove prime sunbathing spots.

Coastal Landforms

Get your bucket and spade ready — it's time to learn about coastal landforms. Wait a minute, where are the sandcastles...

Some **Coastal Landforms** are Caused by **Erosion**

CLIFFS AND WAVE-CUT PLATFORMS

1) **Cliffs** are a common coastal landform. Over time, cliffs **retreat** due to the action of **waves** and **weathering**.

2) Weathering and wave erosion cause a **notch** to form at the high water mark. This eventually develops into a **cave**.

3) Rock above the cave becomes **unstable** with nothing to support it, and it **collapses**.

4) **Wave-cut platforms** are **flat surfaces** left behind when a cliff is eroded.

HEADLANDS AND BAYS

1) **Headlands** and **bays** form where there are **bands** of alternating **hard rock** and **soft rock** at **right angles** to the shoreline.

2) The **soft rock** is **eroded quickly**, forming a **bay**. The harder rock is **eroded less** and sticks out as a **headland**.

CAVES, BLOW HOLES, ARCHES AND STACKS

1) Weak areas in rock (e.g. joints) are **eroded** to form **caves**.

2) Occasionally, the roof of a cave is **weakened** along a major joint by **hydraulic pressure** and the roof **collapses** to form a **blow hole**.

3) Caves on the opposite sides of a narrow headland may eventually join up to form an **arch**.

4) When an **arch** collapses, it forms a **stack**.

Coastal Landforms

Some **Coastal Landforms** are Caused by **Deposition**

BEACHES

1) **Beaches** are formed when **constructive** waves **deposit sediment** on the shore.

2) **Shingle** beaches are **steep** and **narrow**. They're made up of **larger** particles, which pile up at steep angles. **Sand** beaches, formed from **smaller** particles, are **wide** and **flat**.

Beaches have their own **associated features**:

1) **Berms** are **ridges** of sand and pebbles (about 1-2 metres high) found at **high tide** marks. They're formed by deposition of coarse material at the limit of the **swash**.

2) **Runnels** are **grooves** in the sand running **parallel** to the shore. They're formed by **backwash** draining to the sea.

3) **Cusps** are **crescent-shaped indentations** that form on beaches of mixed sand and shingle. It's **not known** exactly how they form, but they develop in areas where waves break parallel to the beach and where there's a large **tidal range** (the difference in height between **high** and **low tides**).

SPITS

Spits tend to form where the coast suddenly **changes direction**, e.g. across river mouths.

Longshore drift (see p. 21) continues to **deposit** material across the river mouth, leaving a bank of **sand** and **shingle** sticking out into the sea.

Occasional **changes** to the dominant wind and wave direction may lead to a spit having a **curved end** (the fancy name for this is a **recurved end**).

Over time, several recurved ends may be abandoned as the waves return to their **original direction**.

The area **behind** the spit is **sheltered** from the waves and often develops into **mudflats** and **salt marshes** (see p. 24).

Watch out for the spit...

Coastal Landforms

Chaz was a bit annoyed that the bar didn't go right across the river, but he was enjoying the lagoon...

BARS

1) Bars are formed when a **spit joins two headlands together**.

2) This can occur across a **bay** or across a **river mouth** (if the river isn't too strong).

3) A **lagoon** forms **behind** the bar.

SAND DUNES

1) Sand dunes are formed when **sand deposited** by longshore drift is moved up the beach by the **wind**.

2) Sand trapped by driftwood or berms (see previous page) is colonised by **plants** and **grasses**, e.g. marram grass. The vegetation **stabilises** the sand and encourages **more sand** to accumulate there, forming **embryo dunes**.

3) Over time, the oldest dunes migrate inland as newer embryo dunes are formed. These **mature dunes** can reach heights of up to 10 m.

©iStockphoto.com/Eric Gevaert

SALT MARSHES

1) Salt marshes form in areas of **sheltered water**, e.g. river estuaries or behind spits.

2) As **silt** and **mud** are **deposited** by the river or the tide, **mudflats** develop.

3) The mudflats are colonised by **vegetation** that can survive the **high salt levels** and long periods of **submergence** by the tide.

4) The plants **trap more mud** and **silt**, and gradually they create an area of marshland that remains **exposed** for longer and longer **between tides**.

©iStockphoto.com/Linda Steward

Practice Questions

Q1 Name four landforms of coastal erosion and four landforms of coastal deposition.

Q2 Describe where headlands and bays form.

Q3 Briefly describe how stacks are formed.

Q4 What are berms, runnels and cusps?

Q5 Where do salt marshes form?

Exam Questions

Q1 Describe how erosion can create a wave-cut platform. [5 marks]

Q2 Describe how spits are formed. [6 marks]

Man walks into a bar, gets his feet wet...

At AS level, the landforms you have to know are pretty much the same ones you have to know for GCSE (not much help if you didn't do GCSE, I know, but then they're not that hard to learn anyway). You just need to know more detail about the processes involved in their formation. And you thought it was going to be all excitement and glamour once you got to AS level. Sorry.

Coastal Erosion — Case Study

The Holderness coastline in East Yorkshire is the fastest eroding coastline in Europe (what a claim to fame).
If you get a case study question in the exam you need to have a bagful of juicy facts at the ready, so get learnin'.

The Average **Rate of Erosion** at Holderness is About **1.8 Metres per Year**

The Holderness coastline is **61 km long** — it stretches from Flamborough Head to Spurn Head. In some places, e.g. **Great Cowden**, the rate of erosion has been over **10 m/year** in recent years. The main **reasons** for this rapid erosion at Holderness are shown in **purple**. Some of the possible **social**, **economic** and **environmental impacts** of the erosion are also shown.

1) **Easily eroded rock type** — the cliffs are mostly made of **till** (or 'boulder clay'). Not only is till **easily eroded** through **corrasion**, but it's also prone to **slumping** when wet.

2) **Narrow beaches** — beaches slow the waves, **reducing** their **erosive power**. Narrow beaches **protect** the cliffs **less**. Beaches along the Holderness coast are narrow for two main reasons:
- **Flamborough Head stops sediment** from the north replenishing the beaches along Holderness. It's also made of **chalk**, which dissolves when eroded rather than making sand for the beaches.
- **Coastal defences**, e.g. at Mappleton (see p. 30 for why these lead to narrow beaches). This is a **human** cause of erosion.

3) **Powerful waves** — the waves are powerful because of:
- The **long fetch** (all the way from the **Arctic Ocean**).
- The coast faces the **dominant wind** and **wave direction** (from the **north-east**).

1) **Property prices** along the coast have **fallen** sharply for those houses at risk from erosion.

2) Around **30 villages** have been lost since **Roman times**.

3) **Visitor numbers in Bridlington dropped** by over **30%** between **1998** and **2006** (though this could have been due to other reasons).

4) Many **caravan parks** are at risk from erosion, e.g. **Seaside Caravan Park** at **Ulrome** is losing an average of **10 pitches a year**.

5) **£2 million** was spent at **Mappleton** in **1991** to **protect** the coast.

6) The **Gas Terminal** at **Easington** is at risk (it's only **25 m** from the cliff edge). This terminal accounts for **25%** of **Britain's gas supply**.

7) **80 000 m²** of good quality **farmland** is lost each year. This has a huge effect on **farmers' livelihoods**.

8) Some **SSSIs** (Sites of Special Scientific Interest) are threatened — e.g. **The Lagoons** near **Easington** are part of an SSSI. It has a colony of over 1% of the British breeding population of **little terns**. The lagoons are separated from the sea by a narrow strip of sand and shingle. Erosion of this would connect the lakes to the sea and 'The Lagoons' would be destroyed.

Map labels: CHALK, Bridlington, Flamborough Head, Ulrome, Mappleton, longshore drift, BOULDER CLAY, Easington, Humber Estuary, Spurn Head

Practice Questions

Q1 For a named area, briefly describe three impacts of coastal erosion.

Exam Question

Q1 With reference to one named area describe and explain the causes of coastal erosion. [15 marks]

Like easily eroded till, I'll be gone when the morning comes...

You need to know a case study of coastal erosion as well as you know how to make beans on toast. Draw an annotated diagram to refresh your memory... toast, then butter, then beans, er... sorry, I mean label the physical causes, human causes and impacts.

Sea Level Changes

There's a fair bit to learn on these two pages. Just try and keep your head above the water...

Coastal Flooding is Now More Likely Because of Rising Sea Level

1) Sea level **varies** on a daily basis with the **tidal cycle**. **Onshore winds** and **low atmospheric pressure systems** also cause the sea surface to rise **temporarily**.

2) On a much longer time scale, global sea level is rising at almost **2 mm** each year, which is forecast to **increase to 4 or 5 mm** a year by 2100.

3) This will increase both the **frequency** and **severity** of flooding in low-lying coastal areas.

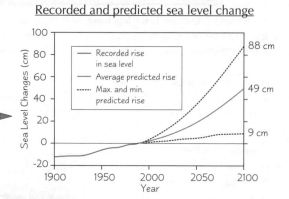

Recorded and predicted sea level change

Sea Level Changes are Either Eustatic or Isostatic

EUSTATIC

Eustatic sea level change is caused by a change in the **volume of water** in the sea, or by a change in the **shape** of the **ocean basins**.

The effects are always **global** and the main **causes** are:

1) **Tectonic movements** of the Earth's crust that alter the shape (and so the volume) of ocean basins. E.g. sea floor spreading **increases** the **volume** of the basin and so **decreases** sea level.

2) **Changes in climate**. Different changes affect sea level in different ways:

- An **increase** in **temperature** causes **melting** of **ice sheets**, which **increases** sea level. It also causes water to **expand**, which **increases** sea level further.

- A **decrease** in **temperature** causes more precipitation to fall as **snow**. This increases the volume of water **stored** in **glaciers** and so reduces the volume of the sea, which **decreases** sea level.

ISOSTATIC

Isostatic sea level change is caused by **vertical movements** of the land **relative** to the sea.

Any **downward** movement of the land causes sea level to **rise** locally, while **uplift of land** causes sea level to **fall**.

The effects are always **local** and the main **causes** are:

1) **Tectonic** (crustal) uplift or depression, which occurs mostly at plate boundaries.

2) **Compression** or **decompression** of the Earth's crust due to accumulation or melting of **ice sheets**. Slow uplift of land can continue for thousands of years after the weight of a **retreating glacier** has gone. **Accumulation of sediment**, mostly at the mouths of major rivers, can also cause **compression**.

3) **Subsidence** of land due to shrinkage after **abstraction of groundwater**, e.g. drainage of marshland.

Sea Level Rise Can Have a Variety of Impacts

1) **More frequent** and **more severe coastal flooding**.
Flooding of low-lying areas has increased with sea level rise and it will increase more with further rises. For example, at the beginning of the 20th century **St Mark's Square** in **Venice** flooded less than **10** times per year, and in **1996** it was flooded almost **100** times.

2) **Submergence of low-lying islands**.
Lots of low-lying islands have **disappeared** as sea level has risen, and loads more are **at risk** of disappearing. For example, if the sea level rises by just **0.5 m** from the current level then most of the **Maldives** would be submerged.

3) **Changes in the coastline**.
As sea levels rise the coastline changes — **islands** are **created** and the **area** of **land** is **decreased**. E.g. over the last 10 000 years sea level rise has separated Britain from mainland Europe. If the sea level rises **0.3 m** from the current level **8000 km²** of land in **Bangladesh** will be lost.

Barry and Ami wish they hadn't delayed their holiday to the Maldives.

Don't forget that all these impacts have **further impacts**, e.g. damage to coastal **infrastructure**, decrease in **tourism**, decrease in **agriculture**, loss of **homes** etc.

Sea Level Changes

Sea Level Rise Results in Coastlines of Submergence

When sea level rises relative to the coast, the sea **submerges** (drowns) the existing coastline. This creates different **landforms**:

① **RIAS** are formed where **river valleys** are partially **submerged**, e.g. Milford Haven in South Wales is a ria. Rias have a **gentle** long- and cross-profile. They're **wide** and **deep** at their **mouth**, becoming **narrower** and **shallower** the further **inland** they reach.

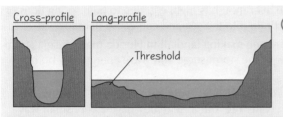

② **FJORDS** are a lot like rias, but they're **drowned glacial valleys** rather than drowned river valleys. They're relatively **straight** and narrow, with very **steep sides**. They have a **shallow mouth** caused by a raised bit of ground (called the **threshold**) formed by deposition of material by the glacier. They're very **deep** further **inland**, e.g. Sognefjorden in Norway is over 1000 m deep in places.

③ In areas where **valleys** lie **parallel** to the coast, an increase in sea level can form a **DALMATIAN COASTLINE**. Valleys are flooded, leaving **islands** parallel to the coastline. It's named after the Dalmatian coast in Croatia.

Sea Level Fall Results in Coastlines of Emergence

When sea level falls relative to the coast, new coastline **emerges** (appears) from the sea. This creates different **landforms**:

1) **Raised beaches** are formed when the fall in sea level **exposes wave-cut platforms** and their **beaches**. Over time, beach sediment becomes **vegetated** and develops into **soil**.

2) The **cliffs** above raised beaches are no longer eroded by the sea, and slowly get covered by **vegetation**. They're called **relict cliffs**. It's not uncommon to see **wave-cut notches**, **caves**, **arches** and **stacks** within relict cliffs. These **raised features** are gradually **degraded** (weathered) over time.

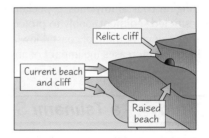

Practice Questions

Q1 State two causes of eustatic sea level change and two causes of isostatic sea level change.

Q2 Give two examples of landforms that show there must have been a drop in sea levels.

Q3 Sketch a diagram showing the cross-profile of a fjord.

Exam Questions

Q1 Describe the possible impacts of sea level rise. [8 marks]

Q2 Describe and explain how coastal submergence can result in a range of landforms. [8 marks]

I'd start moving up onto high ground now...

You need to know that sea levels are rising, and the impacts of sea level rise. Examiners love asking questions about current issues and rising sea levels are a hot topic in the news at the moment — so make sure you're hot on all the details too.

Coastal Flooding

As well as a slow rise in sea level, coastal areas are at risk of flooding because of a number of physical and human causes...

Coastal Flooding *Occurs Naturally Due to* **Physical Causes**

Coastal lowlands (such as coastal plains, salt marshes and deltas) are liable to flooding when the sea rises above normal high-tide level. There are several **physical causes** of this:

1) **Low pressure atmospheric systems** such as **hurricanes** (cyclones) reduce atmospheric pressure on the sea surface, causing it to **rise**. This is called a **storm surge**.

2) **Strong onshore winds** can force water to higher levels along the coast, allowing waves further inland.

3) **Tidal currents** and **surges** may be funnelled into a coastal bottleneck such as the Bay of Bengal, or English Channel, forcing sea levels higher.

4) **High rainfall** may cause **high river discharge**. If sea level at the river mouth is high, e.g. due to high spring tides or storm surges, the large volume of river water may be **unable to drain** into the sea and can cause flooding.

5) When a **combination of the above factors** coincide. E.g. a hurricane making landfall in Florida may cause a storm surge and high rainfall (which may be unable to drain to the sea). The storm surge and wave energy may both be intensified by strong onshore winds.

6) **Tsunamis** are huge ocean waves caused when water is displaced by **landslides**, **volcanic eruptions** or **submarine earthquakes** that shift the ocean floor. When travelling in open water (i.e. out at sea) they have a very small wave height (less than a metre) and travel at hundreds of kilometres an hour. As the waves approach the coast, the bottom of the waves slow considerably due to friction with the sea bed, causing the wave height to increase enormously.

Coastal Flooding *May Also be* **Caused** *or* **Intensified** *by* **Human Activity**

1) **Management of river systems** — some management strategies (e.g. dams) trap sediment and so reduce the amount being deposited at the river's mouth. This causes deltas and salt marshes to shrink, providing less protection against high tides and storm surges.

2) **Management of coastal systems** — some management strategies alter sediment movement, reducing the amount of protective beach material further along the coast. E.g. coastal defences at Barton in Hampshire have reduced sediment transport to the east, allowing Hurst Spit to be breached more often, flooding lowlands behind.

3) **Building on coastal lowlands**, especially sand dunes, has restricted sediment supply to protective beaches and marshes. Development of coastal lowlands, such as Florida, also **increases** the **impact** of any coastal floods.

4) **Reclamation of coastal lowlands**, such as the Dutch polders, and reclaimed marshes along the east coast of England. Draining this land to reclaim it causes the land to shrink to become lower than sea level.

Case Study — *a* **Tsunami** *Struck* **Southern Asia** *on* **26th December 2004**

The **tsunami** that devastated areas of **Indonesia**, **Sri Lanka**, **Thailand** and **India** in December 2004 was caused by a submarine **earthquake** in the Indian Ocean. The earthquake is estimated to have measured **9.0** on the Richter scale, making it one of the **strongest earthquakes** ever recorded. The map below shows some of the countries **most affected** by the tsunami.

The tsunami travelled across the Bay of Bengal at speeds up to 800 kilometres per hour. The waves struck south-eastern India just two hours after the earthquake.

The tsunami reached more than 2 km inland at Trincomalee in the north-east of Sri Lanka.

Waves up to 30 m high struck the Indonesian island of Sumatra within minutes of the earthquake.

The epicentre of the earthquake was off the western coast of Sumatra in Indonesia.

Coastal Flooding

The Tsunami Had Severe Social, Economic and Environmental Impacts

Social

1) It was the **deadliest** tsunami **ever recorded**, with an estimated **230 000 people killed** or **missing**.
2) It's estimated that **1.7 million people** were made **homeless**.
3) Many sources of fresh **drinking water** were **polluted**, either by **sewage** or by **saltwater**.
4) An estimated **400 000 lost their jobs** in **Sri Lanka** alone.

The remains of a house in a destroyed village in Indonesia.

A destroyed fishing boat on a beach in Phuket, Thailand.

Economic

1) Estimates of the **cost** of the initial **damage** caused by the tsunami are between **$8 billion** and **$15 billion**.
2) **Fishing** is a large part of the economy for many of the areas hit by the tsunami. **Boats, nets** and other **equipment** were **destroyed** or **lost**, severely affecting the livelihood of fishermen.
3) **Salinisation** (increase in salt content) of land has severely **reduced soil fertility**. **Crop production** will be **lower** for several years to come.
4) **Tourism** is important to the economy of many of the countries affected. **25%** of hotels in southern **Thailand** were **closed** for at least **6 months** because of damage and the number of **foreign visitors** to the island of **Phuket dropped 80%** in 2005 as the area was perceived to be less safe.

Environmental

1) **8 million litres of oil** were released into the environment after **two oil plants** in Indonesia were **destroyed**. The oil caused widespread **pollution** at sea and **contamination** of the soil, posing **health risks** to humans in the area.
2) **Mangrove forests** as far away as the **East African coast** were **damaged** by the force of the waves, or **covered in layers of silt**.
3) The **high salt content** of the floodwater **destroyed** the natural balance of many **ecosystems**, e.g. the **Karagan Lagoon** in southern **Sri Lanka**.

Mangrove trees uprooted by the waves.

Human Activity Increased the Impact of the Flooding

1) **Mangrove forests** protected parts of the **Sri Lankan coast** by **absorbing wave energy**. Pressure for **tourist development** and the creation of intensive **prawn fisheries** has led to the **destruction** of mangrove forests in other areas around the Indian Ocean. It's estimated that **Thailand** has lost up to **half** of its mangrove forests since **1975**. The lack of protection meant that waves could reach **further inland** and the **flooding** was **much worse** than in areas protected by mangroves.

2) It's thought that healthy **coral reefs** surrounding the **Maldives** acted as a **breakwater** (reducing the power of the tsunami waves) and prevented the complete destruction of the low-lying islands. Illegal **coral mining** and the use of dynamite in explosive 'blast fishing' has **destroyed** many offshore coral reefs in the Indian Ocean. This reduced the level of natural protection from the waves.

Practice Questions

Q1 What is a storm surge?
Q2 Describe how the characteristics of a tsunami change as it approaches the coast.
Q3 Describe three physical and three human causes of coastal flooding.

Exam Question

Q1 Describe and explain the causes and effects of coastal flooding in a named coastal area. [10 marks]

Coastal flooding — it really is no joke...

You can see from these pages the huge impact of coastal flooding on humans and the environment. Make sure you know a case study of the causes and effects of coastal flooding in a specific area — it's one the examiners love to ask you about.

Coastal Management

Coastal management is a complex thing. Fixing up one coastal area can have the unintended effect of messing up another area nearby.

See pages 25 and 29 for some examples of the impacts of coastal erosion and flooding.

Only **Some Parts** of the **Coast** are **Managed**

The aim of coastal management is to **protect homes**, **businesses** and the **environment** from **erosion** and **flooding**.

This is because flooding and erosion of the coastline can have severe social, **economic** and **environmental impacts**.

All coastal settlements want to be defended, but the amount of **money available** is **limited** so not everywhere can be defended. Choosing which places are defended (and how) is based on a **cost-benefit analysis**. The money available is usually used to protect **large settlements** and important **industrial sites**, rather than isolated or small settlements.

There are **Four Options** for **Coastal Management**

1) **Hold the line** — maintain the **existing** coastal defences.
2) **Advance the line** — build **new** coastal defences **further out to sea** than the existing line of defence.
3) **Do nothing** — build **no** coastal defences at all, and deal with erosion and flooding **as it happens**.
4) **Retreat the line** — build no coastal defences, but **move people away** from the coast.

Coastal Defences Include **Hard Engineering** and **Soft Engineering**

Hard Engineering Defences Involve **Built Structures**

Defence	How it works	Cost	Disadvantage
Sea wall	The wall reflects waves back out to sea, preventing erosion of the coast. It also acts as a barrier to prevent flooding.	Expensive to build and maintain	It creates a strong backwash, which erodes under the wall.
Revetment	Revetments are slanted structures built at the foot of cliffs. They can be made from concrete, wood or rocks. Waves break against the revetments, which absorb the wave energy and so prevent cliff erosion.	Expensive to build, but relatively cheap to maintain	They create a strong backwash, as above.
Gabions	Gabions are rock-filled cages. A wall of gabions is usually built at the foot of cliffs. The gabions absorb wave energy and so reduce erosion.	Cheap	Ugly
Riprap	Boulders piled up along the coast are called riprap. The boulders absorb wave energy and so reduce erosion.	Fairly cheap	Can shift in storms.
Groynes	Groynes are fences built at right angles to the coast. They trap beach material transported by longshore drift. This creates wider beaches, which slow the waves (reducing their energy) and so gives greater protection from flooding and erosion.	Quite cheap	They starve down-drift beaches of sand. Thinner beaches don't protect the coast as well, leading to greater erosion and flooding.
Breakwaters	Breakwaters are usually concrete blocks or boulders deposited off the coast. They force waves to break offshore. The waves' energy and erosive power are reduced before they reach the shore.	Expensive	Can be damaged in storms.
Earth bank	Mounds of earth act as a barrier to prevent flooding.	Quite expensive	Can be eroded.
Tidal barrier	Tidal barriers are built across river estuaries. They contain retractable floodgates that can be raised to prevent flooding from storm surges.	VERY expensive	Really, VERY expensive.
Tidal barrage	Tidal barrages are dams built across river estuaries. Their main purpose is to generate electricity. Water is trapped behind the dam at high tide. Controlled release of water through turbines in the dam at low tide generates electricity. They also prevent flooding from storm surges.	VERY expensive	They disrupt sediment flow, which may cause increased erosion elsewhere in the estuary.

Coastal Management

Soft Engineering Defences Involve Coaxing Natural Processes Along

1) **Beach nourishment** is where **sand** and **shingle** are added to beaches from elsewhere (e.g. **dredged** from offshore). This creates **wide** beaches, which **reduce erosion** of cliffs more than thin beaches.

2) **Beach stabilisation** can be done by **reducing the slope angle** and planting **vegetation**, or by sticking **stakes** and **old tree trunks** in the beach to stabilise the sand. It also creates **wide** beaches, which **reduce erosion** of cliffs.

3) **Dune regeneration** is where sand dunes are **created** or **restored** by either nourishment or stabilisation of the sand. Sand dunes provide a **barrier** between land and sea, **absorbing wave energy** and preventing flooding and erosion.

4) **Land use management** is important for dune regeneration. The vegetation needed to stabilise the dune can easily be **trampled** and destroyed, leaving the dune **vulnerable** to **erosion**. Wooden **walkways** across dunes, and **fenced-off areas** that prevent walkers, cyclists or 4×4 drivers from gaining access to the dunes, all **reduce vegetation loss**.

5) **Creating marshland** from mudflats can be encouraged by **planting** appropriate vegetation (e.g. **glassworts**). The vegetation **stabilises** the sediment, and the stems and leaves help **reduce the speed** of the waves. This **reduces** their **erosive power** and **how far** the waves reach **inland**, leading to **less flooding** of the area around the marsh.

6) **Coastal realignment** (also known as **managed retreat**) involves breaching an existing defence and allowing the sea to flood the land behind. Over time, vegetation will colonise the land and it'll become **marshland**.

Soft Engineering is More Sustainable than Hard Engineering

Hard engineering is often expensive, and disrupts natural processes. Soft engineering schemes tend to be cheaper and require much less time and money to maintain than hard engineering schemes. Soft engineering is designed to integrate with the natural environment and it creates areas like marshland and sand dunes, which are important habitats for coastal plants and animals. So soft engineering is a more sustainable management strategy than hard engineering because it has a lower environmental impact and economic cost.

Management Strategies for the Future Must be Sustainable

1) **Rising sea level** means **more** coastal management will be **needed** to protect coastal settlements and developments. **Storms** also seem to be getting **more frequent** and **more severe**, increasing the need further.

2) There's growing emphasis on the need for **more sustainable management strategies**, i.e. soft engineering.

3) Deciding how to manage a coastline is now done in a more **integrated** way to **improve sustainability**. For example, a **Shoreline Management Plan** (SMP) is a plan for how the coastline in one **sediment cell** (see p. 20) should be managed. SMPs are developed by **local authorities**. All the local authorities in one sediment cell **co-operate** when planning their coastal management strategy, so that defences in one area don't increase erosion in an adjacent area in the same cell.

4) The **process** of trying to come up with an integrated, sustainable management plan is called **Integrated Coastal Zone Management** (ICZM).

Practice Questions

Q1   What is the aim of coastal management?

Q2   What are: a) gabions,
                b) groynes,
                c) revetments?

Q3   What other options are there for coastal management, apart from hard and soft engineering?

Exam Question

Q1   Explain why soft engineering schemes are more sustainable than hard engineering schemes.   [6 marks]

Do nothing? Retreat? Sounds like a lousy revision strategy to me...

Coastal management sounds like a difficult and unending job. Even after spending hundreds of thousands of pounds on a nice big concrete wall to keep the waves out, and some wooden groynes to hold the beach in place, it can still all go horrendously wrong. When it goes wrong, it costs even more money. These days they try to use sustainable methods instead, but it's still hard.

Coastal Management — Case Studies

You need to know case studies of coastal management. Wait a minute, what's this I see...

Hard Engineering Has Been Used Along Holderness

The Holderness coast is the fastest eroding coastline in Europe. Page 25 outlines the main reasons for the rapid erosion and the social, economic and environmental impacts of the erosion. A total of **11.4 km** of the 61 km coastline is currently protected by **hard** engineering:

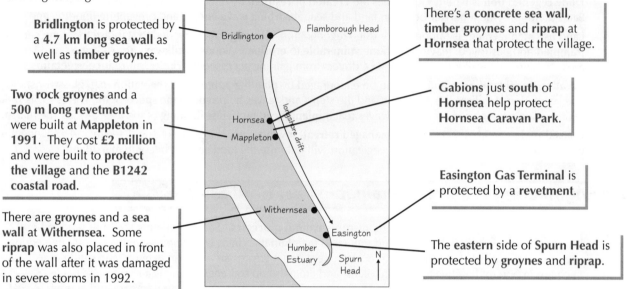

Bridlington is protected by a **4.7 km long sea wall** as well as **timber groynes**.

Two rock groynes and a **500 m long revetment** were built at **Mappleton** in **1991**. They cost **£2 million** and were built to **protect the village** and the B1242 coastal road.

There are **groynes** and a **sea wall** at **Withernsea**. Some **riprap** was also placed in front of the wall after it was damaged in severe storms in 1992.

There's a **concrete sea wall**, **timber groynes** and **riprap** at **Hornsea** that protect the village.

Gabions just **south of Hornsea** help protect **Hornsea Caravan Park**.

Easington Gas Terminal is protected by a **revetment**.

The **eastern** side of **Spurn Head** is protected by **groynes** and **riprap**.

The Schemes are Locally Successful but Cause Problems Down-drift

1) The groynes **trap sediment**, increasing the **width** of the **beaches**. This **protects** the **local area** but **increases erosion** of the cliffs **down-drift** (as the material eroded from the beaches there isn't replenished). E.g. the Mappleton scheme has caused **increased erosion** of the cliffs **south of Mappleton**. **Cowden Farm**, just south of Mappleton, is now at risk of falling into the sea.

2) The **sediment** produced from the erosion of the Holderness coastline is normally washed into the **Humber Estuary** (where it helps to form **tidal mudflats**) and down the **Lincolnshire coast**. Reduction in this sediment **increases the risk of flooding** along the Humber Estuary, and **increases erosion** along the Lincolnshire coast.

3) The protection of local areas is leading to the **formation of bays** between the areas. As bays develop the wave pressure on headlands will increase and eventually the **cost** of maintaining the sea defences may become **too high**.

4) All these problems make the existing schemes **unsustainable**.

Possible Schemes All Have Problems

See p. 31 for more on SMPs.

1) The **SMP** for Holderness for the next 50 years recommends '**holding the line**' at **some settlements** (e.g. at Bridlington, Withernsea, Hornsea, Mappleton and Easington Gas Terminal) and '**doing nothing**' along more **unpopulated stretches**. However, this is **unpopular** with owners of land or property along the stretches where nothing is being done.

2) **Coastal realignment** of businesses has been suggested, e.g. relocating **caravan parks** further inland. This would be a **more sustainable** scheme as it would allow the coast to be eroded as normal without endangering businesses. However, there are issues surrounding how much businesses will be **compensated** by for relocating. Also, relocation isn't always possible, e.g. farmland can't be 'relocated', and there may be no land for sale to relocate buildings to.

3) A **sea wall** has been proposed to better protect **Easington Gas Terminal**. This would cost **£4.5 million**. The problem is that it would reduce sediment flow to the south, **increasing erosion** at the **village of Easington** (with a population of **700 people**). A **longer sea wall** could be built that would protect the village as well as the gas terminal, but that would cost **£7 million**.

4) **Offshore reefs** made from **concrete-filled tyres** have been proposed to protect the coastline. They act like **breakwaters**. Similar reefs have been built in the USA and have reduced erosion. Some people think that the reefs will **harm the environment** though (although there's currently no evidence of this).

Coastal Management — Case Studies

Soft Engineering Has Been Used Along Blackwater Estuary

Blackwater Estuary is part of the **Essex** coastline. Land in the estuary is being eroded at a rate of **0.3-1 m/year**. In some exposed areas (e.g. **Cobmarsh Island**) the erosion rate is **2 m/year**. The area is also **at risk from flooding** as sea level is rising and the **South** of England is **sinking** relative to the sea. There are some hard engineering schemes in the estuary, but these are becoming too expensive to maintain, so **soft** engineering approaches are now being implemented:

Coastal realignment was implemented at **Tollesbury Fleet** in **1995**. An existing **sea wall** was **breached** and **21 hectares** of farmland were flooded to encourage a **marshland** to form. A **new lower sea wall** was built **further back** on higher ground to protect from flooding.

Beaches have been **nourished** along the estuary, e.g. at **Mersea Island**.

Marsh stabilisation has been carried out by planting **stakes** and **brushwood** on the water line to encourage sediment to build up, e.g. at **Ray Creek**.

In **1991** an existing sea wall was **lowered** and **breached** flooding **0.8 hectares** of land at **Northey Island**.

In **1995** a sea wall was **breached** and **40 hectares** of farmland at **Orplands** were flooded as part of **coastal realignment**.

Coastal realignment has been carried out at **Bradwell-on-Sea** by **breaching** an old sea wall.

Cobmarsh Island / Mersea Island / Ray Creek / Tollesbury Fleet / Northey Island / Blackwater Estuary / Bradwell-on-Sea / Orplands

N

The Schemes are More Sustainable than Hard Engineering Schemes

1) The schemes are **more sustainable** in the **long term**. E.g. to repair the sea wall at Orplands would have cost more than £600 000 (and it would only last for 20 years). The 40 hectares of farmland flooded was valued at around £600 000, but the marshland created would defend the coast for **longer** as it's **self-repairing**.

2) The schemes have created **more marshland**, which provides a larger **habitat** for **wildlife**.

3) However, some areas **haven't changed** to marshland (e.g. parts of the Orpland site are still bare mud, which is easily eroded). Also, **grazing land** has been **lost**.

Practice Questions

Q1   List the types of hard engineering used along the Holderness coast.

Q2   List the types of soft engineering used along the Blackwater Estuary in Essex.

Exam Question

Q1   Evaluate the success of a named coastal management scheme.   [15 marks]

More case studies — what a pain in the groyne...

The best thing to do here is learn the annotated map for each case study. Draw them out over and over again until they're practically tattooed on the inside of your eyelids (it'll hurt a lot less than missing a load of easy marks in the exam, I promise).

Distribution of Cold Environments

You're probably thinking that all cold environments are the same — they're all just, well, cold. Well it turns out that there are different types of cold environment, and it's not quite as simple as chilly, cold and blimmin' freezing.

There are **Three** Main **Reasons** Why Environments Might be **Cold**

1) They're at a **high latitude**. High latitudes are **colder** than lower latitudes because they receive **less solar radiation** (the Sun's energy hits the Earth at more of an angle at high latitudes so it's spread over a larger area).

Latitude lines go horizontally round the Earth, like the equator — the higher you go in latitude (either north or south) the further away you get from the equator.

2) They're at a **high altitude**. High altitudes are colder than lower altitudes because **air temperature decreases** with **increasing altitude**. **Less** of the Sun's energy **reflected** back from the Earth is **trapped** at higher altitudes, making it **colder**. Lower **air pressures** higher up also mean temperatures **drop**. It gets between 6 °C and 10 °C colder for every 1000 m you go up.

3) They're in the **middle** of **continents**. The middle of continents are cold because they're **far away** from the **sea**. In the summer, the **land heats** up **quickly** and the **sea** heats up **slowly**. In the winter, the **land cools quickly** and the **sea** cools **slowly**. So, in winter the sea **warms** the land **near the coast**, but **not** the **interior**. This effect is called **continentality**.

These factors control the **distribution** of the different **types** of cold environment — **glacial**, **periglacial**, **alpine** and **polar**.

Different Types *of* Cold Environment *are* Found *in* Different Places

1 Glacial Environments *are* Found at *High Altitudes and* High Latitudes

1) Glacial environments are areas of land permanently **covered by ice**. Land can be covered by **glaciers** or **ice sheets**:

- Glaciers are masses of **ice** that flow **downhill**. There are two main types — **valley** glaciers and **corrie** glaciers. Valley glaciers **fill valleys** and can be **several kilometres long** (e.g. the Franz Josef Glacier in New Zealand is 12 kilometres long). Corrie glaciers are **smaller** glaciers that are found in bowl-shaped hollows high up in **mountains** (e.g. the Lower Curtis Glacier in Washington State, USA).
- Ice sheets are **domes of ice** covering **huge areas** of land, e.g. the Antarctic Ice Sheet.

2) Glaciers and ice sheets only form where it's **really cold**, so glacial environments are found:

- At **high latitudes**. E.g. the **Antarctic Ice Sheet** (in the southern hemisphere), and the **Greenland Ice Sheet** (in the northern hemisphere) are both entirely **above 60°** latitude.

- At **high altitudes** (regardless of the latitude). E.g. glaciers are found in the **Himalayan mountains** even though they're at a **low latitude** (around **30°**). This is because it's the **highest** mountain range in the world. Glaciers even form at latitudes **close to** the **equator** (e.g. the Antizana glacier in Ecuador).

equator

■ = glacial environments

3) Even though it can be really cold on low altitude land in the middle of continents, glaciers don't form as there's not enough snow.

2 Periglacial Environments *are* Found at *High Altitudes and* Latitudes *and in* Continental Interiors

1) **Periglacial** environments are places where the temperature is frequently or constantly **below freezing**, but **not covered by ice**. They contain a layer of **permafrost** (permanently frozen ground) **on** or **below** the surface.

2) They form where it's persistently **below 0 ºC**, so they're found:

- At **high latitudes**. E.g. the northern parts of Asia, North America and Europe are all periglacial environments with large areas of permafrost.

- At **high altitudes**. Periglacial conditions exist **around ice masses** in **mountain ranges**. They're also found on high altitude **plateau** areas, e.g. the Tibetan plateau in Asia, and the Bolivian plateau in South America.

- In the **interior** of land masses. Periglacial conditions exist at lower latitudes and lower altitudes because of the effect of **continentality**, e.g. Siberia, central Asia.

equator

= periglacial environments

Distribution of Cold Environments

③ Alpine Environments are Found at High Altitudes

1) Alpine environments are cold areas of land at an altitude **above** the **treeline**. The treeline is the **limit** of the area that trees can grow in — above the treeline it's **too cold** for trees to grow.

2) Alpine environments are **always** found at **high altitudes**. Alpine conditions can be found above the treeline on **mountain ranges**, e.g. the Himalayas (Asia), the Andes (South America) and the Alps (Europe). They can exist at **any latitude**, e.g. alpine conditions exist along much of the Rocky mountains in North America, which run north to south from above 50° to around 30° latitude.

3) Alpine environments may **include periglacial** and **glacial** conditions. **Temperature decreases** as altitude increases — permafrost (periglacial conditions) may exist above (and below) the treeline, permanent snow and ice (glacial conditions) may exist even higher up.

④ Polar Environments are Found around the Poles

There are **two** polar environments — one around the **North Pole** (the **Arctic**) and one around the **South Pole** (the **Antarctic**).

1) The Arctic polar environment is **cold** because it exists at a **high latitude**.

2) The Arctic polar environment can be defined either by the **Arctic circle** (**66° N**) or by the **10 °C July isotherm** (areas north of this line have an average temperature **below** 10 °C in **July**, the **hottest** month).

3) The area around the north pole is made up of **sea ice** (frozen sea water). The area of sea ice **shrinks** in the **summer**, leaving **open sea**, and **refreezes** in the **winter**.

4) Much of the Arctic polar environment is made up of the **northern land areas** of Asia, **North America** and **Europe**. The land-based polar environment can include **glacial** environments, e.g. the Greenland Ice Sheet, and **periglacial** environments, e.g. northern Russia.

1) The Antarctic polar environment is **cold** because of its **high latitude** — the Antarctic circle (**66° S** latitude) doesn't go all the way round the land mass of Antarctica though, so the polar environment around the south pole can be defined by the **10 °C January isotherm** (the hottest month in the southern hemisphere).

2) Some of the Antarctic polar environment is also cold because it's at a **high altitude** — the ice in some places is so thick it reaches an altitude of over **4000 m**.

3) The **interior** of Antarctica is also **cold** because of the effect of **continentality** — the centre is hundreds of kilometres from the **warming** effect of the **oceans**.

4) A large area around the Antarctic land mass is made up of **sea ice**. The area of sea ice changes throughout the year, **shrinking** in summer and **refreezing** in winter.

5) Most of the Antarctic polar region is on the huge **land mass** of **Antarctica**. The land-based polar environment includes **glacial** environments, e.g. the Antarctic ice sheet.

Practice Questions

Q1 Where are alpine environments found?

Q2 What's the latitude of the Arctic circle?

Q3 Give three reasons why Antarctica is cold.

Exam Question

Q1 Describe and explain the global distribution of glacial and periglacial environments. [15 marks]

So which is better — north or south? Let's take a poll...

It might not seem like it yet, but cold environments are actually pretty interesting. To really get yourself in the mood for these next few pages, try turning the heating off and opening all the windows, and read them with your scarf and gloves on.

Glaciers

Since plenty of cold environments contain glaciers, you need to know a fair bit about them.
I do like a nice glacier. Pity you have to go to the Alps or Norway to see the nearest ones.

Glaciers are Systems

The glacial system has **inputs**, **stores** and **outputs**.

Inputs These include:

1) **Snow** (from **precipitation** or **avalanches**).

2) **Condensation** of water vapour from the air (which then freezes).

3) **Sublimation** of water vapour from the air directly to ice crystals.

4) Bits of **rock** collected when the glacier carves away at the landscape, and rocks that have fallen onto the glacier from above.

Sublimation involves a direct change of state from a gas to a solid without passing through the liquid stage.

Stores

1) The main store is obviously **ice**.

2) **Meltwater** is a small part of the glacier. It can be found **on the ice**, **in the ice** or **below the ice**.

3) Glaciers also carry **debris** (rocks, gravel and sand).

Meltwater is considered a store when it's actually in the glacier. When it's flowing down the valley well away from the glacier, it isn't a store in the system any more.

Outputs Outputs are the **losses** from a glacier.

1) Ice can **melt** and **flow out** of the glacier as **meltwater**.

2) Surface snow can **melt** and **evaporate**.

3) Ice and snow can **sublimate** to water vapour.

4) Snow can be **blown away** by strong winds.

5) With glaciers that end at the **sea**, blocks of ice fall from the **front** (the snout) of the ice mass into water to create **icebergs**. This is called "calving" — as if the glacier were a big old ice cow giving birth to a little ice calf. It can also happen where there's a **lake** at the front of the glacier.

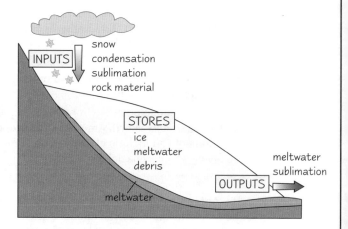

A *Glacial Budget* is the *Balance* between a Glacier's *Inputs* and *Outputs*

The glacial budget is sometimes called the "mass balance".

1) **Accumulation** is the **input** of snow and ice into the glacial system. Most accumulation is snow.

2) **Ablation** is the **output** of water from a glacier.

3) The **glacial budget** is the balance between accumulation and ablation over a year — it shows whether the volume of water in the glacial system has **increased** or **decreased**. This determines whether the **front** of the glacier **advances** forwards or **retreats** back.

4) You get **more accumulation** than ablation in the **upper** part of a glacier — so it's called the **zone of accumulation**.

5) You get **more ablation** than accumulation in the **lower** part of a glacier — so it's called the **zone of ablation**.

6) The place where accumulation and ablation are **equal** is called the glacier's **equilibrium point**.

7) If there's **more accumulation** than ablation over a year, the glacier has a **positive regime** (or a positive mass balance). The glacier grows and **advances** (moves forward).

8) If there's **less accumulation** than ablation over a year, this is a **negative regime** (or a negative mass balance). The glacier shrinks and **retreats** (moves back).

9) If there's the **same amount** of accumulation and ablation over a year, the glacier stays the same size and the position of the snout **doesn't change**.

Glaciers

The Glacial Budget *Changes* Throughout the *Year...*

1) You get **more ablation** during **warmer** times of the year — which makes sense, as more ice melts when it's warm.

2) During the **colder** months, there's **more accumulation** than ablation.

3) Over the year, this might **balance out** — the glacier **advances** in winter but **retreats** in summer, so overall the volume of water in the glacier **stays the same**.

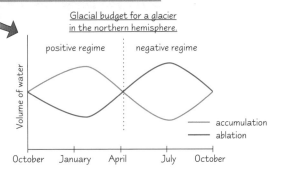

Glacial budget for a glacier in the northern hemisphere.

positive regime   negative regime

Volume of water

—— accumulation
—— ablation

October   January   April   July   October

Hannah and Betty had a very positive regime.

...and Over *Several Years*

Changes in **global temperature** over long periods of time affect the glacial budget.

1) Temperatures in the **19th century** were **colder** than in the 18th century, so in general there was more accumulation than ablation. This meant that many glaciers **advanced** because they had a positive regime.

2) In the **20th century**, global temperature **increased** so glaciers tended to have a negative regime and **retreated**.

Glaciers Form when Snow *Accumulates* and *Turns Into Ice*

1) First, **snow settles**. It has a loose, fluffy, snowflakey consistency at this point.

2) The **weight** of **more snow** falling on top turns the snow into a denser, more granular kind of snow called **firn**.

3) **Air** is squeezed **out**, and particles of ice are **compressed together** by the continuing accumulation of snow and ice.

4) Water also **melts** and **refreezes** in the **air spaces**, making the ice **more dense**. Et voilà — a glacier is formed.

Glaciers can be *Cold-Based* or *Warm-Based*

Glaciers can be classified according to the **temperature** of their **base** (the bit where the ice touches the valley floor).

> The melting temperature of ice at the base of a glacier is slightly lower than the normal melting point of ice (O °C), because of the pressure of all the ice on top of it.

1) In **warm-based glaciers**, the base is **warmer** than the melting point of ice. It's warmer because of heat from **friction** caused by the glacier moving, or because of **geothermal heat** from the Earth. The ice at the bottom of the glacier melts, and the **meltwater** acts as a **lubricant**, making it easier for the glacier to move downhill. Ice at the **surface** also melts if the temperature reaches 0 °C, and meltwater moves down through the glacier, lubricating it even more. Lots of movement means **lots of erosion**.

2) In **cold-based glaciers**, the base is cold (the temperature is usually well **below** the ice's **melting point**) so there's very **little melting**. The ice is frozen to the base of the valley, so there's **very little movement**. There's hardly any melting at the surface either, even in summer. This means that cold-based glaciers **don't** cause very much **erosion** at all.

Practice Questions

Q1 What are the main inputs, stores and outputs in a glacial system?

Q2 What are accumulation and ablation?

Q3 How does the glacial budget change throughout the year in the northern hemisphere?

Exam Questions

Q1 What is a glacial budget? Explain how a glacial budget shows whether a glacier is advancing or retreating.   [3 marks]

Q2 Describe the main differences between warm-based and cold-based glaciers.   [5 marks]

Brrr. Might need an extra jumper on...

Nope, you're not reading an accountancy revision guide by mistake — glaciers have budgets too. Glacial budgets are all about the ins and outs of the glacier. Stuff comes in mainly in the form of snow, and goes out mainly as meltwater. If more comes in than goes out then the glacier advances, and if more goes out than in it retreats — not so hard after all.

Glacial Processes

Glaciers are moving all the time — they don't stop to think about the erosion they might be causing...

Glaciers Move Downhill under their Own Weight

1) **Meltwater** underneath a glacier allows the glacier to **slide** over the ground. This is called **basal sliding**, and it's the main way that warm-based glaciers move.

2) There's **more melting** around bits of **rock protruding** from the valley floor, because there's **more pressure** on the ice (so the ice melts at temperatures lower than 0 °C). Meltwater can **refreeze** downstream of the obstruction where there's less pressure, so the flow tends to be faster around the obstruction, and slower downstream.

3) Glaciers move in an **arc shape** when they're in a **hollow** (by basal sliding). This is called **rotational flow** (which is a bit weird as it isn't really rotation as in "going round and round").

4) **Internal deformation** is where the ice **bends** and **warps** to flow downhill like a liquid. It's caused by ice crystals shifting past each other. It's the main way **cold-based** glaciers move.

5) At the **head** of a glacier the valley is steep, so there's a strong **gravitational force** pulling the ice downwards. This makes the ice **move quickly**. When ice moves quickly there's more **tension** (pulling apart forces), which causes the ice to **fracture** into thick layers. The **layers** then **slip downwards** — this is called **extensional flow**.

6) **Lower down** the glacier the ice is moving more **slowly** because the valley is less steep. The faster ice from the head of the glacier **pushes down** on the slower ice and **compresses it**. The **high pressure** causes the ice to **fracture** into layers, and the layers **slip forwards** — this is called **compressional flow**.

- The main things that determine the **speed** at which a glacier flows are the **gradient** of the valley floor, the **thickness** of the ice and the **temperature** at the base of the glacier.

- The **steeper** the valley, the **faster** the glacier will flow. The **thicker** the **ice** the **faster** it will flow — in a **warm-based** glacier thicker ice exerts **more pressure** on the valley floor, causing **more melting**, which makes it flow faster. In a **cold-based** glacier thicker ice means there's **more internal deformation**, which makes it flow faster. The **warmer** the **base** of the glacier the **faster** it will flow (see p. 37).

- Ice **moves faster** near the glacier's **surface** than at the **base** — **friction** at the base slows the glacier down.

- Ice also moves faster near the **middle** than at the **edges**.

Glaciers Crack as they Move Down the Valley

1) Stresses and strains cause cracks called **crevasses** to form in the glacier.

2) Stress can be caused by **extensional** and **compressional flow**, **calving**, or **tension** between the ice attached to the **valley sides** and **back wall** and the rest of the glacier.

3) The tension caused by the glacier pulling away from the ice attached to the **back wall** produces a big **semicircular crevasse** at the back of the glacier called the **bergschrund**.

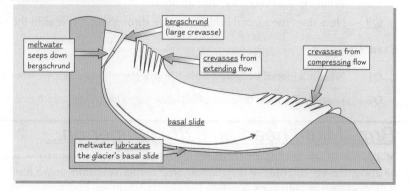

Glacial Processes

Glaciers **Erode** the **Surrounding Rock**

Glaciers erode the valley floor and sides by plucking and abrasion

1) **Plucking** — ice in contact with rock surfaces can thaw slightly then **refreeze around rocks** protruding from the valley sides and floor. When the glacier **moves forward**, it **plucks** the rocks away from the valley sides and floor.

2) **Abrasion** — **debris** carried along by the glacier can **scrape** material off the valley walls and floor.

frost shattering breaks bits of rock off the mountain face

plucking breaks bits of rock off the mountain face and makes the back wall steeper

abrasion grinds and gouges the valley floor

Meltwater erosion shapes the valley floor

Glaciers can produce huge quantities of **meltwater**, making streams that are powerful enough to erode the valley floor and sides by normal **fluvial (river) processes** (see p. 6).

The **amount** and **rate** of erosion is increased in areas of **less resistant rock**, and if the glacier is **thick** or if it's **moving quickly**. It's also increased if there's **lots** of **debris** or if the debris is made of **resistant rock**.

Weathering also contributes to the shaping of the glacial valley

Frost shattering breaks rocks off the **back** and **side walls** of the valley. **Meltwater** from snow gets into **cracks** in the valley walls and then **freezes** — when it freezes it **expands**, so it exerts **pressure** on the rock and bits of the rock get broken off. These bits of rock often **fall onto**, or **into**, the glacier (adding to the debris that **abrades** the valley).

Glaciers **Transport Debris**

1) Glaciers carry large loads of **debris** — this is material that the glacier has gathered by plucking, or bits of rock that have been broken off the back wall or valley sides and fallen onto (or into) the glacier. Debris ranges from **fine sediment** to **huge boulders**.

2) There are **three** main ways debris is transported. **Supraglacial** material is carried **on top** of the glacier's surface. **Englacial** material is carried **within** the body of the glacier. **Subglacial** material is moved along **at the base** of the glacier.

Glaciers **Deposit** their Load as they **Move** and as they **Melt**

1) The **unsorted** mixture of material **deposited** by the glacier is called **till** (it's sometimes called "boulder clay" too). It includes everything from massive boulders down to pebbles and clay. Glaciers drop any size of till anywhere.

2) **Lodgement till** is spread onto the valley floor beneath the ice by **moving** glaciers.

3) **Ablation till** is dropped by a glacier as it **melts**. The till is mainly deposited close to the glacier snout because this is where most ablation happens — the glacier drops debris as the ice around the debris melts.

4) Till **points** in the **direction** that the glacier is flowing.

5) Till is often **deposited** as landforms called **moraines** (see p. 41).

Practice Questions

Q1 What is rotational flow?

Q2 How is a bergschrund formed?

Q3 What are the main ways that debris is transported by a glacier?

Exam Questions

Q1 Explain what is meant by extensional flow. [4 marks]

Q2 Name and explain the two methods of glacial erosion. [4 marks]

Glaciers move r e a l l y s l o w l y — bit like you on a Sunday morning...

Alright, I'll admit that these two pages are slightly harder than the last two. It can be tricky at first to get your head around the different ways that glaciers move. Try reading over the first page a couple of times, then at least you'll know that rotational flow isn't a dance move. Don't forget that glaciers erode valleys in two different ways — by plucking and by abrasion.

Glacial Landforms

These pages are about the landscapes that glaciers leave behind them. Mountain climbers and geography teachers get very excited about the beauty of glacial landscapes. Whether or not they move you, you still need to learn about them.

Glaciers Create Basins called Corries (also called Cirques or Cwms)

1) Glaciers normally form on one side of a mountain peak — the side that gets **least sun** and the **coldest winds**. That's where there's **most accumulation** and **least ablation**.

2) Snow collects in hollows and turns to **ice**. **Basal sliding** (rotational flow) with **abrasion** and **plucking** deepen the hollow into a **corrie** (a bowl-shaped hollow).

3) When the ice in the hollow is thick enough, it **flows** over the lip and downhill as a glacier. Frost shattering and plucking **steepen** the back wall of the corrie.

Cross-section of a glacier forming a corrie
Bergschrund — frost shattering on exposed rock
Corrie lip
plucking
abrasion (grinding of valley floor)

Glacial Erosion Changes the Landscape of Valleys

Glaciers moving through valleys produce **erosional landforms**, which change the way valleys **look** after the ice has **gone**.

1) An **arête** is a steep-sided **ridge** — it's formed when two glaciers flow in parallel valleys. The glaciers erode the sides of the valley, which **sharpens** the mountain ridge **in between** them.

2) A **pyramidal peak** is a pointed mountain peak with at least **three sides**. It forms where **three** or more **corries** form **back to back** (their back walls make the mountain peak).

3) **Glacial troughs** (also called **U-shaped valleys**) are **steep-sided valleys** with **flat bottoms**. They're formed by the erosion of **V-shaped river valleys** by glaciers. As the glacier erodes through the V-shaped valley it makes them **deeper** and **wider**.

4) **Hanging valleys** are valleys formed by **tributary glaciers** — they erode the valley floor much less **deeply** because they're **smaller** than the main glacier. So, when the glaciers melt, the valleys get left at a **higher level** than the glacial trough formed by the main glacier. You get **waterfalls** from hanging valleys into the main glacial trough.

> A tributary glacier is a smaller glacier that flows into the main glacier.

5) **Truncated spurs** are formed when **ridges of land** (spurs) that **stick out** into the main valley are **chopped off** (truncated) as the main valley glacier moves past.

6) **Valley steps** are (funnily enough) steps in the glacial trough. They're formed when the glacier erodes the valley floor **more deeply**. This happens when **another glacier joins** it or where there's **less resistant** (softer) rock.

7) **Tarns** are **lakes** that form in **corries** after a glacier has retreated.

8) **Ribbon lakes** are long, thin lakes that form after a glacier retreats. They form in **dips** caused by erosion of bands of **less resistant** rocks, or **behind dams** of **debris** left by the glacier.

9) **Fjords** are long, deep inlets that form when a valley that's been eroded by a glacier is **flooded** by sea level rise after the ice has **melted**.

10) A **roche moutonnée** is a **resistant** (hard) mass of rock on the valley floor. The **upstream** (stoss) side is **smooth**, because it was smoothed by **abrasion** as the glacier went over it. The **downstream** (lee) side is steep and **rough** where the glacier **plucked** at it.

ice flow →
smoothed by abrasion
3 m
plucking
8 m

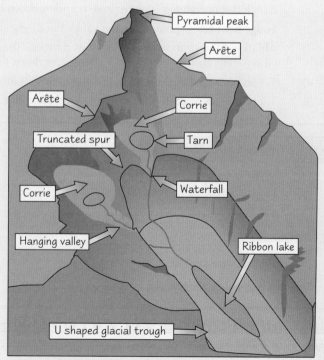

Pyramidal peak
Arête
Arête
Corrie
Truncated spur
Tarn
Corrie
Waterfall
Hanging valley
Ribbon lake
U shaped glacial trough

Glacial Landforms

Glaciers Form *Moraines* by Depositing Till

Moraine is the name for different formations of **till** deposited by a glacier as it melts. There are **three** different types of moraine:

1) **Lateral moraine** is deposited where the **sides** of the glacier were.

2) **Medial moraine** is deposited in the **centre** of the valley where two glaciers **converge** (the two lateral moraines join together).

3) **Terminal moraine** builds up at the **end** of the glacier, and is deposited as semicircular hillocks of till.

Till is all the stuff that a glacier leaves behind — unsorted boulders, stones and clay (see p. 39). Moraine is the name given to particular formations of till.

Till can also be Deposited as *Hills* called *Drumlins*

direction of ice flow

100 m

1500 m

A drumlin faces the opposite way to a roche moutonnée.

1) **Drumlins** are **half-egg shaped hills** of till, up to 1500 m long and 100 m high. The **upstream** (stoss) end is **wide and tall**, and the **downstream** (lee) end is **narrow and low**.

2) Nobody's really sure **why** drumlins are egg-shaped — it may be that till got stuck around a rock or a little hill sticking out into the glacier. It may be that an original mound of dropped till got streamlined when the ice **readvanced** over it.

3) Drumlins often form in **groups**. There are drumlins in the **Ribble Valley** in Lancashire. There are also a whole bunch of drumlins under the water level in Clew Bay, Ireland.

Erratics are *Boulders* that have been *Carried* a *Long Way* by Glaciers

1) Erratics are rocks that have been **picked up** by a glacier or an ice sheet, **carried along** and **dropped** in an area of **completely different geology** (rock type).

2) For example, in the Yorkshire dales at Norber, loose black **Silurian** rocks sit on top of white **Carboniferous** limestone.

3) There are erratics in **Eastern England** that were originally picked up by an ice sheet in **Norway** and carried all the way to England during the Ice Ages.

Les was good at long-distance boulder carrying, but not quite as good as a glacier.

Practice Questions

Q1 What is the name of the ridge formed by two glaciers in parallel valleys?

Q2 Name three erosional features of glaciated valleys.

Q3 What is the name for rocks that are transported by a glacier or an ice sheet and dropped into an area with a different rock type?

Exam Questions

Q1 Describe and explain the landforms shown in the photo on the right. [8 marks]

Q2 Describe the three different types of moraine. [3 marks]

Corries? I'm more of an Emmerdale fan myself...

There are a fair few features to learn here, but don't let that get you down. You just need to learn the names of the features, what they look like and how they're formed. Even the names of the features are a bit tricky though — cirque, arête, roche moutonnée... anyone would think this was a French exam. At least you don't need to know how to pronounce them.

Fluvioglacial Processes and Landforms

The sad news for all you glacier fans is that glaciers don't always stay around forever. But don't worry, they don't go down without a fight — even when they're melting, they still manage to change the landscape.

Meltwater Streams Erode the Landscape

1) When glacial ice melts, water runs out and forms streams of **meltwater**. **Warm-based** glaciers and **retreating** glaciers produce **lots** of meltwater.

2) **Surface** meltwater **filters** through the glacier (e.g. through crevasses) and flows through **tunnels** underneath the glacier, before running out of the snout of the glacier.

3) Meltwater streams cause **erosion** in the same way as normal rivers — but they cause **more** erosion than rivers of the same size. This is because the pressure of the ice means that meltwater streams flow very **quickly** — so they can carry **lots** of material that **erodes** the landscape.

4) Meltwater streams form deep **troughs** in the landscape called **meltwater channels**. Because meltwater streams have a lot of **erosive power**, the meltwater channels they produce are very **wide** and **deep**. After the glacier has **retreated**, the deep meltwater channels are left with very **shallow streams** running through them.

Fluvioglacial Deposits come from Glacial Meltwater

1) Glacial meltwater carries a **large load** of **sediment** of various sizes (from inside, on top of and underneath the glacier).

2) Meltwater streams **deposit** their load on the **valley floor** as they flow away from the glacier.

3) Meltwater streams are often **braided** — they split into lots of mini streams that cross over each other. This is because when the meltwater is flowing more **slowly** (e.g. in winter, when the amount of meltwater is lower) it can't carry its load — so it **deposits** the sediment on the ground, and **splits** into two streams to get round it.

4) There's a difference between **glacial deposition features** formed by **glaciers** dropping debris as they melt (see p. 41) and **fluvioglacial deposition features** formed by **meltwater** carrying debris, then depositing it away from the glacier.

5) **Fluvioglacial** deposits are **sorted** — the fine sediment is **separated** from the larger sand, which is separated from the gravel, and so on. **Glacial** deposits are **unsorted**.

Melting Glaciers leave Outwash Plains and Kettle Holes

1) An **outwash plain** is a layer of gravel, sand and clay that forms in **front** of where the snout of the melting glacier used to be. Meltwater flows out of the glacier, and carries the sediment with it.

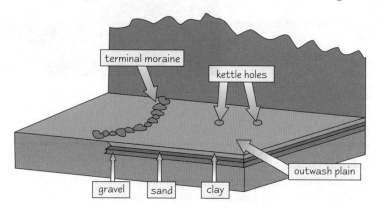

2) Sediments on outwash plains are **sorted** into layers. **Gravel** gets dropped **first** because it's **heavier** than sand and clay, so it forms the **bottom layer** of the outwash plain. **Clay** is dropped **last** and gets carried furthest away from the snout because it's the lightest sediment — it forms the **top layer** of the outwash plain.

3) **Blocks of ice** that have broken off from the front of the glacier can get surrounded and partly buried by the **fluvioglacial deposits**. When the blocks of ice **melt**, they leave **holes** in the outwash plain, called **kettle holes**.

Fluvioglacial Processes and Landforms

Meltwater Streams Deposit **Kames** and **Eskers**

1) **Eskers** are long, winding **ridges** of sand and gravel that run in the **same direction** as the glacier. They're deposited by meltwater streams flowing in **tunnels** underneath the glacier — when the glacier retreats and the stream dries up, the load remains as an esker. Eskers show you where the glacial tunnel used to be.

2) **Kames** are **mounds** of sand and gravel found on the valley floor. Meltwater streams **on top of** glaciers collect in depressions and **deposit** layers of debris. When the ice **melts** the debris is dumped onto the valley floor.

3) **Kame terraces** are piles of deposits left against the **valley wall** by meltwater streams that run between the glacier and the valley sides. They look like lateral moraine, but they're **sorted** into layers — meltwater streams deposit their **heaviest** loads first, so kame terraces have **gravel** at the **bottom** and **sand** on **top**.

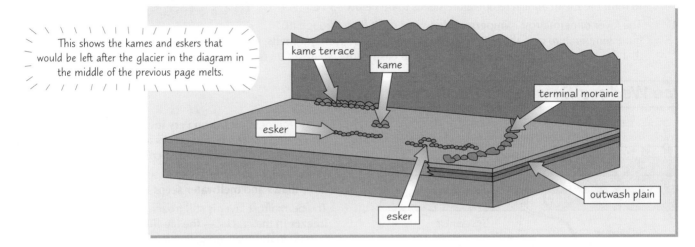

This shows the kames and eskers that would be left after the glacier in the diagram in the middle of the previous page melts.

4) Lakes (called **proglacial lakes**) can form in front of glaciers, e.g. when the flow from meltwater streams gets dammed by the terminal moraine. As meltwater streams flow into a proglacial lake, they **slow down** and **deposit** their sediment on the ice — these deposits are known as **deltas**. When the ice melts, these deltas are dumped on the valley floor, forming **delta kames**.

Practice Questions

Q1   What are meltwater channels?

Q2   What's the main difference between glacial deposits and fluvioglacial deposits?

Q3   What is an outwash plain?

Q4   How are kettle holes formed?

Q5   What are eskers?

Exam Questions

Q1   Describe how kame terraces are formed.   [2 marks]

Q2   Explain how delta kames are formed.   [4 marks]

I'm melting! Meeeeeelting!

Well, this is just typical of glaciers if you ask me. Not content with ripping bits of rock out of mountains and scattering them all over landscapes, glaciers then have to go and melt, and wash all kinds of bits of rock all over the place. If only they didn't have to be so, well, <u>messy</u> about it — then you wouldn't need to know what a kame or an esker was. Oh well, tough luck, eh.

Periglacial Processes and Landforms

Periglacial areas are cold areas that aren't covered in ice.
There's usually ice in the soil though — I knew it'd be there somewhere.

Permafrost is Permanently Frozen Ground

1) **Periglacial** areas contain **permafrost** — **permanently frozen ground** with a top layer that can **melt** in the **summer** (called the **active layer**). 20-25% of Earth's land surface is **permafrost**.

2) Areas of permafrost can be **continuous** (**all** the ground is frozen), or **discontinuous** (only **patches** of the ground are frozen).

3) For **discontinuous** permafrost to form the **mean annual temperature** needs to be **below 0 °C** for at least **2 years**. For **continuous** permafrost to form the mean annual temperature needs to be **below –5 °C**.

4) The layer of permafrost is **impermeable** (water **can't** flow through it). If the temperature gets **above 0 ºC** in the summer, the active layer **melts**, but the water can't go anywhere. This means that the active layer gets **waterlogged** and will **easily flow** wherever there's a **gradient**. This flow is called **solifluction**.

waterlogged active layer flows downhill
whoomph
permafrost layer always stays frozen

Ice Wedges Develop in Permafrost Soil

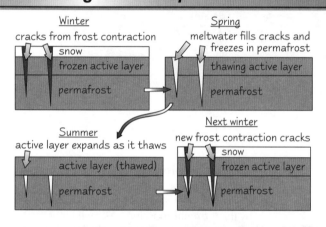

Winter
cracks from frost contraction
snow
frozen active layer
permafrost

Spring
meltwater fills cracks and freezes in permafrost
thawing active layer
permafrost

Summer
active layer expands as it thaws
active layer (thawed)
permafrost

Next winter
new frost contraction cracks
snow
frozen active layer
permafrost

1) When temperatures **drop very low** in winter, the ground **contracts** and **cracks** form in the permafrost. This is called **frost contraction**.

2) When temperatures **increase** in spring, the active layer **thaws** and **meltwater seeps** into the **cracks**.

3) The permafrost layer is still frozen, so the water **freezes** in the cracks — the ice-filled cracks formed in this way are called **ice wedges**.

4) Frost contraction in following years can **re-open** cracks in the same place, **splitting** the ice wedge. More water seeps in and freezes, **widening** the ice wedge. The ice wedge gets **bigger** each time this happens.

Ground Water Freezes causing Frost Heave

1) Water freezing in the ground can make humps on the surface.

2) When the active layer freezes in winter, the ice forms a kind of lens shape.

3) In fine-grained soil (like silt or clay) the ice lifts (heaves) up the surface layers of soil. This is called frost heave.

4) Ice lenses also form underneath stones because stones lose heat faster than the soil around them, so when temperatures drop it's colder beneath the stones.

5) As the ice lenses expand, they push the stones upwards towards the surface of the ground. The ice lenses underneath the stones stop the stones from slipping back down. If the ice thaws, fine material fills in the space where the ice was, so the stones don't fall down. Eventually the stones rise above the surface of the ground.

ice heaves soil upwards
ice forms lens shape
stone
ice lens
ice pushes stones upwards

Patterned Ground is Formed by Frost Activity

Sometimes **stones** on the surface of the ground are arranged in **circles**, **polygons** or **stripes** — this is called **patterned ground**. Patterned ground can be formed in two ways — by **frost heave** and by **frost contraction**:

1) Stones can get pushed to the surface by **frost heave**. Once they reach the surface, they **roll down** to the **edges** of the **mounds** that have formed, so they form **circles** around them (**polygons** form when the mounds are **close together**). If the mounds are on a **slope**, the stones roll downhill and form **lines**.

2) **Frost contraction** causes the ground to **crack** in polygon shapes. The cracks get **filled in** with **stones**, forming polygon patterns on the surface.

stones forming polygon shapes
stones on a slope forming lines

Periglacial Processes and Landforms

Nivation makes Hollows Deeper by Freezing and Thawing

1) When snow gets into a **hollow** in the ground, it can **increase** the **size** of the hollow.

2) The temperature in periglacial environments often **fluctuates** around **0 ºC**, so a lot of **freezing** and **thawing** happens — when the temperature's **above** 0 ºC, the snow **melts**, and when it's **below** 0 ºC, the water refreezes as **ice**.

3) Every time the ice **freezes**, it **expands**, so **frost shattering** eventually breaks bits off the rock at the base of the hollow. When the snow **melts**, the meltwater carries the broken bits of rock (debris) **away**.

4) Slopes **collapse** because they're **waterlogged** and they've been **eroded** — the material is **washed away** by meltwater.

5) Eventually the hollow becomes **deeper** and **wider**. The processes that cause this are collectively called **nivation**, and the hollows formed by nivation are called **nivation hollows**. Nivation hollows can be the beginning of a **corrie**.

Freezing — snow — frost shattering

Thawing — meltwater removes debris

Solifluction Produces Lobe Formations

1) The **waterlogged active layer** of soil **flows** easily over the frozen impermeable layer beneath.

2) Solifluction produces **lobe** formations where one section of the soil is **moving faster** than the soil around it, e.g. because it's on **steeper** ground, so it flows down **further** to create a **tongue** shape.

waterlogged active layer — solifluction lobe — permafrost

Pingos are Ice-Filled Periglacial Hills

1) A pingo is a **conical hill** with a **core of ice**. Pingos can be as large as 80 m high and about 500 m wide.

2) There are **two types** of pingo — **open-system** and **closed-system**.

3) **Open-system pingos** form where there's **discontinuous** permafrost. **Groundwater** is forced **up** through the **gaps between** areas of permafrost (from unfrozen layers lower down). The water **collects** together and **freezes**, forming a **core** of ice that **pushes** the ground above it **upwards**.

4) **Closed-system pingos** form in areas of **continuous** permafrost where there's a **lake** at the surface. The lake **insulates** the ground, so the area beneath it remains **unfrozen**. When the lake **dries up**, the ground is no longer insulated and the permafrost **advances** around the area of unfrozen ground. This causes water to **collect** in the centre of the unfrozen ground. The water eventually **freezes** and creates a **core** of ice that **pushes** the ground above it **upwards**.

5) If the ice core **thaws**, the pingo **collapses**, leaving behind a **pond** of meltwater surrounded by **ramparts** (walls of soil).

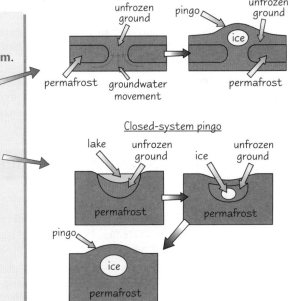

Open-system pingo — unfrozen ground — pingo — unfrozen ground — ice — permafrost — groundwater movement — permafrost

Closed-system pingo — lake — unfrozen ground — ice — unfrozen ground — permafrost — permafrost — pingo — ice — permafrost

Practice Questions

Q1 What is permafrost?

Q2 How do ice wedges develop?

Q3 What's the difference between open-system pingos and closed-system pingos?

Exam Question

Q1 Describe the processes that lead to the formation of patterned ground in periglacial environments. [6 marks]

I always thought Pingo was one of the Beatles...

The trouble with this lot is that there are so many different processes going on, and all of them are to do with water freezing and then thawing. But at least you can sleep soundly now you know that patterned ground is caused by frost activity and not aliens.

Issues in Cold Environments

Cold environments might not be great for beach holidays, but they've still got some great resources. There'll always be people who want to exploit those resources, even if it means damaging the environment in the process.

Cold Environments Contain Valuable Resources, which Attract Development

1) Many cold environments (and the **seas** around them) **contain resources** that **attract development**. These include:
   - **Whales**, **seals** and **fish** — e.g. in **northern Russia** whales and seals are hunted for their skins, meat and blubber, while its **fishing industry** is one of the **largest** in the world.
   - **Minerals** — e.g. the discovery of **gold** in **Canada** and **Alaska** triggered gold rushes and led to the establishment of towns based around mining that still exist today.
   - **Oil** — e.g. **Alaska** has a lot of **oil**, and over the last few decades **oil companies** have moved into the area to **exploit** this resource.

Barry didn't like the sound of 'development'.

2) Cold environments also have **attractive scenery** — this attracts **tourism**. E.g. the number of tourists visiting **Antarctica** each year has risen from **6700** in **1992** to **46 000** in the **2007/2008** season.

3) Some cold environments have the potential for **hydroelectric power production** as they have natural lakes at high altitudes. **Norway** currently supplies **99%** of its domestic electricity through HEP plants.

Cold Environments have Fragile Ecosystems

1) Fragile ecosystems are ecosystems that struggle to **recover** from **damage**.

2) They're fragile because of the **harsh climate**:
   - The **short growing season** (when there's enough **light** and **warmth** for plants to grow) means that plants **don't have much time** to **recover** if they're **damaged**.
   - The **plants** and **animals** in cold environments are **adapted** to the cold conditions, so they find it hard to survive if their **environment changes**.
   - **Decay** is **slow** because it's cold, so **pollution** is **broken down** very **slowly** (and so remains in the environment for a long time).

3) **Tundra** is a fragile ecosystem found in some cold environments, e.g. in periglacial environments.

> **Tundra** is found where it's **too cold** for **trees** to grow, either because of **high altitude** or **high latitude**. **Arctic tundra** is found in Greenland, northern Russia and Canada. **Antarctic tundra** is found in islands around Antarctica, e.g. South Georgia. **Alpine tundra** occurs in alpine environments. Vegetation includes **shrubs**, **grasses**, **mosses** and **lichen**. Animals found there include **seals**, **penguins**, **seabirds**, **hares**, **foxes**, **caribou** (reindeer) and **bears**.

Development in Cold Environments can Damage the Ecosystem

Fishing

1) Fishing can **disrupt food chains**, e.g. **krill** fishing in the **Southern Ocean** is depleting food supplies for **whales** and **penguins**.

2) **Overfishing** of a species can severely **deplete** its **population**, sometimes beyond recovery. Overfishing of the **Patagonian Toothfish** in the **Antarctic** is currently a concern.

3) **Bottom trawling** catches fish by dragging nets along the sea-bed. This **disrupts** the **ecosystem** (by **reducing light levels** through increasing turbidity) and **catches other species** as well as the target one. It's carried out in the **Gulf of Alaska**, the **Greenland Sea** and the **Barents Sea**.

Oil extraction

1) **Oil spills** can occur **during transport** of oil from the area. For example, in **1989** there was a huge **oil spill** off the coast of **Alaska** when the **Exxon Valdez** oil tanker crashed. Over **40 million** litres of oil spilled into the ocean, and over **250 000 birds** and **fish** were **killed**.

2) **Oil spills** can occur if **pipelines leak**. Between **1977** and **1994** there were, on average, **30 to 40** spills a year from the **Trans-Alaska pipeline**. Some of these were caused by **intentional attacks** and **forest fires**.

Hydroelectric power production

1) **Hydroelectric dams** can **block** the normal **migratory path** of fish. This can prevent them reaching **spawning grounds**, and so cause the fish **population** to **decrease**.

2) Hydroelectric dams also **heat up** the water, which can endanger **fish** that are used to **colder** temperatures.

Tourism

1) Large **cruise ships** increase **pollution** in the areas (from the ships and from the tourists).

2) Tourists and tourism developments (e.g. roads, hotels) disrupt **wildlife** and **damage habitats**, leading to **reduced biodiversity**.

Issues in Cold Environments

Mining

1) Mining can lead to **ground** and **surface water contamination**, either by **chemicals** used **during mining** or by the materials **being mined**. E.g. the lead-zinc mine in **Maarmorilik** (Greenland) was closed in 1990 but **lead** and **zinc** are still released, **polluting** nearby fjords.

2) Mining produces both **solid waste** and **wastewater** that has to be disposed of. In some cases, e.g. in the **Red Dog Mine** in **Alaska** and the **Kubaka** mine in **Russia**, the facilities are not built to deal with the quantities produced and the **waste** is **released** into the **environment**.

Development in Cold Environments has Affected the Locals

1) Even though the **climate** in **tundra** areas is very **harsh**, native **tribes** have lived there for **thousands** of years.

2) For example, the **Inuit** people are a group of tribes who live in the tundra in the northern parts of **Canada**, **Greenland** and **Russia**. Their traditional way of life involves **hunting** and **fishing** — they **eat** the **meat** and make **clothes** and **shoes** from the animal **fur** and **skin**.

3) **Newcomers** from Europe and the US started to take an **interest** in tundra areas during the **17th century** because of the opportunities for hunting **whales** and **seals**. **Seals** were hunted for their warm **fur** and their **oil** — the oil was used as **lamp fuel** and to make **leather**. **Whales** were mainly hunted for their **oil**, which was used to fuel **lamps**, make **candles** and also an ingredient in **margarine**.

4) The arrival of the **newcomers** had a very **negative** effect on the people living in the tundra, because they brought new **diseases** with them — many of the Inuit were infected and **died**. E.g. In the late 19th and early 20th century **90%** of the Inuvialuit (a Canadian Inuit tribe) were **killed** by diseases like tuberculosis, measles, smallpox and flu.

5) Also, an increase in **whaling**, **sealing** and **fishing** in the tundra areas **reduced** the **number** of whales, seals and fish available for the Inuit people to catch.

6) So development in tundra areas has had a big impact on the **lifestyles** of the indigenous people. E.g. in Canada:

- There **aren't enough resources** for Inuit tribes to **support themselves** by hunting and fishing (and many young Inuits no longer learn the skills needed for this) so they have to find **paid employment**. This is difficult as the few job opportunities that exist are usually taken by the generally more educated white population.

- With **unemployment** at nearly **50%** amongst some Inuit communities, they have to rely on government help.

- The change of employment has also led to Inuits living in **permanent settlements** rather than being nomadic.

Development in Cold Environments can be Made More Sustainable

For development to be sustainable it has to **not deplete resources** and not cause **long-term environmental damage**. It's pretty **difficult** for development to be totally sustainable, but there are things that make it **more sustainable**. For example:

1) **National parks** have been set up to allow **tourism** whilst **protecting** the environment — e.g. **Denali National Park** in Alaska was set up in 1917, and then expanded in 1980 to include a greater area of land. Cars and private vehicles are **banned** from the park, so visitors have to travel in park buses on approved routes. The most vulnerable parts of the park don't have any **roads** at all, so the ground is **protected** from the damaging effects of vehicles.

2) **Fishing quotas** have been introduced (e.g. in the **Barents Sea**), to **limit** the number of fish caught and **prevent overexploitation** of the resource.

3) **Oil pipes** have automatic **shut-off valves** in order to minimise **oil spills** if the pipelines are damaged.

Practice Questions

Q1 Name three resources that can be found in cold environments.

Q2 What kind of wildlife is found in tundra areas?

Exam Questions

Q1 Describe the impact of development on cold environments. [6 marks]

Q2 Explain how the traditional way of life of native tribes in tundra areas has been affected by development. [6 marks]

Personally, my main issue with cold environments is chilblains...

Exploitation of cold environments is kind of a sad story, but at least it's not too hard to get your head around. Just make sure you learn what kind of resources are found in cold environments, and how exploiting them can damage the environment and affect the lifestyles of the native people. And always check the label on margarine to make sure there's no whale oil in it — urgh.

Issues in Cold Environments — Case Study

You've probably noticed by now that geography teachers love a good case study. Well it turns out that the examiners are just the same — case studies are their absolute favourite thing in the world. So they'd probably love these pages...

The **Antarctic** *is a* **Unique Wilderness Area**

Antarctica is the land mass, 'the Antarctic' is the area within the Antarctic Circle (it includes Antarctica).

1) A wilderness area is an area that has been **unaffected** by large-scale **human activity**.

2) Antarctica is the **largest** wilderness area on Earth — it covers an area about **14 million km²**, so it's **larger** than **Europe**.

3) It contains **90%** of all the **ice** on Earth — around **70%** of all the Earth's **fresh water** supplies.

4) The **Antarctic ice sheet** covers most of the land mass of Antarctica all year round. The **ice sheet** extends into the **sea** — the ice masses that extend out over the sea are called **ice shelves**. The two largest ice shelves are the **Ross Shelf** and the **Ronne Shelf**. Chunks of ice can become detached from the ice shelves and fall into the sea as **icebergs**.

5) There are several **islands** off the coast of Antarctica, e.g. **Elephant Island**.

The **Antarctic** *has a* **Fragile Ecosystem**

1) There's **very little available water** in Antarctica for plants to grow. Inland areas receive **less than 166 mm** of precipitation per year (which is low enough to classify it as a **desert**) and most precipitation that falls is **frozen**.

2) It's **very cold** — the average temperature is **–49 ˚C**.

3) There's also **very little sunshine** in winter (the sun doesn't rise for several months because of the Earth's tilt).

4) This means that **very few** plants and animals **can survive** there, and the ones that do have to be specially **adapted**. Antarctica's plant life is mainly made up of **mosses** and **lichens**, and only **two** species of **flowering plants** grow. There's abundant **bird life**, e.g. **albatross** and **penguins**.

5) The lack of water, warmth and sunlight in Antarctica means that the land environment is very **fragile** — it takes a long time for it to **recover** from **damage**.

6) There's abundant **sea life**, e.g. **fish**, **seals** and **whales**.

7) The **sea ecosystem** is also **fragile** — if the population of one species **decreases** it affects other species in the **food chain**, e.g. if the population of krill decreases it would affect the whale population as some whales feed on them.

The **Antarctic** *has Lots of* **Valuable Resources**

1) Although the Antarctic appears to be **barren** it has a lot of **natural resources**:

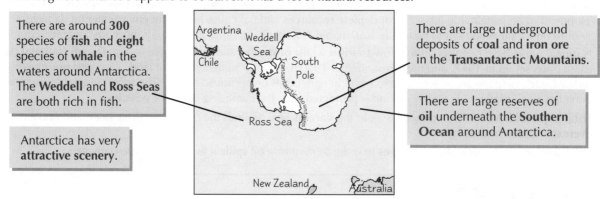

There are around **300** species of **fish** and **eight** species of **whale** in the waters around Antarctica. The **Weddell** and **Ross Seas** are both rich in fish.

Antarctica has very **attractive scenery**.

There are large underground deposits of **coal** and **iron ore** in the **Transantarctic Mountains**.

There are large reserves of **oil** underneath the **Southern Ocean** around Antarctica.

2) These resources mean the Antarctic is an attractive area for **fishing**, **tourism**, **mining** and **oil extraction**.

3) The Antarctic is also very attractive to **scientific researchers** because it's unique.

The **Antarctic** *is* **Protected** *by the* **Antarctic Treaty**

1) Antarctica has **no native people**, so no one can claim the land as their own. This has caused **conflict** over the **ownership** of the region since it was discovered in the 18th century — lots of different countries have **tried** to **claim ownership** of bits of the continent and the right to **exploit** its **resources**.

2) Since the Antarctic has a **fragile** ecosystem the **impact** of any development on the **environment** could be **devastating**.

3) To try and **protect** the Antarctic from environmental damage, the **Antarctic Treaty** was set up **1961**. 12 countries agreed to set aside disputes over who owns Antarctica and came up with **laws** to **protect it**.

4) The treaty includes many **protocols** and **conventions** that **control** or **prohibit** certain activities (see next page for more).

Issues in Cold Environments — Case Study

Oil Extraction, Mining and Whaling are Currently Banned in the Antarctic

OIL EXTRACTION and MINING

1) Due to the **possible** huge **environmental impact** of oil extraction and mining in the area they're currently banned.

2) The **Madrid Protocol** (part of the Antarctic Treaty) came into force in **1998**, banning all mining activity and oil extraction. The ban is in force for **50 years** — it's due to be **reviewed** in **2048**.

3) Some people think the ban may be **lifted** in 2048 due to the **need for minerals** and **oil** (caused by depletion of reserves in the rest of the world).

WHALING

1) Whaling **was allowed** in the Antarctic, but caused a **decrease** in **whale populations**, e.g. it's estimated that there were **250 000 blue whales** in the Antarctic a century ago, now there are fewer than **1000**.

2) In **1994** the whole Antarctic area was declared a **whale sanctuary** and **commercial hunting** was **prohibited** (some whaling is still allowed for scientific research).

Efforts have been Made to Make Other Activities More Sustainable

1) Currently **tourism**, **scientific research** and **fishing** are allowed in and around Antarctica.

2) In the **2007-2008** season **46 000 tourists** visited the area.

3) There are around **5000 scientific researchers** in the Antarctic in **summer**, and about **1000** in **winter**.

4) **Fishing** is huge in the **Southern Ocean**, e.g. over **16 000 tonnes** of **Patagonian toothfish** were caught in **2000**.

5) These activities are controlled to **reduce** their **environmental impact** and to make them **more sustainable**:

Activity	Control
Tourism	• The Antarctic Treaty prohibits discharging of oil or plastics from cruise ships. • Tour operators have to stick to Antarctic Treaty rules, but they're mostly self-regulated by the IAATO (International Association of Antarctica Tour Operators). The IAATO imposes restrictions on tourist activity to reduce the environmental impact, for example no more than 100 passengers are allowed on shore in one place at a time and only one ship is allowed at a landing site at a time.
Scientific research	The Protocol on Environmental Protection came into force in 1998 as part of the Antarctic Treaty. It includes rules that protect Antarctica from damage caused by scientific research, e.g. scientists have to remove most of their waste from the Antarctic, and treat sewage before they dispose of it into the sea.
Fishing	The Convention for the Conservation of Antarctic Marine Living Resources came into force in 1982 as part of the Antarctic Treaty. It includes quotas (limits) on fish catches such as the Patagonian toothfish, krill and icefish.

6) **Not everyone** thinks that **tourism should be allowed**. The number of visitors is expected to increase to **80 000** per year by **2010**, which would **increase** the **environmental impact** of tourism.

7) It's very difficult to police the seas in the Antarctic so a lot of **illegal fishing** occurs despite the quotas, e.g. in the **2003-2004** season it was estimated that **2622 tonnes** of **Patagonian toothfish** were caught illegally.

Practice Questions

Q1   Name three of the resources that are found in Antarctica.

Q2   What is the Antarctic Treaty?

Exam Question

Q1   How is the Antarctic being protected from the impact of development?   [15 marks]

Insert your own Aunt Arctica joke here...

Antarctica seems like quite a lively place considering nobody actually lives there. There's lots to learn on these pages, but at least it's all pretty interesting. Anyway, that's the end of cold environments — I hope you've enjoyed it as much as I have.

Desert and Desert Margin Characteristics

In my mind, deserts are full of towering sand dunes and camels, but in reality they're a bit different to that...

Rainfall is **Low** in **Deserts** and **Desert Margins**

1) **Deserts** are **arid** (dry) environments. Environments are classed as arid if they get **less than 250 mm** of **rainfall** a **year**.

2) **Desert margins** (land at the **edges** of a desert) are **semi-arid** environments. Environments are classed as semi-arid if they receive between **250** and **500 mm** of **rainfall** a **year**.

3) The **aridity** (dryness) of an environment depends on **rainfall** and the **rate of evapotranspiration**.

4) **Not all** deserts are **hot**, e.g. the **Gobi desert** in Asia is a **cold desert**.
You **only** need to know about **hot** deserts for the **exam**.

Evapotranspiration is evaporation and transpiration (evaporation through plants).

Most **Deserts** and **Desert Margins** are **Found**...

① Around **30° North** and **South** of the **Equator**

1) Air moves in **circular patterns** between the **equator** and about **30° north** and **south** of it. These **circular air patterns** are called **Hadley cells**.

2) In a Hadley cell **air rises** at the **equator**. The air cools as it rises, moisture **condenses** and falls as **rain**, leaving the air **dry**.

3) The **dry air descends** around **30° north** and **south** of the equator.

4) In areas where the **air descends** a zone of **high pressure** is created.

5) **Winds** blow **outwards** from high pressure areas — so **no moisture** can be **brought in** by the **wind**.

6) This means that the area has **very low precipitation**, which means desert margins and deserts are found there, e.g. the **Sahara**.

30° north
equator
30° south

② In the **Middle** of **Continents**

1) The **central** parts of **continents** are usually **more arid** than coastal areas.

2) **Moist wind** from the sea **moves inland** and the **moisture** held is **dropped** as precipitation.

3) So when the **wind reaches** the **centre** of a large **continent** it's carrying **very little moisture**, so **very little rain** falls.

4) For example, the **Turkestan** desert exists because it's in the **central** part of **Asia**.

Tropic of Cancer   30°

Equator

Tropic of Capricorn   30°

☐ Desert (arid)
■ Desert margin (semi-arid)

③ **Next** to **Mountain Ranges**

1) Tall mountain ranges **force winds upwards**.

2) As the air rises it **cools** and its ability to **hold moisture** is **reduced**.

3) Any moisture held is dropped as **precipitation** over the mountains, so the wind that moves inland has **very little moisture**, which means that **very little rain falls** there.

4) This is called the **rain shadow effect**.

5) For example, the **Atacama** desert in South America exists because of the rain shadow effect of the **Andes** mountains.

④ **Near Cold Ocean Currents**

1) In some places **cold ocean currents** run along the coastline.

2) Wind is cooled as it travels over the cold water and its **ability to hold moisture** is **reduced**.

3) **Moisture** that's stored in the atmosphere is **released** as precipitation over the ocean **before** reaching **land**.

4) So when the wind **reaches** the **land** there's **very little moisture left**, so **very little rain** falls.

5) For example, the **Namib** desert in **Africa** exists because of the **Benguela Current** (a cold ocean current) that runs up the **west coast** of Africa.

Desert and Desert Margin Characteristics

Hot Deserts are Hot and Have Large Variations in Temperature

1) The **mean annual temperature** of most hot deserts is **high** — usually between **20 and 30 °C**.
2) There are large **seasonal variations** in **temperature** — up to **50 °C** in summer and **below 0 °C** in winter.
3) There are also large **daily variations** in **temperature** — up to **50 °C** in the day and **below 0 °C** at night.
Large variations are due to the dry desert air, which can't **block sunlight** during the day or **trap heat** at night.

The temperature in **desert margins** is a bit lower:

1) The **mean annual temperature** of most **desert margins** is **lower** than in deserts — between **10 and 20 °C**.
2) The **temperature variations** in **desert margins** are usually **less extreme** (between **10 and 35 °C**).

There's Little Vegetation in Hot Deserts

1) The **biomass** (total amount of living matter) in a desert is **low** because the **lack of water** makes it **difficult** for things **to grow**.
2) The amount of vegetation within a desert **varies** — there can be **none** where there are sand dunes, and a **variety** of small **shrubs**, **grasses** and **cacti species** in other areas.
3) Plants are **specialised** to **survive** in the hot and arid conditions, e.g. cacti have special ways to **collect**, **store** and **conserve** water.

The vegetation in **desert margins** is a little different:

1) There's **more** vegetation in desert margins than in deserts.
2) Vegetation includes **shrubs**, **grasses** and **trees**.
3) The **amount** of vegetation generally **increases** the **further away** from the **desert** you go, because there's **more water**.

Adaptations of Cacti

The enlarged stem stores water.

The thick waxy coating reduces transpiration and protects from strong winds.

Small spiny leaves reduce transpiration, and protect them from being eaten by herbivores.

Long, shallow roots absorb water from a large area, whilst longer taproots reach deeper water.

The Soil in Hot Deserts is Very Dry and Not Very Fertile

1) You usually think of deserts as just being made from **sand**, but there are areas of **bare soil** and also **soil underneath** the sand.
2) Desert soils **aren't very fertile** because they don't contain very much organic matter. This is because **few plants grow** there.
3) The soils are often **sandy** (in areas with sand dunes) or **stony** (in rocky areas).
4) The soils are **very dry** due to the **low rainfall** and **high temperatures**.

The soil in **desert margins** is a bit better:

1) The soil in desert margins is **more fertile** than the soil in deserts, because there's more vegetation.
2) The soil contains **more water** than desert soil.
3) The soil is **less sandy** and **stony** than in deserts because there's **more weathering**.

Practice Questions

Q1 How much rainfall do desert margins receive per year?
Q2 Explain how the rain shadow effect causes aridity.
Q3 Why do deserts have large daily temperature variations?

Exam Question

Q1 The graph on the right shows the climate in Riyadh, Saudi Arabia.

a) Describe the climate in Riyadh. [6 marks]

b) Riyadh is 25° north of the equator. Explain how its location leads to low levels of precipitation. [5 marks]

c) Suggest what the vegetation in Riyadh is like, and explain your answer with reference to the climate in Riyadh. [4 marks]

WLTM hot desert — must have a dry sense of humour...

You need to know all about where deserts are, why they formed there and what they're like. So get learnin'. Now, with all this talk of deserts I can't stop thinking about chocolate chip cheesecake. Which reminds me — don't forget it's spelt with one 's'.

Processes in Hot Desert Environments

It's a hard life being a rock in the desert — wind and water erode you and weathering makes bits fall off willy-nilly...

Rocks are Broken Down by Weathering

There are several **different types** of **mechanical weathering** that **break down rocks** in hot deserts. They include:

Thermal expansion and salt weathering cause the most weathering in hot deserts.

THERMAL EXPANSION

1) **Thermal expansion** is caused by **daily extreme temperature variations** in deserts.
2) During the day (when it's **hot**) rocks **expand**, and at **night** (when it's **cold**) they **contract**.
3) Sometimes **outer layers** of the rock **flake off** because they warm up and cool down at a **faster rate** than the inner layers. This is called **exfoliation**.
4) **Individual grains** may also fall off because **different minerals** within the rock expand and contract at **different rates**. This is called **granular disintegration**.

rock expands   rock contracts

SALT WEATHERING

1) **Salt weathering** is caused by **saline (salty) water**, which comes from **rainfall** or from **groundwater** that's **drawn up** to the desert **surface** by **evaporation**.
2) This saline water **enters pores** or **cracks** in desert rocks.
3) The **high temperature** in hot deserts causes the **water** to **evaporate**, forming **salt crystals**. As the salt crystals **form** they **expand**, exerting **pressure** on the rocks.
4) As **more** evaporation occurs the salt crystals **expand** even **more**. This increases **pressure** in the rocks, causing **pieces** to **fall off**.

Rainwater can be slightly salty.

FROST SHATTERING

1) **Frost shattering** (**freeze-thaw** weathering) occurs in areas where there's **moisture** and **temperatures** that fluctuate **above** and **below freezing**.
2) Water from rainfall **enters the joints** and **crevices** in desert rocks.
3) At night, if the temperature **drops below 0 °C**, the water in the cracks **freezes** and **expands**.
4) Over time, **repeated** freeze-thaw action **weakens** the rocks and causes pieces to **fall off**.

ice expands   rock breaks off

WETTING AND DRYING

1) Some desert rocks contain **clay**.
2) When clay gets **wet** (from rainfall), it **expands** and the **pressure** caused by this **breaks fragments off** the rock.

clay expands   rock breaks off

Wind Erodes Desert Rocks and Transports Particles

1) Wind can **erode** desert rocks in **two** ways:

① **Deflation** — the **removal** of **fine, loose particles** from the surface of rocks.

② **Abrasion** — **small particles** being **carried** by the wind **scrape off** particles from the rock surface.

2) It then **transports** the eroded material by **three** processes:

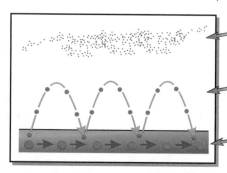

① **Suspension** is when **very small particles** (less than **0.15 mm**) are **picked up** and **carried** by the **wind**.

② **Saltation** is when **small particles** (**0.15-0.25 mm**) are **temporarily lifted** from the ground and **bounce** along.

③ **Surface creep** is when **larger particles** (over **0.25 mm**) are **hit** and **pushed along** the ground by particles being moved by **saltation**.

3) **More particles** are **transported** when the wind is **strong** and comes from a **constant direction**.
4) When there's a **reduction** in **wind speed**, the wind **drops** some of its **load** — this is **deposition**.

Processes in Hot Desert Environments

There are Three Types of River in Hot Deserts

1) **Exogenous** rivers have a **source outside** the **desert margin**. They flow **throughout the year** despite **evaporation** reducing their volume. For example, the source of the **Colorado river** in the **USA** is in the **Rocky Mountains**. It flows through the **Sonoran Desert** and the **Grand Canyon** to the sea.

2) **Endoreic** rivers **terminate inland** in the form of an **inland sea** or **delta**. For example, the **River Jordan** terminates in the **Dead Sea** — an inland sea in the **Middle East**.

3) **Ephemeral** rivers flow **intermittently** or **seasonally** after **rainstorms**. For example, the **Todd River** in the **Simpson Desert** (**Australia**) only flows a few days a year and remains a **dry river bed** for the rest of the year.

Derek promised them an ephemeral river was coming soon...

Flooding Erodes the Desert

Most **rainfall** in hot deserts is **light** and **infrequent**. However, **sometimes** there may be a **sudden**, **high intensity rainstorm** that lasts for a **short period** of time. This can cause **two types** of **flood** in a desert — **flash floods** and **sheet floods**.

Flash Floods

1) A **flash flood** is a **sudden**, **strong** and **rapid** flow of water through a **channel**.

2) They occur because **heavy rainfall** **can't** be **absorbed** by the **dry**, **hard desert soil** — so the **runoff** collects in **channels** and **flows rapidly downhill**.

3) Flash floods have **enough energy** to transport **large pieces** of desert rock by **traction**. They also transport **pebbles**, **gravel** and **sand** by **suspension** and **saltation**. The rocks in the water are **eroded** into **smaller fragments** by **attrition** (rocks smashing into each other).

4) The material carried by flash floods **erodes** the channels by **abrasion**, making them **deeper**.

5) At the **mouth** of a channel, the flash flood waters **spread out**, **slow down** and **soak into** the **ground** (unless they meet another body of water).

See page 6 for more on how water erodes and transports material.

Sheet Floods

1) A **sheet flood** is a **slow-moving**, **even flow** of water **over land** (i.e. it **isn't** confined to a **channel**).

2) Like flash floods, they occur **after** a period of **intense rainfall**, where water **collects** across the **dry**, **impermeable desert floor** and flows down **gentle slopes** as a **sheet** of water.

3) Sheet floods have **less energy** than flash floods, but can still **transport pebbles**, **gravel** and **sand** by **suspension** or **saltation**.

4) The **material** carried by sheet floods **erodes** the **desert surface** by **abrasion**.

Practice Questions

Q1 Name four types of mechanical weathering that occur in hot deserts.

Q2 Describe two ways in which wind can erode desert landscapes.

Q3 What is suspension?

Q4 What is surface creep?

Exam Questions

Q1 Describe the mechanical weathering processes that can occur in hot desert environments. [8 marks]

Q2 a) Describe the three types of river that can be found in hot desert environments. [3 marks]

b) Outline how flash floods and sheet floods can erode hot desert landscapes. [6 marks]

Surface Creep — Grandad's new disco dance move...

There are tons of technical terms to get to know on these two pages — saltation, exogenous, ephemeral... It's tricky enough to get the spelling right, let alone what they mean. But if you shut the book and test yourself a few times you'll soon have 'em sussed.

Landforms in Hot Desert Environments

Wind and water in the desert do really neat things, like sculpting crazy landforms. Ooooooh, aaaaaaaahh.

Wind Erosion Forms Yardangs and Zeugen

Yardangs

Yardangs are **narrow, streamlined ridges** that are usually **three to four** times **longer** than they are **wide**. **Strong winds** (blowing in **one direction**) carry sand in **suspension**, which **erodes rocks** by **abrasion**. **Softer** rock is **eroded faster** than **harder** rock, so **ridges** of hard rock are created (yardangs). The ridges **aren't** always **continuous**.

Zeugen! — That wind is capable of some nifty sculpting.

Zeugen

Zeugen are **long, block-shaped ridges** of rock (a **single ridge** is called a **zeuge**). They're formed in areas where a layer of hard

rock sits **above** a layer of softer rock. If **cracks** form in the **hard rock** due to **weathering** processes such as **frost shattering** (see page 52), the **wind** can **erode** through the **cracks** and into the **softer rock** beneath by **abrasion**. Again, the **softer rock** is eroded **more** than the **hard rock**, and ridges (zeugen) are formed.

Sand Dunes Form When the Wind Deposits Sand

1) **Sand dunes** form when **sand grains** carried by **suspension** are **deposited** as the wind **slows down**.

2) **Vegetation, rocks** and **other dunes** slow wind down, causing it to **drop** its load.

3) The **shape** and **layout** of dunes is affected by several factors:

   See page 52 for more on how wind transports sand.

   • The **speed, direction** and **consistency** of the **wind**.

   • The **amount of sand** being transported — the **more** sand, the **larger** the dune.

   • The nature of the **ground surface** — e.g. **rocky outcrops** or **uneven ground** slow wind down.

   • The **amount** and **type of vegetation** — **deposition** occurs **downwind** from vegetation and **around its base**, **deforming** the shape of dunes. Also, **plant root networks** help to **stabilise sand** and **hold** dunes in place.

4) There are lots of **different types** of sand dune:

Barchan dunes (crescent-shaped)

1) These are **isolated** dunes that develop from mounds of sand. They form in the **direction** of the **prevailing wind** as sand is **deposited**.

2) When the slope of the dune becomes **too steep**, **sand avalanches** occur, depositing sand at the **base** (downwind).

3) **Swirling wind currents (eddies)** help to keep the slope **steep**.

4) The dune **slowly moves forward** in the direction of the wind.

5) If there's a **lot of sand** being deposited, many barchan dunes **connect** with each other to form a **barchanoid ridge**.

Seif dunes (long wiggly lines)

1) **Seif dunes** are **long, wiggly ridges** of sand.

2) They form **from barchan dunes** if a **change** of **wind direction** occurs.

3) When wind blows from **alternate sides** the 'arms' of barchan dunes are **elongated** and form a wiggly line.

Star dunes (urm... star-shaped)

1) Star dunes have **multiple steep faces** caused by winds from **many directions**.

2) As more sand is added they grow in **height**.

Landforms in Hot Desert Environments

Water Erosion Creates Many Different Desert Landforms

The **fast-moving water currents** that follow **torrential rainfall** in the **desert** can create many different **landforms**:

1 Pediments

Pediments are **desert plains** — gently sloping areas of **rock** (usually covered in a thin **layer** of **debris**). They're formed by the **erosion** of rock by **sediment** carried in **sheet floods** or **small streams**.

2 Inselbergs

Inselbergs (e.g. **Ayers Rock**) are **steep-sided hills** that rise up from pediments. They're made of **hard rock** that's more **resistant** to **erosion** than the **surrounding rock**. The surrounding rock is **eroded** by **water**, leaving the harder rock **standing out**. Inselbergs can also be formed by **wind erosion**.

3 Mesas and buttes

A **mesa** is an **isolated, flat-topped, steep-sided** landform found only in **arid** places. They're a **type of inselberg** composed of a **hard horizontal rock layer**. They form in the **same way** as inselbergs. **Buttes** are **smaller** and **narrower** versions of mesas.

4 Salt lakes

Salt lakes form when **desert rivers**, which contain salt, are **endoreic** (**terminate** in an **inland sea**). The water can't **leave** the lake and **evaporation** is **high**, resulting in a lake with a **high salt content** (sometimes higher than **sea water**). Some salt lakes are **ephemeral** — evaporation is **so high** that they **dry up** at certain times of the year, leaving the salt behind to form **salt pans** (**ground** covered with **salt**).

5 Wadis and alluvial fans

A **wadi** is a **gully** or **ravine** that's been eroded by **seasonal rivers**. Depending on the **strength** of the river, a wadi can have **shallow** or very **steep** valley sides. If there's a flat desert plain at the **mouth** of a **wadis** the water **spreads out** on to the plain. This leads to **sediment** being **deposited** as **energy** is **dissipated**, forming an **alluvial fan**.

6 Badlands

Badlands are so called because they're **difficult** and **dangerous** to travel through. Badlands are **vast areas** of **uneven terrain** with **deep, interlocking canyons**, **steep ridges**, **loose sediment** and **deep sands**. **Wadis** and **buttes** can be found there. **Erosion** occurs from **flood waters** and **wind**. **Softer rock** layers and **clay soils erode** to form **canyons**, while **hard rock** layers are **eroded less** to form **ridges**.

Practice Questions

Q1 Give three factors that affect the shape and layout of sand dunes.

Q2 What are pediments?

Q3 Name two features of badlands.

Exam Questions

Q1 Describe and explain the formation of yardangs and zeugen. [7 marks]

Q2 The diagram above shows a desert landscape.

    a) Identify the landforms A, B and C. [3 marks]

    b) Landform D is a mesa. Describe what it is and how it formed. [4 marks]

    c) Suggest what E is and how it formed. [4 marks]

So, the yardangs fight the zeugen and the inselbergs save the world...

...what's that... we're not talking about Star Trek... Oh. Sounded like we were. Best make sure then that you really do know your yardangs from your zeugen, your pediments from your inselbergs — I suggest you get that butte into gear and sha-wadi-wadi.

Desertification

Desertification isn't the cheeriest topic around but it's definitely important.

Desertification *is a Form of* Land Degradation

Desertification is the **degradation** of **semi-arid** land by **human activities** and **changes in climate**. It leaves land **unproductive**. **Africa** and **Asia** are the **worst affected areas** but desertification is a problem across the globe.

1) A **third** of land worldwide is **at risk** of **desertification**. 110 countries have regions that are threatened, with those likely to be worst affected in **Africa**, **Asia** and **Latin America**.

2) **250 million people** across the globe are already affected by desertification, the **largest proportion** of which are in **Asia**.

3) **46%** of **Africa** is **at risk** of desertification (**25%** is at **high** or **very high risk**).

World map of desertification risk

■ Very High ▨ Moderate ▤ Not at risk
■ High □ Low ▣ Dry

Climate Change *is a Physical Cause of Desertification*

Climate change is causing desertification by **reducing rainfall** and **increasing** the **temperature** in some areas:

Lower rainfall

1) Climate change will probably **reduce rainfall** in **sub-tropical regions** (where most semi-arid environments are).

2) If there's **less rain** then **surface water** and **groundwater** will be **reduced** (as it's used up or evaporates but isn't replenished).

3) This means that the volume of **water** available for **vegetation growth** is **reduced**, which leads to the **death** of vegetation.

4) The **roots** of **plants** and **trees bind the soil together**. **Fewer plants** and **trees** mean **fewer roots**, leading to **soil erosion**.

Higher temperatures

1) **Global surface temperature** has **risen** by **0.6 °C** over the last century and is predicted to **continue rising**.

2) As **temperatures increase** the **rate of evapotranspiration** also **increases**.

3) This **dries out soils** and **lowers surface water levels**, leading to soil erosion in the same way as lower rainfall does (vegetation dies).

Human Activity *is the Main Cause of Desertification*

1) **Overgrazing** — **reduces vegetation**, so leads to **soil erosion** (due to lack of **plant roots**). Trampling by large numbers of animals **compresses** and **breaks down** the **structure of soil**, which also makes **erosion more likely**.

2) **Overcultivation** — **reduces soil productivity** as the over-exploitation of the soil leaves it **without** enough **nutrients** to support plants. Without plants (and plant roots) the soil is **easily eroded**.

3) **Deforestation** — removing **trees** and therefore **tree roots** means that (once again) soil is more **vulnerable to erosion**. Forests are cleared to provide **land** for **farming** as well as **wood** for **fuel** and **building materials**.

4) **Irrigation** — can cause desertification in a number of ways:

   - Irrigation **depletes surface water** and may involve **unsustainable pumping** of **aquifers**. As **water levels** are **lowered**, **water availability** for plants **decreases**, leading to **soil erosion**.

   - Some **irrigation techniques** can **erode soil directly**, e.g. surface irrigation, where large amounts of water are added to the soil in a short amount of time, **washing topsoil away**.

   - If **too much water** is used to irrigate crops the excess can **sink** into the soil and **raise groundwater levels**. If the aquifer is **saline** this may bring **high concentrations** of **salt** too close to the surface, **increasing** the **salinity** of the **soil** too much for plants to survive.

   Aquifers are underground rocks containing water that can be extracted.

5) **Population growth** — **increases pressure** on the **land** as more and more **food** is needed to meet the **growing demand**. This leads to **further overgrazing**, **overcultivation**, **deforestation** and **irrigation**, therefore increasing desertification.

Desertification Impacts *on Land, Ecosystems and Populations*

As **fertile topsoil** is **eroded** the land becomes **less productive** (i.e. less can be grown). **Less plant life** means that **less animal life** can be supported and **biodiversity decreases**. If agricultural productivity decreases to the point where farmers **can't feed** their **families** or **earn a living** from the land then they have to **migrate** from the area. This **increases pressure** on the **land** in the **areas** that they **migrate to**. If people are **unable** to move then desertification can lead to **famine**, as families or whole communities are unable to produce the food they need from the degraded land.

Desertification

There are Strategies to Manage Arid Environments

Desertification can be prevented by using strategies that...

...make agriculture more sustainable by reducing overgrazing, overcultivation, and improving the fertility of the soil

1) Leaving areas of land fallow (not cultivated) — this allows the soil to recover from grazing.

2) Adopting nomadic farming — nomadic herders constantly move animals on, which stops areas being overgrazed.

3) Rotating crops — different crops need different nutrients, so rotating crops stops the same nutrients being depleted year after year. This improves soil fertility. Adding compost can also improve soil fertility.

4) Planting legumes (e.g. clover) — these improve soil fertility by increasing the amount of nitrogen present.

...make water use more sustainable by reducing use

1) Growing crops that need little water (e.g. millet, sorghum and olives) — this can reduce water use.

2) Using drip irrigation — this technique adds small volumes of water to the soil at a time. It reduces wastage of water and also prevents soil being eroded by large volumes of water being added in one go.

...increase or maintain the level of vegetation to reduce erosion

1) Planting trees — these act as windbreaks, protecting soil from wind erosion.

2) Using alternative energy sources — technology such as solar cookers can help reduce deforestation to provide wood for fuel. These cookers use the sun's energy to heat food and are cheap and easy to make.

External Aid May be Needed to Implement These Strategies

Implementing strategies to combat desertification costs money, either for equipment (e.g. drip irrigation systems) or for programmes to educate and train local people. In developing countries this money often comes from external aid. For example, in 1988 the International Fund for Agricultural Development funded a programme costing US $1.5 million to combat desertification in Northern Sudan.

Sustainable Strategies Address the Causes of Desertification

1) Most of the strategies above are sustainable because they prevent desertification and once implemented they can be carried on by the local community without external help or money. E.g. once people have been trained how to make a solar cooker, further external aid isn't needed as that knowledge is now within the community.

2) Some strategies just address the problems caused by desertification and so aren't sustainable (as they won't prevent desertification happening again in the future).

3) Examples of unsustainable strategies are transporting water to areas at risk of desertification, and using external aid to provide relief from famine.

4) To address the threat of desertification many countries are drawing up National Action Plans, which aim to prevent desertification using sustainable solutions and involving local communities.

Practice Questions

Q1 What is desertification?

Q2 Describe three strategies that reduce desertification.

Q3 What makes an anti-desertification strategy sustainable?

Exam Question

Q1 Outline the causes of desertification. [10 marks]

Dessertification — now that sounds like a topic I could get on board with...

If a third of land was at risk of being turned into sticky toffee pudding, the world would be a much better place.
Sadly, that's not the case and desertification is causing problems across the globe. The good news is that if you take the time to learn these two pages really well it shouldn't cause you a smidge of a problem in your exam. Every cloud and all that...

58

Desertification Case Study — The Sahel

Down to specifics... The Sahel — it's a real place, with real problems.

Desertification is Already Happening in the Sahel

1) The **Sahel region** is a roughly **3900 km long belt** that runs east to west across **Africa**. It separates the hyper-arid Sahara from the wetter and more fertile savanna further south.

2) The Sahel runs through **10 countries** (see map), which are some of the poorest countries in the world.

3) It receives **200-600 mm** of rain per year, mostly between **May** and **September**, but **rainfall** can **vary** massively from year to year.

4) Some areas are **already suffering** from **desertification**, and others are at **very high risk**.

1. Senegal
2. Mauritania
3. Mali
4. Burkina Faso
5. Algeria
6. Niger
7. Nigeria
8. Chad
9. Sudan
10. Eritrea

The Sahel — Countries of the Sahel

Desertification is Caused by Climate Change, Agriculture and Deforestation

Climate change

1) Between **1968** and **1997** rainfall in the Sahel **decreased** between **29%** and **49%**.

2) Low rainfall led to a **five year drought** from **1968** to **1973** and **droughts** were **common** across the Sahel from then right through to the early 1990s. While drought alone **doesn't cause** desertification (well managed land will recover when the drought ends) it can **contribute** to desertification when the **land** is **badly managed**, as the land will become degraded to a degree that it **can't recover from**.

3) The **average temperature** of the region has **increased** over the last century. This **increases** desertification by **increasing evapotranspiration**, which **reduces ground** and **surface water supplies**.

Agriculture

1) Between **1968** and **1998** the **population** of the Sahel **increased** from **274 million** to **628 million**. As the population increases **more food** has to be produced from the land to feed everyone.

2) At the same time, the **area of good agricultural land** has **reduced**, as more and more land is used as **game parks** for **tourists**.

3) With **less land available** and **more people** to feed the **pressure** on remaining agricultural land has **increased**. This has led to **overcultivation** and **overgrazing**, which has **increased desertification**.

4) The **total** area of land that's used for agriculture has **increased** from **8 million hectares** in **1960** to over **16 million hectares** in **2000**, as land that's **less suitable** for agriculture is used.

5) **Restriction** of **nomadic farmers** (those who move their herds depending on the weather, season or state of pasture) by **border closures** has forced farmers to stay in **one area**, causing **overgrazing**. Some nomads have also adopted a more **settled lifestyle**, which has had the same effect as restricting movement.

6) **Political instability** and **war** has led to **migration** of people to refugee camps, putting huge pressure on the surrounding environment to provide **enough food** for the **enlarged population**. E.g. between **1998** and **1999**, **30 000** people migrated to **Sudan** to escape the war between **Ethiopia** and **Eritrea**.

Deforestation

1) To create **more space** for **agriculture** large areas of **forests** have been **cleared** in the Sahel (usually by burning), leaving the ground vulnerable to **erosion**.

2) **Deforestation** to provide **wood** for **fuel** is a major problem in the Sahel, where **82%** of **total energy** used in homes and for industry comes from **wood**.

3) The demand for fuel wood has led to some people switching **from agriculture to wood collection** to earn a living. As increasing amounts of wood are collected the area of land that's deforested also increases. Wood for use in **Zinder** (a city in **Niger**) is now collected up to **200 km** away from the town.

Desertification Case Study — The Sahel

Desertification Has Environmental, Social and Economic Impacts

1) Erosion of topsoil has **reduced** the **area** of **productive agricultural land** in the Sahel. In **Mauritania** all that's left is a **200 km wide** strip running across the country, whilst in **Niger 2500 km²** of land is lost **each year** to desertification.

2) As land area decreases, so does the **amount of food produced**. E.g. some areas of **Niger** now produce **less than a 20th** of the food they could **40 years ago**. This causes **loss** of **livelihoods** and, in the worst cases, **famine**.

3) Many people have had to **migrate** from areas where the **land can't support them** any longer. E.g. over **2 million** people have migrated from **Mali** and **Burkina Faso** as a result of desertification.

4) With **fertile soil** becoming increasingly **scarce**, **tensions** have grown between **settlement farmers** and **nomadic herders** over use of the land, sometimes leading to **violence**.

5) The **changing conditions** in the Sahel have led to **animal migrations**. E.g. **rodents** from the Sahara are travelling further south, **destroying crops** and bringing **new diseases**.

Strategies to Reduce Desertification are Being Implemented

Some strategies to reduce desertification are **traditional techniques** that have been used for many years. For example:

The plant *Jatropha curcas* is grown as hedges **around food crops** by farmers in **Mali**. It's able to grow in **poor quality soil** and **isn't eaten by animals**. Its roots help **bind soil together** and it **protects** the **soil** from wind and water **erosion**. **Oil** produced from the plant can be **sold**, providing a valuable source of **income**. This strategy has **reduced poverty** and **erosion** in the area. The plant can also be burnt as **fuel**, **reducing** the need for **deforestation**.

Contour bunding is a **low-cost** technique where stones are placed **around agricultural lands** to keep **rainfall** there long enough for it to **soak in**. It's used to **maximise water use** and **prevent soil erosion**. It's **increased** some **yields** by **40%** in **Burkina Faso**, but can only be used in areas with **sufficient stones**.

Other strategies are more **recent** developments and have relied on **external aid** for implementation. For example:

In **Niger**, **Non-Governmental Organisations** (NGOs) are helping farmers to **reduce soil erosion** by providing **free seeds** of plants that are **suitable** for growing in **arid conditions**. These plants grow an **extensive root system** that **holds** the **soil together**. Long roots also mean that the plant can **absorb water** from **deeper** in the ground, so they're **less vulnerable** to drought. This scheme has been successful in **reducing soil erosion** but some people are concerned that it **encourages poor farmers** to continue **agricultural production** that's **high-risk**.

Similar schemes are also run in Sudan and Senegal.

In **Eritrea**, a **more efficient** version of the **mogogo** (a traditional stove) has been introduced. It needs **50% less wood** than the older version and therefore **reduces** the need to **cut down trees** for fuel. **Funding** for the project has come from NGOs and **international aid agencies**. A similar project has been launched in **Chad**, where new stoves run on **manure** rather than wood, therefore **reducing deforestation** and the risk of desertification. The new stoves have **reduced pressure** on **wood supplies** and the number of **respiratory diseases** has **decreased** as they produce **less smoke** than the old ones.

In **Chad**, NGOs have launched schemes to **reduce soil erosion** by **educating villagers** about the importance of maintaining plenty of **vegetation** and by helping them grow and plant seedlings. The schemes also **promote cooperation** between **neighbouring villages** to try to avoid over-exploitation of resources and to **share techniques** for **good land management**.

External aid can have **negative impacts** if the projects they fund aren't managed properly. During the 1968 to 1973 drought thousands of **wells** were built using aid money. Many farmers used the wells to **increase** the **size** of their **herds**, but the land couldn't cope with the **overgrazing** that followed. **Large areas** of land became **desertified** as a result.

Practice Questions

Q1 How is agriculture causing desertification in the Sahel?

Q2 Describe the impact of desertification on the Sahel.

Exam Question

Q1 Evaluate the strategies used to reduce desertification in the Sahel. [15 marks]

I drought you'll have too much of a problem learning this...

Like with all case studies you need to make sure that you learn lots of details and examples. Having a general idea that there are some problems with desertification in the Sahel isn't going to cut it. You need to learn the causes, impacts and the strategies.

Desertification Case Study — Southern Spain

*It's not just developing countries at risk — desertification's causing problems all over the place.
The Med may be fantastic for holidays, but all those tourists have an impact...*

Desertification is Already Happening in Southern Spain

1) **Spain** is in **Southern Europe**, close to North Africa and the Sahara desert.

2) Roughly **50%** of Spain is classified as **arid**, making it the **driest** country in Europe.

3) In 2008 it was estimated that **37%** of Spain is **at risk** of **desertification** (with **18%** of the land at **high** or **very high** risk).

4) The **most vulnerable areas** of the country are in the **south**, e.g. Andalusia and Murcia.

The map on the right shows the vulnerability of different areas to desertification.

Desertification is Caused by Climate Change, Agriculture and Development

Climate Change

1) The **average temperature** in Spain has **risen** by **1.5 °C** in the last century, **increasing** the rate of **evapotranspiration**.

2) **Rainfall** has **decreased** throughout Spain. Between **1991** and **2000** rainfall in **Andalusia** fell by **9.5%**.

3) Higher temperatures and lower rainfall have **reduced surface water resources**. Less water is available to recharge groundwater supplies, leading to **falling groundwater levels**. As there's **less water fewer plants** can grow, meaning **fewer roots** to hold the soil together. This leads to **soil erosion** and desertification.

4) As the climate gets hotter and drier there's **increased risk** of **forest fires**, causing **deforestation** and desertification.

Agriculture

1) **Overcultivation** is causing desertification as the **nutrient content** of the soil is **reduced** to the point that it's no longer productive. **80 million tonnes** of topsoil is **lost** each year in **Andalusia** because of intensive cultivation of **olive trees**.

2) **Overgrazing** is **reducing vegetation cover**, causing desertification.

3) Groundwater resources are being pumped to **irrigate crops**. This is **lowering groundwater levels**. Increasingly more water is being used for irrigation because...

- **Agriculture** is carried out in areas that **aren't** really **suitable** for it. E.g. the region of **Almeria** (in Andalusia) is an important agricultural area as produce grown there for export contributes **$1.5 billion** to the economy each year. Almeria is the driest area in Europe though, so this is only possible with **intensive irrigation**.

- **Crops** that need **more water** than the area can **supply** are being grown for **export**. E.g. Spain is Europe's largest producer of **strawberries**, and **95%** of its exports are grown in **Andalusia**. As Andalusia is so arid **intensive irrigation** is needed to supply the strawberries with the **large amounts** of **water** they need to grow.

Although there are restrictions in place to protect aquifers, many farmers are using **illegal boreholes** to secure water supplies for their crops.

Development

1) There's been a huge **increase** in **tourism** in Southern Spain in the last 50 years. In the last few years an estimated **180 000 holiday homes** have been built along the Spanish coast every year.

2) This is increasing strain on water supplies as there's more and **more demand** for **water** for **swimming pools**, **water parks** and **irrigation of golf courses**.

3) Although there are regulations in place to protect water supplies for agriculture, many developments get around them by **reclassifying** grass on golf courses as "**crops**" or holiday villas as "**farms**". This ensures that, like farms, they get **allocated water**. This contributes to desertification by **depleting water levels**. It also **reduces water availability** for **farms**, **reducing** their **productivity**, which leads to desertification spreading.

Desertification Case Study — Southern Spain

Desertification Has Environmental, Social and Economic Impacts

1) The demand for water to fill swimming pools and irrigate crops and golf courses has led to **conflict** over water. A **black market** for water has developed, supplied by water from **illegal boreholes**. An estimated **40%** of land in some parts of the **Segura basin** (Murcia) is illegally irrigated and **10%** of wells in the **Guadalquivir river basin** (Andalusia) are illegal.

2) Exploitation of groundwaters has led to **loss of habitats**, such as wetlands, and **reduced biodiversity** in the region. E.g. nearly **150 000 ha** of **marshland** surrounding **Doñana National Park** has been **lost** since 1900 — most of which has been deliberately drained for farming.

3) As groundwater levels lower the water can become **salinised** (very salty). When this happens the water is no longer suitable for drinking or irrigation and the **resource** is **lost**. Many wells have had to be abandoned.

4) As **aquifers** become **salinised** so do the **soils** around them, which leads to **further desertification**.

5) Desertification leaves soil **unusable for farming** and deprives farmers of their **livelihood**.

Strategies to Reduce Desertification are Being Implemented

The government's **Programme of National Action Against Desertification** aims to tackle desertification in several ways:

The **National Hydrological Plan** was adopted in **2001** to ensure that water supply meets demand by:

1) **Transferring water** from areas with a **plentiful supply** to areas with **very little**.

2) Building **desalinisation plants** to produce fresh water from saline aquifers at a cost of **€1.2 billion**.

3) **Reducing** the amount of water **wasted** during irrigation by **improving irrigation infrastructure**, e.g. by investing in technology for sprinkling and drip irrigation. The aim is to **reduce** the amount of **water** used for irrigation by **10%** (from 2002 levels), whilst **increasing** the area of **land irrigated** by **7%**.

4) Reducing pressure on water supplies by **introducing management strategies** for **aquifers** and funding awareness-raising activities to **promote efficient use** of **resources**.

The National Hydrological Plan is **controversial** as it's very expensive and some elements **aren't sustainable**. **Raising awareness** and **improving infrastructure** can help **reduce desertification**, but transporting water from one area to another is only a **short-term** solution to the shortage of water (it doesn't tackle the overuse of water that's causing desertification). Irrigation will continue to **increase** and desertification will **spread**.

Areas at **high risk** of **forest fires** are being identified and **defence plans** drawn up for them so that fires can be dealt with quickly. Areas that are destroyed have to be **reforested** and many **new areas** are being planted with trees and bushes. Since the scheme was introduced **550 000 hectares** have been forested.

Reforestation and forest management **reduces soil erosion** and so desertification.

An official **water trading scheme** has been set up that allows farmers to buy water. It costs them three times the normal price but is **lower** than the **black market price** and therefore aims to **reduce illegal exploitation** of **aquifers**.

Water trading can help to reduce **illegal** exploitation of aquifers. If water resources are **sustainably managed** then the scheme could **reduce desertification**, but if resources continue to be **over-exploited** then water trading is unlikely to reduce desertification.

Practice Questions

Q1 Which areas of Spain are most vulnerable to desertification?
Q2 Why has the volume of water needed for irrigation increased?
Q3 Describe two impacts of desertification in Spain.

Exam Question

Q1 Compare the strategies used in Spain and the Sahel to tackle desertification. [15 marks]

Last year I went to sunny Spain — and helped spread desertification...

You know the drill by now — learn all the specifics, don't skimp on the examples, blah blah blah. The more information you know the more marks you can get. And once you've learnt these pages, you're done with deserts and arid environments. Finally.

Population Change Basics and the DTM

Populations are dynamic — they're always changing. These pages will help you understand how and why — it's all to do with birth and death rates and population migrations. And don't forget the famous DTM.

There are **Loads** of **Terms** and **Definitions** to Learn

1) **Birth rate** — the **number** of live **births** per 1000 people, per year.

2) **Death rate** — the **number** of **deaths** per 1000 people, per year.

3) **Fertility rate** — the **average number of children** a woman will have between the ages of **15** and **44** (**reproductive** age).

4) **Infant mortality rate** — the **number** of **children** (out of every 1000 born **alive**) who **die before their first birthday**.

5) **Life expectancy** (longevity) — the **average age** (in years) a person can **expect to live**.

6) **Migration rate** — the **difference** between the **number** of people who **migrate in** (**immigrants**), and the number of people who **migrate out** (**emigrants**) per **100 000** (or 1000) of the population, per year.

7) **Population density** — the **number** of people per **square kilometre** (km²).
It's the **total population** of an area **divided** by the **size of the area** (in km²).

Migration is the movement of people between or within countries.

8) **Changes in the population over time:**

- **Natural change** — the change in population (**increase** or **decrease**) because of the **difference** between **birth rate** and **death rate** (not including changes due to **migration**). For example, when **birth rate > death rate**, the population will **grow naturally** (if migration rate is **zero**). When **death rate > birth rate**, the population will **fall** (unless enough people **migrate in**).

  < means 'less than'
  > means 'more than'

- **Zero growth rate** — the population is **neither increasing** nor **decreasing** (e.g. **birth rate = death rate**).

The **Demographic Transition Model (DTM)** Shows **Population Change**

The **demographic transition model** (**DTM**) shows how the **population** of a country **changes** over time through **five stages**. The model shows changes in **birth rate**, **death rate** and **total population**.

'Demographic' means it's to do with human populations.

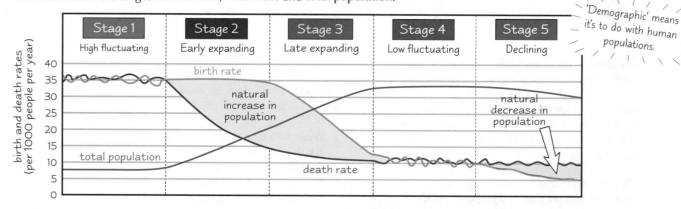

As Countries **Develop** They **Move Through** the **Stages** of the **DTM**

As countries become **more developed** their birth rate and death rate **change**, which causes the **total population to change**.

Stage 1 — high birth rate and high death rate

Birth rate and death rate **fluctuate** at a **high level** — the population remains **stable** but **low**. There **aren't any countries** in **Stage 1**, but some **tribes** in the rainforests of **Brazil** are in this stage.

1) **Birth rate is high** because there's **no birth control** or **family planning**, and **education is poor**.

2) It's also high because there's **high infant mortality**, so people have **more children** to replace those who've **died**.

3) **Death rate is high** and life expectancy is low because there's **poor health care**, **sanitation** and **diet** — leading to **disease** and **starvation**.

    Birth rate — around **35/1000**   **Death rate** — around **35/1000**

The values for the birth rate, death rate and population for each stage are just rough estimates, not exact figures.

Population Change Basics and the DTM

Stage 2 — high birth rate, death rate falls

Death rate **falls**, but birth rate remains **high** — the population **increases rapidly**.
Countries like **Nepal** and **Afghanistan** are in **Stage 2**.

1) **Birth rate** is still **high** as there's still **little birth control** or **family planning** and **education is poor**.

2) Birth rate also stays **high** for **labour reasons** — family members (including **children**) all have to **work**, e.g. on **farms**. A **larger** family can tend to a **larger** farm, helping to bring in **more food** and **money**.

3) **Death rate falls** and **life expectancy increases** due to improved **health care**, **sanitation** and **diet**.

Birth rate — around **35/1000**   **Death rate** — falls to around **15/1000**

Stage 3 — birth rate falls a lot and death rate falls slightly

Birth rate **declines rapidly**, while death rate **falls slowly** — the population **increases** at a **slower rate**.
Countries like **Egypt** are in **Stage 3**.

1) **Birth rate decreases** due to the **increased** use of **birth control** and **family planning**, and **improvements** in **education**.

2) The **birth rate** also **drops** as the **economy** moves towards **manufacturing** — **fewer children** are needed to **work** on farms, so having a **larger family** isn't as **advantageous** as it once was.

3) **Birth rate falls** further still as **more women work** rather than stay at home to have children.

4) Some countries introduce **government population policies** to try to **reduce the birth rate**.

Birth rate — falls to around **13/1000**   **Death rate** — falls to around **10/1000**

Stage 4 — low birth rate and low death rate

Birth rate and death rate **fluctuate** at a **low level** — the population remains **stable** but **high**. Most **developed countries**, e.g. most of **Europe** and the **USA**, are in **Stage 4**. **Birth rate stays low** because **increased access** and **demand** for **luxuries** like **holidays** and **material possessions** means there's **less** money available for having children (they're **expensive** to raise). Also, there are **fewer advantages** to having children, e.g. they're **not needed** to work for the family.

Birth rate — falls to around **10/1000**   **Death rate** — around **10/1000**

Stage 5 — birth rate drops below death rate

Birth rate begins to **decline** further while death rate remains **stable** — the population begins to **decrease**. Some **highly developed** countries, e.g. **Japan**, are in **Stage 5**.

1) The **birth rate decreases** because children are **expensive** to raise and many people have **dependent** elderly relatives, so lots of people choose **not** to have children.

2) **Death rate** remains **steady** as there are **more elderly people** so more people die (of **old age**) despite **advances** in health care.

Birth rate < **Death rate**

Hmm, have children or buy myself a shiny new car...

Practice Questions

Q1   Define fertility rate.
Q2   Define population density.

Exam Question

Q1   The table shows some population data for a country since 1600.
With reference to the DTM, describe and explain the changes in the population shown by the data.   [10 marks]

Date	Birth rate (per 1000 per year)	Death rate (per 1000 per year)	Population (millions)
1600	38	37	2
1700	35	34	3
1800	35	18	7
1850	26	15	15
1900	18	12	21
1950	12	10	26
2000	8	10	28

Rabbits never seem to get much past Stage 2...

You're expected to know your way around the DTM. Make sure you understand the diagram and how all the different rates change over time. You need to be able to explain why the rates change too. Then you can apply it to any country or set of stats.

Applying the DTM

So you're now a dab hand at the ol' DTM and how the stages differ from one another.
It's a nice model but it doesn't work for every country, and you get to learn why. Joy.

Most MEDCs are in Stages 4-5 of the DTM

1) **Most countries** that are classed as MEDCs (More Economically Developed Countries) have **passed through** Stages 1, 2 and 3. They have **low birth and death rates, long life expectancies** and **slow population growth**.

2) During Stages 2 and 3 their **rapid population growth** was accompanied by **industrial growth, farming improvements** and **increasing wealth**. This is where they **changed** from being **LEDCs** (Less Economically Developed Countries) to **MEDCs**.

3) Some MEDCs are in Stage 5, e.g. **Italy, Japan** and **Germany**. Birth rate is **lower** than death rate, causing the population to **shrink**. The population is also **ageing**, as **more people** live for **longer** — a greying population.

4) Being in Stage 5 can cause **problems** for a country:

   • There are too **few children** to **replace** the current, ageing **workforce** — the workforce may not be large enough to carry out the work, which could cause the **economy** to **slow down** or **stop growing**.

   • A **smaller population** means a **reduction in spending**, which could also cause the **economy** to **slow or stall**.

   • There are **fewer taxpayers**, so there's **less money for services**. This is made worse by the **increasing cost of services** for the elderly — **more old people** means **more money** is needed for **pensions and health services** (carers etc.).

Most LEDCs are in Stages 2-3 of the DTM

1) Most countries classed as **LEDCs** are in **Stage 2** (e.g. **Afghanistan**) or **Stage 3** (e.g. **India**).

2) Lots of countries entered **Stage 2** in the **1950s**, e.g. **Kenya** and **Bangladesh**. **Improved health care** and **sanitation** led to a **reduced death rate**, while birth rate **stayed high**. Many of these countries have become **overpopulated** — they don't have the **resources** (e.g. **money** or **services**) to **cope** with the expanding population.

3) Some **former LEDCs** have moved into **Stage 3** in the last few decades, e.g. **Newly Industrialised Countries** (**NICs**) like **Malaysia** and **Taiwan**. The **death rate** is still **falling**, leading to **increasing populations**. Some **governments** have introduced **policies** to reduce **birth rate** and **prevent** overpopulation, e.g. **one-child** policies.

You need to be aware that although most countries used to be classified as either MEDCs or LEDCs, it's now thought that this system is too simplistic — there are too many stages of development to divide countries into only two categories.

The UK's Demographic History Matches the DTM Model

Stage 1 (prehistoric times to about 1760)

Total population was **small** — e.g. **6 million in 1700**. **Poor diet** and **hygiene**, as well as **wars** and **diseases** such as the **Black Death** and **cholera**, caused a **high death rate**, which **cancelled out** the **high birth rate**.

Stage 3 (1880-1940)

The population was still **growing**, but at a **slower rate** — **47 million** by **1941**. **Birth control** improved and was used **more frequently**, so the **birth rate fell**. **Death rate continued to fall** (except during **World War 1**) as **food supply, medicine** and **hygiene** continued to **improve**.

Stage 2 (1760-1880)

The population **grew quickly** — it was **5 times** bigger by the **1880s** (6 million in 1700 to **30 million** by 1881). Improvements in **farming** and **medicine** reduced **starvation** and **disease**, so **death rate fell**. **Birth rate** remained **high** and the **economy grew** quickly. **Urban populations** grew particularly **rapidly**.

Stage 4 (1940-today)

Population growth has **slowed down** — **56 million** by **1981**. **Death rate** was **low**, except during **World War 2**, and **birth rate** was also **low**, except for **baby booms** (large increases in birth rate) after **World War 2** and in the **1960s**.

Stage 5 (today+)

Death rate today is **almost** exactly the same as birth rate and the population is **ageing** — pensioners **outnumber** children and it's been estimated that by **2030**, a **quarter** of the UK's population could be **over 65**. The population could begin to **decline** if birth rate **drops below** death rate because there are too few young people, or death rate becomes larger than birth rate because the large population of elderly people **die**.

Look back at the last two pages to refresh your memory of the DTM.

Applying the DTM

The DTM is Useful...

1) The **DTM** gives a good **generalised** picture of how a **population** can **change** over time.

2) It's easy to **compare** a **country** with the DTM — if you know a bit about how the **population** and **birth** and **death rates** of a country have changed, you can analyse what **stage** of the DTM it's in.

3) You can then **forecast** how its population may change — which can help governments decide on **policies** such as **one-child limits** and **immigration laws**.

Winning major sporting events is often linked to mini peaks in birth rate — I blame it on the short shorts.

...But It Has Limitations

1) The **original data** used to **create** the DTM was from **more developed**, richer countries (e.g. **European** countries, **Japan** and the **USA**). This means it might **not** be a **valid model worldwide** — what happened in these countries might not be the **same** as what's happening in others, e.g. countries in **Asia** or **Africa**.

2) The original DTM **didn't** have **Stage 5** — it's been **added** since some countries have moved **out of Stage 4**.

3) The DTM doesn't take things like **education** and the role of **women** into account separately and these affect **birth rate** quite a lot, e.g. **increased higher education** means more people **delay** having a family.

4) The **population** in countries with **different customs** may change in different ways, e.g. the **Catholic** church **condemns contraception**.

5) **Extreme poverty** and **low levels of development** may cause a **lack of population growth** and **prevent** many **LEDCs** from passing through **all** the stages.

6) The DTM **can't predict** exactly **when** countries will **reach** each stage, or **how long** each stage will **last**.

7) It doesn't consider **migration** — **international migration** can have a large effect on **population change**.

8) **Other factors** can also affect the population so a country **no longer fits** the DTM:

Population control policies (e.g. France and China)

High levels of **population growth or decline** have forced some governments to introduce **population policies** — **discouraging** or **encouraging** larger families. For example, population growth in **France** is very **low**, so the government has introduced things like **subsidised childcare** to encourage **larger families**. In **China**, the **opposite** is occurring. The government has tried to **reduce** birth rate using a **one-child per family policy**.

Infectious disease (e.g. HIV/AIDS, Malaria)

Some countries may have particularly **high levels** of **infectious disease**, which keeps the **death rate high**, **reducing** the population or stalling population **growth**. For example, some **African countries** like **Nigeria** and **Botswana** have very **high HIV/AIDS** rates, leading to **high death rates**.

Civil War (e.g. Rwanda, Sierra Leone, ongoing in Sudan)

War leads to an **increased death rate** and **decreased birth rate**, especially if **large numbers** of men and women of **reproductive age** are **killed** or **involved** in the conflict. Also, **civil war** often leads to **emigration**, decreasing the population, as people **flee** the fighting. For example, thousands of people **died** during the civil war in **Sierra Leone (1991-2002)** and thousands more **fled** to **neighbouring countries**.

Practice Questions

Q1 Describe two problems faced by countries in Stage 5 of the DTM.

Q2 In 1800, what stage of the DTM was the UK in?

Q3 Describe one factor that can affect the population size so that a country no longer fits the DTM.

Exam Question

Q1 Discuss the uses and limitations of the DTM. [15 marks]

Baby boom — the noise babies make as they break the sound barrier...

OK, so not the greatest CGP pun ever, but at least I'm trying. You better be trying to learn all these DTM facts — my blood, sweat and tears have gone into this page. Well tears anyway — that joke really isn't great, it's a 'must try harder' for sure.

Population Structure and Migration

Population structure pyramids are very exciting — not as exciting as cheerleader pyramids, but still better than nowt.

Population Structure is How the Population is Made Up

Population structure is the **number** or % of **males** and **females** in different **age groups** within a population. **Population pyramids (age-sex pyramids) show** population structure. You can **learn** a lot about the **demographics** of a place from its population pyramid. For example, the pyramid below shows the **population structure of France:**

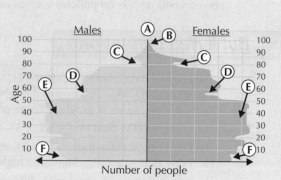

Ⓐ Some people are living to be **100**, which shows a **high life expectancy**.

Ⓑ **Women** are living **longer** than men.

Ⓒ There are **fewer** people aged **75-85**, because there was a **low birth rate** when they were **born** (around **World War 1** – WW1) and they've suffered from a **high death rate** (lots killed in WW2).

Ⓓ There are also **fewer** people aged **50-60**, also because of a **low birth rate** when they were born (around **WW2**).

Ⓔ There are **lots** of people aged **25-50** because of a **baby boom** after WW2.

Ⓕ There are **fewer** people aged **0-10** because of a **low birth rate** for the last 10 years.

Population Structure Varies from Place to Place and Over Time

1) Population pyramids for **different countries** vary because of different **demographic factors** — **birth** and **death rates**, fertility rates, wars, migration etc.

2) A country's population structure **changes** through **time** as it moves through the **stages** of the **DTM** (see page 62).

3) This means a **population pyramid shape** can show **which** stage of the DTM a country is in:

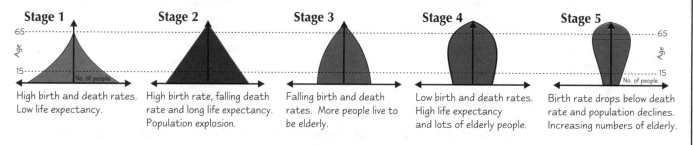

Stage 1 — High birth and death rates. Low life expectancy.

Stage 2 — High birth rate, falling death rate and long life expectancy. Population explosion.

Stage 3 — Falling birth and death rates. More people live to be elderly.

Stage 4 — Low birth and death rates. High life expectancy and lots of elderly people.

Stage 5 — Birth rate drops below death rate and population declines. Increasing numbers of elderly.

Migration Can Change Population Structure

Migration is the (often permanent) movement of people **between** or **within** countries. **Immigration** is the movement of people **into a country** (or area) and **emigration** is the movement of people **out of a country** (or area). Migration can **alter population structure**, which can be seen in the **population pyramids** for the areas affected. Migration can affect **any part** of the population pyramid — it depends **how old** the migrants are.
Here are some examples:

1) **Internal migration (migration within a country)**
Internal migration from **rural** areas to **urban** areas often affects the number of **young adults** (people of **working** and **reproductive age**). They **move away** from the countryside **into** the cities to find **jobs**. This is called **rural-urban migration**. This can **affect birth rate** too as the migrants are of reproductive age.

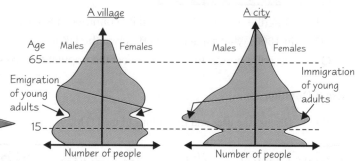

Population Structure and Migration

Before emigration

Age
65 ----

15 ----

Number of people

Emigration of elderly people

After emigration

Number of people

2) <u>**Emigration away from countries at later DTM stages**</u>

Emigration **away** from countries at **later DTM stages into** other countries **decreases the population** of the country they've left. E.g. **elderly people** in the **UK retiring and emigrating** to other countries. This **reduces** the number of elderly in the UK, but **increases** the number in the countries they **move to**.

3) <u>**Immigration into countries at later DTM stages**</u>

Immigration **into** countries at **later DTM stages** (e.g. MEDCs) **from** those at **earlier DTM stages** (e.g. LEDCs) **increases the population** of people of **working** and **reproductive age**. This **increases** the population of young people and **increases birth rate**. For example, immigration **into** the **UK** (Stage 4).

Before immigration

Age
65 ----

15 ----

Number of people

Immigration of young adults

After immigration

Increased birth rate

Number of people

Migration Occurs Because of Push and Pull Factors

The **reasons** for migration can be divided into **push** (**negative**) and **pull** (**positive**) factors:

Push factors — these are things that **make** people want to **move out** of the place they're in. They're **negative factors** about the place they're **leaving**, e.g. **lack of jobs** or **poor living conditions** and **services**, fear of **political persecution**.

Pull factors — these **attract** people to a **new place**. They're **positive factors** about the place they're **moving to**, e.g. **better jobs** and **more job opportunities**, **better living conditions** and **services**.

Migration is also affected by **obstacles** and **opportunities**:

Obstacles — these are things that make migration **more difficult**, e.g. the **cost** of moving.

Opportunities — these are opportunities individuals **encounter** that mean they **stop** before they reach their **intended destination**, e.g. **Polish** migrants heading for **Ireland** for **work** might stop in **London** because there are plenty of **jobs** there.

Hmm, he's got his own boat, but it's a shame about the beard. I'll give him a pull factor of 5.

Practice Questions

Q1 What is population structure?

Q2 What do population pyramids show?

Q3 What is internal migration?

Q4 How does immigration into a country at a later DTM stage affect the population of young people?

Q5 How do obstacles and opportunities affect migration?

Exam Question

Q1 Describe what is meant by push and pull factors. [4 marks]

Large, shiny tractors — rural pull factors...

The diagrams on these pages might look horribly complicated, but they're a good visual way of showing how populations change (plus the colours look nice). I'd bet they make great revision aids and pretty handy additions to exam answers. Hint hint...

Impacts and Management of Population Change

Some countries are full of old people, some are full of young people, and some are full of little green men...

The **Dependency Ratio** Shows **How Much** of the **Population is Dependent**

The **dependency ratio** gives the **proportion** of the population that has to be **supported** by the **working population** (aged **15-64**). **Young people** (aged **0-14**) and **older people** (**over 65**) are generally **dependent** on the working population — they need to be **looked after** or **supported financially**. The **equation** for the dependency ratio is given below:

A **high dependency ratio** means there's a **greater proportion** of dependent people, e.g. **Uganda** has a **high dependency** ratio of **1.1** — there's **more than one** dependent person for **each** working person.

$$\text{Dependency ratio} = \frac{\text{Young people (0-14)} + \text{Old people (over 65)}}{\text{Working age population (15-64)}}$$

There are **Social** and **Economic** Impacts of an **Ageing Population**

An **ageing** (or **greying**) **population** means the **proportion** of older people is **increasing**, which causes an **increase** in the **dependency** ratio. This has **social** and **economic effects**:

Social

1) **Increased pressure on public services** — there's **greater demand** for services like **hospitals** and **hospices**. **More** people are needed to **care** for the elderly, so **more carers** and **nurses** will need **training**. Also, more people will act as **unpaid carers** to their **own** elderly family members, putting pressure on them **socially** and **financially**.

2) **Unequal distribution of older people** — e.g. **Eastbourne** in the UK is a **resort** with a high proportion of **retired**, older people. Areas like this may have **inadequate facilities** for **young people**, e.g. **bars** or **youth clubs**.

3) **Reduced population growth or population decline** — the working population may have **fewer children** because they already have older dependants, leading to a **reduction** in **birth rate**.

4) **Longer working life** — the **state pension** is **low** because there are **so many** retired people. It's often **not enough** to support people in their retirement so some may have to **work beyond** normal **retirement age** — to build up **personal pensions** or **savings**, or to **add to their income** from the state pension.

Economic

1) **Reduced work force** — a **smaller proportion** of the population is working, which may **slow economic growth**.

2) **Increased taxes** — **pensions** and **services** are paid for by **taxes**. A greater proportion of older people **claiming** pensions and support could mean **higher taxes** for the working population.

3) **Spending** — the elderly have **savings** and **pensions** to spend (the **grey pound**).

There are **Social** and **Economic** Impacts of a **Youthful Population**

A **youthful population** means there's a **large** proportion of **young people** in the population. This has **social** and **economic effects**:

Social

1) **Increased pressure on public services** — greater demand for services like **schools** and **childcare**.

2) **Rapid population growth** — the large numbers of children grow up and have **families** too, **increasing** the population. This may lead to **overpopulation** if there **aren't enough resources** to cope with the number of people.

Economic

1) **Too few jobs** — there **aren't enough jobs** for young people when they grow up. **More unemployed** means more people are dependent on **government support**.

2) **Increased poverty** — **more** young people are born into families that are **already poor**, so there are **more people** in **poverty**. Some children may have to **work** to help **support** their large family, so they **can't go to school**, which means they can't **break out of poverty**.

There are **Political Impacts** of Ageing and **Youthful Populations**

Whether a population is getting **older** or **younger**, the impact on **politics** is the same — it changes what's important in **elections** and how people **vote**, and it affects **policies** such as **immigration laws** and **taxes** and **pensions**.

1) **Ageing population** — elderly issues will be important to **voters**, e.g. changes to **national pensions** or **heating allowances**. **Immigration laws** may be **relaxed** to encourage people of **working age** to **enter** the country.

2) **Youthful population** — youth issues will be important, e.g. **student loans** and **childcare provision**. The government may need to **increase teacher salaries** to **encourage** more people into the **profession**.

Impacts and Management of Population Change

There are Strategies to Manage Ageing Populations

1) **Encouraging larger families** — e.g. the **Swedish government** makes having children more **manageable** by giving **both** parents **18 months' paid leave** when they have a child. Encouraging larger families should result in a **larger working population** when the children grow up, which can provide **more taxes** for **better pensions and services**.

2) **Raising retirement age** — the **working population** is made **larger**, so **more people contribute** to the **state pension fund** and to personal pensions for **longer**. People will also **claim** the state pension for **less time**.

3) **Encouraging the immigration of working-age people** — e.g. in recent years **Japan** has **increased** its number of **foreign workers** because there **aren't enough** working-age Japanese people to fill the jobs **available**. This **increases** the **working-age population**, which helps to support the ageing population by **paying taxes**.

4) **Increasing health care provision** — large numbers of older people puts pressure on **health care systems**. This **doesn't** manage the **population change** but it could help ease the problem of **poor health** in the **elderly**.

There are Strategies to Manage Youthful Populations Too

1) **Controlling birth rate** — some countries that are **overpopulated** try to **slow** further growth by introducing policies that **limit** the number of children couples can have. For example, **China** introduced a **one-child policy** for some couples in **1979**. It's thought this has **prevented** more than **300 million births** since it was introduced.

2) **Limiting the immigration of younger people** — **limiting** the number of immigrants of **reproductive age** (15-44) would mean birth rates aren't **made any higher** by immigrants having children.

3) **Encouraging family planning and the use of contraception** — governments can offer **sex education** and **free** contraception, allowing couples to **plan** and **limit** the number of children they have.

4) **Increasing childcare provision** — countries can **invest in more** and **better childcare** so parents can **work** instead of caring for children. This **doesn't** manage the population change, but helps to address some of the **problems caused** by a younger population.

Management Strategies Should Aim Towards Sustainable Development

Sustainable development is all about developing and **growing** to meet the **needs** of people **today**, without **hindering** the ability of people in the **future** to meet their **own** needs. It involves **getting** what we need now without **damaging** or **altering** the **environment** in an **irreversible** way.

Generally, the **strategies** to manage growing elderly or youthful **populations** don't help sustainable development **on their own** — achieving sustainable development requires **lots of strategies** in lots of **different** areas.

1) **Encouraging larger families** — this creates an **even larger population** that'll need **housing, transport, food** etc. This **isn't** sustainable unless the population's **needs** are met in a **sustainable way**, e.g. **carbon-neutral homes**, **low** or **no** emission transport, food that's produced in an **environmentally friendly** way with **few food miles**.

2) **Encouraging the immigration of working-age people** — on its **own** this doesn't help towards sustainable development. E.g. **more** working people require **more jobs**, which could be in **heavily polluting industries**, or in **offices** that use **electricity** etc. Unless **these needs** are met in a **sustainable way**, this strategy on its own isn't sustainable.

3) **Controlling birth rate** — this **helps towards** sustainable development as the population **won't** get much **bigger**. But if the needs of the population still **aren't** met in a sustainable way, then it **just** stops the problem getting any **worse**.

Practice Questions

Q1 What does the dependency ratio tell you about a country or area?

Q2 Describe one strategy used to manage the effects of a youthful population.

Exam Question

Q1 Describe and explain the social and economic impacts of an ageing population. [15 marks]

This book'll have a social impact on you — you'll have to stay in and revise...

I'm sorry about this geography stuff taking up your valuable time, but think of it as an early warning. The population's ageing, so there'll be a lot of people for us to look after, and believe it or not, we'll all be old one day too so these strategies better work.

Managing Populations — Case Studies

And you thought I'd forgotten about the case studies. Case studies are good for you — you should have some for your tea.

The **UK** Has an **Ageing Population**

Like most **wealthy** and **developed countries**, the population of the UK is **ageing** (it's a **greying population**) — people **over 65** make up a **large part** of the population and it's **increasing**. In **2005**, **16%** of the population of the UK were **over 65**. This is expected to rise to **25%** by **2041** — here are a few reasons **why**:

1) **Increasing life expectancy** — between **1980** and **2006** life expectancy **rose 2.8** years for **women** and **4** years for **men**. It's currently **81.3** for **women** and **76.9** for **men**. As people live **longer**, the number of older people **increases**.

2) **Baby booms** — **lots of babies** were born in the **1940s** and **60s**. These large generations are starting to **retire, increasing** the number of elderly people.

3) **Falling birth rate** — there are **fewer** young people, so the **proportion** of older people is **greater**.

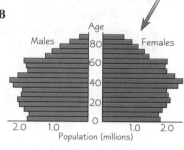

The **Ageing UK Population** Causes **Problems**

1) **Pressure on the pension system** — there aren't enough people of **working-age** to pay for an **adequate pension** for the **retired** population. **State pensions** are paid for by the **working population** through **taxes**.

- Today, **60%** of the population (the people of **working-age**) are paying taxes that go towards the pensions of **19%** of the population (the people of **retirement age**).

- By **2030**, only **56%** of the population will be of **working-age** but the taxes they pay will have to pay for the pensions of the **27%** of the population of **retirement age**.

2) **More elderly people living in poverty** — the state pension **isn't very large**, and many people don't have **other savings**. The working population **isn't large enough** to provide a **better pension** (see above).

3) **Pressure on the health service** — older people often need **more medical care** than younger people, e.g. the average stay in hospital in **2005** for people **over 75** was **13** nights, but only **8** nights for the UK population **as a whole**.

Different **Strategies** Aim to **Manage Ageing Populations**

1) **The age of retirement has been increased** — retirement age in the UK is currently **65** for men and **60** for women, but it will be raised to **68** for everyone by **2050**. Increasing the retirement age means people have to work for **longer, increasing** the size of the **working population**.

2) **Encouraging immigration of working-age people** — the UK has allowed **unlimited immigration** of people from countries who joined the **EU** in **2004**, e.g. **Poland**. In 2004, around **80%** of immigrants that came to the UK from the **new EU** countries were **34 or under**. This also **increases** the size of the **working population**.

3) **Encouraging more women to have children** — new UK **pension** proposals mean **women** won't lose out on **state pensions** if they take **career breaks** to have children. This could encourage women to have children. **Working family tax credits** support women (and men) who go back to **work** once their children are born, which might also encourage **more couples** to have children.

Strategies Need to Work Towards **Sustainable Development**

As mentioned on the **previous page**, strategies to **manage** ageing populations should support **sustainable development**. But usually they can't do this on their **own** — other actions need to be taken to help **achieve** sustainable development.

1) **Increasing retirement age** — this **helps towards** sustainable development because it **doesn't increase** the population. But it might mean **more jobs** are needed, as people work for longer. This could **hinder** sustainable development if the **new jobs** aren't provided in a way that works towards **sustainability**, e.g. **building** and **working** in new **coal-powered** power plants versus **wind-turbine** power plants.

2) **Allowing immigration** — this is only **sustainable** if the **needs** of the new people are met in a sustainable way. E.g. meeting the **increased energy demand** by increasing energy production from **renewable sources**, building new **energy-efficient** homes with **good insulation** and **natural heating systems**.

3) **Encouraging more children** — this could **increase** the **population** of a country, and so is similar to immigration.

Managing Populations — Case Studies

Uganda Has a Youthful Population

Like many **poorer** and **less developed** countries, **Uganda** has a **youthful population**. In **2007, 50%** of the population were **under 15** and only **3%** were **over 65**. The population is becoming **more youthful** — here are a couple of reasons **why**:

1) **High birth and fertility rates** — every year there are **48** babies born for every 1000 people, and women have an average of **7 children** during their reproductive years (15-44).

2) **Low life expectancy** of around **52** years — there are **very few** older people, which means the **proportion** of the population made up of young people is **very high**.

The Youthful Population Causes Problems for Uganda

The main problem caused by a **youthful population** is **overpopulation**, which is caused by a **high birth rate**. The population of Uganda is currently around **30 million**, but by **2025** it's thought it will grow to about **56 million**. When there are **too many people** for the **resources** the country has, things like the **health service** and levels of **employment** suffer:

1) **Pressure on the health service** — around **6000** women already **die** each year in **childbirth**. When the youthful population reaches **reproductive age** the pressure on the health service will be **even greater**, potentially leading to **more deaths**. The health service is also **stretched** because of **HIV/AIDS** (a deadly disease). It's passed on from **mother to child** and through **unprotected sex**, so HIV/AIDS may **spread** further when the youthful population start to have children, putting **even more strain** on the health system.

2) **Unemployment could get much worse** — in **2003** unemployment in **Uganda** was **3.2%**. However, 50% of the population are under 15 and so weren't **counted** in these figures. When the **large youth population** reaches working age there **won't be enough jobs** for them all, so unemployment will **rise further**, causing **poverty** to **increase**.

Some Strategies Have Been Introduced to Address These Problems

1) **Encouraging the use of contraceptives and family planning** — the use of contraceptives among married women is less than 25%. New policies **encouraging** the use of **contraceptives** allow women to plan **how many** children they have and **when they have them**, e.g. the government has brought in **free contraceptives like condoms**. However, family planning clinics **aren't widespread**, so many people don't have **easy access** to birth control. Since 1991, **birth rate** has **increased**, suggesting this population management method **isn't working**.

2) **Policies to combat the spread of HIV/AIDS** — in the late 1980s a programme of **education** called the **ABC approach** was used (**A**bstain from sex until marriage, **B**e faithful to one partner and use **C**ondoms). This strategy **worked** — HIV infection rates **fell** from **15%** of all adults in **1991** to **5%** in **2001**.

These Strategies Should Help to Achieve Sustainable Development Too

1) **Encouraging contraception** — this should **reduce birth rate** and help prevent **overpopulation** from getting any worse. This means the country can **focus** on sustainable development for the current population, without the population **increasing dramatically** and putting **pressure** on sustainable development strategies.

2) **Reducing the spread of disease** — this **relieves** pressure on the **health care system**, which **frees up** money to be used elsewhere, e.g. in **developing sustainable** irrigation techniques for **rural farming** communities.

Practice Questions

Q1   Describe one problem caused by the ageing population in the UK.

Q2   Describe one problem caused by the youthful population in Uganda.

Exam Question

Q1   With reference to a named example, evaluate the strategies used to manage population change.   [10 marks]

Youthful populations — not exactly like Neverland...

You're all too old, you're all too young — hang on, nobody's the right age here. Population structures are constantly changing, causing lots of different problems. Just think, one day the youthful populations will be old, then they'll be ageing populations.

Urban and Rural Characteristics

For anyone who thinks that urban characteristics is a dance beat with a groovy bass line — read on...

Urban and Rural Areas Have Different Characteristics...

Urban areas can be divided into **zones** based on the **major land use** in each area. In **developed** countries, as you **move away** from the **town** or **city centre**, the **major urban zones** are: the **inner city**, the **suburbs** and the **rural/urban fringe**. Each of these urban zones, and the **rural area** beyond them, have their own characteristics. The table below shows the **typical characteristics** of a large urban area in the UK:

Characteristic	Inner city	Suburbs	Rural/urban fringe	Rural area
Housing	High-density terraced housing built in the 19th century and high-rise blocks of flats built in the 1960s. Some old warehouses may have been redeveloped into luxury apartments.	A mix of 20th century detached and semi-detached houses with gardens. Closer to the inner city, a high proportion of properties will be council-owned. Further out, properties will be privately owned and larger, with garages and driveways.	Low-density, high-quality private housing. May also be higher density outer-city council estates.	Larger, privately owned housing and new estates with privately owned houses.
Ethnicity	High proportion of ethnic minorities.	\u2192 Proportion of ethnic minorities tends to decrease as you move out of the city.		Majority white.
Age structure	High proportion of younger people (students and young professionals).	Mostly families with children.	Mostly families with children. More elderly people.	Higher proportion of elderly people.
Wealth	The poorest sections of the urban population tend to live here. You also get more wealthy people living in redeveloped areas.	\u2192 Wealth tends to increase as you move out of the city.		Wealthiest residents who've moved out of the city. Also, some less wealthy original rural residents.
Employment	High proportion of students, unemployed and unskilled or semi-skilled workers. Some young professionals living in redeveloped areas.	More employment in tertiary sector (e.g. services, clerical and professional) and skilled manual workers.	\u2192 Proportion employed in tertiary sector tends to increase.	High proportion of workers in professional and managerial sectors (e.g. doctors, lawyers and bankers). Also agricultural workers.
Provision of services	Today, often an area of urban decay with derelict warehouses and industrial sites. But it's close to the city centre, which has lots of shops and services.	Some local shopping parades. Good transport routes to city centre and good availability of public transport.	The location for out-of-town shopping complexes, airports and recreational facilities such as golf courses.	Village shops may have closed as more residents shop in urban areas on their commute to work. Lack of public transport facilities.

...Which Affect the Welfare of the People Living in Each Zone

As you **move out** of the urban area **towards rural areas**, there tend to be **fewer environmental**, **social** and **economic problems**. These problems are **factors** affecting the **social welfare of people** living in each zone.
In **general**, these problems and social welfare **improve** as you **move away** from the inner city:

Environmental

1) Old, **poor quality housing**, often in a state of **disrepair**, creates a **poor living environment** in the **inner city**.
2) **Graffiti** and **vandalism** levels are **highest** in the **inner city** where there may be many **empty** and **derelict buildings**. Vandalism can also be high in the **suburbs** where there's a larger population of **children** and **teenagers**.
3) **Air pollution** is highest in the **inner city** due to remaining **industrial sites** and the **high volume of traffic**.

Social

1) There can be **tension** between people of **different ethnicities** in the **inner city** because of the **higher proportion** of **ethnic minorities**. This can occur in **rural areas** too if **large numbers** of immigrants move there.
2) The **crime rate** is **high** in the inner city — possibly due to the high levels of **unemployment** and **poverty** in this area. There are often **poor relationships** between the **police** and the **community**. Crime rates tend to **fall** as you **move away** from the inner city.
3) **Rural areas** can also experience social problems, e.g. a **lack of public transport** services can **isolate** people, particularly the **elderly**, and out-migration can lead to the closure of services like **shops** and **post offices**.

Economic

1) **Industrial decline** and **lack of investment** can lead to **high levels** of **unemployment** in the inner city. Although **employment levels** are generally **higher** as you **move away** from the inner city, there is **increasing unemployment** in **rural areas** because of **agricultural decline**.
2) **Poverty** is highest in the **inner city**. This can lead to **higher death rates** and **poorer general health** due to **poor nutrition**, **poor education** and a **lack of access** to services.

Remember, environmental, social and economic problems all affect social welfare.

Urban and Rural Characteristics

Population Change and Migration Have Affected Urban and Rural Areas

The **character** of **urban** and **rural areas** can be affected by **population change** and **migration** (including both **rural-urban migration** and **immigration**).

Housing
1) In **developed countries**, most migrants occupy the **cheaper**, **run-down** areas of housing in **urban areas** such as those found in the **inner city**.
2) In **developing countries**, **rural-urban migration** has resulted in the growth of **shanty towns** — **unplanned** and often **illegal** settlements, usually on the **outskirts** of the urban area, where people build their **own homes** out of whatever they can **find**. Theses areas have **limited services** such as clean **water** and **power**.

Ethnicity
1) High numbers of **immigrants** can change the character of areas by bringing their **existing culture** and **customs** with them. If they **fail to integrate** into the existing community, then 'ghettos' may form — areas of cities where members of an **ethnic minority** group live, **segregated** from the rest of the city.
2) Although most immigrants move to **urban areas**, some move to **rural** areas seeking **work** in **agriculture**. This can have a **greater impact** on the **character** of small rural **villages** than it does on a large city, especially if all the migrants are from one country. E.g. Polish workers moving to the UK countryside might open Polish **shops** and **cafes** in small **villages**, which may have **few shops** for the **original residents** already.

Age Structure
1) In **developed countries**, rural areas have increasingly ageing populations due to the **out-migration** of **younger people** and the **inward migration** of **retired people**.
2) The **provision of services** will be affected by this **changing age structure**, e.g. in **rural areas** schools may close due to reduced demand, whilst there may be **increased** demand for **services for the elderly**, e.g. nursing homes.

There's more about the effects of changing age structure on p. 68

Wealth
1) In **developed countries**, increasing numbers of **second-home owners** and **commuters** increases the **wealth of rural areas**. This leads to **rising house prices**, which can force **younger residents** to leave as they **can't afford housing**.
2) As young, **wealthy professionals** move to **redeveloped urban areas**, they **increase** the **wealth** there. This can **improve inner city areas**, but can also mean **younger original** residents **can't afford** to buy houses there.

Employment
1) **Unemployment** will **increase** if **many people** move to urban areas without there being **enough jobs** available.
2) This is a big problem in **developing countries** as there's often a very **high rate** of **rural-urban migration** for work.
3) In rural areas, the large number of people **moving away** for work could eventually lead to a **lack of available workers**.

A lot of these effects are linked, e.g. a lack of available workers in rural areas can lead to more immigrants moving to rural areas, which can affect age structure and social welfare too.

Services
1) **Shops and services** in rural areas suffer because **residents who commute** may use shops **closer to their work**. Services like **bus routes** can also close as the **newer residents** tend to use **cars** instead. This could be a problem for the **original residents** of the rural areas if they rely on **public transport** to get about.
2) As people of **reproductive age** move to an area, there'll be increased need for **childcare services** and **schools**. When **elderly residents** move to an area, it **increases** the need for **carers**, **home help** and **health care**.

Practice Questions

Q1 How does the proportion of ethnic minorities in each zone change with distance from the city centre?
Q2 In which zone would you expect to find 19th century terraced housing?

Exam Question

Q1 Explain how population change and migration can affect the character of urban areas. [6 marks]

My barber gave me a rural/urban fringe — that affected MY social welfare...

Wow, there's quite a lot on these two pages — make sure you know the different characteristics of urban and rural areas and how they affect the welfare of the people who live there. As if all that wasn't enough, you also need to know how these characteristics can be affected by population change and migration. Look on the bright side though — it could be worse... probably...

Urban and Rural Characteristics — Case Study

Now it's time to take all that lovely theory and apply it to the real world — that's what geography's all about.

Different Areas in Preston Have Different Characteristics

The map below shows **four areas** in and around **Preston**, a city in the **North-west** of **England**. The areas correspond to **wards** (areas of roughly **equal-sized population** defined by the **city council**). There's **one area** from **each of the zones** discussed in the table on page 72. The characteristics of **housing** and the **provision of services** are **different** in **each of the areas**:

LEA — an area on the **rural/urban fringe**. It has large **semi-detached** and **detached** houses with **gardens** and **driveways**. Many of the houses are built on **modern estates**. There are **no out-of-town shopping centres**, but there are small shopping **parades** and a **supermarket**. There's a regular **bus service** to the city centre and there's also a **golf course** in this ward.

FISHWICK — an **inner city** area. Here there's mainly **high-density**, 19th century **terraced housing** built during the **industrial revolution** when Preston's **cotton industry** was at its peak. It has a few **corner shops** that sell convenience goods (e.g. **bread and milk**), but it **doesn't have** any **parades of shops** or **shopping centres**. Residents travel to the **city centre** for these services.

Map of Preston area

UK
Ireland
Preston urban area
Riversway
City centre

ASHTON — a **suburban** area. It has **terraced housing** to the east of the ward. To the west, there are **larger detached** and **semi-detached** houses with **gardens** that border **Ashton park**. The **Lane Ends** shopping area has over 40 shops and there are many **bus stops** with **frequent services** to the city centre.

LONGTON — a **rural area**. Many new **housing estates** have been built here since the **1960s**. Housing consists of **large detached** and **semi-detached** properties with **gardens** and **garages**. The **A59 Longton By-Pass** provides easy **access** to Preston city centre for **commuters**. Longton village has a **supermarket** and many **shops** and **services**.

These Areas Fit the Expected Pattern for Urban and Rural Zones...

The table below shows **data** from the **2001 census** about the **characteristics** of the **population** in each ward. The **four areas** of Preston fit the **generalised** characteristics for **different zones** (as described on p. 72) quite well:

The % of privately owned houses **increases** as you **move away** from Fishwick (inner city).

Characteristic	Statistic	Fishwick	Ashton	Lea	Longton
Housing	% of houses privately owned	60.5	81.5	81.7	92.7
	% of houses without central heating	17.5	17.5	5.6	3.7
	% of houses with 1+ occupant per room	4.8	0.5	0.6	0.3
Ethnicity	% of population in ethnic group 'white'	66.5	93.2	95.7	99.2
Age structure	Average age (years)	32.9	38.4	35.6	43.4
	% of population aged 60 years or over	15.0	20.4	15.8	28.4
Wealth	% of households owning at least 1 car	57.4	75.7	86.2	88.5
Employment	% of 16-74 year olds unemployed	5.9	2.1	2.0	1.1
	% of working population employed in management or professional sector	15.7	28.3	30.8	30.7

The proportion of **ethnic minorities** **decreases** as you **move away** from Fishwick.

The % of **elderly** residents roughly **increases** as you **move towards** Longton (rural area).

The proportion of people **employed generally increases** as you move **away from** Fishwick. Also, more people are employed in **tertiary sector jobs** as you move away from Fishwick.

There's **no direct** data on **wealth**, but **car ownership** can be used as a rough **indicator** of the **wealth** of an area — the **greater the %** of car ownership, the **greater the wealth**. The number of people owning cars **increases** as you move **towards Longton**.

Urban and Rural Characteristics — Case Study

... *But There are **Some Exceptions***

There are a **couple** of ways in which these areas **don't** fit the generalised characteristics:

1) There are **no** out-of-town **shopping** centres in **Lea** (**rural/urban fringe**). This could be because of the **huge redevelopment** of **Preston Docks** in the neighbouring ward of **Riversway**. This has provided shopping and **leisure** facilities (such as a **cinema**, **bars** and **restaurants**). The residents of Lea can **travel** here easily, resulting in **less demand** for these services **within** Lea itself.

2) There are **more services** in **Longton** than might be expected for a **rural area**. Many commuters use the regular **bus service** from Longton to **Preston**, rather than **driving** into the city centre. This could be because of the **difficulty** of parking in the **centre**. Because the bus services are used **more frequently**, they're less likely to get **cancelled**. It also means that commuters are more likely to do their **shopping** in **Longton**, rather than **carry** it home on the bus. This might explain why there are **lots of shops** and a **supermarket** in Longton.

The **Different Characteristics** Have **Implications** for **Social Welfare**

The **social welfare** of people living in and around Preston is **affected** by the **characteristics** of the different areas. **Social welfare** tends to be **worse** in the **inner city**, and improve as you move **further towards** rural areas:

1) **74%** of people in **Lea** described their **general health** in the 12 months leading up to the 2001 census as '**good**'. In **Fishwick**, only **65%** described their general health as '**good**'. This may be because a **higher percentage** of people in Fishwick live in houses that are likely to be **cold and damp** due to the **lack** of **central heating** (see table). Also, the **higher occupancy rate** in Fishwick means that **germs** spread more easily from person to person, **aiding** the spread of **disease**.

2) The **Preston Crime Audit** found that there were **161 crimes** per 1000 people in **Fishwick** between 2003 and 2004, compared to **52** in **Lea**. The high levels of **unemployment** and **low levels of wealth** in inner city areas like Fishwick can lead to **higher crime rates**. **Theft of vehicles** and theft **from** vehicles are also **higher** in Fishwick. This could be because most of the houses **don't** have **driveways** or **garages**, so vehicles are **less secure**.

3) The level of **education** is **lower** in Fishwick than it is in other areas — in **Ashton**, **21.4%** of the population have **no qualifications**, but in Fishwick it's **44.7%**. **Fewer** people are in **higher education** in Fishwick too — **10.3%** of the 18-74 year old population in **Ashton** are classed as **students** in **full-time education**, but this is only **6.2%** in Fishwick. Lower levels of education mean residents can't apply for **more highly skilled** or **professional work** (see data table).

4) **Less skilled workers** are usually paid **lower wages** than highly skilled professionals — this affects the **wealth** of the area. In the table, **car ownership** (i.e. wealth) **increases** towards Longton, **as the proportion** of **managers** and **professional** sector workers **increases**. A **lack of wealth** in an area can lead to other social welfare **problems** such as **increased debt**, and less money for **entertainment** and **sporting activities**, which can add to **health issues** such as **depression** and **obesity**.

Practice Questions

Q1 Name four wards found in the Preston area.

Q2 Which ward in Preston consists of mainly 19th century terraced housing?

Q3 Describe the general pattern of ethnicity for wards in the Preston area.

Exam Question

Q1 For a named region, choose **two** of the following areas:
- inner city
- suburb
- rural/urban fringe
- rural area

For these two areas, compare their characteristics and explain how they affect the social welfare of the resident population.   [15 marks]

It's been a long-ton coming but you prest-on and got to the end...

Hurrah — that's the end of Population. Well, not the end of population as in the end of the world — that wouldn't be anything to cheer about. But that's the Section finished. It might have been tough at times, but you 'pressed on' and got there in the end.

Global Food Distribution

This section is all about one of my favourite topics of conversation — grub. So tuck in.

Global **Food Production** is **Unevenly Distributed**

Some countries produce **large amounts** of food and some countries produce **very little**. The map below shows the production of barley by country from 2000 to 2002. The production of other food follows a similar pattern.

Metric tonnes (1000s)

■ 9001 — 17200   ■ 1501 — 4000   ☐ 0 — 500
■ 4001 — 9000   ☐ 501 — 1500   ☐ No data

East Asia, **North America** and **Europe** produce a lot of food due to:

1) **Climates** that are **good** for farming.
2) Lots of **investment** in farming.

South America and **Africa** only produce small amounts of food due to:

1) A **lack of resources** and **funding** for farming equipment.
2) Large areas of **land** that are **unsuitable** for farming as they are either **mountainous**, have **poor quality** or **little soil**, e.g. the Sahara desert.
3) **Unsuitable climates** — **low rainfall**, **too hot** or **too cold**.

There are **Several** Different **Food Production Systems**

1) **Commercial** farming — the production of crops or livestock to make a **profit**.
2) **Subsistence** farming — when just enough food is grown to **feed the family**. It's common in Africa and Asia.
3) **Intensive** farming — **produces as much as possible** from the land. There are **two types** of intensive farming:
   - **Capital-intensive** farming has a high input of capital (money), and a low input of labour for the area of land. It often involves using fertilisers, pesticides and labour-saving machinery.
   - **Labour-intensive** farming doesn't involve much capital but uses a lot of labour.
4) **Extensive** farming — the **opposite** to intensive farming. It has a **low capital** and **labour input** for the area of land so produces **less food** than intensive farming. Small numbers of livestock grazing large areas of land is an example. Extensive farming has **less impact on the environment** and provides **better animal welfare** than intensive farming.
5) **Arable** farming — **plants** are grown for food, fuel, animal feed or materials (e.g. wood).
6) **Livestock** farming — **animals** like sheep, pigs or cows are raised for food or for materials (e.g. leather).
7) **Mixed** farming — farming of **plants and livestock**.

Global **Food Consumption** is Also **Unevenly Distributed**

Food consumption, like production, **varies** between countries. The map on the right shows the **daily calorie intake** of people in different countries.

1) **More developed** areas like **North America** and **Europe** **consume a lot**. They can afford to import a large variety of foods, have a **culture** of **consumerism**, and many people have **high disposable incomes** so can **afford more food**.
2) **Less developed** areas like **Africa**, **South America** and parts of **Asia consume less food** per person as they **can't afford** as much.
3) **China** and other **newly industrialised countries** are **consuming more** as their **wealth increases**.

Large populations consume more than small populations but this map shows consumption per person.

Daily calorie intake per person (2001-2003)

■ Over 3600   ■ 2600 to 3100   ☐ 1520 to 2100
■ 3100 to 3600   ☐ 2100 to 2600   ☐ Not estimated

Food is **Traded Between Countries**

1) Countries that are able to **produce lots** of food often **export** it to those that can't.
2) North America, Europe, Australia, Argentina and Brazil all **export large amounts** of food.
3) Africa, Japan and Middle Eastern countries such as Saudi Arabia all have to **import large amounts** of food.

Global Food Distribution

Trans-National Corporations Play an Important Role in the Food Industry

Trans-National corporations (TNCs) are companies that operate in **more than one country**.
Many TNCs play a **major role** in the **production**, **processing** and **distribution** of food.

E.g. Cargill™ is a TNC based in the USA. It's the largest privately owned company in the world and operates in **66 countries**.

1) **Production**: Cargill™ **sells products** like fertilisers, equipment and seeds to farmers to help them grow crops. It then **buys** the crops from them. It also **produces its own** food, e.g. palm oil in Papua New Guinea.

2) **Processing**: It **owns processing plants** across the globe, e.g. soya bean processing plants in Paraguay, corn processing plants in China and cocoa processing plants in Ivory Coast.

3) **Distribution**: The worldwide distribution of many Cargill™ products is run from an office in Switzerland. It has its **own distribution network** in some countries, e.g. Venezuela, and **employs local people** to trade products in others, e.g. Pakistan.

ADVANTAGES OF TNCs

1) **Lots of foods can be produced cheaply.**
2) The **range of foods available is increased**.
3) TNCs **provide jobs** and **improve economic security** in countries where they operate.
4) They **invest in research** and **development** of new products and technologies that can increase farming yields.

DISADVANTAGES OF TNCs

1) They **control** the **price** of products such as seeds, fertilisers and machinery, the cost of processing and distribution, and the price of foods produced. If these prices are too high **some countries can't afford them**.
2) **Smaller companies can't compete** and **go bankrupt**. This causes supplies of food to become **delocalised** (countries have to buy from TNCs instead of local companies), leading to **less self-sufficiency**.
3) The **intensive farming methods** of TNCs can cause **environmental problems** (see page 80).
4) It can take a long time to process and transport the food — **reducing** its **nutritional value**.

The Geopolitics of Food Involves Different Issues

1) Food production and trade are **very important** to all governments for many reasons.
2) All countries want 'food security' — they want to make sure that **their supply** of food (either from their own country or from another) **isn't disrupted** by things like poor yields, wars, or other political issues.
3) If their food supply **is** disrupted it can result in **food shortages**. These can cause serious **health issues** as well as **social** and **political instability** in that country. Not good.
4) Also, food production can account for a **huge proportion** of a country's **economy**.
5) So, countries make **agricultural policies** that **protect** their **home production** and **control** the **import** of food (see pages 82-83 for more).

Practice Questions

Q1 Why is food production in Africa low?
Q2 What is subsistence farming?
Q3 Describe the global pattern of food consumption.

Exam Questions

Q1 Compare the main characteristics of intensive farming and extensive farming. [5 marks]

Q2 Discuss the advantages and disadvantages of the involvement of TNCs in the global food industry. [8 marks]

Food fights — a serious threat to the even distribution of food...

OK, I'm fully aware that your main interest in food is probably the part where you shovel it into your mouth — but you do need to learn all the bits that lead up to that. So take the time to learn these pages properly — you could get asked about any of it.

Changes in Demand

Back in yesteryear, olden times and days of yore people had to eat whatever they could grow,
which I imagine made mealtimes a trifle dull. Luckily for you and me, all that has changed...

In the Last 50 Years the **Food Industry** Has Become **Globalised**...

Before the 1960s the food we ate was usually grown in our **own country**, and was often from the local area.
Since then there has been an **increase** in the **global trade** of food to satisfy **rising levels of consumption** and the increasing
demand for a **wide range** of foods **all year round**. This increase in global trade is called **globalisation**.

...Which Has Had a **Negative Impact** on the **Environment**

Countries can make a lot of **money** by **exporting food** so it's in their interests to **produce large amounts**.
Unfortunately, producing and transporting all this extra food can be damaging to the environment:

See page 80 for the damaging effects of intensive farming methods.

1) Countries that **export food** want to **produce as much as possible**. This means that they want
   more land for **farming**, which often leads to **deforestation** to provide the land.

2) The **greater** the **area** of land that's farmed, the **bigger** the **environmental impact** of farming.
   Growing food for export can also mean a change to more environmentally damaging **intensive farming methods**.

3) As **food exports increase**, so does the amount of **transportation** needed and the amount of **carbon dioxide** released by
   vehicles. Carbon dioxide is a greenhouse gas, so the more that's released the bigger the contribution to the **greenhouse
   effect** and **climate change**. 'Food miles' is the distance food travels from **producer** to **consumer** and gives an indication
   of **how much** carbon dioxide is **released** as the food is transported.

The **Type of Food** That's in **Demand** Has **Changed**

1 Demand for **SEASONAL PRODUCTS ALL YEAR
ROUND** has **INCREASED**...

1) In the 1960s most of the fruit and vegetables on
   sale in the UK were **locally produced** and **seasonal**.
   Seasonal food isn't available all year round —
   you can only buy it during the months that it grows.

2) Today, you can buy seasonal products at
   any time of year.

3) This is because fruit and vegetables are **imported**
   from **abroad**. E.g. peaches grow in the UK from
   August to September, but are imported all year
   round from Spain, Italy, France and Greece.

2 ...and so has demand for **HIGH VALUE FOOD
EXPORTS** from **POORER COUNTRIES**.

1) **High value foods** are, unsurprisingly, foods
   that have a **high value**. They include things
   like exotic fruits and vegetables, coffee and
   chocolate.

2) Between 1980/1 and 2003/4 **high value
   food** exported from **poorer** countries to
   richer countries **quadrupled** — from $26
   billion to $106 billion.

Crops that are grown for export are called cash crops.

Both these changes in demand were caused by...
1) A rising culture of **high consumption**.
2) **Rising incomes** in developed countries, which means more people
   can afford to buy the imports.
3) The **increasing popularity** of **exotic** products.

Dave was thrilled
to discover his
favourite vegetables
were now available
all year long.

There are **negative** effects of importing seasonal and high value food:
1) There are **food safety** and **agricultural health concerns** because standards vary between countries.
2) Importing food **increases food miles**, which increases the **negative impact** of transporting food on the
   environment.
3) There's **less food produced** in developed countries because it becomes cheaper to import food than produce it.
   This leads to **lower food security** as countries rely more and more on imported foods.
4) Many people are concerned about the fairness of **workers' pay** in developing countries, and that these
   countries are selling their best produce abroad at cheap prices.
5) The **best land** is often used to grow **high value foods** for exportation. This may leave **little** or **poor quality land**
   to grow **food** to feed the local population, which can lead to **food shortages**.

Changes in Demand

 Demand for ORGANIC food has INCREASED...

Between 1993/4 and 2003/4 **organic food sales** in the UK **increased** over **10 times** — from £105 million to £1119 million.

This trend is caused by people's concern that...

1) **Intensive farming damages** the **environment.**
2) Eating food that may contain **pesticide residues** is **harmful.**

There are negative effects of organic produce:

1) It's more vulnerable to **pests** and **disease.**
2) It's more **expensive** to produce and buy.
3) There's **not enough** organic produce grown in the UK to **meet demand** so some has to be **imported**, which **increases food miles.**

 ...and so has demand for LOCAL PRODUCE.

From 2005 to 2006 the number of UK shoppers buying **local produce increased** by 6%.

Reasons for this change in demand include more awareness of...

1) **Environmental issues**, i.e. food miles.
2) **Social issues** — the possible exploitation of workers in the developing world.

The negative effects are:

1) Local foods can be **more expensive** to produce and buy.
2) If we **import less** from the **developing world**, the **producers** there may **suffer.**

Foods Can be Produced in a *More Sustainable Way*...

For food production to be **sustainable** it has to **not damage** the **environment** and **not deplete resources.** Hardly any food production systems are totally sustainable, but there are ways to make them **more sustainable:**

1) **Relocalising food supplies** (buying food produced locally). This would **reduce food miles.**
2) Replacing intensive farming with **organic farming.** This would reduce the impact on the environment.
3) Using **less food packaging.** This would **reduce energy use** and **waste.**
4) Using **fair trade systems.** This would give growers in developing countries **fair pay** and improved **social** and **environmental** standards.

... But There are *Challenges* to Doing This

1) Food **can't** always be **grown locally** — the land might not be suitable for farming.
2) **Organic** farming methods are usually **less productive** than intensive farming methods — so **more land** is required to produce the same amount of food.
3) **Climate change, soil degradation** and demand for **biofuels** is **reducing** the area of **land** available for farming.
4) Also, in many areas where the **land** available for **farming** is **reducing**, the **population** is **increasing** and therefore **more food** is needed.
5) So, with **less land** available and **more people** to feed, it would be very **difficult** to **produce enough food** using **only organic farming methods** as they're **less productive** than **intensive farming methods.**

Practice Questions

Q1 What are high value food exports?

Q2 List the negative effects of the growth of high value food exports from developing countries.

Q3 List some of the ways that food could be produced in a more sustainable way.

Exam Questions

Q1 Describe and explain the changes in demand that have driven globalisation of the food industry. [4 marks]

Q2 Describe the environmental impacts of the globalisation of the food industry. [8 marks]

'Newsflash: Jet-setting vegetables to destroy planet.' Just as I suspected...

The key thing here is to be able to explain yourself. It's all very well knowing how our food supply has changed but if you can't explain why, you're going to come unstuck, which is never good. So read these pages through, scribble the details down, and you'll be able to explain to all and sundry why you can buy peaches in December. Whether they want to know is a different issue.

Increasing Food Production

So, there's no shortage of demand for good food, which leads us seamlessly on to the fact that...

Global **Food Production** Needs to **Increase**

Food production needs to increase to cope with **population growth** and **increasing consumption** in countries with increasing wealth, e.g. China, India and Brazil.

There are a Range of **Strategies** That **Increase Food Production**

1) The **Green Revolution** Increased the Use of **Technology** in Agriculture

The green revolution began in the 1940s and spread the use of technology and intensive farming methods across the world.

Food production increased through the use of:

1) **Higher yielding crops** and animals (developed by selective breeding).

2) **Monocultures** — growing just one crop over a large area.

3) **Irrigation technologies**, e.g. groundwater pumping, electric sprinklers.

4) **Agrochemicals**, e.g. fertilisers, pesticides and herbicides.

5) **Mechanisation**, e.g. use of machines for sowing, harvesting, weeding and spraying.

The **negative impacts** of the green revolution are:

1) Bankruptcy of **small farms** that **can't afford** the **technology**, leading to **rural unemployment** and **food shortages**.

2) **Lower food security** — monoculture crops can be wiped out by a single pest, drought or disease, and there's no alternative crop to rely on.

3) The **intensive farming methods** of the green revolution can **damage** the **environment**:

- Monoculture **reduces biodiversity**.

- Over-irrigation can lead to **lower ground water levels**, **waterlogging** and **salinisation** (increase in saltiness) of soil and water.

- Agrochemicals can cause **pollution**.

- Mechanisation and over exploiting the land leads to **reduced soil fertility** and **increased soil erosion**.

- Using pesticides could lead to the evolution of "**superpests**" that are resistant to pesticides, which could result in **more damaging pesticides** being used.

Example

India began a green revolution programme in **1961**. It **financed agrochemicals**, **developed irrigation systems** and **imported high yielding** varieties of **wheat** and **rice**. Productivity increased rapidly as a result, e.g. **rice yields tripled** by the **1990s**.

2) **Genetic Modification** is a **High Technology** Approach

Genetically modified (GM) crops are crops that have been altered by the addition of genes that give them **beneficial characteristics**. They were introduced in the 1990s.

Crops can be modified to make them:

1) **Produce pesticides** — making them **resistant** to some **pests**.

2) **Herbicide** and **pesticide tolerant** — this means farmers can use these chemicals without harming the plant.

3) **Resistant to disease**.

4) **Higher yielding** — either by increasing their size, or their rate of growth.

5) **Longer lasting**, i.e. with an increased shelf-life.

6) **Resistant to harsh** environmental **conditions**, e.g. drought or frost.

All of these modifications **increase food production**.

A small number of **GM animals** are also being developed, e.g. quick to mature salmon, cows that produce enriched milk, and pigs that produce lower fat bacon.

Because GM is a new technology it's still unclear what all of its **disadvantages** are. Some concerns include:

1) If crops are grown that are resistant to agrochemicals farmers might be tempted to use **more agrochemicals**, which can **damage** the **environment**.

2) Some GM crops are able to **cross-pollinate** and **transfer** their **genes** to other plants. This could lead to a gene for herbicide tolerance being transferred to a weed, which would then be difficult to kill.

3) The pesticides produced by some GM crops could **harm non-pest species**, e.g. butterflies.

Example

'**Bt maize**' and '**Bt cotton**' contain a **gene** from bacteria that enables them to produce a **toxin** poisonous to insect pests (called Bt toxin). **20% less insecticide** is needed on these crops.

Increasing Food Production

③ Land Colonisation and Land Reform Provide Agricultural Land

Land colonisation and reform can increase food production by giving people access to land to grow food.

Land colonisation is when humans move to an area of land that hasn't been used before, e.g. rainforests.

The disadvantages include environmental damage (such as deforestation) and possible conflicts with indigenous populations.

Example

2 million hectares of the Amazon rainforest are cleared each year to make way for subsistence and commercial farms.

Land reform is when land is redistributed, e.g. land owned by the government is given to local people.

Disadvantages include conflicts over who is entitled to the land (or over compensation for previous landowners). Human rights violations are also a concern if the previous landowners were forcibly removed.

Example

In Albania in the 1990s 216 large state farms were redistributed to create 380 000 small farms owned by former state farm workers.

④ Commercialisation is the Change from Subsistence Farming to Commercial Farming

Commercialisation increases production through the use of capital-intensive green revolution technologies. Commercial farms produce high value food for export and produce cash crops.

Example

Commercialisation of small farms in Kenya since the 1960s has led to it becoming the world's 4th largest exporter of tea. Tea is now Kenya's main source of foreign income.

There are disadvantages to commercialisation:

1) The best land is usually used to produce food. This can lead to food shortages as there's less high quality land left to produce food for the local population.

2) Also, the move from subsistence to commercial farming involves the use of green revolution technologies and the problems that they cause (see previous page).

⑤ Appropriate Technology Solutions are Low Cost

Appropriate technologies are simple, low cost technologies that increase food production. They're made and maintained using local knowledge and resources only, so aren't dependent on any outside support, expensive equipment or fuel.

Appropriate technology is also known as intermediate technology.

Example

The treadle pump is a human powered pump developed in Bangladesh in the 1980s. It pumps water from below the ground to irrigate small areas of land. This is important in Bangladesh as the main crop (rice) needs lots of water to grow. It costs US $7 to buy. It has increased Bangladeshi farmers' average annual incomes by roughly $100, through increased irrigation and therefore increased crop yield.
Local workshops, village dealers, well drillers and pump installers have all benefited from the business that the local production and distribution of the pump has brought.

The main disadvantage of appropriate technology solutions is that they tend to be labour intensive.

Practice Questions

Q1 How have green revolution technologies increased agricultural production?

Q2 What is the difference between land colonisation and land reform?

Q3 What is commercialisation of agriculture?

Exam Question

Q1 Explain the disadvantages of using green revolution technologies to increase food supplies. [6 marks]

Food glorious food — turns out everybody wants some more...

So there you have it — five ways to increase food production. It isn't edge-of-your-seat stuff, but you could be asked to explain or compare any of these strategies, so you need to know each strategy and its disadvantages really well. Sorry about that.

Controlling Food Production and Supply

Just when you thought you had food production sussed, it turns out there's a lot more to it...

Food Production and Supply Needs to be Controlled

Production and supply of food have to be controlled in order to:

1) Ensure **food availability** and **security**, but **prevent overproduction**.

2) Ensure **fair living standards** for farmers and the **survival** of **rural communities**.

3) Encourage farmers to act as '**stewards of the landscape**' and **preserve** the natural **environment**.

In **Europe** food production and supply is controlled by the **Common Agricultural Policy** (**CAP**). CAP is a set of policies laid out by the European Commission — it controls production and supply through a range of **market** and **non-market policies**.

Market Policies Control How Profitable Products Are

Market policies control food production by controlling **how profitable** it is to farm certain produce. There are several different **types** of **market policies**:

1 Subsidies — Paying Farmers to Produce Certain Products

Subsidies are **payments** made to **farmers** to **grow certain products**. This maintains home grown supplies and **food security**. It also ensures **fair living standards** for farmers.

> **Example**
>
> The EU is the second largest **dairy** exporter in the world due to the **subsidies** that support the industry. **€1 billion** was paid out in dairy subsidies in **2006**.

Negative effects of subsidies:

1) The **cost** of paying farmers.

2) It can cause **overproduction**. This can lead to **export dumping** (when food is sold abroad for less than the cost of production).

3) Export dumping causes **disruption** of **international markets** and **problems** in **developing countries** (because farmers are unable to compete with the artificially low price of the dumped food).

2 Quotas Limit Production and How Much is Imported

Quotas limit the production of some food to **prevent overproduction**.
Import quotas protect the market by **limiting** the amount of **imported produce**.

> **Example**
>
> **Milk quotas** were introduced in the **1980s** following overproduction that created '**milk lakes**' and '**butter mountains**' (huge amounts of produce that couldn't be consumed or exported). Milk quotas have gradually been **increased** as demand has **increased**.

Negative effects of import quotas:

1) They **prevent consumers** obtaining **cheap imports**.

2) They can **influence** international **production** and **trade**.

3 Intervention Ensures Farmers Can Sell Their Produce

1) **Intervention** is when the EU **buys produce** from farmers. It improves food security by ensuring farmers can **sell** their **produce** even when demand is low. Intervention stock is either **stored** for later **resale**, **exported** or **disposed** of.

> **Example**
>
> Currently, the EU will buy up excess stocks of **grain**, **butter** and **sugar**. The EU had over **1.5 million tonnes** of sugar **stored** in warehouses in January 2006.

Negative effects of intervention:

1) The **cost** of **transport**, **storage** and **disposal**.

2) It can cause **overproduction**.

3) The risk of **export dumping** and **disruption** of **markets**.

2) **Intervention** involves **guaranteeing** a **minimum price** for certain products (pricing). It **controls production** by encouraging farmers to **produce** or **stop producing** particular products.

> **Example**
>
> The EU aims to **cut sugar production** by 6 million tonnes by 2010 to allow developing countries to export lower cost sugar. In 2006 the **guaranteed price** for sugar was **cut** by 36% to encourage farmers to **stop producing** sugar.

Negative effects of pricing:

1) **Cost** of paying farmers.

2) **Increased cost** to **consumers**.

Controlling Food Production and Supply

4 Tariffs Protect the Market for Domestic Farmers

Tariffs are **taxes** applied to **imported goods** — they stop imports from **undercutting** domestic produce.

> **Example**
> The EU can produce **94%** of the beef that it needs, but if it was **cheaper** for consumers to buy **imported beef** then it would **not be profitable** for EU farmers to produce it and **production** (and so **food security**) would **decrease**. To prevent this, a **tariff** of 18 to 28% is applied to **imported** beef products, making them **more expensive** than locally produced products.

Negative side effects of tariffs:
1) They **prevent consumers** buying **cheap imported products**.
2) They can **affect international production** (by reducing trade of products with high tariffs and increasing trade of products with low tariffs).

Non-market Policies Control Production Without Affecting Markets

Non-market policies also **control food production**, but **don't affect** how **profitable** certain products are to farmers. There are several different **types** of **non-market policies**:

1 Diversification Schemes Promote Enterprise

Diversification schemes encourage farmers to develop **new enterprises**, reducing dependence on subsidies for agricultural products.

> **Example**
> **Rainton Farm** in Scotland has **diversified** by producing and selling **ice cream**, and providing **tourist facilities** such as a farm shop, tea room, adventure playground, 3D maze and nature trails.

2 Environmental Stewardship Protects Nature

Environmental stewardship involves paying **subsidies** to farmers to use **conservation methods** when farming.

Payments are made for schemes that:
1) Protect **wildlife**.
2) Maintain or enhance **landscape quality**.
3) Protect the **environment** and **natural resources**.
4) Promote **public access** to the **countryside**.

> **Example**
> In the **Lake District** farmers receive subsidies to **restrict cultivation** and grazing, **reduce fertiliser** and **pesticide** use, **manage hedges**, **maintain ditches** and **repair** stone walls.

Benefits of **non-market policies**:
1) They prevent **overproduction**.
2) They prevent **land degradation**.
3) They promote **sustainable farming**.
4) They promote a **sustainable rural economy**.

Negative effects of **non-market policies**:
1) **Cost** of paying farmers.
2) **Reduced productivity** (this can be a benefit if overproduction is an issue though).

Practice Questions

Q1 What are agricultural subsidies?
Q2 Describe the negative effects of intervention.
Q3 What are the benefits of environmental stewardship schemes?

Exam Question

Q1 Describe how EU market policies control the level and nature of agricultural production. [15 marks]

More food, less food, environmentally friendly food, grrrr — enough already

Managing food supplies for a whole continent is tricky stuff — the balance needs to be just right. Luckily for you, you only need to be able to explain these policies — pity the people who actually have to come up with them. Or laugh at them. Whichever.

Managing Food Supply — Case Studies

Two highly interesting, hugely important and crucially contrasting case studies for you.

Case Study 1: Bangladesh — Production Doesn't Meet Demand

1) Bangladesh is a **developing country** with a high poverty rate.

2) Rates of **malnutrition** are **high**.

3) **Food production doesn't meet demand** due to **fast population growth** and **climatic events** that **damage production**. E.g. the annual monsoon and cyclones cause flooding as the country is situated on low-lying river deltas.

Food Supplies are Managed Through a Range of Strategies

Various organisations are working to increase productivity and ensure food supplies are sufficient. These include the government, foreign aid agencies, international research institutions and non-governmental organisations (NGOs). These groups have put a range of strategies in place to increase food supplies:

1 Investment in Technology

The government provides **subsidies** and **loans** for farmers to invest in **green revolution technologies**. The use of **high yielding rice seeds**, **agrochemicals** and **increased irrigation** increased rice production from 11.7 to 23.1 million tonnes between 1974 and 2000. There has also recently been more investment into **appropriate technology solutions**, due to the negative effects of green revolution technologies (see page 80).

2 Free Market Policies Encourage Food Imports

The government has **removed** many **subsidies**, **eliminated quotas**, and **reduced import tariffs** to **encourage imports**, which are essential to feed the population. **Disadvantages** of this strategy include **susceptibility to rising food prices** — in 2008 the rising price of grain pushed 4 million people below the poverty line.

3 Diversification is Encouraged

Bangladesh relies heavily on **rice**, which needs four times more water than most crops to grow — a problem in a country with falling water levels. **Food security**, **nutrition** and **health** would all improve if a **greater range of foods** was produced.

Diversification is encouraged in several ways:

1) **Small and medium businesses** are **supported** by projects that provide expertise and training.

2) **Financial incentives** are given to livestock farmers, e.g. tax holidays and duty exemptions.

3) **EU trade preferences** allow goods to be exported to Europe **without duties** or **quotas**.

4 Investment in Infrastructure

There's been **investment** into **infrastructure** that **supports food production**:

1) **Maintaining** and **building roads** to improve the transport of produce. Between 1995 and 2000 the US funded the construction of 15 000 km of farm-to-market roads.

2) **Increasing electricity supplies** — between 1977 and 2000 over 80 000 irrigation pumps were electrified.

3) **Building flood defences** and **improving water flow** to allow damaging flood water to recede quickly.

5 Food Aid is Provided Where it's Needed Most

The government and other organisations operate **schemes** to **provide food**. For example:

1) The '**Food for Work**' programme gives people the opportunity to **work for food** on projects that **improve rural infrastructure** or the **environment**.

2) The '**Food for Education**' programme gives food to families who send their children to school instead of work — **increasing education** and **decreasing child labour**.

These Strategies Have Advantages and Disadvantages

Advantages:

1) Diversification and investment in infrastructure are long-term **sustainable** solutions.

2) Strategies such as "Food for Education" provide **health** and **social benefits**.

3) Diversification would **benefit** the **economy**, providing a wider range of export goods.

Disadvantages:

1) All these strategies cost **money** to initiate.

2) Food imports and food aid are **not sustainable** solutions.

3) Some technologies **damage** the **environment**.

Managing Food Supply — Case Studies

Case Study 2: China — Priority is Self-sufficiency

With 1.3 billion citizens China is the world's **most populated country**. It has had a **history** of **food shortages** so its **goal** is to be **self-sufficient**. It aims to achieve this through focusing agricultural policy on **grain production**. China currently produces 90% of its own grain, despite having only 7% of the planet's arable land and 20% of its population.

Food Supplies are Managed Through a Range of Strategies

1 State Control of Grain Production

Grain production and **distribution** are **controlled** by the **central government**. Farmers are required to produce at least 50 million tonnes of grain that are sold at **government controlled prices** and 40 million tonnes that are sold to the government at **negotiated prices**. This grain is distributed to **urban areas** and sold at **low prices**.

2 Incentives to Grow Grains

Provincial governments are responsible for making sure **enough grain** is produced. Provinces that **don't produce enough** have to **buy produce** from those that have a **surplus**. **Incentives** put in place by the provinces to encourage grain production vary but include **subsidies**, **guaranteed minimum prices**, **tax exemptions** and **free education**.

3 Modernisation of Agriculture

There's been **investment** into **modernising agriculture**:

1) **Transportation infrastructure** has been **improved**, speeding up transport of produce (slow distribution has caused famine in the past).
2) **Losses** during **processing** and **distribution** have been **reduced** using Western technology in packing, refrigerating and canning.
3) **Agricultural research** and **development** have become a **priority**. Research into rice breeding, biological pest control and genetic engineering have been funded with the aim of **improving crop yields**.

4 Domestic Supplies are Protected

China is cautious, **protecting** its **supplies** by:

1) **Stockpiling surplus grain**. In 2008 China held a reserve supply equivalent to 30 to 40% of its annual consumption (the UN regards 17% as a safe minimum).
2) **Limiting grain imports**. This protects the domestic market for home-grown produce.
3) **Reducing grain exports**. In 2007 a global shortage of grain resulted in soaring prices worldwide. Exports to many countries were stopped to protect domestic supplies.

These Strategies Have Advantages and Disadvantages

Advantages:

1) Modernisation of agriculture is a **long-term investment**.
2) Prioritising self-sufficiency leaves **less chance** of **disruption to food supplies** by external events.

Disadvantages:

1) **Urbanisation** is **reducing** the area of **arable land** so food **self-sufficiency** may **not** be **sustainable** as a policy.
2) The focus on grain **prevents farmers** from **growing high value foods** for export, **increasing rural poverty**.
3) **Reducing grain exports** can **adversely affect food supply** in **countries** that **depend** on **imports**.

Practice Questions

Q1   Why doesn't agricultural production meet demand in Bangladesh?
Q2   What strategies are used in Bangladesh to increase food production?
Q3   How has agriculture been modernised in China?

Exam Questions

Q1   Discuss the sustainability of strategies to manage food supplies in Bangladesh.   [10 marks]

Q2   Compare the management of food supply in Bangladesh and China.   [15 marks]

Chinese agriculture — just like the good life, but on a slightly larger scale...

These case studies are mega important. Loads of questions ask you to give examples to back up your points and there's tons of specifics here. So pick out some quotable statistics and learn them — then go over them again. And again. And again.

Energy Resources

What with the palaver over climate change and petrol prices energy is a hot topic these days.
So here's a whole section devoted to it, just for you, to help you do stunningly well in your exams.

There are **Different Types** of **Energy**

Energy comes in many different types (e.g. heat, electrical, light, chemical, potential), and although it can't be created or destroyed, it can be **converted** from **one type** to **another**. Energy can be classified as either **primary** or **secondary energy**:

1) **Primary energy** is released from a **direct source**, e.g. heat energy is released from burning coal.

2) When primary energy is **converted into a different form** it becomes **secondary energy**, e.g. when heat energy from burning coal is used to generate electricity.

Primary Energy Resources can be *Renewable* or *Non-renewable*

Renewable Resources

1) A **resource** is **renewable** if it can be **replenished** at a **similar rate** to which it's **used**.

2) Renewable resources are also known as **flow resources**. There's a constant energy transfer occurring, which if balanced will be sustainable.

3) **Tidal energy**, **wind energy** and **solar power** are all renewable resources because you can't use them up.

See pages 92-93 for more on renewable resources.

Non-renewable Resources

1) **Non-renewable resources** can **run out** and **can't be replaced** in the **foreseeable future**.

2) They're also known as **stock resources** as the planet has a limited 'stock', which when used up won't be replaced.

3) **Fossil fuels** (**coal**, **oil** and **natural gas**) and **nuclear energy** are non-renewable resources.

See pages 90-91 for more on non-renewable resources.

Some Resources are only *Renewable* if *Carefully Managed*

Whether a resource is renewable or not depends on **how fast** the resource is being **used compared** to **how fast** it's **replenished**. If the rates are **roughly equal** then it's a **renewable resource**.

1) Some resources are clearly renewable and will be available no matter how much we use, e.g. solar power.

2) Other resources have to be carefully managed if they're to be considered renewable. For example:

   • Wood — if too much wood is used in a short space of time the natural cycle of replenishment is disrupted and the resource is used up. If wood is managed carefully (using techniques like coppicing and replanting) to ensure that it's replaced at roughly the same rate that it's used, then it can be considered renewable.

   • Geothermal reservoirs — tectonic heat is used to turn water into steam at geothermal power stations, but if the power station is too large for the site then continually pumping water into the ground will end up cooling the ground. This means the resource is lost, so it's not renewable.

3) Some non-renewable resources can be replaced but aren't considered renewable because of the timescale involved, e.g. fossil fuels. Fossil fuels are hydrocarbons that have formed under high temperatures and pressures beneath the Earth's crust. This process hasn't stopped (fossil fuels are still being made), it's just that they take many millions of years to form and we're using them much faster than they are being replaced. So because they can't be replaced in the foreseeable future they're not a renewable energy source.

Energy Resources

The **Primary Energy Mix** Describes the **Sources** of Energy a **Country Uses**

1) Countries need energy for industry and transport, as well as for use in homes.

2) Many countries **aren't able to supply** all of their **energy needs** from **one source**, or they might not want to for energy security reasons. They use a **variety** of sources instead.

3) The **amount** of **each resource used** is called the **energy mix** and it's usually shown as **percentages**.

Solar and wave energy were the ideal mix to satisfy Sam's energy needs.

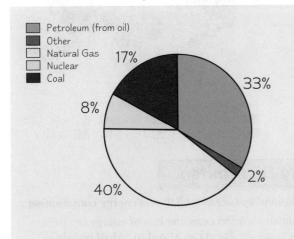

Legend:
- Petroleum (from oil)
- Other
- Natural Gas
- Nuclear
- Coal

17%
33%
8%
40%
2%

The pie graph on the left shows the **UK's energy mix** in **2008**.

1) **Over 70%** of the UK's energy supply is provided by **oil and gas**, which makes sense as the UK has **reserves** of both.

2) Since the early 1970s the UK's **consumption of oil increased** due to the discovery of North Sea oil in 1969 and the growing demand for transport fuel.

3) Use of **natural gas** has **increased** by **85%** since 1990.

4) Despite having **large reserves**, use of **coal** has **fallen** by **40%** since 1990, due to closure of mines and the move to using less polluting oil and gas.

5) Use of **renewable resources** has **increased**, as the government aims to move towards a more sustainable energy supply. It's still below the EU average of 6% though.

The pie graph on the right shows **France's energy mix** in **2004**.

1) France has **limited coal and oil reserves** and most of their supplies have to be **imported**. Coal mining stopped completely in France in 2004 so energy production from coal is low. Energy production from oil remains high though, due to the demand for transport fuel.

2) The proportion of **natural gas** that France uses has **increased** by over 50% since 1990, but is still below the EU average of 24%.

3) As it has limited fossil fuel resources France began investing in **nuclear power** in the 1970s in order to **secure energy supplies**. **41%** of France's energy supply now comes from **nuclear power**. It's the biggest producer of nuclear power in the EU, and the second biggest in the world.

4) Most of France's renewable energy comes from **hydropower** and **biomass**.

Legend:
- Petroleum (from oil)
- Other
- Natural Gas
- Nuclear
- Coal

5%
33%
41%
6%
15%

Practice Questions

Q1 What is the difference between primary and secondary energy?

Q2 What is a fossil fuel?

Q3 What is meant by 'primary energy mix'?

Exam Questions

Q1 Explain the difference between renewable and non-renewable resources. [6 marks]

Q2 Describe the energy mix of one named country and explain how it has changed recently. [6 marks]

50% pizza, 30% cake, 20% chocolate — the perfect energy mix...

The important thing to learn here is what the words renewable and non-renewable mean and why the boundary between them is a bit blurry. A good way of testing how well you understand this is to try explaining it to someone else. So once you think you know it well, pick a victim and explain away. This also doubles up as a handy way of getting rid of people you don't like.

Global Energy Distribution

With 6.6 billion people in the world, supplying everyone with energy isn't simple.

Global **Energy Production** is **Unevenly Distributed**

The map on the right shows energy produced from fossil fuels, per country 1989-1998.

This map shows the energy produced in each country, not the total reserves of energy.

1) Some countries produce **lots of energy** because they have **large energy reserves** and the **money** to **exploit** them. For example:
   - Iran, Saudi Arabia — large oil reserves.
   - China, Australia — large coal reserves.
   - UK, Russia, Canada — large oil and gas reserves.
   - USA, Indonesia — large coal, oil and gas reserves.

2) Some countries produce **little energy** because they have **few resources** or are **unable** to **exploit** their resources due to lack of **money** or **political instability**.
   - Angola — politically unstable and lack of money.
   - Spain — small fossil fuel reserves.

Energy produced from fossil fuels (BTUs)
- Over 25.00
- 10.01 – 25.00
- 5.01 – 10.00
- 2.51 – 5.00
- 0.00 – 2.50
- no data

Global **Energy Consumption** is also **Unevenly Distributed**

The map below shows the energy consumption per person across the world in 2007.

Energy consumption per person (tonnes oil equivalent)
- 6.0 and over
- 4.5 – 6.0
- 3.0 – 4.5
- 1.5 – 3.0
- 0 – 1.5

There's a **strong relationship** between **GDP** and **energy consumption**:

1) **Wealthy countries** tend to **consume lots of energy** per person because they're wealthy and **can afford to**. **Most people** in these countries have **access** to **electricity** and **heating**, and use **energy-intensive devices** like cars. E.g. **Australia, Sweden, USA**.

2) **Poorer countries consume less energy** per person as they are **less able to afford it**. **Less energy** is **available** and lifestyles are less dependent on high energy consumption than in wealthier countries. E.g. **Burkina Faso, Mongolia**.

Some countries don't consume much energy per person, but consume a lot overall because they have large populations. E.g. Brazil consumes less energy per person than Ireland, but has a higher total energy consumption.

Energy is Traded Between Countries

Some countries don't produce much energy but still **consume a lot**, and vice versa. This is possible because **energy** is **traded between countries**.

Electricity is traded between neighbouring countries, while coal, oil and natural gas can be transported around the world.

1) Countries that are able to produce a lot of energy **export** it to those that can't.
2) Canada, Saudi Arabia, United Arab Emirates, Denmark and Venezuela all **export large amounts** of **energy**.
3) Ireland, Italy, Spain and Japan all **import large amounts** of **energy**.

Trans-National Corporations Play an Important Role in the Energy Industry

Trans-National corporations (**TNCs**) are **companies** that **operate** in **more than one country**. Many TNCs play a **major role** in world **energy production** and **distribution**.

E.g. **ExxonMobil** is an **oil** and **gas TNC** based in the USA. It's the largest company in the world (based on revenue) and **operates** in **over 200 countries** worldwide, **producing 3%** of the **world's oil** and **2%** of its **energy**.

1) **Production:** ExxonMobil **explores** for oil and gas on every continent except Antarctica. When found the oil is **extracted** and sent to ExxonMobil **refineries** (e.g. in the USA, Norway, Thailand or the UK) for **processing**.

2) **Distribution: After processing** ExxonMobil uses its **own transportation system** to **transport products** to **distribution centres**, either its own or independent ones, e.g. Acculube, TrAchem Ltd. These then **sell** to **customers** such as CATERPILLAR® and Singapore Airlines, as well as to individuals for transport fuel.

Global Energy Distribution

The *Geopolitics of Energy* is a *Big Issue*

Energy security is an **important** issue for **all governments**, for several reasons:

1) **All countries** are **dependent** on **energy supplies**, e.g. for transport, heating, electricity and manufacturing.

2) Global **energy use** is **increasing** and **fossil fuel reserves** are **decreasing**. Many people believe we're coming to an "**energy crisis**", so governments are more concerned than ever about how to **secure future supplies** of energy.

3) To make the situation trickier, the **largest reserves** of **oil** and **gas** are often in areas that are either **politically** or **economically unstable**, e.g. Russia, which means that **energy supplies** are often at risk of being **disrupted**.

4) So in order to **secure supplies**, **agreements** are often reached between **exporting** and **importing regions**. For example, the EU will become increasingly dependent on imports as North Sea oil runs out, so it opened talks with Russia in 2000 to try to guarantee access to Russian gas supplies. In return Russia wanted investment into production of fuel and improved access to EU markets.

5) At times agreements can't be reached and **concerns over energy security** can **lead to conflict** or the **threat of conflict**. E.g. the 1980 Carter Doctrine stated that the USA would use military force if necessary to protect its interests in the Middle East and secure the free movement of oil.

6) As energy consumption increases, so does the **impact** of energy use on the **environment** (see page 90). **International agreements**, e.g. the Kyoto Protocol, are drawn up to try to **address these problems**, but these too can lead to political **conflict** if environmental protection clashes with other national interests, e.g. economic growth.

Patterns of *Energy Production*, *Consumption* and *Trade Can Change*

Changes in Production

1) **Energy production** has **increased** in countries where **new reserves** have been **discovered**, e.g. in **Nigeria** and **Algeria**.

2) There have also been **increases** in places that have become **more politically stable**, e.g. **Angola** (after the end of the civil war).

3) The production of energy has **decreased** in other countries as **resources are used up**, e.g. **North Sea oil** production has declined since 1999, reducing production in the **UK, Norway, Denmark, Germany** and the **Netherlands**.

4) **Production** often **decreases** in areas that become **more unstable**, e.g. **Sudan** oil production decreased due to civil war between 1983 and 2005.

Changes in Consumption

1) **China** has the largest population and one of the fastest growing economies in the world. As **standards of living** and **industrial output increase** China **consumes** more and **more energy**.

2) Other **newly industrialised countries**, e.g. **India, Malaysia** and **Mexico**, are also **using more energy** as they **develop**.

Changes in Trade

As **production** and **consumption** of energy **changes**, so does the **trade of energy**.

1) **Exports** from ex-Soviet central Asian countries like **Kazakhstan** are **increasing**. These countries are attractive as suppliers to the **EU, USA** and **China** because the region is **more stable** than the **Middle East** and **isn't controlled by Russia, reducing dependence** on these two areas.

2) **Brazil** and **Denmark** were once **heavily dependent** on **imports** but are now both **energy self-sufficient**, due to **development** of **renewable energy** and **discoveries** of **domestic oil reserves**.

Practice Questions

Q1 Why do wealthy countries consume more energy per person than poorer countries?

Q2 What role do TNCs play in the energy industry?

Exam Question

Q1 Explain why global patterns of energy production, consumption and trade change. [15 marks]

Revision — a serious threat to the energy reserves of sixth formers...

So there you have it — the energy supply of an entire planet on one double page. Doesn't seem too bad to me — some places have loads of energy and some don't have enough, so politicians pal up and shunt it about a bit. Don't see what the fuss is about.

Impacts of Energy Production

Imagine you're running a country — you've got yourself a nice secure supply of energy, you're feeling pretty smug.
Only thing to worry about now is the impact of the energy on your shiny new country.

Fuel Wood Gathering can Damage the Environment...

Although **fossil fuels** supply **87%** of the **world's energy**, a significant proportion of the world's population use **wood** as an **energy source**, usually to provide energy within the home. Wood that's burnt for fuel is called **fuel wood**.
The **gathering** of **fuel wood** can **damage the environment** in several ways:

1) **Deforestation** — most fuel wood gathering isn't regulated and can seriously deplete local woodland.

2) **Habitat loss** — deforestation can damage or destroy the habitats of a wide range of wildlife.

3) **Soil erosion** — tree roots bind soil together. If the trees are removed the soil isn't held together as well and can be washed away by rain or blown away by winds.

Example	The **Copperbelt** in **Zambia** is a densely populated industrial area that relies heavily on fuel wood. Between **1972** and **2000** an average of **3125**

hectares of woodland were **cleared** each year for **fuel wood**. Heavy **tropical rains** from November to April resulted in dramatic **erosion of topsoil** as there were fewer trees to hold the soil together. This left much of the land **barren** and **unsuitable for agriculture**, as well as **preventing** the **re-growth** of **woodlands**.

...and so can Using Fossil Fuels

The **extraction** of fossil fuels, e.g. by mining, can damage the environment.
Transportation can also cause environmental damage, e.g. through **oil spills**.
The **use** of fossil fuels has **negative impacts** on the **environment** as well, such as **acid rain** and **global warming**.

1   Acid Rain

Burning fossil fuels releases various **gases**. Some of these **dissolve in water vapour** in the atmosphere, which then falls as **acid rain**. Acid rain can:

1) **Kill fish** and other **aquatic life**, which can lead to **reduced biodiversity**.

2) **Kill trees** and other **plant life**, which also **reduces biodiversity**.

3) **Reduce** the **nutrient content** of **soil** so that some species of plants can't grow, or grow more slowly.

4) **Corrode rocks**, e.g. limestone, sandstone.

2   Global Warming

The largest environmental problem created by the use of fossil fuels is **global warming**. **Burning fossil fuels releases** the greenhouse gas **carbon dioxide** into the air. This **enhances** the planet's natural greenhouse effect, **increasing world temperatures** and causing **climate change**. This could lead to:

1) **Rising sea levels** and **increased flooding**.

2) **More frequent** and **severe extreme weather events**, e.g. hurricanes, droughts.

3) **Habitat loss** (which leads to **loss of biodiversity** and the **extinction** of species).

3   Problems Associated with Mining

Coal mining involves disturbing or removing large areas of land, which can lead to:

1) **Wildlife** being **displaced**.

2) **Habitat Loss**.

3) **Reduced air quality** as dust and other particulates are released.

4) **Contamination** of **surface water** with acidic or toxic substances.

4   Oil Spills

Oil spills happen when **pipes**, **oil wells** or **tankers** transporting oil **leak**, dumping oil onto land or into seas or oceans. The effects of oil spills last for a long time and lead to the **death of wildlife**. There are many reasons for this:

1) **Oil reduces** the **ability** of animals to **move freely**, which makes it more difficult for them to swim, fly or forage.

2) **Hypothermia**. When **feathers** and **fur** become **coated in oil** it reduces the animal's ability to control its body temperature.

3) **Consumption of oil**.

The impact of each of these varies depending on the location of the area affected and the severity of the problem.

Impacts of Energy Production

Fossil Fuel Resources Won't Last For Ever

It's **hard to know how long fossil fuel reserves will last**. This is because **new reserves** might be found, or we might find **more efficient ways to use them**. This would **increase** the length of **time** we can **depend on them**.

A 2006 estimation of **proven** reserves suggested that, worldwide, there were:

They might label him a pessimist now, but Rob knew he'd have the last laugh.

- 1000 billion barrels of oil left (enough to last 40 years).
- 150 trillion cubic metres of natural gas left (enough to last 60 years).
- 1000 billion tonnes of coal left (enough to last 250 years).

Eventually **fossil fuels will run out** (or become too difficult to extract) so an **alternative energy source** needs to be found.

Nuclear Power could be an Alternative to Fossil Fuels

In **nuclear power stations heat energy** released from **uranium** or **plutonium** is used to **generate electricity**. The first commercial nuclear reactor opened in 1956 and there are now 439 reactors in 31 countries around the world. They supply 15% of the world's electricity, which is 6.3% of the total energy consumption. There are **advantages** and **disadvantages** of using nuclear power:

Advantages of nuclear power	Disadvantages of nuclear power
1) It has **low carbon dioxide emissions**, so contributes little to global warming.	1) Nuclear waste is **highly radioactive** and has to be **stored carefully** for **thousands of years**. This is very **expensive**. Some people argue that as technology improves this problem will be solved, but there's no guarantee of this.
2) **Less toxic waste** is released into the environment than from fossil fuel plants. (Fossil fuel plants release ash containing heavy metals such as mercury, cadmium and lead).	2) **Accidents** causing **radioactive waste** to **leak** into the environment can have devastating consequences, e.g. **human, animal** and **plant deaths** and **illnesses**, **destruction** of the local environment and **contamination** of **large areas of land**. The damage lasts for a **long time**. The **explosion** of nuclear power **plants** causes similar problems.
3) **Large amounts of energy** are generated from **small amounts of fuel**.	3) There's only **limited amounts** of **uranium** and **plutonium** so it's a **non-renewable** resource.
4) **Electricity** produced by nuclear power is **cheap**.	4) **Decommissioning** power stations at the end of their life is **very expensive**.

Example: In **France 78%** of **electricity** is produced from **nuclear power**. France has the **cleanest air** of any industrialised country and the **cheapest electricity** in Europe.

Example: The 1986 explosion at the **Chernobyl** nuclear power plant in the Ukraine directly caused **56 deaths** and radiation released caused **thousands** of **deaths** and **illnesses**. **Radioactive material** from the disaster was detected as far away as **Ireland**, a **4 km² area of forest** around Chernobyl **died**, **food supplies** (particularly of fish) were affected in **Scandinavia** for several years after the accident and the Chernobyl area is **still heavily contaminated** today.

Practice Questions

Q1 What is meant by the term fuel wood?
Q2 What environmental problems are associated with coal mining?
Q3 Why is nuclear power a non-renewable source of energy?

Exam Question

Q1 Discuss the advantages and disadvantages of using nuclear power as a replacement for fossil fuels. [10 marks]

Fossil fuels are dwindling — they'll be going, going and then gone

So it's either fossil fuels that damage the environment and will run out soon, or nuclear power, which can also damage the environment and will run out. Guess we'll just have to go back to no electricity and wood fires... No, wait, that damages the environment too. But don't despair. It may seem doomy and gloomy on this page, but there could be a solution. Read on...

Sustainable Energy

Sustainable energy is so important there are four whole pages of it coming your way...

Sustainable Energy Sources are Always Renewable

For **energy production** to be **sustainable** it **mustn't deplete resources** or cause any **long term environmental damage**. Energy production using **non-renewable resources isn't sustainable** as it's environmentally damaging and the resource will one day run out. Energy produced from **renewable resources** is **sustainable** as it doesn't usually cause long term environmental damage and the resource won't run out. There are many different types of renewable energy resources:

1. Wind Energy is Harnessed by Wind Turbines

Wind energy is responsible for **1%** of the world's electricity production. **Carbon dioxide** is released during the **production** and **installation** of wind turbines but once that's done **no greenhouse gases** are released and **no fuel** is needed.

1) **Wind turbines** are built in **open exposed areas** where there's a high chance of **strong** and **regular winds**.

2) The energy of the wind turns the blades of the turbine, **converting wind energy** to **mechanical energy**, which is then converted to **electrical energy** by a **generator**.

3) **Large-scale wind power** involves **wind farms** that may have thousands of turbines. The electricity generated is fed into an **electrical grid** that **transports electricity** to consumers. Wind farms can be **offshore** (out at sea) or **onshore** (on land).

4) **Small-scale wind power** involves small turbines that might be connected to a grid but often just **supply one building**.

EXAMPLE

Denmark has been investing in wind power since the 1970s, establishing **wind farms** onshore and offshore. Families are offered **tax exemptions** for generating their **own electricity**, either by investing in community turbines or by buying their own. By 2004 over 150 000 households had joined this scheme. Denmark now produces **19.7%** of its **electricity from wind power**, the highest proportion in the world.

Disadvantages of wind energy:

1) Wind energy is **unpredictable**. The amount of electricity generated varies with wind strength.

2) **Large numbers of turbines** are needed to produce significant amounts of electricity, which takes up **lots of space**.

3) The **most appropriate places for turbines** are often **protected areas** of natural beauty.

4) Wind farms produce a constant humming **noise**, which some people living nearby don't like.

5) Turbines can **kill** or **injure birds** and **bats**.

2. Biomass is Material That's Burnt for Power or Used to Produce Biofuel

1) **Biomass** is material that is or was **recently living**.

2) It includes **wood**, **plants** and **animal waste**.

3) These materials can be **burnt** to release energy.

4) Biomass can also be **processed** to produce **biofuels**, which are then **burnt** to release energy.

5) A common way of producing biofuel is to **ferment sugar cane** to produce **alcohol**, which can then be burnt. **Methane** and **biogas** are also types of **biofuel** produced using fermentation.

6) Using biomass as an energy source can involve a lot of technology (if biofuels are being made), or very little (if biomass is being burnt directly). This means that biomass is a **suitable energy source** for a **wide range of countries**.

7) Biomass energy is released by **burning**, which produces **carbon dioxide**. Biomass **doesn't contribute to global warming** though, as the amount of **carbon released equals** the amount of **carbon taken in** when the material was growing. This means there's **no overall increase** in the amount of **carbon dioxide** in the **atmosphere** from the burning of biomass.

EXAMPLE

Brazil has been running an **ethanol fuel programme** since the 1970s. The ethanol is made by fermenting sugar cane, and any leftover cane is burnt for heating and power. Ethanol supplies **18%** of **transport fuel** and cars either run on **ethanol** or a **petrol and ethanol mix**. This has **decreased** Brazil's **dependence on imported oil**.

Disadvantages of biomass:

1) **Large areas of land** are needed to produce sufficient amounts of biofuels. This **reduces** the **area of land** available to grow **food crops**, which could lead to **food shortages**.

2) Biomass is only a renewable energy resource if it's **carefully managed** (see page 86).

3) **Fossil fuels** are often used to **process** and **transport** biomass.

Sustainable Energy

3. Solar Power Depends on Energy from the Sun

1) **Solar power** comes from the **sun** and can be used in lots of different ways.
2) **Solar water heaters** use **solar energy** to **heat water**, which is then pumped to a storage tank ready for use.
3) **Solar cookers** work by **concentrating sunlight**, converting it to **heat energy** and then trapping it for use in cooking.
4) **Photovoltaic (PV) cells** convert **light energy** into **electrical energy**, which is used in the home or exported to a grid.
5) **Materials** that **absorb** the **sun's heat** during the day and release it at night can be used to **keep houses warm**.

EXAMPLE

In the Chinese city **Rizhao**, **99%** of buildings have **solar water heaters** (it's now compulsory for new builds), over **6000 households** use **solar cookers** and most **traffic** and **street lights** are powered by **PV cells**.

Disadvantages of solar power:
1) **Carbon dioxide** is released in equipment production.
2) PV cells are **expensive**.
3) **Large areas** of solar panels and **sunny climates** are needed to produce **large amounts** of **electricity**.

4. Tidal Energy is a Reliable Source of Energy

1) **Tidal energy** comes from the movement of tides. It's **less variable** than wind or solar energy as tides are regular, unchangeable events. Tidal energy can be harnessed using **tidal barrages** or **tidal stream systems**.
2) **Tidal barrages** (dams) are built across **estuaries**. As the tide flows in and out water passes through gates in the barrage, turning **turbines** that **generate electricity**. Some turbines are only turned by outgoing tides, some by incoming as well.
3) **Tidal streams** are fast-flowing currents caused by the tide. They turn **turbines** placed in their pathway to **generate electricity**.

EXAMPLE

The **Rance estuary** tidal barrage in Northern **France** began operating in **1967**. It's the **largest** tidal power station in the world, producing enough **electricity** for over **19 000 homes**.

Disadvantages of tidal energy:
1) The equipment is **expensive** and making it releases **carbon dioxide**.
2) Barrages **disrupt ecosystems**, and turbines can **kill aquatic animals**.

5. Wave Energy is Created by Wind Blowing over Water

1) **Wave energy** is harnessed by using a **wave generator** — a chamber with a hole at the top that contains a **turbine**.
2) When a wave flows into the bottom of the chamber, the increased mass of water forces **air** in the chamber upwards and through the hole, which **turns the turbine**.
3) The turbine is connected to a **generator** that **produces electricity**.

EXAMPLE

In 2000 **LIMPET** in Scotland became the world's first device that used **wave energy** on a **commercial scale**. It **generates electricity** for the **national grid**.

Disadvantages of wave energy:
1) Wave energy is **unreliable**, as there aren't always waves.
2) The generators are **expensive** and making them releases **carbon dioxide** into the atmosphere.

6. Hydroelectric Power Uses the Energy of Falling Water

Hydroelectric power (HEP) supplies about **20%** of the world's electricity and is responsible for over 60% of all electricity from renewable sources. Once plants are built they **release no greenhouse gases**.

1) At HEP plants **dams** are built to **trap** large volumes of **water**. Tunnels containing **turbines** are built into the dams.
2) The **pressure of the water** above drives water through the tunnels, **turning the turbines**.
3) **Generators** then convert this energy into **electricity**.

EXAMPLE

The **Nurek Dam** in Tajikistan is the tallest dam in the world and has **nine hydroelectric turbines** in it. In 1994 it supplied **98%** of the country's **electricity**.

Disadvantages of HEP:
1) Creating reservoirs can mean **destruction** of **communities** and **habitats**.
2) If the **dam fails** then large areas of land are likely to be **flooded** rapidly.
3) **Ecosystems** and **fish migratory paths** are **disrupted**.
4) The plants are **expensive** and making them releases **carbon dioxide**.

Sustainable Energy

Keep going...

Appropriate Technology is Technology That's Suitable for the Area

1) **Appropriate technologies** are **simple**, **low-cost** technologies.

2) They're **made** and **maintained** using **local knowledge** and **resources** only, so aren't dependent on any outside support, expensive equipment or fuel.

Appropriate Technology can Contribute to Sustainable Development

1) Using appropriate technologies to produce energy **isn't always sustainable**, e.g. they could be dependent on local sources of non-renewable energy.

2) Some **appropriate technologies** do produce energy from **renewable sources** though, so it's **sustainable**. Producing energy in a sustainable way contributes to **sustainable development** — growth in a way that doesn't stop future generations getting what they need (i.e. by not depleting resources or permanently damaging the environment).

Example	In mountainous regions of developing countries **clay stoves** have been introduced as an **appropriate technology** that makes **energy use** for **cooking and heating more sustainable**.

1) In **high altitude** areas of **developing countries** many indigenous people rely on **burning biomass** on **open fires** as their main **energy source**.

2) Fuel is usually **straw**, **crop roots** and **pasture grass**. One family can burn up to 6000 kg a year.

3) At high altitudes the temperature is lower and **plants grow more slowly**, which often means **crops** are **removed faster than they can be replenished**.

4) As energy supplies are depleted there are fewer plant roots in the soil to support it. This causes **soil erosion** and a **decrease** in soil **productivity**.

5) **Burning biomass in this way** is therefore **unsustainable**.

Clay stoves are **more efficient** than open fires and can lead to a **75% reduction in fuel consumption**. This means fuel is **harvested more slowly**, allowing the **crops** to **replenish** themselves. This leads to decreased soil erosion and increased soil productivity. Using a stove rather than an open fire also has **health benefits**, as the smoke from open fires can cause eye and lung diseases.

Clay stoves are an **appropriate technology** as they can be made by **local** craftsmen from metal and clay, providing a source of income for local people. They **reduce** the quantity of **biomass burnt** and therefore help to maintain the **natural cycle of replenishment**. This makes the resource **renewable** (see page 86) and therefore **sustainable**. So, they contribute to sustainable development.

Energy Conservation is Important for Sustainable Supply

Energy supply can be made **more sustainable** by **conserving** as much **energy** as possible. By **reducing overall use of energy** fewer resources are used up and the **environmental effects** of energy use are **limited**, e.g. emission of greenhouse gases. **Homes**, **workplaces** and **transport** can all be **designed** to **conserve energy**:

Buildings can be made more sustainable...

Energy can be **conserved** in **homes** and **workplaces** in several ways:

1) **Reducing** the amount of energy needed for **heating** by installing **double glazing**, **draught-proofing**, **loft insulation** and **cavity wall insulation** to **reduce heat loss**.

2) **Installing energy-efficient boilers**. They're more efficient because a greater proportion of the heat energy they generate is used to heat the water in the boiler and **less energy** is **lost** to the surroundings.

3) Using computers, printers and faxes that **turn themselves off** after a period of time instead of staying on (stand-by mode can consume nearly as much energy as being turned on permanently).

4) Building in **features** that help **absorb** and **retain** the **sun's energy** (e.g. **large south-facing windows**) to provide **heat** as well as **light**.

Iain understood the importance of insulation but this was a step too far. He looked like a fool and he knew it.

Sustainable Energy

5) Using **energy-saving appliances** wherever possible, e.g. **energy-saving light bulbs**.

The **City of Calgary Water Centre** in Canada was designed to conserve energy. Lots of **south-facing windows** let natural light reach all areas, which **reduces the need** for **electric lighting**. The electric lights only come on when they're needed as they're controlled by **light** and **motion sensors**. The **windows** and the **shape** of the building help to **warm the building** in winter, **reducing the need** for **heating**. An **overhanging roof** keeps the heat out in summer so **less energy** is **needed** for **air-conditioning**. A **radiant ceiling slab cooling system** has been built in to **reduce the need for air-conditioning** further. This system draws cold night air through pipes set into concrete, cooling it down. The cooled concrete helps to keep the building cold throughout the next day. These methods have **reduced** annual **energy consumption** by **58%**.

...and so can Transport

Energy can be conserved in **transport** by:

1) Changing to **vehicles that don't need any fuel**, e.g. **bicycles**. Employers receive tax exemptions for loaning or selling bicycles to employees as part of the **Cycle to Work** scheme. This encourages people to switch cars for more sustainable bicycles.

2) Establishing out-of-town **park-and-ride schemes** and **investing in public transport**. This **reduces fuel consumption** by reducing the number of vehicles on the road.

3) Introducing **congestion charges**. This **encourages public transport use** and is used in London, Singapore, Rome and Stockholm.

Example

The **London congestion charge** was **introduced in 2003**. It charges drivers for entering a central zone of the city during normal working hours. It aims to reduce congestion and raise money for public transport improvements. Since the scheme started the **number of vehicles** within the zone has **decreased** by **21%** (70 000 fewer cars each day) and **carbon dioxide emissions** have **decreased** by **20%**. In 2007/2008 £137 million was raised, which was **invested in public transport**. **Bicycle use** has **increased** by **12%** since 2003, and use of **public buses** has **increased** by **6%**. There's been an **increase in congestion** in the area **surrounding the central zone** though and some small businesses within the zone (e.g. shops and restaurants) claim that the charge has **reduced trade**.

Transport can also be made more sustainable by using **technologies** that run off **sustainable energy sources**:

- **Hydrogen fuel cell buses** run on electricity produced from **hydrogen**. The hydrogen that fuels the bus is **made from water**. The process **uses electricity**. So, for hydrogen fuel cells to be sustainable this initial electricity must be produced from **renewable resources**.
- **Electric buses**, e.g. the **Islay Wave Bus** runs off **wave power generated electricity** from LIMPET (see page 93).
- Using **hybrid fuel vehicles** (vehicles that run off a mixture of two fuels). If one fuel is from a **renewable** source then the vehicle is **more sustainable**, e.g. use of **ethanol-petrol hybrid fuel cars** in Brazil (see page 92).

Practice Questions

Q1 How is wind energy harnessed?
Q2 Give three examples of biomass.
Q3 What are the disadvantages of solar power?
Q4 What does HEP stand for?
Q5 What are appropriate technologies?

Exam Questions

Q1 Explain what biomass is and how it's used as an energy source. [4 marks]

Q2 Compare wave energy and tidal energy. [6 marks]

Q3 Explain how energy use in the home can be made more sustainable. [8 marks]

Q4 Describe and explain how transport can be made more sustainable. [10 marks]

Brain chargers and memory plugs — now they're appropriate technologies...

Well done — you made it. I know there's loads to learn here and I'm guessing you're not too happy about it, but I've not put it in for the good of my health (you do need to know all about sustainable energy for the exam). Don't forget to learn the examples as well — the examiners will expect you to be able to spew some up for any questions they ask on this topic. They're evil like that.

Managing Energy — Case Studies

So, you know the different sources and impacts of energy, you're crammed full of interesting facts and impressive knowledge. You just need to make a tiny bit of space in that grey blob for these case studies...

Chad has Very Low Energy Consumption per Person

Chad is a **developing country** in **North Africa**. It's very **unstable politically** and is one of the **poorest** and **most corrupt countries** in the world. Despite having **large reserves of oil**, annual **energy consumption** is very **low** at only **0.005 tonnes of oil equivalent** per person (average consumption in the EU is 3.8 tonnes). **80%** of the **population** live **below** the **poverty line**.

Chad's Main Energy Resources are Oil and Biomass

Chad is an oil exporter...

1) Chad has **large reserves of oil**.
2) TNCs like ExxonMobil, Chevron and Petronas began **exploiting the oil** in 2003.
3) It's **exported** via a **pipeline through Cameroon** to the Atlantic coast. The pipeline was **part funded** by the **World Bank** on the condition that **80%** of the revenue from the oil was **spent on projects to reduce poverty**.
4) The Chadian government **didn't keep to this agreement**.
5) So although oil is an **important source of income** for Chad and **could** help **improve economic** and **social conditions** for Chadians, the **corruption** and **political instability** in the country at the moment mean that **it doesn't**.

...and also an oil importer

1) Chad **can't use its own oil** because it doesn't have any way of **refining** it.
2) Instead, it has to **rely on imports** of refined oil from **Cameroon** and **Nigeria** to supply its only major power station.
3) The cost of doing this means that the **electricity** generated is **very expensive**, and most Chadians **can't afford it** (only 2% of the population have access to electricity).
4) Also, **delivery problems** caused by the **poor transport system** can lead to **shortages**.
5) So importing oil is **expensive**, **unreliable** and **doesn't support** the **energy needs** of most of the population.

Most Energy is supplied by Biomass

90% of Chad's **total energy** and **98%** of household energy is supplied by **wood**. There's no control over wood production or use, so it's **overexploited**. In 1998 the **World Bank** and the **Chadian government** jointly funded the **Household Energy Project** to address this problem by:

1) Using **non-governmental organisations** (NGOs) to **educate** local people about the **need for conservation**.
2) Setting up **village resource management schemes** that **limit** the amount of **wood cut down**. This can involve **charging** people for **collecting wood**.
3) **Giving villages ownership** of the local **resources**. This allows them to **make money** from wood, so makes it a **more valuable resource** to them and **worth conserving**.
4) **Improving energy use** in homes by introducing **more efficient cooking stoves** that use less fuel than open fires (see page 94).

The Household Energy Project **only operates on a small scale** at the moment though (about 100 villages near the capital city).

1) At the moment Chad's **energy supply isn't sustainable**.
2) Chad's oil policy doesn't help it meet its energy needs, and as oil is **non-renewable** it's **unsustainable** anyway.
3) Most energy is provided by **biomass**, which has the **potential to be sustainable** if it's **managed properly**.
4) The **Household Energy Project** could help to make the supply of biomass sustainable but **needs to be implemented more widely**, which takes time and money.
5) There is the potential to do this using money from exporting oil, but political corruption and instability could be a barrier to this.

Practice Questions

Q1   What are Chad's main energy resources?
Q2   Why does Chad have to import oil?

Exam Question

Q1   Discuss the potential for Chad's energy supply to become sustainable.   [15 marks]

Managing Energy — Case Studies

Norway has High Energy Consumption per Person

Norway is a **wealthy**, **developed country** in **Northern Europe**. **Energy consumption** is **high** in Norway, at **6.2 tonnes of oil equivalent** per person, and **electricity consumption** per person is the **highest in the world**. It has **large reserves of oil** and **gas** (located under the North Sea) and utilises its **high potential for hydroelectricity**, with **99%** of **electricity** being generated from hydroelectric plants. Overall, **39%** of its **energy** comes from **fossil fuels** and **61%** from **renewables**.

Norway's Main Energy Resources are Oil, Gas and Hydroelectricity

Norway is an oil and gas exporter

1) Norway is the **5th largest exporter of oil** and the **3rd largest exporter of gas** in the world.

2) These **fossil fuels** are an **important source of income** for the country, with oil alone providing about **25%** of **GDP**.

3) Despite being oil-rich, Norwegian **fuel prices** are among the **highest in Europe** due to **high taxation**. This fits in with Norway's energy policy of increasing the proportion of their energy supply that comes from renewable sources by **discouraging** the **use of oil**.

4) Almost **all** of Norway's **gas** supplies are **exported** as it's not used much domestically.

5) So, like Chad, Norway **exports most of its fossil fuel** resources, but for different reasons. Chad needs the income from exports and can't exploit the resources itself, whereas Norway **chooses to use other sources of energy** and actively discourages the use of oil.

Most electricity is supplied by hydropower

1) With **natural lakes** at **high altitudes** and **lots of rain** Norway is able to generate **99%** of its **electricity** and **50%** of its **total energy** from **HEP**.

2) This makes it the **6th largest producer** of hydropower in the world and the **largest in Europe**.

3) As many lakes are natural the plants have **less impact on the environment** than **artificially created** reservoirs.

4) Whilst Chad's main source of energy (biomass) has the potential to be renewable if it's managed carefully, **Norway's main source** (hydropower) **is renewable** by nature, and is therefore **sustainable**.

Norway is investing in renewable energy

1) One of Norway's energy aims is to **reduce** its **dependency** on **hydroelectric power** by using a **wider range** of **renewable resources**.

2) This is needed to cope with any future rise in energy consumption, as **almost all potential HEP sites** have been **exploited**.

3) **€2.5 billion** was invested in **developing renewable energy** and **energy efficiency** in 2006. One of the main projects is to **triple wind power capacity**.

4) Research into **solar power** aims to **increase the percentage** of the Sun's energy that can be converted **into electricity** from 17% to 50%.

5) The state also provides **funding** for companies to **research and develop biofuels** to use for transport instead of oil, e.g. producing biodiesel from salmon waste.

6) As a **wealthy nation** (unlike Chad), Norway is able to **invest in research** in order to develop a **sustainable energy supply**.

1) Norway is **energy-rich** so doesn't have to worry about **energy security** in the short term.

2) It can concentrate on developing a **long-term sustainable energy supply**.

3) **Some aspects are already sustainable**, e.g. using hydropower for electricity generation, but **others aren't**, e.g. relying on oil for transport.

4) Policies such as **investing in energy efficiency** and **renewables**, and putting **high taxes on oil**, **promote sustainability**.

5) The **political stability** and **wealth** of the country allow it to pursue **energy sustainability**.

Practice Questions

Q1 What are Norway's main energy resources?

Q2 Why is Norway particularly suited to using hydroelectric power?

Exam Question

Q1 Describe how Norway's energy supply is becoming more sustainable. [15 marks]

My energy resources are running a bit low after all that...

So that's energy done. Learn these two pages and you'll be all set for the exam. As long as you can still remember the other pages that is... You might want to look back over them to check... well OK, you might not want to but you should do it anyway.

Global Patterns of Health, Disease and Death

This section's all about global health issues. Where you live in the world affects your health in many different ways.

Health *is* Better *in* Wealthier Countries

1) **Health** is defined as your **physical**, **mental** and **social well-being**, and the **absence of disease**.

2) Health **varies** between different parts of the world.

3) Health is **difficult** to **measure**, which makes it pretty difficult to **compare** the health of people in two places. There are things you **can measure** that **indicate health** though (they're called health indicators... imaginative).

4) An example of a health indicator is **healthy life expectancy** (**HLE**) — this is the **number** of **years** a newborn child can **expect** to **live** in **full health** without major disease. The **global pattern** of HLE is shown on the map below:

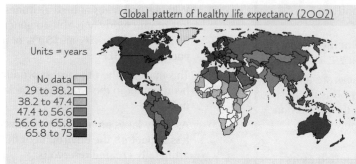

Global pattern of healthy life expectancy (2002)

Units = years

No data
29 to 38.2
38.2 to 47.4
47.4 to 56.6
56.6 to 65.8
65.8 to 75

- The map shows **HLE** is **highest** in **wealthier countries** such as the **UK, USA** and **Australia**.
- HLE is lowest in **poorer countries** such as those in **sub-Saharan Africa**.

Sub-Saharan Africa includes all the countries south of the Sahara Desert.

5) How **healthy** a country is **depends** on how much **disease** there is in the country, and what **types** of **diseases** there are.

Global Morbidity Patterns *are* Different *Depending on the* Type *of* Disease

1) **Morbidity** means **illness**.

2) Morbidity **indicators** include:
   - **prevalence** — the **total** number of **cases** in a **population** at a **particular time**.
   - **incidence** — the number of **new cases** in a **population** during a **particular time period**.

3) You can use these indicators to **compare global patterns of illness**.

4) **Global patterns** of morbidity **differ** depending on the **type** of **disease** you're looking at:
   - **Infectious diseases** (e.g. malaria, HIV/AIDS) — these are often **more common** in **poorer countries**.
   - **Non-communicable diseases** (e.g. cancer, heart disease) — these are often **more common** in **wealthier countries**.

'Non-communicable' means the disease can't be caught from someone else.

① Morbidity pattern of infectious diseases

Global morbidity pattern of tuberculosis (TB) (2005)

Units = new cases per 100 000 of the population

No data
0 to 24
25 to 49
50 to 99
100 to 299
>300

- The map shows the **global morbidity pattern** of the **infectious** disease tuberculosis (**TB**).
- There's **high TB morbidity** in **poorer** countries, e.g. countries in **sub-Saharan Africa**.
- There's **low TB morbidity** in **wealthier** countries, e.g. the **UK, USA** and **Australia**.

The **reasons** for **high infectious disease morbidity** in **poorer** countries include:

1) **Malnutrition** (due to **poor food availability** and **periodic famines**) — **reduces** the body's **ability** to **fight** disease.

2) **Lack** of **clean water** and **sanitation** — **increases** the **spread** of **infectious** diseases.

3) **Overcrowded** conditions in **urban** areas — **increases** the **spread** of **infectious** diseases.

4) **Poor access** to **health care** — people **can't** access drugs to **treat** and **prevent** infectious diseases.

5) **Limited health education** — people **aren't well-informed** about how they can **avoid** infectious diseases.

6) **Disease vectors** (organisms that spread disease) — these are often **more common** in poorer countries, e.g. the **mosquitoes** that spread **malaria** are more common in **tropical** regions of **Africa**.

Global Patterns of Health, Disease and Death

② Morbidity pattern of non-communicable diseases

- The map shows the **global morbidity pattern** of the **non-communicable** disease **breast cancer**.
- There's **high breast cancer morbidity** in **wealthier** countries, e.g. the **UK, USA** and **Australia**.
- There's **low breast cancer morbidity** in **poorer** countries, e.g. countries in **Africa** and **Asia**.

The **reasons** for **high non-communicable disease morbidity** in **wealthier** countries include:

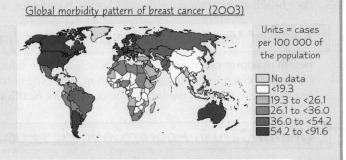

Global morbidity pattern of breast cancer (2003)

Units = cases per 100 000 of the population

- No data
- <19.3
- 19.3 to <26.1
- 26.1 to <36.0
- 36.0 to <54.2
- 54.2 to <91.6

1) **Higher proportion** of **older people** (due to higher life expectancy) — if there are more old people **more** people are **likely** to suffer from **diseases** associated with **old age**, e.g. **cancer** and **heart disease**.

2) **Unhealthy lifestyle** — the **risk** of getting **some diseases** (e.g. cancer, heart disease) **increases** if you're **overweight** or **obese**, eat **unhealthy food** and don't do enough **exercise**. These **factors** are **more common** in **wealthier** countries.

Mortality Patterns Depend on Morbidity and the Ability to Treat Morbidity

1) **Mortality** means **death**. In general, **high morbidity** causes **high mortality**.

2) The **mortality rate** is how many people **die** in a **population** over a **period of time**. You use mortality rates to **compare global patterns of death**.

- The table on the right shows that **wealthier** areas, such as **Northern America** and **Australia**, have a **high mortality** rate for **cancer** (**caused by** a **high incidence** of the disease). But only a **low percentage of cases** result in **death**.

- The **mortality rate** from **cancer** is **lower** in **poorer** areas, such as **Middle** and **Eastern Africa** (**caused by** a **low incidence** of the disease), but the **percentage of cases resulting in death** is **much higher**.

The **risk** of **dying** from a disease is **much higher** in **poorer countries** because of:

1) **Malnutrition** — **reduces** the body's **ability** to **fight** disease.

2) **Poor access** to **health care** — people **can't access** the drugs they need to **treat** the disease.

Global incidence and mortality rates from all forms of cancer (2008)

Area of the world	Incidence rate (cases per 100 000)	Mortality rate (deaths per 100 000)	% of cases resulting in death
Middle Africa	92	76	83
Eastern Africa	123	100	81
Northern Africa	103	78	76
Southern Africa	190	133	70
Central America	134	82	61
Northern America	300	105	35
Northern Europe	269	115	43
Southern Europe	244	112	46
Western Europe	287	108	38
Australia/ New Zealand	313	104	33

Health and Disease are World Issues

1) **Infectious diseases** can **spread** to **other countries** and can even **spread** around the **world** (e.g. **HIV/AIDS** now **affects** people in **all countries**).

2) This means **countries** need to **work together** to help **improve global health** and **prevent diseases spreading**.

3) **Organisations** like the **WHO** (**World Health Organisation**) **work** with **most governments** and in **most countries** to help **eradicate** and **prevent disease**. For example, they run a **programme** of **vaccinations** (**paid** for by **wealthy** countries) to **eradicate polio** (an **infectious disease** mainly found in **poorer countries**).

Practice Questions

Q1 Define health.
Q2 Give an example of how you can measure health.
Q3 What is morbidity?

Exam Question

Q1 Measles is an infectious disease spread by close contact. Use the map to outline the global pattern of measles morbidity. [10 marks]

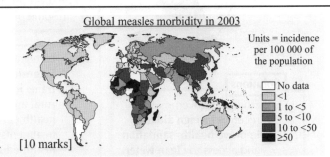

Global measles morbidity in 2003

Units = incidence per 100 000 of the population

- No data
- <1
- 1 to <5
- 5 to <10
- 10 to <50
- ≥50

Disease — it's morbid stuff...

This isn't the cheeriest of sections, I know, but that doesn't mean you can get away with not learning it. Sorry. It doesn't help when they make morbidity and mortality such similar words but with different meanings — that's just asking for trouble. So just remember — morbidity means illness and mortality means death. So what are you waiting for, get on and learn it...

Health Care Approaches

Poor health affects millions of people, both rich and poor. There are lots of ideas for how to improve health, but no easy fix...

Lack of Money *Makes it* Difficult *to* Improve Health *in* Poorer *Countries*

Health in **poorer countries** isn't great, mainly because **infectious diseases** are **common** and **spread easily** (because of issues like **lack** of **clean water** and **poor sanitation**). Helping people become healthier isn't easy — the **key barriers** to improving health include a **lack of money** to provide **effective health care** and **difficulties** in getting health care to **remote populations**.

Health Care *in* Poorer Countries *Focuses on* Treating Disease

1) In **poorer** countries the **national income** is **low**, so **spending** on **health** tends to be **low** too.

2) A **large proportion** of the **money** that's available for health care is often spent on **treating** large numbers of patients with **diseases**. This leaves **little money** available for **preventative care** (like **vaccinations**) and **health education**.

3) **Preventing disease** is often a **more effective** way to **improve health** than just treating disease.

4) Some poorer countries **rely heavily** on **foreign aid** to help with **health care**, e.g. grants and loans, donated medicines and medical equipment, and volunteer doctors and nurses.

5) **Foreign aid** can help poorer countries **improve health care services** in the short-term, but **longer-term solutions** are needed so countries can become **self-reliant**.

Local *Health Care* Training *Can* Improve Health *in* Remote Populations

1) A **key health care issue** in poorer countries is the **lack** of **medical services** in **remote rural populations**.

2) One solution is to **train local people** in **basic health care** and **employ** them to provide basic health care **services** to their **local communities**. Services include **first aid**, **treating common diseases**, providing **medicines** and **vaccinations**, **pregnancy support** and **midwifery**, and **health education**.

3) There are **advantages** and **disadvantages** to training local basic health care workers:

Advantages

1) It's a relatively **inexpensive** way of **improving health care** and **health education** in **rural** areas.

2) It **creates jobs** for **local** people.

3) It **increases the self-reliance** of communities.

4) Local basic health care workers are **unlikely to leave** (professionals, e.g. doctors, often migrate to wealthier countries where pay is better).

Disadvantage

Basic health care workers **can't replace** fully trained **medical professionals**. So **long-term solutions** must improve access to **proper medical facilities** and **fully trained staff**.

Case Study*: Local Health Care Workers in* Ethiopia

ETHIOPIA

Problem

Ethiopia, in Eastern Africa, is one of the world's **poorest** countries. There's widespread **poor health**, e.g. life expectancy is only **52 years** and **infant mortality** is around **8%**. People have **poor nutrition, poor sanitation** and **unclean water**. **Infectious diseases** are very common. There's a **shortage** of **medical professionals** and **health facilities**, especially in **remote rural** areas — in some places there are only **three doctors** per **100 000 people**.

Solutions

1) Ethiopia's government receives **foreign aid** to improve **health, sanitation** and access to **clean water**. Some of the money's spent on **preventative health care** such as **vaccinations** and **contraceptives**.

2) Foreign aid funds the **Health Extension Programme**, which **trains local health care workers** in **rural** areas. Workers deliver **basic health care** (vaccinations, malaria treatments and maternity care) and **health education** (teaching about family planning, prevention of HIV/AIDS, hygiene and nutrition). But **more** health workers are **still needed** by many communities.

3) **Money** is being used to **prevent disease**. E.g. since 2005, millions of **insecticide-treated bed nets** have been given out — a **cost-effective** way of **preventing** the spread of **malaria** by **mosquitoes**. In **one year**, the number of new **malaria** cases **fell by 20%**.

Health Care Approaches

Ignoring Advice Makes it Difficult to Improve Health in Wealthier Countries

1) **Health** in **wealthier countries** isn't that good either, partly because of **ageing populations**. This is when there's a **higher proportion** of **older people** in the population — often due to a **high life expectancy** and **low birth rate**.

2) **More people** suffer from **age-related illnesses**, such as cancer and heart disease. This can put a **big strain** on **health services**.

3) **Lifestyle choices** also affect health. Choosing to **eat healthily**, **exercise**, **not smoke** and **reduce alcohol** consumption can **improve** your **health**.

4) The **key barrier** to improving health in **wealthier** countries is people **ignoring advice** on **lifestyle changes** that would **reduce** their chance of **developing disease**.

Stella tried to cut it down to just a few drinks a day...

Health Care in Wealthier Countries Includes Preventing Disease

In **wealthier** countries a great deal of **money** is spent on **preventative health care**, such as:

1) Providing **vaccinations against diseases** (e.g. measles, mumps, meningitis).

2) **Health awareness campaigns** to **promote good lifestyle choices** (e.g. eating healthily and taking regular exercise).

3) **Providing support services** to help people **improve** their **health** (e.g. services to help people stop smoking).

4) **Early diagnosis** (e.g. cancer screening, antenatal screening and screening for heart conditions).

Case Study: Preventing Cervical Cancer in England

Problem
Nearly **3000 women** are diagnosed with **cervical cancer** each year in **England**, which can cause **death** if left **untreated**. **99%** of all **cervical cancers** are **caused** by a virus called **HPV** (human papillomavirus).

Solutions
1) Some forms of cervical cancer are **preventable** by **stopping infection** with **HPV**. An **HPV vaccine** is now offered to **all girls** aged **12-13** in **England**.

2) **Cervical screening** (a **smear test**) is offered to **all women over 25** in **England**. **Unusual cells** (signs of cancer) can be **detected early**, allowing **treatment** to **prevent cancer**. **Death rates** from cervical cancer have **decreased** by nearly **70% since screening** began.

Practice Questions

Q1 What are the main barriers to improving health in poorer countries?

Q2 What are the advantages of training local people in basic health care in rural areas of poorer countries?

Q3 Why does an ageing population contribute to a country's poor health?

Q4 Give four examples of preventative health care that wealthier countries spend money on.

Exam Question

Q1 The graph shows global differences in public health spending per person.

a) Describe the pattern of public health spending shown by the graph. [2 marks]

b) The amount of money available for public health services can affect the health care approach countries use. With reference to one or more schemes, describe the contrasting health care approaches used in wealthy and poor countries. [10 marks]

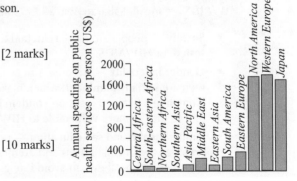

Prevention is the best cure — or so my mum says...

It's not easy to improve the health of populations, in poor or rich countries — you can't just throw money at people. Well, you can, but that'll only help in the short-term. Long-term solutions need to tackle ways of preventing diseases. It's vital that people are educated — this helps people to help themselves. Whether they'll listen or not is another matter...

The Geography of Disease

Different diseases affect different countries — but they all have a big impact...

Diseases Affect Health, Economic Development and Lifestyle

The **cost** of a **disease** to any country includes the following:

HEALTH	**Increased poor health** in the population and in some cases **permanent disability** and **death**.
ECONOMIC DEVELOPMENT	**Slow economic development** due to **increasing death rates** (so fewer taxes go to the government), **decreasing productivity** (due to **days lost** from **work**) and **increasing health care costs**.
LIFESTYLE	**Increased poverty** (due to **days lost** from **work** and **health care costs**), **impaired learning** (due to **days lost** at **school**) and a **downward spiral** as the poorest families are **trapped in poverty**.

Malaria is Common in Tropical Regions such as Sub-Saharan Africa

1) Malaria is an **infectious disease** caused by **parasites**, which are transmitted by **mosquitoes**.

2) Malaria can be **cured** with **anti-malarial drugs**, but **without treatment** it can quickly become **life-threatening**.

3) Malaria can be **prevented** by using **bed nets** and **insecticides** (which kill the mosquitoes that carry the disease).

Distribution of malaria CASES

Most **cases** of **malaria** are found in **tropical** areas, e.g. **sub-Saharan Africa**. In **2006** there were nearly **250 million global cases** of malaria and **86%** occurred in the **poorest** countries in **Africa**. **Reasons** include:

- **Climate** — **mosquitoes** that carry **malaria** can only **survive** in **warm countries** like those in **Africa**.

- **Limited health education** — people **aren't informed** about how to **avoid malaria** (e.g. by using **bed nets**).

- **Poor health care** — people with malaria are **less likely** to be **treated**. This means there are **more infected people** and so **more sources** of the **parasite** for mosquitoes to pick up and transmit.

Distribution of malaria DEATHS

In **2006**, **91%** of **global deaths** from **malaria** were in **sub-Saharan Africa**. **Reasons** include:

- **High number** of **cases**.

- **Poor health care** — **anti-malarial drugs aren't affordable** or **available**, especially to people living in **remote rural populations**.

- **Poor health** and **nutrition** — reduces the body's **ability** to **fight infections**.

HIV/AIDS is Very Common Across Africa but Quite Common Elsewhere

1) **HIV** (Human Immunodeficiency Virus) is a virus that **destroys** the **immune system**. It eventually causes **AIDS** (Acquired Immunodeficiency Syndrome), which causes **death**.

2) HIV is transmitted by **sexual contact**, **sharing needles**, **blood transfusions** and **contaminated medical equipment**.

3) There's **no cure** for AIDS but you can **slow** the **development** of **HIV to AIDS** by using **antiviral drugs**. HIV can be **prevented** by practising **safe sex**, **screening blood donors** and by using **sterile medical equipment**.

Distribution of HIV/AIDS CASES

66% of the **population** (and **90%** of **children**) living with **HIV/AIDS** are in **sub-Saharan Africa**. **Reasons** include:

- **Society** — people are more **reluctant** to get **tested** for **HIV/AIDS**.

- **Gender inequality** — in some African countries men are **socially dominant**, which makes **women** less likely to insist on **condom** use, and so they're **more vulnerable** to **HIV/AIDS**.

- **Limited health** and **sex education** — people **aren't aware** of what HIV is and **aren't informed** of how they can **avoid it** (e.g. by using **condoms** and **sterile medical equipment**).

- **Limited health care** — people with HIV/AIDS are **less likely** to be **diagnosed**, so they're more likely to **pass on** the disease.

HIV infection in adults (2005)

- No data
- <0.1%
- 0.1-<0.5%
- 0.5-<1%
- 1-<5%
- 5-34%

Distribution of HIV/AIDS DEATHS

Over **70%** of **global deaths** from **HIV/AIDS** occur in **sub-Saharan Africa**. **Reasons** include:

- **High number** of **cases**.

- **Poor health care** — **antiviral drugs** that prolong life **aren't affordable** or **available**.

- **Poor health, nutrition** and **hygiene** — **increase** the **risk** of other **infections** that can be **fatal** because HIV **destroys** the **immune system**.

The Geography of Disease

Coronary Heart Disease is Becoming More Common in Poorer Countries

1) Coronary heart disease (CHD) is a disease where the heart doesn't get enough blood. It can lead to a **heart attack**.

2) CHD has **no cure** but it can be **controlled** with **treatment** (e.g. **aspirin**, or **surgery** such as a heart bypass operation). **Early diagnosis** and access to **health care** can **increase life expectancy**.

3) The **risk** of developing CHD can be **reduced** by **lifestyle changes** such as **eating healthily**, **exercising** and **not smoking**.

Distribution of CHD CASES

CHD is a **non-communicable disease** — it's **more common** in **wealthier** countries, e.g. the **UK** and the **USA**. Reasons include:

- **Ageing populations** — your **risk** of developing CHD **increases** as you get **older**.
- **Lifestyle factors** — an **unhealthy lifestyle** and being **obese** or **overweight increases** your **risk** of developing CHD.

Cases of CHD are **increasing** in **poor** and **newly-industrialised countries** though (e.g. countries in **sub-Saharan Africa** and **India**), as their **wealth increases**. Reasons include:

- **Increasing life expectancy** — **more people** suffer from **CHD** because of **ageing populations**.
- **Social**, **economic** and **cultural changes** — people are adopting **Western diets** and **lifestyles**, e.g. smoking.

Distribution of CHD DEATHS

CHD is one of the **world's biggest killers**. It caused **14% of global deaths** in **1997**. Over **80% of deaths** occur in **poor** and **newly-industrialised** areas, e.g. **sub-Saharan Africa** and **India**. Reasons include:

- **Poor health care** — **treatments** (e.g. **surgery**) **aren't affordable** or **available**.
- **Limited health education** — people **aren't aware** of the **effects** of **lifestyle changes** (e.g. **smoking** and **eating fatty foods**).

Death rates are **falling** in **wealthier** countries though, because of **improvements** in **diagnosing** people **at risk** of CHD, developing **effective treatments**, and **awareness campaigns** to **prevent** the disease.

Cancer is Becoming More Common in Poorer Countries

CHD and cancer are non-communicable diseases, see p. 98.

1) **Cancer** is the **uncontrollable growth** and **spread** of **abnormal cells** in the body.

2) If **detected early** enough, many cancers can be **cured** or **controlled** with **treatment** (e.g. surgery). Many cancers are **detected early** through **awareness** of **symptoms** and **regular screening**, e.g. detecting breast cancer lumps.

3) The **risk** of getting cancer can be **reduced** with **lifestyle changes**, such as **eating healthily**, **exercising more** and **not smoking**. Some forms of **cervical cancer** can be **prevented** by having a **vaccination**.

Distribution of cancer CASES

Cancer is another **non-communicable disease** — it's **more common** in **wealthier** countries, e.g. the **UK** and USA. The **most common** types are **prostate**, **breast** and **colon cancer**. Reasons include: ⟹

- **Ageing populations**.
- **Lifestyle factors**.

Cancer is becoming **increasingly common** in poor and newly-industrialised countries — especially **liver**, **stomach** and **cervical cancer**. **Reasons** include:

- **Increasing life expectancy**.
- **Social**, **economic** and **cultural changes** (adoption of a more **Western lifestyle**).

Distribution of cancer DEATHS

Cancer is the **world's second biggest killer**, causing **13% of deaths** in **2007**. **75%** of those **deaths** were in **poor** and **newly-industrialised** countries. Reasons include:

- **Poor health care**.
- **Limited health education**.

Death rates are **falling** in **wealthier** countries though, because of **improvements** in **diagnosis**, **treatment** and **awareness**.

Practice Questions

Q1 Describe the impact of disease on economic development.

Q2 What measures can help prevent the spread of HIV/AIDS?

Q3 Describe the global distribution of coronary heart disease.

Exam Question

Q1 Describe and explain the reasons for the global distribution of malaria and discuss its impact. [10 marks]

Diseases affect the poor and wealthy — but death rates are very uneven...

Irritatingly, any one of these diseases could come up in your exam, so I'm afraid you have to learn them all.
But hey — at least some of the points are similar for the examples of poor and wealthy diseases...

Health and Globalisation

The distribution of disease is affected by some companies, which sounds a bit weird, but it's true (Scout's honour). A lot of these companies now operate at a global level (globalisation) so they have an impact on global health — in both good and bad ways...

Trans-National Corporations *can* Improve Health *or* Add *to* Health Problems

Trans-National corporations (TNCs) are companies that operate in **more than one country**. Some TNCs are **very large**, with **huge budgets** and **powerful political influence**. TNCs affect global health by their **actions**:

1) How they **treat employees** — the **wages** they pay, their **safety standards** and the **health care** they provide.

> **Example** — **Namdeb diamond corporation** runs an **HIV/AIDS awareness programme** in **Namibia** and provides its **HIV-positive employees** with **drug treatment**.

2) How they **market products** — such as **tobacco**, **fatty foods** and **breast milk substitutes**.

> **Example** — There are **concerns** that aiming **fast-food advertising** at **children** may **contribute** to long-term **unhealthy eating** choices and **obesity**.

3) How they **sell products** (such as **tobacco**, **medical drugs** and **medical supplies**) and **how much they charge** for them.

> **Example** — Many **African** countries have to **rely** on the **generosity** of **overseas governments** and **pharmaceutical companies** to **subsidise drugs** because they **can't afford them**.

4) Which **products** they choose to **research** and **develop** — such as **healthy foods** and **medicines**.

> **Example** — **Kraft Foods** are **developing** a **new food** that **kills intestinal worms**. It's aimed at **rural** Africa, Asia and South America, where **intestinal worms** are a **big health problem**.

Pharmaceutical Companies *Affect* Global Health

Pharmaceutical companies **research**, **develop**, **produce** and **distribute drugs** to treat disease.
They affect **world health** because they can choose **which drugs** to develop and what **prices** to charge.

Research and Production

1) There's **more money** in **wealthier countries** so pharmaceutical companies often choose to **research and produce** drugs for diseases that **mainly** affect wealthier countries (e.g. drugs for impotency). This leads to **improved health** in **wealthier countries**.

2) Some pharmaceutical companies use the **profits** they make in wealthier countries to **subsidise research** into diseases that affect **poorer countries** (e.g. malaria vaccines). This leads to **improved health** in **poorer countries**.

Distribution and Sales

1) Drugs cost **a lot of money** to research and develop, which companies get back from the **sale** of their drugs.

2) Pharmaceutical companies have **exclusive rights** for **20 years** to produce new drugs they've developed. This means they can set **any price** for them because you can't get them **anywhere else**.

3) This affects **global health** because some **poorer countries** may not be able to **afford** the drugs they need.

4) Some pharmaceutical companies, often through **deals** with wealthier countries, provide **free or cheaper drugs** for poorer countries (e.g. anti-HIV drugs).

Case Study: *GlaxoSmithKline (GSK)*

GSK is one of the **world's largest pharmaceutical companies**.
It **produces** many different **drugs** and **health products**.

Research and Production

1) GSK produces almost **four billion** packs of **medicines** and health care products **each year**, including **one-quarter** of the **world's vaccines**.

2) It produces products for **wealthy countries** (e.g. Pravastatin-RL™, a drug for CHD), and for **poorer countries** (e.g. polio vaccines).

Distribution and Sales

1) GSK makes a **large profit** from drug sales but also **donates** some drugs to poorer countries for **free**. For example, GSK's donated **750 million albendazole tablets** to treat over **130 million people** with **elephantiasis** (an infectious inflammatory disease).

2) GSK also **invests** a large amount of its profit in **community programmes** to help people in need — **3.8%** of their pre-tax **profits** (**£282 million**) in 2007.

Health and Globalisation

Tobacco Companies Also Affect Global Health

1) About a **third** of the **world's population over** the **age** of **15 smokes**. Although **wealthier countries** are starting to **smoke less**, it's becoming a **huge problem** elsewhere — **80%** of **smokers** live in **poorer countries**.

2) Almost **four million** people **die each year** from **tobacco-related illnesses**, such as **lung cancer** and **heart disease**. **Death rates** are **rising** because most **tobacco-related illnesses** take years or decades to develop.

3) Because tobacco-related illnesses take a long time to develop, they're **traditionally** a health problem associated with **wealthier countries** (because people **live long enough** for the disease to develop).

4) As poorer countries develop and **life expectancy increases**, tobacco-related illnesses are becoming **more common**.

5) In **2003**, the **World Health Organisation** (**WHO**) developed a **treaty** called the 'Framework Convention on Tobacco Control'. The treaty **protects public health** by **restricting tobacco advertising**, **regulating** the **contents of tobacco products**, making sure they're **packaged** and **labelled correctly** and **regulating** who they're **sold to**.

Some people thought tobacco restrictions had gone too far this time.

6) It's hoped these measures will help to **reduce** the number of global **smokers**, **reducing** the number of **tobacco-related illnesses** worldwide.

7) There are **concerns** that some **tobacco companies** are **targeting** countries that **haven't signed** the **WHO treaty**, so have **fewer restrictions**. Companies are accused of **aggressive marketing** to **target vulnerable populations** (e.g. young people), and **exploiting** people's **lack of knowledge** about tobacco's **health effects**.

8) This could result in **increased tobacco-related illnesses** in these countries.

Case Study: Philip Morris International (PMI)

PMI is the **world's largest tobacco company** and **owns** the **world's top selling brand**.

Research and Production

1) PMI **sells** a lot of **tobacco products**. In **2005** it **sold 805 billion cigarettes** worldwide.

2) But PMI does **research** and **develop** some potentially **less harmful tobacco products**, e.g. **cigarettes** that might **reduce the exposure** of the **smoker** to **toxic chemical compounds**. These measures could help to **reduce** the number of **tobacco-related illnesses** worldwide.

Distribution and Sales

1) PMI does stick to the 'Framework Convention on Tobacco Control' in the **countries** that **have signed** it. But it uses a different range of **advertising** and **marketing strategies** in countries that haven't signed up. E.g. PMI **offers** adult **smokers free samples** of **cigarettes** where it's **legal** to do so.

2) PMI does have a 'responsible marketing policy'. It's **agreed** not to **market products** to **children** and to put **health warnings** on all **marketing materials** and all **packaging**.

Practice Questions

Q1 Briefly describe how research carried out by pharmaceutical companies can affect global health.

Q2 Briefly describe how the distribution and sale of drugs by pharmaceutical companies can affect global health.

Q3 Give one possible reason why the number of tobacco-related illnesses is rising.

Exam Question

Q1 With reference to one or more specific examples, explain how transnational corporations can affect global health. [10 marks]

TNC — aren't they a girl band...

Some of the largest TNCs are wealthier than some of the world's poorest countries — seems a little unfair, doesn't it. People have divided opinions about how much these companies should be doing to improve world health. But don't worry, you don't have to come up with the answer to that problem — you just have to get learning these wonderful pages.

The Geography of Health in the UK

Health isn't just different between countries, it's different within countries too. Take the UK for example...

Health is Better in Southern England than in Northern England and Scotland

There are **big differences** in **health** across the **UK**. **Life expectancy** from birth (a measure of health) for **males** born between 2004-2006 is shown on the map.

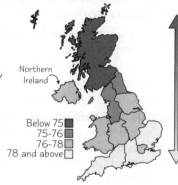

1) The **general health trend** for the UK is a **North-South divide** — people living in the **South** of England are **healthier** than people living in the **North** of England and in **Scotland**.

2) The **highest life expectancy** at birth for **males** (1991-2001) was in **North Dorset**, South-west England (**79 years**) and the **lowest** was in **Glasgow** (**69 years**).

3) The **trend** of **morbidity** (illness) also **varies** — it has a **similar pattern** to **life expectancy**. E.g. **lung cancer** is **more common** in women living in **Scotland** (about **50% higher** than the rest of the UK) and **less common** in women living in **South-west England** (about **40% lower** than the rest of the UK).

*Map legend:*
Northern Ireland
NORTH Lower life expectancy
Below 75
75-76
76-78
78 and above
Higher life expectancy SOUTH

Income Affects Health Patterns in the UK...

There's a **strong link between** how much **money** you earn and how **healthy** you are. In general, **wealthier people** tend to be **healthier** because they have **better access** to **exercise facilities** and **health care**, and are **more educated** about **health issues**. The **pattern** of **household income** in the **UK** broadly **matches** the **pattern** of **life expectancy** (above).

For example, average **household income** (2003/04 to 2005/06) was **highest** in **South-east England** (**£91** a week **higher** than the UK average) and **lowest** in **North-east England** (**£141** a week **lower** than the UK average).

...and so do Age Structure, Occupation Type, Education and Environment

1 Age structure

1) **Older people** are **more likely** to **suffer** from **age-related diseases**, e.g. **cancer** and **heart disease**.

2) **All regions** of the **UK** have an **ageing population**, due to **low birth rates** and **increasing life expectancy**.

3) But, **some areas** have a **higher proportion** of old people than others because **more retired people** choose to live there, e.g. **rural** and **coastal areas** like **Devon**.

2 Occupation type

1) If you do a **manual job** (e.g. a **labourer** or a **cleaner**) then you're up to **three times more likely** to suffer from **poor health** than if you do a **non-manual job** (e.g. a **doctor** or an **accountant**). Reasons for this include a **higher risk of accidents** and **exposure** to **hazardous substances**, e.g. **asbestos**.

2) **More people** do **manual jobs** in the **North of England**, which may contribute to the **higher levels of poor health**.

3) People doing **non-manual jobs** are more likely to suffer from **stress** and **mental health problems**. For example, **London** has the **highest proportion** of people in **non-manual jobs** and the **highest level of self-reported stress**.

3 Education

1) The **better educated** you are, the **more likely** you are to **choose a healthier lifestyle** — such as **eating healthy foods**, exercising **regularly** and **not smoking**.

2) This could be because **poor education** means **poor knowledge** of how to stay healthy.

3) In 2003, **18.8%** of the working-age population in **North-east England** had **no educational qualifications**. Only **10.7%** of the working-age population in **South-west England** had **no educational qualifications**. This might contribute to the **difference** in **health** between the two areas.

Some of these factors are linked together, e.g. people with a poor education are more likely to do manual jobs.

4 Environment and pollution

1) If you live in a **polluted area**, like a **big city** or near a **major road**, then you're **more likely** to suffer from **poor health**.

2) For example, **London** has a particularly **high mortality** rate from **respiratory diseases**, thought to be **caused by the poor air quality** in the city.

3) In contrast, **Devon** and **Cornwall** in **South-west England** are **countryside areas** with much **less pollution**. This may contribute to the **better health** there.

The Geography of Health in the UK

Gender Influences Health Too

Women tend to **live longer** than men but they're **twice as likely** to have **higher morbidity** from **chronic illnesses**, such as **arthritis**, and are **three times more likely** to suffer from **migraines**. **Women** are also **less likely** to take part in **sports** than men (**18.5%** compared with **23.7%**). Some **leisure facilities** have introduced 'ladies only' sessions to **encourage participation**.

Health Care Provision is Affected by Ageing Populations

An **ageing population** requires **more money** to be **allocated** to **certain health care services**, for example:

1) **Specialised wards** — to **care** for the **growing population** of **elderly people** who have **ill health**.
2) **Increased screening** for **age-related diseases** (e.g. cancer and heart disease).
3) **More residential care homes** and **carers**.
4) **More mobile health care services** — to **cope** with the **increasing immobilised elderly population**, especially those in **rural areas** without family support.

More older people in a population means **more people** are **retired** and **fewer people** are **working** — this can result in a **declining tax base** to **pay** for **health** and **social services**.

Case Study: Health in South-west England

The **South-west** of **England** has the oldest population structure in the UK — in **2001**, **21%** of the **South-west's** population was pension age or over (60+ for women and 65+ for men). This compares to **19%** in **England** and **14%** in **London**. This will **increase** as **more people** are reaching **retirement age** and are choosing to **live** in **rural** and **coastal** areas.

An **ageing population** affects the **general health** of the area and the provision of **health care**:

1) **Higher rates** of diseases associated with **age** — in the South-west in **2003**, the rate of **breast cancer** was **7% above** UK average, and the rate of **prostate cancer** was **14% above** the UK average.
2) More **carers** and **health workers** are needed — in **2001**, **11%** of the working population of the South-west worked in the **social and health sectors**, compared to **10%** in **London**.
3) More **care homes** are required — **14%** of care homes in England are located in the **South-west** (only 10% are located in London).

1% extra might not seem like a lot but it's over 22 000 people.

Pumping money into **health care services** might **not** be the **best way** to **improve health** in the South-west:

1) Although the **South-west** has the **oldest population structure**, it's still the **healthiest region** in the UK — which **suggests** that **age isn't** the **most important factor** in poor health. There's **evidence** in the **South-west** that **low income is strongly linked** to **poor health**.
2) **Inland Revenue** figures show that **older people** have **lower personal incomes** than average, so it could be their **low income**, rather than age, that's **mostly affecting** their **health**. So the **most effective way** of **improving health** in the region could be to **focus** on **reducing** the number of **people** living on a **low income**.
3) For example, the **government** provides people **over 60** years old with a **heating allowance** — grants of up to **£4000** to **insulate homes** and make **heating improvements**. This is especially important in the **South-west** because this area has the **highest proportion** of **energy-inefficient homes** in England. The **heating allowance improves health** in the **South-west** because it helps **reduce illness** and **speeds recovery** in the **elderly population**.

Practice Questions

Q1 Describe the general health trend for the UK.
Q2 Why are wealthier people more likely to live healthier lives?
Q3 Name two factors that affect health in the UK.

Exam Question

Q1 Describe how an ageing population in the UK is likely to affect the provision of health care services. [6 marks]

Repeat after me — wealthier means healthier...

So, your health depends on many things but it seems like income's the major factor. Of course, they're all linked — it's hard to afford gym membership and a house by the coast on a low income. Still, there's just no excuse for deep-fried Mars Bars...

A2-Level
Geography

Exam Board: AQA

Plate Tectonics Theory

The ground beneath your feet is moving all the time — but fear not, it's moving really, really, really slowly (about the same speed as your toenails grow. Yuk, toenails). Plate tectonics theory explains this movement...

Part of the Earth's *Mantle* is *Semi-molten*

1) At the **centre** of the Earth is the **CORE**, which is split into an **inner** core and an **outer** core:

- The inner core is a **solid ball** containing lots of **iron and nickel**.
- The outer core is **semi-molten** and also contains lots of **iron and nickel**.

2) Around the core is the **MANTLE**, which is mostly made of **silicate rocks** (rocks that have loads of the element silicon in them):

- The part of the mantle **nearest the core** is **quite rigid**.
- The **layer above** this, called the **asthenosphere**, is **semi-molten** (it can flow).
- And the **very, very top bit** of the mantle is **rigid**.

3) The **outer layer** of the Earth is called the **CRUST**.

4) The **rigid top part** of the **mantle** and the **crust** together are called the **LITHOSPHERE**.

5) There are **two types** of crust — **CONTINENTAL** and **OCEANIC**:

- **Continental** crust is **thicker** (30-70 km thick) and **less dense**.
- **Oceanic** crust is **thinner** (6-10 km thick) and **more dense**.

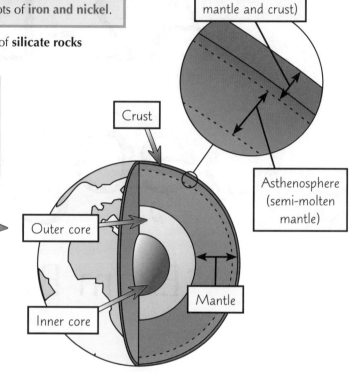

Lithosphere (rigid mantle and crust)

Crust

Asthenosphere (semi-molten mantle)

Outer core

Mantle

Inner core

The **Earth's Surface** is **Separated** into **Tectonic Plates**

1) The lithosphere is **divided** into lots of slabs called **tectonic plates**.

2) The plates are **moving** due to **convection currents** in the **asthenosphere** (see the next page).

3) The places where plates meet are called **boundaries** or **plate margins**.

North American

Eurasian

Pacific

Pacific

African

Philippine

Nazca

South American

Indo-Australian

Antarctic

~ plate boundary

→ direction of plate movement

Pierre really loved continental crust.

4) The idea that the Earth's lithosphere is made up of many plates that are moved around by convection currents is the **theory of plate tectonics**.

Plate Tectonics Theory

The Tectonic Plates **Move** due to **Convection Currents** in the **Mantle**

1) **Radioactive decay** of some elements in the mantle and core, e.g. uranium, generates a **lot of heat**.

2) When **lower parts** of the **asthenosphere heat up** they become **less dense** and slowly **rise**.

3) As they move towards the **top** of the asthenosphere they **cool down**, become **more dense**, then slowly **sink**.

4) These **circular movements** of semi-molten rock are called **CONVECTION CURRENTS**.

5) Convection currents in the asthenosphere **create drag** on the **base** of the **tectonic plates** (which are solid and rigid) — and this causes them to **move**.

The Earth's core is extremely hot — it's over 4000 °C.

Crust is **Created** When **Plates** Move **Apart**

1) **Rising convection currents diverge** (move apart) at the base of the lithosphere.

2) The drag of the convection currents causes the **plates** above them to **diverge too**.

3) **Magma rises up** to fill the gap created, then **cools** to form **new crust**.

4) Over time, the **new crust** is **dragged apart** and even **more new crust forms** between it.

5) When this happens at a plate margin under the sea the **sea floor gets wider**.

6) This **process** is called **sea floor spreading**... imaginative name.

7) It creates structures called **mid-ocean ridges** — ridges of higher terrain on either side of the margin.

8) A similar process of spreading occurs at **land margins** where the plates are moving apart.

9) When plates move together, sometimes the crust is **destroyed** and sometimes it's pushed up into **mountains** (see p. 114 for more).

New crust formation at mid-ocean ridges doesn't happen at the same speed everywhere — at some it's less than 10 mm per year and at others it's more than 100 mm per year.

Practice Questions

Q1 What is the asthenosphere?

Q2 What is the lithosphere?

Q3 Briefly describe sea floor spreading.

Exam Questions

Q1 Describe the structure of the Earth. [8 marks]

Q2 Describe and explain how convection currents cause tectonic plates to move. [8 marks]

Plate tectonics — it's a cracking theory...

What a lovely couple of pages to ease you in gently, but don't think you can get away without knowing this stuff inside out. If you don't get the basics, the rest of this section will be more painful than stubbing your toe on a slab of oceanic crust. A bit of work now will help make the rest of plate tectonics a piece of Victoria sponge. You'd better get learning...

Plate Tectonics Theory

The theory of plate tectonics is widely accepted by scientists. It grew out of the theory of continental drift — which a clever bloke called Alfred Wegener came up with early in the 20th century...

The **Theory of Plate Tectonics** started with **Alfred Wegener**

1) In the **17th centur**y people first noticed that **South America** and **Africa** looked like they could **fit together**, like pieces of a **jigsaw**.

2) There were suggestions that the **continents** might once have been **joined together** before moving apart, but most people believed the continents were fixed in place.

3) In 1912 **Alfred Wegener** proposed the theory of **continental drift**.

4) He suggested that **all the continents** were once **joined** as **one supercontinent** (called **Pangaea**) which drifted apart.

5) Wegener based his theory on **geological evidence** and **fossil records** (see below), but he **couldn't** back it up with a **mechanism** that explained how the continents **moved**.

6) But in the **1950s**, **palaeomagnetism** (see the next page) provided **evidence** that supported continental drift.

7) And in the **1960s** the process of **sea floor spreading** (see previous page) was discovered — it provided the **mechanism** for continental drift.

8) The continental drift theory was **developed further** by scientists after these findings. It grew into the **theory of plate tectonics**.

Ethel and Walter remembered the good ol' days back in Pangaea...

Pangaea, about 250 million years ago

The present day

There's **Plenty of Evidence** for the Theory

Geology

1) Areas of **South America** and **Africa** have **rocks** of the **same age and composition** — if you fit these continents together, the **distribution** of the rocks **matches up**.

2) You can also **match up** the age, rock type and distribution of some **mountain ranges**, e.g. mountains in **Scotland**, **Norway**, **Sweden** and **Finland** are similar to those on the **east coast of North America**.

3) These rocks and mountains must have formed under the **same conditions** and in the **same place** in order to match so well — this would **only be possible** if the **continents were once joined**.

☐ 0.5 billion year old deformed rock
☐ 2 billion year old igneous and metamorphic rock

Fossil Records

1) By fitting land masses together you can **match up** the **distribution** of some **fossils**, e.g. fossils of *Lystrosaurus*, *Cynognathus*, *Mesosaurus* (all reptiles) and *Glossopteris* (a plant).

2) It's **very unlikely** that these species **migrated** across thousands of miles of water, or that they **evolved** in different places.

3) So the fossil records **suggest** that these places were **joined together** when these organisms were alive — **hundreds of millions of years ago**.

☐ *Cynognathus* fossils ☐ *Lystrosaurus* fossils
☐ *Mesosaurus* fossils ☐ *Glossopteris* fossils

Living Species

1) The same living organisms can also be found on **different continents** — like with the fossilised organisms above, it's **unlikely** that some of them **migrated** across the oceans, or **evolved** in different locations.

2) For example, **earthworms** of the family *Megascolecidae* are found in **New Zealand**, parts of **Asia** and **North America**. This suggests that the **continents were once joined**, allowing the earthworms to travel between them.

Plate Tectonics Theory

Climatology

There's evidence that the **past climates** of some continents were **similar**, despite being **thousands of miles apart** now. This suggests that they were **located together** and in a **different place** on Earth to where they are now. Here are a **couple of examples**:

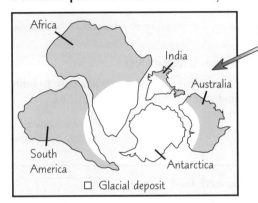

□ Glacial deposit

1) Similar **glacial deposits** are found in **Antarctica, Africa, South America, India** and **Australia**. By fitting these places together you can **match up the distribution** of the deposits, which suggests that they were **joined together** millions of years ago and located **close to the South Pole**.

2) Large **coal deposits** that were **formed in tropical conditions** have been found in **North America** and parts of **Europe**. This suggests these regions were once **closer to the equator** than they are now — they've drifted over time.

Palaeomagnetism

1) **Palaeomagnetism** is the study of the history of the **Earth's magnetic field**.

2) **Once every 200 000 years** or so, the Earth's magnetic field **reverses polarity** (the magnetic north and south poles switch).

3) Palaeomagnetism has provided evidence for the process of **sea floor spreading** (see page 111).

4) As **magma erupts** from mid-ocean ridges, **magnetic minerals** in the molten rock **align themselves** with the direction of the **Earth's magnetic field**.

5) When the new crust has **solidified**, the **alignment** is **fixed**.

6) The magnetic minerals in crust created in periods of **normal polarity** (magnetic north near the North Pole) are aligned in the **opposite direction** to those in crust created in periods of **reverse polarity** (magnetic north near the South Pole).

7) This creates a series of **alternating magnetic stripes** along the sea floor. The stripes show that the **crust** is **older** the **further away** from a **mid-ocean ridge** you go — this means that the **plates are moving apart**.

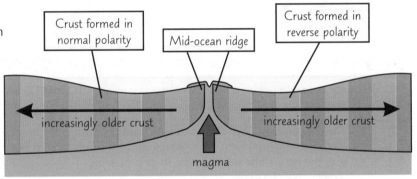

Practice Questions

Q1 Describe the theory of continental drift.

Q2 Name five sources of evidence for the theory of plate tectonics.

Exam Question

Q1 Describe the different types of evidence for the theory of plate tectonics. [40 marks]

Increasingly older crust usually goes hard and grows green stuff...

Two things to bear in mind when you're learning this little lot. Firstly, despite it being called a theory, plate tectonics is pretty much accepted as fact — there's an overwhelming amount of evidence that proves the plates are moving around. Secondly, continental drift takes place over hundreds of millions of years — it's unlikely that the UK will be nestled next to Australia any time soon...

Types of Plate Margin

The next couple of pages build on some of the stuff you should have learnt at GCSE. It's not the most difficult of topics (I'm saving those for later...) but it's vital nonetheless — so put on your favourite revision hat and get ready to take it all in.

Earthquakes and Volcanoes Occur at Constructive Margins

1) A **constructive margin** occurs where two plates are moving **APART** (diverging).

2) The mantle is under **pressure** from the plates above. When they move apart, the pressure is **released** at the **margin**.

3) The release of pressure causes the mantle to **melt**, producing **magma**.

4) The magma is **less dense** than the plate above, so it **rises** and can **erupt** to form a **VOLCANO**.

5) The plates **don't** move apart in a **uniform way** — some parts move faster than others. This causes **pressure to build up**. When the pressure becomes **too much** the plate **cracks**, making a **fault line** and causing an **EARTHQUAKE**. **Further earthquakes** may also occur along the fault line once it's been created.

6) Constructive margins create **two different landforms**, depending on where they are:

~ *A fault line is where a plate* ~
~ *has cracked under pressure.* ~

MID-OCEAN RIDGE

1) Where diverging plates are **underwater**, a **mid-ocean ridge** forms (see page 111). For example, the **Mid-Atlantic Ridge** is where the **Eurasian plate** and **North American plate** are moving apart.

2) **Underwater volcanoes** erupt along mid-ocean ridges and they can **build up** to be above sea level. For example, **Iceland** has been formed by the build-up of underwater volcanoes along the Mid-Atlantic Ridge.

RIFT VALLEY

1) Where plates diverge **beneath land**, rising **magma** causes the continental crust to **bulge** and **fracture**, forming **fault lines**.

2) As the plates keep moving apart, the **crust** between parallel faults **drops down** to form a **rift valley**. For example, the **East African Rift System** is a series of rift valleys that stretches from **Mozambique** to the **Red Sea** — about 4000 km. It's formed because the **Nubian** and **Somalian** plates are diverging. Some parts of the system are hundreds of metres deep and thousands of metres wide.

3) **Volcanoes** are found around rift valleys. For example, **Mount Kilimanjaro** and **Mount Kenya** (the two highest mountains in Africa) are volcanoes in the **East African Rift System**.

Rift Valley | Faults | Mantle

Earthquakes and Volcanoes Also Occur at Destructive Margins

A **destructive margin** occurs where two plates are moving **TOWARDS EACH OTHER** (converging). What happens at these margins depends on the **types of plates** converging:

Oceanic-Continental

1) Where **continental crust** and **oceanic crust** converge, the **more dense oceanic** crust is **forced under** the **less dense continental** crust (it's subducted). This forms a **DEEP SEA TRENCH** (a very deep trench in the sea — e.g. the **Peru-Chile trench** in the Pacific Ocean).

2) **FOLD MOUNTAINS** also form where the plates meet. They're made up of **sediments** that have accumulated on the continental crust, which are **folded upwards** along with the **edge** of the **continental crust**.

3) The oceanic crust is **heated** by **friction** and **contact** with the upper mantle, which melts it into **magma**.

4) The magma is **less dense** than the continental crust above and will **rise** back to the surface to form **VOLCANOES**.

5) As one plate moves under the other they **can get stuck**. This causes **pressure to build up**. When the pressure becomes **too much** the plates **jerk** past each other, causing an **EARTHQUAKE**.

Fold mountains | Volcano | Deep sea trench | oceanic crust | continental crust | subduction zone | magma rising

Oceanic-Oceanic

1) Most of the same processes occur where two plates of **oceanic crust** are moving towards each other — the **denser** of the two will be **subducted**, forming a **DEEP SEA TRENCH** and triggering **EARTHQUAKES** and **VOLCANIC ERUPTIONS**.

2) **Volcanic eruptions** that take place **underwater** (e.g. when two plates of oceanic crust converge) create **ISLAND ARCS** — clusters of islands that sit in a curved line, e.g. the **Mariana Islands**.

Types of Plate Margin

Continental-Continental

1) Where two plates of **continental crust** move towards each other, **neither** is subducted so there **aren't any volcanoes** — but the pressure that builds up between them can cause EARTHQUAKES.

2) FOLD MOUNTAINS form when continental crusts converge. E.g. the **Himalayas** were created in this way.

Only Earthquakes Occur at Conservative Plate Margins

1) A **conservative margin** occurs where two plates are moving **PAST EACH OTHER**.

2) The two plates get **locked together** in places and **pressure builds up**. As with destructive margins, this causes the plates to **jerk** past each other (or to **crack**, forming **fault lines**), releasing the **energy** as an EARTHQUAKE.

3) For example, the **Pacific plate** is moving past the **North American plate**. Many earthquakes occur along this margin and along its fault lines, e.g. along the **San Andreas fault** in **California**.

AERIAL PHOTOGRAPH OF THE SAN ANDREAS FAULT

This is the fault line

Movement of plates

©PETER MENZEL / SCIENCE PHOTO LIBRARY

Here's a Summary for Each Plate Margin — Learn It

Have a look back at the map on page 110 — it'll tell you where the plates are.

Type of margin		Example	Landforms	Earthquakes?	Volcanoes?
Constructive		Eurasian plate and North American plate	• Mid-ocean ridges (when underwater) • Rift valleys (when under land)	Yes	Yes
Destructive	Oceanic-Continental	Nazca plate and South American plate	• Deep sea trenches • Young fold mountains	Yes	Yes
	Oceanic-Oceanic	Pacific plate and Philippine plate	• Deep sea trenches • Island arcs	Yes	Yes
	Continental-Continental	Indo-Australian plate and Eurasian plate	Fold mountains	Yes	No
Conservative		North American plate and Pacific plate	Low ridges	Yes	No

Practice Questions

Q1 Name the two landforms that are created at constructive margins.

Q2 Explain what happens when two continental plates meet.

Q3 Name the two types of plate margin where no volcanic activity takes place.

Q4 Give one example of each type of plate margin.

Exam Questions

Q1 Describe the features of constructive plate margins. [8 marks]

Q2 Compare and contrast margins where two oceanic plates are converging with margins where two continental plates are converging. [8 marks]

Tectonic plates are great — but they do have their faults...

Well that wasn't too bad at all, and you even got out of a 40-mark exam question. Hmm, maybe I've been a bit lenient with you — too much carrot and not enough stick. Right then, before you can move on to the next couple of pages you have to know every little bit about each of these types of plate margin, as well as an example. And yes, I do mean every little bit — get learning.

Volcanic Activity

These pages cover all your classic eruption-style volcanic activity, but they also go that little bit further. Yep, not all lava's the same you know, and we're also talking bubbling pools of mud, fountains of steam and plumes of magma.

Volcanic Activity can be Intrusive or Extrusive

1) The **high pressure** inside the Earth keeps rocks in some parts of the mantle **semi-molten**.

2) When this pressure is **released**, e.g. at constructive boundaries, the rocks become **molten**. The hot molten rock is called **magma**.

3) Because magma is **less dense** than the rock around it, it **rises up** towards the Earth's surface.

4) **Most** magma **doesn't reach the surface**, but some does — the type of **volcanic activity** depends on where the magma ends up:

Once magma erupts from the Earth's surface it's called lava.

INTRUSIVE volcanic activity
- This takes place BENEATH the Earth's surface.
- It includes the formation of **large magma chambers** and **magma** being **forced into the crust** (through cracks in the rock).

EXTRUSIVE volcanic activity
- This takes place **ON** the **Earth's surface**.
- The **major form** of this activity is **volcanic eruptions** of **lava** and other material.
- **Minor types** of extrusive volcanic activity include **hot springs**, **geysers** and **boiling mud pools**.

Intrusive Volcanic Activity forms Dykes, Sills and Batholiths

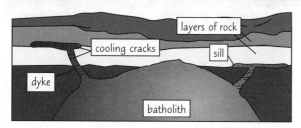

layers of rock

cooling cracks

sill

dyke

batholith

1) When large chambers of magma **cool underground** they form domes of igneous rock called **batholiths**.

2) Where the magma has flowed into **gaps** in the surrounding rock and cooled it forms vertical **dykes** (across the layers of rock) and horizontal **sills** (between the layers of rock).

3) Cracks may form as the magma cools — these are called (wait for it...) **cooling cracks**. In a sill they're **vertical**, and in a dyke they're **horizontal**.

Batholiths (e.g. the Sierra Nevada batholith in the US) can become exposed if the rock layers above them are eroded away.

Lava Eruptions are a form of Extrusive Activity

1) There are **three** main types of lava:

- **BASALTIC lava** is made at **CONSTRUCTIVE** plate margins.
- **ANDESITIC lava** is made at **DESTRUCTIVE** plate margins.
- **RHYOLITIC lava** is made at **DESTRUCTIVE** plate margins.

2) The **different types** of lava have **different chemical compositions** — and it's the chemical composition that controls the **viscosity** (thickness) and **temperature** of the lava:

	BASALTIC LAVA	ANDESITIC LAVA	RHYOLITIC LAVA
Silica content	Low	Medium	High
Viscosity	Low (runny)	Medium	High (thick and sticky)
Temperature of eruption	Over 950 °C (usually 1100 - 1200 °C)	750 - 950 °C	Less than 750 °C

3) **Basaltic lava** has a **low viscosity** so it flows easily and gas can escape from it easily. As a result, eruptions of basaltic lava **aren't violent**. Basaltic lavas usually erupt **frequently** and for **long periods** of time.

4) **Andesitic** and **rhyolitic lavas** have a **higher viscosity** than basaltic lava. They flow less easily, and often form **blockages** in volcanic vents. Also, volcanic gases can't escape easily from viscous lava. **Pressure** builds up because of the lava blockages and trapped gases, until the blockages are cleared by a **violent eruption**. Andesitic and rhyolitic lavas usually erupt **intermittently** (every once in a while) and the eruptions are **short-lived**.

Volcanic Activity

There are Lots of **Different Types** of Volcano

DOME VOLCANO

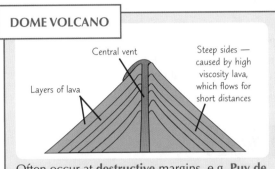

Central vent

Steep sides — caused by high viscosity lava, which flows for short distances

Layers of lava

Often occur at **destructive** margins, e.g. **Puy de Dome** in **France**. The lava from dome volcanoes tends to be either **rhyolitic** or **andesitic**.

CALDERA

Central part of volcano has collapsed as magma chamber below has emptied

Very wide circular crater, which can be several kilometres across

Layers of lava, or lava, ash and cinders

Often occur at **destructive** margins, where they produce **andesitic** and **rhyolitic** lavas, e.g. **Aira Caldera** in **Japan**.

A composite volcano (or stratovolcano) is similar to a dome volcano except that it has layers of lava alternating with layers of ash and cinders.

SHIELD VOLCANO

Central vent

Gently sloping sides — caused by low viscosity lava, which flows for long distances

Layers of lava

Often occur at **constructive** margins or **hotspots** (see p. 118), e.g. **Mauna Loa** in **Hawaii**. Shield volcanoes usually produce **basaltic lava**.

FISSURE VOLCANO

Long, linear vent — it can be a few metres wide but several kilometres long

Layers of lava

Fairly flat surface — caused by low viscosity lava, which flows for long distances

Also called a fissure vent or volcanic fissure. Often occur at **constructive** margins, e.g. **Laki Fissure System** in **Iceland**. Fissure volcanoes usually produce **basaltic lava**.

Hot Springs are Springs... of Hot Water

1) **Springs** are places where **groundwater** emerges at the **surface**.

2) If the **groundwater source** of a spring flows **close** to an area of recent **intrusive volcanic activity**, the water is heated and the spring becomes a **hot spring**.

3) The **temperature** of hot springs varies from around **20 °C** to over **90 °C**.

4) Hot spring water often has a **high mineral content** because hot water can hold a lot of dissolved solids.

5) Hot springs are found **all over the world** and are often popular with **tourists**, e.g. the springs in **Rio Hondo** (Argentina) and **North Island** (New Zealand).

Geysers are Hot Springs where the Water Erupts

Hot springs, geysers and mud pools are often called geothermal features.

1) Geysers are a type of hot spring where **hot water** and **steam** are ejected from the surface in a **fountain**. They form in areas of **intense volcanic activity** — this is what happens:

   - **Groundwater** is **heated** to above **boiling point** by **magma** deep in the crust.
   - The hot water becomes **pressurised** and forces its way to the surface along **cracks** in the rocks. Finally, the hot water and steam spray out from a **vent**.

The Strokkur Geyser in Iceland

©iStockphoto.com/Michel de Leeuw

2) Geysers **erupt periodically**. This is because they only erupt when the **pressure** has built up enough to **force** the water **out of the ground**.

3) Examples of geysers are **Strokkur** (Iceland) and **Old Faithful** in Yellowstone National Park (USA).

Volcanic Activity

Boiling Mud Pools... *you guessed it... are* Pools *of* Boiling Mud

1) A **boiling mud pool** is another type of **hot spring**.
2) They form in areas with **very fine-grained soil** (e.g. soil rich in clay or volcanic ash) — the hot spring water **mixes** with the soil to create a **hot muddy pool**.
3) The pools sometimes contain **brightly-coloured mud** because of **minerals** deposited by the hot water. E.g. iron and sulfur-rich minerals can create purple, orange and yellow colours.
4) Boiling mud pools can be found all over the world, e.g. in **Yellowstone National Park** (USA) and **Iceland**.

Some *Volcanoes* Occur *Away From Plate Margins*

Most volcanic activity occurs at **plate margins**, but there are some areas of **intense volcanic activity** that **aren't** near any plate margins. These areas are called **hot spots**:

1) A hot spot is caused by a **magma plume** — a **vertical column of magma** that **rises up** from the mantle.

2) **Volcanoes** form above magma plumes.

3) The **magma plume** remains **stationary** over time, but the **crust moves** above it.

4) Volcanic activity in the part of the crust that **was** above the hot spot **decreases** as it moves away.

5) **New volcanoes** form in the part of the crust that is **now above** the hot spot.

6) As the crust continues to move, a **chain of volcanoes** is formed.

7) There's a hot spot in **Hawaii** (USA).

Yep, Hawaii's definitely Kevin's idea of a hot spot.

Practice Questions

Q1 What is intrusive volcanic activity?
Q2 Describe how batholiths, sills and dykes are formed.
Q3 Briefly describe the characteristics of the three main types of lava.
Q4 What type of lava is made at constructive plate margins?

Exam Questions

Q1 The diagram shows the names and estimated ages of some of the Hawaiian islands.
Describe and explain the distribution of the islands in relation to hotspots. [7 marks]

Q2 Yellowstone National Park contains many features such as geysers and boiling mud pools.
Explain how these features form. [8 marks]

Mr Basil Tic is one hot guy...

Ooh, lots to learn here — yes indeed. No need to panic though — just take it slowly, one type of volcano and one type of lava at a time. Try quickly scribbling out diagrams of the different types of volcano to get it all clear in your mind. My challenge to you, dear reader, is to know it all before you turn the page. And your prize for knowing every last fascinating scrap of it will be...*

Seismic Activity

Earthquakes happen more often than you think. Obviously there are the big ones that cause loads of damage and make the headlines on the news, but there are also lots of weak earthquakes every year that hardly anyone notices. Sneaky.

Earthquakes are **Caused** by Tectonic Plate Movement

1) Earthquakes are caused by the **tension** that builds up at **all three** types of **plate margin** — see pages 114 and 115.

2) When the plates **jerk past each other** it sends out **SEISMIC WAVES** (vibrations). These vibrations are the **earthquake**.

3) The seismic waves **spread out** from the **FOCUS** — the place **in the** lithosphere where the earthquake **starts**. The focus doesn't have to be a single point — for example, it could be along a **fault line**. Near the focus the waves are **stronger** and cause **more damage**.

4) The **EPICENTRE** is the point **on the Earth's surface** where the earthquake is **felt first**. It's **straight above** the **focus**.

Although **most** earthquakes are caused by movement at **plate boundaries**, there are **other** possible **causes**:

• **Reactivation** of **old fault lines** that have not been active for a long time.

• **Subsidence** (when the ground sinks) as a result of **deep mining**.

• **Pressure on surface rocks** from water in large **reservoirs**.

The focus can also be called the hypocentre.

5) Earthquakes cause **damage** in various ways — they can cause structures to **collapse** (e.g. buildings, bridges), cause **tsunamis** (see next page), **avalanches**, **landslides** or **liquefaction** (where waterlogged soil behaves like a liquid).

There are **Three** Main Types of Seismic Wave

Some seismic waves travel through the **interior** of the Earth:

P (or primary) waves can travel through **solids** and **liquids**. The waves **push and pull** the earth in the **same direction** as the wave is **travelling**. They travel **faster** than other types of seismic wave.

Compression

Vibrations in same direction as wave is travelling

S (or secondary) waves can travel through **solids** but **not liquids**. The waves move the earth at **90°** to the **direction** of **travel**. These waves can cause a **lot of damage** because of their **shearing effect**.

Vibrations from side to side

Wave travelling this way

Others can only travel near the Earth's **surface** (in the **crust**):

Surface waves come in two varieties and travel **more slowly** than P and S waves.

• **Love waves** can only travel through **solids**. They move the surface from **side to side**. These waves also cause a **lot of damage** because of their **shearing effect**.

• **Rayleigh waves** can travel through **liquids** and **solids**. They move the surface in a **rolling motion** — just picture a wave moving across an ocean.

Seismic Activity

Earthquakes can be *Measured* Using *Seismometers*

1) The amount of **energy released** by an earthquake can be measured using a **seismometer**.

2) Seismometers measure the **magnitude** (strength) of earthquakes — the amount of energy they release. They also measure the **duration** and **direction** (horizontal or vertical) of the **vibrations**.

3) **Seismic records** have been built up over time, which allow us to look at the **frequency** of earthquakes in different areas.

Seismometers are also called seismographs or seismoscopes.

©iStockphoto.com/hakan dogu

There are *Two Different Scales* for *Measuring Earthquakes*

THE RICHTER SCALE

1) The **Richter scale** measures the magnitude of an earthquake.

2) It doesn't have an upper limit and it's **logarithmic** — this means that an earthquake with a magnitude of **5** has an amplitude (wave size) **ten times greater** than one with a magnitude of **4**.

3) Each value on the scale also represents about **30 times more energy released** than the previous value.

4) Most people **don't feel** earthquakes of magnitude **1-2**. **Major** earthquakes are **above 7**.

THE MERCALLI SCALE

1) The **Mercalli scale** measures the **impacts** of an earthquake (see diagram on right).

2) The impacts are measured using **observations** of the event (e.g. reports and photos).

3) The scale is between **1 and 12**, with **1** being an earthquake that's only detected by **instruments**, and **12** being an earthquake that causes **total destruction**.

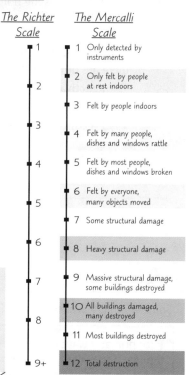

The Richter Scale / _The Mercalli Scale_

1 — 1 Only detected by instruments
2 — 2 Only felt by people at rest indoors
— 3 Felt by people indoors
3 — 4 Felt by many people, dishes and windows rattle
4 — 5 Felt by most people, dishes and windows broken
5 — 6 Felt by everyone, many objects moved
— 7 Some structural damage
6 — 8 Heavy structural damage
7 — 9 Massive structural damage, some buildings destroyed
— 10 All buildings damaged, many destroyed
8 — 11 Most buildings destroyed
9+ — 12 Total destruction

The Kashmir earthquake (see p. 130-131) measured 7.6 on the Richter scale and 10 on the Mercalli scale.

Earthquakes can *Cause Tsunamis*

1) Tsunamis are **large waves** caused by the **displacement** of large volumes of **water**.

2) They can be triggered by **underwater earthquakes**. The earthquakes cause the seabed to move, which displaces water. Waves **radiate** out from the **epicentre** of the earthquake. The **greater** the **movement** of the sea floor, the greater the volume of water displaced, and the **bigger** the **wave** produced.

3) **Volcanic eruptions** and **landslides** that slide into the sea can also displace large volumes of water and **cause tsunamis**.

4) A tsunami will usually be **more powerful** if it starts **close to the coast**. This is because the waves **lose energy** as they travel towards land. So, the closer to the coast the waves start, the less energy they will lose.

5) The waves travel **very fast** in deep water so they can hit the shore **without much warning**. This means that they can cause a **high death toll**.

The word tsunami comes from the Japanese words 'tsu' meaning harbour and 'nami' meaning wave.

Seismic Activity

Tsunami Waves *Increase* in *Height* When They Get *Close To Land*

1) Tsunamis **don't** just affect the **surface** of the water — they affect the **whole column** of water from the surface down to the seabed.

2) In the **open ocean** where the water's **very deep**, the waves travel at **high speeds** of 500-950 km/h. They have a **long wavelength** of about 200 km, and a **small amplitude** (wave height) of about 1 m.

3) **Closer to land** the water gets **shallower**. This causes the waves to get **compressed** (squashed together) and their **energy** becomes **more concentrated**. The waves **slow down** to less than 80 km/h, their **wavelength decreases** to less than 20 km, and their **amplitude increases** to many metres.

4) Just before the tsunami reaches the **coast**, the water **withdraws** down the shore (this is called drawback).

5) The wave then hits with **great force**, but only travels a **short distance inland**.

Aidan was unimpressed with the energy of Santa's wave.

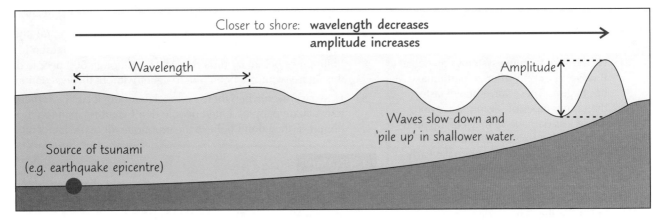

Closer to shore: **wavelength decreases**
amplitude increases

Wavelength

Amplitude

Waves slow down and 'pile up' in shallower water.

Source of tsunami
(e.g. earthquake epicentre)

Practice Questions

Q1 Describe what the focus of an earthquake is.

Q2 What is the epicentre of an earthquake?

Q3 Apart from movement at plate boundaries, give three other possible causes of earthquakes.

Q4 Why are seismic records useful?

Q5 What is the Richter scale?

Q6 What scale is used to measure the impacts of an earthquake?

Exam Questions

Q1 Describe the different types of seismic wave. [8 marks]

Q2 Describe the causes and characteristics of tsunamis. [8 marks]

The Beach Boys' seismometer — great for picking up good vibrations...

The problem with tsunamis is that they travel so fast — even if you knew one was coming, you wouldn't have much time to get out of its way. That's one of the reasons why the Indian Ocean tsunami caused so much loss of life back in 2004. It goes without saying then, that managing the impacts of tsunamis is a tad tricky — which brings us neatly to the next page...

Managing the Impacts of Tectonic Hazards

Dear me, all this talk of volcanoes, earthquakes and tsunamis is a bit alarming. Panic ye not — a bit of management can help.

The **Impacts** of **Hazards** caused by **Tectonic Processes** can be **Managed**

1) A **hazard** is something that's a **potential threat** to **human life** or **property**.

2) **Tectonic hazards** (e.g. **earthquakes**, **volcanoes** and **tsunamis**) are hazards **caused** by **movement of tectonic plates**.

3) Tectonic hazards can have **many impacts** on people and their environment. However, some of these impacts can be reduced by **management strategies** such as **prediction**, **building techniques**, **planning** and **education**.

Predicting When and Where a Hazard Will Occur Really Helps

EARTHQUAKES

1) It's currently impossible to predict when an earthquake will happen, but there can be clues that an earthquake is about to happen, e.g. small tremors, cracks appearing in rocks and strange animal behaviour (e.g. rats abandoning nests).

2) Earthquake warning systems can detect P waves, but only after an earthquake has begun. These waves travel faster than other types of seismic wave and cause less damage so they can be used as a warning for stronger tremors. For example, Japan's Earthquake Early Warning system was set up in 2007 and warns people by TV and radio. However, even far away from the epicentre the warnings may only arrive a few seconds before the strong tremors.

3) It's possible to predict where future earthquakes may happen using data from past earthquakes — these places can prepare themselves for the impacts of an earthquake.

VOLCANOES

1) Unlike earthquakes, it's possible to roughly predict when a volcanic eruption will happen. For example, tiny earthquakes and changes in the shape of the volcano (e.g. bulges in the land where magma has built up under it) can mean an eruption is likely.

2) Prediction allows time for people to be evacuated, e.g. 60 000 people were evacuated from the area around Mt. Pinatubo in the Philippines before it erupted in 1991. Although 800 people died, this figure would've been much higher without the evacuation.

3) However, even when there's enough warning it can be difficult to evacuate people. Often people don't want to abandon their homes or they don't believe the eruption will really happen.

TSUNAMIS

1) Tsunami warning systems rely on earthquake detection systems. If an earthquake occurs in a place that's likely to cause a tsunami (e.g. under an ocean), a warning is issued.

2) There are tsunami warning centres all around the world. For example, The USA's National Oceanic and Atmospheric Administration (NOAA) runs centres in Alaska and Hawaii.

3) Early warnings give people time to evacuate. However, they rely on good communication systems. If people don't receive the warning message they won't evacuate. Also, if an earthquake happens very close to land, the tsunami will reach the coast very quickly and people won't be warned early enough to evacuate.

Building Techniques can Physically Protect People

Building techniques can be used to **protect people** from some of the effects of tectonic hazards. However, they're **more expensive** than standard building techniques.

EARTHQUAKES

1) Buildings can be designed to withstand earthquakes, e.g. by using strong materials like reinforced concrete or building special foundations that absorb an earthquake's energy.

2) Construction laws in some earthquake-prone countries (e.g. Japan and the US) have become stricter in recent years — this means that newer buildings are more likely to be able to withstand earthquakes.

VOLCANOES

1) Buildings can't be designed to withstand lava flows. However, they can be strengthened so they're less likely to collapse due to the weight of falling ash.

2) It's sometimes possible to divert the lava from a volcano away from settlements using barriers. For example, when Etna in Italy erupted in 1983 a rubble barrier 10 m high and 400 m long was built on its slopes, which successfully diverted the lava flow. However, this is only possible where the lava is slow moving and there's sufficient warning.

Managing the Impacts of Tectonic

TSUNAMIS

1) **Buildings** designed with **raised, open foundations** and made of strong materials such as con[?] likely to be damaged by the force of the water during a tsunami.

2) In some places, e.g. Hokkaido (Japan), **tsunami walls** have been built **around settlements** to p[?] They're not always effective though, e.g. some tsunamis have overtopped them.

Planning and *Education* can be *Cost Effective Methods*

1) **Future developments**, e.g. new houses, can be **planned** to **avoid** the **areas most at risk**, e.g. close to an active volcano.

2) **Emergency services** can **train** and **prepare** for disasters. For example, **FEMA** in the USA train emergency personnel to deal with all sorts of disasters.

3) Governments can plan **evacuation routes**. For example, in **Oregon** (USA) leaflets are provided containing evacuation route maps in case of a tsunami.

4) **Governments** and other **organisations** can **educate people** about **what to do** if there's a disaster and **how to evacuate**. For example, earthquake and tsunami **drills** are practised regularly in **Japan**.

5) All these methods are **very cost-effective** ways of reducing the impacts.

Rupert wasn't keen on education. He did have a plan though.

Some Factors can Increase the Severity of the Impacts

DEVELOPMENT LEVEL OF A COUNTRY

1) The impacts are **higher** in **less developed countries** than in more developed countries. The main reason is that they **don't have the money** for disaster preparation or response, e.g. they have no money to spend on training emergency teams.

2) Also, the **buildings** are **poorer quality** than in more developed countries, so are **more easily damaged** by hazards.

3) **Infrastructure** is often **poorer**, making it **more difficult** for **emergency services** to **reach affected areas**.

4) **Health care isn't as good** in less developed countries, so they **struggle** to **treat large numbers** of **casualties**.

5) **Many people depend on agriculture** in less developed countries, which is often badly affected by eruptions or tsunamis.

6) However, the **economic impact** is often **higher** in **more developed** countries as the **buildings** and **infrastructure** damaged are **worth a lot of money**.

POPULATION

1) Obviously, the **more people** in an **area**, the **more people** will be **affected** by a disaster.

2) **Densely populated areas** such as cities have a lot of **buildings**. **Collapsing** buildings pose a big risk to life, particularly during **earthquakes**.

3) It can be difficult to **evacuate large numbers** of people because the **routes** are often **limited**. For example, if everyone in an area tries to drive away from a volcano the roads will quickly become clogged and people will be trapped.

TIMING

1) **When** in the **day** or **year** a disaster happens can have an effect on the severity of its impacts.

2) For example, if an earthquake occurs in the **middle of the night** most people will be **asleep**, so they **don't** get out of buildings as **quickly** and more people are hurt.

3) Also, if an earthquake occurs during **winter**, people can freeze to death before they can be rescued.

Practice Questions

Q1 How can the development level of a country affect the severity of the impacts of tectonic hazards?

Q2 Explain why the timing of a tectonic hazard may affect the severity of its impacts.

Exam Question

Q1 Critically evaluate the strategies used to manage the impacts of tectonic hazards. [40 marks]

If in doubt — run...

These two pages may seem a bit daunting at first, but it's worth putting the effort in to learn it all — this is just the kind of stuff that you could get a long essay question about. In fact, just look at the practice exam question — what are the chances...

Get your brain into gear and get ready to learn some facts and figures — it's case study time.

The **Soufrière Hills** Volcano in **Montserrat** Erupted on **25th June 1997**

Montserrat is a small island in the Caribbean Sea.

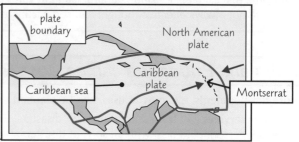

plate boundary

North American plate

Caribbean sea

Caribbean plate

Montserrat

©iStockphoto.com/MichaelUtech

1) The **Soufrière Hills volcano** is a **composite volcano** in Montserrat.

2) Montserrat is above a **destructive plate margin**, where the **North American plate** is being **forced under** the **Caribbean plate**.

3) In **1995**, **earthquakes**, **small eruptions** and **lahars** started. These continued until 1997.

4) On **25th June 1997** there was a series of **small earthquakes**. This was followed by **pyroclastic flows** (fast flowing streams of hot volcanic material and gases).

5) After more earthquakes the **main eruption** happened. About **4-5 million m³** of material was released over a **20 minute period**. **Pyroclastic flows** covered several square kilometres and reached within **50 m** of the airport, which was 5.5 km north of the volcano. The eruption also produced a **large ash cloud**.

6) There were **further eruptions** over the next **few months** and the airport was destroyed by a **pyroclastic flow** on 21st September 1997.

Lahars are mudflows — volcanic material mixed with water.

There were **Many Impacts**

ECONOMIC IMPACTS

1) The **total loss in value** of people's homes and investments was estimated to be about **£1 billion**.

2) Over **20 villages** and **two thirds of homes** on the island were **destroyed** by **pyroclastic flows**.

3) **Tourists stayed away** and **businesses** were **destroyed**, disrupting the **economy**. However, **tourism** on the island is now **increasing** as people come to **see the volcano**.

4) **Schools**, **hospitals**, the **airport** and the **port** were **destroyed**.

SOCIAL IMPACTS

1) **19 people died** and seven were injured.

2) **Hundreds** of people **lost their homes**.

3) **Fires destroyed** many buildings, e.g. local **government offices**, the **police headquarters** and **petrol stations**.

4) The **population has declined** — **8000** of the island's 12 000 inhabitants **have left** since the eruptions began in **1995**. Around **4000** of those came to the UK.

ENVIRONMENTAL IMPACTS

1) **Large areas** were **covered** with **volcanic material** — the capital city **Plymouth** was buried under **12 m of mud and ash**.

2) **Vegetation** and **farmland** were **destroyed**.

3) **Volcanic ash** from the eruption has **improved soil fertility**.

Volcanic Eruption Case Study — Montserrat

Responses *Included Help from the* **Emergency Services** *and* **Aid**

The responses to the eruption were both short-term and long-term:

1) **People** were **evacuated** from the south to **safe areas** in the north. The first evacuations took place in **1995**.
2) **Shelters** were **built** to house evacuees.
3) Temporary **infrastructure** was also built, e.g. **roads** and **electricity supplies**.
4) The **UK** provided **£17 million** of **emergency aid** (Montserrat's an overseas territory of the UK).
5) **Local emergency services** provided support units to **search** for and **rescue** survivors.
6) A **risk map** was created and an **exclusion zone** is in place. The south of the island is **off-limits** while the volcano is **still intermittently active**.
7) The **UK** has provided **£41 million** of long-term aid to develop the north of the island — **new docks**, an **airport** and **houses** have been built with this.
8) The **Montserrat Volcano Observatory** has been set up to try and **predict** future eruptions.

Little Management *Before the Event* Increased *the* Severity *of the* Impacts

1) **Scientists** had studied the volcano in the **1980s** but their report wasn't given a lot of attention.
2) There was **no disaster management plan** for a volcanic eruption. So when the volcano started erupting the **responses** were **slow**.
3) Also, in the **1990s** key **infrastructure** had been built in areas at **risk**, so when the volcano erupted it was **destroyed** — this further hampered the response.

©iStockphoto.com/Sean Hannah

The city of Plymouth in Montserrat buried under ash and mud by the eruption.

Practice Questions

Q1 In which year did the main Soufrière Hills volcano eruption occur?
Q2 What type of volcano is the Soufrière Hills volcano?
Q3 Give two economic impacts of the eruption.
Q4 Give one environmental impact of the eruption.
Q5 Briefly describe the responses to the eruption.
Q6 Describe one way in which hazard management affected the severity of the event.

Exam Question

Q1 With reference to an example you have studied, describe the impacts of a volcanic event and the responses to it.

[8 marks]

Maybe Caribbean islands aren't so idyllic after all...

The scientists at the volcano observatory on Montserrat monitor loads of things all over the volcano. For example, they take thermal images of the dome to see how hot different bits are, they measure earthquakes in the area and they monitor how the ground is bulging using lasers. If things look like they're hotting up they issue alerts so everyone knows to hightail it out of there. Eeek.

Volcanic Eruption Case Study — Mt St Helens

As if one volcano case study wasn't enough, it's time for a second one. It doesn't matter if you've studied different volcanoes in class — if you have, learn those instead. Just make sure you know all about two different case studies.

Mount St Helens *Erupted on* 18th May 1980

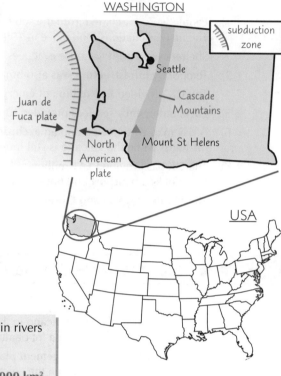

WASHINGTON

subduction zone

Seattle

Cascade Mountains

Juan de Fuca plate

North American plate

Mount St Helens

USA

1) **Mount St Helens** in **Washington** (USA) is one of several volcanic peaks in the Cascade Mountains.

2) The Cascade Mountains are above a **destructive plate margin**, where the **Juan de Fuca plate** is being **forced under** the **North American plate**.

3) Mount St Helens is a **composite volcano**.

4) From March 1980, there were **signs** that an **eruption** could happen soon — there were small **earthquakes**, a **bulge** appeared on the side of the volcano and **ash** and **steam** were released.

5) On **18th May** 1980 there was a **large earthquake** of magnitude **5.1** followed by a massive **eruption of volcanic material** — including **rocks**, **ash**, **hot gases**, **steam** and **lava**.

6) The eruption covered a **600 km² fan-shaped area** north of the volcano (**the blast zone**). Almost all **vegetation** and **buildings** were **destroyed** in the blast zone which reached up to about **30 km** away from the volcano.

7) **Pyroclastic flows**, **lahars** and **floods** (due to material being dumped in rivers and lakes, displacing water) were caused by the eruption.

8) Shortly afterwards there was another eruption of **ash** and **steam**. About **540 million tonnes of ash** were deposited over an area of **57 000 km²**.

The Eruption was the *Most Economically Destructive* Ever in the USA

ECONOMIC IMPACTS

1) The **total cost** of the damage was around **$1.1 billion**.

2) Over **200 homes and cabins** were **destroyed** and many more were **damaged**.

3) **Airports** were temporarily **closed** (some for up to two weeks) because of reduced visibility. Over **1000 commercial flights** were **cancelled**.

4) A lot of money had to be spent on **clearing ash** from roads and runways, e.g. it cost **$2.2 million** to clear the ash in Yakima (a city 135 km from the volcano).

5) **27 bridges, 24 km of railways** and around **300 km of roads** were destroyed.

6) **River traffic** and **shipping** was disrupted, and 31 ships were stranded because **mudflows** dumped huge amounts of **sediment** in rivers.

7) The **timber industry** was severely affected by the destruction of forest.

SOCIAL IMPACTS

1) **57 people** were **killed** — mostly by inhaling volcanic ash.

2) **Hundreds** of people **lost their homes**.

3) **Unemployment** rose tenfold at first — although this did return to normal once clean-up operations began.

4) **Social facilities** and **recreational sites** were **destroyed**.

5) Some people experienced **emotional stress**.

ENVIRONMENTAL IMPACTS

1) Almost **240 km²** of **forest** was **destroyed**.

2) **Wildlife** suffered — around **7000 big game animals** (e.g. deer, elk and bear) and many thousands of **birds** and **small mammals** were **killed**. Around 12 million young salmon were also killed.

3) **Sediment** dumped in **Spirit Lake** raised the lake bottom by over 90 m and the water level by over 60 m.

4) **Water quality** was temporarily **reduced**.

Volcanic Eruption Case Study — Mt St Helens

Responses Included Emergency Shelters and Ash Clearance

Emergency responses were **coordinated** by **FEMA** (Federal Emergency Management Agency) and involved both **national organisations** (e.g. the US Army Corps of Engineers) and **local services** (e.g. local emergency services).

- **Face masks** were distributed in some areas to protect people from breathing in ash.
- **Emergency shelters** were set up for stranded and homeless people.
- **Ash clean-up operations** were organised — around **900 000 tonnes** of ash were removed from **roads**, **buildings** and **airports**.
- **Shipping channels** were cleared of sediment to restore shipping and some **new channels** were cut.
- **45 500 acres** of land have been **replanted** with more than **18.4 million trees**.
- **Domestic water supplies** were monitored to ensure they weren't contaminated.

The ash clean-up operation
near Mount St Helens.

©DAVID R. FRAZIER / SCIENCE PHOTO LIBRARY

Mount St Helens was declared a 'National Monument' in 1982. 445 km² is now a protected and preserved area — it's used for scientific study, education, recreation and tourism.

Good Management Meant That Hazardous Areas Were Evacuated

1) When the earthquakes began in March, the USGS (United States Geological Survey) started a round-the-clock **monitoring system**. It included **gathering seismic data** and measuring the **rate of bulge growth**, **ground temperature** and **sulfur dioxide gas emissions**. Volcanic and seismic activity **reports** were **issued daily**.

2) USGS scientists issued **warnings** to people living in the area and made **recommendations** about the **locations of hazardous zones**.

3) Based on these recommendations, in **March** access to the volcano was **restricted** and the evacuation of around **2000 people** was started.

4) Despite the monitoring data, scientists **couldn't accurately predict** the eruption — on the **day of the eruption** there were **no unusual changes** that could be taken as warning signs.

Practice Questions

Q1 When did Mount St Helens erupt?

Q2 What type of plate boundary is Mount St Helens situated on?

Q3 What type of volcano is Mount St Helens?

Q4 What were the warning signs that Mount St Helens was going to erupt?

Exam Question

Q1 With reference to two volcanic eruptions you have studied, contrast how managing the hazard affected the severity of its impacts. [10 marks]

Hmm, Juan de Fuca — there must be a joke in there somewhere...

When it comes to case studies, it's the details that count. When examiners ask about them, they're looking for answers packed with specific facts and figures — vague waffle just won't cut it, I'm afraid. So go through this case study again and get learning the when, the why, how many, how big, how small, how long, how short, how wide, how narrow, how fast, how slow, how's your father...

Earthquake Case Study — L'Aquila

Italy — the home of pasta, pizza, Pisa... and a surprising number of earthquakes.

The **L'Aquila Earthquake** Happened on **6th April 2009**

1) **L'Aquila** is a city in **central Italy** with a population of around **70 000 people**.

2) The area is **prone to earthquakes** because of a **major fault line** that runs **north-south** along the **Apennine mountain range**. There's also an **east-west fault line** across the centre of Italy.

3) The fault lines are close to the **destructive plate margin** between the **Eurasian and African plates**.

4) The L'Aquila earthquake occurred at **3.32 am** (local time) on **6th April 2009**.

5) It measured **6.3** on the **Richter scale**.

6) The earthquake only lasted a few seconds but it was **felt throughout central Italy**.

7) The **focus** of the earthquake was at a **depth** of about **5 miles** and the **epicentre** was close to **L'Aquila**.

8) It was **caused** by movement along the **north-south fault line**.

9) Several **aftershocks** were felt in the days following the main earthquake — some of them measured around **5** on the **Richter scale**.

ITALY

Apennine mountain range

L'Aquila

Rome

Naples

The **Social Impacts** Were **Bigger Than Expected**

ECONOMIC IMPACTS

1) It's been estimated that the earthquake cost Italy **$15 billion** in total.

2) **Thousands of buildings**, both historic and modern, were **damaged** or **destroyed**. These included part of the city **hospital**, a dormitory at the **university** and **L'Aquila Cathedral**.

3) A **bridge** near the town of Fossa **collapsed**, and a **water pipe** was **broken** near the town of Paganica.

4) **Fires** in some collapsed buildings caused **more damage**.

A house destroyed by the earthquake.

©iStockphoto.com/RanieriMeloni

SOCIAL IMPACTS

1) There were around **300 deaths**, mostly caused by **collapsed buildings**.

2) About **1500 people** were **injured**.

3) **70 000 people** were made **homeless**.

4) The **aftershocks** hampered **rescue efforts** and caused **more damage**.

5) **Thousands of people**, many of them young people, have had to **move away** from the area to other parts of Italy to find **jobs** after buildings were destroyed.

> The timing of the earthquake may have made things worse. It happened at around three in the morning when most people would have been asleep — so they'd have been slow to react.

ENVIRONMENTAL IMPACTS

1) An area of about **1000 km²** was affected by **surface ruptures** (cracks in the ground), **rockfalls** and **landslides**.

2) The **broken water pipe** near the town of Paganica also caused a **landslide**.

3) **Wildlife habitats** were affected by the earthquake.

Earthquake Case Study — L'Aquila

The Responses Included Rescuing and Rehoming People

1) **Camps** were set up for **homeless people** with **water**, **food** and **medical care**.
2) **Ambulances**, **fire engines** and the **army** were sent in to **rescue survivors**.
3) **Cranes** and **diggers** were used to **remove rubble**.
4) **International teams** with **rescue dogs** were sent in to look for **survivors**.
5) **12 000 rescue and support workers** were brought in to help with the response.
6) **Money** was provided by the **government** to **pay rent**. **Mortgage payments**, and **gas** and **electricity bills** were suspended.
7) The Italian Prime Minister promised to build a **new town** to replace L'Aquila as the **capital** of the area.
8) By the end of 2009, **4500 new buildings** had been put up to **house 12 000 people** who had been made homeless.

Some of the Management Strategies Didn't Have Much Effect

Although L'Aquila itself **hadn't** suffered from a **major earthquake** for 300 years, the area around the Apennines experiences regular minor earthquakes. So, there were some **management strategies** in place:

BUILDING TECHNIQUES

Because of the risks, there were **strict building regulations** to ensure that **newer buildings** were **designed** and **built** to **withstand earthquakes**. However, **some** of the newer buildings that were **supposed** to meet the regulations had been **poorly built** and they were **severely damaged** or **destroyed**.

For example, the **San Salvatore Hospital** in west L'Aquila was built in **2000**. It **should** have been able to **withstand** the earthquake, but it actually **collapsed** and the **patients** had to be treated in **tents outdoors**. An investigation was set up to look into why so many modern buildings, like the hospital, collapsed.

PREDICTION

Seismologists were **monitoring** the area prior to the event. Some people felt that the earthquake hazard could have been managed better — in August 2009 a group of **local residents** made a formal complaint that six **seismologists** working in the area **didn't predict** the earthquake. The residents blamed the scientists for the number of people killed and requested a **criminal investigation**. However, it's currently **impossible to predict exactly** when and where an earthquake may occur.

PLANNING

Italy has a **Civil Protection Department** that trains **volunteers** to help with things like **rescue operations**.

Practice Questions

Q1 When was the L'Aquila earthquake?
Q2 Which plate margin is L'Aquila close to?
Q3 What were the social impacts of the L'Aquila earthquake?

Exam Question

Q1 With reference to at least one example you have studied, critically evaluate the strategies used to manage earthquake hazards.

[10 marks]

Darling, did you feel the Earth move... er, yes actually, I did...

L'Aquila wasn't unprepared for an earthquake — Italy experiences quite frequent earthquakes and it had management strategies in place to deal with the impacts. The problem was that when it came to crunch time, those strategies didn't seem to help much.

Earthquake Case Study — Kashmir

Aha, the last case study of the section — no dozing off at the back...

The **Kashmir Earthquake** Happened on **8th October 2005**

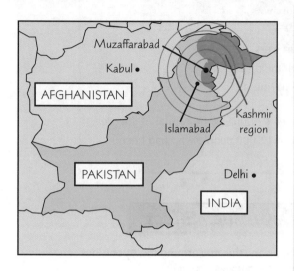

1) The **Kashmir region**, to the north of **Pakistan**, sits on a **destructive plate margin** where the **Indian plate** is being forced under the **Eurasian plate**.

2) An earthquake occurred in the Kashmir region on **8th October 2005**.

3) It happened at **8.50 am** (local time) and measured **7.6** on the **Richter scale**.

4) The **focus** of the earthquake was at a **depth** of about **16 miles** and the **epicentre** was close to **Muzaffarabad**.

5) The earthquake resulted from **movement** along the **plate margin**, which caused a **75 km long** crack in the Earth's surface to form.

6) The earthquake caused **damage** to an area of **30 000 km²** — it was felt as far away as **Kabul** in **Afghanistan** and **Delhi** in **India**.

7) By **27th October 2005** there had been **978 aftershocks** measuring at least **4** on the **Richter scale**.

The **Earthquake** was the **13th Most Destructive** on Record

ECONOMIC IMPACTS

1) It's been estimated that the earthquake cost around **US$5 billion** in **total**.

2) **Whole villages** and **thousands of buildings** were **destroyed**. For example, **80%** of the town of **Uri** was destroyed. Even in some areas up to 25 km from the epicentre, nearly 25% of buildings collapsed and 50% were severely damaged. The **total cost of rebuilding** has been estimated to be **US$3.5 billion**.

SOCIAL IMPACTS

1) There were around **80 000 deaths**, mostly caused by **collapsed buildings**. This is the **13th highest death toll** of any earthquake on record.

2) **Hundreds of thousands** of people were **injured**, including around **6000** in **India**.

3) Around **3 million people** were made **homeless**.

4) **Water pipelines** and **electricity lines** were **broken**, cutting off supplies.

5) **Landslides** buried **buildings** and **people**. They also **blocked access roads** and cut off **water supplies, electricity supplies** and **telephone lines**.

6) **Diarrhoea** and **other diseases** spread due to little **clean water**.

7) **Freezing winter conditions** shortly after the earthquake caused **more casualties** and meant **rescue** and **rebuilding operations** were **difficult**.

ENVIRONMENTAL IMPACTS

1) **Landslides** and **rockfalls** occurred throughout the region. Most landslides were relatively small but there were **two major landslides** that each affected an area of more than **0.1 km²** — one in **Muzaffarabad** and one in the **Jhelum Valley**.

2) The Jhelum Valley landslide was the **biggest** — it was over **1 km wide** and the debris reached over **2 km** from the top of the slide. The debris created a **dam** at the bottom of the valley that **blocked two rivers** where they joined.

3) As a result of the earthquake and surface rupture, the **ground shifted** by more than **5 m** in some areas of Kashmir.

Earthquake Case Study — Kashmir

The **Response** was **Delayed** in **Many Areas**

1) **Help didn't reach** many areas for **days** or **weeks**. People had to be rescued by hand without any equipment or help from emergency services.

2) **Tents, blankets** and **medical supplies** were distributed within a **month**, but **not to all areas** affected.

3) The Pakistani government set up the **Federal Relief Commission** (FRC) and the **Earthquake Reconstruction and Rehabilitation Authority** (ERRA) to **coordinate activities** with other international agencies and non-governmental organisations.

4) **International aid** and **equipment** such as helicopters and rescue dogs were brought in, as well as **teams** of people from **other countries**.

5) Around **40 000 people** have been **relocated** to a **new town**, from the destroyed town of Balakot.

6) **Government money** has been given to people whose homes had been destroyed so they can **rebuild them themselves**.

7) **Training** has been provided to help rebuild more buildings as **earthquake resistant**.

8) New **health centres** have been set up in the area.

The terrain in the Kashmir region and the winter conditions made the rescue operation more difficult.

An estimated $5.8 billion of foreign aid was provided by the international community in response to the disaster. Some of this was for long-term development.

There was **No Hazard Management**

1) There was **no** local **disaster planning** in place.

2) **Buildings** were **not** designed to be **earthquake resistant**. Many **houses** were **structurally poor** because people **couldn't afford** better buildings. However, even **government buildings** in areas such as Muzaffarabad were **structurally unsound** and so were damaged in the earthquake.

3) **Communications** were **poor**. There were **few roads** and they were **badly constructed**.

Practice Questions

Q1 When was the Kashmir earthquake?

Q2 The movement of which two tectonic plates caused the earthquake?

Q3 Give one economic impact of the earthquake.

Q4 Describe three social impacts of the earthquake.

Q5 Give two environmental impacts of the earthquake.

Exam Question

Q1 With reference to at least two examples you have studied, compare and contrast the responses to an earthquake. [10 marks]

Nope, sorry — it's just not very funny...

So, you've reached the end of the Plate Tectonics section. It's really been quite a journey — almost to the centre of the Earth. Well, not really, but 'a journey a bit below the Earth's surface' sounds less dramatic. And, let's face it, this section is all about drama.

Climate Basics

Hurricanes, monsoons, the gaseous composition of the atmosphere — yep, climate's a pretty thrilling topic...

Weather and Climate are Two Different Things

- **WEATHER** is the **SHORT-TERM atmospheric conditions** in a particular place — e.g. temperature, cloud cover, precipitation type, wind speed.
- **CLIMATE** is the **LONG-TERM atmospheric conditions** in a particular place — **average measurements** of temperature, precipitation etc. over a **long period** of time.

The Atmosphere is a Mixture of Gases that Surrounds the Earth

1) The atmosphere contains **dry air** and **water vapour**. **Dry air** is a **mixture of gases**, including **nitrogen** (78%), **oxygen** (21%) and **other gases** such as **carbon dioxide** and **methane** (0.04%).

2) The atmosphere is made up of **four layers**:

Some of the gases present in small amounts have very important roles in the atmosphere — see page 156.

① TROPOSPHERE

- The troposphere extends from the **Earth's surface** to about **12 km** up on average.
- **Temperature decreases** with **altitude** in the troposphere. This is because the Earth's surface warms the troposphere, so the further away from the surface the cooler it gets.
- There's lots of **turbulence** (air movement) because **warm air rises** through the layer and **cool air sinks**.
- The troposphere has lots of **clouds**. This is because there's a lot of **water vapour** that has evaporated from the Earth's surface.
- The **tropopause** is the **boundary** between the **troposphere** and **stratosphere**. **Jet streams** (fast moving currents of air) are found just below the tropopause.

Altitude is the height above sea level.

② STRATOSPHERE

- The **stratosphere** extends from around **12 km** to about **50 km** up.
- **Temperature increases** with altitude in this layer because the **ozone layer** is found in the lower stratosphere — it absorbs UV radiation, which warms the upper stratosphere.
- The stratosphere **isn't turbulent** and there **aren't** many **clouds**.
- The **stratopause** is the **boundary** of the **stratosphere** and **mesosphere**.

③ MESOSPHERE

- The **mesosphere** extends from around **50 km** to **85-90 km** up.
- **Temperature decreases** with altitude in the mesosphere. This is because the mesosphere is **warmed** by the **stratosphere** — the further away from the stratosphere the cooler it gets.
- The **mesopause** is the **boundary** of the **mesosphere** and **thermosphere**.

④ THERMOSPHERE

- The **thermosphere** extends from **85-90 km** to around **1000 km** up.
- **Temperature increases** with altitude in the thermosphere. This is because small amounts of **oxygen** in this layer absorb UV radiation, warming the thermosphere.

Air pressure decreases with **altitude** through the **atmosphere**.

Climate Basics

The *Atmospheric Heat Budget* is *Heat Gained* and *Lost* by the *Earth*

1) We get **energy from the sun** in the form of **shortwave solar radiation**. This is also known as **insolation**.

2) About **50%** of insolation is **absorbed** by the **surface** of the Earth and then released as **longwave radiation**, i.e. **infrared** or **heat energy**. This radiation heats up the **troposphere**.

3) The other **50%** of incoming solar radiation is split three ways:

   - About **25%** is **reflected back into space** by the air and clouds in the **atmosphere**.
   - About **20%** is **absorbed** by the air and clouds in the **atmosphere**.
   - About **5%** is **reflected back into space** by the Earth's **surface**.

The amount of solar radiation reflected by a surface depends on its albedo (its ability to reflect energy).

Four Main Factors Affect How Much Solar Radiation the Atmosphere Receives

1) The **SOLAR CONSTANT** is the amount of solar radiation we get from the sun. It **varies slightly** with the **sun's activity**. When the sun is **more active**, the Earth receives **more solar radiation**.

2) **EARTH'S DISTANCE FROM THE SUN** changes as it orbits. When Earth is **closer to the sun** it receives **more solar radiation**.

3) The **HEIGHT OF THE SUN IN THE SKY** varies with **latitude**:

   - Near the **Equator** the sun is **higher** in the sky and incoming solar radiation is **spread over a smaller surface area**.
   - Near the **poles** the sun is **lower** in the sky and incoming solar radiation is spread **over a larger surface area**. This means there's **less solar radiation per m² at higher latitudes**.

4) **LENGTH OF DAY AND NIGHT.** This varies with the seasons, which are more pronounced at higher altitudes. In **winter** there are **fewer hours of daylight** — so **less solar radiation**.

Incoming solar radiation spread over a <u>large</u> surface area.
Incoming solar radiation spread over a <u>smaller</u> surface area.
Equator

Higher Latitudes and Higher Altitudes are Colder

Latitude is the distance (in degrees) north or south of the Earth's Equator.

1) Higher **latitudes** are colder because:

   - They receive **less solar radiation** because the sun is **lower in the sky** (see above).
   - They receive **less solar radiation** because there are **fewer hours of daylight in winter** (see above).

2) Higher **altitudes** are colder because:

   - The Earth's surface heats the atmosphere through **conduction**, so the temperature is greatest close to the heat source and decreases away from it (upwards).
   - **Air pressure** decreases with altitude — there are fewer air molecules and they move more slowly. This means they create less **heat**, which means lower temperatures.

Practice Questions

Q1 Describe the difference between weather and climate.

Q2 Briefly explain why only 50% of incoming solar radiation reaches the surface of the Earth.

Q3 What are the four main factors that affect how much solar radiation the atmosphere receives?

Exam Question

Q1 With particular reference to temperature, describe and explain the vertical structure of the atmosphere. [8 marks]

Solar radiation won't give you superpowers — just really bad sunburn...

Who'd have thought that something you can't see could be so complicated. I made up a little mnemonic to remember the layers of the atmosphere, it's about a boy I used to know who liked to wear small swimming trunks — we called him Tight Shorts Mike Turner...

Climate Basics

So the Equator gets more solar radiation than the poles, but the Equator doesn't keep getting hotter and the poles don't keep getting colder... I always assumed this was down to the heat elves, but apparently it's wind and ocean currents.

Energy is Redistributed from the Equator to the Poles by Winds...

1) **Winds** are **large scale movements of air** caused by **differences in air pressure**.

2) Differences in air pressure are caused by **differences in atmospheric heating** between the **Equator** and the **poles**.

3) Winds are part of **global atmospheric circulation cells**. These cells have a body of **warm rising air** which creates an area of **low pressure**, and a body of **cool falling air** which creates an area of **high pressure**.

4) Winds move **FROM** the areas of **high pressure TO** the areas of **low pressure**.

5) There are **three main types** of global atmospheric circulation cells — **Hadley**, **Ferrel** and **Polar Cells**.

6) Here's how it all works:

1) At the **Equator** the **sun warms** the Earth, which transfers heat to the air above, causing it to **rise**. Rising air creates **low pressure**, **clouds** and **rain**. This low pressure zone of rising air is called the **Intertropical Convergence Zone (ITCZ)**.

2) As the air rises it **cools** and **moves out** to 30° North and South of the Equator.

3) **30° North and South** of the Equator the **cool air sinks**, creating **high pressure**. **Sub-tropical jet streams** are found here (jet streams are fast moving currents of air).

4) The cool air reaches the ground surface and moves as surface winds either **back to the Equator** or **towards the poles**:

- Surface winds blowing towards the **Equator** are called **trade winds**.
- They blow from the SE in the southern hemisphere and from the NE in the northern hemisphere. At the Equator, these **trade winds meet** (converge) in the **ITCZ**, and are heated by solar radiation. This causes them to rise, condense and form **clouds**.
- Surface winds blowing towards the **poles** are called **westerlies**. They blow from the NW in the southern hemisphere and from the SW in the northern hemisphere.

Winds are deflected to the right in the northern hemisphere and to the left in the southern hemisphere because of the Earth's rotation.

Diagram labels: HIGH Pressure, POLAR CELL, LOW Pressure, Polar Easterlies, 60°, FERREL CELL, HIGH Pressure, 30°, South Westerlies, HADLEY CELL, North Easterly Trade Winds, Equator, LOW Pressure, HADLEY CELL, 30°, South Easterly Trade Winds, North Westerlies, HIGH Pressure, 60°, FERREL CELL, Polar Easterlies, HIGH Pressure, POLAR CELL, LOW Pressure

5) **60° North and South of the Equator** the warmer surface winds meet colder air from the poles. The warmer air is less dense than the cold air so it **rises**, creating **low pressure**.

6) Some of the air joins the Ferrel cell and **moves back** towards the Equator, and the rest joins the polar cell and moves towards the **poles**.

The polar front jet stream is found around 60° North and South of the Equator.

7) At the **poles** the **cool air sinks**, creating **high pressure**. The high pressure air is drawn back towards to the Equator in **surface winds**.

Climate Basics

...and by *Ocean Currents*

1) Ocean currents are **large scale movements of water** caused by **differences** in **water density**. Density depends on **water temperature** and **salinity**.

2) Currents are affected by **surface winds**, the **position of land masses** and **other currents**.

3) Ocean currents **transfer heat energy** from **warmer** to **cooler** regions. **Warm** ocean currents **raise air temperature**, which warms the **land** nearby. **Cool** ocean currents **lower air temperature**, which cools the **land** nearby.

4) Ocean currents form **giant loops** that travel **clockwise** in the **northern hemisphere** and **anti-clockwise** in the **southern hemisphere**. This is because of **surface winds** — e.g. trade winds push water west along the Equator, and westerlies push water east between 30° and 60° North and South.

5) Here's a rough guide to the main ocean currents. **Red arrows** are **warm currents** and **blue arrows** are **cold**.

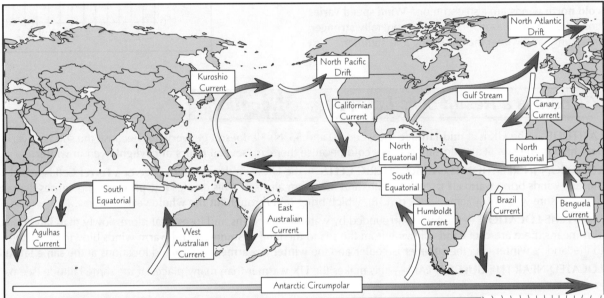

6) Ocean currents **affect the climate** of many regions. For example:

> - The **Gulf Stream** carries **warm** water from the Caribbean Sea along the east coast of America and across the Atlantic to **Western Europe**.
> - The Gulf Stream keeps Western Europe **much warmer** than it would otherwise be.
> - Water in the Gulf Stream **cools** in the northern hemisphere and becomes **more dense**. Some of this water **sinks** and is carried back to the Equator by the **Canary Current**, which **cools** the west coast of Africa.

You don't need to memorise this map, but make sure you learn the main patterns of ocean currents (e.g. the direction the loops move in each hemisphere) and how they move energy (e.g. from the Equator towards the poles along the west side of the oceans).

Practice Questions

Q1 What are winds?

Q2 How is air pressure affected by a) rising warm air and b) sinking cool air?

Q3 Define trade winds and westerlies.

Q4 What causes ocean currents?

Q5 Briefly explain how ocean currents affect climate.

Exam Question

Q1 Describe how energy is redistributed from the Equator to the poles by winds. [8 marks]

I thought current affairs were something completely different...

*The diagrams on these pages are incredibly complicated. Don't worry, you won't be expected to know the diagram on ocean currents in too much detail, but you **do** need to learn the diagram on atmospheric cells. That's all the cells, winds and pressures...*

UK Climate

The climate of the UK is quite temperamental — it ranges from lovely and warm to cold and 'orrible.

UK Climate is **Temperate** — **Cool**, **Wet Winters** and **Warm**, **Wet Summers**

1) **Temperature** in the UK **varies** with the **seasons**. It's **coldest in winter**, it warms up through spring, is **hottest in summer**, and then cools down again through autumn.

2) Temperature ranges from an average of **5 °C in January** to **20 °C in August**.

3) **Rainfall** in the UK is **fairly high all year round**, but it also **varies** with the **seasons**. It's **higher** in autumn and winter (an average of 120 mm in January) and **lower** in spring and summer (an average of 65 mm in May).

4) **Winds** in the UK are mostly **warm south westerlies**, but **cold north winds** are also common. **Wind speed varies** considerably by season — winds are generally **stronger** in autumn and winter than in spring and summer.

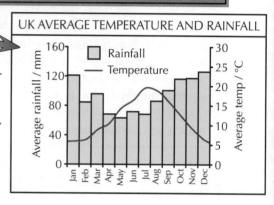

UK AVERAGE TEMPERATURE AND RAINFALL

UK Climate is a **Result** of its **Latitude** and **Location**

1) **LATITUDE** — the UK is at **mid-latitude** (between 50 and 55°N). It **doesn't** get **very hot** because the sun is never **very high** in the sky. It also **doesn't** get very **cold** because there are **several hours of daylight** even in **winter**.

2) **LOCATION IN RELATION TO ATMOSPHERIC CELLS** — the UK is on the northern edge of a **Ferrel Cell** (see p. 134). **Surface winds** bring **warm air** from the south, and the warm air rises. This creates **low pressure** and causes **depressions** (low pressure weather systems — see p. 138), which bring **rain throughout the whole year**. Hooray...

3) **MARITIME LOCATION** — the UK is surrounded by water, which gains and loses heat more slowly than land does. This means there are **cool winds** blowing from the sea to the land in **summer**, and **warm winds** blowing from the sea to the land in **winter**. So, the **summer** is **cooler** and the **winter** is **warmer** than inland locations at the **same latitude**.

4) **LOCATED NEAR THE GULF STREAM** — this makes the UK **warmer** than many places at the same latitude (see p. 135).

Climate **Varies Within** the UK

UK ANNUAL
TEMPERATURE
1971-2000

Average Value (°C)
> 11
10 - 11
9 - 10
8 - 9
7 - 8
6 - 7
5 - 6
4 - 5
< 4

TEMPERATURE

It's warmer in the south because there's **more insolation** (more solar radiation reaching the ground). This is because the sun is **higher in the sky** and there are **more hours of daylight** than in the north (see p. 133). E.g. annual average maximum temperature is 13.6 °C in Cornwall, and 9.3 °C in the north of Scotland.

The UK's maritime setting is important too — the climate is different inland compared to on the coast (see above).

UK ANNUAL
RAINFALL
1971-2000

Average Value (mm)
> 3000
2000 - 3000
1500 - 2000
1250 - 1500
1000 - 1250
800 - 1000
700 - 800
600 - 700
< 600

PRECIPITATION

It's **wetter** in the **west** than the **east**, e.g. annual average rainfall is 871 mm in Blackpool (on the west coast), and 565 mm in Cleethorpes (on the east coast). This is because **south westerly surface winds** bring **warm, wet air** from the **Atlantic Ocean**. The air reaches the **west side** of the UK, and it's forced upwards **over the land**. The **air cools**, the **water vapour condenses** and it **rains**. This is known as **orographic** or **relief rainfall**. The west of the UK is generally **more mountainous** than the east, so the air masses lose most of their moisture in the west. The area to the east of the mountains, where less rain falls, is called the **rain shadow**.

UK Climate

WIND

1) Winds are stronger in the **west**, e.g. the annual average wind speed is 21.7 km/h in St. Mawgan (on the south west coast), and 16.7 km/h in Marham (on the east coast). This is because **south westerly surface winds** come over the **ocean** — the ocean is **flat** so there's **nothing to slow the winds down**. When the **winds hit land**, they're affected by hills and they become weaker.

2) Winds are **stronger** at **higher altitudes** because there are **fewer obstacles to slow them down**.

Average Value (km/h)
- > 45
- 37 - 45
- 28 - 37
- 19 - 28
- 15 - 19
- 11 - 15
- < 11

There are **Five Main Air Masses** that Affect the UK

1) Air masses are **large volumes of air** with a **similar temperature** and **water vapour content**.

2) They cover **large areas** (several hundred km²) and can **travel long distances**.

3) They're classified by the region they form over:

- **Arctic** or **Polar** air masses form at **high latitudes** (so they're **cooler**).
- **Tropical** air masses form at **low latitudes** (so they're **warmer**).
- **Maritime** air masses form over **oceans** (so they've got a **higher water vapour** content).
- **Continental** air masses form over **land** (so they've got a **lower water vapour** content).

4) The UK is affected by **five different air masses**. Each air mass brings a **different type of weather**, which is one of the reasons why the **UK's weather** is so **variable**:

ARCTIC MARITIME air masses form over the Arctic Ocean. They bring **very cold, wet air** which causes **cold weather** and **rain**.

POLAR MARITIME air masses form over the **North Atlantic Ocean**. They bring **cold, wet air** which causes **cold weather** and **rain**.

POLAR CONTINENTAL air masses form over Siberia (in the **Arctic**). They bring **cold, dry air** which causes **very cold, dry weather**. These air masses can bring **snow** if the air picks up moisture from the **North Sea**.

TROPICAL MARITIME air masses form over the **Atlantic Ocean**. They bring **warm, wet air**, which causes **warm weather** and **rain**.

TROPICAL CONTINENTAL air masses form over **Africa**. They bring **warm, dry air** which causes **hot, dry weather**.

Practice Questions

Q1 Describe how temperature and rainfall in the UK vary with the seasons.

Q2 Why is it warmer in the south of the UK than in the north?

Q3 Why is it wetter and windier in the west of the UK than in the east?

Q4 What are air masses?

Exam Question

Q1 Discuss how the climate of the UK is a result of its position on the Earth. [8 marks]

Learn these pages and you'll never be lost for small talk again...

"It's a nice day today, isn't it?", "Yes it is, and here's why... blah blah blah". You can bore the socks off anyone you meet with the information here. Surely that's motivation enough to get revising. And if not, just think about all those lovely exam marks...

UK Weather Systems

*A whole page on depression — I'm feeling pretty miserable just thinking about it. Oh, hang on... depression**s** you say. Well that's a completely different matter — I love a good low pressure weather system. Let's get cracking.*

Depressions are Low Pressure Weather Systems

Depressions form over the **Atlantic Ocean**, then move **east** over the UK. They usually form when the tropical maritime and polar maritime air masses meet. Here's how:

1) **Warm air** constantly moves out of tropical areas, **towards the poles**. A **warm front** is the **leading edge** of a **warm air mass**.

2) **Cold air** moves out of polar regions, **towards the tropics**. A **cold front** is the **leading edge** of a **cold air mass**.

3) Where the air masses **meet**, the **warm air** heading towards the pole **rises** above the cold air heading towards the tropics (because **warm air** is **less dense** than cold air).

4) The rising **warm air** means that atmospheric **pressure** is **reduced**.

5) **Strong winds** blow from surrounding areas of high pressure towards this area of low pressure and the whole system **rotates** as air continues to rise.

6) **Cold fronts move more quickly** than warm fronts, so the cold front **catches up** with the **warm front**.

7) When this happens the **warm air** behind the warm front is **undercut** by the incoming cold front and is **lifted** away from the ground entirely. It now sits **above** the **cold air** — this is an **occluded front**. The warm air rises into the **upper atmosphere** and the depression **dissolves**.

Cold air moving this way

Warm air rises above cold air

Cold front

Warm front

Warm air moving this way

These diagrams show a depression from above.

Low pressure system caused by rising warm air

Wind direction

B

Cold air

Warm air

Cold air undercuts warm air

A

The line between A and B shows how the diagram below (which is a side view of this diagram) relates to this one.

Depressions bring Depressing Weather

As depressions pass over a location they bring a distinct **pattern** of weather, which usually lasts for **two** or **three days**:

(1) Ahead of the warm front, it's **cool** because cold air is **overhead**. **Thin clouds** form high up as warm air is pushed **upwards**.

(2) As the warm front passes, conditions on the ground get **warmer**. The warm air is pushed up over the cold air and **condenses**, forming **low, thick clouds** and **sustained drizzle**.

(3) When the warm air is overhead, it's **warm**. There's no **cloud** because warm air holds a lot of **water vapour**.

(4) As the cold front passes, cool air brings the **temperature down** again. The cold dense **air behind** the cold front **undercuts** the warm air mass in front. This forces the warm air to rise rapidly and condense, **forming clouds** and **heavy showers**. Rapidly rising air makes it **very windy** at the surface.

(5) When the cold front catches up with the warm front, all of the warm air has been **squeezed upwards** so there's **no warm air left** at the bottom. There's **less rain** because the uplift of air has decreased. There is **little condensation**, so **cloud cover decreases**. **Wind speed** also **decreases**, but **air pressure rises** as the dense cold air replaces the uplifted air and the depression dies out.

A ————————————————————————— B

warm moist air rises and condenses

warm tropical air

heavy rain

(5)

cold polar air (4)

(3)

(2)

cold polar air

(1)

ground surface

	(5) Cold air overhead	(4) As the cold front passes	(3) Warm air overhead	(2) As the warm front passes	(1) Ahead of the warm front
Rain	Showers	Heavy showers	None	Sustained drizzle	None
Clouds	High, broken	Towering, thick	None	Low, thick	High, thin
Pressure	Rising	Suddenly rising	Steady	Falling	Falling
Temperature	Cold	Falling	Warm	Rising	Cool
Wind speed	Decreasing	Strong	Decreasing	Strong	Increasing
Wind direction	NW	SW to NW	SW	SE to SW	SE

UK Weather Systems

Anticyclones are High Pressure Weather Systems

1) The UK also experiences **anticyclones** — areas of **high atmospheric pressure** caused by a large mass of **falling air**.

2) The air falls from the **upper atmosphere**, and **warms** on its way down. This causes humidity to decrease because air masses can hold more moisture as they get warmer. This means **clouds don't develop**, and conditions are very **dry**.

3) In anticyclones there's **not much difference** in **air pressure** between the centre and edges. Because the **pressure is similar**, the winds are weak, and flow gently outwards. In the **UK**, the winds flow **clockwise** around the centre.

4) Anticyclones cause **different weather** in winter than in summer:

WINTER WEATHER

- **Low** temperatures during the day (from below freezing to 5 °C), because the sun is at a **low angle**.
- **Extremely cold** overnight temperatures (below freezing) with frosts, because clear skies allow **loss of heat** through **radiation**.
- **Low level cloud** and **radiation fogs** — radiation fog forms overnight. As the ground cools, moisture in the air close to the ground condenses, forming fog.
- **High levels of atmospheric pollution** in urban areas — pollutants are trapped by **temperature inversions** (when the air at **higher altitudes** is **warmer** than the air at **lower levels**). A lack of wind means pollutants aren't dispersed.

SUMMER WEATHER

- The **absence of clouds** leads to intense **insolation**, which means it's **hot**, **sunny** and there's **no rain**.
- Rapid **radiation** at night can cause **temperature inversions**, dew and morning mist.
- **Coastal areas** may get **fogs** and **strong breezes**. Highlands may experience **strong winds** due to heating of valley sides, which causes a **pressure gradient**.
- After **several days** there's a risk of **thunderstorms**, due to large amounts of rapidly rising warm air.

5) Some anticyclones are described as **'blocking'**. Blocking anticyclones can sit over the UK and remain there for **many days**. Depressions that would normally travel across Britain are forced around the upper edge of the anticyclone. **Extreme weather conditions** are likely, e.g. heatwaves in summer and dry, freezing weather in winter.

Make Sure You can Read Synoptic Maps

Synoptic maps have **lines** called **isobars**. These **link** together **points** of **equal atmospheric pressure**, which is measured in **millibars** (mb). Here are **two synoptic charts**, one showing a **depression** and the other an **anticyclone**.

A depression is a low pressure system so the isobars show decreasing pressure towards the centre.

A cold front (the leading edge of a mass of cold air) is shown by the line with blue triangles.

An occluded front is shown by the line with alternate blue triangles and red semi-circles.

A warm front (the leading edge of a mass of warm air) is shown by the line with red semi-circles.

An anticyclone is a high pressure system, so the isobars show increasing pressure towards the centre.

Winds blow almost **parallel** to the **isobars**, not straight across them. This means that winds move in a spiral fashion **into** the **centre** of a depression and **out** of the **centre** of an anticyclone.

Practice Questions

Q1 Write a short description of how a depression forms.

Q2 Give three differences between anticyclones and depressions.

Exam Question

Q1 Describe, and give reasons for, the changes in weather as a depression passes over the UK. [8 marks]

I've been anti-cyclones ever since my house blew away...

*There's **a lot** of information on these pages. Unfortunately it's all important, so you'll have to learn it. You could do some drawing to take your mind off it. How about a nice diagram of a depression cross section? It's doubly fun if you label it too...*

UK Storms

People are scared of things they don't understand. If you're scared of temperate storms then this is the page for you...
You need to know how storms form in temperate climates, and learn the details of one case study of a temperate storm.

Storms that Hit the UK are Temperate Storms

Temperate storms are sometimes called mid-latitude cyclones or extratropical cyclones because they form outside the tropics.

1) Temperate storms occur in **temperate climates** — these are climates that are found at **mid-latitudes**, **30-60° north** or **south** of the Equator.

2) They range from **mild** (e.g. rain showers and 15-30 km/h winds) to **severe** (e.g. thunderstorms and 120 km/h winds). They can bring **strong winds**, **rain**, **hail**, **sleet** or **snow**.

3) They generally cause **less damage** than **tropical storms** (see p. 144). Typical impacts include road closures, power cuts and damage to trees. Occasionally temperate storms can be very severe, with winds strong enough to damage buildings.

4) Temperate storms are caused by **depressions**:

- Depressions often form **over the sea** in **autumn** when the water is warm — **warm surface water** leads to warm, moist air which rises. When this **warm** air meets the polar front it rises rapidly above the **cold polar air** creating an area of **low pressure**, along with **condensation** and **heavy rain**.

- A steep **pressure gradient** between the two air masses drives **strong winds**, which **spiral around the depression**.

- **Steep temperature gradients** in a depression affect the storm's strength — a strong temperature gradient means there is also a stronger **pressure gradient** (warm air has lower atmospheric pressure than cold air) which drives **strong winds**.

"Shall I compare thee to a temperate storm? Thou art more stormy and less temperate."
"Ooh Trevor, you're such a romantic."

The Great Storm Hit the UK in 1987

On the night of the **15th October 1987** the **UK** and **France** were hit by a severe **temperate storm**...

The Storm was Caused by a Depression with Rapidly Falling Air Pressure

1) The depression began over the Bay of Biscay (north of Spain and west of France) as **south westerly** winds carrying **warm**, **wet air** from the **North Atlantic** met **north easterly** winds carrying **cold air** from the **Pole**.

2) The depression **deepened rapidly** due to unusually warm sea surface temperatures in the Bay of Biscay and a steep **temperature gradient** between the two air masses. Low atmospheric pressure in the core of the depression led to the development of **very strong winds**.

3) The **polar front jet stream** was located **further south** than normal, so the depression formed over northern France and southern England, rather than to the north of Scotland.

4) On the 15th October, pressure in the **centre** of the depression **fell** from 970 mb at midday to 953 mb at midnight (much lower than the average air pressure in the UK — 1013 mb).

5) The storm hit the **south coast** of **Cornwall** and **Devon** shortly after midnight, moved **across the Midlands**, and reached the **Humber Estuary** on the **east coast** at around 5.30 am on the 16th October.

6) The **South East** suffered **especially severe winds** between 3 and 6 am, with gusts up to 196 km/h at Gorleston in Norfolk. The highest hourly mean wind speed was recorded at Shoreham-by-Sea, where winds of 136 km/h blew for 20 minutes continuously.

7) After 6 am the depression began to weaken and **moved away** over the **North Sea**.

THE COURSE OF THE GREAT STORM OVER THE UK (WITH PRESSURE READINGS)

16th Oct 12 noon

16th Oct 6 am

16th Oct 12 midnight

15th Oct 12 noon

15th Oct 6 pm

1987 Track Points Pressure (millibars)
- 953
- 956
- 959
- 964
- 970

UK Storms

Impacts included **Deaths, Infrastructure Damage** and **Economic Costs**

SOCIAL IMPACTS

- **18 people died** in England, and another **4** in **France**.
- **Power** and **telephone lines** were knocked down (mostly by falling trees). **150 000 homes** lost their **telephone connection**, and **several hundred thousand** people had **no electricity** for more than 24 hours.
- Some **historical buildings** were **damaged** or **destroyed**, e.g. Shanklin pier on the Isle of Wight was destroyed by waves.

ECONOMIC IMPACTS

- Over **1 million buildings** were **damaged**. Insurance claims totalled **£1.4 billion**.
- **Transport** was **disrupted** as fallen trees **blocked roads** and **railways**.
- **Gatwick airport closed** because it had lost power.
- Thousands of **boats** were **wrecked**. MV Hengist, a cross channel ferry, was **beached**.

ENVIRONMENTAL IMPACTS

- About **15 million trees** were blown down.
- Some areas lost **97%** of their trees, causing a **loss** of woodland **habitat**.

Responses included **Clean Up Operations** and **Improved Forecasting**

1) During the storm **emergency authorities** (e.g. fire, police, ambulance, and coastguard) dealt with huge numbers of emergency calls — four months' worth of calls in one night.

2) After the storm a massive **recovery** and **clean up operation** began:

- **Phone companies** and **electricity boards** worked round the clock **repairing** and **replacing equipment** until phone lines and power were restored.
- **Highways agencies** began **clearing roads**, and **railway companies** cleared **railways**.
- **Forestry workers** began **collecting the fallen trees** in forests (around 4 million m³ of timber needed recovering). It took hundreds of workers **over two years** to collect and store all the timber.
- The **Forestry Commission** established the **Forest Windblow Action Committee** to help woodland owners **recover fallen trees** and offer advice on **replanting**.

3) The **Met Office** were **criticised** for how they **forecast** the storm and **issued warnings**:

- **Severe storm warnings** were only issued about **three hours** before the storm hit.
- The **Ministry of Defence** were only warned that **military assistance** might be needed to help deal with the impacts of the storm at around 1 am on 16th October.

4) There was an **inquiry**, and changes were made:

- **More observations** of weather systems are now made by **ships**, **aircraft** and **satellites**.
- **Improved computer models** are now used to forecast weather.
- The **government** established a **national severe weather warning service** to improve the way severe weather warnings are made and issued.

Practice Questions

Q1 What sort of weather system causes temperate storms?

Q2 What types of weather might a temperate storm cause?

Q3 Describe some of the typical impacts of temperate storms.

Exam Question

Q1 Describe the impacts of, and responses to, one temperate storm that you have studied. [10 marks]

The Great Storm — not so great, and actually quite scary...

Even if you're using a different case study, these pages are a good guide to the kind of facts and figures that you'll need to remember if you want to do well in the exam. Those examiners love specific details, so give them what they want.

Tropical Climates

For your exam you need to learn about the climate of one tropical region. There are three examples here — pick the one you've studied in class and revise that. "Just one?" I hear you cry... Sorry, but knowing all three won't get you any extra marks.

All Tropical Climates are Hot, and Most are Wet

1) They're hot because the sun is **overhead** (high in the sky) — lots of **solar radiation** reaches the surface.

2) They're usually wet because they're affected by the **ITCZ** (**Intertropical Convergence Zone**). In this zone, NE and SE **trade winds** meet and create a **low pressure zone** of rising air that **cools** and **condenses**, forming **frequent heavy rainstorms**.

3) They're also wet because of travelling low pressure systems such as **subtropical cyclones**. Subtropical cyclones are **spinning storms** with a **low pressure centre** that form **outside the tropics**. They often move towards the Equator, bringing cooler air, winds and rain. (Tropical cyclones form in the tropics and are covered on p. 144-145.)

Equatorial Climates are Hot and Wet All Year

Equatorial climates are found **between the Equator** and **5° north** and **south** of the Equator.

> **Characteristics** of an Equatorial climate include:
> - **Hot temperatures** all year round (about 26-32 °C). Often the daytime temperature doesn't vary by more than about 2 °C, although it can drop by up to 10 °C at night.
> - **High rainfall** all year round (about 1600-3600 mm a year), with a fairly **even distribution** throughout the year. It rains **every day**, usually in the **afternoon**.
> - **Winds** are mostly **warm trade winds**, and vary in strength over the year.

Iquitos in Peru has an equatorial climate. Temperature varies from 25.2–26.6 °C. Rainfall is 2879 mm a year, and is always over 150 mm a month.

The climate is like this because:

1) The sun is **overhead all year** round.

2) The **ITCZ** influences the weather **all year round**, bringing **rain** every day.

3) **Strong convection** (heating of surface air) causes **regular afternoon rains**. The sun warms the ground, which warms the air above it and evaporates surface water. The warm, wet air rises, cools again, and the water vapour condenses into rain.

Tropical Savanna Climates are Hot with a Wet Season and a Dry Season

Tropical savanna climates are found between **5** and **20° north** and **south** of the Equator, between the **ITCZ** and zones of **subtropical high pressure**.

> **Characteristics** of a tropical savanna climate include:
> - **Hot temperatures** all year round (between 18 and 30 °C). Often daytime temperature doesn't vary by more than about 2-4 °C (although it can drop by 10-15 °C at night).
> - **Medium annual rainfall** (from around 500 mm to over 1700 mm a year). Rainfall is **seasonal** — **most** of the rain falls in the **wet season**, and **little** falls in the **dry season**.
> - **Winds** are mostly **trade winds**.

Lagos in Nigeria has a tropical savanna climate. Temperature varies from 24.9–28.2 °C. Rainfall is 1740 mm a year, and it varies from 25 mm in December to 414 mm in June.

The climate is like this because:

1) The sun is **overhead all year** round.

2) The wet and dry seasons are caused by a **seasonal shift** in the position of the **ITCZ**:

- In January, the ITCZ moves **south**. The northern hemisphere tropical savannas lie under the **high pressure zone**, so they get **little rain**.

- In July, the ITCZ moves **north**. This brings **low pressure** and **heavy rainfall** to the tropical savannas in the northern hemisphere.

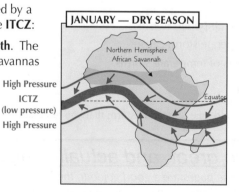

Tropical Climates

Monsoon Climates have Hot, Wet Summers and Cooler, Dry Winters

Monsoon climates are found in **coastal regions** between **5** and **20° north** and **south** of the Equator,
between the ITCZ and a zone of **subtropical high pressure.**

Characteristics of a monsoon climate include:

- **Hot temperatures** all year round (about 18-30 °C), varying by up to 10 °C between summer and winter.
- **Rainfall is high** (around 3000 mm a year). **Most** of the rain falls in the **wet season**, and little falls in the dry season.
- **Winds change direction with the seasons** — in the wet season the winds blow towards the land and in the dry season they blow towards the sea.

Chittagong in Bangladesh has a monsoon climate. Temperature varies from 19.9–28.4 °C. Rainfall is 2796 mm a year, and it varies from 6 mm in January to 818 mm in July.

The climate is like this because:

1) The sun is **overhead all year** round.
2) Seasonal changes in **rainfall**, **temperature** and **wind direction** are caused by a **seasonal shift** in the position of the **ITCZ** and zones of **high pressure**. E.g. on the Indian subcontinent:

In the **cool, dry** season:

- The ITCZ moves **south**. Northern hemisphere tropical monsoon areas lie under the **high pressure zone**, so they get **little rain**.
- The ITCZ is **over the ocean**, and a zone of high pressure is **over the land**. This forces winds **from the land** to the ocean.
- The land is cooler than the ocean (land cools down faster than water), so these NE winds are **cool** and bring lower temperatures.

JANUARY — DRY SEASON

High Pressure

ICTZ (low pressure)

High Pressure

JULY — WET SEASON

High Pressure

ICTZ (low pressure)

High Pressure

In the **warm, wet** season:

- The ITCZ moves **north**. This brings **low pressure** and **heavy rainfall** to the tropical monsoon areas in the northern hemisphere.
- The ITCZ is **over the land**, and a zone of high pressure is **over the ocean**. This forces the winds **from the ocean** to the land.
- The ocean is warmer than the land (water cools down slower than land), so these **SE winds** are **warm** and bring higher temperatures.

Practice Questions

Q1 Why are tropical climates hot?

Q2 What is the ITCZ?

Q3 What type of weather does the ITCZ bring?

Q4 What type of weather do subtropical cyclones bring?

Exam Question

Q1 Describe and explain the climate in one tropical region.   [8 marks]

I like my women how I like my tropical climates... [insert punchline here]

Ah the tropics — white sand beaches, azure seas, swaying palm trees, monsoon rain... Hmmm, the holiday brochure didn't mention that last one. Maybe I'll just stick to sandy sandwiches and a can of pop in the good old British drizzle...

Tropical Revolving Storms

The weather in tropical areas is generally a darn sight better than it is here, but things can get ugly...

Tropical Revolving Storms Form Over Warm Water in the Tropics

1) Tropical revolving storms are **huge spinning storms** with **strong winds** and **torrential rain**.

2) They develop over **warm water**. As warm, moist air **rises** and **condenses**, it **releases energy** that increases wind speed.

3) Scientists don't know exactly **how** they're formed but they do know the **conditions needed**. These include:

- A **disturbance** near the sea-surface that triggers the storm (e.g. an area of low pressure).
- **Sea water** that's **warm** (above **26.5°C** to **at least 50 m** below the surface), so lots of water will evaporate.
- **Convergence of air** in the **lower atmosphere** — either within the ITCZ or along the boundary between warm and cold air masses. This forces warm air to **rise**.
- A location at least **5° from the Equator**. They **don't form 0-5° either side** of the Equator because the **Coriolis effect** isn't strong enough to make them spin.

The Coriolis effect is a force caused by the Earth's rotation. It deflects the path of winds but it's weak at the Equator.

4) So tropical revolving storms form in the **tropics** because the water there is **warm enough**.

5) They occur in the **Caribbean Sea** (where they're called **hurricanes**), in the **Bay of Bengal** (where they're called **cyclones**), in the **China Sea** (where they're called **typhoons**) and in **Northern Australia** (where they're called **willy-willies**).

6) Tropical revolving storms **lose strength** when they move **over land** because their supply of warm, moist air is cut off.

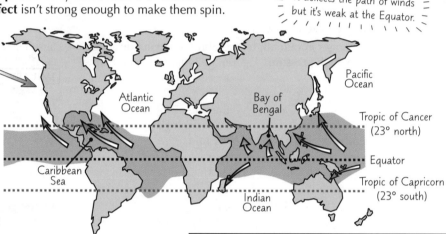

7) They initially **move westwards** due to the **easterly winds** in the **tropics**, e.g. the trade winds move cyclones west across the Atlantic Ocean.

8) They **move away** from the **Equator** because of the **Coriolis effect**.

Tropical Revolving Storms Have a Lot of Impacts

The **strong winds**, **high rainfall** and **storm surges** that come with tropical storms can cause havoc. High rainfall and storm surges cause **flooding** (and heavy rain can make hills unstable, causing **landslides**). Here are a **few examples** of the **possible impacts** of these things:

Storm surges are large rises in sea level caused by the low pressure and high winds of a storm.

ENVIRONMENTAL IMPACTS

1) **Beaches are eroded** and **coastal habitats** (e.g. coral reefs) are **damaged**.

2) **Environments are polluted** by all sorts of things, e.g. salt water, oil, chemicals spilled from factories damaged by the storm.

ECONOMIC IMPACTS

1) **Buildings, bridges, roads, railways, ports** and **airports** are **damaged** or **destroyed**. These cost a huge amount to **rebuild**.

2) **Business premises** are **damaged** or **destroyed**, so they **can't trade**.

3) **Agricultural land** is **damaged**, affecting **commercial farming**.

SOCIAL IMPACTS

1) People may **drown**, or be **injured** or **killed** by **debris** that's blown around or carried in flood water.

2) People are left **homeless**.

3) **Electricity supplies** are **cut off** because cables are damaged.

4) Flooding causes **sewage** overflows which **contaminate water supplies**.

5) The **shortage** of **clean water** and **lack** of proper **sanitation** makes it easier for **diseases** to spread.

6) In **poorer countries** there's often a **shortage** of **food** because **crops** are damaged and **livestock is killed**.

7) **Unemployment increases** because **businesses** are damaged or destroyed.

8) **Damaged roads** make it very difficult for **aid** and **emergency vehicles** to get through.

Tropical Revolving Storms

The Impacts are Usually Higher in Less Developed Countries

There are several reasons why the impacts of a tropical storm are **higher** in **less developed countries**:

- They **don't have the money to respond**, e.g. there is little money for flood defences or training emergency teams.
- The **buildings** are **poorer quality** compared to more developed countries, so are **more easily damaged** by storms.
- **Evacuation** can be **difficult** to organise, particularly when there is **limited access to transport** or when **rural populations** live in **remote areas** with poor communications.
- **Health care isn't as good** in less developed countries, so they **struggle** to **treat large numbers** of **casualties**.
- **Many people depend on agriculture** in less developed countries, which is often badly affected.
- **Infrastructure** is often **poorer**, making it **more difficult** for **emergency services** to **reach affected areas**.

However, the **economic impact** is often **higher** in **more developed** countries, as the **buildings** and **infrastructure** damaged are **worth a lot of money**.

Learn the Main Responses to Tropical Revolving Storms

EVACUATION

1) **When** and **where** tropical storms will hit land can be **predicted**. Scientists use **data** from things like **radar**, **satellites** and **aircraft** to **track** the storm. **Computer models** are then used to **calculate a predicted path**. For example, the **National Hurricane Center** in the USA tracks and predicts hurricanes using these techniques.
2) Predicting where and when a tropical storm is going to strike **gives people time** to **evacuate**. It also gives them time to **protect** their **homes** and **businesses**, e.g. by **boarding up windows** so they don't get smashed.
3) Evacuation can be a **very effective** response, e.g. a cyclone in Bangladesh in 1997 only killed around 100 people because of a successful evacuation. However, it's not effective if people don't receive the evacuation order.
4) Also, if forecasters get it wrong and areas are **evacuated unnecessarily** it **wastes a lot of money**.

PLANNING and EDUCATION

1) **Future developments**, e.g. new houses, can be **planned** to **avoid** the **areas most at risk** (e.g. right on the coast).
2) **Emergency services** can **train** and **prepare** for disasters. For example, in the USA **FEMA** (Federal Emergency Management Agency) train emergency personnel to deal with disasters such as floods and hurricanes.
3) Governments can plan **evacuation routes** to **get people away from storms quickly**. For example, in **Florida** evacuation routes are signposted all along the coast.
4) **Governments** and other **organisations** can **educate people** about **how to prepare** for a tropical storm (e.g. by stockpiling water and food) and **how to evacuate**.
5) All these methods are very **cost-effective**.

BUILDING TECHNIQUES

1) Buildings **can be designed** to **withstand tropical storms**, e.g. by using **reinforced concrete** or by **fixing roofs securely** so they don't get blown off. Buildings can also be **put on stilts** so they're safe from floodwater. For example, homes along the **Gulf Coast** of the USA are built on stilts.
2) **Flood defences** can be built **along rivers** (e.g. levees) and **coasts** (e.g. sea walls).
3) These methods **are effective**, but **don't guarantee** buildings **won't be damaged**. For example, levees in New Orleans broke during Hurricane Katrina, flooding the city.

AID

Aid sent by **governments** or **organisations** can be **very effective**, but there are often **problems** with **getting the aid to the people who need it**, e.g. due to **damaged roads** or **political problems**. For example, Burma's government initially refused to let aid workers in after Cylone Nargis in 2008.

Aid includes lots of things, e.g. tents, food, medicine, rescue teams.

Practice Questions

Q1 Give two social impacts and two environmental impacts of tropical revolving storms.

Q2 Give three reasons why the impacts of tropical revolving storms are usually higher in less developed countries.

Exam Questions

Q1 Describe the characteristics of tropical revolving storms. [7 marks]

Q2 Comment on the effectiveness of responses to tropical revolving storms. [8 marks]

My response to this page is aaaaaaaaaaaaagggggggggggghhhhh...

There's a whopping amount to learn on these two pages, so stop eyeing up the TV remote (I saw you) and get learnin'.

Tropical Revolving Storm Case Study — Katrina

And now time for the inevitable case studies — first up, a little madam called Katrina...

Hurricane Katrina Struck the South East USA on 29th August 2005

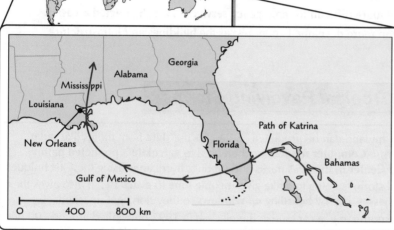

1) A storm **formed** over the **Bahamas** on the **23rd August**.

2) It moved **north west** and **strengthened into a hurricane** just before it went over the southern tip of **Florida** into the **Gulf of Mexico**.

3) As it travelled over the warm water of the Gulf of Mexico it **strengthened** from a **Category 1** hurricane to a **Category 5** hurricane.

> Hurricanes are classified using the Saffir-Simpson Scale, which is based on wind speed. Category 5 is the strongest (with winds over 250 km/h) and 1 is the weakest (with winds of 120-150 km/h).

4) On the night of the **28th August** it **weakened** to a **Category 3** hurricane.

5) On the **morning** of the **29th** it struck land, bringing winds of around **200 km/h** and **200-250 mm** rainfall in **Louisiana** and a **storm surge** of up to **8.5 m** in **Mississippi**.

6) It **travelled over 240 km inland** before the winds dropped enough for it to be **downgraded** from a hurricane to a storm.

The Hurricane had a Huge Economic Impact

1) The coast of **Louisiana** and **Mississippi** bore the brunt of the hurricane, but south Florida and Cuba were also affected. The city of **New Orleans** was very badly damaged. The storm surge and heavy rainfall **overwhelmed the levees** which should have **protected** the city. This caused **widespread flooding** (over **80%** of the city was **underwater**) which hugely increased the **number of deaths** and **level of damage**.

2) The **high winds**, **storm surge** and **flooding** had the following impacts:

SOCIAL IMPACTS

- **1836** people were **killed**.
- **300 000 houses** were **destroyed**.
- **Hundreds of thousands** of people were made **homeless**.
- **3 million** people were left **without electricity**.
- One of the main routes out of New Orleans was closed because parts of the **I-10 bridge collapsed**.
- **Water supplies** were **polluted** with sewage, chemicals and dead bodies. **Five people died from bacterial infections** caught from the contaminated water (although this was far less than feared).
- The **education** of hundreds of thousands of children suffered when schools were damaged or destroyed, e.g. **18 schools** in **New Orleans** were **destroyed** and **74** were badly **damaged**.

ECONOMIC IMPACTS

- **230 000 jobs** were **lost** from businesses that were damaged or destroyed.
- The total **cost of damage** is estimated at around **$300 billion**.
- **30 oil platforms** in the Gulf of Mexico were **damaged** or **destroyed** and **nine oil refineries** had to **close**, disrupting the oil industry.
- **5300 km²** of **forest** was destroyed in **Mississippi**, severely affecting the **logging industry** (the loss of income was estimated to be about **$5 billion**).
- Many **ports** were **damaged**, e.g. **Gulfport** in Mississippi. This disrupted the **shipping industry**.

Damage from Hurricane Katrina.

ENVIRONMENTAL IMPACTS

- **Coastal habitats** such as **sea turtle breeding beaches** were **damaged**.
- Some **coastal conservation areas** were **destroyed**, e.g. around **half** of **Breton National Wildlife Refuge** in **Louisiana** was **washed away**.
- Flooding damaged oil refineries in Louisiana, causing massive **oil spills**.
- Permanent flooding of **salt marshes** in **Louisiana** caused loss of habitat.

Tropical Revolving Storm Case Study — Katrina

Effective **Warning Systems** Helped the USA **Respond Rapidly**

WARNINGS

1) The USA has a **sophisticated monitoring system** to **predict** if (and where) a hurricane will hit. The **National Hurricane Center** (**NHC**) in Florida tracks and predicts hurricanes using things like satellite images, and 'hurricane hunter' planes that collect weather data on approaching storms.

2) On **August 26th** the NHC issued a **hurricane warning** for **Louisiana**, **Mississippi** and **Alabama**. It continued to track the hurricane, updating the government on where and when it would hit.

RESPONSES BEFORE IT HIT

1) The Federal Emergency Management Agency (**FEMA**) **coordinated** the **response**.

2) A **state of emergency was declared** in **Louisiana** on the evening of the **26th August**, and in **Mississippi** on the **27th**. FEMA and various other organisations **started preparing** for the hurricane, for example:
   - The **US Coast Guard** positioned **helicopters** and **boats** around the area likely to be affected.
   - FEMA organised teams and supplies, e.g. **mortuary teams** with refrigerated trucks to deal with bodies.

3) On the morning of **August 28th** the mayor of New Orleans ordered a **mandatory (compulsory) evacuation** of the city. It's estimated that around **80%** of New Orleans residents **were evacuated** before the hurricane reached land. This reduced the number of people killed because lots of people had left the areas where the hurricane hit.

4) **Voluntary** or **mandatory evacuation orders** were also issued in **other places** along the coast.

RESPONSES DURING/AFTER

1) Around **100 000 people didn't evacuate**, either because they wanted to **stay and protect their property**, or because they **didn't have enough money** or **didn't have any transport**. Emergency shelters were set up for these people, e.g. the **Louisiana Superdome** in New Orleans sheltered **26 000 people** during the hurricane.

2) The coastguard, police, fire service and army **rescued over 50 000 people** after the hurricane hit.

3) Lots of organisations sent **teams** and **supplies** into the area after the hurricane:
   - **FEMA** sent **search and rescue** teams, **medical** teams, **water, ice** and **ready meals**.
   - 58 000 **National Guard troops** (reserve military troops) were deployed from all over the US and were responsible for rescuing 17 000 people and evacuating 70 000.
   - **Charities** collected over **$4 billion** of donations from the public to provide aid to victims of Katrina, e.g. the Salvation Army provided 5.7 million hot meals to people in and around New Orleans in the days after the storm.

Responses to the Disaster Have Been **Criticised**

The national response **reduced the impact** of the hurricane, but it was subject to **criticism**:

1) Some **emergency shelters weren't properly prepared** for the number of people needing shelter, e.g. the National Guard delivered enough food to the Louisiana Superdome to feed 15 000 people for 3 days, but 26 000 turned up.

2) Widespread **looting** took place in many areas, e.g. in New Orleans, because there **weren't enough police** or **troops**.

3) Most people agree that the evacuations ordered saved many lives, but the evacuations were **criticised** for **not helping people without transport** to get out, e.g. poorer New Orleans residents without a car.

Practice Questions

Q1 On what date did Hurricane Katrina hit the South East USA?

Q2 Give two social impacts, two economic impacts and two environmental impacts of Hurricane Katrina.

Exam Question

Q1 With reference to one example, discuss how the impacts of a tropical revolving storm are affected by the preparation for and response to the event.

[10 marks]

You need to know what happened, the impacts and the responses...

The US was pretty prepared for a hurricane, but the sheer size and strength of Hurricane Katrina and the fact that New Orleans received a direct hit caused problems. The death toll was way, way higher than anybody expected for such a developed country.

Tropical Revolving Storm Case Study — Nargis

And for your second helping of case study it's... drum roll please... Cyclone Nargis.

Cyclone Nargis Struck Burma on 2nd May 2008

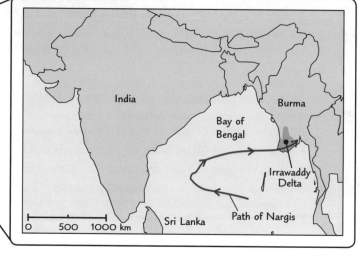

India

Bay of Bengal

Burma

Irrawaddy Delta

Sri Lanka

Path of Nargis

0   500   1000 km

1) A storm **formed** in the **Bay of Bengal** during the **last week** in **April**.

2) On the **28th April** it had **strengthened** enough to be **upgraded** to a **cyclone**.

3) As it **approached the coast of Burma** it strengthened to **Category 4** on the Saffir-Simpson scale (p. 146).

4) On **May 2nd** it **hit the coast of Burma** with **wind speeds** of around **215 km/h** and a **storm surge** of **5 m** (storm waves added another 2 m on top of this).

5) It **weakened** as it **moved inland** and was **downgraded** from a cyclone to a storm on the **3rd May**.

The Cyclone had a Huge Social Impact

1) The **Irrawaddy Delta** in Burma was the hardest hit area because the cyclone hit it head on. A large proportion of it is only just above sea level and over **14 000 km²** of land was **flooded**.

2) **Sri Lanka** was also affected by heavy rainfall, which led to **flooding** and **landslides**.

3) Across the region, the **high winds**, **storm surge** and **flooding** had the following impacts:

SOCIAL IMPACTS

- More than **140 000** people were **killed**.
- **450 000 houses** were **destroyed** and **350 000** were **damaged**.
- **4000 schools** were **destroyed** or severely **damaged**.
- **75%** of **health facilities** were **destroyed** or **severely damaged**.
- Up to **2.5 million** people were left without **shelter**.
- **43%** of **freshwater ponds** (valuable sources of fresh water for local people) were **damaged** by salt water.
- Almost **70%** of the population **had no access to clean water**.
- A lot of people suffered from **diseases** caused by **poor sanitary conditions** and **contaminated water**, e.g. **dysentry, diarrhoea**.
- Many people suffered **mental health problems** afterwards, e.g. up to 30% of the people treated by one aid agency had mental health problems caused by the cyclone.

A house damaged by Cyclone Nargis.

©Reximages

ENVIRONMENTAL IMPACTS

- **38 000 hectares** of **mangrove forests** were **destroyed**.
- The flooding caused **erosion** and **salination** (increased salt content) of land.

Mangrove forests protect the coast from flooding. Unfortunately loads had been chopped down in the decade before Nargis hit to make rice paddies and shrimp farms, reducing the natural protection.

ECONOMIC IMPACTS

- Over **600 000 hectares** of **agricultural land** was damaged, including around 65% of rice paddies in the region.
- **Crops** were **lost**, **200 000 farm animals** were **killed** and over **40%** of **food stores** were **destroyed**. This had a huge impact on the **agricultural industry**.
- **Millions** of people **lost their livelihoods**, e.g. many **fishing boats** were destroyed.
- The **total cost** of the damage was around **$4 billion**.

Tropical Revolving Storm Case Study — Nargis

Burma Wasn't Prepared for Cyclone Nargis

1) **Burma doesn't have** a dedicated **hurricane monitoring centre**. However, **Indian** weather agencies **warned** the Burmese Government that Cyclone Nargis was likely to hit the country **48 hours before** it did.

2) **Burmese weather forecasters** did **give warnings** the cyclone was coming via **TV** and **radio**, but it's claimed that they **didn't** say how **severe** it would be or give any advice about **how to prepare** or **evacuate**. This **increased** the number of people **killed** because people didn't know what to do or where to evacuate to.

3) There were **no emergency preparation plans**, **no evacuation plans** and the country **didn't** have an **early warning system**.

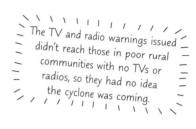
The TV and radio warnings issued didn't reach those in poor rural communities with no TVs or radios, so they had no idea the cyclone was coming.

The Response was Really Slow

1) **Burma's government** initially **refused** to accept any **foreign aid**.

2) On the 9th May they decided to **accept aid donations** of things like food and tents, but **wouldn't** let in **aid workers**. Some countries and organisations sent aid that helped **reduce** the impacts of the cyclone, for example:

- The **UN refugee agency** (UNHCR) sent in 22 tonnes of tents and other supplies from Thailand.
- **Charities** sent aid e.g. **Muslim Aid** distributed water purification tablets, blankets and food parcels.
- **Italy** sent 25 tonnes of **emergency equipment**, e.g. **shelters**, **first aid kits** and **water purifiers**.

3) This helped a lot, but there were **still problems**, e.g. a French Navy ship carrying 1500 tonnes of supplies was refused entry because the Burmese government thought it was a warship.

4) Also, some **aid** was **seized** by the **military**, delaying its delivery to the people who needed it, e.g. two shipments of high-energy biscuits were seized.

5) On the 19th May, **ASEAN** (Association of South East Asian Nations) held an emergency summit to discuss the situation. Following this, Burma decided to **allow aid workers** from **ASEAN member countries** in to help.

6) After talks between the **UN Secretary General** and the **Burmese leader** Than Shwe, **all aid workers** were **allowed in** on the **23rd May** — **three weeks after** the disaster occurred.

7) The **government response** to the disaster has been **heavily criticised** by other countries — the delay in accepting international aid greatly increased the number of deaths because help for some people **came too late**.

Practice Questions

Q1 On what date did Cyclone Nargis hit Burma?

Q2 What category was Cyclone Nargis when it hit Burma?

Q3 Describe the timeline of Cyclone Nargis.

Q4 Which area of Burma was worst hit?

Q5 Give two social impacts, two economic impacts and two environmental impacts of Cyclone Nargis.

Exam Question

Q1 With reference to two examples, discuss how the impacts of a tropical revolving storm are affected by the level of economic development of the country it affects.

[40 marks]

Make sure you learn all about Cyclone Nargis...

Disasters tends to have a higher social impact in less developed countries, and a higher economic impact in more developed countries. This is the same whether you're studying a tropical storm, an earthquake or a volcano, so make sure you understand why it is.

Urban Climate Characteristics

Urban climate characteristics — or 'what the weather's like in cities' to you and me. Geographers and their fancy names...

Urban Areas are Warmer than the Surrounding Rural Areas

1) The phenomenon of urban areas being warmer than rural areas is called the **urban heat island effect**.

2) Urban areas with higher air temperatures than the surrounding rural areas are called **urban heat islands** (UHIs). For example, **London** has a clearly defined UHI.

3) The **highest temperatures** are found in **industrial areas** and in the most **densely built up** areas, e.g. the **CBD** (Central Business District).

LONDON'S HEAT ISLAND

4) There are **pockets** of **cool air** above **parks** and **bodies of water** (e.g. rivers or ponds). These are called temperature '**sinks**'.

5) Areas within the city with the **same land use** (e.g. industry) generally have the **same temperature**. These are called temperature '**plateaus**'.

6) Temperature can **change rapidly** when **land use changes** (e.g. from inner city housing to CBD high rise buildings). Rapid changes are referred to as temperature '**cliffs**'.

There are Four Main Causes of the UHI Effect

Urban surfaces have a low albedo (p. 133) — they absorb lots of energy instead of reflecting it.

1) **ABSORPTION OF HEAT BY URBAN SURFACES:**
Concrete, brick and tarmac surfaces **absorb** and **store heat from the sun** during the **day**. They slowly **release** the heat as **long wave radiation** — this is most noticeable at **night**, when it warms the air.

2) **AIR POLLUTION:**
Air pollution from cars and factories **increases cloud cover** over the city. It also creates a '**pollution dome**' — a layer of pollution over the city. Both these things **trap outgoing heat radiation** and **reflect it back** to the surface.

3) **HEAT FROM HUMAN ACTIVITY:**
Cars, factories, offices, central heating, air conditioning units and people themselves all release heat.

4) **LESS EVAPOTRANSPIRATION:**
When it rains the water's quickly removed by **drainage systems**, so there's **little surface water** to **evaporate**. Also, there isn't much **vegetation**, so there's **little transpiration**. **Evapotranspiration** uses heat energy, so less evapotranspiration means higher temperatures.

Evapotranspiration is the transfer of water from the soil to the air via evaporation and transpiration.

The Effect Varies Seasonally and Diurnally (between Day and Night)

1) The UHI effect is stronger at **NIGHT**. Urban **daytime** temperatures are on average **0.6 °C warmer** than surrounding rural areas, but **night time** temperatures can be **3-4 °C warmer**. This is because rural areas cool down at night, but **urban areas don't cool as much** because **urban surfaces continue to release heat** that they've absorbed during the day.

2) It's stronger in **SUMMER** (in mid-latitude cities like London). Average **winter** temperatures can be **2 °C warmer**, but average summer temperatures can be up to **5 °C warmer**. This is because there's **more solar radiation in summer**, so urban areas absorb more heat.

3) It's stronger when there's an **ANTICYCLONE**. Anticyclones cause **clear skies** and **low winds** (see p. 139). If there are no clouds, **more solar radiation** reaches and heats the ground. **Low winds** mean **warm air isn't blown away**.

Urban Climate Characteristics

Winds are Affected by Buildings in Urban Areas

AIR FLOW AROUND A BUILDING

turbulence

1) **Average wind speed** is usually **lower** in cities than in rural areas. This is because **tall buildings create friction** that slows down the moving air.

2) There are areas where **wind speed** is **zero**, because some areas are **totally sheltered** from wind by **buildings**.

3) You get **turbulence around buildings**. This happens when **wind hits** the **face of a building** — some of it's **deflected down**, some **around the sides** and some **over the top**. When these winds hit other buildings or the ground they causes **vortices** (bodies of swirling air).

4) You get **powerful gusts** of wind when wind is **channelled down streets** — this is known as the **canyon effect**.

The canyon effect has implications for building design and town planning, e.g. positioning of buildings, and the location of doorways on larger buildings.

There's More Rain, Fog and Thunderstorms...

1) It **rains more often** in urban areas than in the surrounding countryside.

2) The rain is also **more intense** and there are **more thunderstorms**.

3) There are **two** main reasons for these things:

- The UHI effect means the air in urban areas is warm, and warm air can hold more water. The **warm, moist air rises** — this is called **convectional uplift**. As it rises it **cools**, the **water vapour condenses** and it **rains**. This type of rain is called **convectional rainfall**.

- Urban areas generate huge amounts of **dust** and **pollution**. Particles of dust and pollution floating about in the air act as **condensation nuclei** (they trigger water to condense around them). This **encourages clouds** to form, rather than allowing the warm, moist air to disperse.

4) The higher concentration of **condensation nuclei** in urban areas also **increases** the **frequency** of fog.

...but Less Snow and Frost

1) It **doesn't snow as often** in urban areas, and when it does snow the **snow melts faster**. This is because it's **warmer** due to the **UHI effect**.

2) Urban areas have **fewer days of frost** for the same reason.

Darn that UHI effect — now I've gone and got my sleigh stuck.

Practice Questions

Q1 What is the urban heat island effect?

Q2 Briefly describe the four main causes of the urban heat island effect.

Q3 Explain why the urban heat island effect is stronger at night than during the day.

Q4 What effect do urban structures have on average wind speed?

Q5 Why is fog more frequent in urban areas than in rural areas?

Exam Question

Q1 Study the table, which shows climate data for two cities. Describe and suggest reasons for the differences between the two urban climates. [7 marks]

	City A	City B
Annual average rainfall (mm)	1200	1300
Average July temperature (°C)	21	23
Average number of thunderstorms per year	18	25
Average number of days with fog	17	23
Average number of days without cloud cover	180	120

UHI — I'm sure you can buy cream for that...

If you know what causes the UHI effect, you should be able to use your common sense to answer any exam question on it, e.g. if you're asked why parks are cooler than built up areas, talk about the fact that they have more vegetation and less tarmac. If you're asked why one city has a stronger UHI than another think about whether it might be more polluted, or more built up.

Urban Air Quality

Urban air pollution causes a range of pretty horrible health problems. Today, *cough* — sorry. Today, most pollution comes from road traffic. Cities all over the world have tried to solve the pollution problem simply by reducing traffic.

There's a lot of **Particulate Pollution** in Urban Areas

1) **Particulates** are **tiny pieces** of **solids** and **tiny droplets** of **liquids** floating in the air.

2) **More** particulates are found in **urban areas** than in rural areas. The concentration of particulates in urban areas is around 10-40 $\mu g/m^3$, compared to less than 10 $\mu g/m^3$ in rural areas.

3) **Sources** of particulates include:

> • **Vehicle exhausts** — they produce very **fine particulates** (0.01 μm-1.0 μm). About **80%** of fine particulates in urban areas are from vehicle exhausts.
>
> • **Burning** of refuse, cigarettes and fuel, e.g. coal — this produces both **fine** and **coarse particulates**, e.g. sulphates, nitrates, soot and ash.
>
> • **Construction**, **mining** and **quarrying** — these activities produce **coarse particulates** (10 μm-100 μm), e.g. tiny fragments of rock, brick and cement dust.
>
> • **Plants and moulds** — also generate **coarse particulates**, e.g. pollen and mould spores.

A microgram (μg) is a one thousandth of a gram and a micrometre (μm) is a one thousandth of a millimetre.

4) Particulates can cause **health problems**. Coarser particulates are usually **filtered out** by the nose and throat, but **finer particulates less than 10 μm** in diameter (often called PM10) can enter the **lungs**. PM10 could **cause** or **make worse** problems like asthma, bronchitis, lung cancer and heart disease.

Other Types of Pollution Lead to **Photochemical Smog**

1) Pollutants such as **nitrogen oxides**, **sulfur oxides** and **hydrocarbons** come from **burning fossil fuels** (e.g. in vehicles and factories).

2) When these **pollutants** come into contact with **sunlight**, the **UV light** causes them to **break down** into **harmful chemicals** (e.g. ozone) which form **photochemical smog**.

3) Photochemical smog is a **problem** in **many cities**, e.g. Los Angeles (USA), Beijing (China), Mexico City (Mexico) and Barcelona (Spain). It's more common in places with **hot** and **sunny climates** because there's **more sunlight**.

4) These locations often have a **temperature inversion** (a layer of warm air trapped below denser cooler air), which keeps the pollutants at **ground level**.

5) Photochemical smog is linked to **health problems** such as **breathing difficulties** (coughing, shortness of breath), **respiratory disorders** (e.g. asthma) and **headaches**.

Smog over Mexico City.

Ozone is useful in the upper atmosphere (protecting us from UV radiation), but when it's in the lower atmosphere it causes health problems.

There are Lots of Different Ways to **Reduce Air Pollution**

Lots of cities have tried to **reduce pollution** by **reducing traffic**. There are various ways that this can be done:

CONGESTION CHARGING

• **People** are charged if they **use their vehicles** in **certain places** at **certain times**.

• This reduces pollution by **reducing road traffic**. In **Central London** congestion charging has reduced traffic and emissions in the congestion zone by **up to 15%** since 2003.

• However, some people **travel around** the edge of **zones** to avoid being charged, which increases traffic in these areas.

• It's difficult to enforce the charge because the **volume of traffic** is so large that it's hard to process all the fines correctly.

PEDESTRIANISATION

• **Vehicles are restricted** from **entering certain places** at **certain times**. It reduces pollution by **reducing road traffic**.

• Many cities have pedestrianised zones — including London, Cardiff, Manchester and Liverpool.

• Pedestrianisation can lead to shops receiving **fewer customers** because people can only get to them on foot.

Urban Air Quality

PUBLIC TRANSPORT IMPROVEMENTS

- Encouraging people to **use public transport** instead of their cars reduces pollution. For example, many cities have:

  - **Improved bus services** to make bus journeys cheaper, faster and more efficient. E.g. many cities have introduced bus lanes so buses don't get caught in slow-moving traffic.
  - **Park and ride schemes** (car parks on public transport routes) to make it easier to **access public transport**.
  - **Trams** and **light railway services** which run on lines, so they don't get caught in **road congestion**. They also **pollute less** than buses. E.g. The Metrolink in Manchester opened in 1992. It links the city centre to the suburbs and has been very successful — the line to Bury and Altrincham has taken about **2.6 million** cars off the roads.

- Public transport improvements are often **expensive** — e.g. construction of the Metrolink has cost over £1 billion.
- New developments can also cause problems — e.g. **park and ride schemes** can shift traffic problems to rural areas.

OTHER SCHEMES FOR REDUCING TRAFFIC

- In **Mexico City** drivers are **banned** from using their cars **one weekday** per week, based on the last digit of their number plate, e.g. number plates ending in 5 or 6 can't be used on Mondays. However, some richer households get around the system by **buying two cars**.
- **Birmingham**, **Bristol** and **London** have council-run **car sharing** schemes to encourage people making the same journey to share a car. However, some people find car sharing inconvenient, or are worried about sharing a car with a stranger.

There are **larger scale** ways of tackling urban air pollution too. For example:

LEGISLATION (LAWS)

Laws aim to **reduce pollution** by **limiting emissions** and setting **air quality standards**. For example:
- The **UK Clean Air Acts** of 1956 and 1968 reduced domestic pollution by introducing **smoke control areas** where only smokeless fuels could be burned, and **reduced industrial pollution** by introducing the use of **tall chimneys** (which mean that pollutants are dispersed higher in the atmosphere, so they're less harmful to people in the city).
- The **Road Vehicles Regulations** reduce exhaust emissions by ensuring cars pass an **emissions test** in their MOT.
- In Scotland, legislation allows local authorities to do **roadside emission tests**, where they can **issue fines** if the vehicle fails. Throughout the UK, local authorities can issue fines to people who leave their engines running unnecessarily.

ALTERNATIVE FUELS

Petrol and diesel are replaced with **cleaner fuels** that **pollute less**. For example:
- **Biofuels** (e.g. **bioethanol** and **biodiesel**) are produced from **plants**. They can **directly replace** petrol and diesel, and have **lower particulate emissions**. However, growing the crops needed to make biofuels can **reduce biodiversity**, e.g. biofuels like corn-based ethanol need a lot of land to grow, which means clearing other vegetation.
- **Liquefied petroleum gas** (**LPG**) is a **gas** produced from **fossil fuels** that has **lower emissions** than petrol or diesel. However, cars have to be **converted** to use LPG, and **service stations** have to be **adapted** to distribute it.
- **Electric vehicles** have **lower emissions** because they run off **batteries**, rather than **conventional fuel**. Electric vehicles need **recharge points**, and **producing** and **disposing** of the **batteries** can cause environmental problems.

Practice Questions

Q1 What are particulates?
Q2 How is photochemical smog produced?
Q3 Why is photochemical smog more common in hot climates?

Exam Question

Q1 Describe how air pollution in urban areas can be reduced. [8 marks]

Country Mouse came to visit Town Mouse... and died due to poor air quality

Ah, the lesser known version of the classic tale. The health and environmental problems associated with urban air pollution really are serious — make sure you learn about the potential solutions and their drawbacks. If only we could all live in the countryside...

Climate Change — Evidence

In the exam you could well be asked to write about climate change and the evidence for it. You need to know specifics, it's no use saying, 'Well, it feels a bit warm today.' Even if it does, you won't make Mr Examiner a very happy man. No sir.

Climate Change *is any* Long Term *change in* Weather

1) **Climate change** is any **significant** change in the **weather** of a region over a period of at least **several decades**. E.g. increasing average **temperature** or **rainfall**, or a change in the usual **wind direction**.

2) The climate **constantly changes**, it **always has**, and it **always will**.

3) For the last 2.5 million years, global temperature has shifted between **cold glacial periods** that last for around 100 000 years, and **warmer interglacial periods** that last for around 10 000 years. We're in an **interglacial period now**.

4) **20 000 years ago** the Earth was cold. Around **15 000** years ago it started to warm up — this was the end of the last glacial period.

5) There was a brief **return** to **cold conditions** between **13 000 and 11 500 years ago**, before a period of **rapid warming**.

6) Over the last **10 000 years** the climate has been **warm** with **minor fluctuations**.

Temperature change in Greenland over the last 20 000 years

Scientists use past temperature from one place, e.g. Greenland, to indicate global temperature.

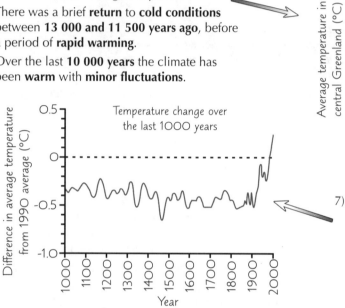

Temperature change over the last 1000 years

7) Over the last **1000 years** the climate has been fairly **constant** with small fluctuations (+/− 0.2 °C) in annual temperature.

8) Over the **last century global temperature** has **increased rapidly**. This is called **global warming**. There's been a **sharp rise** in average temperature (**0.7 °C** between **1900** and **2000**).

9) Global temperatures **rose steadily** from the **early 20th century** until the **1940s** (from **13.5 °C** to **14 °C**), then **dropped**. Scientists thought there would be another **glacial period**, but temperatures have **risen even more rapidly** since the 1970s (from **13.8 °C** to **14.4 °C**).

10) The **temperature increase** over the last century has been **very fast**. There is a **consensus** among scientists that the **changes** in **climate** over the last century are a result of **human activities**.

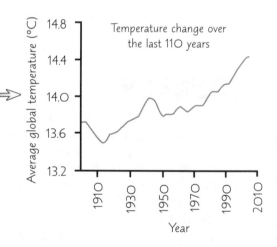

Temperature change over the last 110 years

Evidence *for* Climate Change *comes from* Many Sources

Observations

1) **HISTORICAL RECORDS:**
   - Historical records can **indirectly** show **different conditions** in the past. For example, **agricultural reports** (such as harvest times) show changing conditions throughout **human history**.

2) **WEATHER RECORDS:**
   - Details of **weather conditions** have been consistently **collected since 1861**.
   - These can be used to show detailed **climate changes** over the short time period they've been collected.

Climate Change — Evidence

Physical Evidence

1) **ICE CORES:**
   - Scientists drill deep into **ice sheets** (**huge masses** of **ice**) to extract **cores of ice**. Ice sheets are made up of **layers** of ice — **one** layer is formed **every year**. So the ice at the bottom of the core is really, really old.
   - By analysing **gases** trapped when the ice formed and the **chemistry of the ice** they can tell what the **temperature** was each year and work out how it has **changed over time**. Carbon dioxide (CO_2) and oxygen are key indicators:
     - **High CO_2** levels in ice indicate a **warm climate** at that time.
     - **Oxygen** has two main isotopes — **O-18** and **O-16**. O-16 is **lighter** than O-18. In cold periods there is **less energy** for evaporation, so water molecules containing the lighter O-16 evaporate more **easily**. This O-16 rich water vapour is carried to the poles and falls as snow. This is recorded in ice cores — **high** levels of **O-16** compared to O-18 indicate a period of **cold climate**.

2) **SEA FLOOR SEDIMENTS:**
   - Sediments deposited on the sea floor record the chemical composition of seawater when they were deposited.
   - Like ice cores, sediments contain **oxygen isotopes**. During periods of cold climate water molecules containing O-16 are more easily evaporated, so the ocean becomes **richer** in O-18. This is recorded in sea floor sediments — sediments with **high** levels of **O-18** indicate a period of **cold climate**.

3) **SEA LEVEL CHANGE:**
   - **Sea level** is affected by things like the volume of water **stored as ice**.
   - As the climate warms, ice caps **melt** and sea level **rises**. Some **valleys** formed above sea level are now **submerged** (e.g. Poole Harbour in Dorset and Lough Swilly in Ireland), showing that sea level is **higher** than it used to be.

4) **RETREATING GLACIERS:**
   - Scientists can tell **how big** a glacier was and how far it **extended** by looking at historical photos and at the position of **rocks deposited** by the glacier. These rocks can be **dated** to show when they were deposited.
   - The **distance** of the rocks from the current glacier **indicates climate change**. E.g. if the front of the glacier is now miles away from the rocks it indicates that **temperatures** have **increased** over that period of time.

Biological Evidence

1) **POLLEN ANALYSIS:**
   - **Pollen** is often **preserved** in **sediment**. Scientists study the preserved pollen and **identify** the plant it came from. They also **date** the sediment the pollen is found in so they know when it was **deposited**.
   - Scientists know the **climatic conditions** that plants live in now. When they find preserved pollen from similar plants, it helps them understand what the climate was like when that pollen was **produced**.

2) **COLEOPTERA:**
   - **Coleoptera** are **beetles** whose remains are easily preserved in **sediments**. Different **species** of Coleoptera live in different **climatic conditions**. Scientists can identify the species of Coleoptera in a sediment, and use it to build up a **picture of the climate** when the sediment was laid down.

3) **TREE RINGS (DENDROCHRONOLOGY):**
   - As a tree grows it forms a new **tree ring** each year — the tree rings are **thicker** in warm, wet conditions.
   - Scientists take **cores** and count the rings to find the **age** of a tree. The **thickness** of each ring indicates what the climate was like **each year**. Tree rings can reliably **show** and **date** climate conditions up to **10 000 years ago**.

Practice Questions

Q1 Define climate change.

Q2 Briefly explain what is meant by 'global warming'.

Exam Question

Q1 Outline the sources of evidence for climate change. [8 marks]

All scientists care about is evidence — what about truth, beauty, and love...

All these graphs can be mighty confusing, especially when people manipulate the data to try and show that climate change isn't happening. Basically, the climate has always been changing, but global warming is an unusually large and rapid change.

Climate Change — Causes and Impacts

Pretty much everyone agrees that global warming is a bad thing, but not many people know exactly how wide ranging its impacts could be. Time for you to become one of the privileged few...

Most Scientists *Agree that* Human Activity *is* Causing Global Warming

1) The recent **rise** in **global temperature** (**global warming**) and the **rate** of this increase is **unheard of** in **historical terms**.

2) There's a **scientific consensus** that this temperature rise is **caused** by human **enhancement** of the **greenhouse effect**.

3) The **greenhouse effect** is where greenhouse gases absorb **outgoing long-wave radiation**, so less is **lost** to space. It's **essential** for keeping the planet **warm**.

4) But **too much** greenhouse gas in the atmosphere means **too much** energy is trapped and the planet **warms up**.

5) **Increasing** amounts of **CO_2** and **methane** are the main contributors towards the recent **rise** in **temperature**, but other greenhouse gases include **nitrous oxide**, **water vapour** and **ozone**.

6) **Humans** are increasing the **concentration** of greenhouse gases by:

Ozone is a greenhouse gas in the lower atmosphere. Don't get it confused with the ozone layer higher in the atmosphere.

Burning Fossil Fuels

- **CO_2** is **released** into the atmosphere when **fossil fuels** like coal, oil, natural gas and petrol are **burnt**, e.g. in power stations or in cars.
- Since the industrial revolution in the mid-19th century levels of **atmospheric CO_2** have **increased** from **280 ppm** (parts per million) to **380 ppm**. The level had been **broadly stable** for the previous **10 000 years**.

Deforestation

- **Plants remove CO_2** from the atmosphere and convert it into **organic matter** using photosynthesis. It's also stored in the soil as **dead organic matter**.
- When trees and plants are chopped down, they stop taking in CO_2.
- CO_2 is also **released** into the atmosphere when trees are **burnt** as fuel or to make way for agriculture.

Farming

- Using nitrogen-based **fertiliser** to grow crops increases **nitrous oxide** emissions.
- **Farming** of **livestock** produces a lot of **methane** — cows love to fart...
- **Rice paddies** contribute to global warming, because **flooded fields** emit **methane**.

Things like oceans and plants which store CO_2 are known as CO_2 sinks.

Global Warming *Could Have* Huge Impacts Globally

Temperature is expected to **increase** by **1.4-5.8 °C** between **1990** and **2100**. This would have major impacts:

Global Climate would Change

The **pattern of precipitation** is expected to change:

- **Wet areas** are expected to get **wetter** (e.g. **mid** to **high latitudes**, especially North America and Europe).
- **Precipitation** is expected to **decrease** by 5-20% in **other areas** due to changes in **ocean circulation** and **wind patterns**. **Dry areas** are expected to get **drier** (e.g. the **subtropics**, especially southern Africa, Central America and Australia).

Global warming is a type of climate change, but it can cause other types of climate change as well, e.g. increased temperatures can lead to increased precipitation.

Glaciers, Sea Ice and Ice Caps would continue to Melt and Sea Level to Rise

- Arctic sea ice has **decreased** by **10-15%** since the **1950s**, and there's been **widespread reduction** of **non-polar glaciers** (e.g. in the Alps). This will continue as temperature rises, and many polar and glacial **habitats** could be **lost**.
- Average global sea level is expected to **rise** by 0.09-0.88 m between 1990 and 2100. This will **flood coastal** and **low lying areas** (e.g. areas of **SE Asia** and islands in the **Pacific** and **Indian Oceans**).

More Extreme Weather Events

- **Storms, floods** and **droughts** are likely to occur **more often** and be **more severe** due to **changes in ocean circulation** and **wind patterns**.
- **Less developed countries** are expected to be **worst affected** as they are **less able** to deal with the impacts.

Climate Change — Causes and Impacts

The Incidence of Some Illnesses and Diseases could Increase

- **More people** are likely to suffer from **heat-related illnesses** (e.g. heat stroke) — especially **very old** and **very young** people.
- **Breathing problems** are likely to **increase** as **air pollution** in **cities rises** (higher temperatures cause an increase in photochemical smog — see p. 152).
- **Disease vectors** (e.g. mosquitoes that carry malaria) may **spread** to **regions currently too cold** to support them.
- **Food-borne illnesses** may **increase** as temperature rises.

Conflicts over Water Resources could Increase

- In some areas **higher temperatures** and **reduced rainfall** would **reduce river flow** and **groundwater**, and cause **reservoirs** to **dry up**.
- In some areas water supply is expected to **decrease** by **10%** by 2050. This will affect hundreds of millions or even billions of people.
- This reduction of water supply means it will become a much more **valuable resource**. There may be increased **conflict** over it.

Patterns of Agriculture would Change

- **Agricultural productivity** (how much food farmers can produce) will **decrease in some areas**. E.g. reduced rainfall and droughts in Africa and Australia may reduce productivity.
- **Agricultural productivity** may **increase in other areas**. E.g. increased temperature and rainfall may increase productivity in North America and Europe.
- There may be **changes** in the **types of crops** grown. Crops that **prefer warmer conditions** (e.g. grapes and melons) could be grown further **north**, and crops that **prefer cooler conditions** (e.g. potatoes) would be less successful in their current locations and produce **lower yields**.
- **Agricultural pests** and **diseases** may **increase** in some areas. E.g. the range of the European Corn Borer (a pest of maize) is shifting northwards due to increased temperatures.

Species Distributions would Change and Biodiversity could Decrease

- The **geographical range** of some species will **change**. E.g. the range of some plants, insects, birds and fish will **shift** towards the **poles**, in line with temperature change, as they try to stay in the type of climate they're suited to. Other ecosystems may be damaged by the **invasion** of **new species**.
- **Some species** will **disappear** from some areas as they're **unable to cope** with **changes in climate**.
- **Some habitats** will be **damaged** or **destroyed**, e.g. polar habitats are being destroyed by sea ice melting, and coral reefs and mangrove swamps are threatened by sea level rise.
- Species that are adapted to living in these areas may become **extinct**.

Global Warming will also have *Impacts* in the *UK*

1) **UK CLIMATE WILL CHANGE**:

   - **Temperature** will **increase**. The increase is expected to be greatest in Southern England, where the average summer temperature is projected to increase by 3.9 °C by 2080.
   - **Winter rainfall** is expected to **increase** in many areas — by up to 35% in parts of the western side of the UK.
   - **Summer rainfall** is expected to **decrease** in many areas — by up to 49% in parts of Southern England.

2) **SEA LEVEL WILL RISE** — sea level is expected to rise by 13-76 cm by 2095. The areas **worst affected** by flooding would be towns and cities on estuaries (e.g. Hull, Cardiff, Portsmouth and London) and **low lying areas near the coast** (e.g. large areas of Norfolk). **Housing** and **agricultural land** may be lost in these places and people may have to **move away**.

3) **DROUGHTS MAY INCREASE** — droughts are expected to be more **frequent** and **intense**, especially in **Southern England**.

4) **PATTERNS OF AGRICULTURE ARE EXPECTED TO CHANGE**:

   - **Temperature increase** and a **longer growing season** may increase **productivity of some crops**, e.g. asparagus, onions, courgettes, peas and beans.
   - **Types of farming** may **shift northwards**. E.g. dairy farming and arable crop farming may increase in the north.
   - New **crops adapted** to **warmer climates** could be grown in **Southern England**, e.g. soya, peaches and grapes.
   - **Reduced rainfall** and **droughts** in **Southern England** would increase the need for irrigation and water storage schemes.

5) **HABITATS WILL CHANGE** — some species have already left their original habitats and moved **north** to find **cooler temperatures** (e.g. the comma butterfly). This can affect **ecosystems** and lead to **species extinction**.

Climate Change — Causes and Impacts

Climate will Change in *Tropical Regions*

You only have to learn about **one** tropical region (see p. 142-143).

Equatorial areas

- **Equatorial areas** are expected to get **hotter**, e.g. temperature in the Amazon basin is predicted to increase by 2-3 °C by 2050. The Amazon basin is likely to receive **less rainfall** overall, and rain may be more **seasonal**.
- This would cause **ecosystems** to change — e.g. large areas of the **Amazon rainforest** may **become savanna** due to **reduced rainfall** during the dry season. Species are expected to become **extinct**, so biodiversity will decrease.
- A longer dry season would **decrease agricultural productivity** and increase the risk of **forest fires**.
- Sea level rise along the Amazon delta would increase **erosion** and threaten **mangrove forests**.

Tropical savannas

- **Tropical savanna** areas are also likely to get hotter, e.g. the average annual temperature in Australia is projected to rise by 0.4-2 °C by 2030. This would result in **higher evapotranspiration** and **drought**.
- **Close** to the **Equator**, rainfall is likely to **increase**. This may cause **flooding** and an increase in **water-borne diseases**, e.g. cholera. However, it may also **increase agricultural productivity**.
- **Further** from the **Equator**, rainfall is likely to **decrease**. This would **increase drought** and result in ecosystem changes, including **extinction** of **savanna species**.
- **Rainfall** is likely to become **more variable**, with more extreme events and flooding during the wet season.
- **Increasing sea level** is likely to flood low-lying areas and increase coastal erosion, while **increased sea temperatures** may damage coral reefs due to coral bleaching (see p. 178).

Monsoon areas

- **Monsoon areas** are expected to get **hotter**, e.g. the average temperature in Bangladesh is projected to increase by 2-4 °C by 2100.
- **Seasons** are expected to become more **pronounced**, e.g. Bangladesh could experience **longer winter droughts**, but **more rain** during the **summer monsoon**.
- Intense rainfall may cause flooding, landslides and crop damage.
- **Tropical cyclones** may **increase** in frequency and **intensity**.
- Higher intensity cyclones would cause stronger **storm surges** and more **flooding**.
- **Sea level rise** will flood many islands and coastal areas. E.g. in Bangladesh sea level is predicted to rise by 30-100 cm by 2100, which would submerge up to 18% of the land surface. Millions of people would have to **migrate** from flooded areas. Mass migration, e.g. from Bangladesh to India, would cause **overcrowding** and **tension** between nations.
- **Agricultural productivity**, e.g. rice production, will **decline** due to loss of land caused by sea level rise.
- Areas that suffer from **increased flooding** would be more vulnerable to illnesses such as **cholera** and **hepatitis**.

Paolo was prepared for rapid sea level rise.

Practice Questions

Q1 List three human activities that cause global warming.

Q2 How will global climate change as a result of global warming?

Q3 Explain why global warming may increase agricultural productivity in North America.

Q4 Give two ways in which global warming is likely to affect the climate of the tropical region you have studied.

Exam Question

Q1 Describe the potential impacts of global warming in the UK. [8 marks]

I thought that switching from °F to °C would reduce global warming...

Global warming is a bit of a misleading name — it's not just about temperatures rising. Learn the specifics of the climate changes that will affect the UK and the tropical region you've studied (equatorial, tropical savanna or monsoon). You won't regret it...

Climate Change — Responses

I bet you're sick of hearing about global warming by now, but guess what — there's more. This 'ere bit's about the responses to climate change. There are things the world can do, things that nations can do, and things you can do too...

Responses to Global Warming can be International

The Kyoto Protocol aimed to reduce emissions...

1) The Kyoto Protocol is an **international agreement** formed in 1997. **190 countries** have joined the agreement, which involves pledging to **monitor** and **reduce** greenhouse gas emissions.

2) The agreement divided the countries into two groups — **developed** and **developing**.

3) **Developed countries** agreed to **cut emissions** (by 5% of their 1990 emissions levels) between 2008 and 2012.

4) **Developing countries** didn't have to cut emissions, but needed to **monitor** and **report** their emissions.

5) One of the incentives for countries to reduce their emissions was the introduction of **carbon credits**. Countries and businesses are given a **limit** on the **emissions** they can produce — if they produce **less** they can **sell** the extra carbon credits, if they produce **more** they need to **buy** more credits.

6) They can also gain credits by helping to **reduce emissions** in developing countries — this encourages developed countries to **invest** in developing countries to help them develop in a **sustainable way**.

...but there were problems with it

1) **Four countries** with **high emissions** (the USA, Australia, China and India) **didn't sign up** for the original agreement. The **USA** and **Australia** felt that signing would affect their **economies** and that the developing countries should have targets **as well**. China and India thought it would slow their **rate of growth**.

2) Australia, India and China have now joined the agreement, but there's still lots of **criticism**. Some people think the targets aren't **high enough**, and others think there's no point if the highest polluters **aren't included** (the USA still hasn't **fully** joined). In addition, countries have **failed** to meet their targets — in many cases emissions are actually **increasing**.

The Kyoto Protocol ends in **2012** and world leaders met in 2009 to reach a **new agreement**. The **Copenhagen Accord** was agreed, with each country allowed to set its **own targets** for cutting emissions (e.g. the USA agreed to cut emissions by 17% compared to 2005 levels). However, the accord is **not legally binding** and there are **no penalties** for countries who miss their targets.

Responses can also be Made at a National Level

In the UK, 73% of electricity is generated by fossil fuels, 17% by nuclear power, 8% by renewable energy sources and 2% from other sources.

Changing the Energy Mix of a Country

- The **energy mix of a country** is the mix of energy sources used to meet its energy needs — e.g. **fossil fuels** (oil, gas and coal), **nuclear power** and **renewable energy** (e.g. hydroelectric and wind power). France gets over three quarters of its energy mix from nuclear power, while the UK gets most of its energy from fossil fuels.

- **Replacing** fossil fuels with nuclear power and renewable energy can help reduce climate change by **reducing** greenhouse gas emissions from **power stations**.

- In the UK, around **40%** of emissions reductions by **2020** will be achieved by changing the energy mix. The aim is to generate **30%** of our electricity from **renewable sources** by **2020**.

- More **offshore wind farms** are being built, several **wave and tidal power projects** are planned, and more electricity is being generated using **solar panels**, **wind turbines** and **biomass burning**.

- The UK government is encouraging **small scale renewable energy projects**, e.g. by **relaxing** planning laws to make it easy for people to install solar panels.

BUT...

- There needs to be more investment in nuclear power and renewable energy before these sources can meet all our **energy needs**, so countries still have to rely on **other forms** of energy, e.g. fossil fuels.

- There are also **environmental problems** associated with nuclear power and renewable energy, e.g. nuclear power creates **dangerous waste**, and tidal power can **disrupt coastal ecosystems**.

An offshore wind farm near Barrow-in-Furness, Cumbria.

Climate Change — Responses

Using New Technologies to Cut Emissions from Power Stations

- **Carbon Capture and Storage (CCS)** is a new technology designed to reduce climate change by **reducing emissions** from **power stations**.
- CCS involves **capturing carbon dioxide** and **transporting it** to places where it can be stored safely, e.g. in deep geological formations.
- CCS has the potential to reduce emissions from power stations by **90%**.

BUT...

- The technology is still at the **developmental stage** and several problems have been identified. CCS **uses fuel** and **increases the cost of energy**. There's also the risk of stored **carbon dioxide leaking**.

CCS could reduce emissions from power stations.

Encouraging Energy Conservation at Home

- Encouraging energy conservation **reduces domestic fuel consumption**. This also **reduces emissions** from power stations, because less energy needs to be produced.
- In the UK, around 15% of emissions reductions by 2020 will be achieved by making homes more energy efficient. Government strategies in the UK include **providing energy efficiency grants** to help people pay for energy saving improvements (e.g. new boilers and insulation).
- **Financial incentives** are also being offered to encourage people to **generate their own electricity** from **renewable sources** (e.g. by installing **solar panels** or a **wind turbine**).
- Homes being sold need an **Energy Performance Certificate** that shows how energy efficient the home is, and how efficient it can be. This helps to make people **more aware** of energy use and conservation.

BUT...

- Energy saving improvements can have a **high initial cost** (but this could be **offset** by **reduced fuel consumption**).
- It's **difficult** to work out how energy efficient some houses are.
- There are regulations **restricting** the improvements that can be made to **listed buildings**.

Reducing Emissions from Transport

- In the UK, around 20% of emissions reductions by 2020 will be achieved by **reducing emissions from transport**. Strategies include **encouraging people** to **buy lower emissions vehicles**, e.g. **road tax** is free for cars emitting up to 100 g CO_2/km, but costs £475 a year for cars emitting over 255 g CO_2/km.
- **Financial incentives** are also being offered to encourage people to buy less polluting **electric** and **hybrid cars**, e.g. a government grant of up to £5000 is available for people buying cars that emit less than 75 g CO_2/km.

BUT...

- There are still lots of **older cars** with **higher emissions** on the roads, which will stay on the roads for many years.
- **Producing** hybrid and electric cars uses complex technologies, which use lots of **energy** and **produce emissions**.

There are also **Local Responses** to **Global Warming**

Recycling Waste

- Recycling waste helps reduce climate change because it usually requires **less energy** to recycle material than to create a product from scratch. It also **reduces landfill waste** (landfills generate greenhouse gases like methane).
- In the UK, **recycling prevents the release of 10-15 million tonnes** of **carbon dioxide** every year. This is the equivalent of taking 3.5 million cars off the road every year.

BUT...

- There are some **problems** associated with recycling schemes. For example, **transporting products** to be recycled **creates transport emissions**. This is why it is important to develop **local recycling facilities**.

Climate Change — Responses

Using Cars Less

- **Using cars less** (e.g. by **walking** or **cycling** more, using **public transport** and **car sharing**) reduces climate change by **reducing transport emissions**.
- The **average car produces 2.7 tonnes** of **carbon dioxide every year** in the UK. Millions of tonnes of carbon dioxide could be saved every year if people walked or cycled journeys of less than 5 miles.

BUT...

- Many people **prefer using a car** to the alternatives, because they feel **safer** in their car, and it is often **faster** and more **convenient**.

With cars going out of fashion, Elena had to find something new to drape herself over.

Buying Local

- **Buying local produce** reduces climate change by **reducing transport emissions**. Many fruits and vegetables are **flown** to the UK, and **aircraft have very high emissions** per mile compared to other methods of transport, e.g. shipping.
- **Heated greenhouses** (used to grow produce out of season) have a **high energy consumption**. Eating **seasonal products** and **importing less food** could save millions of tonnes of carbon dioxide every year.

BUT...

- Many people like to have access to a **variety** of foods **all year round**.

Local responses are mostly carried out by individuals, but governments and councils can encourage them, e.g. by subsidising buses in rural areas, or improving recycling facilities.

Choosing Energy Efficient Appliances

- Energy efficient appliances **reduce fuel consumption**, which **reduces emissions** from power stations because less energy needs to be produced.
- Many **modern appliances** are **50% more efficient** than **older models**. If everyone in the UK upgraded their fridges and freezers it would prevent the release of around 3.7 million tonnes of carbon dioxide every year.

BUT...

- Throwing away old appliances creates lots of **waste**.
- Making new appliances uses **energy**, which increases emissions.
- People may be reluctant to spend **money** on buying new appliances.

Practice Questions

Q1 How does recycling reduce climate change?

Q2 Why might people choose to use cars instead of public transport?

Q3 How does buying local help reduce climate change?

Q4 What are the problems involved in upgrading appliances?

Exam Questions

Q1 Evaluate one or more international responses to climate change. [8 marks]

Q2 'Replacing fossil fuels with renewable energy is the most effective way for the UK to reduce its greenhouse gas emissions.' To what extent do you agree with this statement? [40 marks]

Responses to weight change — use cars less and buy low-cal...

There's a lot to remember on these pages — for your exam you need to know about responses to climate change on all scales. Unfortunately, these responses are stuffed full of information that you'll just have to learn if you want to bag top marks.

Ecosystem Basics

Don't fret — you haven't picked up your biology book by accident. These two pages cover the basics of ecosystems, so don't skip them unless you want to be exceptionally confused by the end of the section.

Make Sure You Know the **Difference** Between an **Ecosystem** and a **Biome**

- An **ECOSYSTEM** is a set of **relationships** between **all** the **organisms** and **non-living factors** in a particular area, e.g. a forest ecosystem includes the **trees**, **animals** and **microorganisms** as well as the **water**, **soil**, **rock** and **air**.
- The organisms that live there are called **biotic factors** and the non-living objects are **abiotic factors**.
- The **organisms** depend on **physical factors** and **each other** to survive, so **relationships** between organisms are **important**.
- Ecosystems **vary in size** — they can be small (e.g. a pond) or large (e.g. a forest, mountainside or ocean).

- A **BIOME** is an area with a distinctive **climate** and **vegetation**, e.g. a tropical rainforest or arctic tundra.
- Biomes can contain **different ecosystems**, e.g. within a tropical grassland biome there could be areas of open woodland, areas of swamp, lakes and grassland plains.
- Biomes usually cover a **large area**, often spanning multiple countries.

Energy Moves Between the Organisms in an Ecosystem

1) **Energy enters** an ecosystem by **photosynthesis** — plants use **energy** from **sunlight** to **grow** and **reproduce**.
2) The energy is **stored** in the **plant** and **passed** up the food chain when the plant is **eaten**.
3) This process continues throughout the **ecosystem** — when one organism eats another it receives the energy from that organism. This means that **energy flows** between all the **organisms** in an **ecosystem**.

Food Chains and Food Webs Show How Energy Moves Through an Ecosystem

1) Each **stage** in a food chain or web is called a **trophic** (feeding) **level**.
2) **Producers** (autotrophs, e.g. **plants**) occupy the **first trophic level**. They make their own food.
3) **Primary consumers** (**herbivores** or **omnivores**) occupy the next level — they **eat producers**.
4) **Secondary consumers** (**carnivores** and **omnivores**) occupy the next level — they **eat consumers**.
5) **Tertiary consumers** (**top carnivores** and **omnivores**) occupy the next level — they **eat consumers**.
6) **Biomass** (the total mass of living matter) **decreases** at each **trophic level** e.g. a **field of dandelions** feeds a **family of rabbits**, which can all be scoffed by **one hungry fox**.

Herbivores eat plants, carnivores eat meat, and omnivores eat plants and meat.

7) **Food chains** tend to over-simplify the relationships — a lot of **consumers** don't just fit in **one trophic level**, e.g. a bird will eat seeds from a plant and also eat the insects that feed on the plant. **Food webs** are more complicated:

Food chains show one way the energy from a producer is passed to a consumer:

Food webs show **multiple food chains** and demonstrate **different ways** energy flows through an ecosystem:

Dead organic matter is produced at every trophic level (e.g. from organisms dying). It's broken down by insects and microorganisms and recycled as nutrients.

Ecosystem Basics

*Some Energy is **Lost** at **Each Level** in a Food Chain*

As you go up the trophic levels in a food chain, the **amount of energy** at each level **decreases**.
Around 90% of energy is lost at each trophic level. Here are some reasons why:

1 Energy lost between **sunlight** and the **autotroph**

Less than 50% of sunlight is actually used in **photosynthesis**, for example:

- Some will fall on areas of the plant that **don't photosynthesise**, e.g. the stem or trunk.
- The plant can only use certain wavelengths of light.

2 Energy lost by the **consumers**

Only about 10% of the energy stored by the **autotrophs** is passed to the **herbivores**, and 10% of the energy stored by the herbivores is passed to the carnivores:

- **Some parts** of the organisms **aren't eaten**, e.g. the **roots**, **bones** or **fur**, and not all of what is eaten is used for energy.
- Some energy is lost as **waste**, e.g. droppings.
- Consumers use some of the **energy** for **movement** and generating **body heat**, so it's not passed to the next level.

***Nutrients** are Constantly being **Recycled** in Ecosystems*

Living organisms need large quantities of **carbon**, **hydrogen**, **oxygen**, **nitrogen** and **sulfur**, among other things. These elements are constantly being **recycled** through **ecosystems** — they're recycled between plants, animals and the atmosphere.

1) Plants take **carbon dioxide** from the **air** and **nutrients** from the **soil**, e.g. **nitrogen**. They use these to create **plant material**.

2) These nutrients get passed along food chains by **feeding**.

3) When plants and animals die they're broken down by **decomposers** (e.g. bacteria). **Nutrients** (e.g. nitrogen) are **returned** to the **soil** to be used again by plants.

4) Plants, animals and decomposers all release **carbon dioxide** back into the air through **respiration**.

Photosynthesis uses carbon dioxide and gives out oxygen — respiration does the opposite.

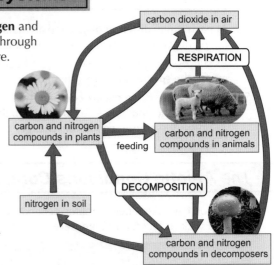

Practice Questions

Q1 What is an ecosystem?

Q2 What is meant by the term 'trophic level'?

Exam Question

Q1 Look at the food web on the right.

Describe how energy is transferred through the food web, and how it is lost.

[7 marks]

I bet Lewis Hamilton has a fair few auto trophies...

Food webs and food chains are the kind of diagrams examiners love. You might be given one to explain in your exam, so make sure you understand them. Remember the arrows show the transfer of energy up the trophic level — in other words, who is eaten by who.

Succession

Leave any surface sitting there for long enough and some plant or other will start colonising it. For your exam you only need to know about one of the ways that this happens, but I'm feeling keen so I've covered four for you here...

Succession is the Process of Ecosystem Change

1) **Succession** is the process by which an **ecosystem changes** over **time**. The **biotic conditions** (e.g. **plant** and **animal life**) change as the **abiotic conditions** (e.g. **water availability**) change.

2) Succession occurs in **stages** called **seres**. There are **two** types of succession:

Primary succession

This happens on land that's been **newly formed** or **exposed**, e.g. where a **volcano** erupts and forms a **new rock surface**.

- The **abiotic conditions** are **harsh**, e.g. there's no soil to **retain water**. **Seeds** and **spores** are blown in by the **wind**.
- The **first species** to colonise the area are called **pioneer species** — this is the **first sere**. Pioneer species can **grow** because they're **specialised** to cope with the harsh conditions, e.g. **marram grass** can grow on sand dunes near the sea because it has **deep roots** to get water and can **tolerate** the salty environment.
- The pioneer species **change** the **abiotic conditions** — they **die** and **decompose**, which forms a **basic soil**.
- This makes conditions **less hostile**, e.g. the basic soil helps to **retain water**, which means **new organisms** can grow. These then die and are decomposed, adding **more** organic material and making the soil **deeper** and **richer in minerals**. This means **larger plants** like **shrubs** can start to grow in the deeper soil, which retains **even more** water.

Secondary succession

Secondary succession happens on land that's been **cleared** of all the **plants**, but where the **soil remains**, e.g. after a **forest fire**. **Secondary succession** happens in the **same way** as primary succession, but because there's already a **soil layer** succession starts at a **later sere** — the pioneer species in secondary succession are **larger plants**, e.g. shrubs.

3) At each stage, **different** plants and animals that are **better adapted** for the improved conditions move in, **out-compete** the plants and animals that are already there, and become the **dominant species** in the ecosystem.

4) As succession goes on, the ecosystem becomes **more complex**. New species move in **alongside** existing species, which means the **species diversity** (the number of **different species** and the **abundance** of each species) tends to **increase**.

5) The **final sere** is the **climax community** — the ecosystem is supporting the **largest** and **most complex** community it can, and the biotic and abiotic factors are **in balance**. This is known as the **climatic climax** and it **won't change** much more — unless the **abiotic conditions change**.

The Abiotic Conditions Control the Type of Community that Develops

Succession can take different routes depending on the **abiotic conditions** at the start of the process. A **lithosere** occurs on exposed rock surfaces, a **psammosere** on sand, a **hydrosere** on water and a **halosere** in saline conditions.

Lithosere example — bare rock to woodland

1) **Pioneer species**, e.g. **lichens**, **colonise** the rocks because they can live with **very little water** and few nutrients. Lichens **break down** rock, which **releases minerals**. As the rock is broken down, its **surface** becomes uneven, which helps to retain **water**.

2) As the rocks get more **damp**, **mosses** begin to grow and **weather** the rock surface. Lichens and mosses **die** and **decompose**, forming a **thin soil**.

3) As the soil **deepens**, **larger plants** that need **more water** move in e.g. **grasses**, **ferns**, **herbs** and **flowering plants**. The soil **gets deeper** as the larger plants die and are decomposed by **bacteria** to form **humus**.

4) **Shrubs**, **ferns** and **small trees** such as **rowan** and **birch** begin to grow. They **out-compete** the smaller plants to become the **dominant** species.

5) Finally, the soil is **deep** and **rich** enough in **nutrients** to support slow-growing **large trees** like **ash** and **oak**. These become the dominant species, and the **climax community** is formed.

The four examples of succession on these pages are all for the temperate climate zone. Different successions occur in different climate zones.

Succession

Psammosere example — bare sand (e.g. coastal sand dune) to woodland

1) Pioneer species colonise the bare sand, e.g. **lyme grass** and **marram grass** have a **high salt tolerance** and leaves that retain **moisture**. The **roots** of these plants **bind** the sand together.

2) The pioneer species **die** and **decompose**, helping to form a **thin soil**. Other species move in, e.g. **sand dune screw moss** and **sand sedge**. At first the soil is very **alkaline** because it contains **shell fragments** and **salt** from seawater.

3) The soil **deepens** and becomes **less alkaline** as more **organic matter forms**. Small plants (e.g. **hawkweed** and **evening primrose**) and larger plants (e.g. **gorse** and **heather**) move in.

4) The soil continues to deepen as larger plants die and decompose. Shrubs and small trees (e.g. **hawthorn** and **elder**) move in and **out-compete** the smaller plants.

5) The soil can eventually **support large trees**. Fast-growing trees (e.g. **pine** and **birch**) move in first, followed by slower growing **ash** and **oak**. These gradually become the **dominant climax species**.

Animals (e.g. rabbits) move in as plant cover increases and their droppings help to improve soil quality.

Hydrosere example — fresh water (e.g. lake) to woodland

1) Pioneer species (e.g. **algae** and floating plants such as **duckweed**) colonise the **water surface**. They die and sink to the bottom, where they accumulate along with other **sediments** (e.g. sediments deposited by rivers).

2) The water gets shallower as sediments and decomposing plant material **accumulate**. Aquatic plants move in, e.g. **elodea** and **starwort**. They are **rooted** in the lake bed and trap and hold **more sediment** on the bottom.

3) The water becomes **very shallow**, and **swamp** and **marsh plants** (e.g. **reeds** and **rushes**) move in. Marsh plants generate lots of leaf litter, which builds up and forms a **wet soil**.

4) Larger plants (e.g. **ferns**) and tree seedlings (e.g. **willow** and **alder**) move in. These plants decrease soil moisture by transpiration, until the soil is no longer water-logged.

5) The **soil deepens** and becomes drier as larger plants die and decompose. This provides suitable conditions for **large climax tree species**, e.g. oak and beech, which become dominant.

Halosere example — salt water (e.g. estuary) to woodland

1) Pioneer species that can tolerate being submerged in saltwater, e.g. **eelgrass** and **cordgrass**, colonise the **intertidal zone** (the bit of the beach exposed at low tide). Their roots **trap mud** brought in by **tidal water**, causing it to accumulate.

2) Pioneer species die and **decompose**, forming a **thin soil**. This **accumulation** of decaying material and mud makes the ground level **rise** above all but the **highest tides**, so less salt water reaches the soil. Species that can tolerate a bit of salt water move in (e.g. **sea lavender** and **sea aster**). Their roots **trap** and **hold more sediment**.

3) The ground level continues to rise and soil **deepens** as more decomposing plant material builds up. Shrubs and small trees (e.g. **rowan** and **alder**) move in and **out-compete** the smaller plants.

4) The **soil deepens** further and **large climax tree species** (e.g. **oak** and **ash**) become dominant.

Practice Questions

Q1 What is the difference between primary and secondary succession?

Q2 What is a pioneer species?

Q3 What is meant by the term 'climatic climax'?

Exam Question

Q1 Describe and explain the characteristic features of one example of a primary plant succession. [8 marks]

I'll have a chicken korma, pilau rice and a vegetable psammosere please...

Each sere follows a similar pattern from bare surface to climatic climax, but it's remembering the details that will get you top marks in your exam — you need to talk about specific species and the abiotic changes they cause, and use the scientific terms correctly.

Succession

When an ecosystem reaches a climatic climax, it settles down and just gets on with life. That is, until humans come along and mess with things, and then succession can take an unexpected turn...

You Need to Know the Characteristics of the UK Climatic Climax

The UK climatic climax is a **temperate deciduous woodland** biome. It has these characteristics:

The **canopy layer** is made up of **trees** (e.g. oak, elm and beech) that grow to around **30 m** tall. These are the dominant species.

Trees grow wider at the crown (top) and have **broad** leaves.

The **trees** are **deciduous**, which means they **lose** their **leaves in autumn**. This **reduces water loss** from leaves in the winter months, when roots struggle to take **water** from the **frozen soil** and when **low light** slows the rate of **photosynthesis**.

Epiphytes, e.g. **lichens** and **mosses**, grow on the **trunks** and **branches** of trees in **all layers**.

— 30m

CANOPY LAYER

— 20m

SHRUB LAYER

— 5m

HERB LAYER

At the **shrub layer** there are **smaller trees**, such as hazel, rowan and hawthorn. They're about **5 to 20 m** tall and tend to be fairly shade-tolerant.

At **ground level**, **mosses** and **leaf litter** create a thick carpet on the forest floor. This is broken down by **decomposers**, e.g. **bacteria**, living in the soil. This returns the **nutrients** to the soil and keeps it **fertile**.

If enough light gets through, the undergrowth can be **dense** with shade-tolerant plants, e.g. **grasses** and **ferns**. **Flowering plants** (e.g. **bluebells**) can grow on the forest floor in the spring, because the trees have not yet **re-grown** all their leaves. This period of time before the canopy develops fully is called the **spring window**.

Human Activity Can Stop or Deflect Succession

Human activities can **stop succession** or **redirect** it towards a different climax. When this happens a climax that's different to the normal **climatic climax** forms — this is called a **plagioclimax**. For example:

Human activity	Why it's carried out	Why it prevents the climatic climax being reached	Characteristics of the resulting plagioclimax
Deforestation	To get **wood** for **timber** or **fuel**, or to make **space** for **farming**.	Removing trees **reduces soil quality** because it takes nutrients out of the ecosystem that would otherwise be returned to the soil by **leaf fall** or **tree death**. **Fewer** types of **plants** can **grow** in the poor soil.	**Hardy shrubs**, e.g. heather.
Animal grazing	Domesticated **animals** kept for **meat** (or other **products**) often **graze** for their food.	**Small plants** and saplings are **eaten** or **destroyed** by trampling before they get a chance to grow.	**Fast** growing **grasses** and **plants** (e.g. dandelions). Very few trees and shrubs.
Clearance by fire	To **clear** an area for **farming**, to **control** the **plants** growing in an area, or to **improve** the **soil** in an area (ash is a fertiliser).	All the **plants** are **destroyed**, and the **fastest growing** types of plants **re-colonise** the area.	**Fast-growing plants**, whose roots aren't damaged by fire, e.g. heather.
Afforestation (planting trees)	To plant trees for **timber**.	The **trees** in an area may be **cleared** to make way for the **new saplings**. Only **one species** is planted and managed (monoculture), so this species **dominates**.	In **managed areas** like forestry plantations **humans control** the **plagioclimax**, e.g. a planted pine forest.

Succession

Plagioclimax Case Study — North York Moors: Heather Moorland

Heather moorland is an area of **open country** mostly covered in **heather**. It's a **plagioclimax** because it's created by human activity. The **North York Moors** are the **largest area** of heather moorland in England, covering **1436 km²** of land.

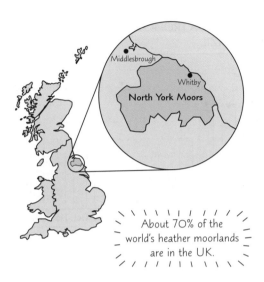

About 70% of the world's heather moorlands are in the UK.

The moors were **created** by human activities:

1) The moors used to be an **oak forest** (a temperate deciduous woodland biome), where only **small amounts** of **heather** grew at ground level.

2) Up to about **5000 years ago** people hunted and gathered in the woodland for food. As the population grew, people began to **clear** the most fertile areas of **woodland** to keep animals and **grow crops**.

3) From around **4000 to 2000 years ago**, the remaining woodland was cleared. Clearing trees **reduced soil quality** — when an area was no longer fertile enough for farming, people moved on.

4) Few types of plants were able to grow in the **poor quality soil**. Heather is a **hardy shrub** — it was able to grow, and it flourished because there was **less competition** from other plants.

5) Around **1000 years ago**, sheep **grazing** became a major form of agriculture in North Yorkshire. This **prevented the re-growth** of other plants (as saplings were eaten or trampled before they got a chance to mature), which **reduced** the level of **competition**. Heather is **fast growing** so it was able to cope with being grazed, and soon it dominated the area.

The moors are also **maintained** by human activities:

1) The **North York Moors** are a **national park** and the moorland is carefully maintained for **environmental** and **economic** reasons. The moors are an **important habitat** for **rare plants**, e.g. sundew and common spotted orchid, and **birds**, e.g. merlin and golden plover. The moors are also used for **sheep grazing** and **grouse shooting**.

2) Without **active management** the heather moorland would eventually return to a **temperate deciduous forest**, and the **moorland plants** and **animals** would **lose their habitat** and **move on** or **die out**.

3) Although **sheep grazing** helps to maintain the moorland, **controlled burning** is the primary management technique. A few sections are burned each year in an **8-15 year rotation**. If left alone heather becomes **tough** and **woody** and eventually collapses, but burning **encourages** new heather shoots to **grow**, which provides better grazing for sheep and grouse. Burning also **destroys less fire-resistant plants**, which helps to ensure that the heather remains **dominant**.

Heather moorlands in Yorkshire.

©iStockphoto.com/Robert Crum

Practice Questions

Q1 Name the three layers in the temperate deciduous woodland biome.

Q2 What is a plagioclimax?

Q3 Give three ways in which human action can prevent a climatic climax being reached.

Exam Question

Q1 With reference to one plagioclimax you have studied, explain how it was created, and how and why it is maintained.

[10 marks]

A plagioclimax on both your houses...

Ecosystems are made of pretty stern stuff — you can burn them down, flood them out or plant trees all over them and they just keep coming back for more. It's a bit like you and this revision guide really, you just can't keep away (because it's so great, obviously).

Tropical Ecosystems — Characteristics

You need to know about one tropical biome. The next few pages cover tropical rainforests — if you've covered another biome in a tropical region in class, dig out your notes and have a look at them instead.

The **Climate** in **Tropical Rainforests** is **Hot** and **Wet** All Year

1) Tropical equatorial rainforests have a distinctive climate.

2) It's hot (mean monthly **temperature** is generally between **20-28 °C** and only varies by a few degrees over the year). This is because tropical rainforests are found near the **equator**, where the sun is **overhead all year** round.

3) **Rainfall** is **high all year round**, around 2000 mm per year. It rains every day (usually in the afternoon) because the high temperature creates **convectional rainfall**:

- The sun **warms** the ground, which conducts this heat to the air above and **evaporates** surface water.

- The **warm air** can hold lots of **water vapour**.

- The warm, wet air **rises** — and as it rises it **cools**.

- The cooler air can hold **less water vapour**, so water condenses to form clouds and then **rain**.

4) The **soil moisture budget** (the balance between water inputs and outputs in the soil) is high, because **precipitation** is higher than **potential evaporation**.

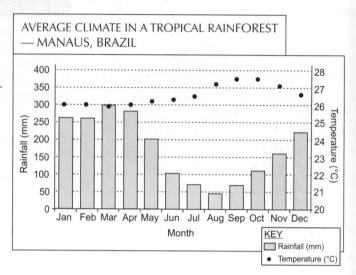

AVERAGE CLIMATE IN A TROPICAL RAINFOREST — MANAUS, BRAZIL

KEY
▢ Rainfall (mm)
● Temperature (°C)

Tropical Rainforests have **Four Layers** of **Vegetation**

Tropical rainforests have a **layered structure**. Different amounts of **sunlight** reach the **different levels** of vegetation. The **trees** have differently **shaped crowns** to absorb **as much light** as they can.

The **canopy layer** is a **continuous** layer of **trees** around **30 m** high. It absorbs about **80%** of **incident light** (direct sunlight that hits the leaves) and **shades** the rest of the forest.

The **tallest trees** are called **emergents**. They can reach around **40 m** and poke out of the main canopy layer. They have **straight trunks** and **widely spaced branches** only at their **crown** where **most light** reaches them. This makes them look **umbrella-shaped**. The emergents receive the **most direct light** of all the layers in the rainforest.

The **shrub layer** is nearest the ground at around **10 m** high. **Only 5%** of **direct light** reaches this layer, so shrubs have very **large, broad leaves** to absorb as much of the **available light** as they can.

Trees in the **undercanopy** layer are about **half the height** of the canopy layer.

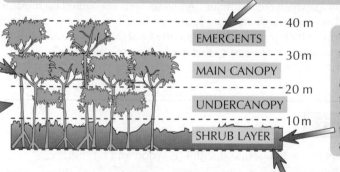

— 40 m
EMERGENTS
— 30 m
MAIN CANOPY
— 20 m
UNDERCANOPY
— 10 m
SHRUB LAYER

Rainforest soils are known as **latosols**. They are **very nutrient poor** because:

1) Although there is a constant supply of new **leaf litter** and **dead organic matter** onto the soil surface, it is broken down **very quickly** because the **warm, wet climate** is ideal for micro-organisms.

2) The growing season continues all year, so as soon as **dead organic matter** is broken down the nutrients are **re-absorbed** by plants. This means that few nutrients remain in the soil.

3) Nutrients are also **leached** down the soil column by heavy rainfall.

There is a **thin layer** of nutrients in the **top layer** of soil, where organic matter is **decaying**. Trees make the most of this by keeping their **roots** very close to the **soil surface**.

Tropical Ecosystems — Characteristics

The *Organisms* that Live There are *Adapted* to the *Abiotic Conditions*

PLANT ADAPTATIONS

1) Plants are **adapted** to the **heavy rainfall** — they have thick, waxy leaves with **pointed tips** (called **drip-tips**). The drip-tips channel the water so it **runs off** quickly to prevent **fungi** and **bacteria** growing on the leaves.

2) Some plants, e.g. Anthurium, have leaves that **rotate** to follow the sun, so they can absorb as much **light** as possible.

3) Tree trunks **only** have **branches** and **leaves** at the top of the canopy where they can absorb **sunlight**. They **grow quickly** to reach the sunlight. Plants in the lower layers have **broad leaves** to maximise **photosynthesis**.

4) Tall trees have big roots called **buttress roots** to keep them upright.

5) The trees are **deciduous** — they **drop** their **leaves** throughout the year because there is **no winter season**. This means they can keep on growing **all year** round.

6) **Lianas** root in the soil and **climb** up trees, while **epiphytes** like orchids and bromeliads grow **on the trees**. These adaptations help plants to reach the **light**.

7) Organisms such as bacteria and fungi are adapted to take **nutrients** from **dead organic matter**. There's lots of dead organic matter in the rainforest because of **high rates** of leaf fall. In return, these organisms make **nutrients** (e.g. **carbon** and **nitrogen**) **available** to the **other organisms** in the ecosystem. The **rainforest nutrient cycle** depends on these species **recycling nutrients**, because the quality of the **soil** is so **poor**.

Buttress roots of the Santinay tree.

When organisms support one another and depend on the existence of the other to survive it is called a symbiotic relationship.

ANIMAL ADAPTATIONS

Smoky and Mr Jump had definitely drawn the short straw in their symbiotic relationships.

1) Many animals are adapted to living in the **canopy** because there's plenty of food there (e.g. **plants** and **fruits**). For example, **red-eyed tree frogs** have **suction cups** on their toes to help them climb trees, and **flying squirrels**, **flying geckos** and **flying lemurs** have **flaps of skin** that they use for **gliding** between trees. These adaptations also help them to **escape predators**.

2) **Jaguars**, **sloths** and **vampire bats** are **nocturnal** — they sleep through the day and are active during the night. This means they can **save energy** by hunting and feeding at night when it's **cooler**.

3) **Camouflage** is an important way of **avoiding predation** for some animals, e.g. **leaf-tailed geckos** are the same colour and texture as tree bark. **Predators** are also camouflaged to help them **hunt**, e.g. tigers' stripes make them less visible in the shadows.

4) Some animals are adapted to the **low light** conditions in the undercanopy. **Tapirs** and **anteaters** have **excellent senses** of hearing and smell, so they can **detect predators** without **seeing** them.

5) Many **rainforest** animals can **swim**. This allows them to **cross river channels** and cope with **flooding** of the forest floor. For example, **pond turtles** have **webbed feet** to help them move through water.

Practice Questions

Q1 Briefly describe the climate of a tropical rainforest.

Q2 What are the four layers of vegetation in a tropical rainforest?

Q3 Name one plant that is adapted to living in the rainforest, and explain how it is adapted.

Exam Question

Q1 Explain how climate affects the organisms living in a tropical region that you have studied. [10 marks]

Very few species in the rainforest are adapted to exam conditions...

All these adaptations are certainly very clever, but no matter how webbed your feet are or how good your hearing is, you won't do well in your exam unless you take a bit of time to learn all the snazzy ways that plants and animals cope with life in the jungle.

Tropical Ecosystems — Human Activity

Rainforests are one of the most important biomes on Earth — they produce oxygen, provide habitats for countless species and they're a great place to make a nature documentary. But human activity is a serious threat in all sorts of ways.

Deforestation *is the* Main Threat *to* Tropical Rainforests

There are lots of reasons why rainforests are chopped down:

Small scale farming — trees are cleared to set up small **subsistence farms**. Often the "slash and burn" technique is used — **vegetation** is **cut down** and left to dry, then **burnt**. Increasing **populations** mean more forest is being cleared.

Cattle farming — forest is cleared to make room for **cattle grazing**.

Commercial agriculture — trees are felled for planting **crops** like **palm oil** and soya.

Other — for example, land is cleared for **mineral extraction** (e.g. of gold and iron ore) and for **new settlements**. Building **dams** to generate **hydroelectric power** floods large areas of forest.

Commercial logging — wood is used for **timber, pulp** and **paper**. **Road building** for logging also makes new areas of forest accessible for **agriculture**.

Deforestation *has* Environmental*,* Social *and* Economic *Impacts*

ENVIRONMENTAL

1) **Deforestation** causes **habitat loss**. This **reduces biodiversity** — if organisms can't **move** or **adapt** they may **become endangered** or **extinct** (e.g. in **Brazil** the number of **endangered species** grew from **218** in **1989** to **628** in **2008**).

2) Deforestation causes increased **surface run-off** and **flooding**. In **deforested areas** there is no tree canopy to intercept rainfall, so more water reaches the ground surface. There is too much **water** to soak into the soil. Instead the **water** moves to rivers as **surface run-off**, which increases the risk of **flooding**.

3) Deforestation degrades the **rainforest soil**. Without **roots** to **hold the soil** together, heavy rain **washes away** the **nutrient rich** top layer of soil.

4) Deforestation **removes nutrients** from the ecosystem. Most of the nutrients in the rainforest are **stored** in the trees and plants. When these are removed, nutrients are **lost**. There is also less **leaf litter**, so humus isn't formed. These changes mean the soil cannot support **new growth**.

5) Deforestation reduces the **rate** of **evapotranspiration** (see p. 150) — this means less water vapour reaches the atmosphere, **fewer clouds form** and **rainfall** is **reduced**. This means there's an increased risk of **drought**.

6) **Deforestation** is a major cause of global warming. Trees **remove** CO_2 from the atmosphere and store it, so fewer trees means more atmospheric CO_2, which enhances the greenhouse effect (see p. 156).

SOCIAL

1) **Quality of life** for some local people improves as there are **more jobs**.

2) The **traditional livelihoods** of some local people are **destroyed** — deforestation can cause the loss of the **plants** and **animals** that they rely on to make a living. For example, **Brazilian rubber tappers** have lost their livelihoods as **rubber trees** have been **cut down**.

3) Some **native tribes** are **forced to move** when their land is cleared, e.g. the **Guarani** tribe in **Brazil** were evicted so their land could be used for **cattle ranching** and **sugar plantations**.

4) Local people are at **risk** because they're not **immune** to **western diseases** introduced by incomers. E.g. the population of the **Nukak** people in the rainforest of the **Amazon basin** has been more than **halved** since **1988**, after outsiders brought in **flu** and **malaria**.

5) There can be **conflict** between native people, landowners, mining companies and logging companies over **use of land**. In **Peru** more than 30 **native people** were **killed** in 2009 in riots over **rainforest destruction**.

ECONOMIC

1) Logging, farming and mining **create jobs**, e.g. at least **50 000 people** are employed in **gold mining** in Peru.

2) A lot of money is made from selling **timber, mining** and commercial **farming**. E.g. in 2008, Brazil made **$6.9 billion** from **cattle trading**.

3) In the long term, deforestation destroys the **resources** that countries depend on, e.g. timber.

Tropical Ecosystems — Human Activity

Humans are Damaging Tropical Rainforests in Other Ways too

OVERHUNTING

- **Indigenous people** living in the rainforest have always hunted and fished for their **own use**. For many people living in the rainforest, meat from wild animals (**bushmeat**) is an **important** part of their diet.

- As populations **increase**, there is a higher demand for bushmeat.

- Hunting is becoming **commercialised**, e.g. people working in the logging industry have access to **weapons** and **transport**. This means they are **equipped** to hunt and take bushmeat to towns outside the forest **to sell**.

POACHING

- Poaching is when **wild animals** and **plants** are taken or killed **illegally**, e.g. for food or as pets.

- Tropical rainforests are home to a huge variety of animals. Many of these species are attractive to poachers because their **skins**, **tusks** and other body parts are **valuable** for sale as **ornaments** or **medicines**.

- Poaching is a big problem in many areas. For example in the Bouba N'Djida conservation reserve in Cameroon **200 elephants** (half the population in the reserve) were killed for their ivory in January 2012.

CLIMATE CHANGE

1) **Climate change** can severely impact tropical rainforests. In some areas **temperature** is increasing and **rainfall** is decreasing, which leads to **drought**. The **Amazon** had **severe droughts** in **2005** and **2010** — the worst in 100 years.

2) **Plants** and **animals** living in tropical rainforests are adapted to **moist conditions**, so many species die in dry weather. **Frequent** or **long periods** of drought could lead to **extinction** of some species. **Drought** can also lead to **forest fires**, which can **destroy** large areas of forest.

3) Scientists predict that a **4 °C** temperature rise could **kill 85%** of the Amazon rainforest.

Poaching and Overexploitation Impact Biodiversity

1) **Poaching** and **overexploitation** (overhunting and overfishing) leads to the **decline** and **extinction** of some species, which reduces biodiversity (see p. 178). For example:

   In Malaysia the tiger, Malayan tapir, Asian elephant and clouded leopard have all become **endangered** as a result of **poaching**.

A clouded leopard.

2) Many organisms are **highly adapted** to their environment and **rely** on symbiotic relationships for survival (see p. 169). This means that the **loss** of a **species** can impact **other species** and the ecosystem as a **whole**. For example:

   The **brazil nut** is an important food source for the **agouti** (a rodent native to Central America) — the agouti breaks open the hard seed pod to eat the nut inside. Sometimes the agouti bury the nuts and forget about them — these **germinate** and **grow**, which is only possible because the nut has been removed from its **thick pod**. If the agouti became **extinct** the brazil nut would be **severely affected**.

Practice Questions

Q1 Give four causes of deforestation.

Q2 Give two environmental impacts of deforestation.

Q3 What effect might climate change have on rainforests?

Exam Question

Q1 Assess the impacts of human activity in a biome that you have studied. [10 marks]

Why is it hard to play cards in the jungle? There are too many cheetahs...

Wow, we humans really aren't doing the rainforest any favours. The stuff on these pages can be pretty disheartening, but you still need to learn it. Make sure your know all the different human activities in the rainforest and their impacts. Luckily there are some solutions to these problems so it's not all doom and gloom — turn over to the next page to find out more...

Tropical Ecosystems — Sustainable Management

These two pages are packed with great ideas about how we can make the most of the rainforests without destroying them. Unfortunately carrying out these ideas isn't always as straightforward as it sounds...

There are Ways to Make **Human Activity** More **Sustainable**

1) It's important to **conserve** tropical rainforests in order to protect the **environment**, enable **native people** to survive and preserve **renewable resources** (p. 179).

2) However, many **people** living in tropical rainforests **rely** directly on them for **food** and **shelter**. In addition, many **developing countries** depend on **resources** produced from the **rainforest** or from **deforested land** (e.g. agriculture, logging, mining) to boost their **economies** and fund **development**.

3) Rainforests need to be managed in a way that's **sustainable**. Sustainability is about **balancing** social, economic and environmental needs so people **today** can get the things they need, **without stopping** people in the **future** from getting what they need. There are lots of ways this can be done.

Deforestation can be **Managed More Sustainably**

Selective Logging

1) Only **some trees** (e.g. just the oldest ones) are **felled** — most are left standing.

2) This is **less damaging** to the forest than felling **all the trees** in an area. If **only a few trees** are taken from each area the **forest structure** is kept — the canopy is still there and the soil isn't exposed. This means the forest is able to **regenerate**.

3) **Dragging** felled trees **out** of the **forest** using **horses** or removing them with **helicopters** is less damaging than using heavy lorries.

Replanting

1) **New trees** are planted to replace the ones that are **cut down**. For example, **Peru** plans to replant more than **100 000 km²** of forest before 2018.

2) It's important that the **same types of tree** are planted that were cut down, so that the **variety of trees** is kept for the future.

3) However, these projects can be very **expensive**. They tend to be used more in **developed countries**, where more funds are available for conservation. For example, in **Australia** replanting projects are taking place in **Queensland**.

4) For example, Greenpeace sponsor schemes in **Papua New Guinea**, where landowners are trained to select, fell and transport trees with as **little damage** to the surrounding **environment** as possible. It's estimated that these projects give local people **ten times more profit** than **commercial logging** operations.

5) However, **selective logging** can still **damage** the rainforest:

   • When a **single** tree falls it can damage as many as **30 others**.

   • **Selective logging** can cause a **patchy canopy**, which doesn't give the same **protection** to the soil as a **full canopy**.

Ecotourism can Benefit the **Economy** and the **Environment**

1) Ecotourism is tourism that **doesn't harm** the **environment** and benefits **local people**.

2) Only **small numbers** of **visitors** go to an area at a time, and staff and visitors are encouraged to **minimise** environmental impact by, for example, **conserving water** and disposing of **waste properly** to prevent **pollution**.

3) It provides a source of **income** for **local people**, e.g. they act as guides, provide accommodation and transport. It also raises **awareness** of conservation issues in tropical rainforests, which can bring **funding** for rainforest **conservation**.

4) When local people are employed in tourism they **don't have to log** or **farm** to make **money**. If a **country's** economy relies on **ecotourism**, there's an **incentive** to **conserve** the environment.

5) In some places ecotourism has been very successful, e.g. in **Costa Rica** ecotourism brings in about US$1.6 million a year and provides jobs for local people. As a result of ecotourism, **25%** of the country is **protected** from development.

6) However, **ecotourism** does **not necessarily** help with the development of the **local community** or the **host country**:

   • **Ecotourism** is often run by companies in the home countries of the visitors, so only a **small amount** of the money is actually **received** in the **host country**.

   • Many jobs in tourism are **menial** and low-paid.

Ecotourism lodges are designed to have a low environmental impact.

Tropical Ecosystems — Sustainable Management

Areas of Rainforest can be Legally Protected

Environmental Law

1) **Environmental laws** can help **protect rainforests**. For example:
   - Laws that **ban** the use of wood from forests that are not managed **sustainably**.
   - Laws that **ban excessive logging**.
   - Laws that control **land use**, e.g. the **Brazilian Forest Code** says that landowners have to keep 50-80% of their land as forest.
2) However, enforcing these laws can be difficult — it's hard to monitor **large areas** with **scattered populations**.

Protection

1) Many countries have set up **national parks** and **nature reserves** to protect rainforests. For example, the **Central Amazon Conservation Complex** in Brazil (see p. 182) is a UNESCO World Heritage Site.
2) Within national parks and nature reserves, **damaging activities** such as logging, hunting and poaching can be **monitored** and **prevented**. **Local people** can be employed as rangers to enforce the restrictions. This provides them with jobs and money, and educates them about the **importance of conservation**, so they're less likely to **overexploit** the rainforest's **resources**.
3) However, it's difficult to **enforce** restrictions, particularly over **large areas** of **dense rainforest**. Many of the people living in the rainforest depend on the rainforest for their **livelihood**, so unless they can make money in another way they will continue to **exploit** its resources.

The International Community Can Help Rainforest Conservation

Reducing Demand for Hardwood

1) **Hardwood** is wood from **certain tree species**, e.g. mahogany and teak. The wood is used to make things like **furniture**.
2) There's a high **demand** for hardwood in more **developed countries**, which means that some **tropical hardwood trees** are becoming **rarer**.
3) Some richer countries are trying to **reduce demand** so fewer trees are cut down.
4) Strategies to reduce demand include charging lots of tax on **imported hardwood** or **banning its sale**.
5) Some countries with tropical rainforests also **ban** logging of hardwood species. E.g. **Brazil banned** mahogany logging in **2001**, and **seizes timber** from illegal logging companies.

Reducing Debt

1) A lot of tropical rainforests are in **less developed countries**.
2) Less developed countries often **borrow money** from richer countries or organisations (e.g. the World Bank) to fund **development schemes** or to **cope with emergencies** like floods.
3) This money has to be paid back, with **interest**.
4) These countries often allow **industrial activities** in rainforests to help to pay back the debt.
5) Debt can be **cancelled** by countries or organisations. This would mean countries wouldn't have to rely on exploiting the rainforests, so they could be **conserved** for the future.
6) However, a system is needed to make sure the money is spent on **conservation**. In a **conservation swap** part of a country's debt is paid off by someone else in **exchange** for investment in **conservation**. For example, in 2008 the **USA** reduced **Peru's debt** by $25 million in exchange for conserving its rainforest.

Practice Questions

Q1 What is ecotourism?
Q2 Give three ways that environmental law can help protect rainforests.
Q3 Give two strategies that can reduce the demand for hardwood.

Exam Question

Q1 Discuss methods of sustainable management and their effectiveness in a biome that you have studied. [10 marks]

Conversation swap — you talk about ducks, I'll talk about biscuits...

That word 'sustainable' keeps popping up all over the place — it seems to be the answer to everything. If you manage your revision sustainably you'll do well in your exams now, whilst preserving exam success for future generations. Or something.

Urban Ecosystems

The Big Smoke. Concrete jungle. The Bright Lights. Cities don't sound like they'd be very comfortable places for wildlife to set up shop. But urban areas, and the areas surrounding the city, can be a home to loads of plants and animals.

The **Expansion** of **Urban Areas** Creates **New Niches**

An organism's '**niche**' is its **role** in an **ecosystem** — it includes its habitat, what it lives off and what it's eaten by.
As a city gets bigger, and the urban ecosystem gets more complicated, there are **more niches** for organisms to occupy.
Some examples of organisms and their **urban niches** include:

- **Plants** growing in **cracks** in the pavement, on **wasteland** and in **gardens**.
  They're eaten by **insects**, **mammals** and **birds**.
- Invertebrates such as **woodlice** living **under paving stones** and in rubble.
  They eat dead plant material and provide a food source for **small mammals** and **birds**.
- **Birds** (e.g. herring gulls) living near **waste dumps** feed on human food waste.

The **Growth** of **Urban Areas** Supports **Small-scale Ecosystems**

Urban areas are home to lots of different **small-scale ecosystems** or '**distinctive ecologies**'. For example:

Urban Gardens and Parks

1) Gardens and parks have a large variety of plants (e.g. **grass**, **flowers**, **shrubs** and **trees**). Gardeners increase **biodiversity** by planting both native and exotic species.
2) Lots of **invertebrates** (e.g. insects, slugs and bees) live in or feed off the plants.
3) Birds feed on **invertebrates** and **plant seeds**, and **nest** in shrubs and trees.
4) Some gardens and parks have **ponds**. Aquatic insects, fish and amphibians (e.g. **frogs** and **newts**) live in these.
5) **Mammals** (e.g. **squirrels** and **hedgehogs**) live in or visit urban gardens and parks.

Exotic species are plants and animals that have been introduced to an area.

Sports fields

1) Sports fields are **dominated** by **grass** because they're mowed, but there are also small plants (e.g. **daisies** and **dandelions**).
2) Lots of invertebrates (e.g. **insects**, **spiders**, **worms** and **butterflies**) live off the plants.
3) **Birds** visit to feed on seeds and insects.

Roads

1) **Plants** grow by the roadside. Cars carry seeds to **verges**, and **exhaust fumes** are rich in nitrogen, which boosts **growth**.
2) Vegetation is often **managed**. **Mowing reduces** biodiversity, but **planting** trees as noise screens or flowers to make the road more attractive can **increase** biodiversity. The plants support **invertebrates** (e.g. insects and butterflies).
3) **Birds** often **nest** in the vegetation. Birds of prey may **hunt** along the roadside, and carrion birds (e.g. crows) **scavenge**.
4) Insects, birds and mammals feed by the roadside and some animals use the verges to **travel** between different areas. This is called a **wildlife corridor**.

Roads and railways are routeways. Routeways are man-made paths and tracks that host ecosystems.

Railways

1) Many different **plants** are found along railways (e.g. **Oxford ragwort** and **clover**) because trains bring seeds from a wide area as they travel.
2) Patches of **wetland plants** (e.g. **rushes**) grow along the sides of the railway. This is because railway beds **drain water** away from the tracks, creating mini wetlands.
3) **Hardy shrubs** (e.g. **gorse**, **hawthorn** and **brambles**) grow at the side of the tracks. This is because **railway companies** cut vegetation back, and these shrubs **grow back quickly**.
4) The variety of plants supports lots of different **invertebrates**, which act as food for **birds**.
5) Lots of **mammals** live along the railway (e.g. **mice**, **hedgehogs** and **badgers**). They feed on plants, invertebrates or smaller mammals. Railways are **fenced off**, so animals are rarely disturbed, and they can use the railways as **wildlife corridors**.

Urban Ecosystems

Urban Growth *Affects Ecosystems* in the *Rural/Urban Fringe*

1) The '**rural/urban fringe**' is where an **urban area** meets a **rural** area.

2) It has a variety of **land uses** — e.g. **residential** (housing estates), **commercial** (out of town shopping centres), **industrial** (factories), **agricultural** (farmland), **recreational** (golf courses, nature reserves), and **routeways** (roads, railways).

3) The variety of land uses means there's a **variety of ecosystems**. Both **rural ecosystems** (e.g. woodland, grassland, farmland) and **urban ecosystems** (e.g. gardens, sports fields, routeways) can be found in the rural/urban fringe.

4) As urban areas **grow**, ecosystems in the rural/urban fringe are affected:

- As the **population** of urban areas increases there is often **new development** in the rural/urban fringe, which can destroy ecosystems. E.g. a higher demand for **water** might mean that grassland is **flooded** to create a **reservoir**.

- Rural ecosystems can be **broken up** by new developments. For example, new developments may gradually surround a wood, **cutting it off** from other rural areas. This can **separate populations** of organisms from each other, and from important feeding grounds.

> The impact of new development can be reduced by greenbelts (land around an urban area that is protected from building and development). These can connect ecosystems and act as wildlife corridors.

- Increased human populations cause more **air** and **water pollution**, which can damage ecosystems. E.g. **water pollution** from industrial or domestic waste **reduces biodiversity** in water courses, which can affect bird populations because it reduces their food supply.

- Lots of people **visit** the rural/urban fringe to do **recreational activities** (e.g. nature walks, mountain bike trails). Visitors can disrupt ecosystems by **disturbing wildlife** and **increasing soil erosion** along paths and trails. Some visitors cause more serious problems:

  - **dropping litter** and **fly-tipping** (dumping big bits of rubbish, e.g. mattresses) — animals and birds can be injured or killed if they get trapped in pieces of litter.

  - **destroying wildlife** — e.g. picking flowers means their seeds are not distributed, so the plant can't reproduce.

  - **vandalism** — e.g. knocking down dry stone walls can disturb birds' nest sites.

  - **starting fires** — e.g. barbecues can start accidental forest fires which damage large areas of woodland.

Cheryl was starting to regret asking the hairdresser for a rural/urban fringe.

5) Some developments can create **new** ecosystems, e.g. the creation of a **wetland** on a **derelict industrial site**. Others have a **positive effect** on existing ecosystems, e.g. the creation of a **wildlife trail** that preserves the ecosystem along an **old railway line**.

Practice Questions

Q1 What is a niche?

Q2 Give three examples of organisms and their urban niches.

Q3 Describe one small-scale ecosystem that could be found in an urban area.

Q4 What is a wildlife corridor?

Q5 Give four land uses that are typically found in the rural/urban fringe.

Exam Questions

Q1 Describe the distinctive ecologies of routeways and explain how they support wildlife. [8 marks]

Q2 Outline the impacts of urbanisation on ecosystems in the rural/urban fringe. [8 marks]

I found a small-scale ecosystem after I didn't brush my teeth for a week...

Think of an ecological niche as what an organism does for a job. Instead of being a butcher, baker or candlestick-maker, an organism's niche is more about the role it plays within its ecosystem and how it being there is important for other species in the ecosystem. My niche is to make a marvellous revision guide so you can pass your exams — I know *sigh* I'm just give, give, give...

Urban Ecosystems

Introduce a species of spider to the new environment of your mum's living room to see these pages in action. No, don't really...

The **Introduction** of **New Species** in Urban Areas Can **Cause Havoc**

1) **Introduced species** (also called **exotic** or **non-native** species) are organisms living in an ecosystem that's not their natural home. The introduction of new species can be **planned** (deliberate) or **unplanned** (accidental).

2) In the UK, species have been **deliberately introduced** for lots of reasons, for example:

- **Farming** — e.g. wheat was introduced from the Middle East as a food crop about 5000 years ago, and American mink were introduced from the USA for fur farming in the 1920s.
- **Game** — e.g. rainbow trout and Canadian geese are from North America.
- **Forestry** — e.g. Douglas fir was introduced as a timber crop.
- **Biological control** — e.g. the Japanese knotweed psyllid (an insect that feeds on the plant) is being released in parts of the UK to control the spread of Japanese knotweed.
- **Novelty** — e.g. grey squirrels were introduced from North America in the 19th century because they were a curiosity.

3) **Unplanned** introductions can occur in various ways, e.g.:

- **Spreading from gardens** — e.g. Oxford ragwort was introduced as an ornamental plant but has spread to the wild.
- **Escaped animals** — e.g. ring-necked parakeets in south east England are descended from escaped pets.
- **Imported** — e.g. the harlequin ladybird is thought to have arrived on imported flowers.

4) The introduction of species can have **negative impacts** on **ecosystems**. These harmful species are called '**invasive**':

- **Non-native** species can **out-compete native** species. E.g. **grey squirrels** out-compete native **red squirrels** — they are bigger, hardier and less timid than red squirrels, so they can gather more food and survive through winter.
- Native plants can be **damaged**, e.g. grey squirrels **strip bark** off trees and **eat shoots** before they can grow.
- **Farm ecosystems** can be **disrupted**, e.g. Canadian geese can damage **crops**, and Oxford ragwort is **toxic** to livestock.
- Non-native species may **eat** native species, e.g. American mink eat water voles and birds.
- They may **transfer diseases** to native species, e.g. the grey squirrel carries **Squirrel Pox**, which is fatal to red squirrels.

5) However, many introduced species have **no significant negative impacts**, and some might even have a **positive impact**, e.g. Buddleia (a flowering shrub which colonises wasteland) provides a food source for butterflies and bees.

Wasteland in Urban Areas is Quickly **Colonised**

1) **Wasteland** is an area of land that has been **abandoned**, e.g. because of **deindustrialisation** (decreased industrial activity). Wastelands are often in **poor condition** with no water supply, high pollution levels and very acidic or alkaline soil.

2) Wastelands can provide a base for **ecosystems** to form through **succession**. The **characteristics** of the wasteland can affect the **sere** that develops on it, e.g. **drainage** (water availability), **acid/alkali conditions** and **pollution** levels. For example:

Succession in a disused quarry or an abandoned car park:

- **Mosses and lichens** start to grow on **bare rock**, **rubble** or **concrete** as they can cope with very little water. They extract nutrients from the bare material, and energy from photosynthesis, and form a thin soil.
- The next stage is **flowering plants** such as **Oxford ragwort**. Seeds blow in on the wind, and germinate in **cracks** in the rock (cracks retain water and soil). As the plants die, they rot down and produce **humus**, which slowly makes the soil more **nutrient rich**.
- Bigger, taller plants can grow in the soil, e.g. **Rosebay willowherb**. **Grass** also starts to grow at this stage, and over time the area becomes a weedy grassland, with invasive plants like Japanese knotweed.
- As the soil thickens, weeds and grass are replaced by **shrubs** and **trees**, e.g. **sycamore** and **rowan**. Plants like **brambles** that can put roots into deep cracks in the rock below the soil also thrive.

See p. 164-165 for more on succession.

3) Roadside verges and railway sidings are **colonised** in much the same way, except the succession usually starts at a **later stage** because the **soil** is already **established**. Seeds are blown in by passing vehicles.

Urban Ecosystems

Some Cities Have *Ecological Conservation Areas*

Ecological conservation areas are areas of land that have been granted a **protected** status to ensure that the ecosystems that exist there are **preserved** and **enhanced**. Developments in ecological conservation areas are **strictly controlled**. For example:

1) The **Mersey Forest** is a network of **woodlands** and **green spaces** in Cheshire and Merseyside.

- It's managed by a partnership of **public**, **private** and **voluntary** organisations, including 7 local authorities, landowners, The Forestry Commission, charities and local community groups.
- The Mersey Forest includes a **range of habitats** — oak and pine woodlands, grasslands, coastal salt marshes, coastal mudflats and rivers. These varied habitats are home to a **huge number of species**.
- The aims of the Mersey Forest are to provide **green space** for local people to enjoy, to **protect** the ecosystems in the area and preserve **biodiversity**, and to bring **money** to the local area through sustainable forestry and tourism.

2) There are many **conservation projects** in and around the Mersey Forest. For example:

- An introduced species, the **Spanish Bluebell**, is **out-competing** the native **British Bluebell** throughout the UK. The **Bluebell Recovery Project** has been **protecting** and **replanting** the native bluebell population of the Mersey Forest since **1996**, using **bulbs** that have been grown from **local British Bluebell seeds**.
- The **Friends of the Woodlands** initiative funds and advises **10 community conservation groups** in Merseyside and North Cheshire. These groups do voluntary work in the Mersey Forest area, e.g. clearing litter, running woodland art workshops and setting up projects to produce woodland products.

3) The Mersey Forest also runs projects in **urban areas** to get **people** involved in conservation and to bring local **communities** together. For example, the **Green Streets** programme sets up **community groups** to plant and care for **trees** in their neighbourhood. The trees improve air quality, make streets more attractive and provide habitats for birds.

4) Altogether, the Mersey Forest projects have created **3000 hectares** of new woodland by planting more than **8 million trees**. This conservation effort has benefited the local environment and the community in various ways:

Environmental benefits:	Social benefits:	Economic benefits:
• Protecting woodland and planting trees **creates habitat** for woodland wildlife, and increases **biodiversity**. • **800 hectares** of **non-woodland habitats** have been created, including **90 km of hedgerows**. • A **reduction** in **pollution** (e.g. urban tree planting improves air quality). • Planting trees **reduces soil erosion**. • **Wildlife corridors** are created.	• **60%** of the 1.5 million **local residents** use the woodlands for **recreation**. This improves **health** by promoting exercise and reducing stress. • A range of environmental **education** activities are offered, encouraging people to explore the forest.	• An **improved image** of the area has **boosted** the economy — e.g. house prices in St Helens have increased by a total of £15 million. • **Sustainable forestry** has created **150 new jobs** since 1994. • An increase in **tourism, leisure** and **recreation** creates jobs and brings money to the area.

5) The Mersey Forest has been **very successful** so far, but some urban areas in the north west still lack green space, e.g. parts of **Liverpool**. The Mersey Forest wants to improve the **landscape** in the city by planting trees on **derelict sites**.

Practice Questions

Q1 What is an introduced species?

Q2 Give two negative impacts of introduced species on ecosystems.

Q3 Briefly describe the process of succession on wasteland in the UK.

Exam Question

Q1 For an ecological conservation area you have studied, discuss how effective the conservation strategies have been. [10 marks]

A little less conversation, a little more conservation please...

You don't need to go off to the rainforest to experience an ecosystem — it seems urban areas provide habitats for all kinds of wildlife. So keep your eyes peeled when you're out and about in town and you may be treated to an urban safari...

Global Ecosystem Issues

Now you've had an introduction to some of the smaller ecosystems it's time for the big boy. All the ecosystems on Earth are part of the global ecosystem. Human activities have an impact on the global ecosystem and conserving it is a tricky business.

Human Activity Generally Reduces Biodiversity

1) **Biodiversity** means the **variety** of organisms living in a particular area — all the different **species**, **habitats** and **ecosystems**.

2) Globally, biodiversity is **not evenly distributed**. It generally increases from the **poles** towards the **equator** — around **50%** of all the world's **plants and animals** live in tropical rainforests. This is because closer to the equator the climate is **warmer**, more **moist**, and more **stable**. This means **plants grow better** and can support more species higher up the food chain.

3) **Human activities** tend to reduce biodiversity. For example:

> - **Deforestation** (e.g. for farming) results in habitat loss.
> - **Draining wetlands** (e.g. for building) results in habitat loss.
> - **Pollution** can damage habitats and harm species.
> - **Global warming** changes the abundance and distribution of species.
> - **Rising sea levels** due to climate change leads to habitat loss.
> - **Overexploitation** (e.g. overfishing, overhunting and overharvesting) reduces the population of certain species.

Litter left by humans causes water pollution.

4) It's important for **ecosystems** to maintain a **high level** of biodiversity:

> - **Having** a range of species helps **maintain** the **ecosystem** — e.g. insects pollinate plants and animals disperse seeds. If **one species dies out**, it affects the **whole ecosystem**.
> - Biodiversity helps ecosystems **adapt** to **changing physical conditions** — e.g. if the **climate changes** in an ecosystem with low biodiversity all the species may die. When biodiversity is **high**, there's a better chance that some of the species in an ecosystem will be able to **adapt** to the **new conditions** and survive.
> - Biodiversity creates **feedback loops** that maintain biodiversity. For example, high biodiversity increases the **fertility** of the **soil** because there's a greater **variety** of **decaying matter**. Fertile soil means that a greater range of plants can grow, so the ecosystem remains biodiverse. If these feedback loops **collapse** the ecosystem may not be able to recover.

5) **Reducing biodiversity** threatens ecosystems and can be **unsustainable**. Humans rely on ecosystems to supply important **natural resources** such as food and fuel — when **biodiversity** is **reduced**, ecosystems are **less able** to **produce** these resources. This means that **future generations** will not be able to make use of them to meet their needs.

Lots of Fragile Environments on Earth are Being Damaged

1) **Fragile environments** are ecosystems that are **easily disturbed** and **can't adapt** to change, e.g. coral reefs, coastal wetlands, polar environments, savanna grasslands (p. 180) and tropical rainforests (p. 182).

2) Fragile environments are easily **damaged** by changes brought about by **human activities**, e.g. loss of habitat due to deforestation, species loss due to overfishing or damage to habitats due to water pollution.

3) Changes in the **natural environment** also affect fragile environments, e.g. extreme weather events like floods and droughts, or longer term changes such as increasing or decreasing erosion or sedimentation.

4) **Small changes** can cause **a lot of damage** to fragile environments, for example:

> - **Coral reefs** are sensitive to changes in **water temperature** and **quality** — they grow in salt water between 21 and 29 °C. If temperatures increase the coral can become 'bleached' — this is when the coral can't provide enough nutrients to support the algae that live in it, and forces them out instead. The coral needs these algae to provide oxygen and nutrients — without them the coral will eventually **die**.
> - **Polar environments** are sensitive to **temperature changes** — small increases can **melt** vast areas of **ice**, which can **destroy habitats** and **threaten species**. E.g. polar bears need sea ice to hunt seals, which are their main food source. As ice melts, polar bears cannot feed and their numbers **decline**.
> - **Coastal wetlands** are sensitive to **changes in sea level** and **sedimentation** — species are adapted to live in certain depths of water and soil, and small changes can **destroy** many species' **habitats**.

5) Once a fragile environment is damaged, it is **extremely difficult** to **repair** the damage.

Global Ecosystem Issues

Managing Fragile Environments Isn't Easy

1) **Fragile ecosystems** are often rich in **natural resources**, e.g. ingredients for medicines, and often have high biodiversity. There is a conflict between using natural resources (**exploitation**) and preserving them for future generations (**conservation**).

2) A single **ecosystem** often has many uses. For example, the Amazon rainforest:

- Provides the resources to feed **subsistence farmers** and **native people** who hunt and fish.
- Provides **renewable resources** for export, such as rubber and ingredients for medicines (e.g. the periwinkle plant is used to treat cancer).
- Is important for countries that depend on **exploiting** its resources to develop their **economies**.

3) Managing fragile environments involves striking a **balance** between **conservation** and **exploitation**. This can be very **difficult** because:

- Some fragile environments cross **international borders**. For example, the Amazon rainforest covers an area which includes parts of **nine** different countries — this makes it very **difficult** to agree on and carry out a **management strategy** across the whole area.
- Many fragile environments are located in **less developed countries** that **lack** the **money** or the **expertise** needed to conserve them properly.
- Countries that depend on **natural resources** from **fragile environments** for income are reluctant to stop these activities, because it would damage their economy and slow development. E.g. in Brazil the mining industry damages the rainforest, but brings money to the country — the leading mining company brought in almost $9 billion in 2006.
- People who live in a fragile environment may exploit it because they have **no alternative**, or because they **don't understand** the need to conserve it.
- In some areas there is a need to introduce **non-native species** (e.g. as a food crop), but these can **out-compete** native species, and be extremely difficult to remove. For example, in Arizona an invasive plant, Tamarisk, was introduced as a windbreak, but it out-competes native plants and is difficult to control, making it a threat to the desert ecosystem.

Marcus was pretty sure he could sort out these fragile ecosystems given half a chance.

4) In some cases people are trying to **restore** fragile environments, for example the Indonesian government has invested in **replanting** areas of rainforest, and the Coral Restoration Foundation has set up **coral nurseries** and **restoration projects** in many areas where reefs have been damaged. However, restoration of fragile environments can be **difficult**:

- Some fragile environments **cannot be restored** because they have already been so **badly damaged** by human activity. For example, clearing land in a rainforest causes **soil quality** to decline. Even if the land is replanted, the degraded soil means that rainforest vegetation **can't easily regrow**.
- **Natural hazards** (e.g. floods, droughts, volcanic events) can cause **damage** to fragile environments which will only fully recover over long timescales. For example, the **Indian Ocean Tsunami** in 2004 destroyed areas of **coral reefs** and **mangrove swamps**. Although some countries affected by the tsunami are undertaking schemes to **replant mangroves** it could take hundreds of years for the ecosystems to fully recover.

Practice Questions

Q1 What is biodiversity?

Q2 Give three examples of human activities that reduce biodiversity.

Q3 What is a fragile environment?

Exam Question

Q1 Discuss the difficulties associated with the management of fragile environments. [8 marks]

Biodiversity — it's the spice of life...

Ecosystems supply us with all sorts of useful things and it's sometimes too easy to take advantage of them. Managing ecosystems requires a balance between making the most of the resources and preserving the ecosystem for future generations. Many ecosystems are already in decline due to human activities, so we're at a critical time in global ecosystem management.

Global Ecosystems Case Study — Serengeti

It's time for another case study — hurrah. Pack up your binoculars and your safari hat because we're off to the Serengeti...

Poaching *is a* Big Problem *on the* Serengeti

The **Serengeti** is a **savanna grassland ecosystem** covering 30 000 km² in Tanzania and south west Kenya. The plantlife is dominated by grasses and shrubs with occasional trees (e.g. acacia). It supports herds of **grazing animals** (wildebeest, zebra, buffalo etc.) and their **predators** (lions, leopards, cheetahs). There are four main **environmental problems**:

HUNTING AND POACHING

1) Historically animals have been **hunted** by visitors for **sport**, as well as by local people as a **source of food** or for products like **ivory** and **rhino horn** to sell.

2) During the 1970s and 1980s poaching for ivory and rhino horn was a huge problem and caused the **black rhino** population in the Serengeti to fall to **two animals**.

3) **Legislation** like the **1989 ban** on the **international trade of ivory** has helped to reduce elephant poaching in recent years, but **local people** hunting illegally for meat is still a problem.

INCREASING POPULATION

1) The human population in the Serengeti is increasing. This creates **land use** conflicts. Land is needed for **settlements**, for growing **crops** and for **grazing** farm animals.

2) As areas of the Serengeti have been colonised and farmed, natural **habitats** have been **lost**.

3) **Increasing population** has also led to increased **hunting**.

FIRE

1) **Controlled fires** during the dry season help to sustain the savanna environment.

2) Fire **prevents woodland** growth, burns off **dead grass** on the surface, leaving the **roots** intact, and **fertilises** the soil. **New shoots** grow through in the **wet season** and are a source of **food** for grazing animals.

3) However, **uncontrolled fires** (sometimes started to clear land for farming) can **damage** trees and destroy grass roots, so grasses can't grow back.

INVASIVE SPECIES

1) **Invasive plant species** can cause damage. For example, the **Mexican poppy**, which was accidentally introduced with imported wheat, **out-competes native plants** and crops, making some areas **unsuitable for farming**.

2) **Animal species** can spread **disease**, e.g. in 1994 canine distemper virus spread from **domestic dogs** killed **a third** of the population of **Serengeti lions**.

Managing *the* Serengeti *involves* Working *with* Local People

The **Serengeti National Park** covers an area of around **15 000 km²** in northern Tanzania. It was established in 1951 to **preserve wildlife** and **reduce environmental damage**. The park is managed by **Tanzania National Parks** (TANAPA). The management strategy aims to balance conservation of biodiversity with the needs of local people, through a number of different schemes:

1) **Monitoring** the **ecosystem** through aerial wildlife surveys, water quality monitoring and monitoring of invasive species.

2) Protection of **priority species**, e.g. rangers monitor the black rhino population and carry out **anti-poaching patrols**.

3) **Disease monitoring** and **vaccination programmes** — domestic dogs in a zone around the park are vaccinated against rabies and canine distemper virus to try to stop these diseases spreading to wild animals.

4) **Controlled burning** is carried out to stop a build-up of dry grass, which could cause damaging wildfires.

5) **Conservation education projects** — the park supports conservation clubs in 74 local primary schools, holds teacher training workshops, and informs local people about work in the park. Involving local people in conservation means they are more likely to **protect the ecosystem** themselves.

6) Four **Wildlife Management Areas** (WMAs) were created, which have a **community based conservation approach**. For example, the **Ikona Community WMA**, an area of **450 km²**, is managed by communities from five villages. They work together to manage the wildlife, and are allowed to use the resources from the area within sustainable limits — either through hunting for their own use, or making money from tourism (e.g. selling local produce or guiding safaris).

7) **Tourism** brings **money** to the local area, but strict **regulations** are in place to make sure it doesn't **damage** the ecosystem, e.g. driving is only permitted in designated areas, and access into the park is only allowed at certain points.

Global Ecosystems Case Study — Serengeti

Management Strategies have Helped the Environment and Local People...

Local **conservation education** projects have improved **understanding** between local people and the National Park:

1) The **WMAs** have been successful in lots of ways. They provide local people with a **food source** and income from **legally traded** animal products and tourism, and help to **reduce** illegal **poaching**.

2) **Poaching** has **declined** in recent years, and the populations of **most species** are steadily **increasing** — e.g. the elephant population increased from 500 in 1990 to 2100 in 2011.

3) Money from tourism goes back into the National Park to help pay for conservation projects. It also **boosts** the **local economy** by creating jobs and a market for local produce. The increased **ranger presence** for tourism has also helped **reduce poaching**.

4) **Disease monitoring** and vaccination has helped **prevent** damaging outbreaks of disease. E.g. in 1996 an outbreak of rinderpest (a disease which affects hooved animals like cattle) was stopped from entering the Serengeti due to a programme of cattle vaccination in the districts of the Park closest to the affected area.

...but there are still Threats to the Ecosystem

It's still proving difficult to balance **wildlife conservation** with the **needs of local people**:

1) The **human population** around the park is still growing, and more settlements and farms are built near the park each year. There can be **conflicts** between agriculture and conservation, e.g. elephants sometimes raid crops such as sorghum and maize, which can make conservation **unpopular** with local people.

2) Some **local people** are reluctant to become part of a **WMA**, because they have **doubts** about what they'll gain from it. Others have **refused** to stop **farming** or **hunting** within the WMAs, so some areas are still being over-exploited.

3) Outside the WMAs, **poaching** is still a **problem** in the Serengeti — **40 000 animals** are killed each year for **meat** and other **products**. These are mostly wildebeest and zebra, but other animals often get caught in poachers' snares or traps. If the human **population** around the park continues to **increase**, it could lead to a **rapid decline** of the **wildebeest population**.

4) **Tourism** can have a number of **negative impacts**:

A traffic jam of safari vehicles in the Serengeti.

- **Construction** and use of roads, trails, campsites, hotels and other buildings have an **environmental impact** through increased erosion and loss of habitat.
- Road **vehicles** and **aeroplanes** cause air and noise **pollution**.
- **Waste disposal** from accommodation can be a problem, e.g. if food waste isn't disposed of properly it can attract pests such as rats and cockroaches.
- Tourists can **disturb** and sometimes **distress** animals.
- Tourism increases the **demand** for **water**, which can lead to **water shortages**.

A clear **code of conduct** and **limits** to **tourism** have been set by the National Park to try and reduce these impacts.

Practice Questions

Q1 How has poaching damaged the Serengeti ecosystem?
Q2 What effect has human population growth had on the Serengeti ecosystem?
Q3 What are Wildlife Management Areas (WMAs)?
Q4 Give two positive and two negative impacts of tourism on the Serengeti ecosystem.

Exam Question

Q1 Discuss the effectiveness of a management strategy in a fragile environment you have studied. [10 marks]

Right, time to geti your head down and learn some stuff...

The Serengeti is a great example to pull out in your exam — there's a lot of stuff to talk about and examiners love answers that are backed up by a truckload of facts. Unfortunately that also means there's a lot to remember, so make sure you know it really well.

Global Ecosystems Case Study — Amazon

The Amazon Rainforest is another example of a fragile environment. You have to know two case studies for your exam, so you need to learn these pages as well as the ones on the Serengeti. Just thinking about it makes me feel a bit fragile to be honest...

The **Amazon Rainforest** is under **Threat**

1) The **Amazon** is the world's largest **tropical rainforest** and covers 40% of the South American landmass.

2) It's one of the most **biodiverse** regions on **Earth** and is home to up to **1 million plant species**, over **500 species** of **mammals** and over **2000 species** of **fish**. The Amazon is also home to many **endangered species**, including the Amazonian manatee (an aquatic mammal), black caiman (a reptile) and the pirarucu (a fish).

3) There are two main threats to the environment:

Climate change is also a serious threat to the Amazon. It could lead to drought, forest fires and species extinction.

Deforestation

1) **Deforestation** is the single biggest **threat** to the rainforest — **13%** of the original forest has been **cleared**.

2) There are a number of **reasons** for **deforestation** (see p. 170). In the Amazon, mining, logging and subsistence agriculture all contribute to deforestation, but **cattle ranching** is the biggest problem — it was responsible for **more than 60%** of all deforestation between **2000** and **2005**.

3) The impacts of deforestation are **wide** (see p. 170). In the Amazon there have been problems with increased **forest fires** and **soil erosion**, and decreased **biodiversity** caused by habitat loss.

Overhunting and overfishing

1) Most of the **local people** still live a **traditional lifestyle** and rely on hunting, fishing, foraging and small-scale farming for food.

2) **Population growth** in recent years has caused an **increase in subsistence hunting** and **fishing** by local people.

3) Hunting primates for **bushmeat** is a big problem — in the Brazilian Amazon **local people** consume between 2.2 and 5.4 million primates per year. This is **unsustainable** because primates **reproduce slowly** and many species are **endangered**.

4) The loss of certain species can have knock-on effects on other species (see p. 171).

The **Central Amazon Conservation Complex** is in the **Brazilian Amazon**

1) The **Central Amazon Conservation Complex** (**CACC**) was established in **2003** by bringing together four reserves in the Brazilian Amazon — **Jaú National Park**, **Anavilhanas Ecological Station**, **Mamirauá Reserve** and **Amana Reserve**.

2) It aims to protect the **biodiversity** of this area of rainforest, with a focus on protecting endangered species, and to maintain the various **ecosystems** while allowing local people to continue using the forest for their livelihood in a **sustainable way**.

3) The complex covers an area of **49 000 km²** and it includes a **variety of habitats** — dry (unflooded) rainforest, rivers, lakes, seasonally flooded forest and dry grasslands.

4) The complex is managed by several organisations, including the **Brazilian Institute of the Environment and Natural Resources** (IBAMA), local government, research institutes and representatives from the mining and tourism industries.

5) The management approach uses a number of **schemes** to try to balance **conservation** and **sustainable development**:

1) The complex is divided into zones — **total protection, buffer zones, sustainable use, rehabilitation** and **experimental use**. Activities within these areas are **strictly controlled**:
   - In areas of total protection access is heavily restricted — for example only **researchers** and **authorised visitors** are allowed in **Jaú National Park**.
   - In areas of sustainable use there are **quotas** to limit **logging, hunting** and **fishing**.

2) Two **Sustainable Development Reserves** (SDRs) have been created where **hunting** and **logging** is only allowed for **subsistence**, and there are **limits** to the numbers of **animals** and **fish** that can be caught.

3) **Economic Alternatives Programs** have been set up. These are **sustainable schemes** run by **local people** who receive a **direct income** from their work — communities are involved in **fisheries management, ecotourism, sustainable agriculture** and **handicraft** production. For example, the Fibrarte Project supports local people who use natural fibres to make handicrafts, which they can **sell**.

4) **Education projects** have been set up to educate local people about the environment and how to manage it.

5) Projects have been set up to **increase community involvement** with conservation. In Mamirauá, **60 communities** take part in **monitoring wildlife**. **Local representatives** meet every two months with local government and non-government organisations to discuss ways of **managing** the environment and **conserving biodiversity**.

Global Ecosystems Case Study — Amazon

Sustainable Development Initiatives have been Successful...

A black caiman lurking in shallow water.

1) The creation of the **conservation complex** has protected the surrounding area from **major developments** that might have impacts on the CACC — there are no dams, pipelines, mines or commercial logging activities and currently **none are planned** for the future.

2) The **SDRs** have improved **biodiversity**. Populations of many key species have increased — since the creation of the CACC the **black caiman** population has **increased by 100%** and the **pirarucu fish** population by over **300%**.

3) **Economic Alternatives Programs** promote **sustainable activities** and have **reduced poverty** — average **household income** has **increased** by 50-99% in some areas. Local farmers and craftsmen belong to **producer's associations**, which means they can sell their goods directly to buyers, rather than trading through 'middle men' who charge a commission.

4) **Ecotourism** provides a **source of income** for locals and promotes **conservation** — in **Mamiraúá** a low environmental impact **ecotourism lodge** has been built, which recycles waste and uses solar power. The lodge brings **jobs** and **money** to the local community, and invests money into **conservation** and **community** projects.

5) **Local education** and **health improvement** projects have been **successful**:

- Local people have been trained as **health workers**, and better **rainwater collection technology** means local communities have access to clean drinking water. These changes have **improved** the **quality of life** of the local population, shown by a **53% drop** in **infant mortality**.

- **80 teachers** from local schools have been trained to educate children about the **environment**. As a result, around **1800 children** have had classes on conservation.

...but Protecting such a Large Area is Difficult

1) The reserves are large and understaffed, which makes it difficult to monitor and control illegal activities, e.g. hunting. 150 people are employed in the Amana and Mamiraúá reserves and there are 100 volunteer guards, but more volunteers are needed to cover the large area effectively.

2) Restricting access to areas of total protection is very difficult because of the size of the zones and the limited number of staff. For example, in Jaú National Park there are only four permanent staff, so poaching of fish and turtles is still a problem. 26 volunteer guards have been trained, which may improve the situation.

3) Population growth in the area puts stress on the ecosystem, and some areas still suffer from intensive fishing and hunting, especially of monkeys and manatees.

4) Population growth across the region means deforestation around the edges of the CACC continues. Deforestation around the edges of the complex results in habitat loss and fragmentation (when forested areas are split up so animals can't move between them). It also makes the complex more accessible, which increases the risk of illegal overhunting and overfishing in the complex.

Practice Questions

Q1 Name two threats to the Central Amazon Conservation Complex.

Q2 What are SDRs?

Q3 Give one example of how SDRs have been successful.

Q4 Give one reason why restricting access to the zones of total protection is difficult.

Exam Question

Q1 Compare and contrast the management schemes in two different fragile environments you have studied. [40 marks]

Well you can't say conservation isn't Complex...

So there you have it — another jolly little case study, if you can call the largest protected area in the Amazon basin 'little'. The trouble with the Central Amazon Conservation Complex is that it's such a large area, with so many different habitats, that it's very difficult to come up with a management scheme that addresses all the issues. That's what makes it great to write about in the exam.

Urban Areas and Urbanisation

Ahh cities, at last. This is the section that I know you've all been waiting for. Now don't get too excited and rush on to the best bits (retailing will still be there when you get to it), you need to get a few basic things into your brain first...

You Need to Know About **Millionaire**, **Mega** and **World Cities**

More than **50%** of the world's population live in **urban areas**. This number is increasing, particularly in **developing countries**. Population growth in urban areas has increased the number of **big cities** in the world:

1) A **millionaire city** is an urban area with **over a million people** living there, e.g. Budapest in Hungary.

2) A **mega city** is an urban area with **over 10 million people** living there, e.g. Mumbai in India.

3) A **world city** is a city that has an **influence** over the **whole world**. World cities are centres for **trade** and **business**, and they also tend to be hubs of **culture** and **science**, e.g. London, New York and Tokyo.

Millionaire, mega and world cities are more common in the northern hemisphere and are often located on a coastline or large river.

GLOBAL DISTRIBUTION OF MILLIONAIRE AND MEGA CITIES, 2012

● = millionaire city   ● = mega city

Millionaire cities — there are more than **400**. In the past, millionaire cities were mostly found in the **developed world**, but **increasingly** they are found in the **developing world**.

Mega cities — there are more than 20. More than two thirds of mega cities are in developing countries.

The exact number of **world cities** is hard to define. World cities tend to be in **developed countries**. Over time it's likely that more cities in **developing countries** such as India and China will become world cities.

Four **Processes** Affect the **Populations** of Cities

1) There are **four processes** that involve the movement of people in and out of **urban areas**:

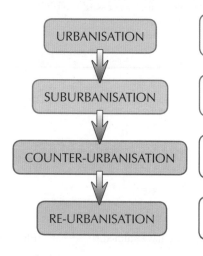

URBANISATION

Urbanisation (see p. 185-187) is the **growth** in the **proportion** of a **country's population** that lives in urban areas.

SUBURBANISATION

Suburbanisation (see p. 188-189) is the movement of people from the **city centre** to the **outskirts**, or **suburbs**.

COUNTER-URBANISATION

Counter-urbanisation (see p. 190-191) is the movement of people from **cities** to **rural areas**.

RE-URBANISATION

Re-urbanisation (see p. 192-193) is the movement of people **back** to the **city centre**.

As people move from one area to another, economic activities (services and industry) move with them.

2) These processes may happen **one after the other** as a country **develops** — this is called the **cycle of urbanisation**.

3) However, in many cities **all four processes** are happening at the **same time** but in different parts of the city.

Urban Areas and Urbanisation

Urbanisation is Mainly Caused by Rural-Urban Migration

1) Urbanisation is caused by **rural-urban migration** and a **naturally increasing population**.

2) As people migrate to cities the **urban population** increases. The migrants tend to be **young people** looking for work. They may then have **children**, which **further increases** the urban population.

3) Rural-urban migration takes place because of **push** and **pull factors**.

   - **Push factors** are the things that push people **away** from a rural area. In **developing countries**, push factors are often linked to **poverty**.

   - **Pull factors** are the things that **attract** people to an urban area.

4) At the moment rural-urban migration is taking place in many **developing countries**. Here are the reasons why:

Every day Cilla dreams of rural-urban migration.

In developed countries, rapid urbanisation occurred in the 18th and 19th centuries, and now the processes of suburbanisation, counter-urbanisation and re-urbanisation are more important.

PUSH FACTORS

1) Human activity and changes in climate can cause **desertification** (when fertile land becomes barren desert). If land becomes **unproductive** it **cannot** provide enough food to support the population, and people are forced to **move away**.

2) Some farmers take out **loans** to help them **improve their yields** (e.g. by buying fertiliser or building irrigation systems). If their **crops fail** they may be **unable** to pay these loans back, and may **lose their land**.

3) **Conflict** and **civil war** may cause people to **flee** their homes. If many people are **killed** or **injured** in a war, there will be less people to work the land and there could be food shortages.

4) **Natural disasters** such as earthquakes and floods may damage homes and farmland, which people cannot afford to **rebuild** or **repair**.

5) **Changes in land use** in rural areas can drive people out. E.g. farmland may be flooded when **dams** are built to generate **hydro-electric** power.

6) **Mechanisation of agriculture** means fewer people are needed to work the land, so there's a lack of jobs.

PULL FACTORS

1) There are **more jobs** available in urban areas.

2) **Jobs** in urban areas are usually **better paid** than jobs in rural areas.

3) There may be better access to **health** and **education** services.

4) **Other family members** may have already moved to the city. They may be able to help migrants find **homes** and **jobs**.

5) There is often a **perception** that **quality of life** will be better in a city.

The expectation of a better quality of life in a city is often wrong — see p. 186-187.

Practice Questions

Q1 What is the difference between a millionaire city and a mega city?

Q2 What is meant by the term 'urbanisation'?

Q3 What are push and pull factors?

Q4 Give one pull factor which attracts people to urban areas.

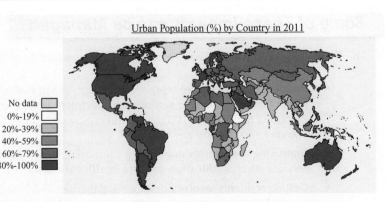

Urban Population (%) by Country in 2011

No data
0%-19%
20%-39%
40%-59%
60%-79%
80%-100%

Exam Questions

Q1 Look at the map showing urban population by country. Describe and comment on the pattern of urbanisation shown. [7 marks]

Q2 Discuss the causes of urbanisation. [8 marks]

Pull factors — quality of dance moves, use of deodorant etc...

As developing countries, errr, develop, people ditch country living and flood to cities. It's well worth knowing the push and pull factors that convince them to make the move — don't turn over until you can rewrite the lists above while standing on your head.

Urbanisation

You might've already worked out that loads of people migrating to a city is going to cause a few issues...

Urbanisation has Impacts in Urban Areas

1) As **urban populations** grow there is increased **demand** for space (e.g. for houses), **resources** (e.g. water), and **services** (e.g. schools). If these increased demands **cannot** be met, it can lead to **poor quality of life** for the people living in the area.

2) Many **developing countries cannot afford** to meet these extra demands or cannot **keep up** with the **rapid** rate of urbanisation, so urbanisation has a number of **negative impacts**:

> 1) When migrants move to a city there are often **not enough houses** for them, or they **cannot afford** to rent or buy.
>
> 2) Some migrants are forced to **live on the streets** or in **shelters**, e.g. in 2009 there were more than 13 000 homeless people in São Paulo, Brazil.
>
> 3) Migrants often **build their own houses**, leading to the unregulated growth of **slums** or **shanty towns**. The houses are often **poorly built** using cheap materials. Shanty towns have a number of problems:

A shanty town (favela) in São Paulo.

> * They're often built on land that isn't suitable for construction, e.g. **steep hillsides** at risk of **landslides**, or **flood risk** areas.
>
> * There is often a **lack of basic services** like clean water and sewage disposal. This means that there is a **high risk of disease** (e.g. dysentery and typhoid).
>
> * Children growing up in a shanty town often **don't** have access to **education**, or need to **work** to earn money for their families. This makes it **difficult** for them to get a **well paid job** and **move out** of the shanty town as they grow older.
>
> * The **difference in wealth** between people living inside and outside the shanty town can cause tension and lead to **social problems** (e.g. crime and violence).
>
> 4) There is often high **competition** for good jobs in the **formal sector** (where workers receive regular wages from an employer and have set hours of work). Migrants may have to accept **low wages, poor working conditions** and **little job security** (e.g. not being on a contract, so they could be dismissed at any time).
>
> 5) Migrants who can't find formal work may be forced to work in the **informal sector**, doing unskilled jobs (e.g. car washing), that **don't** tend to **pay well**, offer **no job security** and can be **dangerous**. People dependent on this type of irregular income often live in **poverty**.
>
> 6) Rapid population growth increases the pressure on **roads** and **railways**, increasing **congestion** and **air pollution**.

Some of These Impacts can be Managed

1) There are **several ways** to tackle poverty and improve quality of life in **urban areas**. Here are some examples:

> * **Building new housing** to replace slums. E.g. in **São Paulo** in 1995 the government-run **Cingapura Housing Project** aimed to **replace** favelas with **apartment blocks**, which locals could rent **cheaply**. However, only 14 000 of the planned 100 000 apartments were built — the scheme was **scrapped** because many people couldn't afford to pay any rent at all.
>
> * **Improving the services** available in slums. E.g. in **São Paulo** the Monte Azul Community Association provides services such as **education** and **free health care** in the Monte Azul favela.
>
> * Getting **residents involved** in improving their local areas. E.g. in Rio de Janeiro, the **$300 million Favela-Bairro** project made improvements in 73 favelas across the city (e.g. supplying electricity and clean water, and running adult education classes to improve adult literacy). **Residents** chose what improvements they wanted in their own favela, so they felt **involved** with the development. New services (e.g. daycare centres for children) were **staffed by local people**, which gave them an **income** and an opportunity to **learn** new skills.
>
> * **Redeveloping** whole areas of slum into new **independent townships**, e.g. in **Dharavi**, Mumbai (see next page).

2) Although schemes like this can help to **decrease poverty** and **increase quality of life**, the **scale** of the problem is so large that tackling it can be extremely **difficult**.

Urbanisation

Mumbai in India has Experienced Rapid Urbanisation

1) **Mumbai** (formerly Bombay) is a **mega city** (see p. 184) on the west coast of **India**.

2) Mumbai is **globally important** — it is a major **port** on the Indian Ocean, India's **financial centre** and a hub of **industry** and **services**. The city is also a **cultural centre** — it's home to the **Bollywood** movie industry.

3) Migrants from **rural** areas all over India have moved to Mumbai in search of jobs. As a result, the population of Mumbai **increased rapidly** from **5.9 million** in 1971 to **12.5 million** in 2011.

4) The city has struggled to handle the **rapid urbanisation** caused by immigration — **more than half** of the population live in **poverty** in slums, which cover large parts of the city.

Dharavi is one of the largest slums in Mumbai and is home to more than 1 million people.

5) Urbanisation has created a number of **issues**:

IMPACTS

- **Living conditions** in the city's slums are poor — the homes are **cramped** and **poorly built**, often without water supply or sanitation. The **lack of toilet and sewage** facilities is a risk to **health** (e.g. raw sewage spreads disease).

- **Health care** services cannot meet the needs of the increased population — it's estimated **public health care** only reaches **30%** of the urban poor. As a result, outbreaks of disease (e.g. **malaria** and **dengue fever**) are common and the **infant mortality rate** (see p. 206) is high (40 deaths per 1000).

- The increased population adds to the **demand** for water. Mumbai's water supply is dependent on the **monsoon rains**, and in dry years water has to be strictly **rationed**.

- The **road network** in Mumbai carries **millions** of people each day. It cannot cope with this level of traffic and there are problems with **long journey times**, **congestion** and **air pollution**.

- An increasing population produces **more waste**. This can cause problems, e.g. in the eastern neighbourhood of Chembur waste on open rubbish dumps is burnt, which causes **air pollution**. This has health impacts on local residents — **25%** of deaths in Chembur between 2007 and 2008 were caused by **respiratory problems**.

Steps have been taken to **manage** some of these issues:

MANAGEMENT

- In 2004 the government first announced a **redevelopment project** to clear the Dharavi slum and create a new **independent township**. Plans include **building new apartments**, a water and sewage system, hospitals and schools. Some residents of Dharavi are **strongly against** the redevelopment — it's an established community with successful industries, e.g. **recycling rubbish** from all over the city. Residents are worried that the redevelopment will destroy their **livelihoods** and the **community spirit** of the area.

- The **Slum Sanitation Program** was started in 1995 by a group of Non-Governmental Organisations (NGOs). It built 330 new **communal toilet blocks** in slums in Mumbai.

- To try and reduce the demand for water, the local authority has made **rainwater harvesting** systems (collecting rainwater from rooftops) compulsory on all **new residential buildings** in Mumbai on plots larger than 300 m². However, since 2007 only **half** of the eligible buildings have actually installed rainwater harvesting plants.

- People are using **alternative forms of transport** (e.g. scooters and mopeds) to avoid being stuck in traffic and reduce their journey times. This helps to reduce congestion, but these vehicles add to the poor air quality.

- The **public transport** system is being upgraded — a **Metro system** with over 140 km of new rail lines is being developed in the city. The first line is set to open in **2013**, but the system will not be completed until **2021**.

Practice Questions

Q1 Give two impacts of urbanisation.

Q2 Give one management strategy used to tackle the impacts of urbanisation.

Exam Question

Q1 "For every problem caused by urbanisation there is an effective solution."
To what extent do you agree with this view? [40 marks]

Poverty management strategy #12 — win 'Who Wants to be a Millionaire'...

Phew — the first case study of the section and it's a bit of a whopper. Mumbai is a big city with some big problems — make sure that you learn the issues and management strategies off by heart. Oh, and everything else on the pages as well...

Suburbanisation

Suburbanisation is caused by cheaper housing on the edges of cities, better transport links and dreams of home grown veg.

Suburbanisation is Taking Place in the Developed World

Suburbanisation is the movement of people from **city centres** to the **outskirts** (see p. 184).
There are a number of reasons **why** people move:

PUSH FACTORS

1) Some **housing** in cities is **poor quality**, e.g. in the UK in the 1940s, many houses in inner cities were small and some **lacked basic services** like indoor bathrooms and central heating.

2) As countries develop, governments often **clear** low quality city centre housing and provide **new houses** outside the city for residents. E.g. **slum clearance** took place in much of **England** between **1950 and 1970**. People were moved to **council estates** on the **outskirts of urban areas**.

3) **Deindustrialisation** in city centres (when manufacturing moves out of an area) leads to people losing their jobs.

4) As **unemployment** increases in the city, people have **less money** to spend there, so local shops and services may be forced to close (see p. 194). This means there are **fewer local services** for people living in the city centre.

PULL FACTORS

1) Planning laws may be **more relaxed** outside city centres, so it's **easier** to build houses. In the UK, until the 1950s developers took advantage of relaxed planning laws and built **new housing estates** on the edge of urban areas. They offered large, modern houses in a **spacious**, **green environment**.

2) Improvements in **public transport** and **increasing car ownership** mean that people can live further from work and **commute** in to the city each day.

3) As **businesses** and **shops** move out of city centres to take advantage of **cheaper rents** on the outskirts, more **jobs** and **services** become available in the suburbs.

Suburbanisation has Impacts on the City Centre and the Suburbs

IMPACTS ON THE CITY CENTRE

- As people and businesses **move out** to the suburbs, buildings in the city centre are **abandoned** and may become **derelict**. These processes can lead to the city centre becoming **run down**.

- As businesses leave **unemployment** increases, which leads to **lower living standards** and **poverty**.

- **Wealthier middle class people** may move to the **suburbs** where there is a **better quality of life**. The people left behind are **poorer** and are often **foreign immigrants**. This can lead to economic and ethnic **segregation**.

- Some people from the suburbs may still **commute** into the city to work, which increases **congestion** and **pollution**.

IMPACTS IN THE SUBURBS

- **New housing estates** are often built on open countryside, which affects **wildlife habitats**.

- As **urban areas** spread, more ground is **concreted over**. This can increase **surface run-off** and the risk of **flooding**.

- Most people who live in the suburbs **own cars**. This means that the number of cars on the roads **increases**, causing **congestion** and **air pollution**.

There are Ways of Managing the Impacts of Suburbanisation

1) **Redevelopment schemes** encourage some **people** and **businesses** to move back to city centres (re-urbanisation — see p. 192-193) by improving **brownfield sites** in the city centre. E.g. the Birmingham Big City Plan, launched in 2011, aims to redevelop five inner city areas of Birmingham. The proposals include space for businesses, shops and cultural uses, as well as 5000 new homes and 50 000 new jobs.

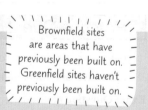
Brownfield sites are areas that have previously been built on. Greenfield sites haven't previously been built on.

2) Many urban areas are surrounded by a **greenbelt** (an area of countryside with restrictions on land use and development) to prevent the **urban areas** getting too large. This protects the countryside from **development**.

3) Some schemes have aimed to **reduce traffic congestion** in the **city centre**. For example, after the London congestion charge (see p. 152) was introduced in 2003, the volume of traffic in the congestion charging zone fell by 15%.

4) Some towns have improved their **flood defence schemes**, e.g. in Shrewsbury in Shropshire, the council has built a system of **flood barriers** and **pumping stations** to reduce the flood risk to newly developed urban areas close to the River Severn.

Suburbanisation

Surbiton is a London Suburb

1) **Surbiton** is an area of **south west London** in the borough of **Kingston upon Thames**. The population of the borough increased from 141 000 in 1971 to 160 000 in 2011 as a result of suburbanisation from the centre of London. **Surbiton** has been the focus for much of this **growth**.

GREATER LONDON AREA

SURBITON

Kingston upon Thames

2) People move to Surbiton because:

- **Transport links** into the **centre of London** are excellent, so it is popular with commuters — the fastest trains reach London Waterloo in **18 minutes**. It is also close to the **A3** — one of the main road routes into the city.
- There is a variety of **good quality housing**, e.g. semi-detached houses and flats.
- It is a wealthy area with plenty of **shops** and **restaurants**.
- The area has good state **schools** and a number of **parks**, so it's popular with families.

3) Suburbanisation has caused **problems** in Surbiton:

1) Lots of people **own cars** (about 70% of households own at least one car), and roads often have a large number of parked cars. This causes congestion and can make it difficult for **larger vehicles** (e.g. buses) to get through.

2) Surbiton is currently in **London travel zone 6**. This means that fares into central London are **expensive** and many commuters choose to **drive** — about **40%** of the working population in **Surbiton** drive to work. This further increases congestion and air pollution, especially along the roads connecting Surbiton to the A3.

The train stations in London are divided into six zones. Zone 1 is in the centre of the city and zone 6 covers stations on the edge of London.

3) **House prices** are **high** in Surbiton — the average selling price in **April 2012** was **£406 000** (compared to a UK average of £226 000). This makes it **harder** for people on **lower incomes** to **move** to the area, which could lead to **economic segregation** — people on higher incomes living in different areas from those on lower incomes.

4) There are some strategies in place to **manage the problems** in Surbiton:

1) The **Improvement Strategy for Surbiton Town Centre** was launched in **September 2009**. It proposed **widening roads**, building a **new access road** to Surbiton station and having **set delivery times** for local shops, so that delivery bays in the town centre can become **parking bays** at other times of the day. These measures will help **combat congestion** and make it easier for traffic to **pass** parked cars.

2) The **Surbiton Neighbourhood Committee** has been set up to involve the residents of Surbiton in **local decision making**. The committee can make decisions about how to make **improvements** (e.g. traffic management) within the area.

3) There is currently a campaign to **reclassify Surbiton station** as being in London travel **zone 5**. This would mean that commuters would **pay less** to travel into **central London**, which would encourage more people to use the train.

4) **Secure bicycle storage units** have been installed at the station and there are plans to **improve pedestrian access**, which should **encourage** more people to cycle or walk to the station rather than driving.

Josh and Pierre had their own way of clearing congestion in Surbiton.

Practice Questions

Q1 Give two reasons why suburbanisation occurs in developed countries.

Q2 Give two strategies that have been used to manage problems caused by suburbanisation in Surbiton.

Exam Question

Q1 Outline the impacts of suburbanisation. [8 marks]

I think it's time to rename the town Suburbiton...

Poor Surbiton is often the butt of jokes about suburbanisation, but that's just because it's such a great example. So get it learnt.

Counter-urbanisation

You might think counter-urbanisation is when you build a LEGO® house on your kitchen work top — well, you'd be wrong. It's the movement of people away from large urban areas to smaller settlements and rural areas.

There are **Lots of Reasons** for **Counter-urbanisation**

A lot of the push and pull factors for counter-urbanisation are the same as for suburbanisation.

PUSH FACTORS

- Many people move out of urban areas to escape the **air and noise pollution** of towns and cities.
- Suburbs and city centres often have problems with **congestion** and **parking**.
- As **suburban** areas become more popular **house prices** rise. People feel they are not getting **value for money** and move further from the city. E.g. in Surbiton **£300 000** would only buy a **two** bedroom house, but in St Ives (see next page) it would buy a **four** bedroom house.

Bob enjoyed country living, but he couldn't shake off his craving for a skinny caramel latte.

PULL FACTORS

- **Houses** in **smaller settlements** and **rural areas** are often less **densely packed** than those in city centres and the suburbs. This means houses are often **bigger** and have more **outside space**.
- People think that living somewhere **quieter** and with **more open space** will improve their **quality of life**. This is especially true for **retired** people and **families** with children.
- Improved **communication services** (e.g. high-speed internet connection) make it easier for people to live in rural areas and **work from home**. E.g. workers can remotely access their office computer at home.
- **Technological improvements** also mean that some companies **no longer** need to be in a city centre to do business and can move to **rural areas** where land is **cheaper**. This creates **jobs** in rural areas.
- As in suburban areas, increased **car ownership** and improved **rail services** mean that people can live **further** from the city and **commute** to work.

Villages with key services and good access to commuter routes are sometimes called suburbanised villages.

Counter-urbanisation has **Impacts** on **Rural Areas**

There are **positive** and **negative impacts** of counter-urbanisation in rural areas:

POSITIVE IMPACTS

1) Some services see an **increase in business** (e.g. pubs that have restaurants). This is because the newer residents are often **professionals** or **retired people** who have **higher disposable income**.
2) In some villages the existing houses are **improved** as farm buildings are **renovated** and **upgraded**. Farmers are able to make money by **selling unwanted land** or **buildings** for housing developments.
3) In some rural areas schools have **closed** due to a lack of pupils. If **families** move to a rural area then schools can **stay open**, and children of existing residents can continue to go to school locally.

NEGATIVE IMPACTS

1) Development (e.g. unattractive new housing developments) can affect the **character** of rural settlements.
2) Some **rural shops** and **services** (e.g. bus services) **may close** — wealthier residents who own cars are more likely to travel to use **shops** and **services** in **urban areas**.
3) **Rural roads** and **infrastructure** may struggle to cope with the **additional traffic**. This can cause **congestion** and **increase air pollution** in rural areas.
4) **Schools may close** if the new residents are **older people** rather than families with **children**.
5) There is more demand for houses, so **house prices increase**. Younger people **may not be able to afford** to buy a house, which can mean the **population** is dominated by older people.

Have a look back at the impacts of suburbanisation (p. 188) — counter-urbanisation has similar impacts.

There are things that are being done in rural areas to **manage** the negative impacts:

1) In some areas, developments are only allowed if they're **in keeping** with the **rest of the area**, e.g. the houses must be built using certain materials.
2) Some companies offer **mobile services** that visit **rural areas**. E.g. NatWest Bank has mobile banking units that visit rural communities in Cornwall, Devon, Cumbria and South Wales each week.
3) In some rural areas there are **local occupancy clauses** on houses. E.g. in parts of Cumbria some relatively low-cost houses can only be bought by people who have lived in the area for **at least three years**. This means that local people on **low incomes** can stay in the area.

Counter-urbanisation

St Ives *is a Great Example of* Counter-Urbanisation

1) **St Ives** in Cambridgeshire is about **70 miles north of London**. The town has grown through counter-urbanisation. In 1961 its population was just **3800**, by **2010** it had reached **16 400**.

2) It has good **road access** and **rail links** to Cambridge and London. Many people commute into **Cambridge** and around a **quarter** of the working population **commute into London** each day.

Counter-urbanisation has had Impacts *in* St Ives

- **Traffic congestion** is a problem, particularly during rush hour on the **A14** (the main **commuter** route from St Ives to Cambridge).

- The **average price** of a detached house in St Ives **rose from £130 000** to **£291 000** between **2000** and **2010**. Commuters often earn **higher wages** than people **working locally**, so they are better able to **afford** higher prices.

- St Ives is on the River Great Ouse and has a history of flood problems. As the **demand for housing** has grown, new developments have been built on the south **river bank** in the centre of town, and on the **floodplain**. This puts more residents at risk of flooding — **1000 properties** in St Ives are at risk of flooding from a 1 in 100 year event.

- There are now more **shops** and **services** in the town. For example, in addition to everyday food and grocery stores there are shops selling other goods, e.g. clothes and antiques, as well as more cafés and restaurants.

- The movement of families to St. Ives has changed its **population structure**. The original population was **ageing**, but the influx of younger people means that there are now more people under the age of 16 than over the age of 65. This has put **pressure on schools**, and **more pre-school** and **primary school places** are needed in the town.

Management Strategies Include More Affordable Housing *and* Better Transport

- Plans were approved in 2010 to build **200 new homes** in St Ives. At least **75** of these will be **affordable housing** aimed at people on lower incomes, e.g. **social rents** (houses that are rented out at low rates by councils or housing associations) and **low-cost ownership** (which enables people to e.g. buy a house at a discounted price or buy a share in a house and rent the rest).

- There are plans to expand **primary schools** in St Ives to make **240 more places** available.

- After flooding in 1998 and 2003, **flood protection works** costing **£8.8 million** were completed along the River Great Ouse in 2007. **New embankments** and **flood walls** were constructed in St Ives.

- A **£116 million guided busway** which links St Ives to Huntingdon and Cambridge has been built. It's hoped that this will **reduce congestion**, as many commuters no longer need to drive along the A14. There are also plans to **extend the busway** to a new train station in Cambridge, from which journey times to London will be quicker than from Huntingdon. This should **reduce** the number of London commuters who use Huntingdon station.

A guided busway is a track for buses to drive on.

Practice Questions

Q1 What is counter-urbanisation?

Q2 Give three reasons for counter-urbanisation.

Exam Question

Q1 With reference to at least one example, discuss the impacts of counter-urbanisation. [8 marks]

It sounds like a St Hive of activity...

Hopefully you know the drill with these pages by now. Learn the causes and impacts of counter-urbanisation and the management strategies that have been used to deal with it. Don't turn over until you can repeat the whole lot off by heart.

Re-urbanisation

Re-urbanisation is the movement of people back into urban areas — and it's the last of the urbanisation processes.

Re-urbanisation Involves Movement Back to City Centres

PULL FACTORS

1) The movement of industry and businesses **out of** cities as a result of suburbanisation, counter-urbanisation and deindustrialisation (see p. 188) may leave **land derelict**. **Government policies** often **favour redevelopment** of **brownfield sites** in city centres over development of greenfield sites. People are **attracted** back to the city by **new developments** (e.g. high quality apartments).

2) **Urban Development Corporations** (**UDCs**) were set up in the UK to regenerate derelict urban areas and provide a more attractive environment for people to live and work. They have the power to **buy land in a city** and plan how the land should be used in order to encourage businesses and people to **move back** into the regenerated areas.

3) Most **universities** are based in urban areas, so young people move there for **education**.

4) **Young single people** often want to live **close to their work** in areas with **good entertainment services** (e.g. bars and nightclubs). For example, Notting Hill in London has been **gentrified** (see p. 194) and attracts young, affluent workers because it is a **lively area** that is well connected to the city centre. Young couples may choose to **stay** in the urban area where they have settled when they have **children**.

5) Once re-urbanisation has **started** it tends to **continue** — as soon as a few businesses invest and people start to return, it encourages other businesses to invest.

PUSH FACTORS

1) There may be a **lack of jobs** in some rural or suburban areas.

2) Rural areas provide fewer **leisure** or **entertainment** facilities (e.g. nightlife).

3) Counter-urbanisation may cause high **house prices** in rural areas (see p. 190).

There's more information about regeneration on pages 194-197.

Re-urbanisation has Impacts on the City Centre

POSITIVE IMPACTS

1) As people move back into the city centre, **new shops** and **services** open, which **boosts the economy** in the city.

2) As shops and businesses return, **jobs** are created. This means there is **less unemployment**, which can help to **reduce** certain types of **crime**, e.g. theft.

3) **Tourism** in the city may **increase** if the city centre is improved. Increased tourism brings **money** into the city which can be spent on **improving** the area even more, e.g. building new attractions or improving public transport.

4) Local state **schools** can benefit from the increased number of students. However, **wealthier people** moving into an area may choose to send their children to **private schools** or **better-performing schools away** from the city centre.

NEGATIVE IMPACTS

1) Original residents in the area being re-urbanised are often on **low incomes** and may not be able to **afford housing** as prices increase. They may have to move to **cheaper areas** of the city.

2) There may be **tension** between the **original residents** and the **new residents**, which could lead to crime or violence.

3) **Jobs** created in new businesses may not be **accessible** to the original residents, many of whom are **unskilled** or **semi-skilled**.

4) **Shops** and **services** catering to the newer, more wealthy residents (e.g. cafés and designer clothes shops) may **replace** shops and services **targeted** at **original residents** (e.g. grocery stores and launderettes). For the original residents, the new shops may be **too expensive** or not stock the products they want, which means they may have to go **elsewhere** to shop.

Re-urbanisation can impact rural and suburban areas too, e.g. as young people move out, an ageing population may be left. Services can also be affected as demand for them falls.

Some of the Impacts can be Managed

1) Re-urbanisation projects can include **guarantees** to bring **affordable housing** to an area. For example, a redevelopment programme in Camden (North London) guaranteed that 25% of the new homes on the site would be made **affordable** for council tenants and people on low incomes.

2) Some charitable projects aim to improve the **skills** of the existing population to increase employment levels. E.g. **City Gateway** is a charity set up in the **London Docklands**. They work with disadvantaged young people from the area, running training courses to help them learn **new skills** so they can get into **employment**.

Re-urbanisation

Redevelopment Caused Re-urbanisation in the London Docklands

1) The **London Docklands** are on the **River Thames** in the east of the city. During the **19th** and **early 20th centuries**, the docks were **globally important** and there was a lot of **economic activity** in the area, e.g. warehouses and shipping offices.

2) From the **1960s** onwards the docks began to **decline** because of changes in the shipping industry — larger container ships became common and the London docks were not **large** or **deep** enough to accommodate them.

3) By **1980** large areas of the Docklands were in a **derelict state**. **150 000 people** had lost their jobs and **20%** of the housing was **not suitable** for living in. The Docklands had **poor public transport**, so it wasn't well linked to the rest of the city.

4) The **London Docklands Development Corporation** (LDDC) was a UDC that was set up in 1981 to redevelop the area. The LDDC redevelopment plan focused on a number of key areas, and had **positive impacts**:

- **Economy** — part of the area was made an **Enterprise Zone** from 1982 until 1992. By 1998, there were **2700 businesses** trading in the Docklands and the area had attracted **£7.7 billion** of **private investment**. The new businesses created jobs — by 1998 **85 000 people** worked there.

  > Enterprise Zones are areas where taxes are lowered and planning restrictions are relaxed to encourage businesses to locate.

- **Housing** — **24 000 new homes** were built, including **6250** housing association or local authority houses.
- **Transport** — the **Docklands Light Railway** opened in 1987, which cut journey times to **Central London** to less than 20 minutes. New **pedestrian** and **cycle routes** made travel within the area **easier** and **safer**.
- **Community** — new **public facilities** were built, including a **sailing and watersports centre** and the **Surrey Quays** shopping complex. Five new **health centres** were built and existing ones were **refurbished**.
- **Education** — **new schools** and colleges were built and existing schools were **improved**, e.g. by buying new IT equipment.
- **Environment** — the docks were **refurbished**, providing a pleasant environment for local residents. New **outdoor spaces** were created, including an ecology park at Bow Creek and a wildfowl sanctuary at East India Dock.

5) **Redevelopment** of the Docklands caused **re-urbanisation** — since 1980 the population has **doubled**.

6) However, re-urbanisation has had some **negative impacts** in the Docklands:

- There was some **conflict** between **original residents** and **newer, more affluent residents**. This was because some of the original residents felt that the LDDC **favoured** luxury developments rather than affordable housing.
- Many of the original residents were **unable** to find work in the new businesses. This was because the jobs on offer were often **skilled** positions in the service industry (e.g. banking) and many of the original residents were not qualified for this type of work (e.g. in 1981, **36%** of people in the Docklands were either **unskilled** or **semi-skilled**).

7) There have been attempts to **manage** these impacts:

- In some areas of the Docklands (e.g. Shadwell Basin and Wapping), the LDDC asked for **40% of new housing** to be sold at an **affordable price** to the original residents.
- Centres were set up to provide **training** in **basic literacy**, **numeracy** and **IT**, e.g. **£1.5 million** was spent on an IT centre, which opened in 1984. It trained **unemployed 16-18 year-olds** in basic electronics and computer programming, giving them **work experience** with local businesses and a **qualification** at the end of the course.
- The LDDC also supported **Skillnet** — a **job agency** which worked with training providers and employers to provide people with the **skills** they needed to find work in the area (e.g. in construction).

Practice Questions

Q1 Give two positive impacts of re-urbanisation.

Q2 Give two impacts of re-urbanisation in an area you have studied.

Exam Question

Q1 Look at the photograph. Comment on the evidence that re-urbanisation has occurred in this area.   [7 marks]

©iStockphoto.com/Pavel Losevsky

Redeveloping the Docklands was Quay to re-urbanisation...

Talking about re-urbanisation seems like a great way to impress someone on a date — you can point out high density buildings and improved transportation links as you stroll around a newly-created public space. There's a reason I've never had a girlfriend.

Urban Decline and Regeneration

People piling out of cities can lead to urban decline. But fear not my urban-dwelling friends — regeneration can turn it around.

Urban Decline Usually Starts with a Decline in Industry

Urban decline is when a **decrease** in economic activity in an **urban area** causes it to become **run down**.
There is often a **pattern** to the decline:

> Urban decline usually only takes place in part of the city (e.g. the inner city).

1 DECLINE IN INDUSTRY

1) The **movement of manufacturing overseas** (see p. 216) causes industry to close.
2) Industry may also **move to sites outside of the city centre** where rent is cheaper.

2 INCREASE IN UNEMPLOYMENT

1) If **industry declines** there will be a **loss of jobs** and an **increase in unemployment**.
Some unemployed people will move **out** of the area to **find jobs** elsewhere.
2) The **jobs** available to the unemployed people who are left behind may be **unskilled** or **low paid**.

3 SHOPS AND SERVICES DECLINE

1) If **lots of people** leave the city, there will be **fewer people** to use the **shops** and **services** (e.g. public transport or leisure facilities). The people who remain in the city have **less money** to spend there.
2) The **shops** may be forced to **close down** and **services** may go into **decline**.

4 THE PHYSICAL ENVIRONMENT DECLINES

1) As industry, people and services move out, they leave **empty buildings** (e.g. factories, houses and shops), which may become **derelict**. Derelict buildings have problems with **vandalism** and **graffiti**.
2) **Recreational areas** (e.g. parks) are **neglected** and may develop problems with crime (e.g. drug dealing).
3) As the area becomes **unattractive**, **decline continues** because fewer people want to live there.

There are **three different processes** that **regenerate** urban areas —
gentrification, **partnership schemes** and **property-led regeneration schemes**.

> These processes are covered in more detail on the next few pages.

Gentrification is Regeneration by a Wealthier Group

1) **Gentrification** is when **wealthier people** move into a **run down area** and regenerate it by improving their **housing**.
2) It often causes **social changes** in the area — **lower income groups** are **replaced** by more affluent people.

POSITIVE IMPACTS

1) **Housing is improved** as wealthy newcomers regenerate old buildings.
2) The **value of housing** in the area **increases**. This means that **existing homeowners** in the area are able to sell their homes for **more money**.
3) **New businesses** (e.g. bars and restaurants) move into the area to cater for the **wealthier newcomers**. This creates jobs.
4) **Crime rates** may **fall** — as housing is improved there are **fewer derelict buildings** that attract graffiti and vandalism.

Max had completed the gentrification process.

NEGATIVE IMPACTS

1) The **high demand** for housing can cause problems. E.g. **tenants** in the area may be **forced out** of their homes because **landlords** want to sell the house while its value is **high**.
2) Increased house prices mean that the **children** of the original homeowners may be **unable to afford** to buy or rent nearby, and may be forced to **move** elsewhere.
3) Original residents may **lose the shops and services** they **need** (e.g. launderettes and charity shops) as these are **replaced** by **up-market shops** aimed at the wealthier residents (e.g. coffee shops).
4) All of these problems can contribute to **tension** between the **local people** and the **new residents**.

Urban Decline and Regeneration

Islington in London has Been Gentrified

1) **Islington** is a borough in **north London**. There are lots of **large Georgian** and **early Victorian houses**, which were originally occupied by **wealthy residents**.

2) In the **late 19th century**, the railways expanded and made access to the city easier, so the wealthier residents left Islington and **moved out** to the **suburbs**.

3) **Poorer residents** from central London **moved into** the area, which became overcrowded. They couldn't afford to **maintain** the housing and the area became **run down**.

4) In the **1960s middle class** people began to buy properties in Islington because:

Georgian Housing along Regent's Canal in Islington.

- Across the city, there was an **increase in jobs** in the **service** sector (e.g. in law and the media) and a **decrease in jobs** in the **manufacturing** sector. People working in the service sector tended to be young, well paid and work long hours, so they wanted to live **close to the city centre**.

- Islington was **well connected** to the city centre by nearby Angel underground station.

- Houses in Islington were **large** and **attractive**, and much **cheaper** than in wealthier areas of the city. Many of the houses were in a poor state, so people could **renovate** them to suit their own tastes.

- Once the gentrification process **began, more and more** wealthier people were encouraged to move there.

Gentrification has had a Number of Impacts on Islington

1) The impacts of gentrification have been both **positive**...

- Improved **housing** — wealthier residents **renovated** and **improved** many of the Georgian and Victorian properties (e.g. restoring original features and repainting exterior walls).

- New **businesses opened**, e.g. wine bars and restaurants, bringing **money** and **jobs** to the area.

... and **negative**:

- Increased **house prices** — the average house price in Islington increased from around **£130 000** in 1996 to **£430 000** in 2008. This made it difficult for people on **lower salaries** to live in the area. Many people were forced out of the area or into **social housing** (which accounted for nearly **50%** of housing in 2008).

- There is **wealth gap** between the **richest** and the **poorest** residents, e.g. the richest 20% earn more than £60 000 a year while the poorest 20% earn less than £15 000 a year. In 2007, Islington was the **8th most deprived area** in England — it had the second-highest rate of child poverty in England, a high crime rate and high unemployment.

- Some **businesses** have **closed**, e.g. traditional pubs and convenience stores.

2) The negative impacts of gentrification are being **managed** by projects that aim to **tackle deprivation** in the area:

- Islington businesses are being encouraged to pay all of their staff the **London living wage** of **£8.30 an hour**. This gives low-skilled workers a **larger income** and helps them to cope with the **high cost of living** in Islington.

- **Charities** work in poorer neighbourhoods to **improve education**. E.g. Light Project International run practical maths classes for unemployed people over the age of 16 and adult education classes in languages.

Practice Questions

Q1 Name the four stages of urban decline.

Q2 What is gentrification?

Exam Question

Q1 With reference to an area you have studied, discuss the changes that have taken place due to gentrification.   [10 marks]

My favourite regeneration programme is Dr Who...

It seems to me that people just can't make up their minds. First they move to the city, then they realise they want to live outside of the city, and then they move back again to get another taste of urban living. Still, I guess it's good news for removal men.

Urban Regeneration

Two more urban regeneration schemes to learn I'm afraid — partnership schemes and property-led regeneration. Alright, we both know they don't sound like they'll be a barrel of laughs but don't give me that look — I'm only a book.

Partnership Schemes Involve Councils and Businesses

Peter and Lara's partnership scheme was heading straight for divorce.

1) **Partnership schemes** involve **local councils** working with **businesses** and **local communities** to come up with a **regeneration plan** for an area.

2) The schemes often try to improve the **economy** and **environment** in the area. They also aim to make **social improvements**, e.g. by building community centres.

3) In the UK, partnership schemes such as **City Challenge** aimed to regenerate urban areas:

> **31 City Challenge Partnership Schemes** ran in deprived urban areas between **1992** and **1998**. The government provided **£1.14 billion** of funding for these schemes and they attracted a total **investment** of around **£7.58 billion**. Cities competed with each other for this funding which aimed to regenerate **deprived** areas by improving the **physical environment, economy** and **quality of life**.

Hulme in Manchester was Regenerated by a City Challenge Partnership

1) In the 19th and early 20th century Hulme provided housing for people working in **Manchester's industries**. By the mid 19th century it was **overcrowded**, with many people living in **poor quality housing** with few facilities (e.g. no indoor toilet). The whole area was **cleared for redevelopment** in the 1960s.

2) People were moved out of their homes into flats in new **tower blocks** and **apartment buildings**, which had problems with **pest infestation** and **poor heating**. Many residents felt **isolated** and suffered from **depression** and **poor health**.

3) By the early 1990s, many **families** had moved **out** of Hulme. Many of the flats were **unlivable**, the area was **poor** and there were problems with **unemployment** and **crime**.

4) In 1992 the **Hulme City Challenge Partnership** was formed. Manchester City Council worked with private companies to design a **£37.5 million** regeneration package to redevelop the area. It aimed to create a **strong community feel** by building a mixture of housing, businesses, shops and community spaces, and improving **transport links** to connect Hulme to the city centre and surrounding communities. The main improvements were:

- Tower blocks were **demolished** and a variety of **new houses** were built. New housing was a **mixture** of council-owned and private to provide for **existing residents** and encourage **outsiders** to buy into the area.
- The main **shopping area** was **refurbished** to include a range of shops, a covered market hall and a supermarket.
- The creation of the **Zion Centre** — an arts venue and community centre which runs arts projects for local people.
- A **business park** was built at **Birley Fields** to encourage **private investment** in the area. Several **high profile businesses** occupy the offices, including the construction company Laing O'Rourke and Colgate Ltd. This has created **jobs** and brought **outsiders** working for these companies into the area.
- **Hulme Park** was created to provide a safe, outdoor green space for residents.

The Hulme City Challenge Partnership has been Successful in Some Ways

1) The new housing and services have made Hulme a much **more attractive place to live** — its population **grew** by an estimated 3.3% between 1992 and 2002, compared to 0.2% across the city as a whole.

2) From 1997 to 2002 Hulme and neighbouring Moss Side received around **£400 million** of private and public **investment**. **Jobs** were created in **new industries** and **services** that moved to the area. Unemployment fell from 32% in 1989 to 6% in 2010.

3) However, not all Hulme's problems have been resolved:

> Social housing is owned and rented out by councils or housing associations.

- Hulme is still a **poor area** and 47.5% of the population live in **social housing**.
- **House prices** have **increased**, which has made private housing **unaffordable** for local people on low incomes.
- Unemployment is still **high** compared to the rest of Manchester.

Urban Regeneration

Property-led Regeneration is being used in the London Thames Gateway

1) **Property-led regeneration schemes** involve **building** or **improving property** in an area to change its **image** and improve the local **environment**. These changes encourage further investment and the return of **people** and **business**. They are often set up by **UDCs** (see page 192), who plan and coordinate the development.

2) The **London Thames Gateway** is a **large area** stretching for 40 miles along the Thames to the **east** of London.

3) The area was once important for **manufacturing**. However, manufacturing industries **declined** from the 1960s onwards, and the area became **run down**. The London Thames Gateway Development Corporation (**LTGDC**) is a **ten-year programme** that was set up in **2004** to regenerate the part of the Thames Gateway to the **north** and **east** of the London Docklands. Its **aims** are:

- To make sure **land** and **buildings** are being used and not left derelict.
- To **encourage** existing and new **industry** and **business** to **develop**.
- To create an **attractive environment**.
- To **improve housing** and **social facilities**, so people want to live and work in the area.

4) The LTGDC is supporting a number of projects across East London, and has invested **£209.6 million** up to April 2011. Projects include:

- Building **new town centres** in Canning Town and Custom House with retail, business and leisure space, an improved **road network**, improved **pedestrian** and **cycle access**, and a new **crossrail** station.
- Renovation of schools and improvements in **education services** — the University of East London and Birkbeck (part of the University of London) are working together to establish a **new campus** in Stratford, which will open in 2013.
- A sustainable housing development at **Barking Riverside** to provide more than 10 000 new homes along with health centres, schools, leisure facilities and extensive green space, including an ecology park. **Barking train station** and **local roads** are being upgraded and existing bus routes will serve the area to make it more accessible.

Crossrail is a new railway service that will run east to west across London. It is due to open in 2018.

5) The project is **ongoing**, but it's had a number of **successes** so far:

- The population of the area is growing, e.g. between 2001 and 2011 the population of the borough of Barking and Dagenham rose by **12%**.
- Renovation of schools has led to improvements in pupils' educational achievement. E.g. a **£40 million** renovation at St Pauls Way Trust School has improved science, drama and sports facilities. As a result, the number of students at the school getting **5 A* to C grades at GCSE** improved from **29%** to **46%** in one year.

6) However, there are some **concerns** about the **redevelopment**:

- The LTGDC has been accused of **not listening** to residents' **opinions**. For example, the LTGDC gave planning permission for a temporary **nightclub** to be erected close to the Olympic Park during the summer of 2012, despite objections about noise and disruption from local residents and Tower Hamlets Council.
- There were **objections** to a proposed tower block at Virginia Quay, which local councillors thought didn't provide enough **affordable housing**, would cause **over-crowding** of the area, **parking problems** and **loss of open space**.

Practice Questions

Q1 What is a property-led regeneration scheme?

Q2 Give the aims of a property-led regeneration scheme that you have studied.

Exam Question

Q1 Evaluate the success of a partnership scheme you have studied which has tried to promote urban regeneration. [10 marks]

Maybe it's because I'm a Londoner, that I love the LTGDC...

Mmm, tuneful. The LTGDC is certainly my favourite example of a property-led regeneration scheme — all those wonderfully exciting aims, projects, successes and concerns. If you learn it well it may become yours too, you lucky badger...

Retailing

We all love to shop, but the way that people are shopping has changed over time — that's what these pages are all about.

Retailing and Other Services are Decentralising

1) In the 1950s and 1960s shops selling **high-order goods** (e.g. furniture, jewellery) were in **town** and **city centres** and attracted customers from a wide area. Shops selling **low-order goods** (e.g. food) provided for customers **locally** within their neighbourhoods.

2) This traditional shopping pattern began to **change** in the **1970s** — shops (e.g. supermarkets and DIY stores) began to move to the outskirts of towns. This process is called **decentralisation**. Nowadays most cities have large **out-of-town retail** complexes.

3) There are a number of **reasons** for the growth of **out-of-town** retailing:

> *High-order goods are expensive items that you only buy occasionally. Low-order goods are inexpensive items that you buy regularly.*

- Increased **car ownership** means more people **drive** to the shops. Out-of-town locations are often close to **motorways**, so they are easy to get to by car, and usually have fewer problems with **congestion** than town centres.
- **Parking prices** are **high** in city centres — at out-of-town shopping complexes customer parking is usually free.
- The use of cars and **home freezers** also means people can do **one weekly food shop** rather than only buying what they can carry home and use immediately. This means people are more likely to shop at out-of-town supermarkets where they can **park directly outside** and get **everything** they need under one roof.
- **Increased road building**, particularly of motorways and bypasses, makes out-of-town shopping centres easy to access and attracts **customers from further away** because driving on motorways reduces journey times.
- It's **cheaper** to build retail parks out-of-town than it is to rent or buy premises in the city centre. Retail parks are often built on **reclaimed derelict land**, so it's easy for developers to get **planning permission**.

"Sure you can do a week's shopping here. You like grapefruit, right?"

4) It's **not just shops** that have moved to out-of-town retail parks. Many large retail centres also offer **services**, e.g. **leisure facilities** such as bowling, cinemas and restaurants. This helps them to attract **more customers** by making a trip to a shopping centre a **social** and **family** activity. It also encourages people to spend **more time** there.

Decentralisation Affects City Centres and the Rural-Urban Fringe

Out-of-town retail parks have impacts on nearby **city centres**:

Negative impacts

- Out-of-town shopping centres **compete** with city centre shops, so **fewer people** shop in the city centre. This can force shops in the city centre to **close**, so people **lose their jobs**.
- The **decline** in the number of people coming to the city centre to **shop** also **decreases** the number of customers using **services** (e.g. restaurants and cafés), and may force them to **close**.
- A **decline** in **business** and **retail** can lead to a more general **decline** in the area — **investment** in the city centre **decreases** and it becomes run down. This can increase problems like **vandalism**.

Positive impacts

- Local councils and the government sometimes **invest** money to **improve** the city centre and **attract customers** back (see p. 200). Improvements may include creating **pedestrian zones**, **renovating** older shopping malls and **organising** events (e.g. festivals).
- **Congestion and pollution** may **decrease** as fewer people drive to the city centre to shop.

They also have impacts on the **rural-urban fringe** (see p. 175) where they are located:

Negative impacts

- Out-of-town complexes require a lot of **construction**, e.g. building tramways to improve transport connections. Although this provides **jobs** in the short term, it creates **noise pollution** and could add to **congestion** if roads are disrupted.
- Most people drive to out-of-town retail centres, which causes **congestion** and air pollution.

Positive impacts

- Out-of-town shopping complexes **create jobs** for people living in the suburbs.
- Retail parks are often built on **brownfield sites** that would otherwise be left empty. E.g. Bluewater in Kent is built in a **former quarry**.
- Houses that have easy access to the shopping centre may **increase in value**.

Retailing

The Trafford Centre is a Large Out-of-town Retail Park near Manchester

1) The **Trafford Centre** opened in **1998**. It was built on a brownfield site in the industrial area of Trafford Park, 5 miles west of Manchester. The site covers 150 acres and it cost **£600 million** to complete.

The Trafford Centre is close to many large towns and cities in northern England.

2) The Trafford Centre has the **largest catchment area** of any shopping centre in the UK — **5.3 million people** (more than 8% of the UK population) live within a **45 minute drive**. More than 30 million people visit the Trafford Centre each year.

3) The Trafford Centre is popular for a number of reasons:

- The Trafford Centre offers a **range** of activities. As well as **over 200 shops**, there is a **1600 seat food court**, a **20 screen cinema**, **crazy golf**, **ten pin bowling**, **laser quest** and an indoor **climbing wall**.
- It is **well connected** by road. The centre is close to the **M60** for customers coming from outside of Manchester, and to the **M602** into the **city centre**. There are lots of **buses** that go **direct** from Manchester to the Trafford Centre.
- It has **11 500 free parking spaces** and a **traffic control system** to reduce congestion and car park waiting times.
- It is **indoors** and **air conditioned** to protect customers from the weather all year round.
- It has **long opening hours** — shops are open until 10pm Monday to Friday, 8pm on Saturday and 6pm on Sunday.

The Trafford Centre has had an Impact on the Surrounding Area

Negative impacts

- Most visitors drive to the centre, which causes **congestion** and **pollution**, particularly at **busy periods**, e.g. Christmas.
- The Trafford Centre has had an impact on shopping in **surrounding towns**. **Fewer people** go to these **town centres** to shop or for leisure activities, because they cannot compete with the **advantages** offered by the Trafford Centre (e.g. free parking). Altrincham has suffered particularly badly — **37%** of shops were **vacant in** 2010 (nearly 3 times the **national average** of 13%).

Positive impacts

- The Trafford Centre supports **local community projects** and charities, e.g. Royal Manchester Children's Hospital, through fundraising and donations.
- The centre provides **work experience** for local school students studying Retail Business.
- **8000 people** are **employed** at the Trafford Centre — they receive **benefits** such as health care and childcare vouchers.
- The Trafford Centre is growing, so that it offers a wider **range** of services, which attract more customers and bring **more economic benefits** (e.g. jobs). For example, LEGOLAND® Discovery Centre opened in 2010.

There are some schemes in place to help **manage** the **negative** impacts:

- The centre is investing in **improving public transport**, **cycle** and **pedestrian** routes to help **reduce** traffic. There are now **40 bus services an hour** to and from the Trafford Centre and a **shuttle bus** to the Metrolink tram system.
- In 2011, **Altrincham Forward** (a board made up of local business owners, residents and councillors), produced the **Altrincham Town Centre Action Plan**. This plan outlines strategies to draw **people** into the town, including establishing an annual calendar of **events** in the town and **reducing parking charges**.

Practice Questions

Q1 Give two reasons for the growth of out-of-town shopping centres.

Q2 Give one positive and one negative impact of out-of-town retail parks on city centres.

Exam Question

Q1 With reference to at least one example, outline the characteristics of out-of-town retail centres. [8 marks]

Want a break from retail? Try some re-tell therapy...

Just because these pages are about retail it doesn't mean that going shopping counts as revision. Instead, have a good read through all this information and then tell your friends everything you can remember. It'll do you the world of good, and they'll love it...

Redeveloping Urban Centres

These pages are all about what happens to poor city centres that fall into decline when people start shopping elsewhere *sob*.

Redevelopment of City Centres Can Help Bring Back Shoppers

1) Before the development of out-of-town retail centres, the central business district (**CBD**) was the hub of a city — where most of the **shops** and **entertainments** were, and where many businesses had their offices.

2) In some cities this is **still true**, but in others there has been a **decline** in the CBD when shops and businesses have closed down or relocated (see p. 198). Shops are left **empty**, which is **unattractive** and can lead to **vandalism**.

3) There are often problems with **crime** (e.g. mugging), particularly at **night**. If people don't **feel safe** in an area they won't go there. As fewer people go to the city centre to shop and for entertainment, **investment is likely to decrease** because business owners don't think it is worth opening shops or services there. This leads to **further decline**.

4) **Government** and **local councils redevelop** city centres to draw people and investment back.
There are different strategies for redevelopment:

- Making shopping areas **more attractive** by creating **pedestrian zones**, adding benches and planting trees and flower beds. **Pavements** are also **improved** to make it easier for people with prams and wheelchairs.
- Building **new shopping malls** (e.g. Liverpool One) or **renovating old ones** (e.g. the Arndale Centre in Manchester). These have plenty of **parking spaces** and many shops under one roof to **compete** with out-of-town retail centres.
- Opening **street markets** to improve the **atmosphere** and encourage people to shop in the city centre by increasing the range of products available, e.g. farmers' markets selling local food.
- Improving **public transport** into the town centre to decrease **congestion**, e.g. park and ride schemes (see p. 153).
- Installing **CCTV** and **security alarms** and improving **street lighting** to reduce crime and make the CBD **safer**.
- Increasing opening hours to include **late night** and **Sunday shopping**.
- Conserving **historic buildings** in the city centre to attract tourists.

Some Cities are Developing Other Functions to Revive the CBD

To compete with the **range** of facilities available at out-of-town shopping centres, some cities are investing in **entertainment** and **leisure facilities** and **cultural events** in their CBD, and others are building **new housing**. For example:

- More **cafés, bars, restaurants** and **entertainment venues** (e.g. cinemas and theatres) to bring people into the city centre. Overall, this helps to **reduce crime and vandalism** because the city centre is **busier**, but can produce **other problems** (e.g. drunkenness) that mean more police are needed on the streets at busy times (e.g. Saturday nights).
- Promoting **free cultural entertainment** in the city centre, e.g. cultural festivals or street theatre. In Liverpool, the **Liverpool Light Night** is a **cultural evening** where galleries and museums stay open late and offer free entry to visitors. There is street theatre, light displays and live music all around the city centre.
- Opening **flagship attractions** — these are major visitor attractions that draw **people** in from a wide area and act as a focal point for **tourism** and **regeneration**. For example, the Lightbox in Woking is a gallery and museum which hosts visiting art exhibitions and runs workshops for schools and community groups. People come to **visit these attractions** and then may **visit shops** and **restaurants nearby**.
- The establishment of **theme areas** such as the gay village in Manchester, where a number of **bars** and **restaurants** have opened in former cotton factories and warehouses along the Rochdale Canal. These theme areas are often attractive to **tourists** as well as local people.
- The development of more **residential property** — building new apartments and renovating old industrial buildings. If more people **live in the CBD** they are more likely to **use the facilities** there.

Canal Street in the heart of
Manchester's gay village.

All these projects are helping to bring more people into the city centre, particularly when they are combined with wider **re-urbanisation** (p. 192-193) and **gentrification** (p. 194) in urban areas. Bringing more people into the CBD means **shops** and **businesses** are more likely to invest there and the **community feel** of a town or city centre is preserved.

Redeveloping Urban Centres

Manchester City Centre has been Redeveloped

1) Manchester was an **important industrial city** throughout the 19th and early 20th centuries. However, from the **1960s** onwards industrial activities began to decrease and people began to **move out** of the city centre.

2) The building of the **Arndale Centre** (a large shopping arcade) in **1975** brought people into the city to **shop**. However, the city centre population was still **declining** and in the 1980s it fell to **less than 1000** as people moved out to the **suburbs**. As people moved out, the centre became **run down**.

3) In **1996** an IRA **bomb** damaged much of **Manchester's CBD**, including the Arndale Centre and the Royal Exchange Theatre.

4) Redevelopment was needed to **repair the damage** done in the bombing and to bring people back into the **city centre**, particularly as the **Trafford Centre** (see p. 199) was about to open outside the city and could threaten the city's retail sector.

5) **Manchester Millennium Ltd**. was formed weeks after the bombing to **design** and **manage** the redevelopment. It aimed to:

- **Re-design** and **rebuild** large parts of the CBD to create a **safe**, **accessible centre** for the whole north west region, where people would come to **live**, to **shop**, and for **entertainment**.
- Make sure that the **success** of the city centre would **last** and would cause **long-term investment**.

6) The **main developments** were in the areas of the city centre damaged by the bombing:

- Old buildings were renovated, e.g. the **Corn Exchange**, a listed building which was occupied by **temporary shops**. It was rebuilt internally and is now an **upmarket mall** selling designer clothing and jewellery.
- **Run down** and **unattractive** buildings (including the Arndale Centre) were **rebuilt** and **restyled**.
- **Upmarket department stores**, e.g. Selfridges, opened.
- Large areas were **pedestrianised**, including Exchange Square, an open area where people can meet and socialise.
- The **Printworks entertainment complex** was built on the site of an **old printing press**. It has a multi-screen IMAX cinema, a gym, restaurants, bars and a night club.
- **Urbis**, an exhibition centre that now hosts the National Football Museum, was built in the Cathedral Gardens.
- Other buildings were constructed or renovated, including new **shops**, **bars**, **restaurants** and **luxury apartments**.
- Old industrial buildings (e.g. warehouses) were turned into **new residential properties**.

Redevelopment of Manchester City Centre has been Successful

1) The redevelopment of Manchester City Centre is an **ongoing process**. So far the redevelopment has been successful in many ways. For example between 2003 and 2009:
- The population of the **city centre doubled** to over 19 000 people.
- Manchester became the third most popular **tourist destination** in the UK — tourism contributed **£5 billion** to the economy each year.
- Retail in the city centre made an extra **£300 million a year**.

2) However, there are still **problems** in the city centre and the redevelopment hasn't benefited everyone. In 2001, **16%** of the population were on **low incomes** — some of these people felt **excluded** from city centre living, because they **couldn't afford** to use the new facilities.

Check out p. 192 for more on the negative impacts of re-urbanisation.

Practice Questions

Q1 Give one strategy for redeveloping city centres.

Q2 What is a flagship attraction?

Exam Question

Q1 Evaluate the success of a redevelopment scheme in an urban centre you have studied. [10 marks]

Get the defibrillator — we need to revive the CBD...

Manchester is a bit of a redevelopment fairy tale — the developers came along and gave the city the kiss of life, and it all ended happily ever after. You need to learn the ways cities can revive their CBDs and how redevelopment has happened in Manchester.

Sustainability in Urban Areas

I know, I know. It's the 'S' word again. These pages aren't rubbish, they're just about waste management...

It can be **Difficult** for **Urban Areas** to be **Sustainable**

Sustainability means meeting the needs of people **today** in a way that doesn't **damage** the environment or **use up** resources, so people can continue to meet their own needs in the **future**. Sustainability is often **difficult** to achieve in urban areas:

1) Urban areas have **large, dense populations**. This causes **environmental problems** because more people create **more waste** which has to be disposed of, drive **more cars** which cause air pollution, and use **more resources** (e.g. water, fuel).

2) The schemes that have been set up to **manage** the impacts of urban growth are often the easiest or cheapest in the **short term** (e.g. disposing of waste in landfill sites, see below) rather than the most sustainable.

Managing Waste can help **Urban Areas** to Become **More Sustainable**

1) **Managing waste** is an important way of improving urban sustainability. By generating **less waste** and **changing** the ways that the waste we do produce is **disposed** of, we can reduce the amount of resources we use and our **impact on the environment**.

2) In 2010 **each person** in the UK produced **452 kg** of waste. A lot of this waste goes into **landfill**, which is unsustainable (see below).

3) However, waste management in the UK is becoming **more sustainable** — landfill is **decreasing** and recycling is **increasing**. E.g. in 2004 **33%** of waste was recovered (e.g. recycled or composted) compared to **45%** in 2008.

4) There are national and EU targets to make waste disposal **more sustainable**, e.g. the EU wants **50%** of household waste to be recycled by 2020.

5) There are **lots** of different methods of **waste management**:

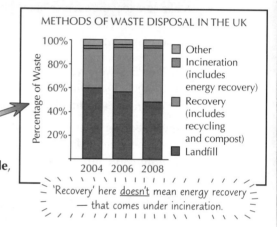

METHODS OF WASTE DISPOSAL IN THE UK

- Other
- Incineration (includes energy recovery)
- Recovery (includes recycling and compost)
- Landfill

'Recovery' here doesn't mean energy recovery — that comes under incineration.

LANDFILL

Landfill is when rubbish is **buried** (often in former quarries). Landfill is **cheap** in the short term but it is **not sustainable**:

- Landfill sites release **carbon dioxide** (CO_2) and **methane** (greenhouse gases — see p. 156). In the UK, landfill sites produce 36% of all methane emissions. This is not sustainable because greenhouse gases cause climate change (see p. 156). However, there are **new technologies** that allow the gases produced to be **captured** and **used**, e.g. as a bio-fuel. In 2008, a landfill site in Mumbai, India was closed and covered — methane produced by the site is used to **generate electricity**. This scheme should reduce greenhouse gas emissions by **2.2 million tonnes** of CO_2 equivalents by 2028.

- Landfill can **pollute groundwater** — new landfill sites can be specially lined to prevent this.

- Dumping waste in landfill sites **wastes valuable materials** that could be **reused** or **recycled**.

- In developing countries, people often **live and work** on landfill sites, scavenging for materials to **sell**. E.g. in Manila, Philippines, **10 000 families** lived on or next to the Smokey Mountain dump until it was closed in 1996. Although this gives people an **income**, it's not sustainable because it doesn't **meet their needs** (e.g. it puts them at risk of disease).

COMPOSTING

In the UK, household waste contains around **38%** organic material (e.g. vegetable peelings). Organic material is **biodegradeable** (it can be broken down by micro-organisms), so it can be composted, either by **individuals** or on a **larger scale**.

- If householders compost in their own gardens it **reduces the costs** to the local authority for waste disposal.

- **Large-scale composting** involves collecting compost from people's **homes** and from **public waste** (e.g. cuttings from pruning trees in parks). The material is transported to **reactors**, where microbes break it down anaerobically (without oxygen). It produces **two useful products** — **biogas** (a mixture of methane and CO_2 which can be combusted to generate heat and electricity), and a nitrogen-rich **fertiliser**.

- Composting is **sustainable** because it **decreases** the amount of waste going to **landfill**, and biogas is a **renewable energy source** that doesn't rely on burning fossil fuels.

- Composting has to be **managed properly** to succeed, for example waste must be **sorted** properly to ensure there are no contaminants, e.g. metals. If the compost is contaminated it can't be sold on for agricultural use because it would **pollute** the soil and could be **harmful** to people eating the crops.

Sustainability in Urban Areas

RECYCLING

Recycling is when waste materials are made into **new products** or **materials**, e.g. plastic bottles are made into fleece jumpers. There are many **advantages** to recycling:

Ulrika liked this recycling lark — she'd made her favourite doily into a snazzy hat.

- Producing goods from recycled materials is often **quicker** and **cheaper** than making them from scratch.

- Recycling materials uses **less energy** than making new things, e.g. it uses **20 times more energy** to manufacture aluminium cans from **raw materials** than recycled materials. Some materials (e.g. glass and aluminium) can be recycled **many times**.

- Recycling **reduces demand** for raw materials. Using fewer raw materials reduces the **environmental impacts** that occur when they're extracted, e.g. deforestation. It also **reduces** the amount of waste going to **landfill** and the **problems** associated with that.

However, there are some **difficulties** with making recycling work well:

- Recycling **relies on individuals**, and some people don't bother. Some local councils encourage people to recycle by letting them put all their recyclable waste **in together** (so they don't have to sort it), or by offering **incentives**. E.g. residents in Windsor, Berkshire were invited to join a trial scheme which gave **rewards** (e.g. points that could be used to pay for goods) for recycling. 70% of those invited signed up to the scheme, and recycling rates for the participants increased by **35%**.

- Recycling costs money — **initial investment** is needed to set up recycling plants, and collection can be **expensive**.

- Lots of the UK's material for recycling is **sent abroad** for processing, e.g. 55% of paper for recycling was sent to China in 2007. Transporting materials **produces emissions**, but generally **less** than would be produced by making new materials.

ENERGY RECOVERY

Energy recovery is when waste that **can't** be composted, reused or recycled is burnt to generate **heat** and **electricity**.

- Energy recovery **reduces** use of fossil fuels, but it is not **fully sustainable** because it produces CO_2 and other **emissions**.

- Energy recovery is used to generate electricity from household waste in Sheffield:
  - The **Energy Recovery Facility** (ERF) provides heat for **140 buildings** in the **city centre**, including Sheffield City Hall. Without ERF, heating these buildings would produce an extra **21 000 tonnes** of CO_2 every year.
  - ERF also provides **17 MW** of electricity to the national grid and **reduces** waste going to **landfill**, e.g. only **15%** of Sheffield's waste goes to **landfill** sites.

- **Other local councils** are looking into ERF. **Leicestershire County Council** has given planning permission for the construction of an energy recovery facility that will produce enough electricity to power **42 000 homes**.

REDUCE AND REUSE

- As well as improving waste management, the overall **amount of waste** produced can be **reduced**. This can be done by **individuals**, e.g. by registering with the Mail Preference Service to reduce the amount of junk mail received, and **businesses**, e.g. by reducing packaging on food.

- Waste products can also be **reused**. This is easier for **some products** than it is for others, e.g. plastic bottles are easily reused, but aluminium cans are not.

- Reusing materials tends to be easier for **individuals** than on a **large scale**. Only certain products can be **successfully reused** on a large scale, e.g. in Germany, drinks companies charge a **deposit** for drinks in **refillable** glass or plastic bottles, which customers get back when they return the bottle to a designated collection point.

Practice Questions

Q1 Name three methods of waste disposal.

Q2 Give two reasons why it is difficult to make recycling successful.

Exam Question

Q1 Explain how different methods of waste management can improve the sustainability of urban areas.   [8 marks]

Reduce, reuse, recycle, revise...

We can all do our bit towards sustainable waste disposal — you could write your revision notes on scrap paper and then recycle them once you've passed your exam. Just make sure you read them carefully in the meantime...

Sustainability in Urban Areas

Managing transport can improve the sustainability of urban areas by reducing emissions, pollution and use of fossil fuels.

Increasing Urban Populations *Mean There is* More Traffic *in* Urban Areas

1) In urban areas the number of cars on the road is **increasing**:

  - As urban areas grow, more people live on the outskirts of cities and **commute** to work in the centre.
  - If businesses and offices **move out** of the city centre (see p. 198), more people are employed on the outskirts. Generally public transport is not as good outside the city centre, so more people **drive** to work.
  - In developing countries, **increasing wealth** means **more people own cars**.
  - As urban areas grow there are more vehicles delivering to a growing number of shops and businesses.

2) Driving cars **isn't sustainable** — it causes **air pollution** which can reduce people's **quality of life**, **greenhouse gas** emissions which damage the environment, and **congestion** which means journeys take longer and people's transport needs aren't met.

3) **Improved public transport** makes cities more sustainable because it produces **less emissions per passenger** than cars.

4) To encourage people to use public transport, it needs to be **reliable**, **cheap** and **easy** to use.

5) Improving public transport isn't the only way to reduce the number of cars on the road — encouraging other **sustainable methods of transport** (e.g. cycling and walking) can help too.

There are Many Ways *to Make* Transport More Sustainable

Lots of **different** schemes are used in cities to make transport **more sustainable**. Most of them aim to reduce **congestion** and **pollution** by reducing the **number of cars** on the road.

Look at the schemes on p. 152-153 as well.

Road schemes

  - **Bus lanes** encourage people to use public transport because buses can **bypass traffic jams**, so travelling by bus is quicker than by car. In Curitiba (a city in Brazil), each of the **main roads** into the city centre has been widened to incorporate a two-way **express lane** for buses. This makes the bus service **reliable** and **efficient**. However, in some cities bus lanes are created without widening the road. This can **increase congestion** for other road users, as the roads are narrower.

  - **Cycle lanes** can speed up travel for cyclists and make it safer to cycle in cities. In 2005, 6 towns in the UK became **Cycle Towns**, which received extra government funding to provide facilities for cyclists (e.g. signed cycle routes, cycle storage) and start cycling initiatives (e.g. events in schools to encourage children to cycle more). Across these towns there was a **27% increase** in cycling between 2005 and 2008.

  - **High Occupancy Vehicle** (HOV) lanes can only be used by vehicles with a **minimum number** of occupants (usually **two** or **three**). They tend to operate during rush hour, and encourage **car sharing**, e.g. in **Toronto, Canada** the opening of HOV lanes on Highway 403 led to an increase in car sharing from 14% to nearly **40%** in three years.

Integrating transport systems

  - **Integrating transport systems** means **coordinating** different types of public transport, e.g. making train arrival times match bus departure times. This makes it **easy** for passengers to transfer between different types of transport. It also **reduces journey times** because people don't have to wait for a connection. These factors mean people are **more likely to use** public transport.

  - Integrating public transport systems is also about making public transport **accessible** to pedestrians and cyclists, e.g. in Tempe, Arizona all the buses have **bike racks** so people can easily cycle and use the bus in one journey.

  - **Curitiba** has an **integrated** public transport system. There are around 1600 buses in operation and passengers can buy **one ticket** for any journey throughout the city. **70%** of commuters use the bus system and Curitiba uses **30% less fuel per capita** than it would without it. As a result air pollution in the city is one of the **lowest in Brazil**.

Congestion charging is an important road scheme that's been used in London. Look at p. 152 for more about it.

Traffic management

  - **Bypasses** can be built so people can go **around** city centres instead of **through** them.
  - **Park and ride schemes** run in many UK cities, e.g. York, Cambridge. They allow people to **park outside the city** and catch a shuttle bus into the centre. This is usually **cheaper** than parking centrally.
  - Although park and ride schemes and bypasses can reduce traffic in the city centre, they won't necessarily **reduce** the number of cars across the **whole urban area**.
  - Bypasses and car parks for park and ride schemes are often built on **open countryside** in the rural-urban fringe. This can have environmental impacts (e.g. destruction of woodland) and cause **conflict** (see p. 230).

Sustainability in Urban Areas

Increasing the use of more **sustainable vehicles** can help to **reduce emissions** in cities:

Low carbon vehicles

- These include hybrid, hydrogen and electric vehicles, and vehicles that run on biofuels. These may run on **renewable energy** sources and produce significantly **less emissions** than standard petrol or diesel vehicles. E.g. in 2010, **Singapore** started using hydrogen-electric buses. The buses are powered by hydrogen and lithium-ion batteries, and **only emit water**.
- Using low carbon vehicles improves **air quality** because emissions of **pollutants** (e.g. sulfur oxides) are reduced.
- However, these vehicles are usually **expensive to buy** and can be **difficult to refuel** if the facilities aren't available. Although vehicles that run on electricity have fewer **environmental impacts** in urban areas where they are used, the **electricity** they use has often been generated by **burning fossil fuels**.

The **German** Government has Made **Transport** More **Sustainable**

1) Between 2000 and 2008, Germans walked, cycled and used public transport for more than **40%** of journeys. This reduces air pollution and greenhouse gas emissions, which increases **environmental sustainability**.

2) In Germany, the government encourages people to buy fuel efficient cars and to drive less (e.g. by putting high taxes on fuel). There are also incentives to use **public transport**, e.g. significant discounts are offered on weekly, monthly and annual train tickets that make it **economical** to use public transport to commute to work.

3) **Freiburg** in south west Germany is the country's **most sustainable** city in terms of transport facilities. From the 1970s onwards the city has built up an **efficient** public transport system:

   - The transport system is **integrated**, e.g. buses are timetabled to match train times. Public transport is also integrated with **walking** and **cycling** routes, e.g. there are designated, secure bike parking spots at public transport **'bike and ride'** facilities to encourage people to cycle to train and bus stations.
   - A **unified ticketing system** means that passengers only have to buy one ticket even if a journey takes them on several routes and different types of public transport.
   - A **light rail system** (the Stadtbahn) was built that is within easy walking distance (300 m) of **65%** of residents. The light rail trains run every 7.5 minutes and are **fully integrated** with the city's 26 bus lines.

     Light rail trains are a bit like trams — they run on special tracks, often alongside road traffic.

   - Buses and light rail trains have **priority** at traffic signals, which makes journeys on public transport faster.
   - The whole city centre is a **pedestrian zone** with vehicles banned, which makes walking safer.
   - In 177 **'home zones'**, the streets have low speed limits and priority is given to pedestrians and cyclists.
   - Cyclists are allowed to travel **in both directions** on half of the city's 120 one-way streets. This **shortens** journey times for bikes compared to cars.

4) These measures have had impacts on the city's **environmental sustainability**:
   - Between 1982 and 2007, the **proportion** of journeys travelled by **car** fell from **38%** to **32%** — **68%** of all journeys in Freiburg are done on foot, by bike or on public transport.
   - The **distance** each person travelled **by car declined** by **7%** on all roads and **13%** on residential roads from 1990 to 2006.
   - Between 1992 and 2005 CO_2 **emissions** per capita from transport **fell** by **13%**.

5) The public transport system requires **little financial input** from the state — passenger fares cover **90%** of the running costs.

Practice Questions

Q1 Give three reasons why the number of cars is increasing in urban areas.

Q2 Give one benefit to passengers of an integrated transport system.

Exam Question

Q1 With reference to specific examples, discuss the ways that transport systems in urban areas can be made more sustainable.

[10 marks]

Life would be so much easier if someone would just invent teleportation...

Sustainable transport is about getting people out of their cars and walking, cycling or using public transport. Talking of public transport, I heard a great joke about a bus driver, a flamingo and a pot of emulsion — shame there isn't enough space to tell you it...

Development Basics

When a country develops it basically gets better for the people living there — their quality of life improves (e.g. their wealth, health and safety). Right, that's development done... oh wait, there's a bit more you need to know about...

As a **Country Develops** Lots of **Things Change**

1) **Economic changes** — the **wealth** of a country **increases** as it develops. **Gross Domestic Product** (GDP) and **Gross National Income** (GNI) are two **measures** of a country's **wealth**:

> GDP is the **total value of goods** and **services** a **country produces** in a year.

> GNI is the **total value of goods** and **services people of that nationality produce** in a **year** (i.e. GDP + money from people living abroad).

As a country becomes **wealthier**, the number of **people living in poverty** (without basic human needs like water, food and shelter) usually **decreases**.

GNP (Gross National Product) is very similar to GNI and is usually used in the same way.

2) **Social changes** — these affect people's **quality of life**. Social change can be measured by the **infant mortality rate** (IMR) and the **number of people per doctor**. These both **decrease** with development:

> IMR is the number of **babies** who **die under 1 year old, per thousand babies born**.

> **People per doctor** is the **average number** of people for **each doctor**.

An **increase** in **access to safe water** and **literacy rate** shows an **increase** in **development**:

> **Access to safe water** — the **percentage** of people who can get **clean drinking water**.

> **Literacy rate** is the **percentage** of adults who can **read and write**.

3) **Demographic changes** — **birth rate** and **death rate** are measures of development. They both **decrease** with development:

> **Birth rate** is the **number of live babies born per thousand** of the population **per year**.

> **Death rate** is the **number of deaths per thousand** of the population **per year**.

Development can also be shown by an **increase** in **life expectancy**:

> **Life expectancy** is the **average age** a person can **expect to live to**.

4) **Political changes** — changes to a country's political system can also be a measure of development:

> For example, a country is **developing** if it **changes** from a **dictatorship** (where a leader makes all the decisions for a country) to a **democracy** (where the people decide on things, e.g. by voting).

5) **Cultural changes** — as a country develops, the way people live their lives (e.g. their **behaviour** and **beliefs**) may change:

> For example, in some cultures **women** are **not treated as equal** to men, e.g. they're **not** allowed to be **educated** or their **only job** is to **provide children**. As a country **develops**, the **role** of women **changes**. This can be shown by an **increase** in the **female literacy rate** (which shows women are **being educated**) and a **decrease** in the **birth rate** (which can show that women are **working** and they have **less time** to **raise children**).

Development Measures have **Limitations** When **Used On Their Own**

1) The different measures of development can be **misleading** when used **on their own** because they're **averages** — they don't show up **elite groups** in the population or **variations** within the country.

2) They also shouldn't be used on their own because as a country develops, **some aspects develop before others**. So it might seem that a country's **more developed** than it **actually is**.

3) Using a compound measure called the **Human Development Index** (HDI) **avoids these problems**:

> HDI is a **number** that's calculated using **life expectancy**, **literacy rate**, **education level** (e.g. degree) and **income per capita**. As a country **develops**, its **HDI** gets **higher**.

'Per capita' means 'for each person'.

Development Basics

There are **Lots of Ways** to **Classify How Developed** a Country is

1) In the late 1960s, countries were classified into the **First**, **Second** and **Third Worlds**:

   - The **First World** included the developed **capitalist countries** such as the **USA** and western European countries.
   - The **Second World** included **communist countries** such as the **former Soviet Union** and eastern European countries.
   - The **Third World** included **every other country**.

2) In the 1980s countries were classified into two categories based on how **economically developed** they were.

3) **Richer** countries were classed as **More Economically Developed Countries** (MEDCs) and **poorer** countries were classed as **Less Economically Developed Countries** (LEDCs).

4) **MEDCs** were generally found in the **north**. They included the USA and European countries, but also Australia and New Zealand.

5) **LEDCs** were generally found in the **south**. They included India, China, Mexico, Brazil and all the African countries.

6) In the **1980s** the **Brandt Report** discussed the **north/south divide** — the **Brandt line** was used to show the divide.

7) But this simple classification **can't** tell you which countries are **developing quickly** and which **aren't** really developing at all.

> *In a capitalist country resources belong to individuals — only they can profit from what they own. In a communist country, the ownership of resources and any profit that comes from them is shared between everyone.*

Brandt line — MEDCs — LEDCs

8) Nowadays, countries are classified into **more categories** to show the **continuous spectrum** of economic development between the least developed countries and the most developed countries — this is the **development continuum**:

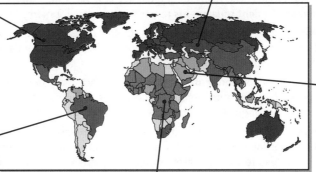

Rich industrial countries — these are the **most developed** countries in the world. For example, the UK, Norway, USA, Canada, France.

Former communist countries — these countries **aren't really poor**, but **aren't rich either** (they're kind of in the middle). They're **developing quickly**, but not as quick as NICs are. For example, the Czech Republic, Bulgaria, Poland.

Oil-exporting countries — these are **quite rich** (they have a high GNI) but the **wealth** often **belongs to a few people** and the rest are quite poor. For example, Qatar, Kuwait, Saudi Arabia.

Newly Industrialising Countries (NICs) — these are **rapidly getting richer** as their **economy** is moving from being based on **primary industry** (e.g. agriculture) to **secondary industry** (manufacturing). For example, China, India, Brazil, Mexico, South Africa.

Least Developed Countries (LDCs) — these are the **poorest**, **least developed** countries in the world. For example, Ethiopia, Chad, Angola.

Practice Questions

Q1 What is the Human Development Index?

Q2 What is an NIC?

Q3 Name two examples of LDCs.

Exam Question

Q1 Outline the changes associated with the development of a country. [8 marks]

Exams — the most feared measure of memory development...

What a delightful pair of pages — get all this learnt because it'll help make the rest of this development stuff easier to handle.

Least Developed Countries

The LDCs are the poorest, least developed countries in the world. You need to know all about their characteristics and the issues they face. I'm afraid that means these aren't the cheeriest pages in the world.

Life Isn't Easy in the Least Developed Countries

1) A lot of the Least Developed Countries are found in **Sub-Saharan Africa**, e.g. **Ethiopia**, **Gambia**, **Rwanda**, **Uganda** and **Zambia**. A few are found outside Africa, e.g. **Afghanistan** (in Asia), and **Haiti** (in the Caribbean).

2) There's a massive **gap** in **development** between the LDCs and the most developed countries, e.g. in terms of the global economy, the richest fifth of the global population have 80% of the world's income and the poorest fifth have only 1%.

3) The **difference** in the level of development between **more** and **less developed countries** is called the **development gap**.

4) To understand **how big** the gap is and **why** there is one, you need to know all about the **characteristics** of the LDCs and the **issues** that they face...

1 ECONOMIC

> Take a look at the causes of poverty on pages 244-245 — it's also pretty relevant to this development gap stuff.

- **Low incomes** — in LDCs the GNI per person is less than $745, e.g. in **Ethiopia** in 2010 the **GNI** per person was **$380**.

- **Poor trade links** — many LDCs have **little involvement** in world trade — the poorest 49 countries make up **10%** of the world's population, but only account for **0.4%** of world trade.

- **High levels of debt** — many LDCs **borrow money** from more developed countries for development projects, e.g. building dams and roads. The loans are large and many have **high interest rates** — lots of LDCs are forced to spend money on **debt repayments** rather than on development.

- Trade in **low profit goods** — many less developed countries rely on the **export** of **primary products** — e.g. **agricultural products** (such as sugar and cotton), **timber** and **minerals** (such as iron ore). The price paid for these products is **low**.

- **Trade deficit** — many LDCs **spend more** on **importing** goods than they **earn exporting** goods. They sell **low profit** primary products to more developed countries, who manufacture goods from these products. More developed countries then sell the manufactured goods to less developed countries at **high prices**.

- **Economic instability** — the economies of many LDCs are **unstable** because they're **based on agriculture** and dependent on exporting **primary products**. So if the crops **fail** (e.g. due to drought), so does the economy. LDCs often also rely on a **narrow range** of exports which makes them **vulnerable** if the price falls. E.g. Ghana heavily relies on the export of cocoa.

2 SOCIAL

Benny wasn't worried about high levels of debt — he knew he looked hot and that was what really mattered.

- **Limited health care** — in LDCs there are thousands of patients per doctor. E.g. in Ethiopia there are over 30 000 patients for every doctor compared to around 360 patients for every doctor in the UK.

- **High IMR**, e.g. in Ethiopia in 2010, there were 75 deaths per 1000 live births compared to 5 deaths per 1000 live births in the UK.

- High levels of **malnutrition**, e.g. in Ethiopia, between 2004 and 2005, 46% of the population was undernourished, and malnutrition was responsible for over half of all deaths of children under 5.

- High numbers of people **infected by diseases**, e.g. an estimated 9 million people in Ethiopia contract malaria every year (around 10% of the population).

- **Low levels of education**, e.g. primary school attendance in Ethiopia was 45% between 2005 and 2010.

- **Low literacy rates**, e.g. the adult literacy rate in Ethiopia in 2010 was 30%.

- Lack of access to **clean water** and **sanitation** (toilets and safe disposal of human waste), e.g. in Ethiopia in 2006 only 42% of people had access to clean water and 11% had access to sanitation.

Least Developed Countries

3 DEMOGRAPHIC

- **Low life expectancy**, e.g. life expectancy at birth in Ethiopia in 2012 was 56, compared to 80 in the UK.
- Many LDCs have a much **higher birth rate** than **death rate**, e.g. the birth rate in Ethiopia in 2012 was 42 per 1000 people per year and the death rate was 11 per 1000 people per year. Having a much **higher** birth rate than death rate causes **rapid population growth** which can lead to other problems, e.g. food shortages.

4 POLITICAL

- Many LDCs don't have a **democratic** government, e.g. up until 1994 Ethiopia was a communist state.
- **Political corruption** is a problem in many LDCs, e.g. at general elections in Ethiopia in 2005, allegations of vote rigging led to hundreds of people being arrested and imprisoned for treason. Some governments of LDCs have also been accused of **keeping money** the country has received as **loans**, rather than spending it on **development**.
- Many LDCs are badly affected by **war** and **conflict**, e.g. tens of thousands of people were killed between 1998 and 2000 in the conflict between Ethiopia and neighbouring Eritrea. During times of conflict, **less money** is spent on **development** (as so much is spent on the conflict itself).

Don't be absurd — I paid for both my gold house and my rocket car with my own money.

5 CULTURAL

Inequality — between **men** and **women**, or between other **social** or **ethnic groups**. E.g. in Ethiopia men and women are not treated equally — between 2005 and 2010, **30%** of **males** were attending secondary schools compared to only **23%** of **females**.

All these characteristics contribute to a **low quality of life** for the **people** living in LDCs. The **HDI** (see p. 206) is a good indicator of quality of life. HDI is much **lower** in LDCs than in more developed countries, e.g. Ethiopia is ranked **174th** in the world with an HDI of 0.363 (1 is the maximum). In comparison, the UK is ranked **28th** with an HDI of 0.863.

Practice Questions

Q1 What is the development gap?

Q2 Give an economic characteristic of an LDC.

Q3 Give a social characteristic of an LDC.

Q4 Give a political characteristic of an LDC.

Q5 Give a demographic characteristic of an LDC.

Exam Question

Q1 The table shows data for three countries. Use the data to comment on the level of development of the countries shown. **[7 marks]**

	Angola	South Africa	Denmark
Birth rate (per 1000 people)	39.36	19.32	10.22
Literacy (% men over 15 years)	82.7	87	99
Literacy (% women over 15 years)	58.1	85.7	99
% of GDP from agriculture	9.6	2.5	4.5

Please mind the gap — it really is massive...

The characteristics of LDCs show you why there's such a huge gap between them and the most developed countries. There are a whole load of characteristics to get your head around here so it's a lot of work, but believe me, examiners love asking about LDCs and the development gap so no skiving off now. Never mind, you're nearly at the end of the section... really you are...

Global Groupings and Development

Nations get together in groups for mutual benefit (and because everyone likes to have friends).

Nations Group Together for a few Different Reasons

1) Nations group together because it will **benefit** all of their **economies**:

- Groups can agree to **reduce barriers to trade** (e.g. import or export taxes, known as tariffs) between the member states, which helps to **increase** the **amount of trade** between members. For example, the USA, Canada and Mexico make up the North American Free Trade Agreement (NAFTA). They've agreed to abolish many tariffs which has increased trade and benefited all three economies.

- Being in a group where there's free trade between members also means there's a **larger market** for businesses, which allows them to **increase trade**.

- **Comparative advantage** — countries can **specialise** in producing the things they're good at making and trade for the things they're not good at making (it's easier to trade for all the different things a country needs, because trade is less restricted). **Production will increase** in each member country because they're concentrating on what they do **best**.

2) Nations group together because it can help to **promote development**:

Countries in a group can **work together** to tackle **development issues**, e.g. disease epidemics, poverty, education issues etc. This can benefit the **members** of a group, or the group can work together to tackle issues of **global concern**. For example, the UN is an international organisation with 193 member states. In 2000 it set eight Millennium Development Goals (MDGs), which highlighted the key global development issues and allowed progress in the development of lots of countries to be measured.

See page 246 for more on the MDGs.

3) Nations group together to **increase security** and **promote peace**:

Countries that are working together in a group are **less likely** to go to **war** with each other as it will badly affect their **economies** and **development** (see above). Countries in a group can also **agree policies** between them that increase **regional** and **global security**, e.g. the Association of South East Asian Nations (ASEAN) is a group of 10 countries that have made agreements to ban nuclear weapons.

There are Consequences to Global Groupings

Check out the next page for an EU case study...

Positive consequences

1) **Increased economic development** for the nations in a group, e.g. due to **increased trade** (see above).

2) Increased economic development can lead to **increased quality of life** for many people in a group.

3) The group can **provide support** for **declining regions** or **industries**, e.g. the EU's rural development policy gives funding to member states to be spent in rural areas to improve the rural economy and the quality of life of people living there.

4) Within some global groupings people looking for **work** can move freely **between member countries** to **find a job**.

5) There can be **better global representation** for smaller nations who join a larger group. E.g. some of the tiny islands of the Caribbean have a greater global presence because they're members of the **Caribbean Community** (CARICOM).

6) Reduced **risk of conflict** (see above) and **better international relations** between nations.

7) Also, groups of nations can **improve global security**, e.g. NATO (the North Atlantic Treaty Organisation) has an international force of soldiers who carry out various duties including peacekeeping in conflict zones.

Negative consequences

1) In some groups, decisions are made **centrally** so member states may **lose control** over some aspects of how they **run their country**.

2) Individual countries may **lose out** when they have to **share resources** with other member states, e.g. fishing grounds.

3) Trade agreements made within a group increase trade between member countries, but can **reduce trade** with countries **outside** the group. This is particularly damaging for **LDCs**, whose **development** can be affected by lost trade.

4) Sometimes being a member of a global group can **damage** a country's economy — **richer member states** may have to support **poorer member states** financially if they are in economic crisis, e.g. the UK contributed around £4 billion to the EU bailout of Portugal in 2011.

Global Groupings and Development

Case Study — the European Union (EU)

1) European nations first formed a group to help Europe to **recover** after the **Second World War**. Their aims were to **ensure peace** and improve **economic development** by making the countries more closely **integrated**.

2) This group has grown from **6 members** in 1957 to **27 members** in 2007. It was **named the EU** in 1993.

3) It's a closely integrated **economic** and **political** group. For example:

   • **Goods**, **services**, **people** and **money** can move **freely** between most member states without barriers.

   • 17 of the 27 members of the EU have adopted a **single currency** — the **Euro**.

   • Member states have agreed to have **common laws** and **policies** on things like agriculture and fisheries.

4) There are **positive** impacts of the EU:

   • **Trade has increased** between European countries. E.g. in 1970 just over 12% of the UK's GDP came from trade with European countries. After the UK joined the EU in 1973, this percentage increased rapidly — in 2002, around 23% of the UK's GDP came from trade with EU countries.

   • The **Euro** has made **trade easier** between some countries because there is no need to **exchange money**. Prices are more **consistent** because there is **no uncertainty** in exchange rates.

   • The EU **supports** some industries. E.g. the **Common Agricultural Policy (CAP)** includes **subsidies** for EU farmers and adds **import tariffs** and **quotas** on agricultural products from outside the EU. This gives farmers a reasonable standard of living, secures food supplies and ensures a good price for consumers.

   • Being in the EU gives members **increased security** from **external threats**. E.g. the EU counter-terrorism policy protects all member states from the threat of terrorism by measures such as introducing biometric passports to increase border security.

   • Most EU residents are **free to move around** the EU — they can **work** or **live** in most other EU countries.

5) There are also **negative** impacts of the EU:

   • **Joining** the EU can be **expensive**. To become an EU member state a country must meet **certain criteria**, e.g. high standards of environmental protection. Meeting these criteria can require a **lot of investment**.

   • Countries have to **share some resources** with other member states. For example, countries joining the **EU** come under the **Common Fisheries Policy**, which means their **fishing grounds** become **open** to fishing by **other member states**.

   • Policies like the **CAP** can have a **negative impact** on the economies of countries **outside** the EU. EU countries may trade with other countries **less**, because it's cheaper for them to trade with **each other**.

   • Increased immigration **within** the EU has resulted in a **lack of skilled workers** in some eastern European countries because so many have moved to Western Europe to seek better wages.

   • Joining the EU can **reduce independence** — EU countries agree to **obey** EU policies even if it **conflicts** with their **national policies**.

Brian was getting his catch in early — he'd heard about the Common Fisheries Policy and he wasn't taking any chances.

Practice Questions

Q1 Give three reasons why different countries might group together.

Q2 Give three examples of global social and economic groupings.

Exam Question

Q1 Discuss the consequences of the grouping of nations, with particular reference to the EU. [10 marks]

Countries form groups for the same reason ageing rockers do — money...

For a long time being a member of the EU was seen as a golden ticket to success — it provided better trade opportunities and helped its members to develop socially and economically. However, since the start of the 2008 economic crisis things have started to go up the spout. Now the future of the EU and particularly the Euro is a bit uncertain — oh heck...

Development Issues

The next four pages cover three important development issues and there's a stunner of a case study for each one.

Becoming Economically Sustainable can be Disastrous for the Environment

1) **Sustainable development** means **developing** to meet the **needs** of people **today**, without **affecting** the ability of people in the **future** to meet their **own needs**. Here's how **economic** and **environmental** sustainability fit in to the whole idea:

- **Economic sustainability** means making sure the economy keeps running and growing in the future, even if resources **run out** or the **population grows**.

- **Environmental sustainability** means using the environment in a way that doesn't permanently **damage** or **alter it**, so that future generations can still get what they **need** from it.

2) Becoming economically sustainable often **reduces** environmental sustainability because **economic activities** often have **negative environmental impacts**. For example, many industries will:

- **Use resources** — industry relies on **natural resources**, e.g. burning fossil fuels for energy. Using up natural resources **faster** than the environment can **replace** them means they won't be **available** to future generations.

- **Produce waste** — industrial waste can cause **pollution** which can **irreversibly alter** the environment — so it isn't the same for future generations.

Case Study — Sarawak

Sarawak is a state in Malaysia which has experienced **rapid economic growth** since the 1980s, but this growth has come at an **environmental cost**:

TIMBER INDUSTRY

1) Sarawak is one of the **world's largest** exporters of **tropical hardwood** timber. Timber exports rose from 4.2 million m³ in 1971 to 18.8 million m³ in 1990, and the timber industry became very important to the **Malaysian economy**.

2) **Intense logging** in the 1980s and 1990s caused **large scale deforestation** — an estimated **70%** of Sarawak's original forests **disappeared**. This caused **habitat loss** and other problems such as **soil erosion** and **flooding**.

3) By the 1990s the rate of logging was both **economically unsustainable** (the timber would run out and the industry would collapse) and **environmentally unsustainable** (the forests were being totally destroyed).

4) Since the late 1990s the Malaysian government has taken **action** to improve the **sustainability** of the industry. They have created **forest management plans** to control the logging and promote **sustainable management**, e.g. felling trees in a 25 year cutting cycle which allows the forest to **recover**. These actions are **helping** to increase sustainability, but illegal **deforestation** is still continuing.

COMMERCIAL AGRICULTURE

> Commercial agriculture is large-scale farming of crops or livestock to be sold in bulk around the world.

1) Since the 1990s there's been a rise in **commercial agriculture** in Sarawak. **Palm oil** is the main commercial crop — in 2008 it accounted for nearly **6%** of Sarawak's exports. It's used to make processed food and biodiesel.

2) The **palm oil** industry has a number of **environmental impacts**. It causes **deforestation** because forests are cleared to make room for plantations. **Monoculture** (growing just one plant) **reduces biodiversity** and the use of **agricultural chemicals** and the **waste** from palm oil production causes **water** and **soil pollution**.

3) Despite the environmental issues, there is continuing **investment** in commercial agriculture. There are plans to **raise** agricultural productivity because the **demand** for **palm oil** is **rising** (for use as a **biofuel**). This means the **palm oil industry** could aid **economic sustainability**, but may continue to **harm** environmental sustainability.

OTHER INDUSTRIES

1) Since 2000, there's been **increased investment** in **manufacturing**, **construction** and **high tech industries**. E.g. aluminium and steel industries, shipbuilding and marine engineering.

2) Many of these industries require **power**. In 2011 construction of the Bakun hydroelectric dam was completed and a number of **coal power stations** are being built. These projects are environmentally damaging — the dam has caused **habitat loss** and **disrupted river ecosystems**, and the power stations will increase **air pollution** and **use up resources**.

3) Many industries also **deplete raw materials** (e.g. aluminium ore) and **create waste products** that pollute.

4) The growth of these industries promotes **economic sustainability** because they provide a source of income **now** and in the **future**, but they are not **environmentally sustainable**.

Development Issues

Some people think **Sustainable Tourism** could be the **Answer**

1) Tourists come to experience the **environment** and **culture** of a place (e.g. a tropical rainforest or a city centre).

2) Too many tourists can **damage** or **permanently alter** an area though, and spoil it for **future generations**. E.g. building hotels and other tourist facilities can destroy the habitats of plants and animals that the tourists have come to see.

3) **Sustainable tourism** is tourism that **doesn't damage** the environment people have come to see, e.g. by **limiting** the number of tourist developments or only permitting tourist activities in **designated areas**. It also benefits **local people** by generating **employment**, and **allows** income to be put back into **conservation** to protect the area.

4) Some people think that tourism can **never** be **truly** sustainable. Tourism is about attracting people to an area to **generate profit** or **income** for the **local economy**, so the more tourists there are, the **better** it is for the local economy. But, more tourists makes it **more difficult** to reduce the **environmental impact** the tourists have.

5) For sustainable tourism to **succeed** certain things need to be done, e.g. **tourist numbers** may need to be tightly controlled and tourist activities **carefully monitored** to make sure they don't damage or alter the environment.

Case Study — The Great Barrier Reef

1) The Great Barrier Reef is the **largest coral reef system** in the world. It lies off the **NE coast** of **Australia** and supports a range of wildlife including many **vulnerable** and **endangered** species.

2) In the 1980s and 1990s improved access led to a **rapid rise in tourism** — visitor numbers increased by about 30% every year in the 1980s.

3) Today, tourism is the **largest commercial activity** around the Great Barrier Reef — it accounts for **87%** of the reef's **economic output**. It is a major source of income for the **local** and **national economy**, generating over **AU$5 billion a year**.

4) Tourist activities can have **negative impacts** on the Great Barrier Reef area:

- Coral reefs are easily **damaged** by **pollution**, which also affects the species dependent on them. The tourist industry creates pollution in several ways, e.g. through waste disposal, litter and pollution from boats.
- Coral can be **damaged** by **boat anchors** and by **poor diving practices** (e.g. divers stepping on coral and breaking pieces off).
- Tourists can **disturb wildlife**, e.g. by disturbing nesting sea birds. Many seabirds nest on the ground and when disturbed the parents leave the nest, exposing the young or eggs to predators.
- The reef is **culturally** and **economically** important to **local indigenous islanders**. Tourism limits where these people can fish or carry out ceremonial activities.
- Developments for tourism along the coast damage **coastal ecosystems** (e.g. mangrove forests and estuaries) which are important for **maintaining** the reef (estuaries feed important nutrients into the reef from land).

The Great Barrier Reef is an example of a fragile environment. See pages 178-179 for more on these.

5) The **Great Barrier Reef Marine Park Authority** (**GBRMPA**) manages a large area of the Great Barrier Reef. The GBRMPA works with the **Queensland Parks and Wildlife Service**, **government agencies**, the **tourist industry** and other groups to ensure that tourism on the reef is managed to so that it's more **environmentally sustainable**:

- In 2003 the GBRMPA established a **zoning system** that describes where certain tourist activities can take place. This helps to protect the **most sensitive areas** and limits all tourism activities to more sustainable levels.
- Some activities, such as **fishing**, are **strictly regulated**. Tourist operators have to obtain **permits** from the GBRMPA for them. The number of permits is capped and there are restrictions on **group numbers** and **boat sizes** in sensitive areas.
- Most tourist operators **pay an Environmental Management Charge (EMC)** of around AU$3.50 per visitor per day to the GBRMPA. This money funds **research**, **education** and **management** of the marine park.
- Tourist operators and tourists are **encouraged to contribute** to **research** and **monitoring** of the reef — such as reporting on the extent of coral bleaching (see page 178). This encourages tourists to take interest in the **protection** of the reef and helps to monitor any **decline** in the reef ecosystem so that something can be done to **repair** any damage that's being done.

Development Issues

Trade and aid are two ways of helping a country to develop. Increasing trade in (and with) a developing country helps encourage economic growth. Giving aid allows it to invest in its own social and economic development. How marvellous...

Aid can help Developing Countries Improve People's Quality of Life

1) Aid is given by one country to another country in the form of **money** or **resources** (e.g. food, doctors).

2) There are **two** main **sources** of aid from donor countries — **governments** (paid for by **taxes**) and **Non-Governmental Organisations** (**NGOs** — paid for by **voluntary donations**).

3) **Governments** can give aid directly to the recipient country (**bilateral aid**) or **indirectly** through an **international organisation** that distributes the aid (**multilateral aid**).

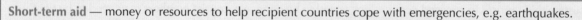 *International organisations include the UN and the World Bank.*

4) There are different types of aid:

> **Short-term aid** — money or resources to help recipient countries cope with emergencies, e.g. earthquakes.
>
> **Long-term aid** — money or resources to help recipient countries become more developed, e.g. to improve health care.
>
> **'Top-down' aid** — when an organisation or government receives the aid and decides where it should be spent. This is usually the case on large infrastructure projects, e.g. building dams for hydroelectric power.
>
> **'Bottom-up' aid** — when money is given directly to local people, e.g. to build a well — this is often used by NGOs.

5) **Aid** is important for **development** because it allows recipient countries to invest in things that improve people's **health** and **quality of life**, e.g. improving access to drinking water. There are **problems** with aid as a route to development though:

- Some recipient countries don't use aid **effectively** because they have **corrupt governments**, who spend the money for their **own purposes**. The money doesn't get to the people who **need** it, so it doesn't help development.

- **Delivering** aid isn't easy, particularly in countries with **poor infrastructure**, e.g. establishing education projects in rural areas with poor road access is difficult. If the distribution of the aid is patchy, then only some areas benefit from it.

- Bilateral aid can be **tied** — this means it's given with the **condition** that the **recipient country** has to **buy** the **goods and services** it needs **from** the **donor country**. However, if the goods and services are **expensive** in the donor country, the aid **doesn't go as far** as it would if the goods and services were bought **elsewhere**.

- Countries can become **dependent** on aid so that they aren't able to function or develop without it.

Trade can Stimulate Economic Growth and Development

1) Trade is the **exchange** of **goods** or **services** (both buying and selling). Increasing trade **within** a developing country and **between** it and other countries **promotes development** by:

- Increasing **economic growth** — increased trade creates **employment** and generates **wealth**, which leads to a rise in the **GDP** of the country and the **living standards** of the population.

- Increasing the amount of money a country has to spend on **social development**, e.g. health and education.

- Increasing the amount of money a country has to spend on **development projects**, e.g. transport infrastructure.

2) But there are **problems** with trade as a route to development:

- Less developed countries often can't **compete** in a **global market**. If they don't have the money to **invest** in **technological developments** that reduce the cost of production, they can't **match** the prices of countries that can.

- Less developed countries may also struggle to trade in a global market because of **other problems** such as **HIV/AIDS** or **conflict**. E.g. money has to be spent on these issues, so there's less money available to invest in developing trade, and things like conflicts can make the supply of goods unreliable.

- Trade can have **negative** social impacts. E.g. to keep **prices low**, wages and working conditions may be very **poor**. This means that increased trade won't necessarily improve **quality of life** for everyone.

- Less developed countries often export **primary products** (see p. 208). This can be an **unreliable income** because things like crop yields **vary**, i.e. because of the weather. These products are also very **low profit**, so don't produce a huge amount of income to improve development.

- Countries are often dependent on trading one thing, e.g. coffee or cotton. If the demand for that commodity falls the producer country has **nothing** to fall back on and **development** is stalled.

> The general opinion is that most countries need a **combination** of **AID** and increased **TRADE** to promote **development**.

Development Issues

Case Study — Sudan

1) Sudan is one of the **poorest countries** in **Africa**.
It has experienced long periods of **civil war** and **conflict** is still
one of the biggest challenges to its development (see p. 236-237).

As a result of ongoing conflict a new country, South Sudan, formed in July 2011.

2) The Sudanese economy has been **growing** rapidly in recent years (the country's GDP grew by 4.7% in 2010), but these changes haven't led to increased **living standards** for everyone.

3) **Poverty** is **widespread** — 46.5% of the population live below the poverty line of $1 a day.

4) Sudan receives **large amounts of aid** each year:

- In 2007 Sudan received **over $2 billion of aid** (equivalent to 4.7% of its GNI). **70%** of this aid was **humanitarian** — to help cope with severe **food shortages** caused by **conflict** and **droughts**.
- Aid comes from different sources — **individual governments** (e.g. US, UK), **international organisations** (e.g. the UN), and **NGOs** (e.g. Save the Children).
- Sudan receives a lot of **food aid** — in 2008 the World Food Programme provided food aid to 6 million people in Sudan. This helps people to **survive** in the short term, but doesn't help the country to **develop** in the long term.
- Some aid is used to **promote development** by attempting to **prevent conflicts**, **rebuild infrastructure** and invest in **education** and **health services**. E.g. the US Agency for International Development has funded the construction or refurbishment of 140 primary schools and 5 secondary schools in Sudan.
- There are **lots of problems** getting aid to where it's needed though, because of **conflicts** and **corruption**.

5) Growth of the oil industry is boosting **trade** and **economic growth**:

- In the 1990s, lots of Sudan's exports were **low profit agricultural goods**, e.g. cotton, nuts and livestock. Sudan had a **trade deficit** (it **spent more importing** goods than it **earned exporting** them). **Production** and **trade** of these goods has **decreased** due to conflicts and droughts.
- In 1999 Sudan started **exporting oil** and as a result the country had its **first trade surplus** (it **earned more** from exports than it **spent** on imports). Over the last decade oil has become the **main export**, and the trade surplus reached $1.4 billion in the first few months of 2011.
- The growth of the oil industry has helped development because it brings **economic growth** and **improves international relations** (e.g. trade agreements have been made with the US, the EU, Egypt and Libya).
- There are concerns that profits from the oil industry **aren't funding development** though, because of **corruption** in the government.
- **Agriculture** is still **important to the economy** — it accounts for 40% of GDP, and 80% of people are employed in agriculture. However, agricultural trade is **low profit** and **unreliable** (see previous page) so it is **difficult** for Sudan to develop while it is still highly dependent on it.
- It's difficult for Sudan to make a lot of **profit** because of **barriers** to trade, e.g. in 2012 average import tariffs were around **20%**. However Sudan is in the process of joining the **World Trade Organisation** (WTO) which will make international trade easier, and give the country access to a **wider market** for its **exports**.

Practice Questions

Q1 What is sustainable development?

Q2 Give three problems with aid as a route to development.

Q3 Give three ways that trade helps promote development.

Exam Question

Q1 Below are three development issues. With reference to a country you have studied, discuss **one** of the issues.
- **either** "Economic sustainability versus environmental sustainability"
- **or** "Sustainable tourism, myth or reality"
- **or** "Trade versus aid" [40 marks]

And the winner is... Traid. The secret love child of both aid and trade.

Nobody knows for definite the best way to promote development, but a combination of both trade and aid is a good bet. It makes answers easier to write too — you can weigh up the pros and cons of both before concluding that a mixture of the two is best. Hooray!

Globalisation Basics

In the last few decades it's become a lot easier to communicate with people around the world, and a lot easier to move around. This is causing globalisation, and it affects pretty much everyone. Including you. Yes, you... with the hair...

Globalisation is the Process of Countries becoming more Closely Integrated

1) Globalisation is the process of the world's **economies**, **political systems** and **cultures** becoming more strongly **connected** to each other.

2) If there was **no** globalisation there wouldn't be any **interaction** between different countries. If there was **complete** globalisation, the whole world would act like **a single community**. The real world is somewhere **in between**, but countries are becoming more and more **closely integrated**.

3) Globalisation is caused by the **movement** of **capital** (money that's invested, see below) and **people** between different countries, as well as **businesses** locating their operations and selling their **products** and **services** in more countries.

4) People have been **moving between countries** and **international trade** has been going on for ages, but most people think that globalisation as we know it today really started to **accelerate** in the **1980s**. Here are a few reasons why:

Globalisation rocks Jamie-Lou's world.

- Improvements to **telephone networks** have made **global communications** cheaper and easier. **Mobile** and **satellite phones** allow people to communicate even when they don't have access to a telephone line.

- The development and rapid spread of **e-mail** and the **internet** allow large amounts of information to be exchanged instantly across the globe. This makes working across long distances very efficient.

- **Global transport** has been improved by the development of high speed rail networks, larger and faster ships, larger cargo planes and low cost airlines. These developments have made it easier for **people** and **goods** to move quickly and cheaply around the world. They have also meant that companies can get **supplies** from all over the world, and **sell their products** to people all over the world.

There are Four Factors which Promote Globalisation

Flows of Capital

1) Capital is money that's **invested** — it's spent on something so that you get an **income** or **increased profit** from it.

2) Historically, capital was mostly invested **within a country**, e.g. companies would expand by doing things like building new factories, or setting up new branches within their country of origin.

3) Over time though, the amount of capital invested in **foreign countries** has increased — this is **Foreign Direct Investment** (FDI). E.g. global FDI increased from $3000 billion in 1996 to $12 000 billion in 2006.

4) Improvements in **information and communications technology** (ICT) have encouraged flows of capital round the world — it can **instantly** be moved around the world via the internet.

5) Increasing **flows of capital** are making the world more **interconnected**, e.g. most countries' economies are now **dependent** on flows of investment to and from other countries.

Have a peek at the next page (and below) for more on how companies divide up the parts of their business round the world.

Flows of Production

1) Historically, manufacturing industries were located in **more developed** countries.

2) The products being produced were also **sold** in the country where they were **made**.

3) In recent decades, manufacturing has **decreased** in **more developed countries**, e.g. the number of people employed in manufacturing in the UK fell from more than 5 million in 1985 to less than 3 million in 2009.

4) Lower labour costs overseas have caused many companies to **relocate** the production **side** of their business **abroad**, they then **import** the products to the countries where they're **sold**. E.g. the vacuum manufacturer Dyson moved the production and assembly part of its business to Malaysia in 2002, but the vacuums are still sold in the UK.

5) As a result of these changes, **international trade** in manufactured goods is **increasing**, e.g. the UK imported £200 billion of manufactured goods in 1990, and £550 billion in 2008.

6) Changing **flows of production** are making the world more **interconnected**, e.g. many of the manufactured products we now buy have been produced in other countries, and then imported to the UK.

Globalisation Basics

Flows of Services

1) Services are economic activities that **aren't** based around producing any **material goods**, e.g. banking and insurance.

2) Improvements in **ICT** have allowed services to become **global industries** in recent decades. Things like banking and insurance depend on **communication** and **transfer of information**. Improvements to ICT mean that services can **locate anywhere** in the world and still be able to serve the needs of **customers anywhere else** in the world.

3) During the 1970s and 1980s there was also **deregulation** (removal of rules to increase competition) and **opening up** of national financial markets to the rest of the world, e.g. in the USA and UK. This meant that it was made **easier** for banks and other financial institutions to **do business** in other countries.

4) Services can be split into **low level** (e.g. customer service) and **high level** (e.g. financial services). **High level services** tend to be concentrated in cities in **more developed countries** (e.g. London and New York). Companies are increasingly **relocating** low level services to **less developed countries** where labour is **cheaper**, e.g. call centres (see p. 224).

5) Increasing **flows of services** are making the world more **interconnected**, e.g. people are connected to other countries just through having a bank account — many banks are huge international organisations.

Flows of People

1) More people are moving to different countries, e.g. international migration has doubled since 1975.

2) Some people move because they have to (e.g. to escape conflict zones) but many people choose to move for work.

3) Some migrants are highly skilled workers (e.g. ICT and medical workers), moving to more developed countries where wages and working conditions are better. Others are unskilled workers who move to more developed countries to look for work because of unemployment or poor wages in their own countries.

4) Increasing flows of people between different countries is making the world more interconnected, e.g. people bring aspects of their culture with them when they move, and countries are connected together because people have family all over the world.

Marketing is Becoming More Global

1) Marketing is the process of **promoting** and **selling products** or **services**.

2) Nowadays, many products and services are sold **all over the world**, rather than just in the country where they are produced. So marketing has had to become **global**.

3) Global marketing involves treating the world as **one single market** (a fully globalised world, see previous page) and using **one marketing strategy** to advertise a product to customers all over the world.

4) Global marketing gives **economies of scale** — it is **cheaper** to have one marketing campaign for the whole world, rather than having a different campaign for every country.

5) Marketing needs to be **adapted** to regional markets though — different populations still have **different laws** and **cultural attitudes**, e.g. different countries have different laws and attitudes about consuming alcohol.

Practice Questions

Q1 What is globalisation?

Q2 Give one example of something that has caused globalisation to accelerate since the 1980s.

Q3 What is global marketing?

Exam Question

Q1 Discuss how changes in patterns of production have promoted globalisation. [10 marks]

Imagine by John Lennon — an ode to globalisation if ever I've heard one...

Don't believe me? Check out the lyrics... Let me simplify these two pages for you — basically globalisation makes some things in life easier... it's easier to talk to your pal in Argentina and easier to flog rubber ducks to your man in Hawaii. If only globalisation made it easier to pass exams...

Trans-National Corporations (TNCs)

Trans-National Corporations (TNCs) are worldwide companies that are bringing countries together by spreading themselves, and their cash, all over the world. Unfortunately, they don't seem to have spread any cash into my bank account.

TNCs are **Companies** that Operate in **Two or More Countries**

1) TNCs are companies that **produce**, **sell** or are **located** in **two or more** countries, e.g. **Sony**® manufacture **electronic products** in **China** and **Japan**, and **sell** many of them in **Europe** and the **USA**.

2) They play an **important role** in the **global economy** — in 2010, TNCs accounted for around a **quarter** of **global GDP**.

3) TNCs operate in **all types** of industry:

   • **Primary industry** (extracting natural resources) e.g. Shell extracts and trades oil and gas.
   • **Secondary industry** (making material goods) e.g. Toyota manufactures vehicles.
   • **Tertiary industry** (providing services) e.g. Aviva™ provides insurance services.

4) TNCs bring lots of **investment** into countries, spread **new technologies** and can promote particular **cultures**, e.g. McDonald's brings Western-style fast food to other countries.

5) **Potential investment**, the **creation of jobs** and access to **new technology** means TNCs can have **political influence**.

6) They're one of the **main driving forces** behind globalisation because of the economic, political and cultural **interactions** that occur **between** the countries where they operate.

7) TNCs also **connect** countries together because of how they are **structured**:

McDonald's and Starbucks
in Chiang Mai, Thailand.

   • **Headquarters** are usually located in **big cities** in more developed countries (e.g. New York). These cities are well connected in terms of global **transport** and **communications**, and there is a supply of **highly skilled workers**.
   • **Research and development** (R&D) facilities tend to be located in cities and towns where there's a supply of **highly educated** people, e.g. scientists, engineers and technicians. They are often in the **same country** as the headquarters.
   • Some TNCs have **regional R&D** facilities located closer to the markets they are selling to, so they can make products that are specifically **for that market**. E.g. South Korean TNC Samsung has an R&D centre in Warsaw, Poland.
   • **Factories** are often located in NICs where **production costs** (e.g. labour, materials, land etc.) **are lower**, e.g. Samsung has factories in China.
   • Many TNCs also have **factories** in the country where **their market** is, e.g. Nissan™ have a factory in the UK. If a product is made in the country where it is **sold**, the TNC can avoid paying **import** and **export taxes** and can **reduce transport costs** (especially on large items, e.g. cars).

TNCs have **Grown Rapidly** In Recent Years

1) TNCs have increased in **size**, **wealth** and **number** since the **mid 20th century**, e.g. in 1970 there were 7000 TNCs, in 2012 there were more than 80 000.

2) Increasing numbers of companies have **grown** to become TNCs. Here are a few reasons why:

   • TNCs can make products **cheaply** because they can move production to countries where **costs are low**, e.g. they can take advantage of cheap labour in less developed countries.
   • TNCs can take advantage of differences in **government policies**, e.g. they can move where **taxes are low**, or where **subsidies** and **grants** to promote manufacturing are available.
   • They can operate in countries where **labour** or **environmental laws** are **less strict**, so they can carry out higher intensity production.
   • A TNC can expand to access new **growing markets** in developing countries.
   • By growing internationally they can reach a size where they can gain from **economies of scale**, which increases **profit**.
   • They can get around **trade barriers** by manufacturing in the **same country** that they are selling (see above).
   • TNCs can **shift** production between locations to **maximise profits**, e.g. they can move production from one country to another if it will save them money.
   • TNCs can control their **supply chain** to maximise profits. E.g. they can **buy** companies that supply them with components, or make components themselves to **cut costs**.

Economies of scale is where companies produce lots more of an item, so the cost of producing each individual item is reduced and they make more profit.

Trans-National Corporations (TNCs)

TNCs have *Positive* and *Negative Impacts* on their Country of *Origin...*

Economic

- **Profits** from activities abroad come back to **shareholders**. Money from **taxes** on the TNC's income also goes to the government of the country of origin.
- **Skilled employment** — even if the TNC moves some activities elsewhere, **highly skilled jobs** (e.g. in R&D and finance) remain in the country of origin.
- Some TNCs move **manufacturing** abroad. In the country of origin, this can cause **unemployment** for employees of the TNC and for the TNC's suppliers.
- Increased unemployment can lead to **wider decline** in an area — people have a **smaller disposable income** so they spend less money, causing shops and businesses to **close**.

Social

- Increased **range of products** available in shops. Large retail TNCs produce many things in **bulk**, which means that they can stock products which smaller companies **couldn't afford** to produce or stock.
- **High unemployment** caused by the closure of factories can lead to **social problems**, e.g. increases in **crime**.

Environmental

Decline in local **manufacturing industry** may **reduce pollution**.

...and on their *Host* Countries

Economic

- Increased employment creates **increased wealth** for local people and the local economy — people have more to spend in local shops.
- Increased economic activity can generate even **more** economic activity (called the **multiplier effect**). E.g. the creation of jobs brings wealth to a region, so more businesses are attracted there and even more jobs are created.
- TNCs can cause local businesses to **shut down** by out-competing them.
- A lot of the **profits** can be sent back to the **country of origin**, so they don't reach the host country.

Social

- TNCs may invest in **social development** (e.g. education), in host countries to create a **more skilled workforce**.
- They may bring **new technologies** and **working methods** into the country, which will also create a more skilled workforce.
- TNCs are sometimes accused of **exploiting** their **workforce**, particularly in developing countries where the workers are prepared to work for **low wages** in **poor conditions**.
- **Managerial positions** are likely to be filled by candidates from the **country of origin**.
- TNCs can cause **urbanisation** as people come from rural areas to work in urban factories.
- **Decisions** made by the TNC are often made in the country of origin with **little consideration** for the needs of the host country.

Environmental

- TNCs may use or invest in **environmentally friendly technologies**, e.g. renewable energy sources.
- Manufacturing can cause **pollution**, particularly in some less developed countries where **environmental laws** are often **less strict**.
- **Agricultural land** or **wildlife habitats** can be lost when TNCs buy areas of **land**, e.g. for building factories.

Practice Questions

Q1 What is a TNC?

Q2 Give three reasons for the growth of TNCs.

Exam Question

Q1 Discuss the social, economic and environmental impacts of TNCs on their host countries. [10 marks]

TNCs — aka Terribly Nasty Companies...

TNCs are often seen as the big baddies of globalisation, but in reality they're not all bad. For your exam you need to know the positive impacts of TNCs as well as the negatives ones — A2 Geography examiners love nothing more than a balanced argument.

TNC Case Study — Wal-Mart

Get over here y'all. It's time for a case study and we're heading stateside (and beyond — that's kinda the point of TNCs...)

Wal-Mart® is a Retail TNC with Headquarters in the USA

Wal-Mart is a chain of discount **department stores** (including ASDA in the UK). It's one of the **largest** TNCs in the world and the largest **retail** TNC (many of the top TNCs are **oil companies**).

1) Wal-Mart began in 1962 when **Sam Walton** opened the first store in **Arkansas, USA**.

2) More stores opened across Arkansas, then across the USA, and more recently across the globe via the **acquisition** of other retail companies. E.g. **Seiyu** in Japan, **ASDA** in the UK and **Bompreço** in Brazil.

3) Some Wal-Mart stores continue trading under their **own name**, e.g. ASDA, while others are **re-branded** as Wal-Mart.

4) Wal-Mart **divides** its **labour** across different countries. Its headquarters are still in Arkansas, but most manufacturing is carried out where costs are **lower** (cheaper labour and resources), e.g. electronic goods are made in China and clothing is made in India.

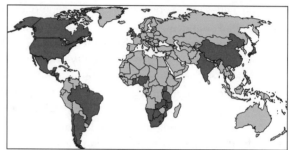

■ = Location of Wal-Mart stores in 2012

5) Wal-Mart is starting to **expand** into **NICs** like India, which have huge **new markets**. For example, Wal-Mart and an **Indian** company called **Bharti Enterprises** are opening new retail outlets **together** in the **style** of Wal-Mart stores.

Wal-Mart® Helps to Accelerate Globalisation

Like other TNCs, Wal-Mart helps to **accelerate globalisation** — it **links** countries together through the flow of **money**, **people**, **trade** and **information**. It also brings the **culture** of its country of origin (**USA**) to other countries.

In the USA, Wal-Mart gives customers all they need in **one building** at **low cost**. They've **successfully** introduced this in other countries, e.g. ASDA now stocks more non-food items. This hasn't been **successful** in all countries. They're trying a **different approach** in **India** where people like to shop in **traditional markets** rather than supermarkets.

Although Wal-Mart is a global brand it's retained a **local approach** by buying **local companies**. Its stores **aren't** all exactly the **same**, though many of the **products** are, e.g. **George** clothing supplies ASDA in the UK and Wal-Mart in the USA. Selling the **same products** globally helps to create **common patterns of consumption** between different countries.

Wal-Mart® has Impacts in the USA...

Social

- Wal-Mart provides consumers with a **wide choice** of goods, e.g. the 'supercenter' stores sell things like garden furniture and car tyres as well as food and clothing.
- Many Wal-Mart stores are open **24 hours a day**, so consumers are able to shop **when they like**.
- Many jobs at Wal-Mart stores are **poorly paid** with **few benefits** (e.g. health care), so employees have to rely on **state benefits**. E.g. in California in 2004, it's estimated that the state paid $86 million to support Wal-Mart employees.
- Wal-Mart has been accused of having **poor working conditions**. E.g. in 2005 Wal-Mart had to pay $172 million compensation because employees had been denied meal breaks.

Economic

- **Employment** — each **new store creates jobs**, e.g. Vineland (USA) opened in 2009, creating 700 jobs.
- **Low prices** — Wal-Mart is one of the **cheapest supermarkets** in the USA.
- **Decline** in **manufacturing industry** — Wal-Mart buys a lot of products from suppliers outside the USA, e.g. electronic goods are made in China and Malaysia, which has caused a loss of manufacturing jobs in the USA.
- **Loss of local businesses** — Wal-Mart stores can cause smaller shops in the area to **shut down** as they can't **match** the low prices.
- This can cause the loss of **local jobs**, e.g. it is estimated that for every **100 jobs created** at a new Wal-Mart, **50 retail jobs are lost** from local businesses over the next 5 years.

Environmental

- Wal-Mart produces huge amounts of **greenhouse gases** but it has opened '**green stores**' that run on **renewable energy**.
- **Domestic stores** are often **very large and out-of-town** — building them takes up **large areas of land** and people **driving** to them **causes traffic** and **pollution**.

TNC Case Study — Wal-Mart

...and in its **Host** Countries

Because Wal-Mart is such a large TNC, it has a **lot of host countries**, with **stores** and **factories** based **all over the world**. It has **positive** and **negative** impacts on these host countries:

Economic

- Wal-Mart creates lots of jobs in **construction**, **manufacturing** and **retail services**. E.g. in Mexico, Wal-Mart employs over 209 000 people.
- **Local companies** and **farmers** supply goods to Wal-Mart. E.g. in Canada, Wal-Mart works with over 6000 Canadian suppliers, creating around $8 billion of business for them each year.
- **Local suppliers** to Wal-Mart may be able to expand their business by starting to **export** their goods to Wal-Mart stores in other countries.
- Wal-Mart has been criticised for forcing its suppliers to accept **low prices** for their products.
- **Local companies suffer** in **competing** with Wal-Mart. Wal-Mart stores cause **smaller shops** in the area to **shut** — they **can't compete** with the **low prices** and **range of products** on sale.
- People from the host country spend their money in the Wal-Mart stores, but **most** of the **profits** are sent back to the **USA** rather than contributing to the host country's economy.

Wal-Mart might have low prices but Glenda's customers receive a unique shopping experience.

Social

- Wal-Mart offers **skilled jobs** in **less developed countries**. E.g. all the Wal-Mart stores in China are managed by local people, not by candidates from the USA.
- In its poorest host countries, working for Wal-Mart can offer a **more reliable** wage than other jobs, e.g. subsistence farming.
- **Working conditions** may be **poor**. For example, some Wal-Mart suppliers have **long working hours** — Beximco in Bangladesh supplies clothing to Wal-Mart and although Bangladesh has a **maximum 60 hour working week**, it's claimed that Beximco employees **regularly work 80 hours** a week.
- Wal-Mart **donates** hundreds of millions of dollars to improve things like **health** and the **environment** in countries where it operates. E.g. in 2008, Wal-Mart in Argentina **donated $77 000** to local projects focusing on reducing hunger, and supported **29 soup kitchens** feeding nearly **12 000 people** across the country.

Environmental

- Wal-Mart invests in **environmentally friendly technologies** and **sustainable development**. E.g. in Puerto Rico, 23 Wal-Mart stores are having solar panels fitted on their roofs to generate electricity.
- Wal-Mart stores use **large areas of land** for factories and stores. For example, the largest Wal-Mart store in Hawaii covers over **29 000 m²**.

Practice Questions

Q1 Explain one way in which Wal-Mart has accelerated globalisation.

Q2 Give three social impacts that Wal-Mart has had on the USA.

Exam Questions

Q1 The map shows the location of the operations of a TNC that makes designer sportswear. Describe and comment on the distribution shown.

[7 marks]

☐ Global headquarters   ● Countries where
■ Research and design   products are sold
◕ Manufacturing

Q2 With reference to at least one example, assess the impacts TNCs have on their countries of origin and their host countries.

[8 marks]

Is it a bird? Is it a plane? Nope it's yet another Wal-Mart...

Wal-Mart is a great example of a TNC that has grown all over the world. Whatever you choose as your case study for a TNC, make sure you pick up lots of facts and details to use in the exam — that's the whole point of case studies. Most of the positive and negative impacts for TNCs will be the same, but the specifics will be <u>different</u>. There's nothing for it but to learn, learn, learn. Fun, fun, fun...

Newly Industrialised Countries (NICs)

Newly Industrialised Countries are exactly what it says on the tin...

NICs are Countries that have Recently Undergone Rapid Industrialisation

1) NICs are countries that are **rapidly getting richer** as their economies change from being based on **primary industry** (e.g. agriculture) to **secondary industry** (e.g. manufacturing) and in some cases to **tertiary industry** (e.g. IT services).

2) **Hong Kong**, **Singapore**, **South Korea** and **Taiwan** were the first generation of NICs. They began to rapidly industrialise in the 1960s, and were later nicknamed the **Asian Tiger** economies (see below).

3) The Asian Tigers have since become **more wealthy** and **developed** — many people **no longer** consider them to be NICs.

4) In 2012, the countries that most people considered to be NICs were Mexico, Brazil, South Africa, Turkey, India, China, Malaysia, the Philippines and Thailand.

NICs are more developed than LDCs but less developed than countries like the US and the UK.

The Asian Tiger Economies grew very Rapidly

1) An **important** factor in the growth of the Asian Tigers was **investment** from **TNCs**.

2) **TNCs** (particularly from Japan) set up the **manufacturing** parts of their business in the Asian Tigers because there was:

- A **cheap** workforce.
- **Low cost** and **availability** of raw materials and land.
- A reasonable standard of **infrastructure**, e.g. roads and ports.
- Favourable **government policies**, e.g. subsidies or grants to attract investment.
- **Reduced trade tariffs**, making importing and exporting cheaper.
- Less strict **environmental**, **labour** and **planning** laws than in developed countries.
- **Expanding domestic markets** — the populations of the NICs were becoming wealthier so the **demand** for material goods within the NICs was **increasing**.

3) The first manufacturing industries had **low production costs** (cheap raw materials and low technology production) and were **labour intensive**, e.g. manufacturing toys.

4) As manufacturing became **successful**, companies invested in **developing** the industries, e.g. improving **technology** to make the manufacturing process more **efficient**. Manufacturers then started to produce **higher value goods** that were more **expensive to make** but more **profitable when sold**. For example, Hong Kong started manufacturing electronic goods.

5) The Asian Tigers became **specialised** in these industries — the workforce became **highly educated** and **skilled**.

6) The continued success of manufacturing led to **rapid economic growth** and **development**, e.g. Hong Kong's GNI per capita grew from $1800 in 1973 to $32 950 in 2008.

7) There have been **benefits** and **disadvantages** of this rapid growth. The **wealth** and **living standards** of the population have generally **improved** (e.g. better health care and access to education). However in some places working conditions are **poor** (e.g. South Korea has one of the highest accident at work rates in the world), and rapid industrialisation has caused **environmental damage** (e.g. Victoria Harbour in Hong Kong is badly polluted).

As NICs get Richer, Industry moves to Cheaper Places, Creating New NICs

1) As the Asian Tiger economies got more **wealthy**, it became more **expensive** to produce things there, e.g. because wages became higher.

2) To continue keeping costs **low**, the TNCs began to **move** their production to other, **less developed** countries, e.g. Malaysia, Thailand and the Philippines.

3) Also, **new TNCs** grew out of the Asian Tiger economies, e.g. Samsung originated in South Korea. These TNCs set up their manufacturing in less developed countries as well.

4) The growth of manufacturing into **less developed countries** from both new and established TNCs created a **second wave** of NICs.

As TNCs moved manufacturing elsewhere, the service sector grew in the Asian Tigers and they continued to develop.

Newly Industrialised Countries (NICs)

China is a Rapidly Growing NIC

1) Since the 1970s there has been **rapid economic growth** in China — GNI per capita rose from around $180 in 1978 to $2940 in 2010 with a growth rate of around 10% a year.

2) Until 1978, the government **controlled** all of China's productive assets (e.g. agricultural land, mines and factories). Since 1978, a number of **economic reforms** and changes in **government policy** have led to economic growth:

- Encouraging **imports** and **exports** by reducing tariffs and taxes — exports rose 19% per year between 1981 and 1994.
- Encouraging the growth of **private business**, e.g. agriculture was partly privatised, allowing farmers to sell their own produce (rather than giving it to the state to sell).
- **Foreign investment** was encouraged — **special economic zones** were set up where foreign companies would receive tax breaks if they invested in manufacturing (e.g. by building factories).
- There was greater **investment** in **education** to create a workforce that is more attractive to TNCs.
- There was greater **investment** in **infrastructure** to make it easier for manufacturers to operate.
- In 2001 China joined the **World Trade Organisation**. This further opened China's markets to foreign investors and allowed Chinese businesses to export more easily.

3) As a result of these reforms (and the large supply of **cheap labour**), both **Chinese** businesses and **foreign TNCs** invested in manufacturing in China.

4) Manufacturing industries (e.g. textiles, toys, electronics, cars) **boomed**, which brought **rapid** and **continuing** economic growth for the whole country.

5) This growth has led to increased **wealth** and **improved living standards** in China.

6) However, there have been **negative consequences** of this rapid industrialisation:

- A wider **gap** between the rich and the poor. Much of the development has been in big **cities** along China's coast (where it's easiest to import and export goods), leaving the **agricultural interior** of the country relatively **poor**.
- **Environmental problems**, e.g. air pollution and acid rain in industrial areas because of increased emissions.
- **Working conditions** are poor in some areas. E.g. in 2010, over 130 workers were injured by a toxic chemical at a factory in Suzhou (near Shanghai) making products for Apple Inc.

Some NICs have Developed into Service Centres

1) Many service industries such as **financial services** (e.g. banks and insurance companies), **IT services** (e.g. software development) and **sales services** (e.g. marketing) have become **globalised** (see p. 217).

2) Because many services can be located **anywhere** in the world, the economic growth in some **NICs** (e.g. India, see next page) is based on investment in **service industries** (rather than manufacturing) by TNCs. Here are a few things that make some NICs attractive to investment in services:

- They have a **skilled**, **educated workforce**, particularly in terms of technically skilled workers (e.g. computer programmers) or workers that speak different languages (e.g. to work in international call centres).
- **Low labour costs**, especially of skilled workers compared to more developed countries.
- Good **communications** links, e.g. improved telephone networks and internet availability.
- Favourable **government policies** that attract businesses.
- Expanding **domestic markets** — as wealth increases there is a demand for more services, e.g. advertising, personal financial services and the media.

Skilled... educated... I'm good looking too by the way.

Newly Industrialised Countries (NICs)

India's Growth has been Based on Service Industries

1) There has been **rapid economic growth** in India in recent years, e.g. the economy has grown by an average of 7% per year since 1997.

2) In the 1990s India made **economic reforms** to reduce barriers to trade and encourage Foreign Direct Investment. Unlike in other NICs though, growth has focused on **service industries** rather than manufacturing.

3) Growth in the service industries **succeeded** in India for a number of reasons:
   - There are plenty of **highly educated** and **technically skilled** workers, e.g. at present, around 3 million people graduate from Indian universities every year, including 500 000 engineering graduates.
   - English is **widely spoken** and **understood** — this is important for many TNCs from English-speaking countries, e.g. they can establish customer service call centres in India.
   - **Low labour costs**.
   - There is an extensive **communications network**, e.g. for telephones and the internet.

4) There are two main ways the service industry has grown in India:

   1 **Local companies** in the **service industries** (e.g. IT services) grew as they **supplied foreign TNCs**.

   - In the 1980s and 1990s, some young Indian **IT professionals** migrated to the UK or US to work for western companies. When they came back to India, they understood the **IT needs** of more developed countries, and set up their own businesses to **supply** those needs.
   - The **low cost of labour** in India meant that these Indian companies could provide the same service as their competitors in developed countries, but at a **lower price**.
   - As the service industries grew in India, more and more western TNCs began to **outsource** (give contracts to outside businesses rather than do the work themselves) to Indian companies because it was **significantly cheaper**.

   2 **TNCs** relocated **service areas** of their business to India (e.g. telephone call centres).

   - The availability of a **skilled, English-speaking** workforce means India can offer a range of other office-based services (so called 'back-office functions') to foreign TNCs, e.g. customer service call centres.
   - By moving their services to India, TNCs can save a lot of money — the average salary in an Indian call centre in 2003 was **£1200 a year** compared to **£12 500 a year** in the UK.
   - Other examples of services transferred to India include **IT technical assistance** and **financial administration**. E.g. KPMG is a financial consultancy TNC. It employs people in ten cities in India, including Delhi and Mumbai.

5) The service sector has become an **important** part of the Indian economy — in 2011 it accounted for around 56% of GDP.

6) The growth of service industries in India has increased **wealth** and **employment** and improved **living standards**.

7) However the growth of the service industries has had **negative** impacts too:
   - A large proportion of the growth is from foreign investment by TNCs so the **profits leave the country**.
   - The benefits and employment opportunities are mostly only available to the **educated middle classes**, which increases the **poverty gap** between them and the lower classes.

Practice Questions

Q1 Which countries are the Asian Tiger economies?

Q2 Give three reasons why NICs attract manufacturing industries.

Q3 Give two reasons why India has experienced growth in the service sector.

Exam Question

Q1 With reference to one or more countries you have studied, explain the economic growth of NICs. [10 marks]

Awww, I really love Newly Industrialised Countries — they're just so NICe...

You like them, I like them and examiners really like them. Your exam board thinks NICs are the bee's knees, so make sure you learn all the stuff on these pages, then when you write a fabulous answer in your exam you'll be the bee's knees too...

Growth in the 21st Century

Economic growth is a continuous process, so don't think for a second that it'll stop in the 21st century...

New Markets are Emerging

1) The opening up of **new markets** is an important factor driving economic growth in the 21st century.

2) **New** (or **emerging**) **markets** are countries which are **opening up** to international trade and investment, e.g. by removing trade barriers such as tariffs. Examples of new markets include **NICs** (e.g. China, India and Brazil), wealthy **oil-producing** countries (e.g. the United Arab Emirates (UAE) and Saudi Arabia) and countries that have recently shifted from a closed market to an **open market** (e.g. Russia).

3) Some new markets, e.g. China, India and Brazil, have very **large populations**. As these countries **develop** and become more **open** to **international trade**, the **wealth** of their populations increases.

4) This creates a **growing demand** in these countries for **material goods**, e.g. luxuries such as electronic goods and cars, and **services**, e.g. entertainment and leisure facilities such as restaurants and cinemas.

5) This has allowed **more developed countries** such as the UK to grow economically — new markets provide opportunities for companies from these countries to increase profits.

6) New markets are increasingly important for the **global economy**, e.g. China has been responsible for 20% of global economic growth since 2000. As new markets become more and more important in world trade and investment, some people think the balance of **world power** could move **away** from North America and Europe into **new market countries**.

New Technologies give Opportunities for Investment

1) **New technologies**, especially in IT and communications (e.g. the internet), have also been one of the main driving forces behind **world economic growth** in recent years.

2) New technologies have led to **growth** in many areas of the world economy. E.g. improved computer hardware such as **CAM** (Computer Aided Manufacturing) has increased **manufacturing efficiency** — work done by computers and robots is faster and more consistent than people doing the same job.

3) Huge profits have been made from the **production** of new technologies and their **sale** and **distribution** to existing and new markets, e.g. laptops, tablet computers and smartphones.

4) There are high levels of **investment** in **creating** new technologies (e.g. 3D televisions), which creates growth in areas such as research and development.

5) There are many new technologies currently **being developed** that could create **more economic growth** in the future, e.g. wireless power transmission, robotics (e.g. the automation of transport) and new energy sources (e.g. fusion reactors).

Mitch wasn't interested in new technology. He had his reliable old desktop and that was just fine thank you very much.

Practice Questions

Q1 What is a new market?

Q2 Give three examples of new markets in the 21st century.

Q3 Give three examples of new technologies in the 21st century.

Exam Question

Q1 Outline the impact of new markets and new technologies on global economic growth in the 21st century.   [8 marks]

Maybe in a few years time we'll all be flying to school...

Sadly this book doesn't have any extra technological functions — it won't play music, show videos or text your friends, but it will help you pass your exam. All you have to do is read the stuff on this page again and again until it's as fixed in your head as your smartphone is in your pocket. Just make sure your phone isn't still fixed in your pocket when you go into your exam though.

Causes of Conflict

If you think that a thumb war with your brother is a serious conflict, then I'm afraid you've got a fair bit to learn...

Conflict *is* Disagreement *between* People

1) People often have **different interests**, **needs** and **points of view**.
2) This can lead to **disagreements** (**conflicts**).
3) Unless conflicts are **resolved** they can lead to **tension**, **violence** or **war** (see page 228).

No doubt about it, Petal and Bob were in serious conflict.

There are *Many Causes* of Conflict

Identity

1) **Identity** is the set of **characteristics** that makes **you who you are** — they might include **where you're from**, your **language**, your **religion** and your **culture**.

2) If **groups** of people have **different identities** it can lead to **conflict**. A common **reason** for conflict is the level of **power** and **independence** each group has — conflicts are often about **political** power and independence.

3) Identity conflicts can be caused by **nationalism**, **regionalism** and **localism**. **Nationalism** is having a strong identity related to the **country** you're from. **Regionalism** relates to a **regional identity** and **localism** relates to a **local identity**. For example:

> *A region is a large area within one or more countries (e.g. a county). A local area is a specific place (e.g. a village or a town).*

- **Nationalism** — **Scottish nationalists** want Scotland to have **greater political independence** from the **UK**. In **1998**, some **powers** were given to a newly-created **Scottish parliament**, but nationalists still want **full independence** from the UK.

- **Regionalism** — in **France**, the **Mouvement Région Savoie** campaigns for Savoie and Haute Savoie (small administrative divisions) to come together as a **larger political region** within France. They used to make up the region of **Savoy**, and at present are part of the larger Rhône-Alpes administrative region.

- **Localism** — in 2012, a **holiday chalet** was proposed close to **Ullswater** (a lake in the Lake District, UK). This caused conflict locally with **environmental groups** who believed that the area should **remain undeveloped**.

Ethnicity

1) **Ethnicity** is a part of **identity**. It can include things you're born with (e.g. **nationality** and **race**) as well as things that are **passed down** from one generation to the next (e.g. **language**, **culture** and **religion**).

2) Your ethnicity **doesn't** have to be the **same** as your **nationality**. For example, people **born in the UK** have a **British nationality** but they can belong to many **different ethnic groups** (e.g. Black Caribbean, Indian, Chinese, etc.) Some people with a **mixed family background** belong to **more than one** ethnic group.

3) **Ethnic conflict** is conflict between **ethnic groups**. It can be the result of an ethnic group wanting **more political power**. Sometimes it can be the result of a **belief** that one ethnic group is **superior** to another.

> For example, in **Rwanda** there's a long history of conflict between the **Tutsi** and **Hutu ethnic groups**. In **1994** this led to a **genocide** (the mass killing of people belonging to a particular national, ethnic, racial or religious group). Around **800 000 people** (mostly Tutsis) were **killed** (mostly by Hutus) within **100 days**.

Culture

1) **Culture** includes many things that relate to **how you live your life**, e.g. foods, customs, clothing, traditions, language, art, attitudes, beliefs and values.

2) For example, culture can be **linked** to **ethnicity** (e.g. African culture), **religion** (e.g. Jewish culture), **gender** (e.g. male or female culture), **age** (e.g. youth culture) or **where you live** (e.g. urban or rural culture).

3) **Cultural differences** can result in **conflicts** — especially when people from different cultures don't fully **understand** or **respect** each other's differences.

> For example, **whale meat** is considered to be a **traditional food delicacy** in Japan. This causes **conflict** with people who are worried about whales becoming **extinct** because **too many** are being caught.

Causes of Conflict

Resources

Conflicts can occur when people are **competing** for the same **resources**, such as:

1) **Territory** — e.g. **sovereignty** (authority) over the **Falkland Islands** in the South Atlantic Ocean has been **disputed** for a long time. In **1982 Argentina** and the **UK** fought over the islands in the **Falklands War**.

2) **Water** — e.g. the **Nile River** is a source of water for **10 countries** in North East Africa. There's conflict between the **downstream countries** (Egypt and Sudan) that use **most** of the **water**, and the **upstream countries** (including Uganda, Rwanda, Ethiopia and Tanzania) that **want to use more water**.

3) **Buildings** — e.g. the **Dome of the Rock** in Jerusalem was **constructed** by **Muslims** on the site of a **Jewish Temple** in the 7th Century. There's been a long conflict over the Dome, as it is **important** to **both religious groups**. Non-Muslims currently have limited access to the Dome and items such as Jewish prayer books are banned.

4) **Oil** — e.g. there's been a conflict between **Russia** and **Norway** over polar oil rights for over 40 years. Recently the countries made an **agreement** that **divided** the **Arctic Ocean** into **zones** where each country can **extract oil**.

Ideology

1) An **ideology** is a **set of ideas** about how **society** should be. For example, an ideology might include ideas about the **form of government**, **economic system**, **education system**, **social welfare system**, **health care system**, **justice system** and **environment**.

2) Groups of people with **different ideologies** can have different ideas that can result in **conflicts**.

For example, the governments of **North Korea** and **South Korea** have different ideologies, which have led to a long history of conflict. **North Korea** has an **authoritarian government** (all political power is held by a few people) and a **communist economic system** (property and production is controlled by the government). **South Korea** has a **democratic government** (there are several political parties and elections) and a **capitalist economic system** (property and production is privately controlled).

Usually There **Isn't** Just a **Single Cause** of **Conflict**

Most conflicts **don't** just have a single cause — they actually have a **mixture** of **some** (or **all**) of these causes. For example, the causes of the **war** between **Iran** and **Iraq** between 1980 and 1988 included:

- **Resources** — there was conflict over **control** of the **Shatt al-Arab** (the **river** that forms the **boundary** between Iran and Iraq). Both countries were also **major oil producers** — this led to **economic competition** between the two.

- **Identity** — the **religion** of Iran was mainly the **Shia** branch of Islam, and the leaders of Iraq followed the **Sunni** branch of Islam.

Practice Questions

Q1 What is conflict?
Q2 What is meant by nationalism?
Q3 Give an example of regionalism.
Q4 Give an example of an ethnic conflict.
Q5 What is ideology?

Exam Question

Q1 Describe how resources can be a cause of conflict. [8 marks]

Look, we can argue over these pages forever...

...but there'll still be lots of stuff on them to learn. Looking at this list of things to disagree about, it's amazing anyone's speaking to each other at all. It's important to realise that conflict doesn't always have to end in wars and violence — many conflicts are resolved by peaceful protests and discussion. In fact, you'll find lots more about that just over the page...

Characteristics and Resolution of Conflict

You may think that conflict is part of everyday life... well, you'd be right. Don't panic though, it can all get sorted in the end.

Conflict can be **International**, **National**, **Regional** or **Local**

Conflicts occur on **different scales** — from small **local disputes** to large-scale **international wars**:

- **International level** conflicts involve **more than one country**, e.g. the **Iran-Iraq war** from 1980 to 1988 (see page 227).
- **National level** conflicts occur within **one country**, e.g. the conflict that began in **Syria** in March 2011 has been fought between the **authoritarian government** and **anti-government** forces who want **democracy**.
- **Regional level** conflicts occur within a region of one or more countries, e.g. in the **Kunar Province** of **Afghanistan**, many rural communities rely on **mountain springs** for **water**. These springs occasionally run **dry**, which can lead to **tension** between the communities as they **compete** for **water resources**.
- **Local level** conflicts occur within **small areas of a country**, e.g. in **2002** a plan to build 27 **wind turbines** on the **Isle of Skye** was approved. Many locals were concerned the wind farm would create **noise pollution**, harm the **tourist industry** and pose a threat to **golden eagles**. Local people who were campaigning **against** the wind farm had their property **vandalised** by people who **supported** the wind farm.

Conflict is **Expressed** in **Many Different Ways**

1) **Non-violent** conflicts **don't** involve **violence** (no, really). For example:
   - **Political activity** includes supporting, opposing or creating a political party.
   - **Debate** is formal discussion to exchange opinions — and it often ends in a vote to make decisions.
   - **Boycotts** involve refusing to do something (e.g. refusing to buy a product).
   - **Strikes** involve refusing to work.
   - **Protests** and **demonstrations** involve groups of people publicly making their opinions heard and drawing attention to issues. They include protest marches (walking through areas) and picketing (gathering in one place).

And just at that moment, Jimmy decided to go on strike...

2) **Terrorism** involves using violence to **intimidate people** — usually with the aim of achieving a **political goal**.
3) **Insurrection** is an organised **rebellion** with the aim of **overthrowing** a government. Insurrection **often** (but not always) involves **violence**.
4) **War** is a **violent conflict** between two or more groups.

Groups that use violence to achieve a political goal might be considered terrorists by some people and freedom fighters by others. These groups are sometimes called 'militant groups' — it's a more neutral term.

There are Lots of Ways to **Resolve Conflict**

Negotiation

1) Negotiation involves **discussing** issues with the aim of producing an **agreement**.
2) Negotiation is used to try to resolve many **different kinds** of conflict — for example, **business** negotiations (businesses and suppliers may negotiate with each other to agree on prices) and **government** negotiations (community groups may negotiate with local government to agree on development plans for an area).
3) Negotiations can be **formal** or **informal**. They may involve **trained negotiators** acting on behalf of a group (e.g. a lawyer may represent a group in legal negotiations).

Diplomacy

1) **Diplomacy** is **negotiation** between countries. It usually involves **trained negotiators** called **diplomats** or **ambassadors**.
2) Most countries have a **diplomatic service** to maintain **international relations** and negotiate **agreements** (e.g. trade agreements), **alliances** (e.g. political alliances where governments work together to solve problems) and **peace treaties** (e.g. to prevent or resolve violent conflicts).
3) **Cultural differences** (e.g. diplomats from different countries following **different rules** and **methods** of discussion, or having **different negotiation styles**) may affect diplomacy, so diplomats are **trained** to act reasonably and follow certain **rules of behaviour** — so they don't cause **offence**.

Characteristics and Resolution of Conflict

Mediation

1) **Mediation** involves the groups at conflict meeting with a mediator (an **independent third party**).
2) Mediators aim to make sure groups **listen to** and **understand each other**.
   They try to find ways of reaching an **agreement**.
3) **All sorts** of conflicts involve mediators — from **local disputes** to **international disagreements**.
4) Mediators of **international conflicts** include **countries** (e.g. Norway mediated the Sri Lankan Civil War), **non-government organisations** (e.g. 'International Alert' is a mediator in Liberia) and **inter-government organisations** (e.g. the UN is a mediator in the Middle East).

Planning Laws can Help Resolve Conflicts Over Local Resources

1) **Proposed developments** (building projects) often cause conflict over **available space** and **local resources**.
2) When a development is proposed, **planning officers** first make sure that the development **sticks to planning laws**. If it doesn't, they can ask for the proposal to be **changed**.
3) Then, **planning committees** discuss the proposals. They must consider:

The Newbury Bypass (see next page) is an example of a proposal with positive and negative impacts.

- The views of **all** of the **interested parties**. This often involves the **people** or **organisation** that made the proposal, and the **local community** who may be affected by the plans.
- Whether the **gains** from the development **outweigh** the **negative impacts** it may cause.
- Whether the proposed development has **wider benefits** outside of the local area (e.g. developing an industrial plant in an area can be good for other companies who will supply materials and components to the plant).

4) The committees take all of these factors into account and then make a **decision** about the proposed development. The plans may be **accepted** or **rejected**, or they may ask for the plans to be **modified** and resubmitted.
5) If plans are **rejected**, the developers can go through an **appeals process** against the decision.

Conflict Resolution May Not Make Everyone Happy

Unfortunately, **not everyone** can **win** all the time when it comes to conflict resolution.
There are **three** possible outcomes when a conflict is resolved:

- a **win-lose outcome** (one side gains while the other loses).
- a **win-win outcome** (both sides gain).
- a **lose-lose outcome** (both sides lose out).

> For example, a conflict about **trade** between two countries could result in a **win-win outcome** (e.g. a trade agreement that benefits both countries), a **win-lose outcome** (e.g. a trade agreement that involves applying taxes that benefit one country and penalise another) or a **lose-lose outcome** (e.g. trade sanctions are applied that reduce trade between the countries).

Practice Questions

Q1 What is a national level conflict?
Q2 Give three examples of how non-violent conflicts can be expressed.
Q3 What is insurrection?
Q4 What is a win-win outcome when a conflict is resolved?

Exam Question

Q1 Outline the different ways to resolve a conflict. [8 marks]

When it comes to diplomacy, it's best not to say exactly what you think...

Oh dear, conflict resolution is tricky stuff — the problem is that everyone tends to have very strong views and no one wants to lose. Think about how tricky things can get between football fans on a Saturday evening — scale it up a few thousand times and you've got some idea of how difficult things can be when whole countries are in conflict.

Local Resource Conflict Case Study — Newbury Bypass

Ah, the Newbury Bypass case study — a staple component of any decent Geography course...

The **Newbury Bypass** was Proposed to Solve **Traffic Problems**

1) In the 1980s the **volume of traffic** passing through **Newbury** in Berkshire was around **50 000 vehicles per day** and **congestion** was a serious **problem** (even though Newbury already had a bypass called the A34).

A bypass is a road that avoids busy town or city centres.

2) In **1982** four possible routes for a **new bypass** to reduce traffic through the town centre were **proposed**.

3) A **public consultation** was undertaken which included **exhibitions** of the possible routes as well as the distribution of **brochures** and **questionnaires**.

4) In **1984** the UK Government's **Department of Transport** announced its recommendation of the **western route** — this would involve building an additional **13.5 km long** section of the **A34** to bypass the town.

There Were Many **Objections** to the **Proposal**

1) Many local people believed the bypass **wouldn't solve** the **traffic problems**, partly because **a lot of** the traffic was **local** (travelling within the Newbury area). They thought that **other methods** could solve the traffic problems, e.g. traffic calming measures, bus lanes, and park and ride schemes.

2) There were many **environmental concerns** over the **route** and its **construction**. For example:
   - The proposed route crossed **three Sites of Special Scientific Interest** (SSSIs) — Snelsmore Common, the River Kennet and the River Lambourn.
   - It crossed **six county wildlife sites** and the Rack Marsh **nature reserve**.
   - **10 000 trees** would be felled.
   - The **habitats** of protected species such as the **dormouse** and the rare **Desmoulin's whorl snail** would be **destroyed**.

3) The bypass also crossed two **civil war battle sites** and 12 **archaeological** sites.

Newbury, Berkshire

People **Campaigned Against** the **Bypass** in Different Ways...

- A group of **local residents** formed the Society for the Prevention of the Western Bypass (SPEWBY). They submitted a **report** to the public consultation in 1982 which described the case against the western bypass, and they also **raised public awareness** of the case using the media.

- In 1994 some local residents formed the **Third Battle of Newbury Group**. This group gained the support of **national organisations** including Friends of the Earth, WWF® and Greenpeace. They raised awareness of the case **nationally**, and got many people across the country to **write protest letters** to the **government**.

- This group also made **formal complaints** to the **EU commission** — they claimed that the **UK government** was **breaking European laws** by approving the bypass without doing an **Environmental Impact Assessment** (EIA). However, **no laws** were **broken** because the bypass was proposed just **before** the law about EIAs was made.

- **Direct action protests** began in **1994**. **Protesters** from all over the country began to set up **camps** along the **route** of the bypass. Some built **tree houses** and others lived in **tents**. There were a few incidents of criminal damage and violence, but the protests were **mostly peaceful**.

- By **February 1996** there were **hundreds of people** in over **30 camps**. Protestors tried to **stop work** to clear the bypass route by **living in the trees**, digging and living in **tunnels**, and **blocking** the path of **heavy machinery**.

- That month, the protest became the **biggest ever anti-road protest** in UK history — **8000 people** marched along 3 km of the route of the bypass.

...But the **Bypass** Also Had **Supporters**

- A **large number** of local residents **supported** the building of the bypass and a group of them formed the **Newbury Bypass Supporters Association**. They gathered a **petition of 6000 signatures** of people who **supported** the bypass.

- The **four local councils** in the area **supported** the bypass (although some objections were expressed, e.g. Berkshire County Council's archaeological officer raised concerns about the route going through the Kennet River Valley SSSI).

- The **local MP** (David Rendel, a Liberal Democrat elected in 1993) was a **strong supporter** of the building of the bypass.

Local Resource Conflict Case Study — Newbury Bypass

A *Public Inquiry* and a *Review* Were Held

To try to resolve the conflict, the government held a **public inquiry** and a **review**.

1) The public inquiry was held in **1988**. This involved **147 witnesses** giving evidence to a **government appointed inspector**.
   - **Support** for the bypass was expressed by the **four councils** and the **Newbury Bypass Supporters Association**.
   - **Opposition** to the bypass was expressed by **SPEWBY**, a group of **local farmers**, a **parish council**, the **National Trust** (who owned one of the woodlands) and the **National Rivers Authority**.

2) In **1990**, following the inquiry, the **government** announced the bypass would **go ahead** despite the opposition.

3) The conflict continued, so in **1994** the transport minister announced a **review** by the **Highways Agency** where **alternatives** to the bypass would be considered. Again it was decided that the bypass would **continue**.

Work Began on the Bypass in *1996*

1) After the review, **preparations** to clear the bypass route **began**.

2) The **Highways Agency** obtained **eviction** orders to remove the direct action **protestors** from their camps. The evictions began in 1996.

3) Two **police forces** (Thames Valley and Hampshire), over **600 security guards** and professional **climbers** were used to remove the protestors and their camps.

4) It took around **five weeks** to evict all the protestors.

5) **Security costs** on the bypass reached over **£30 million** — originally only £7 million had been allocated for security.

6) Over **900 protestors** were **arrested**.

The *Bypass* was *Built* But the *Conflict* Goes on

1) The bypass was **completed** in **1998** but the anti-bypass campaign continues and there have been several **reunion rallies** at Newbury.

2) Campaigners still work to **raise awareness** of the **negative impacts** of the bypass. E.g. some people say the bypass has actually **increased** the amount of traffic in the area.

3) There is ongoing **environmental assessment** of the impacts of the bypass. For example, **pollution** in habitats along the bypass route is **monitored**.

Jonny protested by making the Newbury Bypass Bypass.

4) Although the bypass was built, the **anti-bypass campaign** had some **successes**:
   - The campaign highlighted **environmental issues**. As a result nearly **200 000 trees** and **shrubs** were planted and attempts were made to **relocate wildlife** such as dormice, snails, bats, slow worms, voles and badgers.
   - The campaign also **raised awareness** of the fact that road building may not be the solution to **traffic problems**. As a result, many new **road building schemes** were **scrapped**.

Practice Questions

Q1 What was the cause of the conflict in Newbury?

Q2 What groups were involved in the conflict?

Q3 Why did some people object to the bypass?

Q4 What was the outcome of the conflict?

Exam Question

Q1 Give an example of a conflict over a local resource you have studied and evaluate the processes which operated to resolve it.

[10 marks]

If only they could have bypassed the conflict...

There's loads to learn here, I'm afraid — the Newbury bypass conflict is an example of a local dispute that just ran and ran. It became a national campaign and even made some of its main campaigners household names around the UK.

International Conflict Case Study — Gaza and the West Bank

This is the first of three case studies about international conflicts. Ready, get set, go.

Israel, the **West Bank** and **Gaza** Were Created from **Palestine**

1) **Palestine** was an area in the **Middle East** that used to cover the area that is now Israel, Gaza and the West Bank.

2) Historically, this area has been settled by both **Jews** and **Arabs**.
   - The **Jews** hadn't had their **own state** for around 2000 years.
   - They saw the **biblical land** of **Palestine** as their natural home.
   - Many Jews **set up communities** in Palestine in the early part of the 20th century. Jews also **fled Europe** and moved to Palestine around the time of **World War 2** (due to anti-semitism — the hatred of Jews).
   - Conflict developed between the **Jews** and the **Arabs** who lived there (called **Palestinians**) over who had the **right to the land**.

3) In **1947** the UN proposed a plan to **divide Palestine** into a Jewish state, an Arab state and Jerusalem (a holy city important to both Jewish and Muslim people).

4) The Jews **accepted** the plan, but the Palestinians and the **Arab states** (Jordan, Egypt, Lebanon, Syria and Iraq) **didn't**. **War** broke out, and in 1949 **three states** were created in an attempt to end the conflict:

   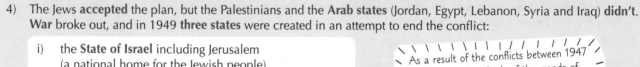

   i) the **State of Israel** including Jerusalem (a national home for the Jewish people),

   ii) the **West Bank** (an Arab territory controlled by Jordan),

   iii) **Gaza** (an Arab territory controlled by Egypt).

   > As a result of the conflicts between 1947 and 1949, hundreds of thousands of Palestinians living in Israel became refugees and fled to the West Bank and Gaza.

5) Many Palestinians still **did not agree** with this solution. In the **1960s** the **Palestinian Liberation Organisation** (PLO) was formed with the aim of making the whole former area of **Palestine** an Arab state. An armed conflict began between the PLO and Israeli forces.

6) In response to attacks from the PLO, **Israel invaded** and **seized control** of the **West Bank** and **Gaza** in 1967.

7) **Conflict** between **Israelis** and **Palestinians** continued. E.g. in 1987 Palestinians began **demonstrating** against the Israeli occupation of the West Bank and Gaza in an uprising called the **First Intifada**.

8) There were peace talks in 1993 to end the First Intifada. They resulted in the **PLO** recognising **Israel's right to exist** and Israel giving **control** of the **West Bank** and **Gaza** to **Palestine**.

9) However, this **didn't end the conflict**. Between **2000** and **2005** there were more violent conflicts in a Second Intifada (Palestinian uprising against Israel).

10) In 2006, **elections** were held in Gaza and the West Bank — they were won by **Hamas**, a Palestinian group with a **history of violence** against Israel. They **refused** to accept Israel's right to exist and **fighting continued**.

The **Conflict** is **Ongoing**

1) There have been **many peace talks** to **try to resolve** the conflict, e.g. the 1993 peace talks (see above). These have been **mediated** by **countries** and **international organisations** including the **USA**, the **EU**, the **UN**, the **Arab League** and **Russia**.

2) Issues that are proving **hard to agree on** include:

   - **Control of Jerusalem** — e.g. some people are concerned that access to holy places may be restricted.
   - The **location of certain settlements** — e.g. some people would like Israeli settlements removed from Palestinian areas, and vice-versa.
   - The **rights of the Palestinian refugees** from the 1947-1949 conflicts (and their descendants) to return to Israel. This includes at least 4 million people currently living in refugee camps.
   - **Freedom of movement** of Palestinian people. E.g. the borders around Gaza are tightly controlled — Palestinian people are not allowed to pass freely into Israel or Egypt.

3) In **2010 new peace talks** began, mediated by the USA.

International Conflict Case Study — Gaza and the West Bank

The Conflict Over *Israel*, the *West Bank* and *Gaza* Has Had Many *Impacts*

Social Impacts

- **Hundreds of thousands** of people live at risk of **military attacks**.
- Since 1948 there have been **tens of thousands of deaths** caused by the conflict. There were an estimated **50 000-100 000 military deaths** and **10 000-50 000 civilian deaths** between **1948** and **1997**.
- **Tens of thousands** of people have been **injured** as a result of the conflict.
- During the **1948 war**, around **700 000 Palestinians** were forced to leave their homes and become **refugees**. These people and their descendants (now at least 4 million people) still live in refugee camps (mostly in Jordan, Lebanon, Syria, the West Bank and Gaza).
- Some people have **human rights concerns**, e.g. over the treatment of civilians and political prisoners.
- There have been many **cultural losses**, e.g. places of worship have been destroyed (both Jewish synagogues and Muslim mosques).
- Many **unexploded land mines** litter the landscape. They pose a risk to civilians and livestock.

Environmental Impacts

- Large **military structures** have been **built** that have **affected the environment**. E.g. Israeli military bases and large security walls in the West Bank and Gaza have damaged agricultural land, affected drainage patterns and destroyed natural habitats.
- The **loss of agricultural land** has led to **overgrazing** in some areas, which has led to **desertification**.
- Some areas have been **damaged** and **polluted** by **explosions**, e.g. a wastewater plant bombed in 2009 contaminated water resources and the surrounding land.
- The **Mediterranean sea** is being **polluted** as 80 000 m³ of partially treated or untreated **sewage** is being pumped out from the Gaza strip **every day** (caused by a lack of investment in infrastructure due to the ongoing conflict).

Economic Impacts

- It's difficult to estimate the cost of such a long conflict but it's likely to have cost many **trillions** of US$ since **1948**.
- The conflict has **hindered economic growth** in the region, e.g. because large amounts of money are spent on security instead of development.
- The **majority of Palestinians** live in **poverty** — around 40% are unemployed.
- Because the **Palestinians** have no country, they **can't trade internationally**.
- The **Palestinians** rely on large amounts of **international aid**. E.g. at least 4 million people currently living in refugee camps are supported by a UN refugee fund.

Practice Questions

Q1 What was Palestine divided into in 1949?
Q2 What is the PLO?
Q3 Who won the election in Gaza and the West Bank in 2006?
Q4 Give four social impacts of the conflict.

Exam Question

Q1 Describe the economic and environmental impacts of a major international conflict you have studied. [8 marks]

Hmm, Gazza and Jordan — what can go wrong...

You'll probably have heard about this conflict in the news, but you may not have known the social, economic and environmental impacts of it. Get those details learnt — it's all about using facts and figures to back up your point when it comes to case studies.

International Conflict Case Study — Afghanistan

Here's another case study about an international conflict — this one's about the ongoing war in Afghanistan.

There's a **History** of **Conflict** in **Afghanistan**

1) In **1979**, the **Soviet Union invaded Afghanistan** and supported the installation of a communist government.

2) At the time, the **US** was in a **conflict** with the **Soviet Union** — so the US began **funding** rebel groups opposed to the Soviet Union (the Mujahideen).

3) In **1989** the Soviet Union **left** Afghanistan — but **conflicts continued** between the Mujahideen and the government, and between different groups **within** the Mujahideen.

4) In **1996** the **Taliban** (one of the Mujahideen groups) took **control** of the **government**.

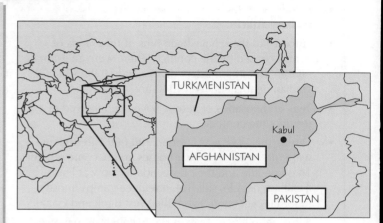

5) **Al-Qaeda** (an extreme Islamic group from the Middle East) had links with the Taliban and a base of operations in **Afghanistan**. In **1998**, the US launched **missile attacks** on bases that they believed were used by **Osama Bin Laden** (the leader of al-Qaeda).

The **US Invaded** Afghanistan in **October 2001**

1) On **September 11th 2001** there was a **terrorist attack** in the **US** — hijacked planes were flown into the **World Trade Centre** and the **Pentagon**. The attacks are widely believed to have been carried out by **al-Qaeda**.

2) The **US** wanted to bring **Osama Bin Laden** to **trial** for the attack. They issued a series of **demands** to the Taliban government of **Afghanistan** (including the immediate handover of Osama Bin Laden), but they were **refused**.

3) In **October 2001** the **US invaded Afghanistan**. They were supported by an **international coalition** that included the UK, Canada, Australia, Germany and France, as well as an Afghan opposition force (the Northern Alliance).

4) The coalition wanted to **prevent further terrorist attacks**, so their **aims** in Afghanistan were:

   - To bring **Osama Bin Laden** (and other leading members of al-Qaeda) to **trial**.
   - To destroy **al-Qaeda**.
   - To ensure that Afghanistan could no longer be used as a **safe haven** for **terrorists**.

5) By **December 2001** the **Taliban** government had been **removed** from power and a **new government** had been set up. US and **coalition troops** remained in Afghanistan in conflict with al-Qaeda and Taliban forces.

6) In **2006 NATO** took over the command of the **US-led coalition force**, which included soldiers from more than 40 different countries.

7) On the **2nd May 2011**, a **US-led** operation stormed a compound in Pakistan and Osama Bin Laden was shot and **killed**. Both al-Qaeda and the Taliban vowed to **avenge** his death.

NATO stands for the North Atlantic Treaty Organisation. It's a military and political alliance between the US, Canada and some European governments.

8) In **2012**, there were around **130,000** coalition troops still serving in Afghanistan.

There's Lots of **Debate** About How to **Resolve** the **Conflict**

1) Many people think that **military action isn't** the **best way** to resolve the conflict — they want **diplomatic talks** that include the Afghan government, the Taliban, other groups in Afghanistan and the neighbouring countries.

2) Others think that **military action** is **necessary** to prevent civil war and to **prevent** the Taliban returning to **power**. Some believe that the Taliban would create a regime that abuses human rights.

3) In 2009 **President Obama** (of the US) described a **new strategy** in the war — sending **33 000 more US troops** to Afghanistan to **train** the **Afghan army** and **police forces**. The US and the UK plan to **fully withdraw** their troops from Afghanistan by the **end of 2014**.

235

International Conflict Case Study — Afghanistan

The War Has Had Many Impacts

Social Impacts

- An estimated **11 000 Afghan civilians** were **killed** between 2001 and 2009 — both the Taliban and the coalition troops were responsible for the deaths.
- **1832 coalition troops** were **killed** between 2001 and 2010 (including 1115 US troops and 300 UK troops).
- Many soldiers suffer from **Post Traumatic Stress Disorder** — an anxiety condition which can cause sleep problems and feelings of isolation.
- By 2010, an estimated **3 million refugees** had fled Afghanistan to neighbouring countries, e.g. Iran and Pakistan. Many ended up living in **refugee camps**. There was a **lack** of **basic supplies** (e.g. tents and food) for the refugees and there were outbreaks of **disease** within the refugee camps (e.g. cholera and tuberculosis).
- The ongoing conflict has contributed to widespread **poverty** and **malnutrition** in Afghanistan.
- The war also **prevented** the growth of **health** and **education** services (that were already limited before the conflict).
- The **availability** of **safe drinking water** has **decreased** due to damage to infrastructure and contamination — this has caused **health problems**.
- The presence and behaviour of **coalition troops** has caused **distress** to many people — for example, air strikes and night raids spread **fear**.
- Many groups in Afghanistan have been accused of **human rights abuses** — e.g. the Taliban, local security forces and US soldiers have all been accused of **torturing prisoners** and treating them inhumanely.
- There are **safety** and **security problems** in many areas — this can lead to high levels of crime.

Environmental Impacts

- **Explosives** have **polluted** the air, soil and water with chemicals that are **toxic** to both humans and wildlife.
- The area of Afghanistan covered by **forest** has **halved** during the last few decades of conflict. The forests have been cleared by **illegal logging** as well as logging for fuel and cooking purposes.
- **Water supplies** from rivers and groundwater have been **polluted** due to a lack of adequate sanitation and waste management. Years of conflict have **destroyed** much of the **infrastructure** and reduced the country's ability to **manage waste**.
- **Hunting** of wild animals for **meat** and **furs** has increased.

Economic Impacts

- **Many countries** are **paying** for the war — especially the **US** who had spent an estimated **$740 billion** by the end of 2010. The **UK** spent **£11.1 billion** on the war up to March 2010.
- Fears over **terrorist attacks** as a result of the war have led to **increased spending** on **security** in countries like the US and UK (e.g. on **airlines** and at large **political** and **public events**).
- The conflict has **prevented** the **economic growth** of **Afghanistan**. It's one of the **poorest countries** in the world and it relies heavily on **international aid**.
- **Rebuilding** the **infrastructure** of Afghanistan following the conflict will have a **high economic cost** — e.g. roads, water and communication infrastructure, health services, manufacturing and agricultural industries all need investment.

Practice Questions

Q1 When did the US invade Afghanistan?
Q2 Give two reasons for the US invasion of Afghanistan.
Q3 Give three environmental impacts of the conflict.

Exam Question

Q1 With reference to at least one case study, discuss the social impacts of international conflict. [10 marks]

So, Afghanistan — nope, nothing funny here at all...

Even though those lists of impacts are pretty long, you really need to store the lot in your memory so you can write a stonking answer in the exam. And that's well worth doing if you want your Geography teacher to be as proud as your Mum on results day.

International Conflict Case Study — Darfur

This is the last of the three case studies. Once again, get stuck in with learning those details.

Rebel Groups Attacked the Government in 2003

1) **Darfur** is a region in the west of **Sudan** in Africa.

2) For **many decades** there have been tensions and **conflicts** between **nomadic Arabs** in the region and **black African farmers** over land and grazing rights.

3) In **February 2003** rebel groups attacked government troops. The main rebel groups were the **Sudan Liberation Army** (SLA) and the **Justice and Equality Movement** (JEM). They accused the government of **oppressing black Africans** in favour of Arabs.

4) **Sudan's government** responded to the attacks using **official military** and **police forces**. A **war** began between the **government** and the **rebel groups**.

5) However, a **third faction** was also involved in the conflict — the **Janjaweed**. They are pro-government **nomadic Arabs**.

6) The **Janjaweed** have been accused of **murdering** black Africans and trying to **drive them out** of large areas. Some groups believe that **genocide** has taken place (the killing of people belonging to a particular national, ethnic, racial or religious group).

7) The Sudanese **government** has been accused of **financially supporting** and **working with** the Janjaweed — but the government **denies** this.

8) A **peacekeeping force** from the **African Union** entered the region in **2004** — but they had little success preventing conflicts.

9) The **UN** had tried to get peacekeepers into the region — but the **Sudanese** government initially **rejected** the offer. In **2007** they **accepted** and a combined **UN-African Union** peacekeeping force (called UNAMID) began working in the region.

10) The **conflicts** and the **accusations of genocide** have continued. In **2008** the International Criminal Court (ICC) issued an **arrest warrant** for **President Bashir** (the head of the government) for **war crimes** and **crimes against humanity**. He strongly **denies** the charges and the ICC has **no power** to arrest him unless he leaves Sudan.

> As a result of a wider national conflict, Sudan was split into South Sudan and Sudan in 2011.

Map showing Africa with an inset of the region around Sudan, labelled: Libya, Egypt, Chad, DARFUR, SUDAN, Central African Republic, Ethiopia, SOUTH SUDAN.

> The African Union is a group made up of 54 African countries.

Peace Deals and Ceasefires Haven't Worked

1) Since the conflict began many groups have helped to arrange **peace negotiations** — including the **African Union**, the **Arab League**, **Chad** and the **UN**.

2) In **May 2006** a **ceasefire** between the **government** and the **SLA** was agreed — but **JEM** rejected the deal.

3) In **February 2010** a **ceasefire** between the **government** and **JEM** was agreed. Shortly afterwards, JEM accused the government of **breaking the ceasefire** by carrying out air strikes and they **boycotted** further negotiations.

4) In **April 2010** elections were held. **President Bashir** won but there were accusations of **fraud** and **election rigging**.

5) In **July 2011** the **government** signed a peace deal with the **LJM** (Liberation and Justice Movement) — a collection of rebel groups. Some refugees **left** refugee camps and began to **return** to villages in Darfur. However, JEM and the SLA **did not sign** the deal, and outbreaks of fighting have **continued**.

The **conflict in Darfur** was caused by disagreements over **local resources** (land and grazing rights). However, it's also part of a wider **national conflict** related to **political power**, **control of natural resources** (especially oil), and **religious and ethnic differences** between people in different parts of the country.

A refugee camp in Sudan.

International Conflict Case Study — Darfur

The War Has Had Many *Impacts*

Social Impacts

- An estimated **300 000 people** had been **killed** in the conflict by **2008** due to the combined effects of **war**, **famine** and **disease**.
- By 2010, **2.7 million people** had become **refugees** — many living in camps near Darfur's main towns. Around **200 000** of these **refugees** fled to neighbouring **Chad**, where they live in camps along the border.
- Many **villages** and **refugee camps** have suffered **violent attacks** involving murder, rape and theft.
- The murder of farmers and the destruction of farming communities has led to a **decrease** in **food production** in the region. As a result, lots of people have suffered from **malnutrition**.
- People living in refugee camps have **limited** access to **clean water** and **health facilities** (the camps are **massively overcrowded** so local resources cannot meet the demand).

Environmental Impacts

- **Desertification** (which causes land to become unsuitable for growing vegetation) is happening **around refugee camps**. Refugees are **stripping the land** of vegetation to use as fuel — the soil then becomes more **exposed** to wind and rain and is **eroded away**.
- Refugees are also putting **increased pressure** on **local resources** as they use up the available **firewood**.
- **Refugee camps** are **polluting water resources** (as they generally have poor waste disposal infrastructure).
- **Uncontrolled deforestation** is taking place as different groups participate in **logging** to **fund the conflict** and for **construction**. E.g. the UN estimate that 52 000 trees are being felled each year to be used in the production of bricks (wood is used as a fuel in brick kilns).
- **Wildlife** has been **killed**, **injured** and **disturbed** by weapons (including bombs).

Economic Impacts

- The **total cost** of the war to Sudan is difficult to estimate — it is likely to be many **billions of dollars**. This is especially damaging because Sudan is such a **poor country** (see p. 215) and this money could have been spent on **development**.
- The **trade of livestock** in Darfur is important to Sudan's economy. **Millions of pounds** of livestock have been lost due to the effects of conflict in the region.
- The conflict has **prevented** the **economic growth** of the region, e.g. productive farmland has been abandoned and many of the available natural resources haven't been developed.
- The conflict has contributed to widespread **poverty** and **slowed the development** of Sudan's **infrastructure**. **Rebuilding** the infrastructure that has been damaged during the conflict will also have a **high economic cost**, e.g. water infrastructure, health services and agricultural industries all need investment.

Practice Questions

Q1 Why did rebel groups first attack government troops?
Q2 Name the rebel groups involved in the conflict.
Q3 What has been done to attempt to resolve the conflict?
Q4 Give three social impacts of the conflict.

Exam Question

Q1 For an international conflict you have studied, examine the impacts of the conflict on the area involved. [40 marks]

... or here

These last few pages haven't really been the cheeriest, but then I don't suppose you read the conflict section for a bit of light-hearted jollity. If that's the kind of thing you're after, I can only recommend that you hire a bouncy castle.

Separatism

Not everyone wants to follow the crowd, you know. Some people are separatists...

Separatism Involves Breaking Up a Group

No amount of separatism could break up this group.

1) **Separatists** support the **separation** of a **smaller group of people** from a **larger group**.

2) The **groups** involved in separatist movements can **vary in size**. For example, the larger group could be a **single country** or **several countries**.

3) Separatism often involves **smaller groups** wanting **more political independence** from the larger group, so they can meet the needs of their people.

4) Separatism occurs because small groups feel **alienated**, **discriminated against** or **oppressed**. It can also occur if they feel they are at risk of **losing their identity**.

5) There are a number of **possible reasons** for these feelings:

- **Economic independence.** E.g. the state of Western Australia is rich in minerals such as iron ore. It accounts for a high percentage of Australia's GDP, but has a smaller population than the eastern states. Some people think that Western Australia would be much more wealthy if it was an independent country.

  GDP is the total value of the goods and services produced by a country in a year.

- **Historical allegiances.** E.g. Quebec is a province of Canada colonised by the French in the 17th century. It has a French speaking majority and a French-influenced culture. Quebec separatists want it to become a separate country.

- **Peripheral location.** E.g. Scotland and Wales are located away from the political centre of the UK (London), which can make some people living there feel that the government doesn't look after or understand the specific needs of the regions. Scottish and Welsh nationalists campaign for greater independence from the rest of the UK.

- **Religious differences.** E.g. India and Pakistan used to be one country. On the basis of the two main religions (Islam and Hinduism), it was split into an Islamic nation (Pakistan) and a Hindu nation (India) in 1947.

- **Cultural differences.** E.g. Chechen people mostly live in Chechnya — a region of the Russian Federation. They have a unique culture which has been shaped by living in isolated farming communities in a mountainous region. Chechen separatists want political independence from Russia.

- **Language differences.** E.g. Catalonia is a region of Spain with a unique language (Catalan) and culture. Catalan separatists want greater political independence.

  Separatism is almost always caused by a combination of several of these reasons.

Separatism Can Have Serious Consequences

The **consequences** of separatism can be **peaceful** or **non-peaceful**. For example:

PEACEFUL

1) **Establishing or maintaining a separate cultural identity.** E.g. the Bretons (people who live in the region of Brittany in France) maintain a separate culture to the rest of France through traditions, customs, festivals, foods and music.

2) **Language preservation.** E.g. the Welsh language is being preserved in several ways — a Welsh TV channel (S4C) was launched in 1982 and most road signs are in both languages. Laws made in the 1990s ensure that public sector literature is published in Welsh and English, and since 1999 it's been compulsory to teach Welsh in schools.

3) **Greater political independence.** E.g. devolution of the UK government in 1998 gave some political powers to the newly-created Scottish Parliament, National Assembly for Wales and Northern Ireland Assembly.

4) **Settlements that redistribute land, wealth and resources.** E.g. the Maori Party is a political party that seeks to support and protect the rights of the indigenous people of New Zealand. The Maori people lost a lot of land when Europeans began settling in New Zealand in the 18th century. Since the 1990s government negotiations have resulted in the Maori being given financial compensation and large areas of forest land.

5) **Civil disobedience** (refusal to obey certain laws or government demands). E.g. Lithuanian separatists in the 1980s ignored Soviet Union leaders and held mass meetings (rallies) and protests before gaining independence in 1990.

NON-PEACEFUL

1) **Terrorism.** E.g. the Baloch Liberation Army (BLA) is a separatist group that seeks to establish the independence of Balochistan (a region that spans parts of Pakistan, Iran and Afghanistan). The group has admitted using terrorist methods — such as bomb attacks in markets and on railway lines.

2) **Civil War.** E.g. the Sri Lankan Civil War (1983-2009) involved a separatist group (the Tamil Tigers) that wanted to establish an independent Tamil state. The military defeated the Tamil Tigers in 2009.

3) **Genocide.** E.g. Russia has been accused of committing genocide against the Chechen people.

Separatism

There's a **Separatist Movement** in the **Basque Country**

The Basque Country is a region that includes parts of **south western France** and **northern Spain**. Basque separatists want the **region** to become an **independent state**.

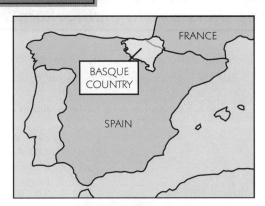

Basque Separatism has Many **Causes**

The Basque people have a **unique identity** which they want to **protect**:

- The Basque people have a **long history** going back to before Roman times.
- The Basque people have a **unique culture** and **language** that's different to **French** or **Spanish**.
- The language (**Euskera**) is one of the **oldest** in Europe and has **no clear links** with other **European languages**. Today, around **30%** of the 2.5 million Basque people speak the language.
- The Basque region occupies a **distinct geographical area** on the borders of **France** and **Spain**.

Both the **Spanish** and **French governments** have in the past tried to **suppress** the Basque **culture** and **language**.

There have been **Peaceful** and **Non-Peaceful Consequences**

PEACEFUL CONSEQUENCES

- The Basque people **preserve their culture** through traditions, clothing, foods, festivals, marches and public storytelling sessions.
- The **language** is being **preserved** through **school policies** and the **media**.
- **Political parties** (e.g. the Basque Nationalist Party) have formed — they aim to get **greater political independence** for Basque.
- **Some** political independence has been **gained**. **Areas of Basque** that are in **Spain** have their own **parliament** and **police force**, control over **education** and **collect** their own **taxes**. While some Basque separatists are happy with this, others want **full independence**.

NON-PEACEFUL CONSEQUENCES

- The **separatist group ETA** (Euskadi Ta Azkatasuna) has used **violence** in its campaign for independence, e.g. assassinations, sniper attacks and bomb attacks.
- It formed in **1959** to **oppose** a **dictatorship** in **Spain** that banned the Basque language and suppressed their culture.
- ETA have **killed over 800 people** since they formed, including policemen, politicians, journalists and businessmen.
- They were **most active** in the **1970s**. But **terrorist activities** have occurred in **recent years** — in **1997** ETA kidnapped and killed a politician and in **2006** they were responsible for a **bomb** in **Madrid Airport** that killed 2 people.
- In 2010, ETA declared a **ceasefire** and in 2011 it announced that it had decided to **end all armed activity**. However, ETA have **broken** ceasefires in the past and the Spanish government still want ETA to **disband** completely.

Practice Questions

Q1 What is separatism?

Q2 List three possible causes of separatism.

Exam Question

Q1 With reference to at least one case study, discuss the possible consequences of separatism. [10 marks]

They also preserve their culture through sport — Basquetball...

There are loads of examples of separatism out there. Although separatist movements can involve relatively small numbers of people, the consequences can be pretty big — just look at what's going on in the Basque Country.

The Challenge of a Multicultural UK

Over the years, there's been a flurry of people moving to the UK from all over the world, and there are lots of reasons why.

The **UK** is a Fairly **Multicultural** Place

1) A **multicultural society** contains people from many different **national, cultural, religious** and **linguistic** backgrounds.
2) The **UK** is an **example** of a multicultural society.

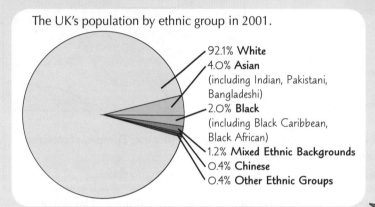

The UK's population by ethnic group in 2001.

92.1% **White**
4.0% **Asian**
(including Indian, Pakistani, Bangladeshi)
2.0% **Black**
(including Black Caribbean, Black African)
1.2% **Mixed Ethnic Backgrounds**
0.4% **Chinese**
0.4% **Other Ethnic Groups**

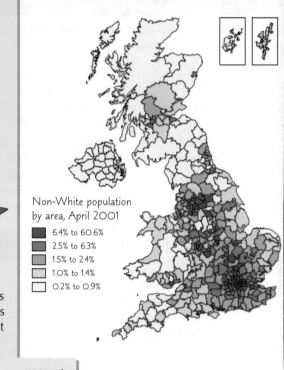

Non-White population by area, April 2001

- 6.4% to 60.6%
- 2.5% to 6.3%
- 1.5% to 2.4%
- 1.0% to 1.4%
- 0.2% to 0.9%

3) Ethnic groups **aren't evenly distributed** across the UK. For example:

- **More** people from ethnic minority groups live in **England** than in **Scotland, Wales** or **Northern Ireland**.
- **Ethnic minority groups** tend to live in **larger urban areas** such as London and Birmingham. E.g. 45% of the UK's ethnic minorities live in London, where they make up 29% of the population. But less than 4% of the UK's ethnic minorities live in the south west of England, where they make up only 2% of the population.
- Different **ethnic minority groups** have **different distributions** — e.g. 78% of the UK's Black Africans and 54% of the UK's Bangladeshis live in London.

Immigration Has Been **Encouraged** In The Past

The UK is a **multicultural society** because of **immigration**:

1) The **British Empire** existed from the **17th century** to the early **20th century**. During that time there was some **immigration** from British **overseas colonies** to the UK.
2) Between the **1940s** and **1960s** there were **large waves** of **immigration** to the UK:

- Around **World War Two** there were **labour shortages** so the government **encouraged immigration**.
- New **laws** allowed people from countries of the **former British Empire** to **live** and **work** in the **UK** without a visa. This included people from India, Pakistan, the Caribbean, South Africa, Kenya and Hong Kong.
- As a result, many people came to the UK. For example, more than **60 000 Indians** and **Pakistanis** had moved to the **UK** by **1960**.

3) Since the **1960s** there have been other **waves** of immigration. For example:

- In **1972** the **Ugandan dictator** General Idi Amin **expelled 80 000** African Asians from the country. Uganda had been part of the **British Empire** until 1962 so many Ugandans held **British passports**. **28 000** of those who were expelled came to the **UK**.
- In the **1970s** and **1990s** many **Ethiopians** and **Somalians** came to the UK **fleeing civil war** in East Africa.
- Since **2004** there has been an **increase** in immigration from **Eastern Europe** after several **new countries** joined the European Union. This is because **EU citizens** can live and work in **any EU country**.

The Challenge of a Multicultural UK

Most Immigrants Move to Urban Areas

Retail therapy — yet another reason to move to an urban area.

1) The vast **majority** of **immigrants** to the UK have settled in **industrial cities** and towns where there is a **demand for workers**. For example, in the 1950s and 1960s many immigrants moved to **Birmingham** (where there were jobs in **manufacturing** and **engineering** industries) and other cities and towns in the **Midlands** and **northern England**, e.g. Manchester, Liverpool, Nottingham, Leicester and Coventry.

2) **Few** immigrants have settled in **rural areas** because there **aren't** as many **jobs** available.

3) Immigrant workers have found **employment** and **accommodation** and then **helped others** from their family or community abroad to **join them** in the UK. They often move to the **same areas** and set up **communities** of ethnic minorities (see p. 242). This is known as **'chain migration'**.

4) **Large numbers** of immigrants have always settled in **London** because it is a **global hub** — a place that lots of people visit, pass through and where many international organisations and businesses operate. There are also jobs in **manufacturing**, **transport**, **hospitals** and the **tourism** industry.

Some Ethnic Minority Populations Have Spread Out a Bit More

1) Many ethnic minority populations are still **concentrated** in certain **urban areas**.

2) However, some ethnic minority populations have **spread out** more across the UK.

3) This is mainly due to the **children** and **grandchildren** of immigrants **moving away** from their **place of birth**. Here's a bit about **why** this has happened:

Take a look back at the previous page to see the distribution of ethnic minority populations in the UK.

- The **decline** of many **traditional industries** in the late 20th century has led to **high unemployment** in many **old industrial towns**. As a result, people have **moved** to areas where **employment prospects** are **better**.

- Many children and grandchildren of immigrants have lived in the UK all their lives — so they often feel **more comfortable** moving to areas with **lower ethnic minority populations** than their parents or grandparents might have done.

- Many have gone to **universities** in towns or cities away from their place of birth, then **settled** in their **university town**, or in a town or city where more **graduate jobs** are available.

- **Inter-marriage** between people from **different ethnic groups** can cause them to leave their established communities and move to a **new area**.

Practice Questions

Q1 What is a multicultural society?

Q2 Why were there large waves of immigration to the UK in the 1940s, 1950s and 1960s?

Q3 Why do many immigrants settle in London?

Exam Question

Q1 The graph shows the percentage of the UK's ethnic minority population that live in different regions.

Describe and comment on the graph. [7 marks]

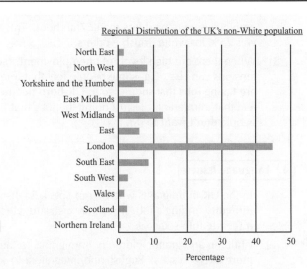

Regional Distribution of the UK's non-White population

Waves of immigration — surfboards not usually involved...

When you look outside and it's bucketing down, it's hard to think why so may people actually want to end up living in the UK. The reasons behind the spread of immigrants throughout the UK are a lot more logical though — so no excuses for not learning the lot.

The Challenge of a Multicultural UK

There aren't any challenges associated with the UK's multicultural society, surely... oh, alright, there are a couple then...

There are **Issues** Associated with **Multicultural Societies**

1) Racial, Ethnic and Religious Tensions

1) **Racial, ethnic, religious** and **language differences** can lead to **tensions** between groups — often because groups **lack understanding** of each other.

2) **Racial violence** can be a problem. E.g. after the London bombings on 7th July 2005 **assaults** on Muslims increased in the **UK**.

3) Sometimes there's **opposition** to certain **customs** and **religious practices**. E.g. in the UK there has been some debate about **banning** the **burqa** (the full Islamic face veil) in some public places. Some people say wearing it violates **women's rights**, but others believe that a ban **violates** the **human right** to **freedom of expression**.

2) Housing and Assimilation Issues

1) Many immigrants have **low paid** jobs in **inner city** areas. As a result, many immigrants live in **low cost housing** where **poor living conditions** and **overcrowding** are an issue.

2) The **children** of immigrants can become **trapped** in low cost housing and find it **difficult** to **move away**. It's often much easier for them to rent housing **cheaply** within the community, e.g. in Rochdale 96% of the Pakistani community live within the central area, which is among the most deprived areas in the North West.

3) Many ethnic minority populations prefer to **live in communities** where they can **socialise** with members of their own ethnic group and have **access** to **facilities** important to their culture (e.g. **places of worship** and **shops** that sell ingredients required for traditional cooking). **Individuals** may also feel **safer** and **less isolated** in these communities.

4) However, ethnic minority populations living in groups can create **ethnic segregation** within an area — and this can result in **racial tensions** (see above).

5) When ethnic minority groups **spread out more** it can lead to them **adopting** the culture of a **larger group** — this is called **cultural assimilation**. The members of an ethnic minority group can feel like they're **losing** their **own culture**.

3) Economic Issues

1) Immigrants claiming **state benefits** for unemployment and housing and putting increased pressure on **public services** can cause **resentment** among other members of the population.

2) In the UK, many immigrants work **long hours** for **low salaries** compared to UK-born people. E.g. from 2008 to 2010 almost 50% of Pakistani and Bangladeshi employees were paid less than £7 an hour. This figure was 25% for white British workers.

3) When there are high levels of **unemployment**, racial tensions can **rise**. E.g. some people feel that immigrants are **taking jobs** that should go to **UK-born people**. Others feel that immigrants are just doing the jobs that UK-born people **don't want to do**.

4) Language Issues

1) In the UK, immigrants who **do not** speak English often have **difficulty** finding a job. They may also struggle to fully **integrate** into society.

2) Children and grandchildren of immigrants to the UK are **more likely** to speak English and integrate into society. This can cause **tension** within the ethnic group as older members of the group may feel their culture is being **eroded**.

5) Education Issues

1) At some schools (e.g. in inner city areas) **most** of the children come from one or more ethnic minority groups, and these students may need **extra help**. E.g. some ethnic minority **children** do not speak English and schools may need to provide special **English** lessons for them.

2) **Faith schools** have developed in some areas to teach children according to a particular **religion**. Some people argue that this can cause **segregation** between different groups.

3) **Holiday patterns**, **school meals** and **school timetables** may need to be altered for ethnic minority groups. E.g. some schools in Manchester and London have had to close to allow **Muslim** pupils to have time off to celebrate the festival of **Eid**.

Cultural challenges for Gordon and his chums were all about who could stay awake for the longest in the art gallery.

The Challenge of a Multicultural UK

Bradford *is a UK City with a Multicultural Society*

Bradford is a city with a **diverse mix** of **cultures**. There are **places of worship** for **many** different religions and a large number of different **cultural** and **religious festivals** are celebrated in the city. There are also shops and markets that sell many **international foods**.

The pie chart shows the **population** of Bradford by **ethnic group** in 2001:

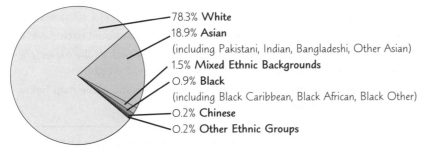

78.3% **White**
18.9% **Asian**
(including Pakistani, Indian, Bangladeshi, Other Asian)
1.5% **Mixed Ethnic Backgrounds**
0.9% **Black**
(including Black Caribbean, Black African, Black Other)
0.2% **Chinese**
0.2% **Other Ethnic Groups**

BRADFORD

There are Lots of Reasons for this Ethnic Mix

- Bradford became an important international centre for the **textile industry** in the **19th century**. There was lots of **immigration** as people came to work in the **mills** — especially **white workers** from **Europe**.
- From the **1940s** to the **1960s** the government encouraged immigration to meet **labour shortages**. Immigrants came to **Bradford** to work in the textile industry (where there was a **high demand** for **workers**). Many people came from **Pakistan**, the **Caribbean** and **East Africa**.
- Around **70%** of the ethnic minority population in Bradford is **Pakistani**. This is largely due to **chain migration** (see p. 241) — early settlers from Pakistan helped other Pakistanis to come to Bradford.

There are Many Issues with Bradford's Multicultural Society

- Economic issues — Bradford's employment rate is **76%**, but only **49%** of ethnic minority **men** and **23%** of ethnic minority **women** are employed.
- Housing issues — Ethnic groups in Bradford are **concentrated** in particular areas. E.g. many Pakistanis living in Bradford live in the **Manningham** area, where **overcrowding** is a problem.
- Racial, ethnic and religious tensions — Relations between ethnic groups are **generally good**, but in **2001** there were **riots** after a demonstration by the Anti-Nazi league against the National Front.
- Education issues — Some schools in Bradford, with a **mix** of children from **different ethnic backgrounds**, have to have **specialist language** staff to help teach students who can't speak English.

The National Front is a political party that is against immigration of non-white people to the UK. The Anti-Nazi league was set up to oppose groups like this.

Practice Questions

Q1 Give one reason why Bradford has a multicultural society.

Q2 Give one issue caused by Bradford's multicultural society.

Exam Question

Q1 Using examples from the UK, discuss the issues related to multicultural societies. [10 marks]

Multicultural Challenge — your starter for ten...

Nothing in Geography ever seems to come without issues and multicultural societies are no different. Start by learning the bread and butter issues on the left hand page and then add the lovely jammy filling that is the Bradford case study. Is it lunchtime yet?

The Challenge of Global Poverty

These final few pages are all about global poverty. First up there's the distribution and causes to get your head around.

Poverty *is* Unevenly *Distributed* Across *the* World

1) Poverty means being **unable** to **afford basic things** such as safe drinking water, food, shelter, sanitation, health care and education.

2) There are **different** ways of **measuring poverty** worldwide. For example:

   - **Economic indicators** can be used, such as gross domestic product (GDP) or the international poverty line (the percentage of the population living on less than a certain amount each day).

   - Indexes such as the **Human Poverty Index** can be used — it includes several measures such as life expectancy, adult literacy, access to safe drinking water and the proportion of children who are underweight.

The international poverty line used to be less than $1 a day. In 2008, the World Bank set it at less than $1.25 a day.

3) All of the measures of poverty show that it is **unevenly distributed** across the world. For example, the map below shows the **percentage** of people living on **less than $1 per day** in 2004.

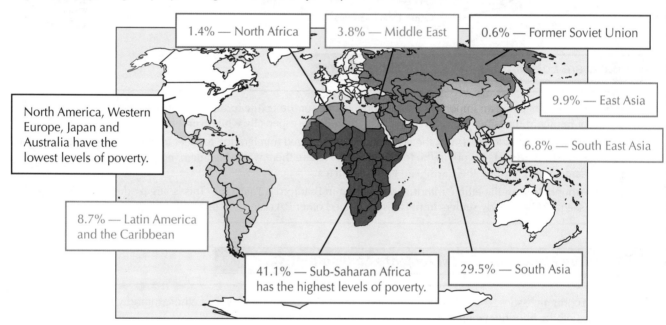

1.4% — North Africa

3.8% — Middle East

0.6% — Former Soviet Union

North America, Western Europe, Japan and Australia have the lowest levels of poverty.

9.9% — East Asia

6.8% — South East Asia

8.7% — Latin America and the Caribbean

41.1% — Sub-Saharan Africa has the highest levels of poverty.

29.5% — South Asia

There are *Many Causes* of Poverty

Here are a few of the things that can **cause poverty**:

These pages cover a few examples of things that can cause poverty, but take a look at pages 208-209 as well — there's a bit more on why entire nations are in poverty.

BAD GROWING CONDITIONS

- **Physical factors** affect how easy it is to **grow food**. Plants need **water** and **fertile soil**, and animals need plants to graze on.

- Many poor countries have **low quality soil**, which can be made worse by **bad farming practices** (e.g. overgrazing). These **degrade** the soil, reduce **agricultural productivity** and **increase poverty**.

- Many of the **poorest countries** in the world have climates with **little** or **seasonal** rainfall, which makes it difficult to grow crops and rear animals. If it **doesn't rain**, or if it rains **less than usual**, it can lead to **food shortages** or **famine**.

Famine is when a large percentage of the population doesn't get enough food and they become malnourished.

SUBSISTENCE FARMING

- **Subsistence farmers** only produce enough food to **feed themselves** and their **families**. They are particularly at **risk of poverty** because they depend on the food they produce to **survive**.

- The growth of their crops relies on the **climate**, so they're **vulnerable** to extreme weather events that **reduce production** (see next page).

- Subsistence farmers usually **don't have surpluses** which they can sell or trade — so they have **no income**. This means they are unable to **escape poverty** because they **can't afford** adequate health care, education or better technology to **increase food production**.

- Subsistence farming occurs in **Sub-Saharan Africa**, **South East Asia** and parts of **Latin America**. E.g. in **Zambia** most of the population relies on subsistence farming to survive. There are **few irrigation systems** so most farmers rely on seasonal rains. However, **droughts** in the 1980s and 1990s **reduced production** and resulted in **famine**.

The Challenge of Global Poverty

OVERPOPULATION

- Overpopulation is when there **isn't** enough **space**, **food**, **water** or other **resources** to support the population.

- It can result from **population increase**, the **reduction of resources** — or from a combination of **both**.

- Overpopulation causes **poverty** because there is too much of a strain on **resources** (e.g. water, food and housing). E.g. **India's population** is over **1 billion** and increasing rapidly. 35% of people in India are living on less than $1 a day. The number of people living in poverty may **increase** as the population continues to **grow**.

- The areas with **high levels** of overpopulation (e.g. Sub-Saharan Africa, and South Asia) also have the highest levels of **poverty**.

WAR

- War can **damage** or **destroy property**, **infrastructure** and **crops**. This can cause poverty by creating **shortages** of safe drinking water, shelter, food, sanitation, health care and education.

- When a country is at war, **productivity** often **decreases**. **Industrial** and **agricultural activity** can be **disrupted** and **trade** with other countries may **decline or stop**. E.g. because of the First Gulf War (1990-1) the **GDP** of Iraq **fell** from $2304 per capita in 1989 to $938 in 1990.

- People become **refugees** during times of war when they **flee their homes**. Many end up in **refugee camps** which often have a limited supply of food, water, shelter and health care.

- **War** in parts of the **Middle East** and **Africa** in recent years has **increased poverty** in these areas.

NATURAL HAZARDS

- **Natural hazards** (e.g. floods, droughts) can **cause poverty** by **damaging or destroying** property, infrastructure and crops.

- **Floods** can reduce access to **clean water** and **sanitation**. They can also cause **loss of property** and **reduce crop yields**. E.g. floods in Bangladesh in 1998 made 25 million people homeless. 2 million tonnes of rice were lost, clean water became scarce and diseases (e.g. cholera) spread.

- **Drought** reduces **water supplies** and can increase **soil erosion**. This can result in reduced crop yields, crop failures and the death of livestock. For example, drought and crop disease contributed to a famine in Ethiopia in 1984 that left 8 million people starving.

- Many of the **poorest** areas of the world are **heavily affected** by natural hazards, e.g. Sub-Saharan Africa, South Asia and South East Asia. Some hazards can occur **every year** (e.g. tropical cyclones in Bangladesh), which means people struggle to break out of poverty.

Poverty Usually Has a *Mixture* of *Causes*

Poverty is usually the result of a **combination** of **causes**. The causes of poverty are often **linked to each other** and can create a **cycle of poverty** that becomes difficult to break. For example:

1) **Drought** can lead to **famine** and **poverty** as water and food resources decline.

2) This can cause a **war over natural resources**. War increases poverty (e.g. by causing destruction and reducing productivity).

3) War can also result in **refugees**, who may move to an area where they contribute to **overpopulation** and put further pressure on resources.

Practice Questions

Q1 What is poverty?

Q2 Give three causes of poverty.

Exam Question

Q1 The map shows the percentage of children who are less than five years old and underweight. Using the map, describe and comment on the global distribution of poverty. [7 marks]

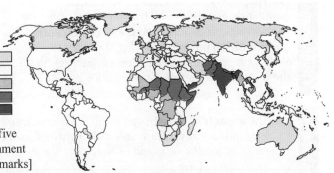

% of Children Under 5 who are Underweight

Data not available	
0%-20%	
20%-30%	
30%-40%	
More than 40%	

Poverty — pretty serious stuff, I'm afraid...

Nearly half the children in the world live in poverty and one third of deaths in the world are due to poverty — that's 50 000 people every day. You need to have a good grip on what's causing it all, so scribble the points on these pages out a few times.

The Challenge of Global Poverty

Poverty is a global problem — it affects people in countries all over the world. So, it needs some international solutions...

International Agencies can help to Reduce Poverty

1) **International agencies** play an important role in **reducing** global poverty. For example:

In 2000, the UN agreed eight Millennium Development Goals (to be achieved by 2015) to tackle global poverty:

- Eradicate extreme poverty and hunger
- Achieve universal primary education
- Promote gender equality and empower women
- Reduce child mortality

- Improve maternal health
- Combat HIV/AIDS, malaria and other diseases
- Ensure environmental sustainability
- Develop a global partnership for development

The MDGs are intended to highlight the areas that need to be addressed, and to give the UN a way of measuring the progress that's been made in reducing global poverty.

To date, the success of the MDGs has varied. Some progress is being made, e.g. in Sub-Saharan Africa there has been an 18% increase in primary school enrolment between 1999 and 2009. But little or no progress has been made in other areas, e.g. in Africa the number of children with stunted growth due to malnutrition has actually increased between 1990 and 2010.

The last goal basically means that countries need to work together to help each other develop.

2) Other **international agencies**, such as the World Bank and the World Health Organisation, and **international charities** (e.g. Oxfam and the Red Cross) are also working to **reduce global poverty**.

Poverty can be Reduced in a Number of Ways

To **reduce poverty**, international organisations are doing things to address the **causes of poverty** (see pages 244-245).

Bad growing conditions
- Growing crops that can **withstand** harsh environmental conditions helps to **increase crop yields**. For example, the $39 million Water Efficient Maize for Africa (WEMA) project aims to develop drought-tolerant types of maize to be grown in Sub-Saharan Africa.
- Reducing overgrazing helps **maintain soil quality**. For example, in central Tanzania the HADO project encouraged farmers to grow hay to feed cattle. This reduced grazing and provided reliable food for animals all year round.

Subsistence farming
- Subsistence farmers need to **improve productivity** so they can **generate an income**.
- **Loans** could enable farmers to increase productivity by **buying equipment or animals**. E.g. as part of a UN programme, a Kenyan business is offering small loans to 100 000 farmers in Kenya to help them buy livestock, seeds and equipment which they can use to improve their farming methods and produce more food.
- Increased agricultural productivity also reduces the risk of **famine** by **improving food security**. Food security is when **all people** have access to **sufficient food** at all times. E.g. a UN programme in 2012 aimed to increase the area of irrigated farmland in Afghanistan by 15% (by upgrading old irrigation systems) and increase crop yield by 20%.

Overpopulation
Overpopulation is sometimes due to **rapid population growth** caused by a **high birth rate**. This can be reduced by increased use of **contraception** and **education programmes**. E.g. the UN and WHO ran programmes in Ethiopia which doubled the use of contraception between 2005 and 2010.

War
Diplomacy could resolve many conflicts before they escalate to **war** (see page 228). For example, the Union of South American Nations was set up in 2008. One of its aims is to improve security in South America by building stronger diplomatic links between the nations.

Natural hazards
- The **impacts of drought** can sometimes be reduced by strategies such as **water collection and storage** schemes, **irrigation** schemes or the use of **drought-resistant GM crops**. E.g. a UN-led programme has installed water storage tanks on the Pacific island of Nauru, so homes still have access to water during a drought.
- The impacts of **floods** can be reduced by improving **prediction and warning systems**, e.g. UNESCO (part of the UN) has set up a project to improve flood prediction and warning systems in Pakistan following the 2010 floods. This allows people to make better **plans** to prepare for floods, and to **protect their property** when floods occur.

The Challenge of Global Poverty

Poverty, Security and Development are all Tied Up Together

1) Poverty is **closely linked** to the **level of development** of a country (see pages 206-207). **More developed** countries tend to have **lower levels of poverty**.

2) So a country **needs to develop** to reduce its level of poverty.

3) In order to develop, countries need **security**. This means a few **different things**:

- **Economic security** involves a country's economy being **stable** and **sustainable**, as well as all individuals having a reliable **basic income**.
- **Food security** involves having access to a reliable source of **sufficient food**.
- **Health security** involves having **protection from diseases** and access to **health care**.
- **Personal, community** and **political security** involves being **protected** from violence, crime and human rights abuses.

I know, I know, it's confusing. But think how upset you'd be if CGP hadn't explained this stuff so well.

4) Countries **can't develop without security**. For example, if a country has a low level of economic security, (e.g. because it has a high level of debt), then it can't afford to invest in development.

5) But, countries **can't get security without development** either. For example, if a country is at a low level of development, then it can't generate the money it needs to pay off debts and create economic security.

6) If you thought we'd forgotten about a case study for this stuff... think again.

Poverty, Security and Development are Problems in Afghanistan

1) There have been **conflicts** going on in Afghanistan for a long time (see pages 234-235).

2) The conflicts have contributed to Afghanistan being at a **very low level of development**:

- It is **economically poor** — in 2011, the GDP per capita was $1000 (in the UK it was $36 600).
- The **birth rate** is **high** — in 2011, each woman had an average of 5.64 children.
- There are **high levels of gender inequality** — in 2000, the male adult literacy rate was 43.1%, but the female adult literacy rate was only 12.6%.

3) They've also meant that Afghanistan has **very little security**:

- **Economic security** is low — the unemployment rate was 35% in 2008.
- **Food security** is low — in 2008, 29% of the population did not get enough calories every day.
- **Health security** is low — there is 1 doctor for every 5000 people.
- **Personal security** is low — in 2008 there were 2118 civilian deaths caused by war.

4) Afghanistan can't get **security** without **investing** in projects to improve its level of **development**, such as building roads, hospitals and schools etc. These projects would create security by providing **jobs**, **health care** and **education**.

5) But money can't be **invested** in **development projects** while things like **personal** and **political security** are so low, e.g. there is no guarantee that new roads, hospitals and schools won't be destroyed by the ongoing conflict.

6) So, Afghanistan can't get security **without development**, but it can't develop **without security** either. To break this cycle Afghanistan may need **help** (e.g. money or military assistance) from **international agencies** and **other countries**.

Many countries are trapped in poverty because they can't overcome this problem.

Practice Questions

Q1 What are the eight UN Millennium Development Goals?

Q2 What is security?

Exam Question

Q1 'No development without security, and no security without development.' Discuss this statement. [40 marks]

Eight goals? One way to make sure that England finally score...

Ah, a conundrum to end the section with. You need development to reduce poverty, but you can't get development without security and you can't get security without development. It's a bit of a chicken and egg situation...

Answering Questions

Figuring out what exam questions are actually asking you to do is a bit of a dark art — whether you're in a duel for supremacy with your AS or your A2 exams. Here are some tips to help you decipher exam speak and produce some top notch answers...

1 Make Sure You Read the Question Properly

It's dead easy to **misread** the question and spend 10 minutes writing about the **wrong thing**.
A few simple tips can help you avoid this:

There are loads of hints about how to answer the questions in this book in the Answers section at the back.

1) <u>Underline</u> the **command words** in the question (the ones that tell you **what to do**):

Answers to questions with 'explain' in them often include the word **'because'** (or **'due to'**).

E.g. for the question 'Explain why GDP alone is not a reliable measure of development', your answer would include '... GDP may be misleading because it is an average...'.

'Assess', 'Evaluate' and 'Discuss' all mean pretty much the **same thing**. They're all about **weighing something up**, e.g. how **successful** responses to a tectonic hazard were. You need to give a **balanced** answer — talk about all the **different viewpoints** on the subject.

Command word	Means write about...
Describe	what it's **like**
Explain	**why** it's like that (i.e. give **reasons**)
Compare	the **similarities AND differences**
Contrast	the **differences**
Distinguish	the **differences**
Assess	the **advantages** and **disadvantages OR** the **arguments for** and **against**
Evaluate	
Discuss	
Examine	describe **AND** explain
Outline	describe **AND** explain
Define	the **meaning** of the word

If a question asks you to describe a **pattern** (e.g. from a map or graph), make sure you identify the **general pattern**, then refer to any **anomalies** (things that **don't** fit the general pattern).

E.g. for the question 'Describe the global distribution of volcanoes', you first need to say that they're mostly on plate margins, *then* mention that a few aren't (e.g. Kilauea in Hawaii).

When writing about differences, use **comparative words** like '**larger**' or '**more severe**', e.g. 'Temperature has risen more steeply in the last century than at any time in the last 1000 years'.

'Examine' and 'Outline' are pretty similar. The main difference is that you do **more explaining** for '**Examine**' and **more describing** for '**Outline**'.

2) <u>Underline</u> the **key words** (the ones that tell you **what it's about**), e.g. glaciers, conflict, global warming.

3) **Re-read** the question and your answer **when you've finished**, just to check that your answer really does address **all parts** of the question being asked. A **common mistake** is to **miss a bit out** — like when questions say 'use data from the graph in your answer' or 'use evidence from the map'.

2 Figure Out Your Structure Before You Start

1) For any **longer answers**, you need to think carefully about how to **structure** your answer. Jot down the **order** you're going to cover things in.

2) **Label** your **plan** and **answer** clearly so the examiner knows which is which.

3) **Don't cross out** your plan — the examiner might look at it to see what you've included, especially if you run out of time.

Q1 <u>Describe</u> how <u>energy flows</u> through an <u>ecosystem</u>.

PLAN

1. Intro — define 'ecosystem'. Energy flows through system as organisms are eaten.

2. Where energy comes from — plants (autotrophs) photosynthesise using sunlight.

3. Energy flow — primary, secondary and tertiary consumers (give examples).

4. Loss of energy — 90% at each level. Lost through waste, movement etc.

ANSWER

An ecosystem is a set of relationships...

3 Include Relevant Geographical Terms

Use the **proper geography words** for things, e.g. say 'herbivore' rather than 'plant eater', and 'aid' instead of 'help'.

Don't Forget all the Usual Rules

1) Your answer should be **legible** (you won't get many marks if the examiner can't read it), use **correct grammar**, and **everything** should be **spelt correctly** (double-check jazzy geography words).

2) **Use diagrams** where they're appropriate — drawing a diagram can be way **quicker** than describing the same thing in words.

3) If you're **running out of time** at the end of the exam, **don't panic** — just write what you can as **bullet points**. You'll still get some marks for doing this.

Answering Questions

There are loads of different types of question that can come up in Geography exams. If you know what they all are you'll stand a better chance of writing a cracking answer, and if you write a cracking answer you'll get a top grade. Happy days.

You Might Have to **Interpret** a **Resource**

1) Whichever options you choose in your exams, some of the questions will probably include a **resource** for you to look at. This could be, for example, a graph, a map, an aerial photo or a data table.

> *Watch out for log scales (see p. 252).*

> If you're given a **GRAPH**, make sure you read the **scale** carefully — use **working lines** to help you read off values accurately. Start by looking for **general trends** in the data, e.g. whether values increase or decrease overall, and whether they change smoothly or in stages. Then look for any **anomalies** — points that don't fit the pattern.

> If you're given a **MAP**, have a good look at the **key** to work out what it shows. Be **specific** when you're writing about maps — if you're referring to a particular place or feature, give the **grid reference**. Make sure you use **compass points** (e.g. west) rather than words (e.g. left). There's more about how to read maps on pages 254-255.

> *When you're writing about a graph or a data table, quote specific data to back up your points, and manipulate it if you can (e.g. by working out the difference between two values).*

> If you're given a **PHOTO**, study it really carefully. Scribble down a **list** of all the relevant things you spot in it, and use the list to plan your answer.

> If you're given a **DATA TABLE**, start by looking for **patterns** in the data — e.g. if the table gives data for two different areas, look for major **similarities** and **differences** between the two places.

2) You might be given **two** resources (e.g. two maps showing the distribution of ethnic groups in an area at two different times) and asked to **compare** them. Pick out **similarities** and **differences** between the resources.

3) Read the question carefully and think about how it **relates** to the resource, and which **bits** of the resource will be helpful to you. E.g. if you're given a map of a town and asked about the **social and economic** impacts of flooding there, you can **ignore** any possible **environmental** impacts.

4) Make sure you use your **knowledge** from the **course** in your answers, particularly if the question asks you to **analyse** or **interpret** the resource, or suggest **reasons** for a particular feature.

Include Lots of **Facts** and **Figures** in **Case Study** Questions

1) You'll often have to include a **case study** in your answers. Case study questions won't necessarily include the words 'case study', so you need to know how to spot them. Look out for **phrases** like 'with reference to one named area' or '... that you have studied'.

2) **Plan** what you want to include before you start writing, so your answer has a **clear structure**.

3) Remember to include loads of **specific details** in your answer — place names, dates, statistics and so on.

4) Make sure they're **relevant** though — there's no point giving the exact number of people killed in a war if the question is about the **causes** of the war.

5) Drawing an **annotated map** might help you show how your points **relate** to the **area** you're talking about.

Essay Questions Are Worth **Lots** of **Marks**...

> *Re-read the question a couple of times whilst you're answering it, to make sure you're sticking to the question.*

1) For the Unit 3 exam at A2-level you'll have to do an **essay question** worth a **lot of marks** (40, since you're asking).

2) They usually ask about **one** topic, but you'll be expected to bring in your **wider knowledge** of Geography too.

3) However the question is worded, you'll need to include specific **examples** or a **case study**. Have a good read of the **advice** about case study questions above — the same tips apply to essay questions.

4) Essay questions will often use words like '**evaluate**' or '**discuss**', so you have to look at **both sides** of an issue.

5) If a question uses the phrase '**To what extent...**', you need to form a sensible **opinion** about the subject. It doesn't matter whether you agree with what the question is saying or not, as long as you give a **balanced argument** and **justify** your views.

6) Write a plan to make sure your essay has a sensible **structure**, and **link** your points together so your answer **flows**. Use words and phrases like 'however', 'in contrast' and 'in addition' to link your sentences.

7) For essay questions you should **always** write a **conclusion** — **sum up** the different viewpoints and then say what **you think**. You could also briefly mention how and why the issue you're discussing may **change** in the **future**.

Investigative Skills

*This page covers useful stuff about fieldwork for **Unit 2 at AS-level** and **Unit 4A at A2-level**. If you're doing **Unit 4B** for A2-level, you can ignore this stuff and go straight to the next page (hurrah!). Don't forget to look at the pages on graph and map skills (p. 252-255) once you're done here — they're important for your Geography fieldwork too.*

You Need to Have an *Aim* and a *Hypothesis*

1) When you're doing fieldwork and research you won't get very far without an **aim**, and a **hypothesis** to test.

2) An aim is **what you want to find out**, e.g. 'To see if coastal defences at Holderness affect the rate of erosion of the coastline'.

3) A hypothesis is a **testable statement**, e.g. 'Coastal defences at Holderness increase the rate of erosion downdrift of the defences'.

4) Both your aim and hypothesis need to be **specific**. E.g. the above aim is better than 'To see if coastal defences affect erosion', and the hypothesis above is better than 'Coastal defences do affect erosion'.

You Need to *Collect* Your *Data Carefully and Safely*

1) When you know exactly what you want to find out, **plan** what **data** you'll need and how to **collect** it. Think about what data would be most **useful** and what you can **realistically** (and **safely**) collect.

2) There are two types of data — **primary** and **secondary**. **Primary data** is data that you collect yourself during your fieldwork. **Secondary data** is data that someone else has collected.

3) When collecting primary data, think about your **sampling strategy** — when you're studying a large area like a city or a river, you **can't** collect data for the whole thing, so you have to select **sites** to study. Make sure these sites are **representative** of the whole area and aren't biased. E.g. if you're studying how channel characteristics change along the course of a river, you need to select sites at different stages along the course of the river, from source to mouth.

4) When you're doing your **fieldwork** you need to be **careful**. **Identify** any **risks** there might be and **take action** to reduce the risks.

5) Risks basically include any way you could **get hurt**. Here are a few examples: ⟸

Area	Risk	Action
City	Being run over	Cross roads using pedestrian crossings where possible.
	Abuse (verbal and physical)	Be polite.
		If you're asking people questions, introduce what you're doing and give them an opportunity to refuse to answer.
River	Drowning	Don't go into deep water (e.g. past knee height).
		Don't tread on slippy rocks (e.g. ones with moss on them).

Analyse and Interpret Your Data and Reach a Balanced Conclusion

1) When you've collected all your data, you need to **present** and **analyse** it. Plotting data on **graphs** and **maps** and applying **statistical analyses** can help you to see **patterns** — have a look at pages 252-259 for some ideas.

2) You need to use your analysis to draw a **conclusion**. Think about what your data **shows** in relation to your **original aim** and **hypothesis**, e.g. whether it supports the hypothesis or not.

3) Your conclusion needs to be **balanced** — e.g. if you've studied a potential bypass that might be built around your town, don't just discuss the negative impacts of it, make sure you mention the positive impacts too.

4) Your results might not give you a **clear-cut** conclusion, but that's fine — it gives you more to write about.

5) You also need to **evaluate** your study, e.g. think about the **limitations** of the study and suggest ways that it could be **improved**. You should think about how your study could be **extended**, e.g. what extra data could be collected.

You Have to Answer Questions About Your Fieldwork in the Exam

1) For **both** Unit 2 and Unit 4A, you will be asked questions about **your own fieldwork investigations** and about **new data** that you're given in the exam.

2) For Unit 2, the new data you get will be related to one of the **core topics** (Rivers, Floods and Management or Population Change). For Unit 4A, it could be based on **anything** from the **AS** and **A2** course.

3) For both your own investigations and the new data, you might be asked about things like: ⟸

- The **aim** of the investigation.
- The **method** of data collection.
- The **risks** associated with data collection.
- How the data was **analysed** and **presented** (for the new data you're given, you might have to present or analyse the data in the exam).
- The **conclusion** that was drawn.
- The **limitations** of the investigation.

Unit 4B — Geographical Issue Evaluation

*For A2-level, you'll either do Unit 4A or Unit 4B. If you're doing **Unit 4B**, this page is for you. If you're doing Unit 4A or you're an AS student, you need to look at the stuff on the previous page. Blimey, this is all very complicated — I think I need a sit down.*

Unit 4B is All About *Analysing* and *Interpreting Information*

1) If you're doing **Unit 4B** for A2, you'll be given an **Advance Information Booklet (AIB)** a couple of months before the exam. It contains loads of material about a geographical issue.

2) The issue could be based in the **UK** or **elsewhere** and could vary in **scale** from **local** (e.g. the management of a single ecosystem) to **international** (e.g. the expansion of a transnational corporation).

3) You need to study **all** the information **carefully**, work out what it all **means**, how it **fits** together and how you might **investigate**, **present** and **analyse** it.

4) In the exam you'll have an hour and a half to answer questions about the **issue**, using the **data** you're given as well as your existing knowledge of Geography.

"If only I'd studied A2 Geography," sighed Martha as the others pored over their AIB for the seventeenth lunchtime in a row.

The Information in the AIB Will All Relate to a *Single Issue*

1) The AIB could include several different **types** of information, such as **reports**, **data tables**, **maps** and **graphs**. All the information will be **related** in some way — e.g. you might be given a report on a proposed out-of-town shopping centre, photos of the town's high street and a data table about employment in the area.

2) The AIB might also direct you to some **secondary data sources**, such as **websites** — make sure you look at these before the exam, as questions are sometimes **directly based** on information from these sources.

3) The information you're given will give you some **clues** about the type of **questions** that might come up. E.g. if the booklet has a table of development indicators in two countries it's pretty likely that you'll have to compare them in some way.

4) As well as looking at the information you're given, have a think about how you might **collect more data** — you could get a question about what **fieldwork** or **extra research** could be carried out to investigate the issue further.

Think About How You'd *Present* and *Analyse* the Data

1) In the exam, you might have to **choose** a technique for **presenting** or **analysing** data (see pages 252-259), then justify **why** you chose that technique. Look at **each** piece of data that you're given and think about how it might best be **presented** or **analysed** — this'll save you time in the exam.

2) If the data you're given are quite **complex**, and contain lots of figures, try **different methods** of plotting them on graphs or maps before your exam. This will help you understand what the information shows.

3) You also need to think about possible **problems** with the data. For example:

- How **reliable** are the data sources? Are they **biased** or **unbiased**?
- How **big** was the sample? Is it **representative** of the population?
- Are there important points of view that are **missing**?

'Population' here just means all of the data available.

Use *All* the Information to *Form Opinions* About the *Issue*

1) Once you've got your head around all the information, you need to **link it all together** and form an **opinion** about the issue.

2) You're likely to be asked to **argue** a point of view using the information, e.g. suggesting how an area could best be managed to meet the needs of everyone involved. There's **no single right or wrong** answer — but you need to be able to **justify** your argument, so make sure you can **use the data** to support it.

3) Whatever your view is, you need to give a **balanced argument**. Try to think of potential **economic**, **political**, **social** and **environmental impacts** of the different sides of the argument, and how any negative impacts could be **reduced**.

4) It's likely to be a **complex** issue with lots of different parties involved, so you need to think about possible **conflicts** that your solution might cause and how they could be **resolved**.

Graph and Map Skills

The examiners could spring any type of graph or map on you in your exam (they're sneaky like that). For A2-level, you need to know all the different types of graphs and maps on these pages. For AS-level, you only need to know some of them. Luckily for you I've marked the ones that you only need to know for A2 — sometimes I just don't know what you'd do without me...

There are Loads of **Different Types** of Graphs and Maps

1) There are some types of graphs and maps that you'll have come across lots of times before. These include **line graphs**, **bar charts**, **pie charts**, **scatter graphs**, **atlas maps** and **sketch maps**.

2) Some graphs and maps are trickier than others, so the next four pages are full of tips to help you interpret the tougher ones.

3) When you're **interpreting** graphs and maps you need to remember to **read** the **scale** or **key really carefully**.

4) If you have to read from a graph **draw working lines on** to help you get an accurate figure.

Triangular Graphs Show **Percentages** Split into **Three Categories**

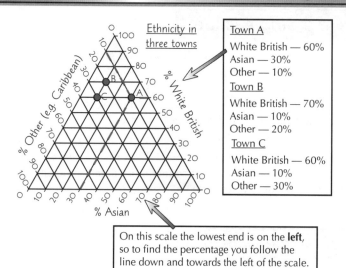

Town A
White British — 60%
Asian — 30%
Other — 10%

Town B
White British — 70%
Asian — 10%
Other — 20%

Town C
White British — 60%
Asian — 10%
Other — 30%

On this scale the lowest end is on the **left**, so to find the percentage you follow the line down and towards the left of the scale.

1) To read a triangular graph start by **finding the point** you want on the graph.

2) **Follow** the **line** that goes **down** from the **point** to the **lowest end** of the **scale** and record the percentage.

3) Then **turn the graph around** so that the next axis is at **the bottom**, **follow** the **line** down to the lower end of the scale and record that percentage.

4) Do the same for the **third axis**.

5) The three readings should **add up to 100%**.

6) The graph on the left shows the ethnicity of people in three towns. There are **three ethnic groups** so a triangular graph can be used. **Each point** represents **one town**.

Logarithmic Scales are Used When the **Data Range** is **Large**

1) The **intervals** on logarithmic scales are **not fixed amounts** (e.g. they don't go up by 5 every time).

2) Instead, the **intervals** get **increasingly larger** at the top end of the scale (e.g. 10, 20, 40, 80).

3) This lets you fit a **very wide range** of **data** onto one **axis** without having to draw an enormous graph.

4) The graph on the right uses a **logarithmic scale** on the **vertical axis** to show how the population of four cities changed over 40 years.

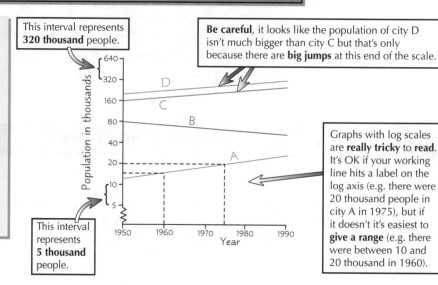

This interval represents **320 thousand** people.

Be careful, it looks like the population of city D isn't much bigger than city C but that's only because there are **big jumps** at this end of the scale.

This interval represents **5 thousand** people.

Graphs with log scales are **really tricky** to **read**. It's OK if your working line hits a label on the log axis (e.g. there were 20 thousand people in city A in 1975), but if it doesn't it's easiest to **give a range** (e.g. there were between 10 and 20 thousand in 1960).

Graph and Map Skills

Dispersion Diagrams Show the Frequency of Data

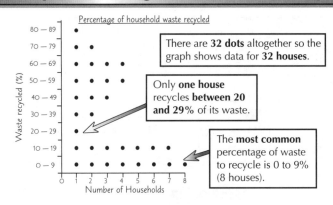

Percentage of household waste recycled

There are **32 dots** altogether so the graph shows data for **32 houses**.

Only **one house** recycles **between 20 and 29%** of its waste.

The **most common** percentage of waste to recycle is 0 to 9% (8 houses).

1) Dispersion diagrams are a bit like a cross between a **tally chart** and a **bar chart**.

2) The **range** of **data that's measured** goes on one axis. **Frequency** goes on the other axis.

3) **Each dot** represents **one piece** of **information** — the **more dots** there are in a particular category, the **more frequently** that event has happened.

4) The dispersion diagram on the left shows the **percentage** of **household waste** that's **recycled** for **houses** in a **particular village**.

Radial Plots Often Show Directional Data

1) **Radial plots** always appear as a **circle**.

2) The points on the **outside** of the circle usually show **direction** (compass points), but they can show other things, e.g. months of the year.

3) The **bars** coming out from the centre show another variable — the **distance** they reach from the centre shows the **size** of the variable.

4) The most common radial diagram is a **wind rose**. The bars point in different directions to show **which way** the wind is blowing **from**. How **far** the bar reaches from the centre shows how **often** winds blow from that direction.

5) This diagram also shows a third variable — each bar is split into different coloured sections to show the **frequency** of different **wind speeds** from each direction.

The wind blows from the west about 14% of the time.

Roughly 6% of winds blow from the west **and** have a speed of 0-4 m/s.

Winds from the south and west are more common than from the north and east.

Kite Diagrams Usually Show the Distribution and Abundance of Organisms

You only need to know about **kite diagrams** for **A2-level**. You can skip this bit if you're doing AS-level.

1) **Kite diagrams** are usually used to plot **species distribution** along a **transect**, e.g. in the diagram below of a transect along a **coastal sand dune**, marram grass is found between 0 and 10 m along the transect.

2) They can also show the **abundance** of different species along a transect. E.g. in the diagram below the scale on the left shows the **percentage cover** of each species. At 2 m along the transect marram grass covered 20% of the surface.

A transect is a line — you count the number or percentage cover of organisms at fixed points along it.

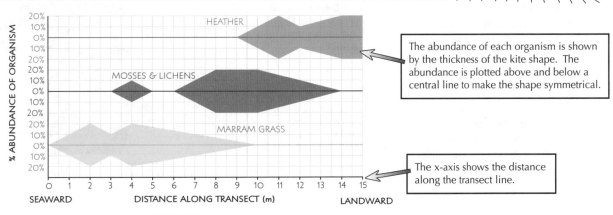

The abundance of each organism is shown by the thickness of the kite shape. The abundance is plotted above and below a central line to make the shape symmetrical.

The x-axis shows the distance along the transect line.

Graph and Map Skills

Choropleth Maps Show Information Using Colours and Patterns

1) Choropleth maps show how something **varies** between **different areas** using colours or patterns.

2) The maps in exams often use **cross-hatched lines** and **dots**.

3) They're straightforward to read but it's **easy to make mistakes** with them as the patterns can be very similar.

4) If you're asked to talk about all the parts of the map with a **certain type of hatching**, look at the map carefully and put a **big tick** on each part with that hatching, to make them all **stand out**.

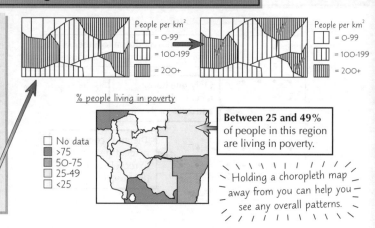

% people living in poverty

☐ No data
■ >75
▨ 50-75
☐ 25-49
☐ <25

Between 25 and 49% of people in this region are living in poverty.

Holding a choropleth map away from you can help you see any overall patterns.

Dot Maps Show Distribution and Quantity Using Identical Symbols...

1) Dot maps use **identical dots** to show how something is **distributed** across an **area**.

2) Use the **key** to find out what **quantity** each dot represents.

Location of factories

● = 10 factories

Most dots, and therefore **most factories**, are in the **north east**.

A cluster of **three dots** shows **thirty factories**.

Individual dots show **ten factories**.

...Proportional Symbol Maps Use Symbols of Different Sizes

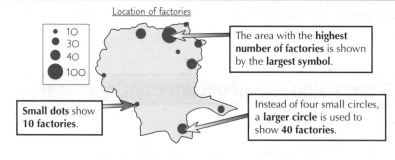

Location of factories

● 10
● 30
● 40
● 100

The area with the **highest number of factories** is shown by the **largest symbol**.

Small dots show **10 factories**.

Instead of four small circles, a **larger circle** is used to show **40 factories**.

1) **Proportional symbol maps** use symbols of **different sizes** to represent **different quantities**.

2) A **key** shows the quantity each symbol represents. The **bigger** the **symbol**, the **larger** the **amount**.

3) The symbols might be **circles**, **squares**, **semi-circles** or **bars**, but they're always read the **same way**.

Flow Line Maps Show Movement

1) Flow line maps have **arrows** on, showing how things **move** (or are moved) from **one place to another**.

2) The map on the right shows the movement of people **into** and **out of** a region.

3) It's also a **proportional symbol map** as the size of the arrows show **how many** people are moving.

The **largest flows** of people are **to Region A**, as these are the **largest arrows**.

Roughly the same number of people are **immigrating to Region A from Regions B and C**. This is shown by the arrows, which are the **same size**.

Some of the flows of people to and from Region A

Region B
Region A
Region C

Key
■ Urban area
☐ Rural area
▷ Emigration
▷ Immigration

The **smallest flows** of people are **out of Region A**, as these are the **smallest arrows**.

Graph and Map Skills

Isoline Maps Show Where Conditions are the Same

1) **Isolines** are lines on a map **linking** up all the **places** where something's the **same**, e.g. on **weather maps** isolines show places that are the **same air pressure**.

2) If the place you're being asked about lies **on** an isoline you can just **read** the value off the line.

3) If the place is **between** isolines you have to **estimate** the value.

4) For A2-level, you also need to know a bit more about **weather maps** — see page 139 for more.

Helsinki and Lecce both lie **on** this line so both have a pressure of **996 mb**.

Madrid lies **between** the lines for **988** and **992**. It's pretty much in the middle of the lines, so has a pressure of roughly **990 mb**.

Map of low pressure system

Town Centre Plans Show Detailed Information of Urban Areas

Town centre plans are **A2-level** territory. You can skip this bit if you're doing AS.

Roads

Park (obviously)

School and college (also obvious)

Railway track

Rows of **houses** — the little plots of land are **gardens**

Fields and woods

1) When you get a plan, start by looking at the **types of buildings** and what's **around** them.

2) **Small buildings** are probably **houses** or **shops**. **Bigger buildings** are probably **factories** or **schools**.

3) Work out what kind of **area** it is — lots of **car parks** and **shops** mean it's a **Central Business District (CBD)**, **houses with gardens** mean a **residential area**.

4) The plan to the left shows a **residential area**.

Ordnance Survey Maps Show Detailed Information of All Areas

1) Ordnance Survey® (OS®) maps use lots of **symbols**. It's a good idea to **learn** the most common ones.

2) You can find places on OS maps using **grid references**.

3) **Four-figure grid references** direct you to a 1 km × 1 km **square** on the map, e.g. for **1534** go **across** to the number **15** (the **eastings** value) and then **up** to the number **34** (the **northings** value). This grid reference refers to the **square above** and to the **right** of the point 1534.

4) **Six-figure grid references** are more precise and can direct you to a more **exact spot** (a 100 m × 100 m square). E.g. for 155341 the eastings value is 155, so go across to 15 again and then a further **5 "tenths"** across the square. For the northings value of 341 go up to 34 and a further **1 "tenth"** of that square. The spot you're looking for is where the easting and northing values **cross**.

5) Every map has a **scale** so that you can work out the **distance between points**. If the scale is **1:25 000**, it means that every **1 cm** on the map represents **25 000 cm** (250 m) in real life.

6) **Altitude** (height above sea level) is shown on OS maps using a type of isoline called **contour lines**. The **closer together** the contour lines are, the **steeper the gradient** is. Sometimes, the altitude of specific **spot heights** is also given.

Common OS Map Symbols

— Railway
▢ Building
+ Place of worship
⚓ Place of worship, with a tower
⚓ Church with a spire, minaret or dome

═══ Motorway
━━━ Main (A) road
═══ Secondary (B) road

◀● Bus station
PO Post office
PH Pub
–·–·– County boundary
═══ National Park boundary
------- Footpath

Grid reference: 1534

Grid reference: 155341

Getting your northings and eastings mixed up can cause havoc — Chaz thought he was heading to the bus station.

Altitude rises from **200 m** to **250 m**.

Altitude rises from **200 m** to **300 m**.

The contour lines on the right are closer together and show a **steeper slope** (there's a **greater increase in height** over the **same distance**).

Statistical Skills

The next few pages may look as terrifying as your Geography teacher in their underwear, but I'll bet my lucky stapler that some statistics will crop up in your exams, so get learnin'.

There are **Different Ways** of Finding the **Average** Value of a Set of Data

1) The **mean**, **median** and **mode** are different ways of finding the **average** value of a set of data.

2) You find the **mean** by **adding up** all the numbers in a set of data, then **dividing** by the number of **sample points**, **n**.

Take a look at the data in this table:

Location	1	2	3	4	5	6	7	8	9	10	11
Temperature in °C	3	7	4	3	7	9	9	5	5	7	6

n = 11, so the mean temperature is: $\dfrac{3 + 7 + 4 + 3 + 7 + 9 + 9 + 5 + 5 + 7 + 6}{11}$ = **5.9 °C**.

3) The **median** is the **middle value** in an ordered set of data. So you need to **sort the numbers into order**, then work out which one is in the middle. So for the data above the median is **6 °C**.

$$3\ 3\ 4\ 5\ 5\ (6)\ 7\ 7\ 7\ 9\ 9$$

If there are an even number of sample points the median is the mean of the middle two numbers.

4) The **mode** is the **most common value** in a set of data. So for the data above the mode is **7 °C**.

$$3\ 3\ 4\ 5\ 5\ 6\ (7\ 7\ 7)\ 9\ 9$$

Sometimes there isn't a mode, and sometimes there's more than one.

The **Interquartile Range** is a **Measure of Dispersion**...

1) The **interquartile range** (**IQR**) is the range of values covered by the **middle 50%** of a set of data.

2) To find the interquartile range you first need to find the median of the values **to the left** of the median. This is called the **lower quartile** (**LQ**). Next find the median of the values **to the right** of the median. This is the **upper quartile** (**UQ**). Then you just **subtract** the **LQ from the UQ** to give you the **IQR**.

3) So, for the data above, the **LQ** is **4** and the **UQ** is **7**, and the interquartile range is UQ – LQ = 7 – 4 = **3 °C**.

LQ   Median   UQ
$$3\ 3\ (4)\ 5\ 5\ (6)\ 7\ 7\ (7)\ 9\ 9$$
IQR

4) The interquartile range tells you about the **spread** of data **around** the **median**. If it's a **big** number, it shows that the numbers are pretty **spread out**. And yep, you've guessed it — a **small** number means that a lot of the data is pretty **close** to the **median**.

...and so is **Standard Deviation**

1) The **standard deviation** is a bit trickier to calculate than the IQR, but it's often a **more reliable** measure of dispersion (spread). The symbol for it is σ.

The formula is $\sigma = \sqrt{\dfrac{\Sigma(x - \bar{x})^2}{n}}$

Σ just means 'sum of', and x̄ is just a way of writing 'mean'.

2) To calculate it, it's easiest to **work out** the **individual bits** in the formula **first**, e.g. the mean. It's a good idea to **draw** a **table** to help you. Below is a simple example for the set: 5, 9, 10, 11, 14.

- For these numbers, the **mean** is (5 + 9 + 10 + 11 + 14) ÷ 5 = **9.8**. This is shown in the 2nd column in the table.

- For each number, **calculate x – x̄** (3rd column in the table).

- Then **square** each of those values (4th column) — remember that the square of a **negative number** is always **positive**.

- Then **add up** all the squared numbers you've just worked out — this will give you $\Sigma(x - \bar{x})^2$.

- Now just **divide** your total by **n**, then take the **square root**.

- In this example, n = 5, so $\sigma = \sqrt{\dfrac{42.8}{5}}$ = **2.93** (2 d.p.)

x	x̄	x – x̄	(x – x̄)²
5	9.8	−4.8	23.04
9	9.8	−0.8	0.64
10	9.8	0.2	0.04
11	9.8	1.2	1.44
14	9.8	4.2	17.64
		Σ	42.8

Standard deviation can be represented by σ or s.

3) If the standard deviation is **large**, the numbers in the set of data are **spread out** around the **mean**. If it's **small**, the numbers are **bunched** closely around the mean.

Statistical Skills

Make Sure You Know How to Find *Spearman's Rank Correlation Coefficient*

The Spearman's Rank correlation coefficient is a test to find out whether two sets of numbers are **correlated** (there's a **relationship** between them). The example below uses the test to see if **GDP per capita** ($) and **life expectancy** (in years) are correlated.

1) The bad news is that it's a bit of a pain to calculate. The first step is to give a **rank** to each number in both sets of data. The **highest** number is given rank **1**, the second highest is given rank 2... you get the idea.

2) Then you **calculate 'd'**, the **difference** between the ranks for each item, e.g. if the ranks for Country F are 4 and 6, the difference is 2.

3) Next you **square 'd'** and **add up** the **d² values** to give $\sum d^2$, which you use in the formula below.

4) Finally you need to work out the **Spearman's Rank Correlation Coefficient** (known as **r$_s$**).

The formula is: $r_s = 1 - \dfrac{6\sum d^2}{n^3 - n}$

Country	GDP per capita ($)	GDP rank	Life expectancy	Life expec. rank	d	d²
A	14 000	5	72	5	0	0
B	19 000	4	71	6	2	4
C	9000	9	67	8	1	1
D	6000	11	61	11	0	0
E	21 000	3	75	3	0	0
F	13 000	6	74	4	2	4
G	22 000	2	76	2	0	0
H	35 000	1	78	1	0	0
I	5000	12	60	12	0	0
J	7000	10	65	9	1	1
K	11 000	8	64	10	2	4
L	12 000	7	69	7	0	0
					$\sum d^2$	14

5) So for the example above, $\sum d^2 = 14$ and n = 12. So $r_s = 1 - \dfrac{6\times14}{12^3-12} = 1 - \dfrac{84}{1716} = 1 - 0.05 = \mathbf{0.95}$.

6) The number you get is always **between –1** and **+1**.

7) A **positive number** means the variables are **positively correlated** — as one variable **increases** so does the **other**. The **closer** the number is to 1 the **stronger** the correlation.

8) A **negative number** means that the two sets of variables are **negatively correlated** — as one variable **increases** the other **decreases**. The **closer** the number is to –1 the **stronger** the correlation.

9) If the coefficient is **0**, or near 0, there probably isn't much of a relationship between the figures.

10) The value of r$_s$ in the example above was **0.95**, which is **close to 1**, so there's a **strong positive correlation** between the **data** for GDP per capita and life expectancy.

You *Have To Check* the *Correlation Is Significant* Though

1) A **Spearman's Rank correlation coefficient** might tell you that **two sets of numbers** are **correlated**. But you need to check whether this is evidence for a **genuine link** between the two quantities you're looking at. (You sometimes get correlations between sets of data **by chance**, even if there's no underlying relationship. For example, there **is** a correlation between GDP per capita and life expectancy **for the data shown above**, but this might have been a fluke and there might be **no real relationship** between the two things.)

2) You can check whether it's evidence for a genuine link by looking at the **probability** that a correlation would happen by chance. If there's a 5% (or higher) probability that a correlation is because of chance then it's **not significant** evidence for a link. If there's a **0.1% or less** chance, then it's **very significant** evidence for a link. (This is what's meant by the **significance level** of a statistical test — it's a kind of 'cut-off' probability.)

3) To test whether the value of r$_s$ is evidence for a relationship between GDP per capita and life expectancy, you'll need a **graph** like the one on the right, or a **table** of critical values. You'll also need to know the **degrees of freedom** (in the example above this is just n – 2, so 12 – 2 = **10**). Since r$_s$ = **0.95**, you can use the graph to find that this correlation has a **less than 0.1%** probability of being due to chance. This means you have **very significant** evidence for a **relationship** between GDP per capita and life expectancy.

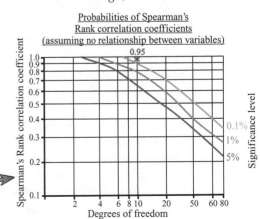

Statistical Skills

*These two pages are for **A2 only**. If you're doing AS, this is the end of the road (well the end of Exam Skills, anyway — yippeee).*

The **Chi-Squared** (χ^2) **Test** tells you whether **Two Variables** are **Linked**

1) There's no better way of explaining the chi-squared test than by showing you an example. So, here we go...

> A student is interested in finding out whether the **number of wells** in three areas of Africa is related to how much **rainfall** the areas receive each year.

2) In this case the two variables are the **number of wells** and the **amount of rainfall**.

3) You always start by making a **hypothesis** and a **null hypothesis**. The hypothesis is your theory about the link between the variables. In this example the student thinks the variables are linked, so the **hypothesis** is:

> **There is a link between the number of wells and the amount of rainfall the area receives.**

4) The **null hypothesis** is **always** that the two variables are **independent** (i.e. there isn't a link between them). E.g.:

> **There is no link between the number of wells and the amount of rainfall the area receives.**

5) First, use the null hypothesis to **predict** a **result** — this is called the **expected result**. In this example, there are 144 wells in total. If there was **no link** between rainfall and number of wells you'd **expect** that there would be an equal number of wells in each area, i.e. **48** (144 ÷ 3 = 48).

6) Next, the experiment is carried out and the **actual result** is recorded — this is called the **observed result**. The **observed** result in this case is the actual number of wells in each area.

7) The chi-squared (χ^2) **test** is then carried out and the **outcome** either supports the **null hypothesis** or allows you to **reject** it.

The χ^2 test uses a complicated looking **formula**.

$$\chi^2 = \Sigma \frac{(O - E)^2}{E}$$

You don't need to remember this equation — you'll be given it in the exam.

	Area A (lower rainfall)	Area B (medium rainfall)	Area C (higher rainfall)	
Expected	48	48	48	
Observed	64	49	31	
$O - E$	16	1	−17	
$(O - E)^2$	256	1	289	
$\dfrac{(O - E)^2}{E}$	5.33	0.02	6.02	**11.37**

Put your observed values (**O**) and expected values (**E**) into this **equation** to work out chi-squared (χ^2) one step at a time:

- First calculate **O − E** (**subtract** the **expected** result from the **observed** result) for each area, e.g. 64 − 48 = 16.
- Then **square** each of the resulting numbers, e.g. $16^2 = 256$.
- Next, **divide** each of these figures by the **expected result**, e.g. 256 ÷ 48 = 5.33.
- Finally, **add** the numbers for Areas A, B and C together to get χ^2. 5.33 + 0.02 + 6.02 = 11.37, so $\chi^2 = $ **11.37**.

Compare Your Result to the **Critical Value**

1) The χ^2 value shows whether there is a **significant difference** between your observed and expected results. If there **is** a significant difference, this suggests your two variables are **linked** (and you can **reject** the null hypothesis).

2) To find out if there is a significant difference between your observed and expected results you need to **compare** your χ^2 **value** to a **critical value**.

If you're not given the critical value, you might have to look it up in a table.

3) The critical value is the χ^2 value that corresponds to a 0.05 (**5**%) level of **probability** that the **difference** between the observed and expected results is **due to chance**.

4) If your χ^2 value is **smaller** than the critical value then there is **no significant difference** between the observed and expected results. This means your variables are **independent** and you accept your **null hypothesis**.

5) If your χ^2 value is **larger** than the critical value then there is a **significant difference** between the observed and expected results (something **other than chance** is causing the difference). This suggests that there is a link between your two variables and the **null hypothesis** is **rejected**.

6) For this example the critical value is **5.99**. The χ^2 value of 11.37 is bigger than 5.99, so there is a significant difference between the observed and expected results and the **null hypothesis** is **rejected**.

7) Be careful with your conclusions though — your χ^2 value is **evidence supporting** your hypothesis that there is a **link** between the number of wells and the amount of rainfall. However, it **doesn't prove** this link — there could be **other factors** involved that you haven't considered in your investigation.

Statistical Skills

The Mann-Whitney U Test Shows if Two Data Sets are Significantly Different

1) You use the **Mann-Whitney U Test** to work out if two sets of **unrelated** data are statistically different.

2) Take a look at this example:

> A student wants to find out whether **grazing by sheep** reduces the **number** of **plant species** in a field, compared to a field that hasn't been grazed at all. She studies two fields — Field A is ungrazed and Field B is grazed by sheep.

3) The **hypothesis** is that there **is** a **significant difference** in the number of species found in grazed and ungrazed fields.

4) The **null hypothesis** is that there is **no significant difference** in the number of species found in grazed and ungrazed fields.

5) The number of species in ten quadrats in each of the fields were counted. Here are the results:

Number of species	Field A (ungrazed)	17	24	18	26	30	19	31	20	27	26
	Field B (grazed)	16	9	15	10	22	15	21	13	8	12

A quadrat is a square frame of a known size, e.g. 1 m². You count the species inside it.

First You Need to Rank the Data

1) Look at **all** the data together and **rank** them regardless of what group they're in (i.e. Field A or Field B). Start with the **lowest score** (in the example it's 8) and give it a rank of '**1**'. Then the next lowest score gets a rank of '**2**' and so on.

2) If some of the values are the **same**, give them an **average** rank. Here there are two values of 15, so each has a rank of **6.5**.

Number of species	Field A (ungrazed)	17	24	18	26	30	19	31	20	27	26
	(rank)	(9)	(15)	(10)	(16.5)	(19)	(11)	(20)	(12)	(18)	(16.5)
	Field B (grazed)	16	9	15	10	22	15	21	13	8	12
	(rank)	(8)	(2)	(6.5)	(3)	(14)	(6.5)	(13)	(5)	(1)	(4)

Then Add Up the Ranks for Each Group

1) Add up the **ranks** for the ungrazed field group, then do the same for the grazed field group.

> Sum of ranks in **ungrazed field (Field A)** (R_A) = 9 + 15 + 10 + 16.5 + 19 + 11 + 20 + 12 + 18 + 16.5 = **147**
> Sum of ranks in **grazed field (Field B)** (R_B) = 8 + 2 + 6.5 + 3 + 14 + 6.5 + 13 + 5 + 1 + 4 = **63**

When you think about it, if the ungrazed field really did have a **greater number of plant species**, then you'd expect to see more species in the quadrats than the grazed field. This means that the **ranks** of the quadrats in the ungrazed field would also be **higher**.

2) Once you've added up the ranks for each group, you need to put your data into these scary-looking **formulas**:

$$U_A = N_A \times N_B + \frac{N_A(N_A + 1)}{2} - R_A$$

$$U_B = N_A \times N_B + \frac{N_B(N_B + 1)}{2} - R_B$$

N_A is the number of quadrats in Field A
N_B is the number of quadrats in Field B
R_A is the sum of the ranks for Field A
R_B is the sum of the ranks for Field B

$$U_A = (10 \times 10) + \frac{10(10 + 1)}{2} - 147$$

$$U_B = (10 \times 10) + \frac{10(10 + 1)}{2} - 63$$

$$U_A = 8$$

$$U_B = 92$$

You might be given the critical value, or you might have to look it up in a table. For the Mann-Whitney U Test you need to use both N values (N_A and N_B) to find the critical value.

3) Take the **smaller** of these two numbers, 8, and call it '**U**'.

4) U must be **less than or equal to** the **critical value** to be **significant** and for you to **reject** the **null hypothesis**. Here, the critical value of U for a probability of 0.05 is 23.

5) U is **lower** than the critical value, so you can **reject** the **null hypothesis**.

6) Remember, this result is only **evidence** to support the **hypothesis** that there is a **significant difference** in the **number of species** in these two fields. You **don't know** whether that's down to grazing or some other factor.

AS-Level Answers

Unit 1: Section 1 — Rivers, Floods and Management

Page 3 — The Hydrological Cycle

1   Maximum of 4 marks available.
In wet seasons, precipitation exceeds evapotranspiration, creating a water surplus — ground stores fill with water as there's more surface runoff and higher discharge, so river levels rise *[1 mark]*. In drier seasons, precipitation is lower than evapotranspiration — ground stores are depleted as some water is used by plants and humans and some flows into the river channel, but isn't replaced by precipitation *[1 mark]*. At the end of a dry season, there's a deficit (shortage) of water in the ground *[1 mark]*. This has to be paid back in the next wet season (ground store recharge) *[1 mark]*.

Page 5 — River Discharge

1 a) Maximum of 2 marks available.
Lag time = 12 hours *[1 mark]*.
Peak discharge = 35 cumecs *[1 mark]*.

b) Maximum of 4 marks available.
Vegetation intercepts precipitation and slows its movement to the river channel, increasing lag time *[1 mark]*. So deforestation will reduce interception, resulting in a decreased lag time *[1 mark]*. The more vegetation there is in a basin, the more water is lost through transpiration and evaporation directly from the vegetation before it reaches the river channel, reducing peak discharge *[1 mark]*. So deforestation will reduce transpiration and evaporation, causing an increase in peak discharge *[1 mark]*.

Page 7 — River Processes

1   Maximum of 5 marks available.
Erosion by hydraulic action happens as the pressure of the water breaks rock particles away from the bed and banks *[1 mark]*. Abrasion (corrasion) occurs when eroded pieces of rock in the water scrape and rub against the bed and banks, removing material *[1 mark]*. Attrition is when eroded rocks smash into each other and break into smaller fragments *[1 mark]*. Erosion by cavitation occurs as air bubbles in turbulent stretches of water implode causing shockwaves that break pieces of rock off the banks and bed *[1 mark]*. Corrosion erosion (solution) is the dissolving of rock by chemical processes *[1 mark]*.

2   Maximum of 6 marks available. This question is level marked.
HINTS:
   •   Start off by *defining* what the critical erosion velocity curve shows, e.g. 'The critical erosion velocity curve shows the minimum velocity needed to pick up and transport particles of different sizes'.
   •   Then you need to *describe* how it's different for different particle sizes, e.g. 'It's lowest for sand (particles between 0.1 mm and 1 mm), but it's higher for particles that are both larger (e.g. gravel, pebbles and boulders) and smaller (e.g. clay and silt)'.
   •   Finally *explain why* clay and silt require a faster velocity to be picked up and transported than sand (they tend to stick together more, so it takes more energy (velocity) to erode them), and do the same for larger particles (they require more velocity as they're heavier).

Page 9 — The Long Profile and Channel Characteristics

1   Maximum of 3 marks available.
A river's hydraulic radius is a measure of how efficient the river is *[1 mark]*. It's calculated by dividing the river's cross-sectional area *[1 mark]* by the length of its wetted perimeter (the total length of the banks and bed that are in contact with the water) *[1 mark]*.

2   Maximum of 6 marks available. This question is level marked.
HINTS:
   •   It's fairly easy to structure your answer to this question. You can either talk about *each stage* of the river in turn and describe how the processes change. Or you can talk about *each process* in turn and describe how it changes as you go down the river.
   •   The questions says '*outline*' so you need to *describe* what's happening *and explain why*, e.g. 'In the lower stage of a river, there's less erosion because turbulence is lower and sediment particle size is reduced (reducing erosion due to abrasion)'.

Page 11 — River Landforms

1   Maximum of 4 marks available.
Levees are natural, raised embankments formed when a river overflows its banks *[1 mark]*. During a flood, material is deposited across the whole flood plain as the river loses velocity and energy due to increased friction *[1 mark]*. The heaviest material (e.g. sand and gravel) is dropped first, closest to the river channel *[1 mark]*. Over time, this material builds up on the river bank, creating a levee *[1 mark]*.

Page 13 — Causes and Impacts of Flooding

1   Maximum of 6 marks available. This question is level marked.
HINTS:
   •   The question asks you to 'outline' — this means *describe* the physical characteristics and *explain* why they would increase the risk of flooding.
   •   Focus on one characteristic at a time and give a *full explanation*, e.g. 'Drainage basins with impermeable ground (such as clay soils) don't allow infiltration of surface water. This increases surface runoff, which increases river discharge and increases the risk of flooding'.
   •   Cover a *range* of physical characteristics in detail, e.g. sparse vegetation, high drainage density, circular basin, steep slopes, etc.

2   Maximum of 5 marks available.
Urban areas have large areas of impermeable tarmac and concrete *[1 mark]*, so when it rains, surface runoff is very rapid *[1 mark]*. Urban areas also have gutters and drains, which quickly take runoff to the rivers *[1 mark]*. Both of these reduce lag time *[1 mark]*, which increases discharge and so increases the risk of flooding *[1 mark]*.

Page 15 — Causes and Impacts of Flooding — Case Studies

1   Maximum of 10 marks available. This question is level marked.
HINTS:
   •   Focus your answer on the *impacts* of flooding — write about the *effect* flooding has on society, the economy and the environment.
   •   The question asks you to use two named examples, so use *two case studies* you've learnt (e.g. the South Asia flood and the Carlisle flood).

AS-Level Answers

- *'Compare'* means you should describe the impacts that are <u>similar</u> in poor and wealthy countries, and those that are <u>different</u>. For example, 'When South Asia was flooded in 2007 over 2000 people died, but only three people died in the Carlisle floods of 2005. The death toll in South Asia was high for many reasons, e.g. because many people living there rely on agriculture, so were reluctant to evacuate and leave their land and livestock unattended. Also, many children couldn't swim so they drowned in the floods'.

Page 17 — Flood Management Strategies

1 Maximum of 8 marks available. This question is level marked.
<u>HINTS</u>:
- This is a sneaky one — to answer the question you need to know that most <u>soft engineering defences</u> don't use man-made structures.
- <u>Explain</u> how flooding can be reduced using soft engineering defences, and explain how each defence works. For example, 'Flooding can be reduced by restoring the river to its natural state, e.g. by removing man-made levees. This allows the river to flood naturally. The water spreads out over the flood plain, which reduces river discharge and so decreases flooding downstream'.
- You don't need to include weather forecasts and flood warnings, as these don't actually reduce flooding (they only reduce the impacts of flooding).

Page 19 — Flood Management Strategies — Case Studies

1 Maximum of 10 marks available. This question is level marked.
<u>HINTS</u>:
- The question asks you to refer to 'named examples', so you need to write about at least <u>two case studies</u> (e.g. the different approaches used on the Yangtze River and in Abingdon).
- Start off by describing <u>what type of defences</u> have been implemented in each place, e.g. 'Hard engineering defences, such as dams and levees, have been used along the Yangtze river in China'.
- Next write about the <u>success</u> of the schemes — say whether they have reduced flooding and describe any <u>problems</u> they have caused. For example, 'The Three Gorges Dam on the Yangtze River is thought to have successfully reduced major flooding from once every 10 years to once every 100 years. However, it has had many negative impacts, e.g. people have had to relocate as the reservoir behind the dam builds up. It's thought that between 1.3 and 2 million people will have been forced to relocate by the time the reservoir is full'.
- Don't forget to stuff your answer full of <u>specific details</u> about the case studies, e.g. 'There are 3600 km of levees along the middle and lower parts of the Yangtze'.

Unit 1: Section 2 — Coastal Environments

Page 21 — Introduction to Coastal Environments

1 Maximum of 4 marks available.
2 marks available for characteristics of constructive waves, from any of the following points: Constructive waves are flat and gentle *[1 mark]*. They have a low frequency *[1 mark]* of about 6-8 waves per minute *[1 mark]*. Their swash is greater than their backwash *[1 mark]* which carries material up the beach and deposits it *[1 mark]*. 2 marks available for characteristics of destructive waves, from any of the following points: Destructive waves are tall and steep *[1 mark]*. They have a high frequency *[1 mark]* of about 10-14 waves per minute *[1 mark]*. Their backwash is greater than their swash *[1 mark]* and removes beach material *[1 mark]*.

2 Maximum of 6 marks available. This question is level marked.
<u>HINTS</u>:
- 'Outline' means <u>describe</u> and <u>explain</u>, so first you need to list the erosion processes that affect cliffs — these include abrasion/corrasion, hydraulic action, quarrying and corrosion/solution.
- Don't write about attrition — it's not a type of erosion that affects cliffs (it's the erosion of rocks in the water by smashing together).
- Then for each type of erosion you need to <u>explain how</u> it erodes cliffs, e.g. 'Hydraulic action is where air in cracks in cliffs is compressed by waves. The pressure exerted by the compressed air breaks bits of rock off the cliff'.
- For top marks you also need to explain how <u>sub-aerial weathering</u> makes cliffs more vulnerable to erosion, e.g. 'Freeze-thaw weathering weakens cliffs and so makes them more vulnerable to erosion'.

Page 24 — Coastal Landforms

1 Maximum of 5 marks available.
Weathering and wave erosion forms a notch in a cliff *[1 mark]* at the high water mark *[1 mark]*. This eventually develops into a cave *[1 mark]*. Rock above the cave is unsupported and so collapses *[1 mark]*. As this process is repeated the cliff retreats, leaving behind a flat wave-cut platform *[1 mark]*.

2 Maximum of 6 marks available. This question is level marked.
<u>HINTS</u>:
- Spits are formed by <u>longshore drift</u> — to get top level marks you'll need to describe the process.
- Describe <u>where</u> spits are likely to form, e.g. 'Spits tend to form where the coast suddenly changes direction, such as across a river mouth'.
- Explain what a <u>recurved end</u> is, and how it's formed.
- Make sure you include what happens <u>behind</u> the spit, e.g. 'The area behind the spit is sheltered from the sea and often forms salt marshes'.
- Include a <u>diagram</u> (or a series of diagrams, like on page 23) to illustrate the formation.

Page 25 — Coastal Erosion — Case Study

1 Maximum of 15 marks available. This question is level marked.
<u>HINTS</u>:
- The question says <u>one named area</u>. It might sound obvious, but remember to write about a <u>case study</u>, not just the general causes and effects of coastal erosion, e.g. 'Holderness is a 61km long stretch of coastline in East Yorkshire. It's eroding at a rate of 1.8 m/year...'.
- Talk about both the <u>physical</u> and <u>human</u> causes of erosion, e.g. 'One of the most important physical causes of erosion at Holderness is the long fetch (from the Arctic Ocean), which means the waves have a lot of energy when they hit the coastline. Humans are contributing to coastal erosion too. Sea defences built at Mappleton trap sediment and starve down-drift beaches of sediment'.
- You could draw an <u>annotated map</u> in your answer to help illustrate the causes of coastal erosion at Holderness.
- Include plenty of relevant <u>facts</u> and <u>figures</u> in your answer, e.g. 'At Holderness, the coastline is made of till, which is an easily eroded rock type'.

Page 27 — Sea Level Changes

1 Maximum of 8 marks available. This question is level marked.
<u>HINTS</u>:
- The question asks for <u>possible</u> impacts, so you need to write about what the impacts might be in the <u>future</u>.
- Make sure you include all the main impacts — more frequent and more severe flooding, submergence of low-lying islands and changes in the coastline.
- For each impact describe what could happen and <u>give an example</u> to back up your point if possible, e.g. 'Low-lying coastal islands may be submerged if sea level rises, e.g. if it rises 0.5 m, most of the Maldives would be submerged'.
- Don't forget to include that the main impacts have <u>further impacts</u>, e.g. decrease in tourism, damage to infrastructure etc.

AS-Level Answers

2   Maximum of 8 marks available. This question is level marked.
    HINTS:
    • The question asks about *coastal submergence*, so you need to explain how it happens, e.g. 'Coastal submergence happens when the sea level rises relative to the land'.
    • Then you need to explain *how* the rise in sea level may occur, and the difference between eustatic and isostatic change.
    • The question also asks for a *range* of landforms, so make sure you talk about more than one (e.g. cover rias, fjords and Dalmatian coastlines).
    • For each landform, describe *how it's formed* and its *main features*, e.g. 'Rias are drowned river valleys. They are wide and deep at the mouth, becoming narrower and shallower further inland'.

Page 29 — Coastal Flooding

1   Maximum of 10 marks available. This question is level marked.
    HINTS:
    • The question says a *named coastal area*. It might sound obvious, but remember to write about a *case study*, not just the general causes and effects of flooding.
    • Talk about both the *physical and human* causes of the flooding, e.g. 'Coastal areas in south-east Asia were flooded by a tsunami that was caused by a submarine earthquake measuring about 9.0 on the Richter scale off the coast of Indonesia. However, human activity, such as destruction of mangrove forests in Thailand to make way for fish farms, and coral mining in the Indian Ocean, meant that a lot of the coasts' natural protection was missing. This made the effects of flooding worse'.
    • Make sure you know whether each effect is *social, economic* or *environmental* because you *might not always* get asked for *all three*.
    • Include plenty of *facts* and *figures* and make plenty of *place-specific statements* to show that you really know the case study, e.g. 'A quarter of hotels in southern Thailand were forced to close for at least 6 months because of damage from the flooding'.

Page 31 — Coastal Management

1   Maximum of 6 marks available. This question is level marked.
    HINTS:
    • First you need to *describe* what hard engineering defences and soft engineering defences are and give a couple of *examples*. E.g. 'Hard engineering defences are built structures, e.g. revetments, groynes and sea walls'.
    • Then go on to explain *why* soft engineering defences are *more sustainable*, e.g. 'Soft engineering defences usually require much less time and money to maintain than hard engineering defences. They also create habitats like dunes and marshland, e.g. coastal realignment leads to the formation of marshland. Hard engineering defences often disrupt natural processes'.
    • Finish up with a *conclusion*, e.g. 'Soft engineering schemes have a lower environmental impact and a lower economic cost than hard engineering schemes, so are more sustainable'.

Page 33 — Coastal Management — Case Studies

1   Maximum of 15 marks available. This question is level marked.
    HINTS:
    • The command word in this question is *evaluate*, so you need to talk about the costs *and* benefits of your chosen scheme.
    • The question doesn't specify whether you need to write about a *hard* or *soft* engineering scheme, so the choice is yours. Make sure you pick one that you *know loads about*, so you can get plenty of *detail* in your answer.
    • Whatever scheme you choose, the *benefits* are likely to be things like saving land, housing, transport routes, and industry, and preserving natural habitats. The *costs* will include things like the price of setting up and maintaining the defences, the appearance of the defences and the possible effects on adjacent areas of the coast.
    • Examiners love 'specific and detailed reference' to the case study, so it's good to have some *numbers* to back up your points, e.g. '£2 million was spent on two rock groynes and 500 m of revetment at Mappleton in 1991'.

• But don't just scribble down all facts — you need to explain *why* these measures were used and the *effect* that they've had, e.g. 'They were built to protect the village and the B1242 road. The scheme has successfully protected these areas, but the groynes have starved down-drift beaches of sediment, which has caused increased erosion of the cliffs south of Mappleton'.

Unit 1: Section 3 — Cold Environments

Page 35 — Distribution of Cold Environments

1   Maximum of 15 marks available. This question is level marked.
    HINTS:
    • The question only mentions *glacial* and *periglacial* environments, so don't write about alpine or polar environments.
    • Start by *defining* each environment, e.g. 'Glacial environments are areas of land covered by ice (either glaciers or ice sheets)'.
    • Then *describe where* each environment is found (i.e. its *distribution*). Don't forget to *include examples*. E.g. 'Glacial environments are found at high latitudes, e.g. the Antarctic Ice Sheet is above 60°, and at high altitudes, e.g. there are glaciers in the Himalayan mountains (the highest mountain range in the world)'.
    • Then *explain why* they're found there. E.g. 'Glaciers and ice sheets only form where it's really cold. High latitude areas are really cold because they receive little solar radiation. The Sun's energy hits the Earth at more of an angle at high latitudes, so it's spread out over a larger area'.
    • For extra marks explain why glacial environments aren't found on low altitude land in the middle of continents.

Page 37 — Glaciers

1   Maximum of 3 marks available.
    A glacial budget is the balance between accumulation (the input of snow and ice into a glacier) and ablation (the output of water from a glacier) over a year *[1 mark]*. If the glacial budget is positive, accumulation is exceeding ablation, and the glacier is advancing *[1 mark]*. If the glacial budget is negative, ablation is exceeding accumulation, and the glacier is retreating *[1 mark]*.

2   Maximum of 5 marks available.
    In warm-based glaciers, the base temperature is warmer than the melting point of ice, so melting occurs. The meltwater acts as a lubricant, making it easier for the glacier to move downhill *[1 mark]*. Ice at the surface also melts if the temperature reaches 0 °C. Meltwater moves down through the glacier and lubricates it even more *[1 mark]*. In cold-based glaciers the base is cold, so there's very little melting at the bottom of the glacier. The ice is frozen to the valley floor *[1 mark]*. So warm-based glaciers move faster than cold-based glaciers *[1 mark]*, which means they erode the landscape more *[1 mark]*.

Page 39 — Glacial Processes

1   Maximum of 4 marks available.
    At the head of a glacier the valley is steep, so there's a strong gravitational force pulling the ice downwards *[1 mark]*. This makes the ice move quickly *[1 mark]*. The tension created causes the ice to crack into layers, which slip downwards over each other *[1 mark]*. This is called extensional flow *[1 mark]*.

AS-Level Answers

2   Maximum of 4 marks available.
Glaciers pick up debris by plucking *[1 mark]* and abrasion
[1 mark]. Plucking is when ice thaws and then refreezes
around rocks. When the glacier moves forward, it plucks the
rocks from the valley floor or wall *[1 mark]*. Abrasion is when
debris carried by the glacier scrapes material off the valley
walls and floor *[1 mark]*.

Page 41 — Glacial Landforms

1   Maximum of 8 marks available. This question is level marked.
HINTS:
   • Look closely at the photograph and make a quick list of all the landforms
     you can see so you don't miss any out. For example, there's a ribbon lake
     at the top of the photo in the background, an arête, a corrie and a tarn.
   • The question asks you to *describe* and *explain* the landforms. For each
     one you need to describe it and explain how it formed. E.g. 'There is
     a corrie on the right of the photo. A corrie is a bowl-shaped hollow.
     Glaciers form when snow accumulates in a hollow and turns to ice.
     Basal sliding, along with abrasion and plucking, deepens the hollow into
     a corrie. When there is enough ice the glacier starts to move downhill.
     Frost shattering and plucking steepen the back wall of the corrie'.
   • You could include a diagram where it helps illustrate your answer.
     For example a cross-section of the formation of a corrie.

2   Maximum of 3 marks available.
Lateral moraine is deposited where the sides of the glacier
were *[1 mark]*. Medial moraine is deposited in the centre of
the valley where two glaciers converge *[1 mark]*. Terminal
moraine is deposited as semicircular hillocks at the end of the
glacier *[1 mark]*.

Page 43 — Fluvioglacial Processes and Landforms

1   Maximum of 2 marks available.
Kame terraces are piles of sorted deposits that run along
the valley walls *[1 mark]*. They're deposited by meltwater
streams that run between the glacier and the valley sides
[1 mark].

2   Maximum of 4 marks available.
Delta kames are formed when meltwater streams flow into
a proglacial lake *[1 mark]*. When they flow into a proglacial
lake, they slow down and deposit the sediment they're
carrying on the ice *[1 mark]*. These deposits are known
as deltas *[1 mark]*. After the ice has melted the deltas are
deposited on the valley floor, forming delta kames *[1 mark]*.

Page 45 — Periglacial Processes and Landforms

1   Maximum of 6 marks available. This question is level marked.
HINTS:
   • Start by *explaining* what's meant by patterned ground.
   • *State* the two ways that patterned ground is formed — by frost heave and
     frost contraction.
   • *Explain* how each process causes stones to form patterns on the surface of
     the ground, e.g. 'Frost contraction occurs when temperatures drop very low
     in winter — the ground contracts, causing polygon shaped cracks to form
     in the permafrost. The cracks get filled in with stones forming polygon
     patterns on the surface'.

Page 47 — Issues in Cold Environments

1   Maximum of 6 marks available. This question is level marked.
HINTS:
   • The main types of development in cold environments are mining, fishing, oil
     extraction, tourism and hydroelectric power production.
   • For each type of development, *describe how* it can damage the environment
     and give an *example*. E.g. 'Oil spilt when it's being transported can lead
     to the death of birds and marine life. For example, when the Exxon Valdez
     tanker crashed off the coast of Alaska over 40 million litres of oil were spilt,
     which killed over 250 000 birds and fish'.
   • Include that cold environments have *fragile ecosystems*, which means that
     they struggle to recover from damage.

2   Maximum of 6 marks available. This question is level marked.
HINTS:
   • Start by describing the *traditional way of life* of native tribes, i.e. what their
     lifestyle was like *before* development of tundra areas.
   • Then say what development has taken place, e.g. whaling, sealing and fishing
     by newcomers.
   • Finally, explain how this development has *affected* the native tribes, e.g. by
     bringing diseases and depleting their resources.
   • Include any relevant *facts* you can remember, e.g. 'When newcomers arrived
     in Canada in the late 19th century and early 20th century, they brought
     diseases like tuberculosis, which killed 90% of the Inuvialuit tribe'.

Page 49 — Issues in Cold Environments — Case Study

1   Maximum of 15 marks available. This question is level marked.
HINTS:
   • Start off by describing what resources are found in the Antarctic and what
     type of development they attract.
   • Then explain how the Antarctic is being protected by the Antarctic Treaty
     — i.e. it *bans some development* and *controls other activities*.
   • *Describe* which activities are *banned* (mining, oil extraction and whaling)
     and *explain why* they're banned — the possible environmental impact
     of mining and oil extraction could be huge, and the whale population
     has decreased due to whaling. Don't forget to include the *names of the
     protocols* that ban them.
   • Then say which activities are *allowed* but controlled (tourism, scientific
     research, fishing). Explain how they're controlled and how the measures
     reduce their environmental impact and make them *more sustainable*.
   • Finish off by talking about *any issues*, e.g. illegal fishing.

Unit 1: Section 4 — Hot Desert Environments

Page 51 — Desert and Desert Margin Characteristics

1 a) Maximum of 6 marks available. This part is level marked.
HINTS:
   • Start by describing what the *rainfall* is like — say which months have no
     rainfall, which months do, and which month has the highest rainfall, e.g.
     'Riyadh receives no rainfall from June to September. It typically rains from
     October until May, with most rain falling in April (average 29 mm)'.
   • You get higher marks if you *manipulate the data*, so count up the total
     rainfall for the year and say if Riyadh has an arid or semi-arid climate, e.g.
     'The total rainfall in Riyadh is about 100 mm per year, which is less than
     250 mm per year, so it has an arid climate and is classed as a desert'.
   • Next describe the *temperature* throughout the year.
   • Remember to *quote data from the graph* to back up your points.

   b) Maximum of 5 marks available. This part is level marked.
HINTS:
   • First, say that if it's 25° north of the equator it's located in an area of
     circulating air known as a Hadley cell.
   • Then you need to explain how the circulating air leads to low precipitation,
     e.g. 'As air rises at the equator, the moisture that it holds condenses and
     falls as rain. The dry air descends over Riyadh, creating an area of high
     pressure. Winds blow outwards from this area, meaning no moisture can be
     brought in, so there's very little precipitation'.

c) Maximum of 4 marks available.
The total amount of vegetation in Riyadh will be low
[1 mark] because the lack of water makes it difficult for plants
to grow *[1 mark]*. Any vegetation present will be specialised
to collect, store and conserve water *[1 mark]*. Vegetation is
likely to include shrubs, grasses and cacti *[1 mark]*.

Page 53 — Processes in Hot Desert Environments

1 Maximum of 8 marks available. This question is level marked.
HINTS:
- To get full marks you need to describe all four types of mechanical
  weathering that occur in hot desert environments — thermal fracture, frost
  shattering, wetting and drying, and salt weathering.
- Write a brief paragraph about each type of weathering, e.g. 'Thermal
  fracture is caused by the large daily temperature variations in hot
  desert environments. Rocks expand during the day (when it's hot) and
  contract at night (when it's cold). Sometimes outer layers of rock flake
  off because they warm up and cool down more quickly than the inner
  layers (exfoliation). Individual grains can also fall off because different
  minerals within the rock expand and contract at different rates (granular
  disintegration)'.
- Include diagrams to help you explain the processes involved.

2 a) Maximum of 3 marks available.
Exogenous rivers have a source outside the desert margin and
they flow throughout the year despite evaporation reducing
their volume *[1 mark]*. Endoreic rivers terminate inland in the
form of an inland sea or delta *[1 mark]*. Ephemeral rivers flow
intermittently or seasonally after rainstorms *[1 mark]*.

b) Maximum of 6 marks available. This part is level marked.
HINTS:
- Start your answer by describing what flash floods and sheet floods are.
- Then describe how both types of flood transport material. Make sure you
  point out that flash floods have more energy and so can carry larger pieces
  of rock.
- Be specific in your answer — don't just say, 'Flash floods carry large pieces
  of rock', instead say, 'Flash floods carry large pieces of desert rock by
  traction'.
- The question asks about erosion — so make sure your answer includes
  how both types of floods erode the desert surface by abrasion and attrition.

Page 55 — Landforms in Hot Desert Environments

1 Maximum of 7 marks available. This question is level marked.
HINTS:
- You need to describe and explain the formation of both yardangs and
  zeugen to get full marks. Make sure you don't get them confused.
- First explain what yardangs are and how they're formed, e.g. 'Yardangs are
  narrow, streamlined ridges. Strong winds (blowing in one direction) carry
  sand in suspension, which erodes rocks by abrasion. Softer rock is eroded
  faster than harder rock, so ridges of hard rock are created'.
- Then do the same for zeugen.
- You could include diagrams of each to help explain how they're formed.
  For example, draw one like this for yardangs:

2 a) Maximum of 3 marks available.
Landform A is a sand dune/barchan/crescent-shaped sand
dune *[1 mark]*. Landform B is an alluvial fan *[1 mark]*.
Landform C is a wadi *[1 mark]*.

b) Maximum of 4 marks available.
A mesa is an isolated, flat-topped, steep-sided landform found
only in arid places *[1 mark]*. It's a type of inselberg *[1 mark]*
made of hard rock that's more resistant to erosion than the
surrounding rock *[1 mark]*. It's formed when the surrounding
softer rock is eroded away by wind or water, leaving the harder
rock mesa standing out *[1 mark]*.

c) Maximum of 4 marks available.
Feature E could be a salt lake or a salt pan *[1 mark]*. Salt lakes
form when desert rivers are endoreic/terminate inland
[1 mark]. The water can't leave the lake and evaporation
is high, resulting in a lake with a high salt content *[1 mark]*.
Some salt lakes are ephemeral — evaporation is so high that
they dry up at certain times of the year, leaving the salt behind
to form salt pans *[1 mark]*.

Page 57 — Desertification

1 Maximum of 10 marks available. This question is level marked.
HINTS:
- Split your answer into two — first cover the physical causes, then the
  human causes.
- For each cause, explain how it leads to desertification, e.g. 'Climate change
  is causing an increase in temperature in some areas. This increases the rate
  of evapotranspiration, which dries soils out and lowers surface water levels.
  Vegetation dies due to lack of water and so there are fewer roots to hold
  the soil together. This leads to an increase in soil erosion'.
- Make sure you explicitly say how each one leads to either soil erosion or the
  land being less fertile (e.g. because the salt content has increased).
- Don't forget that there are a number of ways that irrigation leads to
  desertification.
- As a final point, include how an increase in population can increase
  overgrazing, overcultivation and deforestation.

Page 59 — Desertification Case Study — The Sahel

1 Maximum of 15 marks available. This question is level marked.
HINTS:
- This question asks you to evaluate the strategies, so you need to say if they
  worked, if they caused any problems and if they had any extra benefits, e.g.
  'Jatropha curcas is being grown around crops in Mali to protect them from
  wind erosion. The strategy has reduced erosion in the area and has also
  reduced rural poverty, as oil from the plant can be sold'.
- Include whether each strategy is sustainable or not.
- As always with case study questions include plenty of relevant details, e.g.
  'Yields of some crops increased 40% in Burkina Faso as a result of contour
  bunding'.

Page 61 — Desertification Case Study — Southern Spain

1 Maximum of 15 marks available. This question is level marked.
HINTS:
- The question asks you to compare strategies, so you need to write about
  the similarities and differences between the strategies used to tackle
  desertification in Spain and the Sahel.
- Start off by describing the similarities in the strategies used in the Sahel
  and Spain, e.g. 'Both the Sahel and Spain are implementing strategies to
  increase the level of vegetation, as loss of vegetation is a major cause of
  desertification in both areas'.
- Then explain the differences in the strategies used, e.g. 'In Spain lots of
  money is being spent on transferring water from one place to another, whilst
  in the Sahel the focus is on working with what little water they have, by
  conserving rainwater (using contour bunding) and growing plants that are
  suited to drought conditions'.

AS-Level Answers

Unit 1: Section 5 — Population Change

Page 63 — Population Change Basics and the DTM

1 Maximum of 10 marks available. This question is level marked.
  HINTS:
  • Write an introduction briefly explaining what the DTM is, e.g. 'The Demographic Transition Model (DTM) shows how the population of a country changes over time through five stages. The model shows birth rate, death rate and total population'.
  • The question asks you to refer to the DTM, so you can use this to structure your answer — start by explaining what stage of the DTM the country was in in 1600. E.g. 'In 1600 the birth rate and death rate were very high (38 and 37 respectively) and the population was low (2 million). The country was in Stage 1 of the DTM. Birth rate was high because there was no birth control or family planning, and education was poor. Also, infant mortality was high, so people had more children to replace those who'd died. The death rate was high because of poor health care, sanitation and diet, which led to disease and starvation'.
  • Next, describe how the data changes and relate the changes to the stages of the DTM, e.g. 'Between 1600 and 1800, the death rate decreased (from 37 to 18 per 1000 per year) and the population had more than tripled, from 2 million to 7 million. The birth rate had dropped very slightly from 38 to 35 per 1000 per year. The country had reached Stage 2 of the DTM'. Don't forget to give reasons for the changes.
  • Make sure you use data from the table in your answer.

Page 65 — Applying the DTM

1 Maximum of 15 marks available. This question is level marked.
  HINTS:
  • Start with an introduction briefly explaining the DTM.
  • The question asks you to discuss the uses and limitations, so you need to talk about the advantages and disadvantages.
  • Write a section on what the DTM can be used for and why it's useful (the advantages), e.g. 'The DTM can be used to forecast how a population may change, which can help governments decide on policies such as one-child limits or immigration laws'.
  • Then explain each limitation of the DTM (the disadvantages), e.g. 'The original data used to create the DTM was from more developed, richer countries (e.g. European countries, Japan and the USA). This means it might not be a valid model worldwide — what happened in these countries might not be the same as what's happening in others, e.g. countries in Asia or Africa'.

Page 67 — Population Structure and Migration

1 Maximum of 4 marks available.
  Push factors are the things that make people want to move out of the place they're in [1 mark]. They're negative factors about the place they're leaving, e.g. lack of jobs or poor living conditions and services, fear of political persecution [1 mark]. Pull factors attract people to a new place [1 mark]. They're positive factors about the place they're moving to, e.g. better jobs and more job opportunities, better living conditions and services [1 mark].

Page 69 — Impacts and Management of Population Change

1 Maximum of 15 marks available. This question is level marked.
  HINTS:
  • First, briefly explain what an ageing population is, e.g. 'An ageing population is a population where the proportion of older people (over 65) is increasing'.
  • Then write a section describing and explaining each social effect. E.g. 'An ageing population means there's increased pressure on public services such as hospitals and hospices. More people are needed to care for the elderly, so more carers and nurses will need training'.
  • Next write about the economic effects, e.g. 'There could be increased taxes for the working population. Pensions and services are paid for by taxes, so if there's a greater proportion of older people claiming pensions and support, there'll be higher taxes for the working population'.

Page 71 — Managing Populations — Case Studies

1 Maximum of 10 marks available. This question is level marked.
  HINTS:
  • Remember, evaluate means you need to talk about whether the strategies have been successful or not.
  • Introduce the named example, and say briefly how the population has been changing, e.g. 'Uganda has a youthful population — in 2007, 50% of the population were under 15 and only 3% were over 65. The youthful population is increasing because the birth rate is high — 48 babies are born for every 1000 people each year'.
  • Next talk about any strategies that have been used to manage the population change, e.g. 'The use of contraceptives and family planning has been encouraged in Uganda to try to slow the increase in the youthful population, e.g. the government has brought in free contraceptives like condoms'.
  • Finally, assess the strategy, e.g. 'Family planning clinics aren't widespread, so many people don't have easy access to birth control. This may explain why the strategy has been unsuccessful — since 1991 the birth rate has increased'.

Page 73 — Urban and Rural Characteristics

1 Maximum of 6 marks available. This question is level marked.
  HINTS:
  • Cover one characteristic at a time and for each one explain how population change and migration can affect it, e.g. 'As young, wealthy professionals move to redeveloped urban areas, they increase the wealth of those areas. This can improve inner city areas, but can also mean that the younger original residents can't afford to live in these areas any more'.
  • Remember that the question says 'explain', so you need to say why population change and migration can affect the character of urban areas, e.g. 'Younger people could migrate into urban areas to look for work, which would affect the population structure of the area. This could also affect the provision of services, as younger people (of reproductive age) require more schools and childcare services'.
  • The question only asks you about the character of urban areas, so don't start talking about how rural areas are affected.

Page 75 — Urban and Rural Characteristics — Case Study

1 Maximum of 15 marks available. This question is level marked.
  HINTS:
  • Start by naming your region and the two areas you've chosen, and describe and compare their characteristics. E.g. 'The wards of Fishwick (inner city area) and Lea (rural/urban fringe) can be found in Preston, a city in the North-west of England. Fishwick has lots of high-density, 19th century housing, whereas Lea has large detached and semi-detached houses with gardens and driveways'.
  • Then for each of the different characteristics, describe and explain any effects they have on the social welfare of the residents in your chosen areas, e.g. '74% of people in Lea (rural/urban fringe) described their general health in the 12 months leading up to the 2001 census as 'good'. This was only 64% for Fishwick. This may be because a higher percentage of people in Fishwick live in houses that are likely to be cold and damp due to a lack of central heating — 17.5% of houses in Fishwick have no central heating, compared to 5.6% in Lea'.
  • Include data from the table on p. 74 in your answer, and don't forget to use appropriate terms such as suburban area, occupancy rate, professional sector.

AS-Level Answers

Unit 1: Section 6 — Food Supply Issues

Page 77 — Global Food Distribution

1 Maximum of 5 marks available.
   Intensive farming produces as much as possible from the land *[1 mark]*. It has a high input of capital or labour relative to land area *[1 mark]*. Extensive farming has a low input of capital and labour relative to land area *[1 mark]*. Extensive farming produces less food from the land than intensive farming *[1 mark]*, but has less environmental impact and offers better animal welfare *[1 mark]*.

2 Maximum of 8 marks available. This question is level marked.
   HINTS:
   • Start by *describing the role* of TNCs in the global food industry, e.g. in production, processing and distribution.
   • To get full marks you need to discuss at least three advantages *and* three disadvantages of the involvement of TNCs.
   • Give *specific examples* where possible, e.g. 'Cargill™ employs local people to trade and distribute their produce in Pakistan, which benefits the local economy'.
   • *Discuss* points from *different angles*, e.g. 'Although some local people benefit from the job opportunities that TNCs provide, local companies that can't compete with the TNCs often go bankrupt, and this causes unemployment in the area'.
   • *Link* points together, e.g. '...and this causes unemployment in the area. Another effect of smaller companies going bankrupt is delocalisation of food supplies'.

Page 79 — Changes in Demand

1 Maximum of 4 marks available.
   The demand for high value food exports from developing countries has increased *[1 mark]*. The demand for seasonal products all year round has also increased *[1 mark]*. 1 mark for each reason up to a maximum of two marks. Reasons include: rising incomes *[1 mark]*, an increasing culture of high consumption *[1 mark]*, increased demand for exotic products in developed countries *[1 mark]*.

2 Maximum of 8 marks available. This question is level marked.
   HINTS:
   • To get full marks you need to describe a *range* of environmental issues relating to the globalisation of the food industry (e.g. deforestation, damaging effects of intensive farming, transporting food / food miles).
   • Write a paragraph for each environmental issue, covering the negative environmental impacts. For example, 'Transporting food releases carbon dioxide into the atmosphere. Carbon dioxide is a greenhouse gas, which contributes to climate change'.

Page 81 — Increasing Food Production

1 Maximum of 6 marks available. This question is level marked.
   HINTS:
   • To get full marks you need to *describe* what the technologies and methods are and *give their disadvantages*, e.g. 'Mechanisation brought in by the green revolution involves the use of expensive machines. Farms that can't afford these machines could go bankrupt, leading to unemployment and food shortages'.

Page 83 — Controlling Food Production and Supply

1 Maximum of 15 marks available. This question is level marked.
   HINTS:
   • This question is about EU *market policies* so don't write about non-market policies.
   • EU market policies include: subsidies, tariffs, intervention (including pricing) and quotas.
   • To get full marks you need to cover at least three EU market policies.
   • For each policy you need to describe *what it is*, then *explain how* it controls the level and nature of agricultural production, e.g. 'Subsidies are payments made to farmers. They can control production by encouraging farmers to produce particular products'.
   • Quote facts and give real-life examples where possible, e.g. 'In 2006 EU farmers were paid €1 billion to produce dairy products' and 'Tariffs of 18-28% are applied to imported beef products'.

Page 85 — Managing Food Supply — Case Studies

1 Maximum of 10 marks available. This question is level marked.
   HINTS:
   • First *describe* the strategies used to manage food supplies in Bangladesh.
   • Strategies include: investment in green revolution technologies, investment in improving infrastructure, diversification, free market policies and food aid.
   • Then discuss the sustainability of each strategy you describe, e.g. 'Investment in green revolution technologies is not sustainable because of the high cost and the environmental impact (falling water tables and soil salinisation due to irrigation, water pollution from agrochemicals, and soil degradation due to overcultivation)'.
   • Quote facts and give real-life examples where possible, e.g. 'Between 1974 and 2000 the use of high yielding rice seeds, increased irrigation and increased use of agrochemicals increased rice production from 11.7 to 23.1 million tonnes'.

2 Maximum of 15 marks available. This question is level marked.
   HINTS:
   • To 'compare' the management of food supplies in the two countries you need to look at the similarities and differences between them.
   • Start by describing and explaining the aim of food supply management in Bangladesh and China, e.g. 'Food supply management in Bangladesh aims to provide enough food for the population, as there isn't enough at the moment. Chinese management is focused on producing enough food within the country to be self-sufficient, as it has a history of food shortages'.
   • Next, describe and explain the *similarities* in the management of food supply in China and Bangladesh, e.g. 'Both China and Bangladesh have invested in transportation infrastructure to improve the transport of produce around the country'.
   • Then describe and explain the *differences* between the two countries, e.g. 'Bangladesh has removed subsidies, eliminated quotas and reduced import tariffs to encourage food imports as this increases the amount of food available to feed the population. In contrast, China limits imports in order to protect the market for local produce, encourage production and improve food security'.
   • Discuss the sustainability of the contrasting strategies, e.g. 'Self-sufficiency may not be a realistic and sustainable strategy in China as the limited amount of arable land available is being reduced as the country becomes increasingly urbanised. Free market policies in Bangladesh may not be sustainable because they increase susceptibility to rising food prices, and maintain reliance on food imports — more sustainable solutions may involve improving local production and reducing imports'.

AS-Level Answers

Unit 1: Section 7 — Energy Issues

Page 87 — Energy Resources

1   Maximum of 6 marks available. This question is level marked.
    HINTS:
    • Start off by describing what renewable and non-renewable resources are.
    • Include examples of renewable and non-renewable resources.
    • Explain why it can be difficult to classify resources as renewable or non-renewable (because some resources are only renewable if carefully managed).

2   Maximum of 6 marks available. This question is level marked.
    HINTS:
    • Start off by explaining what the term 'energy mix' means.
    • Then describe the energy mix of a particular country, e.g. 'In 2008 the UK got 33% of its energy from petroleum (oil), 40% from natural gas, 17% from coal, 8% from nuclear and 2% from other sources'.
    • Finally describe how the amount an energy source contributes has changed and give reasons for the change, e.g. 'The use of coal has fallen 40% since 1990. This is due to the closure of coal mines in the UK and a move to less polluting oil and gas'.

Page 89 — Global Energy Distribution

1   Maximum of 15 marks available. This question is level marked.
    HINTS:
    • Start off by explaining why the amount of energy that a country produces could increase or decrease.
    • Then explain why the amount of energy a country consumes could change.
    • Go on to energy trading next. Explain what energy trading is and why it's needed.
    • Describe how the amount of energy that a country needs to import (or is able to export) could change and how this would affect trade, e.g. 'After Brazil discovered new supplies of oil it was able to become energy self-sufficient and no longer needed to import energy'.
    • Explain why some countries might decide to change their energy supplier, e.g. to reduce their dependence on a particular country or to receive imports from a more stable and therefore more reliable region.

Page 91 — Impacts of Energy Production

1   Maximum of 10 marks available. This question is level marked.
    HINTS:
    • Start off by describing why a replacement for fossil fuels needs to be found, i.e. fossil fuel use is environmentally damaging and they will run out.
    • Describe the advantages and disadvantages of nuclear power in relation to fossil fuels, e.g. 'Accidents at nuclear power plants can cause more serious environmental damage than accidents at fossil fuel plants, as radioactive material can be released into the environment. However, if accidents are avoided fossil fuels cause the more serious environmental problems as burning them leads to global warming and climate change, whereas the environmental impacts of nuclear energy are much smaller'.
    • Using your arguments for and against nuclear power, come to a conclusion on whether it's a suitable replacement for fossil fuels. It doesn't matter whether you think that nuclear power is a good replacement for fossil fuels or not, as long as you can give reasons for your choice.

Page 95 — Sustainable Energy

1   Maximum of 4 marks available.
    Biomass is material that is or was recently living [1 mark]. It can be burnt directly to release energy [1 mark]. Biomass can also be used to produce biofuels like ethanol [1 mark], which are burnt to release energy [1 mark].

2   Maximum of 6 marks available. This question is level marked.
    HINTS:
    • 'Compare' means talk about the similarities and differences.
    • Start off by describing the similarities between wave energy and tidal energy, e.g. they both rely on seas/oceans, they both involve the use of turbines to convert the energy into electricity.
    • Then describe the differences between them, e.g. 'Although both wave and wind energy use turbines to generate electricity, tidal energy is a reliable and constant source of energy (as tides are regular events), but wave energy isn't. If there's no wind no waves are produced and that means electricity can't be generated. This is a big disadvantage of wave energy'.

3   Maximum of 8 marks available. This question is level marked.
    HINTS:
    • Start off by explaining why energy use isn't sustainable (i.e. the energy that we use comes from unsustainable sources), but that there are things that can be done to make energy use more sustainable.
    • Then explain that energy use can be made more sustainable by conserving as much energy as possible.
    • Describe the different strategies that conserve energy in the home, e.g. insulation, energy-efficient boilers, features that absorb the Sun's energy.

4   Maximum of 10 marks available. This question is level marked.
    HINTS:
    • Start by explaining why transport isn't sustainable at the moment, e.g. using oil for transport depletes non-renewable resources and releases greenhouse gases.
    • Explain that energy conservation can make transport more sustainable and describe strategies that can conserve energy, e.g. park-and-ride schemes and congestion charging.
    • Then explain how technologies that run off sustainable energy sources can improve sustainability of transport. Describe at least two and explain why they improve sustainability of transport, e.g. 'Hybrid fuel vehicles use more than one source of fuel. If a vehicle runs on an ethanol and petrol mix then less fossil fuels are used and less greenhouse gases are emitted, making the vehicle more sustainable than those that just run on petrol'.
    • Technologies include hydrogen fuel cell vehicles, hybrid fuel vehicles and vehicles that run off other renewable energies, e.g. wave power.

Page 96 — Managing Energy — Case Studies

1   Maximum of 15 marks available. This question is level marked.
    HINTS:
    • Start by describing Chad's energy resources and its energy mix.
    • Explain which aspects of Chad's energy supply aren't sustainable, e.g. 'Currently, oil is used to generate electricity. This is unsustainable as oil will run out one day and its use contributes to global warming. If Chad is to generate electricity in a more sustainable manner, a different energy source must be used'.
    • Describe aspects of Chad's current energy supply that are sustainable or have the potential to be sustainable, e.g. '90% of Chad's energy is supplied by biomass. This has the potential to be a renewable resource, but at the moment it's overexploited, making it unsustainable'.
    • Then explain how supplies could be made sustainable, e.g. 'If the Household Energy Project was successfully implemented over a larger area, more of the country's biomass resources would be better managed, becoming renewable and therefore sustainable'.
    • Include details of any aspects of Chad's energy supply that are a barrier to sustainability, e.g. 'The revenue from Chad's oil exports could be invested in projects to improve the sustainability of energy supplies, e.g. the Household Energy Project. This doesn't happen though, due to the high level of corruption in Chad, which is a serious barrier to sustainability'.

AS-Level Answers

Page 97 — Managing Energy — Case Studies

1 Maximum of 15 marks available. This question is level marked.
HINTS:
  • Start by describing Norway's current energy supply and briefly explain which aspects of it are sustainable, e.g. '50% of Norway's energy is supplied by HEP which is a renewable source of energy and (once established) is sustainable'.
  • Then explain which aspects of Norway's energy supply are unsustainable and what methods are being used to improve their sustainability, e.g. 'Norway relies on oil for transport, which as a non-renewable resource is unsustainable. Biofuels are being developed to replace oil. This will make energy supply for transport more sustainable as long as the sources of materials used to produce the biofuels are managed properly'.
  • Other methods that Norway is pursuing to improve sustainability include development of wind power and development of solar power.

Unit 1: Section 8 — Health Issues

Page 99 — Global Patterns of Health, Disease and Death

1 Maximum of 10 marks available. This question is level marked.
HINTS:
  • Take your time to study any maps or graphs you get — look carefully at the title, key and units.
  • The map shows the global pattern of measles morbidity (measles cases) — don't get this confused with measles mortality (deaths due to measles).
  • The question asks you to 'outline' the pattern — in other words, you should 'describe and explain' it.
  • When describing the pattern, say what the map shows and quote relevant data for the most and least affected countries. E.g. 'The countries most affected by measles are mostly in Africa — some countries had over 50 cases per 100 000 of the population in 2003. Measles morbidity is low in North America, South America and Australia, which had less than 1 case per 100 000 of the population in 2003'.
  • Give reasons why the pattern is like this, e.g. 'The countries mostly affected by measles are those in poorer areas of the world. There's limited health education in Africa so many people aren't informed about how they can avoid infectious diseases, like measles. Also, overcrowded conditions in urban areas of poorer countries means that measles is more likely to spread to other people'.
  • Remember, the general trend is that poorer countries have higher mortality and morbidity than wealthier countries — but always point out any exceptions to the rule. E.g. 'The map shows that measles also affects wealthier countries like Italy'.

Page 101 — Health Care Approaches

1a) Maximum of 2 marks available.
Public health spending is high in Western Europe, North America and Japan [1 mark] and particularly low in Africa, Asia and South America [1 mark].

b) Maximum of 10 marks available. This question is level marked.
HINTS:
  • To get full marks, you need to describe the differences in health care approaches used in poor and wealthy countries — and refer to at least one scheme (case study).
  • Start with the main difference — e.g. 'Poor countries have less money, which is mainly spent on treating diseases, whereas wealthier countries have more money to spend on treatments, prevention and awareness of diseases'.
  • Give examples of the main approaches to health care used in poor and wealthy countries, and describe at least one specific scheme you've studied. E.g. 'Many people live in remote rural areas in sub-Saharan Africa, so have limited access to health care and medical services. One inexpensive health care approach is to train local people as basic health care workers. For example, the Health Extension Programme in Ethiopia trains people who live in remote rural areas as local health care workers. Workers can then deliver basic health care and education to people in their local communities'.

  • Use statistics where relevant, e.g. 'Insecticide-treated bed nets helped the number of malaria cases to fall by 20% in just one year'.
  • The question doesn't ask you to discuss or evaluate, so don't go on about advantages or disadvantages.

Page 103 — The Geography of Disease

1 Maximum of 10 marks available. This question is level marked.
HINTS:
  • Start off by describing the global distribution of malaria — the main countries affected by malaria (with a statistic) and those least affected.
  • Give reasons for the uneven distribution of malaria cases and explain each reason, e.g. 'Mosquitoes that carry malaria can only survive in tropical climates, such as those found in sub-Saharan Africa'.
  • 'Discuss its impact' means you should explain a range of effects that malaria has on a country's health, economic development and lifestyle. E.g. 'Malaria has a big impact on a country's economic development because of the number of people dying, decreasing productivity due to days lost from work, and increasing health care costs'.

Page 105 — Health and Globalisation

1 Maximum of 10 marks available. This question is level marked.
HINTS:
  • Start off by describing what is meant by a Trans-National Corporation (TNC).
  • Explain how TNCs can improve global health and how they can add to global health problems. E.g. 'Pharmaceutical companies can improve health in wealthier countries by choosing to research and produce drugs for diseases that mainly affect wealthier countries, such as drugs for impotency. However, this can add to health problems in poorer countries because money isn't being spent on life-saving drugs for diseases such as malaria and HIV/AIDS'.
  • To get full marks, you need to give a range of examples of how specific TNCs (like GSK or PMI) affect global health. E.g. 'The pharmaceutical company GSK helps to improve global health by investing a large amount of their profit (e.g. £282 million in 2007) in community programmes to help people in need'.
  • You can take a mixture of examples from different case studies if you want, as long as each example backs up whatever point you're making and doesn't just repeat points you've already made.

Page 107 — The Geography of Health in the UK

1 Maximum of 6 marks available. This question is level marked.
HINTS:
  • Start off by describing what's meant by the term 'ageing population'.
  • To describe how ageing populations will affect the provision of health care services, you need to cover examples of services needed by the elderly. For example, 'An ageing population has different health needs, such as the need for more mobile health care services to cope with the increasing immobilised elderly population. This is a particularly important way of providing health care to elderly people in rural areas who don't have family support'.

A2-Level Answers

Unit 3: Section 1 — Plate Tectonics

Page 111 — Plate Tectonics Theory

1 Maximum of 8 marks available. *HINTS*:
- Start by talking about the <u>centre</u> of the Earth — <u>describe</u> the structure of the <u>core</u> (inner and outer) and say <u>what it's made from</u>.
- Then <u>describe</u> the <u>mantle</u>, e.g. 'The mantle surrounds the core and is mostly made up of silicate rocks. The part of the mantle nearest the core is quite rigid. The layer above this is the asthenosphere. It's semi-molten, which means it can flow. The very top bit of the mantle is rigid'.
- Now <u>describe</u> the <u>crust</u> — make sure you mention the <u>differences</u> between the <u>two types</u> of crust. You should also <u>describe</u> the structure of the <u>lithosphere</u>, and say that it's split up into slabs called <u>tectonic plates</u>.
- Draw a <u>simple, labelled diagram</u> to help explain your answer.
- The question doesn't ask about the <u>movement</u> of the plates, so you <u>don't</u> need to talk about it.

2 Maximum of 8 marks available. *HINTS*:
- Start your answer by briefly saying <u>how</u> it occurs, e.g. 'Tectonic plates are moved by convection currents that flow in the asthenosphere'.
- Then <u>describe</u> and <u>explain</u> how a convection current is <u>created</u> in the mantle and core, e.g. 'Radioactive decay of some elements in the mantle and core, e.g. uranium, generates a lot of heat. When lower parts of the asthenosphere heat up they become less dense and slowly rise. As they move towards the top of the asthenosphere they cool down, become more dense, then slowly sink...'.
- Then <u>describe</u> how a convection current <u>moves</u> a tectonic plate, e.g. 'Convection currents create drag on the base of tectonic plates, which causes them to move'.
- Include a <u>labelled diagram</u> of the convection currents and plate movement to help explain your written answer.

Page 113 — Plate Tectonics Theory

1 Maximum of 40 marks available. *HINTS*:
- This is an essay question, so make sure your answer has a <u>clear structure</u> — you'll need an <u>introduction</u>, a description of each of the <u>different types of evidence</u> and a <u>summary</u>.
- In the introduction define the theory of plate tectonics, e.g. 'The Earth's lithosphere is made up of many plates that are moved around by convection currents in the mantle. This is the theory of plate tectonics'.
- Then talk about how the theory has <u>developed over time</u>, e.g. 'In 1912 Alfred Wegener proposed the theory of continental drift. However, he couldn't provide a mechanism that explained how the continents moved. In the 1950s and 1960s more evidence was discovered to support continental drift. Scientists developed the continental drift theory further to create the plate tectonics theory'.
- Then talk about <u>each type</u> of evidence in turn — aim to cover about <u>four</u> different types.
- Start by <u>describing</u> how the evidence <u>supports</u> the theory of plate tectonics, e.g. 'Areas of some continents have rocks of the same age and type. If you fit these continents together, the distribution of the rocks matches up. These rocks must have formed under the same conditions and in the same place in order to match so well. This would only be possible if the continents were once joined'.
- Then give an <u>example</u> of the evidence if you know one, e.g. 'For example, areas of South America and Africa have rocks of the same age and composition. Joining these continents together allows you to match up the distribution of the rock'.
- Then talk about <u>another type</u> of evidence for the theory.
- Make sure you include <u>labelled diagrams</u> when appropriate, e.g. for palaeomagnetism.

Page 115 — Types of Plate Margin

1 Maximum of 8 marks available. *HINTS*:
- Start by <u>stating what a constructive plate margin is</u>, e.g. 'A constructive margin occurs where two plates are moving apart'.
- Say that constructive margins can occur on <u>land</u> or <u>under water</u>.

- Then talk about <u>mid-ocean ridges</u>, include an <u>example</u> of one and explain how volcanoes form along them, e.g. 'Where diverging plates are underwater, a mid-ocean ridge forms. For example, the Mid-Atlantic Ridge is where the Eurasian plate and North American plate are moving apart. Underwater volcanoes can erupt along mid-ocean ridges. The mantle is under pressure from the plates above and when they move apart, the pressure is released...'.
- Talk about <u>rift valleys</u> and give an example of one, e.g. 'Where plates diverge beneath land, the crust between parallel fault lines drops down and forms a rift valley. For example, the East African Rift System has formed where the Nubian and Somalian plates are diverging. Volcanoes are found along the rift system, for example Kilimanjaro and Mount Kenya'.
- You could also describe how earthquakes occur at constructive margins, e.g. 'Earthquakes are a characteristic of constructive margins. This is because the plates don't always move apart in a uniform way, so pressure can build up. When the pressure becomes too much the plate cracks, making a fault line and causing an earthquake'.

2 Maximum of 8 marks available. *HINTS*:
- This question is asking about specific types of <u>destructive plate margin</u>, so make sure you <u>only</u> talk about them.
- The question asks you to <u>compare</u> and <u>contrast</u> the margins — this means you need to say how they're <u>similar</u> and how they're <u>different</u>.
- Firstly, <u>describe</u> what happens at <u>oceanic-oceanic destructive margins</u>, e.g. 'When two plates of oceanic crust are moving towards each other, the denser of the two will be subducted. This forms a deep sea trench. The subducted crust is heated by friction and contact with the upper mantle, which melts it into magma. The magma is less dense than the crust above, so it will rise back to the surface to form volcanoes. Volcanic eruptions will take place underwater and so create island arcs. These are clusters of islands that sit in a curved line, for example the Mariana Islands. As one plate moves under the other they can get stuck. This causes pressure to build up, and when the pressure becomes too much the plates jerk past each other, causing an earthquake'.
- Then point out how <u>continental-continental destructive margins</u> compare, e.g. 'When continental crusts converge they form fold mountains, but there's no volcanic activity as neither is subducted...'.

Page 118 — Volcanic Activity

1 Maximum of 7 marks available. *HINTS*:
- Start your answer by briefly describing <u>what a hot spot</u> is and <u>what causes it</u>, e.g. 'A hot spot is an area of volcanic activity found away from a plate margin. A hot spot is caused by a magma plume — a vertical column of magma that rises up from the mantle'.
- <u>Describe the distribution</u> of the Hawaiian islands, making sure that you include plenty of relevant details from the map. E.g. 'The oldest island is Kauai, at 6 million years old, and the islands become younger in age as you move towards the south-east'.
- Next, <u>give reasons why</u> the islands are distributed in this way. State that the chain of volcanic islands has formed due to the <u>magma plume staying still</u>, whereas the <u>plate has moved</u> over it in a north-westerly direction.

2 Maximum of 8 marks available. *HINTS*:
- Even though your answer won't be that long (it's only worth eight marks), make sure it's got a clear structure — write a short <u>introduction</u> and a <u>section</u> for each of the features.
- In the introduction state that these features are types of <u>extrusive volcanic activity</u>. Explain that they form when groundwater has been heated by magma underground.
- Next, describe what <u>each</u> of the features <u>are</u> and <u>how they form</u>. The question only mentions <u>geysers</u> and <u>boiling mud pools</u> but it'll help you to describe them if you include some information about <u>hot springs</u> as well. E.g. 'Springs are places where groundwater emerges at the surface. If the groundwater source of a spring flows close to an area of recent intrusive volcanic activity, the water is heated and the spring becomes a hot spring. Geysers are a type of hot spring where hot water and steam are periodically ejected from the surface in a fountain. They form when groundwater is heated by magma deep in the crust to over its boiling point...'.

A2-Level Answers

Page 121 — Seismic Activity

1   Maximum of 8 marks available. <u>HINTS</u>:
    * Start by <u>introducing</u> the <u>different types</u> of seismic wave, e.g. 'There are three main types of seismic wave. These are P (primary) waves, S (secondary) waves and Surface waves. Two types of Surface wave are Love waves and Rayleigh waves'.
    * <u>Describe</u> the first type of wave you introduced. E.g. 'P waves push and pull the Earth in the same direction as the wave is travelling. They can travel through both solids (e.g. rock) and liquids (e.g. sea). They travel faster than other types of seismic wave'.
    * Then describe each of the <u>other waves</u> you introduced in turn.
    * Remember, the question's only asking you to <u>describe</u> the types of wave, so you <u>don't need to compare them in detail</u>.

2   Maximum of 8 marks available. <u>HINTS</u>:
    * Begin your answer by <u>briefly</u> saying <u>what tsunamis are</u>, e.g. 'Tsunamis are large waves caused by the displacement of large volumes of water'.
    * Then describe the <u>different causes</u> of tsunamis. For example, start by talking about <u>earthquakes</u>, e.g. 'Underwater earthquakes can cause the seabed to move, which displaces water. Waves radiate out from the epicentre of the earthquake'. Then, mention other causes — e.g. <u>volcanic eruptions</u> and <u>landslides</u>.
    * Finally describe the <u>characteristics</u> of tsunamis, e.g. 'In the open ocean where the water is very deep, the waves travel at high speeds of 500-950 km/h. They have a long wavelength of about 200 km, and a small amplitude of about 1 m'.
    * Make sure you include some <u>figures</u> in your description of the characteristics. For example, give the wavelengths in open water and close to the shore, and say how the speed of the waves changes.

Page 123 — Managing the Impacts of Tectonic Hazards

1   Maximum of 40 marks available. <u>HINTS</u>:
    * This is a 40-mark essay question so the <u>structure</u> of your answer is really <u>important</u>. It may help you to write a <u>brief essay plan</u> before you begin.
    * Introduce your answer by <u>defining</u> what a <u>tectonic hazard</u> is, e.g. 'A tectonic hazard is a hazard caused by movement of tectonic plates. Earthquakes, volcanoes and tsunamis are examples of tectonic hazards'.
    * You then need to <u>describe the different strategies</u> for managing the impacts of tectonic hazards. You should split them logically — you can do this in two ways. <u>Either</u> talk about a type of hazard and the different strategies used to manage it, <u>or</u> talk about the type of strategy (e.g. prediction or planning) and how it can be applied to the different hazards.
    * After each of the strategies you describe, you should <u>critically evaluate</u> them. This means that you should say <u>how successful a strategy is</u>, e.g. 'Earthquake warning systems can detect P waves, but only after an earthquake has begun. These waves travel faster than other types of seismic wave and cause less damage so they can be used as a warning for stronger tremors. However, even far away from the epicentre the warnings may only arrive a few seconds before the strong tremors. This will not give people enough time to prepare for the earthquake or to evacuate'.
    * Try to <u>include examples</u> of the strategies you write about, e.g. 'Japan's Earthquake Early Warning system was set up in 2007. When a P wave is detected warnings are sent out by TV and radio'.

Page 125 — Volcanic Eruption Case Study — Montserrat

1   Maximum of 8 marks available. <u>HINTS</u>:
    * This is a case study question so make sure you choose to write about a volcanic event you know <u>lots about</u>.
    * Give details of the volcanic event you have chosen — include <u>what happened</u>, <u>where</u> and <u>when</u>, e.g. 'The Soufrière Hills volcano on the island of Montserrat erupted on 25th June 1997. The eruption caused rockfalls and the formation of a massive ash cloud and pyroclastic flows'.
    * Write about the <u>economic impacts</u>, <u>social impacts</u> and the <u>environmental impacts</u>. Make it clear in your answer <u>what kind of impact</u> you're writing about. E.g. 'An environmental impact of the eruption is that large areas of the island were covered with volcanic material. For example, the capital city Plymouth was buried under 12 m of mud and ash'.

* The question also asks you to talk about the <u>responses</u> to the eruption. Talk about a few short-term responses (e.g. evacuation) and a few long-term responses (e.g. setting up the Montserrat Volcano Observatory).

Page 127 — Volcanic Eruption Case Study — Mt St Helens

1   Maximum of 10 marks available. <u>HINTS</u>:
    * You need to do <u>two things</u> in this answer:
      1) Describe how management strategies <u>affected the impacts</u>.
      2) Contrast this for two examples (i.e. point out the <u>differences</u>).
    * Make sure you pick two case studies that are different (otherwise you won't have much to talk about).
    * Begin your answer by <u>briefly introducing your two examples</u> (include when and where the eruptions happened).
    * For the main body of your answer, describe the hazard management strategies for one eruption and explain how they affected the impacts. Then say how it was <u>different</u> in your other example. For example, 'At Montserrat, scientists had studied the volcano in the 1980s, but their report was not given a lot of attention. There was no disaster management plan and this meant that the response to the eruption was slow. This was not the case at Mount St Helens, where the USGS were monitoring the volcano prior to the eruption. Before the eruption, they issued warnings and around 2000 people were evacuated from the area'.
    * Don't forget to include <u>facts</u> and <u>figures</u> to back up your points, e.g. 'Despite the Mount St Helens eruption being well managed, the eruption still caused $1.1 billion of damage and killed 57 people'.

Page 129 — Earthquake Case Study — L'Aquila

1   Maximum of 10 marks available. <u>HINTS</u>:
    * You need to talk about <u>at least one case study</u> — you should have studied at least two. Whichever case study (or studies) you write about make sure you know them well enough to be able to quote <u>facts</u> and <u>figures</u>.
    * Start with a brief description of the event — when it happened, where it happened, how big it was on the Richter scale.
    * The question is asking you to <u>critically evaluate</u> the <u>management strategies</u> — so you need to include <u>whether they were successful or not</u>.
    * The easiest way to do this is to <u>describe the strategy</u> then <u>link it to the impacts</u>. For example, 'There were strict building regulations in place in L'Aquila to make sure that new buildings were able to withstand earthquakes. However, some of these buildings were severely damaged or destroyed by the quake. For example, the San Salvatore hospital had been built in west L'Aquila in 2000 and was supposed to be in accordance with the regulations. But the building wasn't strong enough to withstand the earthquake and it collapsed. This hampered the efforts to treat some of the 1500 people injured in the earthquake as patients had to be treated in tents outdoors'.

Page 131 — Earthquake Case Study — Kashmir

1   Maximum of 10 marks available. <u>HINTS</u>:
    * Begin your answer by briefly <u>introducing the two examples</u> you've chosen and <u>describing some of the impacts</u>. For example, 'L'Aquila (Italy) was struck by an earthquake measuring 6.3 on the Richter scale on the 6th April 2009. It killed around 300 people and caused an estimated $15 billion of damage. A stronger magnitude 7.6 earthquake hit the Kashmir region to the north of Pakistan on the 8th October 2005, killing around 80 000 people'.
    * Write about the <u>responses</u> to the two earthquakes, but make sure you <u>compare</u> and <u>contrast</u> them as you go (i.e. point out where they're similar and where they're different). E.g. 'In response to the L'Aquila earthquake ambulances, fire crews and the army were sent in to rescue survivors. The immediate response to the Kashmir earthquake was much slower. Many areas did not receive help for days or even weeks. People had to be rescued by hand without any equipment or help from the emergency services'.
    * Conclude your answer by briefly stating how the different responses affected <u>the impacts</u>. E.g. 'The slow response to the Kashmir earthquake increased the severity of the social impacts as the millions of people made homeless by the quake had little food, shelter or medical supplies. The faster response to the L'Aquila earthquake....'.

A2-Level Answers

Unit 3: Section 2 — Weather and Climate

Page 133 — Climate Basics

1   Maximum of 8 marks available. _HINTS_:
- Start with an introduction where you _state_ that the _vertical structure_ of the atmosphere is divided into _four layers_ — the troposphere, the stratosphere, the mesosphere and the thermosphere.
- Then _describe_ the _four layers_. For each layer, give its _height_, then _describe_ and _explain_ the _temperature_ (whether it increases or decreases through the layer, giving temperature values in °C) and the _turbulence_ (whether the layer is turbulent or calm).
- You need to give _reasons_ for each of the characteristics in each layer.
- You could _draw_ a _simple, labelled diagram_ to show the position of the four layers.

Page 135 — Climate Basics

1   Maximum of 8 marks available. _HINTS_:
- Write an introduction where you _state_ that _more solar radiation_ is received at the _equator_ than the _poles_, and that _winds_ help _redistribute_ this energy to maintain a balance.
- Describe the way that _winds_ are caused by _differences in air pressure_, and are part of _global atmospheric circulation cells_. _Describe_ these cells, e.g. 'They consist of warm air rising creating low pressure zones, and cool air falling creating high pressure zones, and winds moving from the high pressure to the low pressure zones'.
- Use a _simple diagram_ to show Hadley, Ferrel and Polar Cells — include _arrows_ to show the _direction_ of the _surface winds_.
- Starting at the Equator, _describe_ the _air circulation_, e.g. 'At the Equator the sun warms the air and it rises, creating low pressure. As the air rises it cools and flows out to 30° North and South of the Equator, where it sinks, creating high pressure. When the cool air reaches the ground surface it either returns to the Equator or moves towards to the poles in surface winds'.

Page 137 — UK Climate

1   Maximum of 8 marks available. _HINTS_:
- Start by _briefly describing_ the UK climate, e.g. 'The UK climate is temperate, with cool, wet winters and warm, wet summers'.
- Give the _latitude_ of the UK, and explain _how this affects_ climate.
- Describe the _maritime location_ of the UK, and explain _how this affects_ climate e.g. 'The UK is an island surrounded by water. Water gains and loses heat more slowly than land. This means that in the summer, the sea is cooler than the land, and in the winter it is warmer than the land. This causes cool winds to blow from the sea to the land in summer, and warm winds to blow from the sea to the land in winter'.
- Describe the UK's _location_ relative to _global atmospheric circulation_ cells, and explain _how this affects_ climate, e.g. 'The UK is found on the northern edge of a Ferrel Cell, where south westerly surface winds bring warm air from the south. This warm air is rising, creating a zone of low pressure, causing depressions that bring rain throughout the year'.
- Describe the UK's location relative to the _Gulf Stream_, and explain _how this affects_ climate, e.g. 'The Gulf Stream is a warm ocean current which passes along the west coast of the UK. It makes the UK climate warmer than other places at a similar latitude'.

Page 139 — UK Weather Systems

1   Maximum of 8 marks available. _HINTS_:
- Write an introduction _briefly describing_ how a depression begins to form.
- Give a _brief overview_ of the pressure patterns, isobars associated with a depression and say that it flows anti-clockwise.
- Describe the _different stages_ of a depression in a sensible order (e.g. as the warm front passes, as the warm air is overhead, as the cold air passes etc.).
- For _each stage_ of the depression _describe_ the differences in the weather, give _clear reasons_ for the changes and explain _why they occur_. E.g. 'As the warm front passes overhead temperatures increase and there is heavy rainfall. This is because the warm air rises over the body of cold air and water vapour in the warm air condenses, forming clouds and leading to heavy rain'.

- Make sure that the _links_ between the changing _weather_ and the _reasons_ for it are obvious — don't just list the weather types, make sure the causes match up with them clearly.

Page 141 — UK Storms

1   Maximum of 10 marks available. _HINTS_:
- Introduce the storm you've studied — give the _date_ and _location_ of the storm. E.g. 'Between the 15th and 16th October 1987 the UK and France were hit by a severe storm'.
- Write a section on the _impacts_ of the storm. Divide them by economic, social and environmental impacts, and make sure you've got at least one of each. Include as many _specific details_ as you can, e.g. 'There were 18 deaths; around 15 million trees were blown down' etc.
- Write a section on the _responses_ to the storm. Discuss the _immediate responses_ (e.g. severe weather warnings, emergency responses by emergency services and the military etc.)
- Then discuss _longer term responses after the storm_ (e.g. clean up operations, any improvements made as a result of the evaluation of responses).
- Be as _specific_ as you can when giving examples of responses — include times, dates, organisations involved, relevant data etc. E.g. 'As part of the clean up operation forestry workers collected 4 million m³ of timber from fallen trees. It took over two years for all the timber to be collected and stored'.

Page 143 — Tropical Climates

1   Maximum of 8 marks available. _HINTS_:
- Introduce the region you've studied — give the _climate type_ and the _location_ of the region. E.g. 'Monsoon climates are found in coastal regions 5—20° North and South of the Equator'.
- _Describe_ the climate in the region — include winds, average annual temperature range, average annual rainfall and rainfall variation, and _explain_ why the climate is like that. E.g. 'Monsoon climates are hot all year round (between 18—30 °C), and temperature varies by up to 10 °C between summer and winter. It's hot because the sun is high in the sky, so large amounts of solar radiation reach the surface'.
- Give some _example data_ for the location you've studied. E.g. 'Chittagong (Bangladesh) has a monsoon climate. Temperature varies from 19.9—28.4 °C. Rainfall is 2796 mm a year — and it varies from 6 mm in January to 818 mm in July'.
- _Describe_ and _explain_ how _movements of the ITCZ_ affect the climate of your region, e.g. 'The tropical monsoon climate is affected by the seasonal shift of the ITCZ. It moves north of the Equator in summer and south of the Equator in winter. In the wet season the ITCZ is overhead, which brings low pressure and heavy rainfall. The low pressure is over the land, and high pressure is over the ocean so winds blow onshore. In the dry season...'.

Page 145 — Tropical Revolving Storms

1   Maximum of 7 marks available. _HINTS_:
- Start by _describing_ what tropical revolving storms are, e.g. 'Tropical revolving storms are huge spinning storms with strong winds and torrential rain'.
- _State_ that scientists don't know exactly _how they form_, but they do know the _conditions_ needed. Then list the conditions needed.
- _Describe_ their _distribution_ (including their alternative names in different parts of the world).
- Finish up by _explaining why_ they _move west_, away from the Equator and why they lose strength over land.

A2-Level Answers

2   Maximum of 8 marks available. *HINTS:*
- *List* the main *types of responses* — evacuation, planning, education, building techniques and aid.
- For *each type of response* explain *whether it's effective* or *not*, e.g. 'Prediction of storms is important because it allows people time to evacuate safely before the storm hits. If the prediction is made far enough in advance it can significantly reduce the number of deaths. For example, in 1997 a cyclone in Bangladesh only killed around a hundred people because there was enough time to carry out a successful evacuation'.
- Try to give a *balanced evaluation* of a response's effectiveness. E.g. 'Evacuation is not so effective when it's difficult to communicate the evacuation order, for example in remote areas'.
- Try to include *real life examples* where you can, e.g. levees breaking in New Orleans, or Burma's government initially refusing to let aid workers in.

Page 147 — Tropical Revolving Storm Case Study — Katrina

1   Maximum of 10 marks available. *HINTS:*
- The wording 'With reference to one example' means that this is a case study question.
- The first thing to do is *briefly introduce* the case study, e.g. 'Hurricane Katrina hit the south east USA on 29th August 2005. It was a category 4 hurricane when it made landfall'.
- Then *briefly describe* the impacts, e.g. 'More than 1800 people were killed, and hundreds of thousands were made homeless'.
- *Describe* the preparation and responses, and comment on how they *affected the impacts* of the storm. Try and give as many specific examples as you can, e.g. 'The mayor of New Orleans ordered a mandatory evacuation of the town. Around 80% of residents evacuated, which meant that the death toll was much lower than it would otherwise have been'.

Page 149 — Tropical Revolving Storm Case Study — Nargis

1   Maximum of 40 marks available. *HINTS:*
- The word 'discuss' means you need to weigh something up. In this question it means you need to weigh up *whether* (and how) the *level of development* of a country is *related* to the *severity of the impacts* of tropical revolving storms.
- You need to *discuss* why the social impacts are usually higher in less developed countries using *detail* from the *case studies* you've learnt.
- The *main reason* the social impacts are usually higher in less developed countries is that they *don't have the money* to prepare for tropical revolving storms, but don't forget *other things* like the fact that more people depend on agriculture in less developed countries, and agriculture is often badly affected.
- For *each point* you make, use *examples* from your case studies to either back up the point or contradict it, e.g. 'In less developed countries the buildings are poorly constructed and are more easily damaged by storms. Hurricane Katrina in the USA damaged fewer than 100 schools, whereas Cyclone Nargis (a storm of comparable strength) damaged around 4000 schools. This could have been due to poorer quality construction'.
- Include a *paragraph* about the fact that the *economic impact* is usually *higher* in *more developed countries*, e.g. 'The economic impact is usually higher in more developed countries because the buildings and infrastructure damaged are usually worth more money. For example, when Hurricane Katrina hit the USA it caused an estimated $300 billion of damage, whereas when Cyclone Nargis hit Burma it only caused an estimated $4 billion worth of damage. High value infrastructure damaged by Katrina included oil platforms and international shipping ports'.
- Finish off your answer with a *conclusion*, e.g. 'In general, the severity of the social impacts is much higher in less developed countries than more developed countries. However, when the storm is extremely strong even developed countries suffer badly, as no amount of preparation is enough for the force of the storm. Generally, the severity of the economic impact is....'.

Page 151 — Urban Climate Characteristics

1   Maximum of 7 marks available. *HINTS:*
- You need to *describe* the differences *and* suggest *reasons* for them.
- Take your time to *study the table* and pick out the differences.
- Once you've done that write about *each climate characteristic* at a time — say *what the difference* is and *explain why* they might be different, e.g. 'Annual average rainfall is 100 mm higher in City B than in City A. This could be because City B has more pollution than City A, so there are more condensation nuclei in the air to encourage cloud formation'.
- Try to *manipulate* the data if you can, e.g. 'The average number of days without cloud cover is 50% higher in City A than City B'.

Page 153 — Urban Air Quality

1   Maximum of 8 marks available. *HINTS:*
- Begin by stating that there are lots of *different ways* of reducing air pollution in urban areas. Write that *road traffic emissions* cause the majority of pollution in urban areas — so most pollution reduction policies focus on reducing road traffic.
- *Describe in detail* a few *different* pollution reduction schemes you have studied — e.g. congestion charging, using number plates to restrict car use, clean air acts, construction of tall chimneys, alternative fuels.
- For *each scheme/strategy*:
  - i)   *Describe* how the scheme *reduces pollution*.
  - ii) *Describe* any *problems* associated with the scheme.
  - iii) Give *specific examples* of the scheme, including *data* where you can.
- For example, 'Congestion charging involves charging people to use their vehicles in certain places at certain times. It aims to reduce pollution by discouraging people from driving. Problems with congestion charging include increased traffic outside the zone and difficulties enforcing the charge. Congestion charging in Central London was introduced in 2003 and has reduced traffic and emissions by up to 15%'.

Page 155 — Climate Change — Evidence

1   Maximum of 8 marks available. *HINTS:*
- To get full marks you need to *outline* (*describe* and *explain*) a number of sources of evidence for climate change, e.g. ice cores, pollen analysis and indicators of sea level change.
- Structure the answer to have an *introduction*, then separate sections outlining *each* of the sources of evidence, and finish with a *conclusion*.
- In your introduction, define the *key terms* of the question such as 'climate change', e.g. 'Climate change is any significant change in the weather of a region over a period of at least several decades'.
- For each source of evidence, *describe* it and then explain how it's used to determine past climate, e.g. 'Scientists can drill deep into ice sheets (huge masses of ice) to extract cores of ice. Scientists can analyse the gases trapped in the ice cores, and the chemistry of the ice to tell what the temperature was when the ice formed. For example, oxygen has two isotopes — O-16 and O-18. During periods of cold climate, water containing the lighter O-16 is more readily evaporated from seawater....'.

Page 158 — Climate Change — Causes and Impacts

1   Maximum of 8 marks available. *HINTS:*
- Start by *describing how* global warming will *affect the climate* in the UK — include temperature and rainfall patterns.
- Use *specific examples* and *locations* — e.g. 'Summer average temperature is expected to increase by 3.9 °C in Southern England by 2080'.
- *Describe* the *potential impacts* of climate change — e.g. rising sea levels, increased droughts, changing agriculture, and changing habitats.
- For *each impact*, include *specific examples* and *locations* — e.g. 'Sea level is expected to rise by 13-76 cm by 2095. The areas worst affected by sea level rise will be towns and cities on coastal estuaries (e.g. Hull, Cardiff, and London) and low lying areas near the coast (e.g. large areas of Norfolk)'.

A2-Level Answers

Page 161 — Climate Change — Responses

1   Maximum of 8 marks available. *HINTS*:
   - To evaluate the international responses you need to first *explain what the responses are* and then *assess* their *impacts*.
   - *Describe* the responses, giving *examples* to back up your point. *The Kyoto Protocol* is a good example, because it has had mixed success, so there's plenty to write about.
   - For *each response*, give as much *detail* as you can and then *assess* whether the response is *effective*, e.g. 'Developed countries in the Kyoto agreement have agreed to cut emissions by 5% overall. However, not all developed countries signed up to the agreement. Some of the largest polluters (e.g. the USA) chose to stay out of the Kyoto protocol because it would affect their economies. This means that the response is less effective than it could have been because the largest polluters, who have the greatest effect on global emissions, aren't trying to reduce their emissions in the same way'.
   - Think about other *possible problems* with coordinating the international responses to global warming, e.g. problems with enforcing the agreement.

2   Maximum of 40 marks available. *HINTS*:
   - This question is asking to what extent you agree with *the statement*. You need to decide whether you *agree* or *disagree* and *explain* why. It doesn't matter which way you argue, as long as your answer is *relevant to the statement* and you *give reasons* for each point you make.
   - Start with an introduction which *briefly explains* what greenhouse gas emissions are and why we need to reduce them, e.g. 'Greenhouse gases are produced through the burning of fossil fuels. Greenhouse gas emissions need to be reduced because they are one of the main causes of global warming'. Go on to say that changing the energy mix of the UK to include less fossil fuels is an important way of reducing greenhouse gas emissions, but that there are other ways. Then say whether you agree or disagree with the statement.
   - Go through each of the *reasons* why you agree or disagree in turn. *Explain* each *point* in detail, giving a *balanced argument*. E.g. 'There are other ways to reduce greenhouse gas emissions which could be as important as using less fossil fuels. A switch over from fossil fuels takes time and money to carry out, and in the meantime shorter term solutions are needed. Government schemes such as offering financial incentives to encourage people to insulate their homes or buy lower emissions cars can be very effective at reducing emissions. Although the impact from these changes would not be as large as the benefit gained from changing over to renewable sources of energy, it could significantly reduce greenhouse gas emissions while renewable energy sources are developed'.
   - Even if you agree with the statement you should *discuss* a *range* of ways of *reducing greenhouse gas emissions* and say whether they are *important* or not (e.g. saving energy in the home, recycling waste, reducing emissions from transport, buying local produce).
   - Back up your points with *detail* and *facts* where possible, e.g. 'Reducing the burning of fossil fuels in the UK is very important to reducing greenhouse gas emissions because the burning of fossil fuels is responsible for a large part of the UK's emissions. Of the reductions in emissions in the UK by 2020, around 40% will be due to a reduction in the burning of fossil fuels'.
   - At the end write a short *conclusion* — say *whether* or *not* you *agree* with the *statement* and use a sentence or two to *summarise why*. It's important that your conclusion is related to the rest of your answer and that it completes your argument.

Unit 3: Section 3 — Ecosystems

Page 163 — Ecosystem Basics

1   Maximum of 7 marks available. *HINTS*:
   - Discuss the diagram in *order* of the web's hierarchy. Start with the autotroph and move up through the *trophic levels* to herbivores, carnivores/omnivores and top carnivores.
   - Refer specifically to the diagram, using the *names* of the consumers shown rather than talking about food webs and chains in general.
   - Show that you know which consumer belongs to which trophic level, e.g. 'Greenfly is a primary consumer (herbivore) while a sparrow is a primary and secondary consumer because it is an omnivore'.

   - Explain how energy is *lost* in the process of consuming as well as from the consumer themselves, e.g. 'The sparrow loses some energy through respiration and waste, and the sparrowhawk loses further energy in eating the sparrow, as it cannot digest the bones or the feathers'.

Page 165 — Succession

1   Maximum of 8 marks available. *HINTS*:
   - Choose *one* of the *examples* from these pages. *Explain* what your chosen succession is and where you might *find* it. E.g. 'A lithosere is a succession that starts on bare rock, for example on new ground created after a volcanic eruption'.
   - *Describe* the *main stages* of the succession in turn. For each stage, describe the *abiotic conditions*, the *plants* that move in and *why* they can grow there. E.g. 'At first the rock is dry and has no organic matter. The pioneer species are lichens — they can survive on bare rock because they require very little water and nutrients'.
   - Explain the *effects* the plants have on their *environment*, e.g. 'Lichens break down the rock, and release minerals. They also hold some water, this makes the environment less hostile and enables mosses to grow'.
   - Give *specific examples* of plants wherever you can, e.g. 'At the climatic climax, the soil is deep enough for large tree species like ash and oak trees to grow'.
   - Use *scientific terminology*, e.g. pioneer species, decompose, organic matter, out-compete, dominant species, climax species.

Page 167 — Succession

1   Maximum of 10 marks available. *HINTS*:
   - Describe the characteristics of the area, e.g. 'The North York Moors are heather moorland. This is a plagioclimax characterised by large areas of open country covered with heather'.
   - *Describe* and *explain* how the plagioclimax was *created*. Say what the area used to be (e.g. 'The moors used to be an oak forest'.) and describe the activities that led to the plagioclimax. For each activity explain *why* it was carried out (e.g. 'Areas were deforested to make farming easier'), and *how* the activity prevented the climax being reached (e.g. 'Deforestation reduced soil quality').
   - *Describe* why the plagioclimax is *maintained*. E.g. 'The moors are maintained because they provide grazing for sheep and grouse, and because they are an important habitat for rare plants and animals'.
   - *Explain* how the plagioclimax is *maintained*. E.g. 'The heather is cleared by burning every 8-15 years — a few sections are burned each year in rotation. The oldest heather is burned because it gets tough and woody and eventually collapses. Burning encourages new heather shoots to grow (sheep and grouse graze these younger shoots). Burning also destroys other plants, which helps to ensure that the heather remains dominant'.
   - Explain what would happen if the area was *not maintained*. E.g. 'Without burning the heather moorland would eventually become a temperate deciduous forest again, and the moorland plants and animals would lose their habitat and disappear'.
   - Give *specific examples* of plant and animal life. E.g. grouse, sundew, golden plover.

Page 169 — Tropical Ecosystems — Characteristics

1   Maximum of 10 marks available. *HINTS*:
   - *Describe* the climate of a tropical rainforest, e.g. *temperature* and *rainfall*. Where possible, give *percentages* or *figures* to back up your descriptions.
   - *Show* that the climate creates *abiotic conditions* that affect animal and plant life, e.g. 'Soil moisture budget and humidity levels are high because of frequent heavy rainfall, which means that organisms have to be adapted to these conditions'.
   - Concentrate your answer on explaining *each climatic condition* and listing the *effects* it has on the biotic conditions (the animals and plants living in the rainforest). Show that you understand how biotic factors change to suit the climatic conditions.
   - You might do this for a paragraph on the effects of rainfall in the rainforest:
   - *Explain* that the *high temperatures* encourage evaporation which increases the *humidity* levels in the rainforest. In turn, this promotes heavier *rainfall*. Give details for the amount of annual rainfall in the rainforest.

A2-Level Answers

- Link the heavy and continual rainfall to *plant adaptations* in the rainforest. E.g. 'Plant leaves have drip-tips to funnel water, and trees have buttress roots to stabilise their very tall trunks'.
- Link the heavy and continual rainfall to *animal adaptations* in the rainforest. E.g. 'Pond turtles have webbed feet that let them both walk and swim on the wet forest floor'.

Page 171 — Tropical Ecosystems — Human Activity

1   Maximum of 10 marks available. *HINTS*:
- The question asks you to *assess* the impacts of human activity, so you need to write about *what humans do* and what *effect* their actions have on the tropical rainforest.
- Start with a *brief introduction* saying which *biome* you will discuss in your answer and what its *main features* are. Give a *brief summary* of the *main human activities*. E.g. 'Tropical rainforests are a biome with a hot, wet climate and high biodiversity. The primary human activity is deforestation, but overhunting, overfishing and climate change all have significant impacts on tropical rainforests'.
- For *each* human activity *discuss* the *different impacts* (environmental, social and economic) that this activity has on the *rainforest*, and give *reasons why* it is a problem. E.g. 'Deforestation can have negative impacts on the people living in the rainforest. The plants and animals they rely on to make their living may be destroyed, or they may be forced to sell their land so it can be used for commercial agriculture or logging'.
- Make sure you include *some positive impacts* as well as negative impacts, e.g. 'Deforestation often takes place to clear land for mining or agriculture. These activities can have a positive impact on the local economy by providing jobs for local people'.
- Give as much *detail* and *as many examples* as you can. E.g. 'Deforestation causes habitat loss. This affects biodiversity because species that can't adapt or move face decline or extinction. For example, in Brazil the number of endangered species has nearly tripled from 218 in 1989 to 628 in 2008'.

Page 173 — Tropical Ecosystems — Sustainable Management

1   Maximum of 10 marks available. *HINTS*:
- Start with a *brief introduction* that explains the idea of *sustainable management* and *explains why* it is important.
- The question asks you to discuss methods of sustainable management and their effectiveness. This means you need to give details about *different methods* of *sustainable management* and then say *whether they work* or *not*.
- For *each method* start by *explaining how* it works, and *why* it is *sustainable*, e.g. 'Many countries have established national parks and nature reserves to help protect areas of rainforest. Within these protected areas, activities like logging and hunting are banned or heavily restricted. This means that the biodiversity of that area of rainforest is preserved'. Then go on to say *how successful* the method is and *give details* of any *problems*, e.g. 'It can often be difficult to enforce regulations within protected areas — the parks are huge areas of dense rainforest and there may not be enough funds to employ staff to patrol the whole area'.
- For *each* sustainable management *technique* give *examples* and as much *detail* as you can, e.g. 'Selective logging is less damaging than large scale deforestation, and it is permitted in some protected areas. As well as preserving the rainforest and allowing it to regenerate, selective logging can benefit local people. For example, in Papua New Guinea it's estimated that landowners receive ten times as much profit from selective logging as from commercial logging. However, it can still have serious impacts because it leaves a patchy canopy (so soil erosion can be a problem) and felling one tree can bring down as many as thirty others'.

Page 175 — Urban Ecosystems

1   Maximum of 8 marks available. *HINTS*:
- Introduce the *routeways* you will discuss — e.g. roads and railways. You may also have studied canals in class. Discuss at least two different types.
- Write a section for *each routeway*.
- Describe the *ecosystem* — start with the plants, then the invertebrates, then birds and mammals.

- For each group of organisms, *explain* why they are found there. E.g. 'Many different types of flowering plants are found along railways because trains bring seeds from a wide area. A variety of mammals are found because they use the railways as wildlife corridors, have a rich food source and are rarely disturbed'.
- Use *specific examples* / name species wherever possible. E.g. 'Mammals might include mice, rabbits and foxes'.

2   Maximum of 8 marks available. *HINTS*:
- Write an introduction where you *define* the rural/urban fringe and *describe* what ecosystems are found there. E.g. 'The rural/urban fringe is the area of land between an urban and a rural area. The fringe usually has a variety of ecosystems; both rural ecosystems (e.g. woodland, grassland, farmland) and urban ecosystems (e.g. gardens, sports fields, routeways) can be found there'.
- *Describe* the *changes* that may result from urbanisation.
- For *each of the changes*, give a *specific example* and describe its *wider impacts*. E.g. 'Rural ecosystems can be destroyed by new developments, such as a housing estate being built on an area that was previously woodland. A housing estate would generate air and water pollution, which can damage ecosystems — for example water pollution from domestic waste can reduce biodiversity in water courses, which can affect bird populations by reducing their food supply'.

Page 177 — Urban Ecosystems

1   Maximum of 10 marks available. *HINTS*:
- Write an *introduction* — state what an *ecological conservation* area is, and introduce the area you will discuss. E.g. 'Ecological conservation areas have a protected status to ensure that ecosystems are preserved and enhanced. The Mersey Forest is an ecological conservation area that includes a network of woodlands and other ecosystems in Cheshire and Merseyside'.
- *Describe* how the area is *managed*. E.g. 'The Mersey Forest is managed by a partnership of public, private and voluntary organisations, who work together to protect ecosystems, preserve biodiversity and provide green spaces for local people to enjoy'.
- *Describe* the *ecosystems* and species found in the area.
- *Discuss* how *effective* conservation strategies are. List the environmental, social and economic *benefits* specific to the area. Try to include some *percentages* or *figures* that back up your claims. E.g. 'Over 8 million trees have been planted, which has created habitat for woodland wildlife'.
- *Explain* why the conservation strategies have been *effective* (or *not effective*). E.g. 'The Bluebell Recovery Project is a sustainable conservation strategy because the project team are replanting bluebells using only locally sourced bluebell bulbs. British bluebells are being outcompeted by the invasive Spanish bluebell. By planting local varieties the project is helping to protect the native British bluebell and the natural ecosystem'.
- Try to include *negative points* or areas where the scheme has been *less successful* if you can, e.g. 'The Mersey Forest has brought a huge number of benefits to the area, but there is still a lot more that can be done, especially in urban areas. For example, in Liverpool...'.

Page 179 — Global Ecosystem Issues

1   Maximum of 8 marks available. *HINTS*:
- Write an introduction where you *describe* what *fragile environments* are, and give a few *examples*. E.g. 'Fragile environments are ecosystems that are easily disturbed and not able to adapt to change. Examples include coral reefs (which are very sensitive to changes in water temperature) and coastal wetlands (which are very sensitive to changes in water levels)'.
- *Describe* the *threats* to *fragile environments*, e.g. loss of biodiversity, climate change, pollution, extreme weather. Mention that once a fragile environment is damaged, it is extremely difficult or impossible to repair the damage.
- *Explain* that in many fragile environments there is a *conflict* between *conservation* and *exploitation*. Give an *example* of this, e.g. the need to conserve the Amazon rainforest vs. the economic benefits of logging and farming.
- *Describe* the *difficulties* associated with managing fragile environments. E.g. environments crossing international borders, lack of money or expertise, economic reliance on resources from ecosystems, problems of introduced species.

A2-Level Answers

- Give <u>specific examples</u> where you can, e.g. 'The Brazilian economy is dependent on mining (of e.g. gold and iron) — the main mining company alone brought in $9 billion in 2006. However, clearing land to extract metals damages the environment, whilst access roads open up more land for agriculture and logging'.

Page 181 — Global Ecosystems Case Study — Serengeti

1 Maximum of 10 marks available. <u>HINTS</u>:
- Write an introduction <u>describing</u> the ecosystem you have studied — where it is, what type of ecosystem it is, and why it needs protecting.
- Then <u>describe</u> the <u>management strategy</u> used in the ecosystem. E.g. 'The Serengeti National Park is managed by Tanzania National Parks (TANAPA). The management approach involves trying to balance the need to conserve biodiversity with the needs of local people. Schemes include monitoring the ecosystem, protecting priority species, disease monitoring and vaccination programmes, preventing wildfires, local conservation education projects and the creation of four Wildlife Management Areas (WMAs) where local people legally manage wildlife'.
- <u>Discuss</u> how <u>effective</u> the schemes are. Start with a brief introduction where you <u>summarise</u> how <u>effective</u> the strategy has been overall. E.g. 'The schemes have improved understanding between local people and the National Park, but it is still proving difficult to balance wildlife conservation with the needs of local people'.
- Then go into <u>detail</u> about the <u>effectiveness</u> of different aspects of the scheme — describe things that have worked well and explain why, and things that have not worked so well and explain why. E.g. 'The WMAs are having some success. They provide local people with a food source and income, and have helped reduce illegal poaching. But there are some concerns that the areas are being overexploited. Better monitoring may be needed to ensure they are sustainable'.
- Give <u>specific examples</u> and include <u>data</u> where you can. E.g. 'Poaching has declined, and the populations of most species are steadily increasing - the elephant population has increased from 500 in 1990 to 2100 in 2011. However, 40 000 animals a year are still killed by poachers, and many more are caught in traps'.

Page 183 — Global Ecosystems Case Study — Amazon

1 Maximum of 40 marks available. <u>HINTS</u>:
- This is a 40 mark essay question, so the <u>structure</u> of your answer is really important. It may help you to write a <u>brief essay plan</u> before you begin.
- <u>Introduce</u> the <u>two management schemes</u> you will compare. E.g. 'The Serengeti National Park in Tanzania protects a savanna ecosystem, and the Central Amazon Conservation Complex in Brazil protects a rainforest ecosystem'.
- If you're after top marks, <u>compare</u> the two case studies directly rather than discussing them separately.
- <u>Compare</u> the <u>threats</u> to the <u>two ecosystems</u>, and highlight any <u>similarities</u> and/or <u>differences</u>. E.g. 'Both ecosystems are threatened by habitat destruction from human activities (e.g. the need for agricultural land) and overexploitation of resources from hunting'.
- <u>Introduce</u> the <u>management approaches</u> in the two areas, and highlight any similarities and/or differences. E.g. 'The Serengeti National Park is managed by one organisation (TANAPA), whereas the Central Amazon Conservation Complex is managed by several public and private organisations including research bodies and local government. Both areas have a management approach that involves working with local people'.
- <u>Describe examples</u> of projects within the two areas. For each one <u>discuss</u> the <u>similarities</u> and <u>differences</u> between strategies in the two areas and <u>evaluate</u> how <u>effective</u> each scheme has been with the <u>reasons why</u>. E.g. 'Law enforcement and anti-poaching strategies have been implemented in both areas. In the Serengeti, there are daily anti-poaching patrols by air, vehicle and on foot. In the Central Amazon Conservation Complex rangers and guards have been employed to man entrances to the Complex and carry out patrols. These efforts seem to be more effective in the Serengeti National Park than the CACC. This is probably because the Serengeti National Park (15 000 km²) is much smaller than the Central Amazon Conservation Complex (49 000 km²), and has considerably better infrastructure (i.e. roads). The resources in the Serengeti (e.g. park rangers and their vehicles and equipment) are able to cope with its size, whilst there are not enough resources and employees to cope with the size of the Central Amazon Conservation Complex'.

- <u>Compare</u> the <u>ongoing threats</u> to the two ecosystems, and explain the <u>reasons</u> for them. E.g. 'Both areas are still threatened by overexploitation of resources. This is due to continued population growth within and around the protected areas — these people are generally poor and rely on poaching or fishing to feed themselves'.
- Finish your answer with a <u>short conclusion</u>. You could write a sentence or two <u>evaluating</u> how successful the schemes have been overall and what still needs to be done in <u>future</u> to ensure sustainable management.

Unit 3: Section 4 — World Cities

Page 185 — Urban Areas and Urbanisation

1 Maximum of 7 marks available. <u>HINTS</u>:
- Start by <u>describing</u> the <u>general pattern</u> shown. You'll really impress the examiner if you can link urbanisation with economic development. E.g. 'The lowest levels of urbanisation are found in developing countries, for example in Africa and South East Asia countries typically have an urban population of less than 60%'.
- Remember to <u>use the data</u> in your answer as much as possible and mention <u>any anomalies</u> (countries or areas that don't fit the general overall pattern). It will also help your answer stand out if you can identify <u>specific countries</u> — but only do this if you're absolutely certain that you know which one is which. E.g. 'Although the map shows that countries in the developing world typically have the lowest levels of urbanisation, many countries at lower levels of development in South America do not follow this pattern. The majority of the countries have an urban population of 60% or higher and Brazil, Argentina and Chile all have an urban population higher than 80%'.
- The question asks you to <u>comment</u> on the pattern. This means you need to give some <u>reasons why</u> this pattern occurs, e.g. 'Urban population tends to be high in developed countries, because the process of urbanisation has already taken place'.

2 Maximum of 8 marks available. <u>HINTS</u>:
- You could begin your answer by briefly <u>defining urbanisation</u> and explaining that rural-urban migration is the main cause. E.g. 'Urbanisation is the growth in the proportion of a country's population living in urban areas. It is caused primarily by people migrating from rural areas to urban areas'.
- Then go on to say that the <u>reasons</u> people migrate can be divided into push and pull factors, e.g. 'There are many reasons for rural-urban migration. These can be split into push and pull factors. Push factors are the things that drive people away from the rural area, and pull factors are the things that attract them to the urban area'.
- Then talk about the different <u>push</u> and <u>pull factors</u> that may <u>cause</u> rural-urban migration. The command word in the question is <u>discuss</u>, so remember to talk about the effect of that factor on the population. E.g. 'Agricultural activity can cause problems like desertification. This means that fertile land becomes unproductive. This affects the people who are dependent on the land for food, and can force them to move away to urban areas'.

Page 187 — Urbanisation

1 Maximum of 40 marks available. <u>HINTS</u>:
- It's important to <u>structure</u> your essay. Start with an introduction where you introduce your <u>argument</u>. In the main body of the answer you should go through all the <u>points</u> that <u>support</u> your argument, then finish your essay off with a <u>conclusion</u>.
- In your <u>introduction</u> you should <u>define urbanisation</u> and <u>introduce</u> any case studies that you're going to use, e.g. 'Urbanisation is the growth in the proportion of a country's population that live in urban areas. Urbanisation is occurring rapidly in Mumbai in India...' You also need to <u>introduce your argument</u>. Remember it doesn't matter which way you argue, as long as you answer the question, e.g. 'Although for many of the problems caused by urbanisation there are effective solutions, they do not always work for everyone....'.

A2-Level Answers

- Then discuss the _problems_, their _solutions_ and how _successful_ they've been. E.g. 'More than half of the population of Mumbai live in slums. The slums are cramped and homes are poorly built. Dharavi is one of the largest slums in Mumbai and the 2004 Dharavi Redevelopment Project aimed to address the problems there, but it was not well received by residents. The project aimed to move people out of the slum and build apartments for them to live in instead. However, the scheme has been unpopular with residents who worry that they will no longer be able to run small-scale industries such as recycling, and that community spirit will be lost'.
- You need to _relate each point_ you make back to the _question_, e.g. 'The situation in Dharavi shows that it can be difficult to find a solution that works well for everyone involved'.
- You could bring in information from _different parts_ of the course. For example you could write about Curitiba (see p. 204), e.g. 'Increased congestion and pollution is often an impact of urbanisation. Curitiba is a city in Brazil where a number of different solutions have been found to reduce car use and decrease congestion and pollution, such as creating bus lanes on the city's main highways to make journeys by public transport quicker. The schemes have been successful and air pollution is lower in Curitiba than in other Brazilian cities'.
- In your concluding paragraph you have to say '_to what extent_' you agree with the statement. _Don't_ make any _new points_ in your conclusion, just _summarise_ your argument.

Page 189 — Suburbanisation

1   Maximum of 8 marks available. _HINTS_:
- The question asks about _impacts_ so remember to talk about _different areas_ within the urban environment, such as the suburbs and the city centre.
- The command word is '_outline_', so you should _describe_ the impacts of suburbanisation and _explain_ why they occur. E.g. 'Shops and offices in the CBD may close and move to the suburbs because the rents are usually lower. This can leave empty buildings in the CBD, which can lead to the CBD becoming run down'.
- Even though the question doesn't specifically ask you to use a case study, _you can still use one_. You could use Surbiton or another example you have studied. E.g. 'Suburbanisation can also lead to congestion in the suburb as car ownership is high and lots of commuters drive into the city centre for work. This is the case in Surbiton, where the large number of commuters causes congestion on routes into London'.

Page 191 — Counter-urbanisation

1   Maximum of 8 marks available. _HINTS_:
- You could begin your answer by _defining_ the process of _counter-urbanisation_. E.g. 'Counter-urbanisation is the movement of people from large urban areas to smaller settlements and rural areas'.
- Then discuss the _impacts_ of counter-urbanisation. Remember to use a case study example and include _lots of facts and figures_. You could start with a negative impact, e.g. 'Counter-urbanisation can result in increased house prices in rural areas, which means local people are less able to afford to buy or rent houses. Commuters often earn higher wages, so they can afford to pay more for housing. This has been the case in St Ives in Cambridgeshire, where the average price of a detached house rose from £130 000 to £291 000 between 2000 and 2010'.
- Make sure you talk about positive impacts too, e.g. 'Some local businesses, such as pubs with restaurants, may receive more customers because the people moving to the area have a larger disposal income than the existing residents. This can help improve the local economy'.

Page 193 — Re-urbanisation

1   Maximum of 7 marks available. _HINTS_:
- Look closely at the photograph and think about anything that could be a result of _re-urbanisation_. For example, you could talk about _buildings_, _public spaces_ and _transportation links_.
- For _each piece_ of evidence, _explain why_ it suggests that re-urbanisation has taken place. E.g. 'In the centre of the picture there are modern, high density tower blocks. These look newly built and could have been designed to attract businesses into the area. There are also cranes in the photograph, which shows that new buildings are still being constructed as the area is further regenerated'.

Page 195 — Urban Decline and Regeneration

1   Maximum of 10 marks available. _HINTS_:
- Start your answer by _defining gentrification_. E.g. 'Gentrification is the regeneration of an area by a wealthier group who move into a run down area and improve their own housing'. Then _introduce_ your case study.
- The question asks you to discuss the _changes_ that have taken place due to gentrification, so you need to _describe_ the changes and talk about their _effects_ on the area. E.g. 'Middle class people moving into the area improved the Georgian and Victorian properties in Islington (for example by restoring original features). This increases the quality of the housing in the area, but it also increases house prices. An increase in house prices means that original residents cannot afford to buy or rent in the area and may be forced to move elsewhere or into social housing'.
- Remember the question is asking you to use a _case study_, so use _facts and examples_ from your case study to back up your points wherever you can.

Page 197 — Urban Regeneration

1   Maximum of 10 marks available. _HINTS_:
- _Briefly explain_ what _urban regeneration_ is and why it is needed. Then explain what a partnership scheme is.
- Introduce your _case study_. Give _details_ about _where_ it is and _why_ regeneration was needed.
- Then go on to _describe_ the _aims_ of the partnership scheme and _how_ regeneration was carried out, e.g. 'The Hulme City Challenge Partnership in Manchester aimed to improve living conditions by building a range of new housing'.
- Lastly, you need to _evaluate_ how successful the scheme has been. Make sure you give a _balanced answer_, e.g. 'The Partnership Scheme has had positive impacts in Hulme. Unemployment has decreased because jobs have been created in new industries that have moved to the area. However, Hulme is still a poor area, and 47.5% of the people there live in social housing'.
- Use _details_ and _facts_ in your answer wherever possible, e.g. 'Hulme has become a more popular place to live since its redevelopment — its population is estimated to have grown by 3.3% since 1992, compared to a 0.2% increase in the city as a whole'.

Page 199 — Retailing

1   Maximum of 8 marks available. _HINTS_:
- Introduce your answer by _describing_ what an out-of-town retail centre is and state that shops have moved out of city centres. Briefly describe the general characteristics of out-of-town shopping centres and why they are popular, e.g. 'Large out-of-town shopping centres are easy to access by car, provide free parking, and have many shops all under one roof. This makes them popular with customers'.
- Then introduce your _case study_. Describing _where_ it is, _when_ it was built, how much it _cost_, _who_ comes to shop there etc.
- Now _describe_ the facilities it provides and _why_ it is popular, giving as many _details_ as possible. E.g. 'The Trafford Centre in Manchester has over 200 shops, but it is not just used for shopping — it also has extensive leisure facilities including a 1600 seat food court, ten pin bowling, an indoor climbing wall and crazy golf'.

Page 201 — Redeveloping Urban Centres

1   Maximum of 10 marks available. _HINTS_:
- Introduce your case study. Give some _brief background information_, e.g. where it is, why it needed redeveloping.
- Then go on to _discuss the ways_ in which redevelopment was carried out. Give as much _detail_ as you can, e.g. 'In Manchester city centre a number of old buildings were renovated, for example the Manchester Corn Exchange was refurbished and is now a upmarket clothing mall'.
- The question asks you to _evaluate_. This means you need to say _how successful_ the scheme has been, e.g. 'In Manchester the redevelopment has had a number of positive impacts. An increase in good quality residential property has led to an increase in the population of the city centre. The population doubled between 2003 and 2009. However there are still problems in Manchester...'.

A2-Level Answers

Page 203 — Sustainability in Urban Areas

1 Maximum of 8 marks available. _HINTS:_
- Start by _explaining_ the idea of _sustainability_, and explain why _improving waste management_ is an important way of _improving sustainability_ in urban areas.
- Now go on to talk about _different methods_ of waste disposal. You could start with landfill and _explain why it is not sustainable_, e.g. 'In the UK landfill is still an important method of waste disposal and it accounted for nearly 50% of waste disposal in 2008. Landfill is cheap in the short term, but there are other much more sustainable methods of waste management (e.g. recycling). Landfill is unsustainable for a number of reasons: landfill sites can pollute groundwater if they aren't properly lined...'.
- Then go on to give details about _other types_ of waste disposal — make sure you say _how_ they can make waste management more sustainable.
- Include _facts_ and _examples_ wherever possible, e.g. 'Energy recovery has been used successfully in Sheffield, where 140 buildings in the city centre are heated by ERF, preventing the release of 21 000 tonnes of CO_2 each year'.

Page 205 — Sustainability in Urban Areas

1 Maximum of 10 marks available. _HINTS:_
- Start by _explaining briefly_ what sustainability is. Then explain why an increasing number of cars in urban areas is not sustainable, e.g. 'As populations in urban areas increase, the number of people driving cars increases too. Having lots of people travelling by car in urban areas isn't sustainable because cars produce greenhouse gas emissions and air pollutants which damage the environment. It also increases congestion, which means people's journeys are longer and their transport needs aren't being met'.
- Discuss the _different ways_ of making transport more sustainable. You could start by saying that public transport is more sustainable than private cars because it produces less emissions per passenger.
- Then go on to give details about different improvements to transport which make it _more sustainable_. For each point _give as much detail as you can_ and _examples_ wherever possible, e.g. 'High occupancy vehicle lanes have been introduced in some places to encourage car sharing. In Toronto in Canada, the introduction of high occupancy vehicle lanes to Highway 403 increased car sharing from 14% to nearly 40% in three years. This increases sustainability of transport because people are travelling in fewer cars, so emissions and congestion are reduced'.
- You need to say _how successful_ the schemes have been in the examples you have given, e.g. 'Some urban areas have taken specific measures to encourage residents to cycle instead of drive. In Freiburg in Germany, about half of the 120 one-way streets restrict motorists to travelling one way, while cyclists are allowed to travel in both directions. This reduces journey times for people cycling, but not for people driving, so it may encourage more people to cycle. In addition, there are designated, secure bike parking spots at public transport 'bike and ride' facilities, which makes it safer to leave your bike. These measures have been very successful — the proportion of journeys travelled by car fell from 38% in 1982 to 32% in 2007. Making cycling more popular is a good way of increasing sustainability because cycling produces no emissions and does not cause congestion'.

Unit 3: Section 5 — Development and Globalisation

Page 207 — Development Basics

1 Maximum of 8 marks available. _HINTS:_
- Start by giving a _brief introduction_ about what sorts of things _change_ as a country develops. Say that the changes can be economic, demographic, social, political and cultural.
- Then go on to give _more detail_ about each _type_ of change. You could mention how the change is _measured_, e.g. 'As a country develops, a number of economic changes take place, such as an increase in wealth. This can be shown by measures such as GDP (Gross Domestic Product), which is the value of goods and services that a country produces in a year. Increased GDP means that a country has become more wealthy'.

- The question is asking you to _outline_ the changes, so you could link some of the changes together to _explain_ why they are happening, e.g. 'An increase in wealth as a country develops can cause other social changes to take place. For example, when a country is more wealthy, fewer people are living in poverty (without basic human needs such as water and food)'.

Page 209 — Least Developed Countries

1 Maximum of 7 marks available. _HINTS:_
- The question is asking you to _use the data_. Before you start writing your answer you could _jot down the key points_ that you notice in a short plan.
- The question is asking you to _comment_ on the level of development for each of the countries shown. So, first you need to show what the data says about the level of development of each country, e.g. 'The data shows that Angola has many of the characteristics of a country at a very low level of development, such as a high birth rate. The group of countries that make up the Least Developed Countries (LDCs) all tend to have high birth rates'.
- _Manipulate_ the data wherever you can, e.g. 'In Angola the birth rate is almost 4 times that of Denmark'.
- You also need to _link together_ what the data says about the different countries and _explain_ these differences, e.g. 'The literacy rate in Denmark (99% for both men and women) is considerably higher than in Angola (82.7% for men and 58.1% for women). There is also a discrepancy between the literacy of men and women in Angola: more men are literate than women. This is not true in Denmark, where the percentage is the same for men and women. This is because countries which are less developed tend to have inequalities between men and women...'
- Point out any data that is _anomalous_, e.g. 'As countries develop you would expect less of their income to come from agriculture. So we would expect that Angola would get the most of its GDP from agriculture and Denmark the least. The data actually show that Denmark gets more of its GDP from agriculture than South Africa, even though all the other data suggest that Denmark is a more developed country than South Africa'.

Page 211 — Global Groupings and Development

1 Maximum of 10 marks available. _HINTS:_
- Start your answer with a bit about the grouping of nations — you could _briefly introduce_ the EU to show _why_ it came about and _who_ it involves. E.g. 'The EU is an economic and political grouping of 27 European countries. It formed to help Europe recover after the second world war, and its aims were to promote peace and economic growth for its members'.
- Now go on to _discuss_ the consequences of global groupings. Make sure you support your points with _examples from the EU_. E.g. 'Global groupings can bring economic benefits to their members. For example, the EU has a free trade agreement, which allows members to trade with each other without barriers such as tariffs or quotas. This leads to increased trade and promotes economic development. You can see this in the UK by looking at figures such as the percentage of GDP made up by trade with EU countries...'.
- The question is asking you to _discuss_ the consequences, so give a _balanced argument_, e.g. 'There are negative impacts of trade agreements too. Although they increase trade between member countries, they exclude countries that are not members. For example, in the EU, the Common Agricultural Policy puts quotas and tariffs on trading with countries outside the EU. This makes it more likely that EU members will trade with each other, rather than with countries outside the EU'.

Page 215 — Development Issues

1 Maximum of 40 marks available. _HINTS:_
- Remember, for this question you only have to write about _one_ of the issues.
- The command word is 'discuss'. This means you need to give a _balanced answer_. Briefly plan the points you are going to make before you start writing. To get _top marks_, you should try and discuss the _positive_ and _negative_ points _together_ rather than discussing all the positives and then all the negatives.

A2-Level Answers

- Start by giving an <u>introduction</u> to the issue you've chosen, e.g. for economic sustainability versus environmental sustainability you could say, 'Sustainable development is about meeting the needs of people today, so that the economy can grow, without compromising the ability of people in the future to meet their own needs. For development to be truly sustainable there needs to be both economic and environmental sustainability...'.
- <u>Use your case study</u> to discuss the issue in the question. Give as much <u>detail</u> as you can and make sure that you always <u>link</u> the points you make <u>back to the question</u>, e.g. 'It is difficult for a country to develop in a way that makes its economy sustainable, whilst maintaining environmental sustainability. For example, in Sarawak (a state in Malaysia) one way that the economy has developed has been an increase in commercial agriculture. The main crop is palm oil which is grown for export (it accounts nearly for 6% of Sarawak's exports). Although palm oil cultivation is economically sustainable, because it can continue to bring revenue into the country in the future, it is not environmentally sustainable...'.
- For a 40 mark question like this you need to use your knowledge from the <u>whole course</u>. You could bring in what you've learnt about sustainability from the other topics.
- Finish with a <u>conclusion</u>. Give an <u>overview</u> of your discussion, and say what <u>you think</u> about the issue. Make sure that the conclusion is <u>balanced</u> though — back up what you say about both sides of the discussion with evidence from your answer.

Page 217 — Globalisation Basics

1   Maximum of 10 marks available. <u>HINTS</u>:
- Start with a <u>brief introduction</u> to your answer, e.g. 'Globalisation is the process of the world's economies, political systems and cultures becoming more strongly connected to each other. The movement of manufacturing away from developed countries has been an important factor in globalisation'.
- Then explain <u>what changes</u> in patterns of production have taken place, e.g. 'In recent decades, manufacturing has decreased in developed countries and increased in developing countries. There are a number of reasons for this. Firstly, labour costs are often lower in developing countries. By relocating manufacturing abroad companies can save money...'.
- Now discuss <u>how</u> these changes have promoted globalisation by making countries more interconnected, e.g. 'As production moves away from developed countries, these countries become reliant on goods produced abroad, so international trade increases. This means that less developed and more developed countries become more interconnected through trade'.
- Use <u>examples</u> to back up your points wherever possible, e.g. 'A variety of different products that used to be made in the UK are now made abroad. For example, the vacuum cleaner manufacturers Dyson moved their production operations from the UK to Malaysia in 2002'.

Page 219 — Trans-National Corporations (TNCs)

1   Maximum of 10 marks available. <u>HINTS</u>:
- First, write a short <u>introduction</u> to your answer, e.g. 'Trans-National Corporations (TNCs) are companies that operate in two or more countries. They start in one country (their country of origin) and as they grow, parts of the business, e.g. manufacturing, services and retail, move elsewhere (their host countries)'.
- You need to <u>discuss</u> the social, environmental and economic impacts of TNCs, so first you could write about the <u>positive</u> impacts, e.g. for economic impacts you could say, 'TNCs can provide jobs in host countries. This can create increased economic activity in the host country through the multiplier effect: higher employment means the local population has a higher disposable income which they spend locally. This increased wealth then attracts other businesses, who may provide even more employment'.
- Then you could talk about how TNCs can also have <u>negative</u> economic impacts, e.g. 'However, TNCs can also have a negative effect on employment in host countries. They may out-compete local businesses which can cause them to shut down'.
- Make sure you discuss <u>economic</u>, <u>social</u> and <u>environmental</u> impacts on the host country.

Page 221 — TNC Case Study — Wal-Mart

1   Maximum of 7 marks available. <u>HINTS</u>:
- You should describe the <u>general patterns</u> on the map, but the question is also asking you to <u>comment</u>, so you should try to explain the <u>reasons</u> for the patterns you spot. E.g. 'The manufacturing operations for the TNC are all located in South East Asia, for example, in China, India and Malaysia. It's likely manufacturing is based in these countries to take advantage of the lower labour costs found in newly industrialised countries (compared to wealthier nations such as the USA, where the headquarters are located)'.
- Make sure you describe and comment on <u>all</u> the different types of operations.
- Comment on any <u>anomalies</u> that you see in the general patterns and try to <u>explain</u> them, e.g. 'All the research and design centres are in highly developed countries such as the USA, the UK and Japan except for one which is in China. This is likely to be because the TNC needs to have a research and design centre close to the market where they are selling the products'.

2   Maximum of 8 marks available. <u>HINTS</u>:
- The question is asking you to write about an <u>example</u>, so you need to write about a <u>case study</u>. Give a <u>brief introduction</u> to your case study, e.g. 'Wal-Mart is a retail TNC which started in the USA in the 1960s. It has become the largest retail TNC in the world and operates in North and South America, Europe, Asia and Africa'.
- Discuss the impacts in the host countries and country of origin <u>together</u> but always make it <u>clear</u> which one you are talking about, e.g. 'As Wal-Mart has grown it has bought more and more of its manufactured products from outside the USA. This has had a negative impact on manufacturing in the USA, where the industry has declined and there have been job losses. However, in its host countries this change in production has had a positive impact, providing jobs in manufacturing in countries such as China'.
- Make sure you include both <u>positive</u> and <u>negative</u> impacts.
- The question is asking you to <u>assess</u> the impacts so you could write a short <u>conclusion</u> — write about whether you think the TNC has had an overall positive or negative impact on the host countries and country of origin. Whatever conclusion you reach, make sure you <u>back it up</u> with the points you have made in your answer.

Page 224 — Newly Industrialised Countries (NICs)

1   Maximum of 10 marks available. <u>HINTS</u>:
- Start your answer by <u>briefly describing</u> what NICs are, e.g. 'NICs (Newly Industrialised Countries) are countries that are rapidly developing as their economy moves from being dependent on primary industry to secondary or tertiary industry'.
- The question is asking you to <u>explain</u> the economic growth of NICs, so you need to say <u>why</u> they became wealthier. You could divide your answer between countries that grew because of investment in manufacturing, and countries that grew because of investment in services.
- For both of these you should make sure that you refer to one or more countries that you have studied. E.g. 'The first wave of NICs was the Asian Tiger economies (Hong Kong, Singapore, South Korea and Taiwan) who experienced massive economic growth from the 1960s onwards. For example, the GNI per capita of Hong Kong grew from $1800 in 1973 to $32 950 in 2008. One of the main reasons that NICs grew economically was investment that came from foreign TNCs, who set up the manufacturing parts of their business in these countries. TNCs invested in manufacturing in the Asian Tigers for lots of reasons. There was a large and cheap workforce available...'.

Page 225 — Growth in the 21st Century

1   Maximum of 8 marks available. <u>HINTS</u>:
- The question is asking you to <u>outline</u>, so you need to <u>describe</u> how new markets and new technologies have affected economic growth in the 21st century and also <u>explain</u> a bit about why this has happened.
- Make sure you're really <u>clear</u> about the meaning of the terms you are using, e.g. 'New markets in the 21st century are countries that are becoming more open to international trade and investment, and are often rapidly developing as well'.

A2-Level Answers

- First you could discuss the impact of <u>new markets</u> on economic growth, e.g. 'The emergence of new markets has been an important driving factor in the growth of the global economy in the 21st century. NICs such as China, India and Brazil are all countries that are rapidly developing and have huge populations. As these countries develop, the people who live there become more wealthy. This creates enormous opportunities for global companies to increase their profits and grow by exploiting these new markets'.
- Make sure you discuss <u>everything</u> that's asked for in the question — you also need to discuss the effect of <u>new technologies</u> on global economic growth in the 21st century.

Unit 3: Section 6 — Contemporary Conflicts and Challenges

Page 227 — Causes of Conflict

1   Maximum of 8 marks available. <u>HINTS</u>:
- Write an <u>introduction</u> to your answer — for example, state that conflicts can occur when people are competing for the <u>same resources</u>.
- Include some <u>examples</u> of resources that people might compete for, e.g. territory, water, buildings and oil.
- Then, for <u>each type of resource</u> describe a <u>specific example</u> of a conflict, e.g. 'The Nile River is a source of water for 10 countries in North East Africa. There is conflict between the downstream countries (Egypt and Sudan) that use most of the water, and the upstream countries (including Uganda, Rwanda, Ethiopia and Tanzania) that want to use more water'.
- Include <u>names</u>, <u>facts</u>, <u>dates</u> and <u>figures</u> where you can.

Page 229 — Characteristics and Resolution of Conflict

1   Maximum of 8 marks available. <u>HINTS</u>:
- The question is asking you to <u>outline</u> the <u>ways</u> to resolve a conflict, so you need to talk about a few different methods and <u>explain</u> how they may lead to a resolution.
- You could <u>divide your answer</u> between the ways to resolve <u>different levels</u> of conflict, e.g. international, national, regional and local conflicts.
- Introduce each method <u>one at a time</u>, e.g. 'Diplomacy is negotiation between countries to resolve an international conflict. Diplomats and ambassadors are trained negotiators who can represent a country to negotiate agreements, alliances or peace treaties'.
- Don't just <u>describe</u> the method — outline why it <u>may</u> or <u>may not</u> be successful. 'Diplomats are trained to act reasonably and respectfully, however cultural differences between countries mean that diplomats have to be aware of different negotiation styles and different protocols that countries have'.

Page 231 — Local Resource Conflict Case Study — Newbury Bypass

1   Maximum of 10 marks available. <u>HINTS</u>:
- <u>Introduce the conflict</u> you have studied — include <u>when it started</u>, what <u>caused</u> the conflict and what the <u>local resource</u> involved was, e.g. 'The Newbury bypass was proposed in 1982 to help solve congestion in the town after the volume of traffic had increased to 50 000 vehicles per day. There was conflict between those who supported the proposal and those who objected to it. Many people believed the bypass would not solve the traffic problems and there were many concerns about the impacts the bypass would have on the natural environment around Newbury'.
- <u>Evaluate</u> the processes which operated to <u>resolve</u> the conflict — begin by describing what was done. E.g. 'There was a public enquiry in 1988 where 147 witnesses gave evidence to a government appointed inspector either supporting or opposing the bypass'.

- Then <u>comment</u> on whether the process was <u>successful</u>. E.g. 'In 1990, following the enquiry, the government announced the bypass would go ahead. However, the groups who opposed the bypass still did not agree to its construction and the conflict continued. As a result, in 1994 there was a review by the Highways Agency to consider alternatives. Again it was decided that the bypass would go ahead despite continued opposition. As one side was still unhappy with the proposal it could be argued that the process was not a success'.
- Make sure you include lots of <u>specific information</u>, <u>details</u>, <u>facts</u> and <u>dates</u>.

Page 233 — International Conflict Case Study — Gaza and the West Bank

1   Maximum of 8 marks available. <u>HINTS</u>:
- <u>Briefly introduce the conflict</u> you have studied. The question is about the <u>impacts</u> of the conflict so you <u>don't need to give lots of detail</u> here, but you should give some background. E.g. 'There is conflict in the Middle East between Jews and Arabs over who has the right to the land that was formerly known as Palestine. In 1949 Palestine was divided into three different territories — Israel (a Jewish nation), Gaza and the West Bank (both Arab nations under the control of Egypt and Jordan respectively). Armed conflict was happening between Jews and Arabs leading up to this division, and has been continuing since 1949'.
- Split the impacts into <u>economic</u> and <u>environmental</u> and make sure you <u>write a section for each</u>. E.g. 'It's difficult to estimate the cost of such a long conflict, however it's likely to have cost many trillions of US$ since 1948. This has hindered economic development in the region because large amounts of money have been spent on security instead of development'.

Page 235 — International Conflict Case Study — Afghanistan

1   Maximum of 10 marks available. <u>HINTS</u>:
- Make sure you <u>introduce</u> any case studies you include in your answer, e.g. 'A major international conflict began in Afghanistan in October 2001. As a response to the terrorist attacks of September 11th 2001 (carried out by al-Qaeda), the USA and an international coalition force invaded Afghanistan. Their objectives were to prevent further terrorist attacks by ensuring that Afghanistan could no longer be used as a safe haven for terrorists, destroying al-Qaeda and bringing Osama Bin Laden (the leader of al-Qaeda) to trial'.
- You are only being asked about <u>social impacts</u> — make sure you discuss <u>at least four or five</u> of these in <u>detail</u>. Don't talk about economic or environmental impacts because you <u>won't get any marks</u> for them.
- Remember to <u>give examples</u> from <u>at least one</u> case study you have learnt and include facts and data where you can, e.g. 'The war in Afghanistan has had a wide range of social impacts on both Afghanistan and the other countries involved. For example, the conflict has led to an estimated 11 000 civilian deaths between 2001 and 2009. These deaths were the result of actions by both the Taliban and the coalition forces. Coalition forces themselves have suffered 1832 losses between 2001 and 2010'.

Page 237 — International Conflict Case Study — Darfur

1   Maximum of 40 marks available. <u>HINTS</u>:
- For an answer worth 40 marks it's really important that you <u>plan the structure</u> of your answer <u>before you start writing</u>.
- Begin with an <u>introduction to the conflict</u> you have chosen, e.g. 'Darfur is a region in the west of Sudan in Africa. An international conflict started there in February 2003 when rebel groups attacked government troops. The main rebel groups are the Sudan Liberation Army (SLA) and the Justice and Equality Movement (JEM)'.
- You could mention some of the <u>causes</u> of the conflict too, but you don't need too much detail here — remember that the question is asking about the <u>impacts</u> of the conflict.
- Then, <u>examine</u> the <u>impacts</u> of the conflict. To do this, you need to do more than just describe what the impacts are, e.g. think about how the <u>different groups of people</u> have been affected by the impacts.

A2-Level Answers

• You should also split your answer up into the _different types of impact_ — _social_, _environmental_ and _economic_. E.g. you could write about the social impacts first, 'By 2010, the conflict in Darfur had caused 2.7 million people to flee their homes. Many of these people have become refugees and now live in camps near Darfur's main towns. Living in these camps has lots of negative impacts on people. For example, due to overcrowding they have limited access to clean water and healthcare. This can make other problems worse, such as the spread of disease...'.

Page 239 — Separatism

1 Maximum of 10 marks available. _HINTS_:
• _Begin your answer_ by defining separatism. E.g. 'Separatism is when a smaller group of people want more independence from a larger group of people'.
• _Briefly introduce_ your _case study_. E.g. 'The Basque Country is a region on the borders of France and Spain. The Basque people have a unique history, culture and language (Euskera), so many people in the region want it to become an independent state from France and Spain'.
• Then _discuss_ the _consequences_ of separatism. You could divide your answer up by discussing both the _peaceful_ and the _non-peaceful_ consequences of separatism, e.g. 'Political parties like the Basque nationalist party have formed. They aim to get greater political independence for the Basque Country and they do this peacefully. This is in contrast to the actions of ETA — a separatist group who use violence in their campaign for independence. ETA have killed over 800 people since their formation in the 1960s, and in 2006 were responsible for a bombing at Madrid Airport'.

Page 241 — The Challenge of a Multicultural UK

1 Maximum of 7 marks available. _HINTS_:
• You need to _describe_ the graph, so if there's a _general pattern_, you should mention this first. Then you can move onto the _specific features_ of the graph, such as any _anomalies_ (things that don't fit the general pattern). Remember to _quote figures_ from the graph in your answer. E.g. 'All but two of the regions of the UK are home to less than 10% of the UK's non-white population. London has by far the greatest percentage with around 45%. Next to this, the West Midlands has around 12% of the UK's non-white population. Compared to the English regions, Wales, Scotland and Northern Ireland all have very low percentages of ethnic minorities...'.
• The question is also asking you to _comment_ on the graph, so use your knowledge to _explain_ the reasons for the patterns shown on the graph, e.g. 'London has a high percentage of the UK's non-white population because it has always attracted high numbers of immigrants. People move to London from all over the world because it is a global hub where lots of organisations have offices. Also, there are lots of jobs in manufacturing, transport, hospitals and the tourism industry'.

Page 243 — The Challenge of a Multicultural UK

1 Maximum of 10 marks available. _HINTS_:
• Begin your answer by _briefly explaining_ what a multicultural society is.
• _Describe the different issues_ and _explain_ how they can arise. Remember to give _examples from the UK_ to back up your points. E.g. 'There are economic issues associated with multicultural societies. For example, many ethnic minority groups work longer hours for lower salaries than people who were born in the country. In the UK in 2011, almost 50% of Pakistani and Bangladeshi workers were paid less than £7 an hour, whereas 25% of White British workers were paid this amount'.
• You could _divide up_ the issues you discuss into _different types_ (e.g. economic, housing, education issues etc.) and try to _link them together_ as you discuss them. E.g. 'As a result of many immigrants being in low paid work, a large number of immigrants live in low cost housing where overcrowding is a problem. For example, overcrowding is a problem in the Manningham area of Bradford, where there is a large Pakistani community'.

Page 245 — The Challenge of Global Poverty

1 Maximum of 7 marks available. _HINTS_:
• First briefly _define_ poverty, and talk about _how_ the map shows global poverty, e.g. 'Poverty means being unable to afford basic things such as safe drinking water, food, shelter, sanitation, healthcare and education. The map shows global poverty by showing the percentage of children under five who are underweight. A major cause of being underweight is an inadequate food supply, so areas with lots of underweight children are also likely to be areas in poverty'.
• Then _describe_ the pattern shown on the map in _detail_, using _names of places_ and _figures_. E.g. 'Poverty is unevenly distributed across the world. Central Africa and South Asia have the highest levels of poverty, with at least 30% of under 5s being underweight in a number of countries. India and Bangladesh are the worst affected countries, with at least 40% of under 5s being underweight. This is in contrast to countries such as the USA...'.
• If there are any _anomalies_ to the pattern you've described, then make sure you highlight them in your answer.
• The question is asking you to _comment_ on the global distribution of poverty, so you also need to _explain_ your points. E.g. 'Poverty is high in countries in South Asia, such as India and Bangladesh, for a number of reasons. For example, these countries are heavily affected by natural hazards such as floods and droughts. These hazards can cause poverty by damaging or destroying property, infrastructure and crops'.

Page 247 — The Challenge of Global Poverty

1 Maximum of 40 marks available. _HINTS_:
• Start by writing an _introduction_ to your answer. Introduce both the _key terms_ ('security' and 'development') in the statement, e.g. 'Security for a country means many different things. It can include personal security, which is how at threat the population is from violence or crime, but also economic security, which is to do with how stable the country's economy is and whether everyone has a reliable income or not'.
• Write about the first part of the statement — you should use _examples_ to back up your points wherever possible. E.g. "No development without security' means that it is difficult for a country to develop if it does not have all the different forms of security. For example, in Afghanistan there is very little personal and political security because of an ongoing war. Without this security, Afghanistan can't invest in development projects such as building roads, schools and hospitals as there is no guarantee that they won't be destroyed by the ongoing conflict'.
• Then write about the _second part_ of the statement ('no security without development'), and discuss how it contrasts with your point about the first part of the statement.
• This is a 40 mark essay question, so, wherever it's relevant, you need to bring in your _geography knowledge_ from _other parts of the course_. For example, you could talk about how lots of countries remain trapped at low levels of development because of this problem, then discuss the ways that countries can develop (e.g. through trade and aid) to break this cycle.

Acknowledgements

With thanks to iStockphoto.com for permission to reproduce the photographs used on pages 24, 29, 117, 120, 124, 125, 128, 131, 146, 152, 167, 169, 172, 181, 183, 186, 195, 197, 218 and 236.

Graph on page 26 adapted from Climate Change 2001: The Scientific Basis. Contribution of Working Group I to the Third Assessment Report of the Intergovernmental Panel on Climate Change. Figure 5. Cambridge University Press.

Antarctic diagram on page 35 reproduced from 'Fundamentals of the Physical Environment' by Peter Smithson, Ken Addison and Ken Atkinson, Third edition June 2002, Chapter 24, Polar Environments, Fig. 24.2. © 2007, Routledge, member of the Taylor & Francis Group.

Data used to construct the Riyadh climate graph on page 51 from: http://www.climate-charts.com/Locations/s/SD40438.php © Climate-Charts.com

World map of desertification risk on page 56 and vulnerability to desertification map of Spain on page 60 reproduced from U.S. Department of Agriculture: National Resources Conservation Service, Soil Survey Division, World Soil Resource, Washington, D.C.

Data used to construct the UK population pyramids on page 70 adapted from the Office for National Statistics licensed under the Open Government Licence v.1.0.

Data used to construct the population pyramid for Uganda on page 71, source: U.S. Census Bureau.

Data used to compile the table on Preston on page 74 adapted from the Office for National Statistics licensed under the Open Government Licence v.1.0.

Barley production map on page 76 reproduced with kind permission from the Food and Agriculture Organization of the United Nations, http://oregonstate.edu/instruct/css/330/five/BarleyOverview.htm with data from FAOSTAT, http://faostat.fao.org/default.aspx.

Data used to construct the daily calorie intake map on page 76 from the Food and Agriculture Organisation of the United Nations.

UK energy mix pie chart on page 87 © Crown Copyright licensed under the Open Government Licence v.1.0.

France's energy mix pie chart on page 87 © European Union, 1995-2012

Map of world energy production and consumption of energy on page 88, source: Map projection, Buckminster Fuller Institute and Dymaxion Map Design, Santa Barbara, CA. The word Dymaxion and the Fuller Projection Dymaxion™ Map design are trademarks of the Buckminster Fuller Institute, Santa Barbara, California, ©1938, 1967 & 1992. All rights reserved.

Global Energy Consumption map on page 88 © BP Statistical Review of World Energy 2008, BP p.l.c.

Healthy Life Expectancy map on page 98 reproduced from UNEP/DEWA/GRID-Europe, GEO Data Portal, Healthy Life Expectancy (HALE), 2002, United Nations Environment Programme.

TB map on page 98 © WHO, 2008. All rights reserved. World Health Organisation, http://www.who.int/ith/maps/tuberculosis_2008.jpg

Breast cancer map on page 99 reproduced with thanks to WHO © International Agency for Research on Cancer, March 2003. Data from Stewart B. W. and Kleihues P. (Eds): World Cancer Report. IARCPress. Lyon 2003. http://www.who.int/bookorders/anglais/detart1.jsp?sesslan=1&codlan=1&codcol=76&codcch=16#

Data used to construct the cancer table on page 99 reproduced with kind permission from Cancer Research UK.

Global measles map on page 99 reproduced with thanks to WHO, from the WHO/IVB database, 2004 © WHO 2004. All rights reserved. http://www.who.int/vaccines-surveillance/graphics/NY_graphics/glob_inc_measles_map.jpg

Graph on page 101 © Copyright 2006 SASI Group (University of Sheffield) and Mark Newman (University of Michigan), www.worldmapper.org

HIV map on page 102 © WHO, 2008. All rights reserved. World Health Organisation, http://www.who.int/ith/maps/HIV_infection2005_en.gif

Data used to construct the UK life expectancy map on page 106 adapted from the Office for National Statistics licensed under the Open Government Licence v.1.0.

With thanks to Science Photo Library for permission to use the images on pages 115 and 127.

Graph of UK temperature and rainfall on page 136 © Crown copyright reproduced under the terms of the Open Government Licence.

Acknowledgements

Maps of UK annual temperature, rainfall and wind speed 1971-2000 on pages 136 and 137 © Crown copyright reproduced under the terms of the Open Government Licence.

Map showing the course of the Great Storm with pressure readings on page 140 © 2007 Risk Management Solutions, Inc.

With thanks to Rex Features for permission to use the images on pages 148 and 200.

Graph showing climate change in Greenland over the last 20 000 years on page 154 reproduced with thanks to the NOAA for the graphic and to the Alley (2000) paper for the underlying data.

Last 1000 years of climate change graph on page 154 reproduced with kind permission from Climate Change 2001: The Scientific Basis, Contribution of Working Group I to the Third Assessment Report of the Intergovernmental Panel on Climate Change, SPM Figure 1. Cambridge University Press.

Graph showing temperature change over the last 110 years on page 154 © Crown copyright 2009, the Met Office.

Image of an offshore wind farm near Barrow-in-Furness on page 159 © Copyright David Dixon and licensed for reuse under the Creative Commons Licence.

Data used to construct the Average Climate in a Tropical Rainforest graph on page 168 from the U.S. National Climatic Data Center.

Data used to construct the map showing global urban population on page 185 from the United Nations Development Programme.

Map of LTGDC developments on page 197 adapted from http://ltgdc.org.uk/

Graph of methods of waste disposal in the UK on page 202 © Crown copyright reproduced under the terms of the Open Government Licence.

Data used to compile the table on page 209 © Central Intelligence Agency.

Page 223 — Apple Inc. is a registered trademark in the U.S. and other countries.

Pie chart of the UK's population by ethnic group in 2001 on page 240 © Crown copyright reproduced under the terms of the Open Government Licence.

Map of the UK's non-white population by area in 2001 on page 240 contains National Statistics data © Crown copyright and database rights 2012.

Graph of the regional distribution of the UK's non-white population on page 241 © Crown copyright reproduced under the terms of the Open Government Licence.

Pie chart of the population of Bradford by ethnic group in 2001 on page 243 contains National Statistics data © Crown copyright and database rights 2012.

Data used to construct the map on page 244 from the United Nations Millennium Goals Report 2007.

Data used to construct the map on page 245 © WHO, 2011. All rights reserved. World Health Organisation, http://www.who.int/whosis/whostat/EN_WHS2011_Full.pdf

Mapping data on page 255 reproduced by permission of Ordnance Survey® on behalf of HMSO © Crown copyright (2012). All rights reserved. Ordnance Survey® Licence No. 100034841.

Index

Index

Index

Index

Index